PITMAN OFFICE HANDBOOK

D1269975

SEVENTH EDITION

PITMAN OFFICE HANDBOOK

◆ Joan I. Campbell

PEARSON

Addison
Wesley

Toronto

Library and Archives Canada Cataloguing in Publication

Campbell, Joan (Joan I.)
   Pitman office handbook / Joan I. Campbell.—7th ed.

Includes index.
Fourth ed. written by: Pat Smith, Pamela Hay-Ellis, Joan Campbell.
ISBN-13: 978-0-321-47343-1
ISBN-10: 0-321-47343-4

1. Office practice—Handbooks, manuals, etc.
I. Smith, Pat. Pitman office handbook. II. Title.

HF5547.C23 2007   651   C2006-904870-3

ISBN-13: 978-0-321-47343-1
ISBN-10: 0-321-47343-4

Editor-in-Chief: Gary Bennett
Acquisitions Editor: Karen Elliott
Marketing Manager: Eileen Lasswell
Associate Editor: Kimberley Hermans
Production Editor: Jen Handel
Copy Editor: Nicole Mellow
Proofreader: Karen Alliston
Production Coordinator: Janis Raisen
Composition: Jansom
Photo and Permissions Research: Sandy Cooke
Art Director: Julia Hall
Interior and Cover Design: Monica Kompter
Cover Image: Comstock

Credits: Pages 143–145, Yellow Pages™ directories, Talking Yellow Pages™, and Web Number™ are trademarks of Yellow Pages Group Co. in Canada; page 145, Thanks to Yellow Pages Group Co. for the screen capture of its online directory Canada411.ca; page 162, information on asynchronous and synchronous communication Copyright Jupitermedia Corporation, 2006; pages 465, 466, 467, information on Xpresspost-USA, Small Packets, International Parcel Service, and Xpresspost-International Courtesy of Canada Post. For permission to reproduce other copyrighted material, the publisher gratefully acknowledges the copyright holders listed in the sources throughout the text, which are considered an extension of this copyright page.

2 3 4 5   12 11 10 09 08

Printed and bound in Canada.

HOW TO FIND INFORMATION IN YOUR HANDBOOK

Your handbook is designed to make life easy for you. The first letter of the word(s) in each unit title usually gives you the location code. For example, information on Telephone Techniques and Services has TT1, TT2, etc., as its locators.

There are three ways to find information quickly in this book. Use whichever one best suits your needs.

1. Go to the index at the back of the book. Find the subject that interests you and go to the page.

2. Refer to the table of contents on the next page for section and unit titles, section numbers, unit codes, and the beginning page number for each unit. Use the selected contents listed at the beginning of each unit to find particular topics (using the locator codes).

3. The combined table of contents and unit locator guide provide information about where each unit begins and how each unit is coded. Section and unit titles are aligned using thumb tabs, which are also printed on the outside edge of every text page. Use the tabs to find the unit you want.

CONTENTS

Preface   ix

Section I   Communications and Language Skills   1

Unit 1   The Technicalities of Language   1   T

Unit 2   The Expression of Language   83   E

Section II   Administrative and Office Procedures   116

Unit 3   Interpersonal and Social/Soft Skills   116   IS

Unit 4   Telephone Techniques and Services   134   TT

Unit 5   Electronic Mail   150   EM

Unit 6   Productivity/Time Management Skills   165   PT

Unit 7   Human Resources Management   186   H

Unit 8   Records and Information Management (RIM)   211   R

Unit 9   Copying Processes   240   CP

Unit 10   Meetings, Net Meetings, and Event Planning   249   M

Unit 11   Travel Arrangements   267   TA

Section III   Office Technology   285

Unit 12   Computers: Hardware and Software   285   C

Unit 13   The Integrated Office/New Technologies   314   IO

Unit 14   Keying and Formatting Documents for Processing   328   K

Unit 15   Desktop Publishing   395   DP

Unit 16   Information/Reference Sources/Internet   411   IR

Unit 17   Business Forms and Form Design   439   B

Unit 18   Postal and Shipping Services   455   P

Section IV   Finance   473

Unit 19   Math and Financial Management   473   MF

Section V   Job Search   526

Unit 20   Job Search Skills/Career Planning   526   J

Appendix   549   APPENDIX

Index   565   INDEX

····PREFACE········

Workplaces and work styles are continually changing and presenting new challenges. To help you manage your workload, we have updated and expanded the already comprehensive information in the *Pitman Office Handbook*. Full of productivity tips, soft skills, useful templates, and up-to-date data, the seventh edition continues the tradition of being an ideal "quick reference" tool for anyone working in an academic or business environment.

The *Pitman Office Handbook* has always been easy to use, and the seventh edition retains its familiar format. Among the features that our faithful readers appreciate are

◆ a second colour that highlights headings, illustrations, and examples

◆ a table of selected contents that appears at the beginning of each unit

◆ a comprehensive index for quick reference of terms and topics

◆ coloured tabs that guide readers to specific data

◆ locator codes that help readers find each entry easily

◆ subheadings and concise point-form notes that make it easy to quickly find and retain information

◆ a special Otabind binding that makes it easier to lay pages open and flat

◆ a handy, compact size that makes it both lightweight and portable

In the seventh edition of the *Pitman Office Handbook*, we have reorganized the structure to help ensure that you find the right information quickly and efficiently, by grouping like topics together and promoting a more intuitive order to the units. Students will find an abundance of useful information in the comprehensive Appendix, which has been updated to include important facts about Canada and how we are governed. We have also created a Text Enrichment Site for this text, containing material that supplements the topics in the textbook (for example, information is provided on Micrographics, Almanacs and Yearbooks, Atlases, and Dining and Table Etiquette). Please visit the Text Enrichment Site for this text at www.pearsoned.ca/text/campbell.

The modern workplace relies heavily on technology; therefore, an office is continually striving to keep up with rapid technological advances. Rather than homing in on specific changes to technology, the *Pitman Office Handbook* takes a general approach to inform you about technology's uses and its ability to improve productivity. In this edition you will find updated coverage of computer systems, software, and other office technologies. You will also learn how to use the internet for many daily tasks such as searching for jobs, planning conferences, shipping packages, and other events. Email can be a valuable communications tool in the workplace; therefore, this handbook discusses the pros and cons of email correspondence; offers many suggestions about drafting effective email messages; and provides guidelines regarding online etiquette (netiquette).

Because a day at the office involves much more than "pointing" and "clicking" at your computer terminal, this edition features new and revised coverage of soft skills (Unit 3 and throughout); VOIP, WiFi, and PDAs (Unit 5); substance abuse and violence in the workplace (Unit 6); employee assistance plans (Unit 7); employment standards legislation (Unit 7); information management (Unit 8); new technological definitions such as binary, CRT, Uptime, RAID, and PDF (Units 12 and 15); new business directories (Unit 16); electronic shipping tools (Unit 18).

We have also added "Words of Wisdom" throughout the text, a new feature designed to provide daily advice and thoughts useful to office administrators not only in the workplace, but also at home and in other aspects of life. The following icon accompanies each Word of Wisdom so that they are easily identifiable as you flip through the pages of the text.

Finally, a very important addition to the seventh edition of the *Pitman Office Handbook* is the increased emphasis on soft skills. Employers are looking for people who can do more than perform a set of tasks. They need people who have soft (transferable) skills as well as hard (technical) skills. Hard skills can be acquired through on-the-job training, but soft skills (e.g., a willingness to learn, customer service skills, good communication and problem-solving skills, and getting along with other employees) are much harder to teach. Employers prefer to hire people who already have soft skills. Soft skills are at least as important, and often more important, than technological skills when relating to the success of a project.

Soft skills are becoming a large part of an employee's job performance evaluation as well as a critical area for the hiring/firing process. The seventh edition of the *Pitman Office Handbook* emphasizes soft skills and improvement on these skills throughout the text.

Whether you are an office employee, business administrator, manager, entrepreneur, or student, we hope that you enjoy using the *Pitman Office Handbook*, Seventh Edition. We invite you to share your comments about the handbook with us by writing to webinfo.pubcanada@pearsoned.com.

ACKNOWLEDGMENTS

To compile the *Pitman Office Handbook*, Seventh Edition, we consulted with many people and sources. We would like to express our thanks to the following people and organizations for their help: Bell Canada, Canada Customs, Francine Conn, Canada Post Corporation, Troy Nichols (Technician, Future Shop), David Akin, *The Hamilton Spectator*, Kelly Darling, Hamilton Teachers' Credit Union, Jenny McCartney and Marilyn McDermott of Mohawk College, and Evelyn Kemp, Librarian. Thanks to Yellow Pages Group for the screen captures of its online directories, YellowPages.ca[TM] and Canada411.ca. Thank you also to Debbie Bruce and Veronica Weir of Mohawk College.

Special thanks also goes to members of the editorial and production teams at Pearson Education Canada, including Karen Elliott, Acquisitions Editor; Kimberley Hermans, Developmental Editor; Jen Handel, Production

Editor; Janis Raisen, Production Coordinator; Nicole Mellow, Copy Editor; Karen Alliston, Proofreader; and Julia Hall, Art Director.

We also gratefully acknowledge the assistance of the following reviewers:

Madelaine Befus, *Okanagan College*
Lynn Berry, *Algonquin College*
Shelly Gibson, *Confederation College of Applied Arts & Technology*
Mary Louise Harrison, *North Island College*
Colleen McGavin, *Camosun College*
James Weare, *Conestoga College*
Carolyn Whittaker, *Centennial College*

Dedication

This comprehensive handbook is dedicated to students, office employees, employers, and entrepreneurs who need access to up-to-date basic office or technology reference information for success in college courses or in the business environment.

An educated person is a literate person and is usually successful through hard work and a thirst for knowledge. Knowledge becomes wisdom only after it has been put to practical use. May this handbook be one of the valuable tools that help you to attain success and to meet your goals in all future endeavours.

J.I.C.

WORDS OF WISDOM

*Life is like a smorgasbord—help
yourself to all you can learn!*

T

1 THE TECHNICALITIES OF LANGUAGE

SELECTED CONTENTS

T1	**CHOOSING THE RIGHT WORDS**
T2	Clichés to Avoid
T3	Frequently Confused Words
T4	Misused Words
T5	Double Negative Words
T6	One Word or Two?
T7	Words with Accompanying Prepositions
T8	Words with Unnecessary Prepositions
T9	Spelling
T10	Rules for Spelling
T11	Word Variants
T12	Frequently Misspelled Words
T13	Word Meanings
T14	Gender-Inclusive Language
T15	**GRAMMAR AND USAGE**
T16	The Sentence
T17	Parts of the Sentence
T18	*Subject*
T19	*Predicate*
T20	*Object*
T21	*Phrases*
T22	*Clauses*
T23	Types of Sentences
T24	Sentence Construction Hints
T25	Sentence Flaws to Avoid
T26	The Paragraph
T27	Parts of Speech
T28	Nouns
T29	Pronouns
T30	Verbs
T31	Adjectives

I

T32	Adverbs
T33	Prepositions
T34	Conjunctions
T35	Interjections

T36	**PUNCTUATION**
T37	Apostrophe
T43	Colon
T49	Comma
T68	Dash
T69	Exclamation Mark
T70	Hyphen
T76	Parentheses, Square Brackets, and Brace Brackets
T79	Period
T80	Ellipsis Mark
T81	Slash or Right Diagonal
T82	Question Mark
T85	Quotation Marks
T90	Semicolon
T93	Underscore
T94	Italics

T95	**STYLE MECHANICS**
T96	Abbreviations
T108	Capitalization
T124	Numbers
T137	Word Division

The ability to communicate well is essential to success in business. A successful communication—either oral or written—is one that is understood by the receiver exactly as the sender intended it to be. If the sender puts him- or herself in the receiver's position, uses appropriate language, structures sentences with care, and adopts the right tone, the sender will produce an effective communication.

Clarity in language is becoming increasingly important. Canada is welcoming more and more immigrants and trading more globally than ever before. Considerable care must be taken, then, to ensure that communications are easy to understand for those whose first language is not English.

This unit is concerned with the technicalities or workings of the language. It provides the information needed to help you

♦ choose and spell words with precision

♦ be knowledgeable about the rules of grammar

♦ punctuate accurately

♦ follow the conventions of style

NOTE This unit is not designed to provide you with a detailed analysis of the English language, but rather to increase your knowledge and help you solve day-to-day language problems.

T1 CHOOSING THE RIGHT WORDS

Send clear messages by keeping your words simple and by using them with precision and care. Avoid clichés, slang, and jargon. Stay away from overused and dated expressions. Be very careful to steer clear of ambiguities, redundancies, and inaccuracies.

If in doubt, search it out!

Tap into the richness of the language to make your communications more expressive and effective. A dictionary, a thesaurus, and a handbook of English usage are invaluable reference books (see Unit 16 for details of these and other information resources).

T2 CLICHÉS TO AVOID

Do not use clichés or hackneyed, old-fashioned expressions in the hope they will make a good impression. Let one word do the work of three or four.

Avoid	Use	Example
(We) acknowledge receipt of	Thank you	Thank you for your letter . . .
At all times	Always	We always enjoy our business associations with you.
At an early date	Soon; immediately	We expect to have an answer soon.
At this point in time; at this time	Now; at present	Your representative is here now.
Due to the fact that	Because; since; as	Because the workers are on strike . . .
Enclosed please find; enclosed herewith	We enclose; enclosed is	Enclosed is a cheque for . . .
Encounter difficulty	Have trouble; need help	If you need help, please call us.
For the purpose of	For	The software was needed for inventory control.
In a position to	Can	We can mail the contract today.
In due course	As soon as; when	My client will pay as soon as she can.

(continued . . .)

Avoid	Use	Example
In re	Regarding; about	Your suggestion regarding the annual bonus . . .
In the amount of	For	Your cheque for $100 arrived . . .
In the event that	In case; if	If it rains, the games . . .
In the near future	Soon; shortly	You can expect to hear from us soon.
In view of the fact that	Because; since	Because it was a fair solution, they all agreed.
May we anticipate an early reply?	May we expect	May we expect to hear from you soon?
Of the opinion that	Think	They think this is a good time to buy.
Until such time as	Until	Until an agreement is reached . . .

T3   FREQUENTLY CONFUSED WORDS

The complexity of the English language sometimes causes confusion because some words that sound alike have different meanings. Consult the following chart if you are in doubt about the correct word to choose.

Word	Meaning	Example
accede	agree to	I will accede to the manager's request.
exceed	to go beyond	Please do not exceed the speed limit.
accept	to receive	Please accept this gift.
except	not including	Everyone except the newest member was present.
accent	a distinctive manner of pronunciation	Silvia has a delightful accent.
ascent	act of rising	Climbers take months to prepare for the ascent of Mount Everest.
assent	consent	She gave a nod of assent.
access	entry	The office did not have street access.
excess	too much; surplus	The excess paper was cut off.
ad	abbreviation for advertisement	We placed three ads in the local newspaper.
add	extend; make larger	Let's add Fran's name to the list.
addition	process of adding	The addition was incorrect.
edition	printed copies of a book or newspaper	The seventh edition is in print.

(continued . . .)

T

Word	Meaning	Example
adapt	adjust	Can you adapt yourself to the job?
adept	thoroughly skilled	She proved she was adept on the job.
adopt	accept formally	Council needed to adopt the motion.
		The couple decided to adopt.
adjoin	next to	Canada adjoins the United States.
adjourn	put off to a later time	The meeting did adjourn early.
adverse	hostile	Unemployment has an adverse effect on business.
averse	opposed	Politicians are averse to being blunt.
advice (n.)	recommendation	Their advice was freely given.
advise (v.)	inform; recommend	The lawyer was eager to advise the client.
affect (v.)	influence	Praise will affect an employee's productivity.
	put on, assume	She affected an air of confidence.
effect (n.)	consequence	Meeting the prime minister had a profound effect on Ginette.
effect (v.)	accomplish	We will do all we can to effect speedy delivery.
aid (n.)	help	Send aid to Iraq.
aid (v.)		Will you aid their cause?
aide	helper; assistant	He wants to be a nursing aide.
ail	to feel sick	What is it that ails her?
ale	a bitter beer	He did enjoy a cold ale on occasion.
aisle	a passageway	The supermarket aisle was too narrow.
I'll	contraction for *I will*	I'll be here.
isle	an island	Bermuda is a lovely isle to visit.
allowed	permitted	They were not allowed to go to the club.
aloud	audibly; not silently	Loretta should have kept her thoughts to herself instead of saying them aloud.
altar (n.)	sacred part of a church	The bride and groom approached the altar.
alter (v.)	to change	We had to alter our plans.
alternate	one of two choices	She took the scenic route; we took the alternate one.
alternative	choice of several	He had three alternatives: turn right, turn left, or go straight ahead.
appraise	to estimate	The real estate agent was asked to appraise the property.
apprise	to inform	Please apprise me of the changes.

(continued . . .)

I

Word	Meaning	Example
are (v.)	the plural and second person singular of *to be*	They are going to college.
hour (n.)	sixty minutes	The meeting lasted an hour.
our (adj.)	shows ownership	Our parents live in Toronto, but our aunt lives in Montreal.
assistance	help; aid	Give your assistance to those nurses, please.
assistants	helpers	The managers and their assistants were present.
attendance	presence	Your attendance is appreciated.
attendants (n.)	people who provide a service	The hospital attendants enjoyed helping people.
bail	a security guarantee	Bail was set at $5000.
bale	a large bundle of material	The bale of hay was too heavy.
bare	naked	The winter wind stripped the leaves from the trees, leaving them bare.
bear (n.)	large animal	They went to the zoo to see the polar bear.
bear (v.)	support	The thin ice cannot bear your weight.
bases	plural of base and basis	The bases were loaded.
basis	the main part	The basis of the medicine is an oil. The basis of the cake is flour.
berry	a fruit	We picked berries off the bushes.
bury	put in the earth	Erika wanted to bury the dead mouse.
berth	a place to sleep	They reserved a berth on the train.
birth	being born	She gave birth to a healthy baby boy.
beside	next to; adjacent	Please sit beside me.
besides	also; moreover	Besides a computer, he also wanted a scanner.
biannual	twice a year	The biannual pay period (June and December) was approved.
biennial	occurring every two years	It was a biennial celebration (2004, 2006, 2008, etc.).
bloc (n.)	a group of people	The Quebec bloc attended the conference.
block (n.)	a solid piece of material	Maxine cut up the block of wood.
block (v.)	to prevent passage	The main idea was to block the entrance.
board	a piece of wood	They needed a board for the display.
	group	The board of directors met today.
bored	to be made weary by tiresome behaviour	The audience was bored and began to leave.

(continued . . .)

T

Word	Meaning	Example
brake (n.)	a mechanical part of a vehicle	The brake on the car was found to be defective.
break (v.)	to cause to come apart	How did the child break the vase?
buy	to purchase	What did you buy today?
by	a preposition; near or beside	The theatre is by the lake.
bye	informal for goodbye	She sadly said bye to her friend.
	the odd person/team not required to play a game or match	The team had a bye in the first round and went on to win the cup.
cache	hiding place	The cache was not easy to locate.
cash	money	Mary had $20 in cash with her.
canvas	a strong cotton cloth	We will use the canvas tent when we go camping.
canvass	to solicit subscriptions or votes or to fundraise	It is hard work to canvass door-to-door for charities.
capital	invested money	The company had a huge capital investment in its steelmaking facilities.
	city	Ottawa is the capital of Canada.
	upper case when keying text	Use a capital "O" when keying the word Ottawa.
Capitol (n.)	Congress or state legislature building	The U.S. Congress meets at the Capitol in Washington, D.C.
carat	a measure used for precious stones	The ring had a half-carat diamond.
caret	a proofreader's symbol	A caret symbol (^) indicates an insertion.
carrot	a vegetable	She needed a carrot for the salad.
cast	a group of entertainers	The cast for the new musical started rehearsals right after the holiday.
	a mould	The cast on her broken arm was made out of plaster.
caste	a distinct class of society	He was a member of a Hindu caste.
census	statistics of an area	The census is taken every 10 years.
senses	normal, sound condition of mind	The children quickly came to their senses after hearing the joke.
cent	a unit of currency	His change from the purchase was one cent.
scent	an odour or smell	The scent of the perfume was very pleasant.
sent	dispatched	The letter was sent out two days ago.
cereal	grain food	Cereal is good for breakfast.
serial	arranged in a series	Soap operas are serials.

(continued . . .)

Word	Meaning	Example
choose	select	Which car did you choose?
chose	selected	I chose the newest model.
cite (v.)	to quote from an author	The student did not cite anything by Atwood in her report.
sight (n.)	vision or act of seeing	Glasses or contact lenses help many whose sight is not 20/20.
site (n.)	a position or place	The site for our new home has been chosen.
coarse	rough; common	The unfinished table has a coarse surface.
course	path; way	The safe course has no challenge.
	part of a meal served at one time	We ate the seven-course meal slowly.
	outline of a subject to be learned	The teacher prepared the Grade 11 English course of study.
complement	complete or make perfect	Use these paintings to complement your office decor.
compliment	polite expression of praise	It is kind to pay a compliment.
confidant(e)	friend; counsellor	She was a loyal confidante.
confident	sure of oneself	Tamara was confident she would succeed.
conscience	the sense that one should do right	Her conscience bothered her all day because she had lied.
conscious	aware	The accident victim was still conscious.
core	the central part	The city core was depressing.
corpse	a dead body	The corpse was found that night.
corps	a military body;	Her corps entered the war zone.
	a group of people engaged in a specific activity	He joined the press corps in June.
correspondence	an exchange of letters	Amanda filed the correspondence.
correspondents	people who exchange letters	They were correspondents.
council (n.)	a group of people	They introduced the newly elected council.
counsel (n.)	advice	She sought counsel from her lawyer.
counsel (v.)	advise	A lawyer was called to counsel the group.
consul	an official in a foreign country	One of the Canadian consuls is located in Japan.
credible	believable	Their story was barely credible.
creditable	deserving credit	That was a creditable presentation.
currant	a berry	Carole made delicious red currant jam.
current	a flow of water or electricity	You must cut off the electrical current before repairing the toaster. The current near the dam was dangerous.
current	of or at the present time	Are turtlenecks the current fashion?

(continued . . .)

Word	Meaning	Example
decent	respectable	Study hard to earn a decent salary.
descent	downward movement	The descent from the mountaintop was difficult.
dissent (n. or v.)	disagree(ment)	The dissent among players caused their team to lose.
defective	faulty	The defective computer was returned to the store.
deficient	incomplete	His diet was deficient in protein.
defer	to postpone	Will we defer the meeting until next week?
defer to	respect the opinion of	Young people usually defer to older people.
differ	be unlike	Because their opinions differed, they compromised.
desert (n.)	barren land	Sand is everywhere in the desert.
desert (v.)	to abandon	The leader was deserted by his supporters.
dessert	sweet course	Dessert will be tartufo.
device (n.)	item designed to achieve a particular purpose	A shredder is a very useful device for shredding paper.
devise (v.)	to invent	Let's devise a new strategy for the campaign.
discreet	tactful	Be discreet with your comments.
discrete	separate; distinct	The workshop had three discrete segments.
elicit	to draw out	The teacher tried very hard to elicit the correct answer from the student.
illicit	not legal	As a result of illicit financial dealings, the accountant was dismissed.
eligible	fit to be chosen	Your training makes you eligible for the job.
illegible	unreadable	That person's writing is illegible.
emigrant	person leaving country	Sanjay is an emigrant from Kenya.
immigrant	person entering country	Joe Chan is an immigrant to Canada.
eminent	distinguished	Canada's Governor General is an eminent person.
imminent	about to happen	They were told that a merger was imminent.
emanate	come out (from)	Cooking aromas emanated from the kitchen.
ensure	to make sure or certain	We must proofread carefully to ensure there are no errors.
insure	to protect	They were advised to insure the property against fire and theft.

(continued . . .)

I

Word	Meaning	Example
envelop (v.)	wrap; surround	They let the warm Caribbean envelop them.
envelope (n.)	container for letter	Use a No. 10 envelope, please.
fair	favourable or just	Our instructor is always fair when she marks tests.
	festivity: exhibition of goods or services	The Summerhill Fair takes place every June.
fare	cost of transportation	The bus fare increased in January.
	food	Cucumber sandwiches are dainty fare.
farther	refers to actual distance	He lived three kilometres farther down the road.
further	extending beyond; in addition	Nothing could be further from the truth.
feat	an act of skill	The daring circus feat was breath-taking.
feet	plural of foot	He danced as if he had two left feet.
foreword	preface	A book often contains a foreword.
forward	in front	Veronica was asked to step forward ten paces.
formally	according to form, rule	Please dress formally for the dinner.
formerly	previously	She was formerly an administrative assistant.
forth	forward	Go forth in peace!
fourth	ordinal for *four*	Our company placed fourth in the competition.
golf	a game played with a small hard ball and a club	Mike Weir won the Masters golf tournament on April 13, 2003.
gulf	large bay; ocean	She requested accommodation on the gulf side of the resort.
	large gap	There was a gulf between them.
guessed	formed opinion without knowledge	She guessed his age to be around 50.
guest	a visitor	We had a special guest dine with us on the holiday.
hail (n.)	frozen rain	We had a severe hailstorm.
hail (v.)	to call	She will hail a cab.
hale (adj.)	healthy	For all his 80 years, he was a hale and hearty man.
hall	a passageway	The school hall was bright and cheerful.
haul	to drag or pull	They had to haul the tree from the river.
hear	perceive by ear	Praise is pleasant to hear.
here	in this place	Bring the files here, please.

(continued . . .)

T

Word	Meaning	Example
hole	an open area	He dug a hole in the ground.
whole	complete	It was cheaper to purchase the whole package than one piece at a time.
holy	refers to religion	Christmas is a holy day.
wholly	completely	They were wholly responsible.
incite	stir up	The speaker incited the workers to strike.
insight	understanding	The article provided a useful insight into the possibilities.
its	possessive form of *it*	The lion protects its young.
it's	contraction for *it is*	It's the end of the year on December 31.
key	instrument to lock or unlock	Hard work is one of the keys to success.
quay (pronounced "key")	dock	We'll meet your boat at Queen's Quay tomorrow.
knew	past tense of *know*	Carter knew he had to play ball.
new	recent; not old	This was the new edition of the textbook.
last	final	The last train left at 2:30 p.m.
latest	most recent	What is the latest news on world food supplies?
later	further on in time	The later we dine, the more we will eat.
latter	second of two	Sue and Carol came to the party together; the latter drove.
lay	to set, to place	Please lay the books on the desk.
lie (n.)	a falsehood	He told a lie.
lie (v.)	to recline	He had to lie down.
lead (n.)	a soft metal	Art students sketch using lead pencils.
lead (v.)	to show the way	You lead; I'll follow.
led (v.)	guided	The guide led the group to safety.
lean	not upright	The shed tended to lean to the right.
	thin	The lean dog was begging for food.
lien	a legal claim	There was a lien on the property because the taxes were in arrears.
leased	rented	They leased the property, but they may purchase it next year.
least	less than any other	I paid $20; Jane paid $15; but Betty paid the least, only $10.
lessen (v.)	diminish	Don't lessen pressure on that cut yet.
lesson (n.)	exercise	How was your economics lesson today?

(continued . . .)

I

Word	Meaning	Example
lightening	making lighter	Lightening the load made a big difference.
lightning	a sudden flash of light	Lightning is often followed by thunder during a storm.
loan	a debt	You must pay interest on a loan.
lone	alone	There was a lone wolf out on the ridge.
loose	free	The wheel cover came loose and fell off.
lose	be deprived of	They may lose the contract if their quote is too high.
mall	a public place to shop	The new mall is opening today.
maul	to handle in a rough way	Often a male bear will maul its own cub.
medal	a decoration	Canadians won 24 medals at the 2006 Winter Olympics.
meddle	to interfere	It was hoped that no one would meddle with the display.
might (v.)	expresses possibility	The weather forecaster said it might rain.
might (n.)	a force	The might of the tornado was frightening.
mite	a small bit; small object	It didn't make a mite of difference.
	a small child	Although she was very rushed, the shopper stopped to help the crying mite who had somehow lost his way.
	a small bug	There were mites on the plants and in the carpet.
miner	mine worker	He was a coal miner's son.
minor (n.)	person under legal age	Susie was the only minor in the group.
minor (adj.)	of lesser importance	Luckily, the error was only a minor one.
moral	concerned with distinction between right and wrong	The moral behaviour of children is patterned after that of adults.
morale	mental condition or attitude	The morale in our office is higher with the team approach.
overdo	go too far	If you overdo the exercise, you may become ill.
overdue	late; past the due time	The March payment is long overdue.
packed	wrapped or tied	The luggage was packed for travel.
pact	an agreement	The boys made a pact to be friends forever.
pail	bucket	Donna carried the pail of water for the animals.
pale	whitish in colour	She looked so pale that they asked her to sit down.

(continued . . .)

T

Word	Meaning	Example
pair (n.)	a couple or two	She purchased a pair of shoes.
pare (v.)	to cut or peel	You can pare the potatoes for the dinner.
pear (n.)	a fruit	I had a pear for dessert.
passed	past tense of *to pass*	Every student passed the exam.
past	beyond in time or place	It is now long past midnight.
patience	endurance; tolerance	A teacher needs plenty of patience.
patients	sick clients	My doctor sees 25 patients each day.
peace	peace and quiet	They wanted peace.
piece (n.)	a portion or part	May I please have a piece of pie?
piece (v.)	make or repair	The material needed to be pieced.
peak	top of mountain or hill	They climbed to the peak of Mount Everest.
peek	a quick look	The child took a peek into the sack.
personal	one's own	Each member is entitled to a personal opinion.
personnel	body of workers	All of our personnel are happy.
perspective	viewpoint	Your perspective will influence your decision.
prospective	anticipated	Daniel interviewed three prospective employees.
peruse	examine carefully	Please peruse the report when you have time.
pursue	follow with intent to catch	The wolf pursued the deer.
plaintiff	one who brings legal suit	Jane was the plaintiff in the lawsuit.
plaintive	mournful or sad	The music of the pipes was plaintive, reminding everyone of those lost in battle.
poor (n.)	the needy	A benefit concert was held to help the poor.
pour (v.)	cause to flow in a steady stream	The waiter poured the coffee as he spoke.
pray (v.)	as in worship	They were asked to pray for the sick child.
prey (n.)	a hunted animal	The lion stalks its prey.
precede	go before	*A* precedes *B* in the alphabet.
proceed	go on	Let us proceed with the meeting.
principal (adj.)	chief; major	A principal cause of car accidents is careless driving.
principal (n.)	a sum of money borrowed or invested upon which interest is calculated	She has not been able to reduce the principal on her mortgage.
	head of a school	Go to the principal's office at once.
principle	personal code of truth	His high principles won him the respect of his co-workers.
quay (*see key*)		

(continued . . .)

I

Word	Meaning	Example
quiet	silent	Everyone was quiet for two minutes.
quite	absolutely	That is not quite correct.
	– or –	
	to a considerable degree	I hiked quite a distance.
quit	stop; give up	Did you quit work at 5 p.m.?
real	true	It did not look like a real diamond.
reel	a device for winding	The film was put on a reel.
receipt	proof of purchase	You will need a receipt if you wish to return the goods.
recipe	a set of directions; formula	Please follow the recipe as written.
recent	not long past	Masami was a recent graduate.
resent	feel offended	We resent his constant interruptions.
reign (v.)	to rule	The Queen of England may reign for a long time.
rain (n.)	water drops from clouds	It may rain today.
rein (n.)	bridle part	The rein broke during the race.
right (adj.)	correct	You made the right choice.
right (n.)	fair claim	You have the right to be silent.
rite	ritual; ceremony	Welcoming rites in Guinea are fascinating.
wright	creator; maker	Shakespeare was a playwright.
role	a part in a play	He was wonderful in the leading role.
roll	to move by turning over	She had to roll the bread dough quickly.
root	part of a plant	The root of the tree was rotting away.
route	a course/way in travel	That was the safest route to take.
sail	piece of canvas	The new sail flapped in the breeze.
sale	reduced price	Sophie purchased the sweater on sale.
scene	the time or place	The scene of the crime was close to the lake.
seen	past participle of *see*	Have you seen the latest statistics?
sew	to use needle and thread	She had to sew her torn jeans.
so	in a way; stated	Was that really so?
sole (adj.)	only one	She was the sole heir to the estate.
sole (n.)	the bottom of a shoe	There was a large hole in the sole of his shoe.
	fish	She ate sole for lunch.
soul	spirit	Sabrina put all her soul into the acting role.
stair	one of a series of steps	Please take one stair at a time.
stare	look with a fixed gaze	It is not polite to stare at a person.

(continued . . .)

T

Word	Meaning	Example
stalk (n.)	the stem	She cut the celery stalk into small pieces.
stalk (v.)	follow	Wild animals stalk their prey.
stock (n.)	a supply	We should add to our stock of canned goods.
stationary	unmoving	A statue is stationary.
stationery	writing materials	Most firms have printed stationery.
statue	figure carved or moulded	Michelangelo's *David* is an impressive statue.
statute	a law	A recent statute permits extended opening hours.
straight	not broken	The garment did not have a straight hem.
strait	narrow channel	The sailboat just made it through the narrow strait.
suite	an apartment	The rented suite had a wonderful view.
sweet (adj.)	a pleasant taste	The drink was very sweet.
sweet (n.)	candy	He offered her a sweet.
tail	rearmost part of an animal's body	The dog wagged its tail.
tale	a story	The tale of the two competitors was unbelievable.
tear (n.)	water from the eye	She shed a tear or two.
tear (v.)	to come apart	The mother asked her son not to tear his new shirt.
than (conj.)	used in comparisons	Steve was taller than Troy.
then (adv.)	indicates time	Marnie knew then that the prophecy had come true.
their	possessive form of *they*	Their house is very large.
there	in that place	Take this computer over there, please.
they're	contraction for *they are*	They're late for the meeting.
threw	past tense of *throw*	The winning team threw five touchdown passes.
through	by means of	Their success came through hard work.
	from beginning to end	He came through the entire assignment unscathed.
thorough	complete	Your assistant did a thorough job for us.
verses	literary expressions	The poet wrote several verses for the poem.
versus	against	The trial involved Black versus (vs.) Robinson.

(continued . . .)

Word	Meaning	Example
waist (n.)	middle of the body	You have a small waist.
waste (adj.)	useless material	They inspected the disposal of the company's waste materials.
waste (v.)	to make poor use of	We are advised not to waste electricity.
wait	to stay	It was not necessary to wait for the mail.
weight	heaviness	The weight of the luggage caused the shelf to collapse.
waive	to give up	They decided to waive their rights to the property.
wave (v.)	to make a signal with a hand motion	It was sad to wave goodbye.
wave (n.)	a swell of water	The huge wave almost toppled the boat.
ware (n.)	usually *wares* or part of a compound word; product	Kitchenware is colourful these days.
wear (v.)	put on	Wear your best suit for the interview.
were (v.)	past tense of *to be*	All the managers were friends.
where (adv.)	place at which	Who knows where we're going?
weak	not very strong	The presentation was weak and lacked substance.
week	seven days	They had one week to prepare the report.
weather	atmospheric conditions	The weather forecast called for rain.
whether	which of two alternatives	Whether they come or not is unimportant.
whose	possessive form of *who*	Whose pen is this?
who's	contraction for *who is*	The one who's first gets the prize.
your	possessive form of *you*	Make sure you use your dictionary.
you're	contraction for *you are*	When you're in Spain, speak Spanish.

Word	Meaning	Example
Latin terms:		
per se	by itself; in itself	The list was as per se.
verbatim	word for word	Mr. Martin's speech was printed verbatim in the newspaper.
vice versa	the other way round	Joe blamed John, and vice versa.
vis-à-vis	face-to-face with/ in relation to	All three moves make up for Harper's outsider status vis-à-vis the business world.

T4   MISUSED WORDS

Certain words and phrases are frequently misused. The following is a list of commonly misused expressions and examples of how they ought to be used.

a and an (articles) [see also "Articles," page 44]
Use *a* before words beginning with consonant sounds, including those spelled with an initial pronounced *h* and those spelled with vowels that are sounded as consonants.

> Greg was a historian.
> Sandra had a one-o'clock appointment.
> Marnie had a university degree.

Use *an* before all vowel sounds, including those spelled with an initial silent *h*.

> It was an organization with an excellent productivity record.
> What an honour to be invited to the opening.

accept and except
Accept is a verb that means "to receive."

> Please accept this gift as a token of appreciation.

Except is a verb or a preposition that means "to exclude."

> They were all going to attend except Leonard.

affect and effect
affect (v.) to influence

> The rainy weather did affect attendance at the concert.

effect (n.) result

> The effect of downsizing has been to create unemployment for many people.

effect (v.) to bring about or make happen

> The supplier promised to effect delivery by the date required.

among and between
Use *between* when referring to two items; *among* for more than two.

> The argument is between you and me.
> Please sort out the problem among the six of you.

and etc. and etc.
etc. means "and the rest" or "and so forth"; therefore, *and* is redundant.

> Travel agents can arrange flights, hotels, theatre tickets, etc., on request.

anyplace and anywhere
Use *anywhere* only. *Any* and *place* are always used separately.

> Is there a foreign exchange counter anywhere near here?

I

anyways and *anyway*

There is no such word as *anyways*.

> He had to be present anyway.

As regards and **with regard**

As regards and with regard—concerning or relating to a specific object or subject.

> With regard to the inquiry made on Tuesday, ...
> With regards or regards—warm thoughts, good wishes, or consideration of.
> Give my regards to Aunt Tillie.

at and *to*

At indicates position.

> The branch managers were at the convention all week.

To indicates motion or direction towards something.

> The managers went to the meeting on Wednesday morning.

behind and *in back of*

Use *behind* not *in back of*.

> Place the information sheet behind the test papers.

NOTE *In front of* is correct.

> Place the information sheet behind, not in front of, the test papers.

beside and *besides*

Beside means "by the side of."

> She will sit beside the chairperson.

Besides means "in addition to."

> Do we have any more copies besides these?

bring and *take*

Use *bring* to this place (here); and *take* to that place (there).

> Will you please bring the report when you come?
> Take these books home with you.

can and *may*

Can implies capability; *may* signifies permission sought or granted, possibility, or uncertainty.

> An athlete can usually run very fast.
> May my friend join me at the reception?
> The Games may take place in Canada.

come and *go*

Use *come* when implying "here," *go* when meaning "there."

> The president is expecting 20 guests to come for lunch.
> I am planning to go to Cape Breton Island for my holidays.

T

currently and *presently*

Use *currently* when meaning at the present time or now.

> We are currently using the revised schedule.

Use *presently* when meaning before long or soon.

> The taxi will arrive presently.

different from

Ordinarily, use the preposition *from* after *different* when making comparisons.

> Tony's costume was *different from* Barbara's.

When a clause follows, either *than* or *from* may be used.

> The costume was *different than* (or *from what*) she had expected.

every which way and *in all directions*

Every which way is slang.

> The traffic seemed to be moving *in all directions* at the same time.

from, off, of

From is generally used with persons.

> Did she borrow money from Alice?

Off is used with things. *Off* can only be used with persons when something is physically resting on them and is being lifted away.

> The plane took off as scheduled.
> He was asked to take off his hat.

Never use *of* for *from* after *off*.

> The team ran off the field. *Not* The team ran off of the field.

Never use *of* when you mean *have*.

> Troy could have been more careful with the new car.

good and *well*

The adjective *good* must modify a noun; *well* is used as an adverb or an adjective.

> She did a good job.
> He did well.
> I am well.

have and *of*

Use *have*, not *of*, after helping verbs such as c*ould, should, would, may,* and *might*.

> You should have (not *should of*) told me.

in, into, in to

In means position or movement within a place.

> Sharon has been in hospital for two weeks.

Into means entry or change of form.

> She was asked to take the food into the cafeteria.
> Please convert the figures into table form for the publisher.

In to (two separate words). *In* is used as an adverb; *to* is used as a preposition.

> Please take this report in to Mrs. Rodgers.

in regards to and *in regard to*
In regard to is correct. *In regards to* is *never* used.

> Call me soon in regard to the annual meeting.

lay and *lie*
Lay means to place and requires a direct object; *lie* means to recline and can stand alone.

> Yan was asked to lay the documents on the desk.
> Robert had to lie down every afternoon while recuperating from his illlness.

like and *as*
Like is a preposition; it should not be used as a conjunction to join clauses.

> Her skin felt like sandpaper.

If a conjunction is needed, use *as, as if,* or *as though.*

> Try to proofread as carefully as Keri does.
> Miss Weir smiled as though she knew what was going to happen.

none and *no one*
None is the singular pronoun standing for not one; it should always take a singular verb. *No one* is used in place of not one person; it also takes a singular verb.

> None of those machines is working properly.
> No one was visible in the dense fog.

on, onto, on to
On means position or movement over.

> We were asked to wait on level one for the next performance.

Onto means movement towards or over.

> They can get onto this train or wait for the next one.

On to (two separate words). *On* is used as an adverb; *to* is used as a preposition.

> They were asked to move on to the next platform.

per, a, an
Per is a preposition usually used before Latin nouns or weights and measures.

> The mortgage rates were set at 6 percent per annum. (Latin expression)
> The paper comes in 500 pages per package.

T

NOTE Whenever possible, use *a* or *an* instead of *per*. Never use *per* to mean "according to" or "in accordance with." See page 17.

> He was earning $10 an hour for his time on the job.

real and *really*
Real is an adjective that describes a noun; *really* is an adverb.

> She bought a real Picasso.
> He ran really well.

seeing as how and *since*
Seeing as how is slang and should be avoided.

> Since you like chocolates, here is a large box for you.

shall and *will*
Used in formal English in the first person to indicate future action, *shall* is now so rare as to be almost obsolete. In modern usage, *will* is used to express both future and determination.

> I expect I will have a good trip. (future)
> I will complete this report if it kills me. (determination)

should of—see *have, of* (page 19)

some place and *somewhere*
Some place is incorrect.

> I left my glasses somewhere.

than and *then*
Use *than* for making comparisons; use *then* when referring to time.

> Entrepreneurs usually work longer hours than their employees do.
> First came the soup, then came the main course.

there is and *there are*
Is refers to a singular noun; *are* refers to a plural one.

> There is only one space after a comma.
> There are many voters here today.

to, too, two
To may be a preposition or part of an infinitive.

> Few people walk to work today.

Too is an adverb meaning "also" or "more than enough."

> The summary was far too long.

Two is a number used as a noun or adjective.

> She was told to give two references on her résumé.

who and *which* (relative pronouns)
Who refers to a person; *which,* to a thing.

> The person who delivered the computer was very polite.
> The telephone, which is near the door, is within easy reach.

T5   DOUBLE NEGATIVE WORDS

No, nobody, and other negative words

No is known as a negative word. It is the kind of word used to refuse or deny something or to contradict someone. Other negative words are

◆ *not, nothing, none, nowhere,* and *nobody*

◆ verbs combined with *not: hasn't, don't, wouldn't,* etc.

◆ words combined with un-: *unable, unwilling,* etc.

Avoid using double negative words by following this simple rule:

Rule: To express a negative idea, use no more than *one* negative.

Correct: He does *not* need any money.
                      He needs *no* money.

Incorrect: He does *not* need *no* money.

Correct: I said *nothing.*
                      I *didn't* say anything.

Incorrect: I *didn't* say *nothing.*

Correct: It *doesn't* mean anything.

Incorrect: It *don't* mean *nothing.*

Correct: She is *unwilling* to make any apology.
                      She is willing to make *no* apology.

Incorrect: She is *unwilling* to make *no* apology.

Special negatives

Like *no, not,* and *nobody,* the following are negative words: *never, neither, hardly, neither . . . nor, scarcely, without,* and sometimes *but* and *only.*

Correct: There had *never* been anything like it before.

Incorrect: There had *never* been *nothing* like it before.

Correct: She has *scarcely* anything to show for her effort.

Incorrect: She has *scarcely nothing* to show for her effort.

NOTE   The combination *neither . . . nor* is treated as if it were a single negative.

Rule: *Never, hardly, scarcely,* and similar words follow the same rule as do other negatives. To express a negative idea, use only one negative.

T6   ONE WORD OR TWO?

If you are in doubt, refer to the list below.

Word(s)	Meaning	Example
a lot	many	There was a lot of work left to be completed.
allot	distribute	They had to allot portions of the donations to various charities.
a part	a section or piece; a member	Are you a part of this group?
apart (adv.)	separate from	They stood three metres apart from each other.
a while (n.)	a period of time	Lee Ming worked here for a while.
awhile (adv.)	for a period of time	The candidates had to wait awhile.
all ready	prepared	They are all ready to go.
already (adv.)	past the time	It is already too late for lunch.
all right	acceptable, satisfactory	Everyone agreed that the office layout was all right.
(*alright*: incorrect spelling of *all right*)		
all together	in unison	The choir should sing all together.
altogether (adv.)	entirely	Your holiday was altogether too expensive.
all ways (n.)	all methods	They tried in all ways to win the game.
always (adv.)	at all times	Our members always do a good job.
any body	a noun modified by *any*	Can you reach any body of government?
anybody	indefinite pronoun	Can anybody call that number?
any more	no more	She doesn't want any more.
anymore	now	Bill doesn't live here anymore.
any time	used with a specific time in mind	If you have any time next week, please call.
anytime (adv.)	used when no specific time is intended	You are welcome here anytime.
any way	a way	Is there any way in which we can help?
anyway (adv.)	in any case	Anyway, the job had already been completed.
(*anyways* is not a word)		
burnout	stressed out	The social workers are suffering from burnout.
checkmark	a mark	Please put a checkmark beside each correct answer.
every day	each day	It is good to practise every day.
everyday (adj.)	daily	Meetings are an everyday occurrence.

(continued . . .)

T

Word(s)	Meaning	Example
every one	each person	Every one of them wore casual clothes on Fridays.
everyone	everybody	It's correct to show appreciation to everyone who participated.
filename	name of document	The document's filename was missing.
high school	school of higher learning	Stacey will be going to high school soon.
in to	to a place	All reports are to be handed in to me before the weekend.
into (prep.)	to the inside of	The visitor walked straight into my office.
mailbox	holder of mail	The mailbox was incorrectly labelled.
may be	could be	The children may be going this afternoon.
maybe (adv.)	perhaps	Maybe the children will go out soon.
no body	no substance; no physical structure	No body was found in that murder case.
nobody (pronoun)	no one	Nobody came to work last Saturday.
shortcut	a shorter way	They took a shortcut to school.
some time	a period of time	It will take some time to arrange the conference.
sometimes (adv.)	at times	Sometimes it's difficult to sit up straight.
Touch-Tone	a phone	The Touch-Tone phone comes in many colours.
turnover	a business transaction	A quick turnover of merchandise was necessary to make a profit.
workplace	a place where one works	Safety in the workplace is a major concern.
worksheet	a page on which work is created	Please hand in your worksheet with the test.
workstation	location of equipment/desk	She was asked to clean up her workstation.

T7   WORDS WITH ACCOMPANYING PREPOSITIONS

Certain English words must be accompanied by a particular preposition. In the following examples, the correct prepositions are italicized.

accompanied *by*	She was accompanied by her mother.
according *to*	According to the news, the damage was great.
account *for*	David was unable to account for the missing items.
account *to*	David will have to account to the auditors for the discrepancy in figures.
agree *on/upon*	They could not agree on a settlement.
agree *to*	Did they agree to the terms of the contract?
agree *with*	I agree with your proposal.
capable *of*	Our new recruit is capable of doing that job well.
comply *with*	If you agree, please comply with my request promptly.
concur *in* (something)	Everyone did not concur in that decision.
concur *with* (people)	The president concurred with the manager.
conform *to*	The building does not conform to specifications.
different *from* (not *to* or *than*)	Bill is quite different from Stan.
plan *to* (not *on*)	We plan to expand our office space next month.
superior *to* (not *than*)	One twin is superior to the other in intelligence.
surrounded *by*	That farmhouse is surrounded by fields.
try *to* (not *and*)	Please try to see it my way.

T8   WORDS WITH UNNECESSARY PREPOSITIONS

Omit prepositions that add nothing to the meaning of the sentence.

Examples: Where is he [at]?
Where did that book go [to]?
The car is too near [to] the garage.
Jack's house is opposite [to] hers.
Why don't we meet at about seven o'clock? (Omit either *at* or *about*.)
The box fell off [of] the truck.
Canada comprises ten provinces and three territories. (*Not* Canada is comprised of ten provinces and three territories.)

T9   SPELLING

Because English is derived from so many languages and has undergone so many changes, words are sometimes spelled in unusual ways. Here are some rules to help you become a better speller, as well as a list of commonly misspelled words.

NOTE   Most software is equipped with a spell-check feature. This is extremely useful, but remember that it cannot spot homonyms (words that sound alike) or words that have been correctly spelled but misused.

▶T10   Rules for spelling

A number of rules can help you become a good speller, but there are also many exceptions to these rules. You can improve your spelling if you try to develop a word sense, increase your vocabulary, and become a proficient dictionary user. Use memory aids such as the following:

◆ The **ice** in adv**ice** is a noun.

◆ The **is** in adv**ise** is a verb.

◆ A popular rhyme helps with ei and ie words:
I before *e*
Except after *c,*
Or when sounded as *eh,*
As in *neighbour* and *weigh.*

Normal use:	ach**ie**ve	bel**ie**f	bel**ie**ve	rel**ie**f	y**ie**ld
After c:	conc**ei**t	rec**ei**ve	c**ei**ling		
The eh *sound:*	fr**ei**ght	w**ei**ght	sl**ei**gh		

Common exceptions: counterfeit
forfeit
height
seize
neither
their
weird

Adding suffixes

Adding suffixes to words is a spelling process that seems to cause some difficulty. The standard guideline is simply to add the required suffix to a word, as in these samples:

bulk-y	depend-ent	reason-able	thought-ful
care-less	express-ed	report-ing	
citizen-ship	pack-age	retire-ment	

Several words, however, require special treatment when suffixes are added to them. The following rules will help you form endings correctly.

For one-syllable words ending in a consonant preceded by a vowel, double the final consonant:

| bat batted | drag dragging |
| cut cutting | star starry |

Exceptions: buses
boxed
fixing

For words with two or more syllables that end in a consonant and have the accent on the last syllable, double the final consonant:

control-ler   prefer-ring

Words ending in a silent *e* usually drop the *e* to add the suffix *y* or a suffix beginning with a vowel:

believe	believing	believable
desire	desirable	desirous
ice	icing	icy
propose	proposal	proposition

A notable exception is *mileage*.

NOTE For words ending in *ce* or *ge,* keep the *e* before the suffix *-able:*

charge chargeable   replace replaceable

For words ending in *y* preceded by a consonant, change the *y* to *i* before adding the suffix:

apply applicable   carry carrier   forty fortieth

For words ending in *y* preceded by a vowel, simply add the suffix:

display displayed   enjoy enjoyable enjoyment

For words ending in *c,* add a *k* before the suffix to retain the hard *c* sound:

picnic picnicking   traffic trafficked

▶T11   Word variants

Word variants according to *Gage Canadian Dictionary* (Gage Educational Publishing Company, Toronto, ON), the *Concise Oxford Dictionary of Current English* (Clarendon Press, Oxford, England), and *Webster's New World Dictionary of American English* (Prentice Hall, New York, U.S.):

Words ending in *er* and *re* (all spellings are acceptable)

Gage	Oxford	Webster
calibre	calibre	caliber
centre*	centre	center
litre	litre	liter
lustre	lustre	luster
manoeuvre	manoeuvre	maneuver
metre	metre	meter
sabre	sabre	saber
theatre	theatre	theater

*(Note: the names of most buildings in Canada use *re* in their names, while the U.S. generally uses *er*.)

Examples: Dalhousie Arts Centre
Quebec City Convention Centre
Harbourfront Centre
Saskatchewan Indian Cultural Centre
The Volunteer Centre of North Vancouver
The World Trade Center (U.S.)

(Note: Always use the proper designated name of the building.)

I

NOTE   Corel WordPerfect and Microsoft Word spell-check software redlines the Gage and Oxford spellings.

▶T12   Frequently misspelled words

The words listed here frequently pose spelling problems. If you have difficulties with spelling, consult a dictionary often, refer to this section, or compose your own list of troublesome words (and practise two or three of them every day). Use the spell checker that comes with your software; a spell checker will not always identify situations in which a word is spelled correctly but is the wrong word in that context (e.g., *he* when *her* is intended). Some software with grammar-check features will identify correct word usage, and this is a bonus for the user.

absence	beginning	copyright	eighth
access	believe	concede	eligible
accessibility	beneficiary	congratulate	ellipsis
accidentally	biased	conscience	embarrass
accommodate	bilingualism	conscious	enrolment
achievement	bookkeeper	consolidation	en route
acquaintance	brand name	controversy	entrepreneur
acquiesce	brochure	convenience	environment
acquisition	bulk	correspondence	etiquette
advantageous	bulletin	courteous	exaggerate
advisable	business	courtesy	exceed
affidavit	calendar	criticism	exercise
aggressive	campaign	cursor	exhaustible
aisle	Caribbean	database	extension
all right	carriage	debt	extraordinary
amateur	carriers	deceive	facetious
amortize	catalogue	deductible	facsimile
analyse	category	defendant	familiar
analysis	Celsius	deficit	fascinating
anonymity	chaise longue	definitely	February
apparel	champagne	dependant (n.)	feedback
apparently	changeable	dependent (adj.)	financier
architect	chauffeur	desirable	foreign
argument	chronological	development	foresee
arrears	collateral	dilemma	forty
ascertain	colonel	disappoint	fourteen
assessment	column	discreet	fourth
assistance	commitment	discrete	friend
attendant	committee	dissatisfied	fulfil
attitude	commonplace	dividend	gauge
attributions	communicator	domain	government
bachelor	compatible	drawback	grammar
bankruptcy	competency	efficiency	grateful

(continued . . .)

T

grievance	milestone	practise (v.)	speedy
guarantee	millennium	precede	sponsor
guise	millionaire	preferable	spreadsheet
hacker	miscellaneous	prejudice	status
hacking	mischievous	prerogative	subpoena
handkerchief	miscommunication	preside	substantial
harass	misspell	privilege	subtle
height	mobile	procedure	subtlety
hindrance	modem	proceed	subtly
hors d'oeuvre	mortgage	professor	succeed
hundredth	movable	program	surgeon
hypocrisy	necessary	promissory	surprise
inasmuch as	neighbour	prompt	susceptible
incidentally	neither	pronounce	synonym
incompetent	niche	pronunciation	tariff
indictment	nickel	psychiatric	technique
indispensable	niece	psychology	temperament
innovation	ninety	pursue	temperature
installing	ninth	query	thoroughly
intercede	noticeable	questionnaire	toggle
interfering	nuclear	queue	trademark
interim	obsolescent	receipt	transmit
irrelevant	occasion(ally)	receive	truly
itinerary	occurred	recipient	unanimous
jeopardy	occurrence	recognize	unique
knowledgeable	offered	recommend	usable
laboratory	omission	reference	vacuum
ledger	omitted	regulatory	vast
leeway	ongoing	reinforce	via
liaison	overhead	relevant	vice versa
licence (n.)	oversight	resistance	volume
license (v.)	pamphlet	restaurant	warehouse
lien	paperwork	résumé	Wednesday
lieutenant	parallel	rhetoric	weekend
lightning	patience	rhythm	weird
loose (adj.)	perceive	satellite	whether
lose (v.)	permissible	schedule	wholly
lying	perseverance	scissors	widespread
maintenance	personal	sector	wield
management	personnel	seize	withhold
meantime	persuade	separate	woollen
mediocre	phase	sergeant	worldwide
megabyte	physician	similar	wraparound
microcomputer	playback	simultaneous	writing
microprocessor	possession	sincerely	
microtranscription	practically	skilful	
mileage	practice (n.)	souvenir	

NOTE The word *you* for *your* is one of the most common keyboarding errors.

T13 WORD MEANINGS

Words are formed by starting with a *root* word (**port** = carry) and then adding to it a prefix (**ex**-port = carry out of) or a suffix (port-**able** = able to be carried). Knowledge of the root meaning is the key to understanding the word; also, if you become familiar with common prefixes and suffixes, you will develop greater expertise as a language user. English root words are derived from several other languages. Some common root words are shown below.

Root	Meaning	Words derived from root
ceed	go	proceed, succeed
ject	throw	reject, projection
mit/mis	send	dismiss, remittance
mote	move	demotion, motivate
pend	hang	suspend, depend
port	carry	important, transport
scribe	write	subscribe, transcribe, describe
serve	guard/serve	reserve, service
spect	look	aspect, respect
tend	stretch	attend, extension
vent	come	prevent, adventure
vert	turn	extrovert, conversion

When you first encounter a word and do not know the root meaning, try to think of a familiar word that has the same root. For example, a**pathetic**; think of sym**pathetic**—something to do with feeling; a- (ab = from) and -pathetic = away from feeling. This approach will increase not only your vocabulary but also your enjoyment of English.

Prefixes, which *change the meanings of words,* come largely from Latin, French, and Greek. Depending on usage, the original prefix sometimes changes slightly. Common examples are as follows.

Prefix	Meaning	Word example	Meaning
a/ab	from	absence	being away from
ad	to	advise	give advice to
bi	two	biannual	twice a year
com/con	with	commit	pledge oneself with
		concede	go along with

(continued . . .)

T

Prefix	Meaning	Word example	Meaning
con	against	contest	witness (go) against
de	from	deceive	take from
en/in	in	entrance	coming in
		induce	(lead in) persuade
ex	out	exceed	go out or beyond
pre	before	prejudice	judgment before
pro	for	promise	(send for or on behalf of) assurance
super	over	supersede	(go over) take the place of
trans	across	transport	carry across or over
un/in	not	unable	not able
		inactive	not active

Suffixes, which *do not change the meanings of words,* change the functions of words (i.e., parts of speech). For example, *love* (a verb or noun) can be changed to *lovely* (adjective) without losing the root meaning. Some common suffixes are the following.

Suffix	Meaning	Word example	Meaning
able/ible	able to	(in)dispensable	(un)able to be done without
		permissible	able to be permitted
ance/ence	act or condition/ state	acquaintance	someone known
		correspondence	communication
ant/ent	one who/ that which	defendant	one who is defended
		dependent	that which depends on
ary/ery	one who/that which/state	beneficiary	one who benefits
		archery	using bows and arrows
ful	full of	skilful	full of skill
ion/sion/ tion	condition/ act/ result of	opinion	view held as probable
		possession	ownership holding
		retention	keeping in place
ive	quality of/ tending to	exhaustive	thorough
ment	condition/ quality/state	development	growth
ous/ious	full of/having qualities of	unanimous	agreed by all
		conscientious	ruled by conscience
ure	act/process/being	procedure	actions in a certain order

I

T14 GENDER-INCLUSIVE LANGUAGE

Language that excludes one gender is no longer appropriate. Examples of inclusive and exclusive language follow.

Exclusive (undesirable)	Inclusive (use this)
anchorman	anchor
brotherhood	association
businessman	businessperson or executive
foreman	supervisor
manmade	manufactured; machine-made
saleswoman	salesclerk/salesperson/sales associate
chairman	chairperson

◆ Some words (such as *sportsmanship* and *workmanship*) are difficult to amend. Use completely different expressions in such cases:

Instead of: The dress showed fine workmanship.
Use: The dress was well made.

◆ Terms such as *doctor, lawyer, professor, nurse, teacher* are free of gender discrimination. Do not use such expressions as *male nurse* and *lady doctor* unless there is a reason for doing so, as in

There will be a meeting for all male nurses at 3:30 p.m.

◆ Avoid feminine suffixes (-ess, -ette):

She is a fine actor (*not* actress).
Ask the flight attendant (*not* stewardess).

◆ Constructing sentences that avoid gender discrimination can sometimes result in clumsiness. Use plurals if you can or try to restructure your sentences to avoid the use of "he/she":

Instead of: A teacher can be an excellent role model for his/her students.
Use: Teachers can be good role models for their students.

Instead of: The average Canadian drinks his/her coffee black.
Use: The average Canadian drinks black coffee.

Bias and discrimination

Sensitive people will be careful to avoid, in speaking and writing, all types of biases and discrimination, including racism, ageism, and gender role stereotyping:

Instead of: Leave it with the old man at the desk.
Say: Leave it with the person at the desk.

T

T15 GRAMMAR AND USAGE

Good grammar is the result of choosing the right words and putting them in the right order to produce a clear, correctly phrased message. To help develop your understanding of grammar, this section provides information on the sentence and its parts, types of sentences, and parts of speech.

Phrases and clauses	Sample sentence
Introductory phrase:	In a small business,
Independent (main) clause:	(the owner or manager) {can keep in close touch with everything
Subordinate (auxiliary) clause:	that goes on [in the firm.]}

Parts of a sentence (example indicated within marks shown)	Parts of speech (example indicated by underscoring shown)
Subject ( )	Noun _____
Predicate (verb plus	Adjective ....
complement) { }	Preposition ======= .
Object [ ]	Verb _____
	Pronoun ....
	Conjunction (Connective) =======

Components of grammar, identified in a sample sentence

T16 THE SENTENCE

A sentence is a group of words that contains a subject and a predicate (verb or verb and complement containing an object) and expresses a complete thought. Sentences can include a variety of devices to stress points, create excitement, or evoke a reaction. Well-constructed sentences are the result of correct word choice and careful word order. This unit provides all the details you need to compose interesting, accurate, and effective sentences. It also shows you how sentences are blended and developed into paragraphs.

▶T17 Parts of the sentence

T18 Subject—noun(s) or pronoun(s)

The subject is a noun or pronoun that governs the verb. The verb must agree with the subject in *number* (singular or plural) and *person* (first, second, or third).

Simple (single) subject—one noun/pronoun

The <u>manager</u> is a good administrator. (singular)
Our <u>managers</u> are good administrators. (plural)
<u>I</u> am working hard to qualify for a promotion. (first-person singular)
<u>We</u> were pleased to hear about your promotion. (first-person plural)
Will <u>you</u> deliver the mail, please? (second-person singular)
<u>She</u> deserves a raise. (third-person singular)
<u>They</u> work late nearly every Monday. (third-person plural)

Person	Singular	Plural
1st	I	we
2nd	you	you
3rd	he/she/it	they

Compound (combined) subject—two or more nouns/pronouns combined to make one subject

♦ requires a plural verb whether the combined subject has two singular, two plural, or one singular and one plural noun:

<u>Rebecca and Ali</u> have opened a new store.
Both <u>Jasodra and Kim</u> enjoy accounting.
Our <u>manager and the team leaders</u> will meet on Wednesday.
<u>Males and females</u> alike appreciate a bonus.

Subjects joined by connectives such as "or"

♦ if both words in the subject are singular, use a singular verb:

Either <u>Franco or his brother</u> is coming tonight.

♦ if both words are plural, use a plural verb:

Not only the <u>store managers</u> but also the <u>clerks</u> came.

♦ if the subject consists of one singular and one plural word, the verb must agree with the noun/pronoun nearer to it:

Neither the <u>teacher nor the students</u> work alone.

NOTE   In cases in which sentence construction is awkward because of this rule, rewrite the sentence:

Either Gisele or I am planning to work tomorrow.

Change to: Either Gisele or I will work tomorrow.

Subjects with intervening phrases or clauses

♦ verb must agree with the subject noun/pronoun, disregarding the intervening words:

The <u>manager</u>, along with two assistants, *is* representing our company at the convention. (singular)

All <u>employees</u>, as well as the president, *are* going on vacation next month. (plural)

<u>No one</u> except your parents <u>knows</u> where we're going. (singular)

T19   Predicate

The predicate is a verb or verb and complement (verb phrase) that says something about the subject. Complements may include a direct object and/or an indirect object.

Verb

◆ is an action word (see T27)

◆ must agree with the subject:

All people <u>are created</u> equal.

◆ has present, future, and past tenses

◆ can be used in active or passive voice

◆ has indicative, imperative, and subjunctive moods

Verb phrase (two or more verbs—one principal and one auxiliary— used as one)

Bob <u>will be returning</u> your telephone call tomorrow.

T20   Object

An object is one or more nouns or pronouns. The object receives the action of the verb.

Direct object

◆ follows a transitive verb

◆ answers the question *who* or *what:*

Our client signed the <u>contract</u>.

Object of a preposition

◆ follows a transitive verb:

The chief engineer asked about the <u>plans</u> for the new <u>plant</u>.

Indirect object

◆ must appear with a direct object

◆ answers the questions *to what, to whom:*

Our client gave the signed contract to the <u>president</u>.

– or –

Our client gave the <u>president</u> the signed contract.

Object complement

◆ several words referring to the direct object:

> The president signed the contract <u>consisting of seven pages</u>.

T21   Phrases

A group of words without a subject or predicate—an incomplete thought—is a phrase. Phrases can function as nouns, adjectives, or prepositions. When used as subjects, they always take the singular verb form. Phrases do not contain verbs:

> <u>Completing the project</u> was a relief. (noun)
> The applicant <u>with the best credentials</u> got the job. (adjective)
> The meeting <u>in the boardroom</u> was a success. (preposition)

Phrases are used effectively to introduce a sentence or to emphasize a point:

> <u>In spite of the snow</u>, the convention proceeded on time.
> It was clear, <u>from the voters' reaction</u>, that victory was at hand.

T22   Clauses

A group of words including a subject and a predicate is a clause.

Independent (main) clauses can stand alone because they express a complete thought (i.e., they can be sentences):

> Each staff member was given a 6 percent salary increase.

Dependent (subordinate) clauses—not complete thoughts—usually occur in complex sentences in which they are connected to an independent clause:

> <u>Because everyone had worked so hard</u>, each staff member was given a 6 percent salary increase.

Verb tenses must match. For example, if the verb in the main clause is in the past tense, the verb in the subordinate clause should be in the past tense also:

> Because everyone <u>had worked</u> so hard, each staff member <u>was given</u> a 6 percent salary increase.

If the verb in the main clause expresses necessity, demand, a strong request, or urging, the present tense (without the *s* in the third-person singular) should be used in the dependent clause:

> They insist that she <u>report</u> to work immediately.

If the verb *to be* is used in the dependent clause, use only *be* with all three persons:

> It is essential that I <u>be</u> present at the next meeting.

If a sentence begins with a subject and the verb *to wish*, the subordinate clause should contain a subjunctive verb:

> She wishes she <u>could attend</u> the seminar.
> They wished he <u>were going</u> with them to Ottawa.
> I wished I <u>had been able</u> to stay longer.

▶T23   Types of sentences

A sentence is the most important part of the structure of language. Its shape may be simple or complicated. The writer's language expertise will determine which type of sentence suits the occasion and the reader.

Simple sentences consist of only one independent clause (a main thought) that may contain numerous words and phrases:

> The stock market rallied at the end of the week.

Complex sentences are made up of one independent clause and one or more dependent (subordinate) clauses:

> Although the stock market rallied at the end of the week, the brokers were not optimistic.
> After the stock market had rallied, the brokers, who had spent many sleepless nights, took a holiday.

Compound sentences contain two or more independent clauses (main thoughts):

> The crisis was over, so the brokers went home.

Compound-complex sentences are composed of two independent clauses and one or more dependent clauses:

> The crisis was over, so the brokers went home after they had finished the paperwork.

▶T24   Sentence construction hints

Select your words with care. Use words as precisely as possible. Avoid wordiness.

> *Wordy:* The customer was angry because when he returned the merchandise the clerk was rude and she refused to give him a refund.

> *Better:* When the customer returned the merchandise, he was annoyed at the clerk's rudeness and refusal to refund the money.

Be grammatically consistent. Avoid disagreements in number, tense, or mood.

> *Inconsistency in number:* Each person is responsible for their own assignment.

> *Correction:* Each person is responsible for his or her own assignment.

> *Inconsistency in tense:* The architect designed the city hall, and then the council rejects it.

> *Correction:* The architect designed the city hall, and then the council rejected it.

> *Inconsistency in mood:* We would appreciate it if you can come early.

> *Correction:* We would appreciate it if you could come early.

Use parallel (balanced) structure. Make your writing flow smoothly.

Not parallel: Do you think faxing or a courier would be faster?
(Here, <u>faxing</u> is a participle, <u>courier</u> is a noun.)

Correction: Do you think a fax or a courier would be faster?
(Here, <u>fax</u> and <u>courier</u> are both nouns.)

Position modifiers (descriptive expressions) properly. Closely related parts of a sentence should be placed close together to avoid ambiguity.

Improperly placed modifier: Having lost his job after 15 years of service, the company gave him a good separation package.

Correction: The company gave the man whom they "retired" after 15 years a good separation package.

Use the active voice as much as possible. Give your words energy.

Weak: His name will be seen in lights. (passive voice)

Better: He will see his name in lights. (active voice)

Avoid excessive co-ordination (too many "ands" and "buts").

Too many "ands": I attended a meeting and she stood up and took her time and started a long monologue on her new invention.

Correction: I attended a meeting, during which she stood up slowly and began a long monologue on her new invention.

Place the part to be stressed at the beginning.

Stress improperly placed: One of its major disadvantages is high cost, but our busy sales representatives really feel that the time it saves is worth the expense of a cellular phone.

Correction: Cellular phones save so much time that our sales representatives feel the cost is more than offset.

▶T25 Sentence flaws to avoid

Sentence fragment (incomplete thought):

Although the singer is good.

Correction: The singer is good.

Comma fault (do not separate subject from verb unless a non-restrictive clause is used):

The woman with the broken leg, could not walk.

Correction: The woman with the broken leg could not walk.
(See T54.)

Shifted constructions:

Because of the recession and we are losing money, the plant will have to shut down.

Correction: Because of the recession and a loss of money, the plant will have to shut down.

– *or* –

Because we are suffering from the recession and are losing money, we will have to shut down.

Pronoun-antecedent non-agreement (pronoun must agree with antecedent in number and gender):

Everyone was given their own office.

Correction: Everyone was given his or her own office.

– *or* –

All staff members were given their own offices.

Subject-verb non-agreement (in number):

His contribution to the recycling committees were extremely high.

Correction: His contribution to the recycling committees was extremely high.

The president, as well as her staff, have arrived.

Correction: The president, as well as her staff, has arrived.

Incorrect case (nominative, objective, or possessive):

Me and my brother are telecommuters.

Correction: My brother and I are telecommuters.

We do not approve of them arriving late.

Correction: We do not approve of their arriving late.

NOTE A noun or pronoun preceding a gerund (e.g., *arriving*) is written in the possessive case.

Adjective and adverb confusion:

He did a real good job.

Correction: He did a really good job.

Cheryl played good yesterday.

Correction: Cheryl played a good game yesterday.

– *or* –

Cheryl played well yesterday.

T26 THE PARAGRAPH

A paragraph is a series of sentences developing *one central purpose or idea*. The *topic* sentence opens the paragraph and the *transitional* one (linking the paragraph that follows) ends it.

> Golf is a game that many people play. Most of my friends are golf fanatics, and they particularly enjoy competition. (topic)

> The club in town runs four major tournaments each season to test every golfer's skill. (transitional)

Good paragraphing is an essential element of effective writing. It helps writers to progress logically by forcing them to stay on topic, and keeps readers on track by helping them to focus on one idea at a time.

Paragraphing business letters can sometimes be difficult. Most letters should contain at least two paragraphs, but very short letters, memos, faxes, and email messages are acceptable with only one.

T27 PARTS OF SPEECH

Words are classified according to the jobs they do. These categories are called *parts of speech*. Although most words fall into just one classification, many are versatile and perform several functions. The information that follows is by no means complete. The user who requires full details should consult a more complete source.

Part of speech	Function	Example
Noun	Is a person, place, or thing	president, dog
Pronoun	Replaces person, place, or thing	me, it
Verb	Is an action word, state of being	go, talk, is
Adjective	Describes noun or pronoun	fair (referee)
Adverb	Describes verb or adjective	(talk) softly
Preposition	Connects noun or pronoun to make it the object	under (the window)
Conjunction (connective)	Connects words, phrases	(men) and (women)
Interjection	Is an expressive word	Wow!

►T28 Nouns

◆ are names of persons, places, things, animals, actions, or concepts

◆ are used as the subject or object of a sentence

◆ have singular, plural, and possessive forms

T

Types of nouns

Proper nouns		
Person	*Place*	
Mother Teresa	Canada	
Stephen Harper	Mt. Edziza	
Pierre Berton	Beijing	
Common nouns		
Thing	*Animal*	*Action*
apple	bird	game
desk	dog	labour
tree	lion	race
Abstract nouns (concept)		
hate, love, sympathy		
Collective nouns (groups)		
committee, population, team		

Usage of noun

A noun can act either as the subject or the object of a sentence.

The <u>manager</u> hired two new <u>employees</u>.

    subject (noun)   object (noun)

Forms of nouns

The original form of most nouns is singular (i.e., describing one person, place, etc.). It can be changed to a plural form and to a possessive form.

Plural form of nouns

Most nouns are made plural by adding *s* to the singular:

apple	apples	committee	committees
boy	boys	Henrik Ibsen	the Ibsens
chair	chairs	valley	valleys

Exceptions to this rule include the following:
Nouns ending in ch, s, sh, x, *or* z—*add* es:

box	boxes	church	churches
brush	brushes	class	classes
bus	buses	fizz	fizzes
business	businesses	Jones	the Joneses

Nouns ending in y *preceded by a consonant—change* y *to* ies:

city	cities	country	countries	lady	ladies

Nouns ending in y *preceded by a vowel—add* s:

attorney	attorneys	tray	trays

Nouns ending in o *preceded by a consonant—add* es:

| cargo | cargoes | potato | potatoes |
| hero | heroes | tomato | tomatoes |

Exceptions include some musical terms, abbreviations, and nouns from foreign languages. Check the dictionary if you are in doubt.

| condos | Filipinos | memos | pianos |

Most nouns ending in o *preceded by a vowel form plurals by adding* s:

| radio | radios | rodeo | rodeos |
| ratio | ratios | studio | studios |

Most nouns ending in f *or* fe—*change* f *to* v *and add* es:

| knife | knives | loaf | loaves |
| life | lives | shelf | shelves |

Exceptions: *beliefs, chiefs, reefs. Hoof* and *roof* can be either *hoofs* or *hooves* and *roofs* or *rooves.*

Never *change the* f *to* v *in proper nouns. Simply add* s:

Maple Leaf team
The Maple Leafs played at home last night.

Nouns with the same singular and plural forms:

deer	deer	sheep	sheep
fish	fish	trout	trout
series	series		

Nouns always singular in meaning include:

| measles | news | physics | politics |

Nouns always plural in meaning are:

| clothes | earnings | people | proceeds |

Some nouns have irregular plural endings:

| child children | foot feet | man men | mouse mice |

♦ Compound nouns

Hyphenated and compound words, as a rule, call for pluralizing the principal word:

leave of absence	leaves of absence
officer-in-charge	officers-in-charge
sister-in-law	sisters-in-law

If the compound word is foreign, add *s* to the end of it:

cul-de-sac   cul-de-sacs   (although culs-de-sac is also acceptable)

Unhyphenated words form plurals by adding *s* to the end:

cupful   cupfuls   yearbook   yearbooks

T

◆ Latin and other foreign nouns

Some terms derived from other languages retain their own plurals; others have been anglicized. The following are the preferred plural forms of some commonly used expressions:

alumna	alumnae
appendix	appendices
campus	campuses
criterion	criteria
datum	data (may be used with a singular verb except in formal or technical usage)
formula	formulas
medium	media
memorandum	memorandums
thesis	theses

◆ Abbreviations, letters, numbers, words

Form the plural by adding *s:*

ands and buts	the five *C*s	the pros and cons
in twos and threes	the 1900s	YMCAs
the PCs	the 2000s	

If the plural form is not clear with the simple addition of *s,* use *'s* to remove confusion:

37 B.A.'s and 42 B.Sc.'s
There are two a's in my name

Possessive form of nouns

Nouns in the possessive form indicate ownership. To simplify speech and abbreviate writing, the apostrophe is used to replace the words *belonging to* or *of.* For example, instead of saying, "The workstation of Cindy is untidy," we say, "Cindy's workstation is untidy." Possessive nouns refer to living things rather than inanimate objects.

The walls of our office *– not –* Our office's walls

Basic rule: To make any noun (singular or plural) possessive, add *'s:*

Jack's car is an antique.
The judge's decision was final.
She spent $1000 on her children's clothes.

For a noun that ends in *s,* add only an apostrophe, for ease of pronunciation:

directors	directors' meeting
fathers	fathers' advice
girls	girls' shoes
secretaries	secretaries' desks
Del Marinas	Del Marinas' cottage

Exception: Add *'s* to one-syllable proper names ending in s: James's business. See also "Apostrophe," T37.

Articles

Most languages using an alphabet have a *definite article* and an *indefinite article* preceding nouns. In English, the definite article, which refers to something specific, is *the;* the indefinite article is *a* or *an:*

> The weather is perfect today. (definite article)
> A sunny day makes everyone happy. (indefinite article)
> *An apple a day keeps the doctor away.
> *They waited for an hour.

* **NOTE** *An* is used instead of *a* before a noun beginning with a vowel or a vowel pronunciation.

▶T29 Pronouns

◆ substitute for persons, places, things, and other nouns
◆ are used to avoid repetition of nouns/pronouns
◆ have singular and plural forms
◆ are used as the subject or object (direct or indirect)
◆ have three cases:

Nominative (subjective) (initiates action): *I, he, she, we, they, who:*

> Who can write good reports?

Objective (receives action): *me, him, her, us, them, whom:*

> Give them the printout.

Possessive (ownership): *my (mine), your (yours)*, etc.:

> I use my computer every day.

NOTE Do not use the incorrect pronoun for the verb case (Sandra and me are going to the movies), or when the pronoun is the direct or indirect object of a verb (Sandra came with Bill and I). Use the objective pronoun after prepositions (Sandra came with Bill and me, or Between you and me . . .).

Types of pronouns
Personal pronouns replace persons or things.

Singular		
Subject	*Object*	*Possessive*
I	me	my, mine
you	you	your, yours
he, she, it	him, her, it	his, her, hers, its
Plural		
we	us	our, ours
you	you	your, yours
they	them	their, theirs

T

Impersonal (indefinite) pronouns have no specific relationship to a noun—they are always singular: *one, one's.*

Relative pronouns refer to nouns or pronouns that appear elsewhere in a sentence, usually as the antecedents.

Subject	Object	Possessive
who	whom	whose
which	which	whose
what	what	what
that	that	that

Please give my donation to the <u>person who</u> needs it most.

NOTE *Who* always refers to people. Additional forms of *who, which,* and *what* are also used to reflect or emphasize a noun. These forms are *whoever, whomever, whichever, whatever.*

Reflexive pronouns refer to or stress the subject. The word *self* is always part of this pronoun:

The premier herself attended the rally.

Demonstrative pronouns point to specific nouns or pronouns and do not change their form: *this, that, these, those.*

Interrogative pronouns are used when asking a question: *Who? Whom? Whose? Which? What?*

▶T30 Verbs

- ◆ tell what happens in a sentence
- ◆ are all or part of the predicate
- ◆ are used in first, second, or third person
- ◆ indicate time of action by tenses
- ◆ have active and passive voices
- ◆ have indicative, imperative, and subjunctive moods

Conjugation of verbs

Verbs, which must agree with the nouns that govern them, are conjugated (presented in different forms) in first, second, and third person singular and plural, as follows.

Regular verb (*to work*)	Singular	Plural
First person	I work	we work
Second person	you work	you work
Third person	he/she/it works	they work

| | NOTE | The form changes only with the third-person singular.

Irregular verb (*to be*) (does not follow the pattern of the regular verb)		
First person	I am	we are
Second person	you are	you are
Third person	he/she/it is	they are

Just as words begin with a root, verbs start with the *infinitive,* the basic verb form preceded by *to* (e.g., *to work, to travel*). From this starting point come the other forms of the verb.

Verb tenses

The principal parts of a verb guide you to the time of action (i.e., the *tenses* of verbs).

Infinitive	Present tense	Past tense	Past participle	Present participle
to ask	I ask	asked	(was) asked	(am) asking
to like	I like	liked	(have) liked	(am) liking

The present tense is formed from the infinitive; the progressive present tense, indicating ongoing action, is formed by using the verb *to be* and the present participle (e.g., *I am going; they are planning a trip,* etc.). The past tense of regular verbs adds *ed,* as does the past participle, which is always used in conjunction with the auxiliary verbs *to be* or *to have.* Irregular verbs do not follow this rule. Refer to a dictionary for the principal parts of irregular verbs.

Voice

Verbs can be used in either the active or the passive *voice.* Active voice is used when the subject directs the verb. Passive voice makes the subject the receiver of the action (hence, passive) and thus diminishes the strength of the statement.

> James wrote an excellent program. (active)
> An excellent program was written by James. (passive)

Mood

The *mood* of a verb conveys the feeling of the subject.

Indicative mood shows the ongoing action of the subject:

> Josie is planning a workshop for us.

Imperative mood takes the form of a command:

> Leave the room at once!

T

Subjunctive mood expresses a wish or hope:

If I <u>were</u> younger, I could run the marathon with you.

Types of verbs

Regular verbs form their parts according to the basic rule mentioned under "Verb tenses," on the previous page.

Present tense	Past tense	Past participle	Present participle
open	open*ed*	open*ed*	open*ing*
sail	sail*ed*	sail*ed*	sail*ing*
work	work*ed*	work*ed*	work*ing*

Irregular verbs do not conform to the basic rule. Some examples of irregular verbs, given in the first person singular, are shown below.

Infinitive	Present tense	Past tense	Past participle *(with have or has)*
to be	am	was	been
to begin	begin	began	begun
to bring	bring	brought	brought
to come	come	came	come
to do	do	did	done
to get	get	got	got
to give	give	gave	given
to go	go	went	gone
to have	have	had	had
to know	know	knew	known
to lay	lay	laid	laid
to lie	lie	lay	lain
to ride	ride	rode	ridden
to run	run	ran	run
to see	see	saw	seen
to sing	sing	sang	sung
to speak	speak	spoke	spoken
to take	take	took	taken
to throw	throw	threw	thrown
to write	write	wrote	written

Auxiliary verbs are used in conjunction with other verbs. The auxiliaries are *to be* and *to have* and are used in the following forms, among others: *be, can, could, have, may, might, ought, shall, should, will, would.*

They <u>should</u> arrive at any minute.
You <u>can</u> help Jack in records management if you like.

Transitive verbs require a direct object to complete the meaning of the sentence. Some examples are *believe, catch, cook, lay, play, raise, wear.*

Geese <u>lay</u> large eggs.
Lu <u>plays</u> the clarinet, trombone, and trumpet.

Intransitive verbs do not require a direct object to complete the meaning of the sentence. Some examples are *be, become, grow, lie, rise, stay.*

> My job <u>is</u> very stressful.
> In the tropics, many people <u>lie</u> down at siesta time.

Linking verbs (copula verbs) are non-action words that often connect subject and adjective. Some of these verbs are *appear, feel, look, sound, smell, taste.*

> The office <u>feels</u> cool today.
> Our sales <u>seem</u> to be on target.

Gerunds are the present forms of verbs with *ing* endings and are used as nouns.

> <u>Getting</u> that report out on time was a challenge.

▶T31 Adjectives

◆ describe a noun or pronoun
◆ are classified into three degrees of comparison
◆ can answer the questions *how many? what kind? which one?*

> Ramesh has worked with us for <u>several</u> years.
> If we buy <u>superior</u> equipment, it will last.
> You are invited to our <u>next</u> meeting.

Adjective comparison

Because adjectives modify nouns or pronouns that can be either singular or plural, they must change to match those nouns. Adjectives fall into three categories, called degrees of comparison:

◆ The simple form applies to a singular noun.
◆ The comparative compares two nouns/pronouns.
◆ The superlative compares more than two.

> Our <u>new</u> office is spacious and bright. (simple)
> Your office is <u>newer</u> than ours. (comparative)
> Mr. Finch's office is the <u>newest</u> one in the building. (superlative)

Most adjectives change to the comparative form by adding *r* or *er* to the simple form and to the superlative by adding *st* or *est* to the simple form.

Simple	Comparative	Superlative
brave	braver	bravest
busy	busier	busiest
cold	colder	coldest
old	older	oldest

T

Irregular adjectives do not conform to the regular pattern when changing to comparative and superlative. Most of them are common words; some of them are often misused.

Simple	Comparative	Superlative
bad	worse	worst
good	better	best
little	less	least
many	more	most
much	more	most
well	better	best

Most adjectives of two or more syllables use *more/less* and *most/least* to form comparatives and superlatives.

Simple	Comparative	Superlative
careful	more careful	most careful
descriptive	less descriptive	least descriptive

Compound adjectives are a combination of two or more words used as an adjective to describe a noun. They should be hyphenated if they precede the noun they modify:

> Carter has an <u>old-fashioned</u> printer.
> An <u>18-year-old</u> university student joined us.
> Thank you for your <u>up-to-date</u> report.

– but –

> Please bring your report up to date.

Linking verbs with adjectives

Use an adjective with the verbs *seem, appear, feel, look, smell, sound, taste:*

> Most employees feel <u>satisfied</u> on payday.
> The buffet you have arranged looks <u>impressive</u>.
> Doesn't lobster taste <u>delicious</u>!

▶T32 Adverbs

◆ modify verbs, adjectives, and other adverbs
◆ are used mainly in answer to the question *how?*

> The Canadian team played <u>well</u>.

> It was <u>extremely</u> hot last summer.

> A wise worker evaluates <u>daily</u>.

> Christo writes <u>very</u> quickly.

One clue to identifying adverbs is that they often end in *ly*—the ending that is added to an adjective to change it to an adverb.

Adjective	Adverb
real	really
reasonable	reasonably
special	specially
sure	surely

Many common adverbs, however, do not have the *ly* ending. Some examples are *again, everywhere, here, now, soon, there, very, well.*

Adverbs can never be the subject of a sentence:

Here is the doctor. (<u>doctor</u> is the subject)

A number of adverbs have two forms (the first of which is also an adjective), but only one form can be correct in a sentence. Some examples of these words are as follows:

close	closely	loud	loudly
direct	directly	quiet	quietly
fair	fairly	short	shortly
hard	hardly	slow	slowly
late	lately	wide	widely

The train arrived <u>late</u>.　　Have you read any good books <u>lately</u>?
They took the <u>slow</u> train.　　Please drive <u>slowly</u>.

Conjunctive adverbs

Conjunctive adverbs are connectives that can help semicolons connect independent clauses. Some examples are as follows:

accordingly	however	nevertheless
also	moreover	now
furthermore	neither	therefore

The project is incomplete; <u>therefore</u>, we will have to work on Saturday.
We want to win the contest; <u>accordingly</u>, we will have to increase our efforts.

NOTE　A semicolon precedes a conjunctive adverb and a comma follows it.

▶T33　Prepositions

◆ link a noun/pronoun to show its relationship to another word in a sentence
◆ always make their nouns the objects

Please give this package <u>to</u> Mr. Ho.

That fine illustration was done <u>by</u> Lydia.

Some of the most common prepositions are as follows:

about	as	beside	for	near	over	through
above	at	between	from	of	to	toward
across	before	by	in/into	off	up/upon	against
among	below	down	like	on	with	around

NOTE: Use *me, us,* or *them* after common prepositions, not *I, we,* or *they.*

▶T34 Conjunctions

◆ connect words, phrases, or clauses

Co-ordinating conjunctions link similar grammatical parts (i.e., word to word, phrase to phrase, or clause to clause). The most common co-ordinating conjunctions are *and, but, for, or, nor, yet.*

You <u>and</u> Kathleen share the same workstation.

You enjoy keyboarding <u>but</u> Kathleen does not.

Correlative conjunctions are used in pairs to relate words, phrases, or clauses to each other. Examples of these are as follows:

both .... and	not only .... but also
either............................ or	whether .... or
neither .... nor	

<u>Neither</u> sleet <u>nor</u> snow will hold up the mail.
<u>Not only</u> is the accountant accurate, <u>but</u> he is <u>also</u> conscientious.

Subordinate conjunctions connect dependent clauses to independent clauses. They can also act as adjectives, adverbs, or nouns. Examples are as follows:

after	because	in order that	since	whereas
although	before	otherwise	unless	while
as	if	provided	until	

<u>After</u> the statistics were compiled, the accounting department went home.
You may use our courier service, <u>provided</u> you complete a requisition form.

NOTE While not true conjunctions, *conjunctive adverbs* can help semi-colons join independent clauses (see T32).

▶T35 Interjections

◆ are single, emphatic expressions, usually followed by an exclamation mark:

Oh!   Ouch!   Wow!

I

T36 PUNCTUATION

Punctuation marks give sentences meaning and expression. Properly used, punctuation makes the reading of sentences easier by showing the relationships among the various parts.

Punctuating should not be a difficult matter. If, however, you do have a problem choosing the appropriate punctuation for a sentence, perhaps your sentence has been improperly constructed. Should this be the case, restructure your sentence into a form that you *know* is correct and one that consequently becomes easy for you to punctuate. The information in this section will acquaint you with all the punctuation marks that might be used in a sentence.

T37 APOSTROPHE (')

Use the apostrophe to form contractions, to indicate omissions, to form plurals, to form possessives, and as a single quotation mark.

▶T38   To form contractions

When a letter or number is omitted, use an apostrophe to indicate the omission:

you are	you're	I will	I'll
do not	don't	2008	'08
does not	doesn't		

NOTE Do not use an apostrophe to form the possessive of personal pronouns: *yours* not your's
theirs not their's

▶T39   To show omissions

Use the apostrophe where the noun modified is not shown:

We're going to the Sullivans'. (home implied)

▶T40   In plurals

Although plurals of many single letters or words are formed simply by adding an *s* (see T28), the apostrophe is used before the *s* in cases where confusion might result with the addition of *s* only:

Please dot all the i's.
One can never earn too many *A*'s.

– but –

He understood the five *C*s.
They ordered five new PCs.

▶T41   To form possessives

In singular nouns

To form the *singular possessive,* add an apostrophe plus *s* (*'s*).

T

Singular	Possessive
assistant	assistant's
boy	boy's
witness	witness's
woman	woman's
Charles	Charles's
Joan Haslam	Joan Haslam's

The <u>boy's</u> coat and the <u>woman's</u> shoes were dirty.
<u>Joan Haslam's</u> responsibility is to pay the <u>assistant's</u> salary.
You are invited to <u>Charles's</u> party tonight.

NOTE Where the addition of an apostrophe plus *s* would add a new syllable that would make pronunciation difficult, add the apostrophe only:

goodness   goodness'
For goodness' sake be on time!

Use of *it is* or *it's*

its   is the possessive form
it's   is the abbreviated form of *it is*

TIP   When is it its?
When it's not, it is.
When is it it's?
When it is it is.

With compound words

Add the possessive ending to the last syllable:

She borrowed her <u>father-in-law's</u> car.

In plural nouns

To form the *plural possessive,* add an apostrophe if the plural noun ends in *s;* add an apostrophe plus *s* if it does not.

Plural	Possessive
boys	*boys'
children	children's
men	men's
witnesses	*witnesses'
women	women's
* The *s* after the apostrophe is omitted in most plural words ending in *s* to make pronunciation easier. The words noted above are examples.	

<u>Boys'</u> coats and <u>women's</u> shoes are on special this week.
The two <u>witnesses'</u> testimony continued all day.
The <u>children's</u> bulletin board was blank.

I

NOTE Possessive pronouns are already possessive (see T29). They do not need the addition of an apostrophe:

According to an old cliché, "You can't judge a book by <u>its</u> cover."

To indicate types of ownership

Individual ownership: To show individual ownership when two or more words or names are involved, use an apostrophe after both words to make the meaning clear. The following example clarifies that both Phil and Maya had high marks, but they did not both get the same mark:

Phil's and Maya's marks were good last term.

Joint ownership: Using an apostrophe only after the final name or word indicates that ownership is shared:

Hulan, Emily, and Nadia's apartment is spacious.

In expressions relating to time or measure

They ordered <u>ten dollars'</u> worth of muffins to go.
Justin will be home in <u>two months'</u> time.
She was released with <u>one week's</u> pay.

With gerunds

When a verb form ending in *ing* is used as a noun (gerund), the noun or pronoun that precedes it takes the possessive form:

We were surprised by <u>John's</u> leaving.

NOTE Inanimate objects (non-living things) do not generally use the possessive form. Restructure your sentence to avoid such problems:

The colour of the wall

– not –

The wall's colour

▶T42 As single quotation mark

When a quotation occurs within a quotation, use quotation marks for the main quotation and the apostrophe (single quotation mark) to surround the inner one:

Mr. Stefanopoulos said, "They told me this was a 'rush' order."

T43 COLON (:)

▶T44 With direct quotations

Introduce a quotation of more than three lines with a colon:

When you are feeling downhearted, remember these lines from the poem "Smile":

We know the distance to the sun,
    The size and weight of earth,
But no one's ever told us yet
    How much a smile is worth.

Use the colon to introduce and to separate:

> Kelly was asked to order the following: ten dozen pens, six boxes of paper, four toner cartridges, and an up-to-date dictionary.

▶ T45 With introductory statements followed by lists or series

Use a colon to introduce a list (and, sometimes, examples, as has been done in this book):

> The agenda is as follows: . . .
> They brought the following: . . .
> We still need these dishes for the staff party: stroganoff, rice, salad, and broccoli.

NOTE Use a period rather than a colon if the introductory statement is contained within a preceding sentence:

> Participants will find that the following agenda items will provoke a lively meeting. The items have been carefully selected.
> > Flexible hours
> > Cash bonuses
> > Staff holidays

▶ T46 In business letters

Use a colon after the salutation in business letters when mixed (standard) punctuation is being used (see Unit 14, K18):

> Dear Ms. Chang:

Use a colon to separate the reference initials:

> PHE:PS

▶ T47 In times and ratios

Use a colon to separate hours and minutes:

> 9:56 a.m.

Show ratios with a colon:

> 3:2

▶ T48 In references to publications

Separate the title from the subtitle with a colon:

> *Canadian Business: Its Nature and Environment*

T49 COMMA (,)

The comma is the most common punctuation mark and is often misused and overworked. Apply good sense to your writing by asking yourself if there *is* need for a pause where you have placed the comma. Remember, "When in doubt, leave it out!"

► **T50 In compound sentences to separate independent clauses linked by a conjunction**

Compound sentences contain two or more independent clauses. Independent (main) clauses are complete thoughts that have their own subjects. When these are joined by a co-ordinating conjunction (*and, but, for, or, nor, yet*), use a comma before the conjunction to separate them. An exception is permitted if the sentence is quite short.

> Subject 1
>
> Our former office manager demanded a very high standard of work,
>
> Subject 2
>
> but the new one is more interested in quantity than in quality.

> *Exception:* The former manager demanded high work standards but the new one does not.

> **NOTE** If a conjunction does not separate the clauses, use a semicolon, not a comma. If one or both of the clauses already has internal punctuation, use a semicolon. (See T90 on semicolon usage.)

► **T51 After introductory words, phrases, or clauses**

Place a comma after an introductory word, phrase, or clause:

> <u>Yes</u>, restructuring is essential.
> <u>In the circumstances</u>, it was the best decision.
> <u>Our journey over</u>, we checked into a motel.
> <u>When the convention ended</u>, all the participants flew home.

► **T52 To set off parenthetical expressions**

Parenthetical words and phrases are ones that are not essential to the meaning of the sentence but give added emphasis. Such expressions can occur at the beginning, within, or at the end of a sentence. They should be set off by commas:

> <u>Needless to say</u>, he did not show up.
> The matter, <u>as far as I am concerned</u>, is closed.
> England is a beautiful country, <u>without a doubt</u>.
> Everyone knew, <u>of course</u>, that Adana would win the party leadership.
> The most popular version, <u>however</u>, is out of print.

The following words and phrases are common introductory and parenthetical expressions that are usually set off by commas:

accordingly	however	obviously
also	in addition	of course
as a matter of fact	in fact	otherwise
as a result	in my opinion	personally
besides	in other words	secondly
consequently	in the meantime	that is
finally	meanwhile	therefore

first, first of all	moreover	thus
for example	namely	well
fortunately	needless to say	without a doubt
further, furthermore	nevertheless	yet

▶ T53   To set off appositives

Appositives are words or phrases that rename or explain something about the subject, and should be set off by commas:

> Telemarketing, <u>an effective sales tool</u>, is gaining in popularity.
>
> Kieron, <u>a recent immigrant</u>, is an excellent advertising representative.
>
> Your best friend, <u>Sylvia Harding</u>, won the competition.

NOTE   Restrictive appositives (those that are essential to identification) should not be set off by commas:

> Your employee Yuko Ohga telephoned us.

▶ T54   To set off non-restrictive phrases and clauses

Restrictive phrases and clauses contribute information to the sentence and are *not* set off by commas.

Non-restrictive phrases and clauses do not add essential information to the sentence. The sentence could stand without them, so they are set off by commas:

> Our new computer, <u>which is in constant use</u>, is a major addition to our office. (Commas are used to set off the non-restrictive expression.)
>
> The new computer that we bought last week is much more powerful than our first one. (Commas are not used because <u>that we bought last week</u> is essential to the meaning of the sentence.)
>
> Employees <u>who can operate computers</u> are highly paid. (essential to meaning—restrictive)
>
> Leon, <u>who is a computer operator</u>, obtained a well-paid job. (not essential to meaning—non-restrictive)

NOTE   *That* and *which* are used in very specific ways with restrictive and non-restrictive clauses. *That* introduces restrictive clauses (no comma); *which*, non-restrictive (comma needed).

▶ T55   To set off subordinate clauses

Use a comma to set off a subordinate clause that precedes the main clause:

> <u>Assuming that you will arrive tomorrow</u>, we will schedule the meeting for 2 p.m.

▶ T56   To separate independent adjectives

When two or more adjectives precede a noun or when several adjectives follow the noun they are describing, use a comma:

> He is a <u>punctual, efficient</u> employee.
>
> That employee, <u>punctual and efficient</u>, deserves a raise.

But when the first adjective qualifies the second, omit the comma:

a <u>large, blue</u> binder

a <u>bright blue</u> binder

The test here is to try to use *and* where the comma might be inserted. If *and* would work, use a comma; if it would not, leave the comma out.

▶ T57   To separate items in a series

Insert a comma after all words, phrases, and clauses in a series:

Her favourite colours are green, purple, and orange.
The visitors were expected to behave politely, to ask questions, and to return to the hotel by noon.

NOTE   When commas are used within the items in a series, separate the items with semicolons. (See T90 on semicolon usage.)

Commas are not needed when conjunctions are used in a series:

Her favourite colours are green and purple and orange.

A comma is needed after the final item in the series when *no* conjunction is used:

Green, purple, orange, are her favourite colours.

If *etc.* ends the series, use a comma before and after the *etc.,* unless the *etc.* occurs at the sentence end.

Hockey, baseball, lacrosse, etc., are popular sports.

▶ T58   In dates

Separate the day from the year, and the year from what follows, by a comma, unless using the international date method:

September <u>1</u>, 20– (but 20– 09 01)
Thank you for your letter of September <u>1, 20–</u>, in which . . .
<u>Monday, September 13</u>, is the day we leave.

– *but not when the date is incomplete* –

Mr. Ondaatje retired in June 2000.
The year 2000 was important to me. (restrictive; no commas needed)

TIP   Use the function key in the software you are using to bring in the current date.

Keep the month and day together (use a hard space when keying dates in body or text of document), i.e., April[ ]19, 2007.

▶ T59   In addresses

Place commas after the street address and the town or city when they run on in text, but not before the postal code:

130 Franklin Street, Brandon, Manitoba R7A 5P1

In text, set off the city name and/or province, etc., from the rest of the sentence:

> Calgary, Alberta, is a large city.
> He lives at 136 Bay Street, Toronto, in an apartment.

▶T60   In names and titles

Separate the name from the title by means of a comma:

> T. Ginelli, our sales manager, is retiring.
> J. B. McCumber, Ph.D., is our guest speaker.
> Mr. J. Barry, Jr.,
>
> – *but* –
>
> Roger Aldrich II

Do not separate initials from names in letters or reports (use a hard space to keep together).

▶T61   To set off repeated words or numbers coming together

To avoid confusion, use a comma:

> What the task is, is unknown.
> No, no, that won't do!
> In 2007, 4000 more hectares will be sold.

▶T62   To show omissions

Insert a comma to indicate that one or more words have been omitted:

> He travelled the scenic route; she, the most direct one. (Here, *travelled* is implied after *she*.)

▶T63   Between a statement and a question

Insert a comma to separate the two parts:

> I think she did a good job, don't you?

▶T64   In direct address

Use commas to set off the name of the person:

> Thank you, Mr. Kormos, for paying your bill so promptly.

▶T65   With interruptions, contrasting expressions, and afterthoughts

Set off such expressions with commas:

> Katalin, rather than Gayle, completed the assignment.
> He was, I suppose, guaranteed a refund.

▶T66   With direct quotations

Use commas as illustrated here:

> "I hope," Pierre said, "that you can accept our invitation."

I

▶ T67 Avoiding comma problems

Restrictive clauses and phrases do not require commas because they are essential to the meaning of the sentence:

The man who held the smoking gun was the obvious killer.
The acid rain that fell on the region damaged the crops.

Do not be trapped into using a comma between the subject and the verb unless these are separated by a non-restrictive clause.

Incorrect: The new computer with the high-resolution colour monitor, gave graphics another dimension.
Correct: The new computer with the high-resolution colour monitor gave graphics another dimension.

– or –

The new computer, which had a high-resolution colour monitor, gave graphics another dimension.

T68 DASH (—)

A dash is a separating device that is used to set off certain kinds of parenthetical expressions. Use it to enlarge on a point or to give strong emphasis to a statement. Do not, however, overwork the dash in your writing because you will diminish the special emphasis it provides.

Roger lost a tough battle—and I don't blame him for being disappointed.
The manager—I'm pleased to say—gave them a special commendation.
Keetah plays excellent tennis—she has lost only one match out of twenty this month.
Linda was promoted to Branch Manager—a well-earned promotion.

Use the dash to set off parenthetical expressions that are already punctuated:

He went west—Calgary, Edmonton, and Vancouver—on his last sales trip.

There are two types of dashes:

Em-dash   An em-dash is used to separate parenthetical expressions or non-date items.
En-dash   An en-dash is used to separate years in dates.

NOTE An em-dash is created by keying two hyphen symbols without spaces. Most software will join the two hyphens. Other software permits the user to make the full dash that is shown in the preceding examples.
Always position a dash at the end of a line, never at the beginning.

T69 EXCLAMATION MARK (!)

Use an exclamation mark to indicate surprise, enthusiasm, strong emotion, or a command:

T

Happy birthday, Canada!
Stop, thief!

Use the exclamation mark after the interjections *Ah* and *Oh:*

Ah! What low prices!
Oh! How beautiful!

Use the exclamation mark when a single exclamatory word is used as a sentence:

Help!   Wait!

When exclamations are not strong ones, use a comma or a period rather than an exclamation mark:

No, this is not quite satisfactory.

NOTE   One exclamation mark does the job. *Never* use a string of them in formal writing.

T70 HYPHEN (-)

Use a hyphen to form compound nouns (e.g., *job-sharing*) and adjectives or to indicate word division (see T137).

▶ T71   In compound adjectives

When two or more words are used in combination immediately preceding the noun they modify, join them with a hyphen to form a compound adjective:

They went away for a six-day holiday.
My car has a four-cylinder engine.
These are state-of-the-art computers.
The job involves the development of problem-solving skills.

Do not use a hyphen when each adjective separately describes the subject:

Her brother is a big, strong man.

Do not use a hyphen when an expression is used adverbially:

This is the most up-to-date edition I could find. (adjective)
It is time to bring this edition up to date. (adverb)

Do not use a hyphen after words ending in *ly:*

The beautifully wrapped gift came as a complete surprise.

NOTE   If the compound element consists of an adverb plus participle, such as *a highly valued principle*, then you do not hyphenate. If the compound element consists of an adjective plus participle, as in *a friendly-looking dog*, then it may be hyphenated.

▶T72   In fractions

When fractions standing alone are spelled out, use a hyphen:

<u>Two-thirds</u> of the residents are employed downtown.

▶T73   In numbers

Use a hyphen when the spelled-out number consists of two words:

The band consisted of <u>twenty-nine</u> musicians.

▶T74   With prefixes and suffixes

Most prefixes and suffixes do not require a hyphen. Use them:

◆ to avoid confusion:

Co-op *not* coop
re-cover *not* recover

◆ when the prefix ends and the root word begins with the same letter:

anti-intellectual   pre-empt

◆ after *self* and *ex:*

self-control   ex-officio

◆ when followed by a capitalized word:

mid-Atlantic   pre-Cambrian

◆ with *great* in family relationships (but not with *step* or *grand*):

great-grandfather   stepbrother

◆ with the suffix *elect:*

Mayor-elect

▶T75   In word division

Use a hyphen to divide words (see T137).

NOTE   When a series of hyphenated adjectives modifies one noun, use a hyphen to avoid repetition. Leave a space after the first hyphen:

A *three-* to four-month tour   *– not –*   A *three-month* to *four-month* tour

T76   PARENTHESES (), SQUARE BRACKETS [], AND BRACE BRACKETS {}

▶T77   Parentheses

These are used with parenthetical expressions (i.e., explanatory or supplemental material) made by the author and incidental to the context. Commas and dashes could be used to perform the same functions, but parentheses tend to *de-emphasize* while other forms of punctuation *emphasize*.

Grammar (<u>essential to every student</u>) is high on the priority list.

Parentheses can also be used to set off expressions that require an abrupt change of direction by the reader:

> I saw an ad for a car (it was in the *Vancouver Sun*, I think) and went to look at it.

They are also used to provide references:

> Letter styles (Chapter 3) was the next topic covered.

Use parentheses to set off enumerations in narrative form:

> The reasons I want to leave are: (a) more pay, (b) shorter hours, (c) better prospects.

Use parentheses to set off money amounts or other figures that have been written in words in formal documents:

> Five hundred thousand dollars ($500 000) shall be paid in installments.

NOTE Any needed punctuation must be placed outside the closing parenthesis (unless an abbreviation like "etc." occurs):

> We are leaving on Wednesday (August 13, I think), but we still have much to do.

►T78   Square brackets [] and brace brackets {}

Square brackets are used to set off inserted matter that is incidental to the context. The insertion is usually made by someone other than the author (e.g., an editor's comments or explanations):

> In 1938, he [Best] was involved in one of Canada's most exciting medical research undertakings.

Square brackets are also used to set off parenthetical expressions that occur within parenthetical expressions. Use parentheses for the main expression and brackets for the one that comes within it:

> Some fine Elizabethan literature (written by William Shakespeare [sixteenth and seventeenth centuries] and others) is still enjoyed today.

Brace brackets can be used to enclose words or figures in books or medical journals.

T79   PERIOD (.)

Use a period after a sentence, a polite request, or an indirect question:

> The sun came up very early that day.
> Would you kindly send us your cheque.
> He asked whether we were willing to go.

Use a period with abbreviations:

Mr. S. Eby	a.m.
St. Cecelia's Church	Ph.D.
R.S.V.P.	encl.

I

For organizations known by abbreviations, the current trend is to omit periods:

IBM   YMCA   CBC

NOTE   If an abbreviation closes a sentence, only *one* period is needed at the end of the sentence. If a question mark or exclamation mark closes the sentence, position the mark outside the period:

The goods must have been shipped c.o.d.
Were the goods shipped c.o.d.?

Use a period to indicate decimals:

In money amounts	$17.75
In percentages	1.82%
With decimal fractions	6.667

Use periods in a series (ellipses) to indicate omissions. This device is used with quoted material. (See Unit 14, K57.)

Fowler describes grammar as ". . . the science of language."

T80   ELLIPSIS MARK (. . .)

Use the ellipsis mark to indicate omissions within quotations. (See Unit 14, K57.)

The ellipsis mark consists of

◆ three spaced periods (. . .).

The author says her novel shows "a pattern . . . of how in these small events and in these small lives the world intrudes."

NOTE   Use the ellipsis mark and a period, i.e., four periods, if the omission comes at the end of the sentence:

"The novel quickly moves back in time to the afternoon of the funeral. . . ."

T81   SLASH OR RIGHT DIAGONAL (/)

Use the slash between options and to separate lines of poetry that are run in to the text:

◆ **options:** P/N/F (meaning "Please Note and Forward")
I do not know why the Spring/Summer rates are different.

◆ **poetry:**   Margaret Avison begins "The Swimmer's Moment" with a statement of her universal theme:
"For everyone/The swimmer's moment at the whirlpool comes" (1–2).

T82   QUESTION MARK (?)

▶ **T83 Use a question mark**

◆ at the end of a direct question:

How much does it cost?

T

◆ to express doubt. Place the question mark in parentheses and use it after the doubtful term:

> He was born in 1963 (?).

◆ to add emphasis. The question mark *may* be used after each question in a series of questions within one sentence. In this case, do not capitalize the first letters of the questions and leave only one space after the question marks:

> Which do you think is more important for career success: having good qualifications? being well educated? possessing a sparkling personality?

▶T84 Do not use a question mark

◆ after an indirect question:

> I asked him how much it cost.

◆ after a polite request:

> Will you please find out the cost.

T85 QUOTATION MARKS (" ")

Use quotation marks in the following ways.

▶T86 In direct quotations (the exact wording used by a writer or speaker)

> The man cried, "Stop, thief!" and then called the police.
> He said, "Stop, or I'll call the police."
> Did he say, "Stop, or I'll call the police"? No, he did not.
> "If you don't stop," he said, "I'll call the police."
> "Please lend me ten dollars," said Louise.
> "Steve," said Kelly, "can you help me?"

When a quoted reference contains fewer than three lines, place quotation marks at the beginning and end of the quoted material. When more than one paragraph of quoted material is used, use quotation marks at the beginning of each paragraph and at the end of the final paragraph.

" _____

_____

" _____

_____ "

Long quotations do not need quotation marks because they are indented and set off from the rest of the text. (See Unit 14, K57.)

NOTE Use single quotation marks for the second quotation when a quotation within a quotation must be indicated:

> She said, "I heard him say, 'Come to dinner.'"

Use quotation marks to enclose words used in a particular way:

> Although he was not actually put in jail, he was held in "protective" custody for three days.

NOTE Frequently, the same key is used for both beginning and ending quotation marks. If your software offers you both beginning and ending quotation marks (smart quotes), use them in preference to the indistinguishable type, especially in desktop-publishing applications.

▶ T87   With titles

Parts of magazines, parts of books, articles, essays, sermons, titles of television and radio programs, songs, speeches, and poems are indicated by quotation marks:

> The poem "Ode on a Grecian Urn," by Keats, is famous.
> When you read Chapter 5, "Punctuation," study the section entitled "Comma."

▶ T88   For special emphasis

If you want your reader to be aware that you are using an expression in an unusual way or are attempting to be humorous, use quotation marks for emphasis. Technical terms used in a non-technical way can be emphasized this way also.

> Unfortunately, we committed a "no-no" on our last statement.
> He used the term "input" eight times in the last four minutes.

▶ T89   Punctuating with quotation marks

Current practice is to place quotation marks outside commas and periods (see the examples in T87, above). When used with colons and semicolons, however, quotation marks are placed inside the punctuation:

> Please learn the following verse from "Wildflowers":

Question marks and exclamation marks go inside the closing quotes when they apply only to the quoted matter (see the third example in T86). They go outside when they apply to the entire sentence:

> "It is the east, and Juliet is the sun!"

T90   SEMICOLON (;)

The semicolon is used in a sentence when a stronger break than that provided by a comma is needed.

▶ T91   In compound sentences

Compound sentences consist of two or more independent, related clauses.

Use a semicolon to separate independent, closely related clauses when the second clause is introduced by a transitional expression. Examples of

T

transitional expressions are: *however, therefore, in fact, in other words.* A more complete list is provided in T52.

> Sales are down badly this quarter; in fact, they are at a record-breaking low.

Use a semicolon to separate independent clauses that are not connected by a conjunction, as in this example:

> Fireplaces bring comfort in winter; pools offer cool relaxation in summer.

Use a semicolon before the conjunction (*and, but,* etc.) to separate independent related clauses if one or both already contain punctuation:

> They promised a much leaner, meaner, and more efficient government; and they produced a perfect government.

▶ T92   In a series

Use a semicolon for clarity when a comma has already been used to punctuate items in the series:

> Most of the executives were present: Hugh Fine, president, Ottawa;
> Elisabeth Jacques, treasurer, Trois-Rivières; Todd Taylor, secretary,
> Edmonton; and James Zabig, vice-president, Halifax.

It should be noted that use of the semicolon is decreasing in favour of the comma in business communications. Of the three rules presented in T91, the first is still commonly used, while the other two apply mainly to formal and literary writing. In business, a good rule of thumb is to ask yourself, "Would a comma serve the same purpose as a semicolon, or should a period replace it?" In common usage, a comma could replace a semicolon in the following example:

> The wind was high; the sea was rough.

T93   UNDERSCORE (_)

Use the underscore (underline) in handwritten or keyed material to indicate titles of books, plays, works of art, magazines, newspapers, words that need emphasis, and foreign expressions:

> <u>Hard Times</u> is a fine novel by Charles Dickens.
> The last issue of <u>Maclean's</u> contained an interesting article.
> Have you seen Michelangelo's sculpture the <u>Pietà</u>?
> Please tell Bill that this order is <u>rush</u>.

NOTE   If italic type is available to you, you may use it instead of the underscore.

NOTE   Punctuation marks are not underlined unless they are an integral part of the expression to be underscored.

> <u>Pietà?</u>   – *not* –   <u>Pietà</u>?

I

T94 ITALICS

Italics refers to a printing style as shown in this sentence.

◆ Use italics to give special emphasis:

> The enclosed information is *confidential.*
> Always key *your initials* at the end of documents.

◆ Use italics to set off figures, letters, and words referred to as figures, letters, and words. Usually the word to be defined is italicized and the definition is quoted to distinguish the two elements.

> The word *principal,* meaning "a sum of money on which interest is paid," is often misspelled.
> Remember to spell *accommodation* with two *c*'s and two *m*'s.

◆ Use italics to set off foreign words and phrases that have not been absorbed into the English language:

> What does *caveat emptor* mean?

◆ Use italics to set off titles of complete works published and bound separately: books, poems, magazines, movies, musicals, newspapers, operas, pamphlets, periodicals, and plays. Names of airplanes, ships, spacecraft, and trains are also italicized. Use quotation marks to set off titles of speeches, articles and chapters within books and periodicals, and works of art.

> The motion picture *Gone With the Wind* has become a classic.
> Did you read this month's issue of *Maclean's* magazine?
> We took a cruise to Alaska on the *Nieuw Amsterdam.*
> Mr. Renzella chose "Five Important Steps for Financial Planning Success" as the topic for his presentation.
> She was asked to order a copy of the *Pitman Office Handbook.*

◆ When referring to the title of a book and to a chapter in it, use italics **or** underline the title of the book and use quotation marks for the chapter title.

> Chapter two of *English at Work* is entitled "Writing Styles."

NOTE Another method of keying titles is to use all capitals. This method is often used in correspondence of publishing houses in which titles occur frequently. It is also used in advertising and sales promotion as an eye-catching device. Avoid using this style for general use.

T95 STYLE MECHANICS

Style defines the details—the mechanics—of the writer's craft. Writing styles are constantly changing. Today, productivity is key, clarity is paramount, and simplicity is desirable. As a result, rules and conventions that used to apply no longer do. Organizations are moving more towards styles and conventions that suit their particular purposes. For example, desktop publishing has resulted in changes in rules for spacing following punctuation marks, the reduced use of hyphens in compounds, and more sparing use of capitalization. This section provides a set of suggested standards that are generally acceptable, that are consistent with the practices of most organizations, and that have productivity as a major concern.

T96   ABBREVIATIONS

Generally, abbreviations should be avoided if they might be misinterpreted; however, they are acceptable in statistical or tabulated matter.

◆ Use only common abbreviations that cannot be misunderstood.

◆ Use capitals only if the word being abbreviated is capitalized:

> etc.   *ibid.*   Mon.   Nov.   vs.   i.e.   e.g.

◆ Use the ampersand (&) *only in company names,* never in text matter:

> Braithwaite & Singh   Zimmer & Co., Ltd.

NOTE   Do not change *and* to &. Follow what is printed on the company letterhead.

◆ Pluralize most abbreviations by adding *s*. Where confusion is possible, add *'s:*

> The five *C*s   Dot all the i's.

▶T97   Academic degrees

Academic degrees are generally abbreviated. No space follows the periods in the abbreviation:

> B.Sc.   Bachelor of Science   Ph.D.   Doctor of Philosophy

Capitalize and abbreviate academic titles after a person's name. No title should precede the name if the degree and title mean the same thing:

> June Haskin, Ph.D. – *or* – Dr. June Haskin – **never** – Dr. June Haskin, Ph.D.

(See the Appendix for a listing of academic degrees.)

▶T98   Addresses

Abbreviate terms such as *boulevard, building,* etc., only when essential in inside addresses and envelopes, never in the body of a letter or other text. Permissible abbreviations for provinces and states are given in the Appendix. For acceptable mailing abbreviations, see Unit 14, K8.

▶T99   Broadcasting stations

Call letters are shown in capitals, without spaces. (These are not, in fact, abbreviations.)

> CFRH-TV   CHEX   CHUM

I

▶T100 Business terms (see also the Appendix)

The following standard abbreviations are frequently used in business communications such as forms and tables.

acct. or a/c	account
ad val. or A/V	*ad valorem*—according to value
agt.	agent
a.k.a.	also known as
AP	accounts payable
AR	accounts receivable
ASAP	as soon as possible
assoc. or assn.	association
asst.	assistant
ATM or ABM	automated teller machine or automated banking machine
avg.	average
b.l. or B/L	bill of lading
B/S	bill of sale
C	hundred (roman numeral); Celsius; carbon (science)
c.i.f. or CIF	cost, insurance, freight
c.l. or CL	carload
c.o. or c/o	in care of
Co.	Company
c.o.d. or C.O.D.	cash on delivery
Corp.	Corporation
cr.	credit
dept.	department
do.	ditto
dr.	debit
E. and O.E.	errors and omissions excepted
e.g.	for example
e.o.m. or EOM	end of month
et al.	and others
ETA	estimated time of arrival
ETD	estimated time of departure
FAQ	frequently asked questions
FIFO	first-in, first-out
f.o.b. or FOB	free on board
fwd.	forward; forwarded
F.Y.I. or FYI	for your information
GST	Goods and Services Tax
HST	Harmonized Sales Tax
i.e.	that is to say
Inc.	Incorporated
inv.	invoice
K	thousand (metric); Kelvin (science); karat (also carat)
l.c.l. or LCL	less than carload
LIFO	last-in, first-out
Ltd.	Limited
M	thousand (roman numeral)
mdse.	merchandise
mfg.	manufacturing
mgr.	manager

(continued . . .)

T

misc.	miscellaneous
ms. or MS	manuscript
N.B.	nota bene (note well)
NSF	not sufficient funds
n/c or NC	no charge
No., Nos.	number(s) (use only with numerals)
n/30	net in 30 days
os, O/S	out of stock
pkg.	package
P/N/F	please note and forward
P/N/R	please note and return
P.O.	purchase order
P.O. or PO	Post Office (often with box numbers: P.O. Box 96)
P.S.	postscript
qty.	quantity
PST	Provincial Sales Tax
R.R.	Rural Route or railroad
vol.	volume
W.B.	waybill

▶T101 Company and organization names

For companies, agencies, unions, and societies, use only the abbreviations shown in the legally registered titles (i.e., the abbreviations in that organization's letterhead):

Bros.   Co.   Ltd.

Many companies and organizations are commonly known by abbreviated names. Current practice is to use capital letters and no spaces for such names:

IBM   UNICEF   YMHA   YWCA

▶T102 Compass points

Compass points may be abbreviated in addresses and technical material, but not otherwise:

N   NE   NNW   SSE   SW   W

▶T103 Dates and times

Abbreviate months and days of the week only in tables, and only then if space is limited.

If the abbreviations *B.C.* or *A.D.* are to be shown, use them only when dates are in numerals. *B.C.* is positioned after the year; *A.D.* before it:

A.D. 1936   55 B.C.

Use *a.m.* and *p.m.* when hours are shown as numerals (not to be used when the 24-hour clock is used):

11:45 p.m.   13:30

Use capitals and no periods if time zones are abbreviated:

EST (Eastern Standard Time)   PST (Pacific Standard Time)

▶ T104 Metric measurements

For metric measurements, see the Appendix.

▶ T105 Places

Country, province, and state names should never be abbreviated in text. Province and state names may be abbreviated in addresses.

UK   – *or* –   U.K.
USA – *or* –   U.S.A. – *or* –   U.S.

Country names (except the two shown here) should not be abbreviated in addresses, except on envelopes. Abbreviations are often used, however, in tables, charts, etc.

▶ T106 Publication terms

Standard abbreviations used in referring to printed materials when a number is included are as follows:

Ch., Chap.	Chapter	p., pp.	page(s)
Div.	Division	Sec.	Section
Fig., Figs.	Figure(s)	v., vs.	verse(s)
l., ll.	line(s)	Vol., Vols.	Volume(s)

▶ T107 Titles

◆ after names:

Jr.   Sr.   Dr.   R. Farmer, Jr.

(See T97 for treatment of academic degrees.)

◆ before names (social titles):

Mr.   Mrs.   Ms.   Messrs.   Mmes.

The following professional, military, and civic titles are abbreviated when they precede a family name *and* a given name but not otherwise: *Rev., Hon., Prof., Gen., Col., Capt., Lieut.*

Gen. Lewis MacKenzie   – *but* –   General MacKenzie   Prof. Morley Lazier

Rev. and *Hon.* must be written in full if preceded by *the:*

Rev. Charles Parnell   – *or* –   the Reverend Charles Parnell
– *never* –   Rev. Parnell

T108 CAPITALIZATION

Although the basic conventions of capitalization are common knowledge, there are many specific uses of capital letters for emphasis or clarification

T

of an idea. The general rule is to capitalize proper nouns and words that begin a sentence. Other uses are illustrated in this section.

NOTE A simple, basic guide to correct capitalization is this: When being specific, capitalize; when being general, do not capitalize.

> Prime Minister Greto led the way. (referring to a specific person)
> There was a heated discussion among the prime ministers. (no specific prime minister in mind)
> Vancouver City Hall is an example of fine architecture. (specific building)
> A large city usually has a city hall. (general reference)
> I think Unit 3 is the most interesting. (specific reference)
> Every unit in this book is long. (general reference)

NOTE Some words that were once proper nouns have become common nouns through usage. These should not be capitalized:

arabic numerals	roman numerals
manila envelope	venetian blinds

▶T109 Abbreviations

Capitalize abbreviations only when the words they represent are normally capitalized:

> a.m.   p.m.   Mon.   Nov.

▶T110 Academic field

Capitalize as follows:

Specific course titles   Biology 23   Linguistics I   Spanish 307Y

NOTE Language names are always capitalized in this context. Other non-specific course titles are not.

> Carl enjoyed French and Japanese, but he did not like accounting or science.

Degrees	B.A.	LL.B.	M.Sc.	Ph.D.
Titles	Dr. Yvonne Borden		Professor Chiu	

College diplomas are designated as *Dipl.* or *Dipl.* with a letter or letters that identify the area of study.

◆ two-year diploma programs add *Dipl.* after the name:

> Mary Williamson, Dipl. (Business Diploma)

◆ three-year diploma programs add *Dipl.* and a letter or letters to designate the area of study:

> Warren Kimoto, Dipl.B. (Business)
> June Bourne, Dipl.H.Sc. (Nursing)
> Carol Mulholland, Dipl.T. (Technology)
> Jane Marusiak, Dipl.A. (Applied Arts)

I

NOTE: If after graduating from a community college, you go on to university and obtain a degree, put the university degree first: Marnie Bell, B.A., Dipl.B.

▶T111 Addresses

Capitalize all key words in addresses—names of streets, avenues, buildings, roads, towns, cities, provinces, countries.

▶T112 Advertising trademarks

Capitalize trademarks:

> Shake 'n Bake   Tide   Dove

▶T113 Astronomical bodies

Capitalize astronomical bodies (constellations, planets, and stars):

> the Great Bear   the Milky Way   Venus

▶T114 Dates, seasons, holidays, historical periods

Capitalize days of the week, months, festivals, and holidays:

> Civic Holiday   November   Saint-Jean-Baptiste Day
> Monday   Ramadan   Yom Kippur

Names of seasons, decades, and centuries are capitalized only when they are personified or used as special terms:

> spring sales   – *but* –   Oh! Spring!
> early nineties   – *but* –   Fabulous Fifties
> year 2000   – *but* –   Year of the Children

▶T115 Geographic terms

Compass points should be capitalized only when a specific place is intended. They should not be capitalized when they indicate only a general direction.

> The Joneses went out West for their holiday.
> He drove west from Kenora.
> The golf courses in South Carolina are magnificent.
> How far south do you plan to drive?

Geographic localities should be capitalized when the compass points refer to people:

> Easterners   Westerners

Names of continents, countries, nationalities, bodies of water, provinces, cities, valleys, mountains, regions, and localities should be capitalized:

> the Mackenzie River   Barbados   Lake Athabaska
> Mont Tremblant   Canadians   the Okanagan Valley
> Lake of the Woods   Essex County

T

►T116 Government and political references

Capitalize as follows:

Bodies

Industry Canada

Ministry of the Environment

Royal Canadian Mounted Police

the Saskatchewan Legislature

Supreme Court of Canada

Acts, Treaties

North American Free Trade Agreement

Canadian Charter of Rights and Freedoms

Family Law Act

Maastricht Treaty

Titles

Governor General of Canada

– but –

N. Greco, minister of Transport Canada

►T117 Institutions

Capitalize names of institutions and their divisions:

Beth Tzedec Synagogue

Canadian National Institute for the Blind

Mount Allison University

School of Music

►T118 Nationalities, languages, races

Capitalize nationalities, languages, and races of people:

| Asian | Cree | Hispanic |
| Chinese | French | Latin |

►T119 Organizations

Capitalize names of organizations:

Canadian Broadcasting Corporation

Girl Guides of Canada

NOTE Minor words (*of, the, and,* etc.) in a name are not capitalized unless they start the name:

The Financial Post

►T120 Publications

Capitalize the first and all of the important words in titles of plays, books, articles, newspapers, magazines, operas, songs, poems, reports, works of art:

Canada: A Country to Enjoy

The Importance of Being Earnest

"The Night of the Shower of Stars"

Star Trek

►T121 Punctuation marks

Capitalize the first letter

◆ after a *colon* when an independent clause follows:

Canada is beautiful: Its lakes, mountains, and beaches are popular with tourists.

I

♦ after a *period, question mark, exclamation mark:*

> Please come. If you insist.
> Are you coming? No, thanks.
> Do come! It is not possible.

♦ after the opening *quotation marks* when a complete sentence is quoted:

> The visiting dignitary said, "It's my pleasure to be here."
>
> – *but* –
>
> The visitor's "pleasure to be here" was somewhat dampened by bad weather.

With hyphenated expressions, capitalize only the part that would normally be capitalized:

> cross-Canada   mid-August

▶T122 Religious references

Capitalize words with religious significance. Capitalize names of deities, the Bible, names of books of the Bible, all other sacred books, festivals and holy days, and adjectives derived from these terms:

Buddhism	Good Friday	Protestant
Catholic	Jewish	the Qur'an
God	Judaism	the Nicene Creed

▶T123 Titles

Capitalize titles of relatives when they precede a name. Do not capitalize when these are preceded by a pronoun:

> His uncle left him a small fortune.
> I have invited Uncle Fred for dinner.
> My mother is an important politician.
>
> – *but* –
>
> I asked Mom to help me with my packing.

Capitalize professional, business, civic, military, and religious titles that precede a person's name:

> the Reverend Jim Battye
> Mayor Frank Scarpitti
> General Fletcher

Do not capitalize titles when they follow a personal name or are used in place of a personal name—except in inside addresses. Titles of high-ranking government officials were an exception to this rule at one time but modern usage generally leans towards minimizing capitalization.

> Barbara Bertin, vice-president of Allied Capital, is coming for lunch.
> Stephen Harper, prime minister of Canada, is campaigning in western Canada.

T124 NUMBERS

The question often arises as to whether figures or words should be used to express numerical values. Figures are usually preferred for most business situations because they are easier to read. If in doubt, follow these general guidelines:

◆ Spell out numbers from one to ten and use figures for numbers above ten. Numbers in the millions or higher, however, may be expressed as

> 1 billion   3.5 million (instead of 3 500 000)

◆ If numbers are mixed within a sentence, use figures for all of them or write all of them out:

> Send 15 television sets, 6 CD players, 4 VCRs.
> Of the 12 cats, 6 were tabbies.
>
> – or –
>
> Of the twelve cats, six were tabbies.

◆ Always use figures with symbols and abbreviations:

> 6°C   3 km   No. 68   #68
>
> – but –
>
> 6 percent (use the % symbol only in tables or statistical work)

◆ Make the plural form of figures by adding *s:*

> The 1980s saw the start of the information age.

◆ Hyphenate spelled-out numbers containing two words and any number that is part of a compound adjective:

> Thirty-two people were invited.
> A five-hundred-kilometre journey lies ahead of us.
>
> – or –
>
> A 500-km journey lies ahead of us.

◆ Spell out any number that starts a sentence (but avoid this situation if possible by rewriting the sentence):

> Eighteen children came.   (All 18 children came.)

◆ When two numbers are used consecutively, spell out the lower number:

> Buy twelve 43-cent stamps, please.

◆ Use a comma for clarity when two numbers used together could cause confusion:

> By 2007, 99 branch offices will be equipped with this technology.

The following examples provide further guidelines.

I

▶ T125 Addresses

For house, building, apartment, post office box, and rural route numbers, use figures. (Exception: Spell out "One" in street addresses.)

15 King Street, Apartment 804   R.R. 1   P.O. Box 120

– but –

One Crown Crescent

For street names above ten, use figures. For street names under ten, use words.

402 – 40th Street (insert a space on both sides of the hyphen)

– but –

240 Fifth Avenue

▶ T126 Ages and anniversaries

Use figures with very precise ages:

She will be 2 years, 3 months old on Tuesday.

Use words for less precise and approximate ages:

Lou will be thirty tomorrow.
Frankie is three.
Ilse is almost eighteen.

Use figures for ages stated immediately after names:

Shafig, 27, and Suni, 25, were engaged last week.

Use figures for ages expressed in a statistical or technical sense:

The legal age for marrying in Ontario is 16.
People in the 65-plus age group qualify for pensions.

Use words for anniversaries except when three or more words are required:

It's their fifteenth anniversary.

– but –

Canada celebrated its 125th birthday in 1992.

▶ T127 Dates

Use figures:

February 29, 20– – or – 20– 02 29

NOTE Use of *nd* and *th* and *st* is shown in these examples:

On the 2nd of January, they attended a New Year's luncheon.
On January 2, they attended a New Year's luncheon.
They attended the leap-year party on the 29th of February.
On February 29, they will attend a leap-year party.
On the 1st of March, they checked their finances.
They checked their finances on March 1.

In legal or formal documents, however, spell out figures:

November eighth, two thousand . . .

▶T128 Decimals

Use figures:

0.50   7.3 million

▶T129 Document numbers

Use figures:

Invoice No. 2071   Order No. 26   Policy No. 168-2948   Cheque No. 2345

(Use a hard space/non-breaking space to keep the figure with No., i.e., No.[ ]2345.)

▶T130 Fractions and mixed numbers

Spell out simple fractions when used alone:

Only three-quarters of the group attended.

Use figures for mixed numbers:

His mass increased $1\frac{1}{2}$ times.

▶T131 Metric symbols

Use figures:

3 kg   2 cm   30 km   22 cm × 27 cm   5 L

– *but* –

six kilometres   nine litres

▶T132 Money amounts

As a general rule, use figures for money amounts. Round amounts, however, can be spelled out in text if desired:

twenty thousand dollars

When expressing a series of round amounts in figures, omit decimals and zeros:

$25 $43 $82   ¥21 000   MXN50 000

When expressing a series of amounts that includes cents, use decimals and zeros in all cases, for consistency:

$23.95 $43.00 $9.50   £50.50   € 89.75

Use figures with a series of amounts in cents only (the ¢ symbol may be used in statistical material; the word "cents" is used in text):

17¢   28¢   79¢

– *in text* –

17 cents

I

In a series in which one of the amounts is in cents only, express it as part of a dollar:

$3.50 $0.85 $14.75

For very large amounts, use figures and words:

6.5 billion $5 million

(Use a hard space/non-breaking space to keep number with word, i.e., 6.5[ ]million.)

In legal documents and very formal communications, use words and confirm the amounts in figures in parentheses (note use of capitals):

Two Thousand Dollars ($2000)

NOTE   In some areas (such as banking and accounting), a comma, rather than a space, is used in dollar amounts to prevent fraud and confusion (e.g., $500,000).

▶T133 Percentages

Use figures:

We saved 20 percent or 20 per cent. (accepted as one or two words)
(Remember, use a hard space/non-breaking space to keep number with percent or %. Use % symbol only in tabulations or statistical work.)

▶T134 Ratios and proportions

Use figures:

5:2   – or –   5 to 2

▶T135 Temperatures

Use figures:

49°C   49 degrees

▶T136 Times

Use figures with *a.m.* or *p.m.*:

2:30 p.m.   – or –   14:30
4 p.m.   – not –   4:00 p.m.

When using the term *o'clock*, either figures or words may be used. In a formal context, use words:

The ceremony will take place at three o'clock.
Let's meet at 2 o'clock.

Use figures with exact units of time:

The trip took 1 year, 7 months, 10 days.

T137 WORD DIVISION

Because word-processing software has default settings and automatic wraparound, most routine documents can be produced without requiring any line-end word divisions (or hyphenation). As well, most software offers automatic hyphenation.

Never divide

◆ where only one or two characters would be separated:

largely   mounted   oblique   ready

◆ numbers and amounts (unless they are *very* long) and units of measure:

$2147.75   2[ ]million   500[ ]km

◆ numbers from streets

112[ ]Main Street

NOTE   Use the comma as the natural connector for sums of money or large number amounts:

$1,200,375 $350,000

Remember to use the hard space/non-breaking space when keying in the metric version:

$1[ ]200[ ]375 $350[ ]000

Where to divide words

Always divide words between syllables. Specifically,

◆ as close to the centre as possible:

communi-cation

◆ after prefixes:

contra-dict

◆ before suffixes:

lov–able

◆ between double consonants when the root word does not contain double consonants:

occur-rence   omit-ted   run-ning

– but –

fill-ing   stall-ing

◆ after the vowel when a one-letter syllable is followed by a consonant:

regu-late   sepa-rate

◆ between the vowels when there are two one-letter syllables:

radi-ator   anxi-ety

I

◆ only at the existing hyphen when the term is already hyphenated:

self-control   two-fifteenths

Where to divide related expressions

Avoid dividing parts of a related expression (i.e., parts normally read together) but, if division is essential, choose the logical breaking point.

NOTE   Use the hard space/non-breaking space to keep related expressions together:

Dates: May[ ]24, 20—,   September[ ]5, 20—

Money (very large amounts only): $2[ ]hundred million
Break after: $2 hundred
Do not *break:* 2[ ]hundred

If possible, avoid breaking large sums of money:
$2 600 975

Names: Professor[ ]B. Cormier
Break after: Professor B.

Numbers (very long ones only): 24[ ]000[ ]500
Break after: 24[ ]000

If possible, avoid breaking large number streams (use the comma as the natural connector).

Phone numbers and fax numbers: Do not divide. Use a hard space/ non-breaking space to keep numbers together:

Tel.[ ](905)[ ]238-6074 Fax[ ](905)[ ]238-6075

Addresses: 37[ ]Bayview Avenue
Break after: 37[ ]Bayview

Other: *Do* not *break:* Room[ ]7 Schedule[ ]A Appendix[ ]I

NOTE   Widow/orphan protection: this software function prevents single lines from being separated from a paragraph. You can keep text together on a page in the following ways:

◆ Keep the first or last line of a paragraph from being separated from the paragraph across a page break.

◆ Keep a block of text together on one page (a quotation, tabulation, table, etc.).

◆ Keep a heading together with the text that follows by specifying the number of lines to be kept together.

WORDS OF WISDOM

*It often shows a fine command of
language to say nothing.*

2 THE EXPRESSION OF LANGUAGE

E

SELECTED CONTENTS

E1	**WRITTEN EXPRESSION**
E2	Business Letters
E3	**Letter Samples**
E25	Forms of Address
E27	Memorandums
E28	Press Releases
E29	Reports
E30	**ORAL EXPRESSION**
E31	Presentations
E36	Dictation Techniques

The most effective communications are well organized, clear, concise, courteous, factually accurate, and positively worded. The purpose of this unit is to show you how to produce written and oral communications for most business situations.

E1   WRITTEN EXPRESSION

This section offers help in writing business letters, memorandums, press releases, and reports. Guidelines for the following writing situations are presented in other parts of this book:

◆ advertisements, see Unit 7, H6

◆ formal acceptances, see Unit 3, IS24

◆ job applications, see Unit 20, J13

◆ minutes, see Unit 10, M10–14

E2   BUSINESS LETTERS

Despite the increased use of fax, email, etc., letters are a common form of communication in business. They represent the sender's company and should therefore make a good impression. The following suggestions will help in the creation of any business letter.

Get off to the right start

Collect all the facts and documents you need and do one of these:

◆ Make an outline of the points you wish to cover.

◆ Underline or highlight important facts on a document to which you are replying.

◆ Make notes in the margin about points you wish to cover.

Follow the five Cs

Produce correspondence that is coherent, clear, concise, courteous, and correct.

◆ Coherent: Progresses logically, after starting with a clear statement of purpose

◆ Clear: Is written in simple, easy-to-follow, unambiguous language

◆ Concise: Is short and to the point

◆ Courteous: Uses "you" frequently and is written in a tactful, friendly style that shows concern for the reader

◆ Correct: States all required facts accurately and is always correct in spelling, punctuation, and grammar

---

Dear Sir or Madam:

Would you please send us a copy of *Wordpro Made Easy*, which was previewed in last month's issue of *Office Systems and Technology*. Your booklet seems to be exactly what our department needs.

We would appreciate receiving this by September 17, if possible.

Yours very truly,

A concisely worded business letter

Use a logical development

Introduction

Start in a pleasing way with a clear statement of the purpose of your communication. If you do this, the reader does not have to wonder why you are writing.

Development

◆ Develop the introduction by giving further details (background, anticipated outcome, etc.).

◆ Tailor your language to suit the reader (e.g., do not assume that everyone will be familiar with the specialized vocabulary of your particular business).

◆ Give precise information to avoid confusion.

Ending

◆ Find a friendly way to close the letter.

◆ Ask for action, if this is appropriate.

E

◆ Do not thank in advance because it is an imposition on the reader to assume that he or she will fulfil your request.

Keep it simple
Brevity is the key to quick and effective communication. Focusing on one point at one time leads to easy understanding by the recipient.

Use the "you" approach
Make your readers feel important. Show your consideration by putting yourself in their place when you write. Do not bore them with numerous "I's" or "we's." Be sincere and friendly.

Mean what you say
Be honest in your writing. Stay away from "urgent," "as soon as possible," and similar terms unless you really mean them.

Handle the negatives positively
When you have bad news to impart (e.g., you must close a client's charge account), precede the negative statement with a positive one to soften the blow.

> You have been a valued customer of ours for the past five years. However, your record of slow payment this year has forced us to cancel our credit arrangements with you. We will, of course, be glad to accommodate you with cash purchases.

Take care with appearance
A well-formatted, attractively set-up letter makes a favourable impact. Be a good ambassador for your organization. Follow the formatting instructions provided in Unit 14, K17–K40.

Proofread carefully
A document with mistakes tells the reader that you are careless. Create a good impression by producing error-free communications.

Use shortcuts where feasible
Is a letter really necessary? A short fax or email message might be better.

◆ Email messages can replace interpersonal and intercompany communications of all types: correspondence, memos, meeting notices. They can be sent to one or many recipients at the same time and can preclude telephone tag. (See Unit 5, "Electronic Mail," and consider the advantages offered.)

NOTE   All types of correspondence can be sent (via email) as attachments to email messages.

◆ Instead of a formal letter in reply to a routine request, attaching a compliment slip with the sender's name or a business card will often fulfil the same function and save time.

```
The Sylvia Harding Music Co.
4716 13 Street N.E.
Calgary, AB  T2E 6P1

                Sylvia Harding
                President

(403) 692-9213  Fax. (403) 692-9000
E-mail: sharding@hardingmusic.com
Web site: www.hardingmusic.com
```
Business card

```
                              Compliment slip

The Sylvia Harding Music Co.
4716 13 Street N.E.
Calgary, AB  T2E 6P1

                    With the compliments of
                          Sylvia Harding
                          President
```

◆ Consider a telephone call instead of a letter.

◆ If a very brief answer is required, reply on the bottom of the incoming letter, make a photocopy for your files, and return the original to the sender.

◆ Consider using a form letter rather than creating an original. (See Unit 14, K39.)

▶ E3   Letter samples

Effective business correspondence demonstrates courtesy, conciseness, clarity, coherence, and correctness. The sample letters in this section are offered as guides to achieving best results. For business etiquette practices regarding salutations and their appropriate complimentary closings, see E25 and E26.

E4   Acknowledgment letter (in someone's absence)

If your task is to handle someone's correspondence and certain decisions must wait until that person is able to deal with them (e.g., on returning from vacation), the polite thing to do is to write an acknowledgment.

```
Dear Ms. Belza:

    Thank you for your kind invitation to Mr. Reubens to make the keynote
speech at the Kiwanis Club Annual Meeting on May 10, 20--.
    Mr. Reubens is away on a trip at the moment. He will be returning next
week and will contact you then.
                                    Yours sincerely,


                                    J. McCartney
                                    Administrative Assistant
```

E5   Apology letter

If something more formal than a telephone call is appropriate, write a note giving a reason for your regrets.

E

Dear Mr. Smillie:

Thank you for inviting me to be a panellist at your forum on "Ergonomics in the Workplace" on November 3.

Much as I would relish the opportunity to share my views and discuss them with colleagues, I regret that I must decline the offer because of a previous commitment. Please accept my thanks and my apologies.

I wish you and the Forum success.

Sincerely,

E6   Collection letter

After several statements and reminder notices have been sent without effect, it is time to demand payment for an overdue account by means of letters. Start with a lenient reminder letter.

Dear Sir:

We hope you are satisfied with the personal computer you bought from us three months ago.

At the time of purchase you made a down payment of $500, with a promise to pay the balance in 30 days. However, we have not heard from you.

If you are having a problem with the equipment, please let us know; if not, we would appreciate a cheque for the outstanding amount right away.

Yours truly,

If there is no reply in two weeks, send a more demanding note.

Have you overlooked us? According to our records, your balance outstanding is still $1100.

The amount due is, as you know, nearly four months old. Since we also have to meet our financial commitments, we would appreciate your completing your end of our bargain by putting a cheque in the mail today.

If you have already sent your payment, please ignore this reminder. If you have not, please act now to preclude our taking further action.

Yours truly,

If this firmer request brings no response, the following letter may work.

You have not replied to, nor acted on, our two reminder letters about your outstanding account of $1100. We must inform you, therefore, that unless you send us a cheque for the full amount within one week, we will put your account in the hands of a collection agency.

We regret having to take this step, but you have given us no other choice.

Yours truly,

E7   Complaint letter

If a verbal expression of dissatisfaction brings no results, try a firmly worded but courteous letter. Wait until you are calm before writing, because anger works against you.

Dear Mr. Boehmer:

Our July shipment of frames arrived on schedule but, unfortunately, 100 of them were badly damaged.

We contacted your shipping department twice last week and were told the matter was under investigation; however, we have heard nothing. Since we want to enter a claim with the carrier for the damage and also need replacement frames as soon as possible, we would appreciate your immediate attention to our problem.

Please telephone or fax Ms. Lopez before Friday so that she can proceed with the necessary paperwork.

Yours sincerely,

Reply to complaint letter

Dear Mrs. Ling:

As requested in your letter of July 15 regarding the damaged frames, I telephoned Ms. Lopez to discuss the problem.

I apologize for the delay, but our shipping department had difficulty reaching the carrier for the details you required. Happily, Ms. Lopez now has the information she needs to enter a claim with the transport company. She has also placed an order for 100 frames to replace the broken ones.

Thank you for your patience and courtesy. I hope our future dealings will be trouble-free and mutually beneficial.

Yours sincerely,

E8   To cancel a contract

Dear Mr. Dillon:

On (insert date), I signed a contract in my home to purchase a new vacuum cleaner, Model XYZ, at a price of $2000. Today, I realized that I wish to cancel that contract.

I hereby exercise my right to rescind the contract under the Consumer Protection Act, and ask that the full amount be refunded by cheque or credited to my credit card.

Yours truly,

E9   Congratulatory letter

Make it short and sincere.

> Dear Marcello:
>
> I was delighted to hear of your promotion to the position of national sales manager of Elliott Galleries. After all your years of dedication and service, you certainly well deserve this honour.
> Congratulations, Marcello! I hope you will be happy in your new post.
>
> Most sincerely,

Reply to congratulatory letter
Yes! You need to write one.

> Dear Catherine:
>
> How kind of you to write a note about my recent promotion. Your good wishes certainly added to my delight at being promoted at Elliott Galleries.
> I look forward to a challenging and rewarding future.
>
> Cordially yours,

E10   Donation (response to request for)

Whether your reply is affirmative or negative, be kind.

Affirmative reply

> Dear Ms. Lafontaine:
>
> In reply to your request for a donation towards prizes for the "Games for the Physically Challenged," I am pleased to enclose our cheque for $250. On behalf of the manager and staff, I wish you and your organizers every success.
>
> Yours sincerely,

Negative reply

> Dear Ms. Lafontaine:
>
> Thank you for inviting us to participate in your annual "Games for the Physically Challenged" by means of a donation towards prizes.
> Unfortunately, we cannot assist you because it is our policy to make one major donation yearly to the United Way.
> Please accept our regrets and our good wishes for a successful event.
>
> Yours sincerely,

E

I

E11   Form letters

When routine correspondence is mailed to a large number of people (e.g., advertising a new product, introducing a new salesperson, announcing a change of location, asking repeatedly for payment of an account), the most efficient method of handling this is by keying and saving a master of the body (primary file) and inserting only the variables (secondary file) (date, inside address, salutation, and other pertinent information) at the time of mailing.

Dear

    Enclosed is our cheque for $, which represents the proceeds of your loan. The attached statement shows the terms of your contract.
    Your monthly payments are $, payable on the   of each month, and the first payment will be due on   . It is wise for you to meet your payments on time in order to maintain your good credit rating.
    Thank you for bringing your financial requirements to our company.

                                Very truly yours,

    Standard paragraphs can also be created on a computer for assembling in any order. (See Unit 14, K39.)

E12   Gratitude or thank-you letter

Avoid gushing phrases, but show your genuine appreciation.

For a gift

Dear Armand:

    It was so thoughtful of you to send me the Picasso print for my birthday. I will have it framed to hang in splendour in my office.
    Thank you very much. Perhaps the next time you are in town, you will drop in for lunch and let me show you your generous gift in its new setting.

                                  Kindest regards,

For a favour

Dear Lison:

    Thank you very much for the tickets to the final round of the Canadian Open last week. What an exciting experience it was to see the pros in real life!
    I know that you went out of your way to get the tickets. Your thoughtfulness was very much appreciated.

                              Cordially,

To a speaker

> Dear Dr. Liontos:
>
> It was a pleasure to meet you at our annual board meeting and to hear your thoughts on technology in this decade.
> I know I voice the opinion of all our members when I say a sincere thank you for coming to address our organization. We are all grateful for your interest.
>
> Sincerely yours,

E13   Inquiry letter

When a telephone inquiry is not possible, send a written request for information. Be specific about the information you require.

> Dear Sir or Madam:
>
> Our class is conducting a survey to find out which computer hardware and word-processing and accounting software programs are currently most popular with business firms in our community.
> To simplify the process, we have enclosed a form that we believe is straightforward. If you would complete the form and return it to us by August 28, we would be very grateful.
> We look forward to hearing from you.
>
> Yours truly,

Reply to inquiry letter

> Dear Ms. DiFiore:
>
> Thank you for your letter of August 3.
> We are pleased to take part in your hardware/software survey and hope that the completed form enclosed will give you the information you require.
> Good luck in your endeavours.
>
> Yours sincerely,

E14   Introduction letter

A letter introducing a person may either be mailed directly to the addressee or delivered to the addressee by the person being introduced. It should clearly state its purpose.

> Dear Dr. Shaefer:
>
> Please allow me to introduce my friend, Professor Morley Mazier, whose work in mechanical engineering is probably familiar to you. He is keen to visit your research laboratory and to discuss a matter he believes will interest you greatly.
> I hope your meeting will prove mutually beneficial.
>
> Yours sincerely,

> May I introduce to you Max Von Eben, my colleague of the past five years.
> Max and his family have decided to move out West for business reasons,
> and it occurred to me that you and he might derive some mutual benefit from
> a meeting. I would be very grateful for any assistance or guidance you could
> offer Max.
>
> Sincerely,

E15   Job application letter

See Unit 20, J14.

E16   Job recommendation or reference letter

On occasion you may be asked to write a letter of reference for an
employee or co-worker. Keep it short, positive, and honest.

> Dear Miss Wang:
>
> I am very pleased to recommend Glenn Asano to you as a prospective
> office manager.
> Glenn has worked with our organization for four years as an accounting
> assistant, payroll clerk, and finally, office supervisor. He has been a loyal and
> conscientious worker, and his eagerness to improve, combined with his
> friendly personality, has made him very popular.
> Our loss will be your gain. I know Glenn will be an asset to your com-
> pany, and I wish him every success.
>
> Yours sincerely,

If you do not have an addressee's name, in place of a salutation, use *To
Whom It May Concern*.

Request for job recommendation/reference letter

If you wish a former employer to recommend you for a new position, the
following letter would be suitable.

> Dear Judge Vanek:
>
> Would you please write a letter of reference on my behalf to Mrs. Ayako
> Okamoto of Computemps (business card enclosed), to whom I have applied
> for the position of legal placements officer.
> Mrs. Okamoto has indicated that my qualifications are satisfactory, but I
> feel sure that your confirmation of my capabilities will give added weight to
> my application.
> I would be most grateful for your assistance.
>
> Sincerely,

E17 Job refusal letter

It is courteous to send a brief note when declining a job offer.

Dear Ms. Conrad-Knight:

Thank you very much for offering me the position of . . . with your organization. I have accepted another job offer, however, so regret that I must refuse yours.

I enjoyed meeting you and appreciate the time you spent with me.

Yours sincerely,

E18 Job rejection letter

Letters to unsuccessful job applicants should be brief but kind and should be mailed as soon as possible after selection of the successful candidate. The first example below would be suitable for a person who you feel would never be suitable for your organization.

Dear Mr. Hubel:

I regret to inform you that you have not been successful in your application for a position with our organization.

The decision we had to make was extremely difficult, but we believe we have chosen the best candidate of the many who applied.

Thank you for the time and effort you expended for the interview, and good luck in the future.

Sincerely,

The following letter could be sent to an unsuccessful candidate who might be suitable for another position in your company later on.

Dear Mr. Robinette:

I am sorry to inform you that you have not been successful in your application for the position of administrative assistant with our organization.

A number of strong candidates applied and it was difficult to make a decision. We do feel, however, that a position for which you might be a candidate may become available in the future, and we will keep your application on file for that purpose. We will contact you if such an opportunity arises.

Sincerely,

Response to unsolicited job application

Try not to discourage the writer. Be straightforward in a gentle way.

Dear Mr. Denobrega:

Thank you for submitting an application to join our organization. Unfortunately, we cannot help you at the moment because there are no openings in our accounting department.

If a position to suit you does become vacant, we will contact you. In the meantime, good luck with your job hunting.

Yours sincerely,

E19 Job resignation letter

It is customary to submit a written intent of resignation as well as a verbal one when you wish to leave an organization. Be prepared to depart on a positive note—for your own benefit.

Dear Mrs. Mammone:

It is with sincere regret that I offer my resignation to Financial Associates Inc., to take effect on October 31, 20--.

The past three years have taught me a great deal, but it is now time for me to move on to a new set of challenges. Thank you for your part in my growth at Financial.

I wish you and your organization continued success.

Yours sincerely,

E20 Order letter

When a preprinted order form is not available, send a simple, detailed letter to make your request.

Dear Sirs:

Would you please send the following items to our branch at 16 Sheppard Avenue, Shubenacadie, NS, immediately.

Qty.	Description	Unit Price	Total
1000	No. 204 T hinges, copper plate	$2.00	$2000.00
500	No. 72 corner braces, copper plate	2.25	1125.00
		Total	$3125.00

An unexpected increase in orders means that our supplies are low. We would, therefore, appreciate your rushing this shipment to us.

Very truly yours,

E21   Payment letter

If a letter is required to accompany a payment, give an explanation of the payment.

Dear Sirs:

Enclosed is our cheque in payment of Invoice No. 473.
The amount of $784 on the cheque is equivalent to the invoice total of $800 less your 2% discount if payment is made within 10 days.

Yours truly,

E22   Reservations letter

Although most reservations for convention facilities or hotel accommo-dation are made by telephone, fax, or email, a letter is sometimes neces-sary. Remember to give full details and to address the letter to the reservations manager at the hotel.

Dear Sir or Madam:

Please reserve a three-room suite for September 17 and 18, 20--, for our annual conference of sales managers.
One room should be suitable for informal social meetings, one for prod-uct displays, and one for formal meetings for 15 to 20 people.
The conference will open with a social gathering at 3 p.m., September 17 and close with a brief business meeting at 10 a.m. on the 18th.
An early confirmation of this booking will be appreciated.

Yours truly,

E23   Sales letter

Since the purpose of a sales letter is to sell a product or service, be posi-tive and use the *you* approach.

Dear Mr. Shkuda:

How would you like to increase the efficiency of your office workers by 10 percent this summer? Tests in 100 offices where Iceberg air conditioners were installed proved that worker efficiency improved 10 percent.
Greater efficiency means larger profits for your organization; thus, the Iceberg pays for itself in a short time. Spread the cost of the air conditioner over one, two, or three years if you wish. The money you spend to improve worker comfort and morale and to increase productivity will be a wise investment.
Won't you call us today and let our engineer determine your office air-conditioning needs? Every day without an Iceberg is costing you money.

Yours sincerely,

Covering letter with sales information

Use this letter as a friendly encouragement to a prospective buyer. Make sure you close with a request for action.

Dear Mr. Shkuda:

We are pleased to enclose a catalogue and price list of Iceberg air conditioners as requested by our engineer, Joe Ubelacker, following his visit to your company. Joe has indicated which models are best suited to your office needs.

If you have any questions after you have had an opportunity to look over the catalogue, please give us a call. We know you and your employees will be delighted with the performance of the Iceberg.

We are at your service. Call us now for immediate delivery.

Yours sincerely,

E24   Sympathy or condolence letter

Letters of sympathy should be brief but compassionate.

Dear Miss Jacques:

It was with much regret that I read today about your brother's sudden death. Everyone who knew him will feel the loss.

I realize I cannot offer you much comfort, but please count on me if you need anything in the difficult days ahead.

Most sincerely,

Reply to sympathy letter

Dear Ms. Kordez:

Your thoughtful note and donation to the Heart and Stroke Foundation were very much appreciated by our family.

It is good to be back at the office again, with plenty of work to occupy me. I know that your kind thoughts will help sustain me through the weeks ahead.

Yours sincerely,

E25   FORMS OF ADDRESS

Addresses in business correspondence follow an established pattern (see Unit 14, K6, regarding envelopes). The form of address consists of the addressee plus mailing address (individual's name and title—if known, organization name, address, and postal code), the salutation, and the complimentary closing. The two most common examples are as follows:

E

Mr. B. Machon, President
Machon, Mortimer, and Oxley
296 Landy Lane
Saskatoon, SK S7L 2C7

Eglinton Enterprises Ltd.
495 Eglinton Avenue East
Toronto, ON M5N 3A2

Dear Mr. Machon:

Dear Sirs:

Yours sincerely,

Very truly yours,

In a situation where *the gender of the addressee is unknown* and in cases where *individuals prefer to be addressed without a social title,* use the following:

T. Weazy Leslie
(address)

Leslie Winger
(address)

Dear T. Weazy:

Dear Leslie Winger:

Yours truly,

Yours truly,

Where the *name of an addressee is unknown,* choose from the following:

Human Resources Manager
(company name and address)

Sir or Madam:

– *or* –

Dear Sir or Madam:

Yours truly,

Addressing individuals

Female:

Miss   Misses   Ms.   Mrs.
Mademoiselle (Mlle): French for an unmarried woman
Mesdemoiselles (Mlles): French for two or more unmarried women
Madame (Mme): French for a married or mature woman
Mesdames (Mmes): French for two or more married or mature women

Male:

Mr.
Monsieur (M.): French
Messieurs (MM.; Messrs.): French plural; also sometimes used in English when addressing two or more men:

Messrs. Smith and Weston

I

Addressing organizations

In these situations, the company name appears as the first line of the address. The appropriate salutations are:

Organizations consisting of all women:

◆ Ladies

◆ Mesdames

Organizations consisting of all men:

◆ Gentlemen

Organizations consisting of women and men:

◆ Gentlemen

◆ Ladies and Gentlemen

◆ Gentlemen and Ladies

◆ Dear [organization name]

Although most written communication in business is an exchange between organizations, it is sometimes necessary to contact individuals outside industry or commerce. The correct method of addressing prominent people in all sectors is included in the following section.

FORMS OF ADDRESS CHART

Title	Address	Salutation	Complimentary closing
Armed forces			
Officer			
Lieutenant-General	Lieutenant-General F. Hebert, V.C., O.B.E.	Dear Lieutenant-General Dear General Dear Sir Dear Madam	Yours very truly
Non-commissioned officer			
Sergeant	Sergeant C. Lichten	Dear Sergeant	Yours truly
Diplomatic			
Ambassador or High Commissioner (Canadian)	C. Ronning, Esq. Canadian Ambassador to . . .	Dear Sir Dear Mr. Ronning	Very truly yours
Ambassador or High Commissioner (foreign)	Her Excellency D. Raj Ambassador of . . .	Dear Madam Excellency	Respectfully
Education			
President of university	Joseph L. Billings, LL.D. President, University of . . .	Dear Sir Dear Dr. Billings Dear Mr. President	Very truly yours
Chancellor of university	Mary L. Billings, Ph.D. Chancellor, University of . . .	Dear Madam Dear Chancellor	Very truly yours
President of community college	Mary West-Moynes, President Mohawk College	Dear Madam President Dear President West-Moynes	Very truly yours

(continued . . .)

Title	Address	Salutation	Complimentary closing
Dean of college/faculty	Joseph L. Billings, Ph.D. Dean of . . .	Dear Sir Dear Dean Billings Dear Dr. Billings	Very truly yours
Professor of university	Mary L. Billings, Ph.D. University of . . .	Dear Madam Dear Professor Billings	Very truly yours
Government			
Governor General	The Right Honourable Michaëlle Jean Governor General of Canada	Your Excellency	Yours sincerely
Lieutenant-Governor	The Honourable James K. Bartleman, Lieutenant-Governor of Ontario	Your Honour	Yours sincerely
Prime Minister	The Right Honourable Lesley Billings, P.C., MP* Prime Minister of Canada	Sir Madam	I am, Sir, yours very truly I am, Madam, yours very truly
Premier of province	The Honourable Sir John Billings, MLA* Premier of the Province of . . .	Sir	Respectfully yours Sincerely yours
Minister	The Honourable Mary Billings Minister of . . .	Madam Dear Madam	Respectfully yours Sincerely yours
Mayor	His/Her Worship, The Mayor of [name of city]	Dear Sir/Madam Dear Mr./Ms./Mrs. Mayor	Yours sincerely

*The prime minister and federal cabinet ministers are members of the Privy Council (P.C.).
The Governor General is a Privy councillor (P.C.), as well as a chancellor of the Order of Canada.
All members of the federal Parliament have the designation Member of Parliament (MP) after their names.
Members of provincial and territorial legislatures use the designation Member of the Provincial Parliament (MPP) in Ontario, Member of the National Assembly (MNA) in Quebec, Member of the House of Assembly (MHA) in Newfoundland and Labrador and Nova Scotia, and Member of the Legislative Assembly (MLA) in the other provinces.
To access new government appointments: www.servicecanada.gc.ca or www.pm.gc.ca

(continued . . .)

Title	Address	Salutation	Complimentary closing
Judiciary			
Chief Justice, Supreme Court of Canada	The Right Honourable Mary Billings, Chief Justice of Canada	Dear Madam Madam Dear Madam Chief Justice	I am, Madam, yours very truly I am, Madam, yours faithfully I am, Madam, yours sincerely
Chief Justice, Provincial Supreme Court	The Honourable John Billings, Chief Justice of [name of province]	Dear Sir Sir	Yours sincerely I am, yours very truly
Justice, Supreme Court of Canada	The Honourable Mr. Justice John Billings	Sir Dear Mr. Justice Billings	Yours sincerely I am, yours very truly
Judge (federal and provincial courts)	Her Honour Judge Mary Billings	Madam Dear Judge Billings	Yours sincerely
Judge (district and county courts)	His Honour Judge John Billings	Sir Dear Judge Billings	Yours sincerely
Professional			
Doctor	Dr. B. Borden B. Borden, M.D.	Dear Dr. Borden	Yours sincerely
Lawyer	Mr. N. Jacobi Barrister and Solicitor	Dear Mr. Jacobi	Yours sincerely
(if Queen's Counsel)	N. Jacobi, Esq. N. Jacobi, Q.C.	Dear Mr. Jacobi	Yours sincerely
Religion			
Archbishop (Anglican)	The Most Reverend John Dawes, D.D., Archbishop of . . .	Most Reverend Sir Your Grace	Respectfully yours
Archbishop (Greek Orthodox)	His Eminence the Archbishop of the Greek Orthodox Church	Your Eminence	I am, Your Eminence, respectfully yours

(continued . . .)

Title	Address	Salutation	Complimentary closing
Archbishop (Roman Catholic)	The Most Reverend John Billings, Archbishop of . . .	Your Excellency	Respectfully yours
Bishop (Anglican)	The Right Reverend John Billings, D.D., Bishop of . . .	Right Reverend Sir	Respectfully yours
Bishop (Greek Orthodox)	The Most Reverend Bishop of the Greek Orthodox Church	Right Reverend Bishop	Very respectfully yours
Bishop (Roman Catholic)	The Most Reverend John Billings, Bishop of . . .	Your Excellency	Respectfully yours
Cardinal (Roman Catholic)	His Eminence John Cardinal Billings Archbishop of . . .	Your Eminence	Respectfully yours
Moderator	The Right Reverend Carol Dawson, D.D., Moderator of the . . . Church	Right Reverend Madam / Dear Dr. Dawson	Respectfully yours
Mother Superior (Roman Catholic)	The Reverend Mother Superior, The Congregation of . . .	Dear Madam / Reverend Mother Superior / Dear Mother Superior	Respectfully yours
Pope (Roman Catholic)	His Holiness The Pope	Your Holiness	I have the honour to be, Your Holiness' obedient servant
Rabbi (Jewish)	The Reverend Rabbi Jacob Abrams	Dear Sir	Respectfully yours

►E26 Salutations and complimentary closings

Consult the following chart to ensure that you use the appropriate salutation and complimentary closing in your business and personal correspondence. As a general rule, do everything you can to find a name (this makes the letter more personal and increases chances of a response).

Correspondence	Salutation	Complimentary closing
Formal		
◆ writing to a person of high political, diplomatic, royal, or religious rank	(See the "Forms of Address Chart" in the previous section.)	
◆ writing to a company or organization and addressing no one in particular	Dear Sirs Gentlemen Gentlemen and Ladies Ladies and Gentlemen Dear [company name]	Yours truly
◆ writing to a person whom you have not met but are mentioning specifically in the inside address	Sir Madam Dear Sir Dear Madam	Very truly yours Yours truly Yours very truly
◆ when an attention line is used	Gentlemen Dear Sirs Ladies and Gentlemen Ladies *or* Mesdames (when the company is totally female)	Very truly yours Yours truly Yours very truly
◆ writing to a person but using only a business title (e.g., Sales Manager)	Dear Sir Dear Madam	Very truly yours Yours truly Yours very truly
Less formal		
◆ writing to a person you know but on a business basis only	Dear Mr. Robinette Dear Miss Jones Dear Ms. Chantrelle Dear Mrs. Kuman	Sincerely Sincerely yours Yours sincerely Cordially yours
◆ writing to a businessperson you do not know and whose gender is unknown	Dear Sir or Madam Dear Madam or Sir Dear C. Kreiner	Yours very truly
◆ writing to an unknown address in a form letter	Dear Friend Dear Customer Dear Homeowner	Very truly yours
Personal		
◆ writing to a friend	Dear Maurice My dear Ginette	Cordially yours Most sincerely Kindest regards Best wishes Regards Sincerely
◆ writing to a friend in a business situation	Dear Mr. Bird	Yours very sincerely
◆ writing to a young person	Dear Jonathan	Yours sincerely

E27 MEMORANDUMS

The interoffice memorandum is designed for sending messages within an organization and therefore does not need an inside address, salutation, or complimentary closing. Designed for short, factual communications, one paragraph is acceptable. See Unit 14, K41, for formatting information.

Memo to: A. Palambo, Sales Rep.
From: Debbie Bruce, Sales Manager
Date: Current Date
Subject: May Sales Meeting

The next monthly sales meeting is scheduled for Thursday,
May 13, at 10 a.m. in my office.

A valuable addition to the agenda would be a 15-min presentation by you to
the salespeople on the ad campaign you ran so successfully in January.
Please let me know by Friday if this will be possible.

phe

NOTE   It is not necessary to key in sender's initials if his or her name appears in the From:[   ] line.

E28 PRESS RELEASES

When a new product is introduced, a senior managerial appointment announced, or another notable event occurs, the occasion is often publicized in the media by means of a press release. This is a bulletin sent out to newspapers, trade magazines, and other pertinent journals in the hope of free publication. The press release follows this format:

♦ Key on standard-sized company letterhead.

♦ Use wide margins.

♦ Double-space to allow for editing.

♦ Insert the name, title, telephone and fax numbers, and email address of a company contact person.

♦ Key the story headline in block capitals.

♦ Insert FOR RELEASE ON [provide the date on which the announcement becomes official] or FOR IMMEDIATE RELEASE and the date of transmission underneath.

♦ End the release with –30–.

Contents of the press release

Keep the contents to one page if possible and the writing strictly factual. A well-written release enables an editor to do an accurate précis if one is necessary.

E

The first paragraph should tell a brief story that answers the questions *who*, *what*, *when*, *where*, *why*, and *how*. Subsequent paragraphs amplify or expand on the news. No concluding paragraph is necessary.

PRESS RELEASE

Pitman Office Handbook
Seventh Edition © 2008
Joan I. Campbell

FOR IMMEDIATE RELEASE

May 2007
Contact: Barbara Chen, Publicist
Tel: 416-447-5101, ext. 214
Fax: 416-447-7755

Workplace and work styles are continually changing and presenting new challenges. Full of productivity tips, the *Pitman Office Handbook* is a useful reference book that helps readers keep up with the times with this fully updated and expanded seventh edition.

SOME FEATURES OF THE SEVENTH EDITION

• Locator codes and an expanded index that make it easy to find information quickly

• Expanded coverage of technology including computer systems, company intranets, voice technology, and information on using the internet effectively to conduct job searches, do research, and plan events

• Sound advice about communication, language, and delivery/presentation skills, as well as interpersonal skills, effective telephone techniques, Netiquette, and conflict resolution in the workplace

• Expanded coverage of marketplace terminology and tips about financial management

• Completely reorganized into five major sections

• Testing material for each unit and suggested marking schemes available on Pearson Education website to accompany this handbook

–30–

Representing Pearson Education Canada, a division of Pearson Canada Inc.
26 Prince Andrew Place, Toronto, Ontario M3C 2T8
Tel: (416) 447-5101, Fax: (416) 443-0948
E-mail: phabinfo.pubcanada@pearsoned.com
Visit our website at: www.pearsoned.ca

A press release

E29 REPORTS

Reports come in two broad categories: the *information* report, which provides data, and the *research* report, which outlines a problem, presents facts and findings after research has been carried out, evaluates the data collected, and recommends a solution. The information report is informal and usually brief; the research report is complex and therefore requires a more structured format. (See Unit 14, K42–66, for formatting instructions.)

Preparing a report

Research Before you start writing the report, gather all the facts to be presented. Go to appropriate and, of course, reliable sources for records, figures, dates, and other pertinent information.

Primary research data is information that you gather specifically for the project you are doing. This information can be the result of your own observations or surveys, or can be derived from general reference books or materials.

Secondary research data is information that has been collected and compiled by others on the topic that you are investigating and that exists in printed or electronic form.

"The report notes should be generous in the use of headings throughout the report."

Lanham, Stewart, Zimmer:

Business English and Communication 3rd Cdn. Ed. McGraw-Hill Ryerson, Toronto, 1987 p. 106
Advocates
1. Closely written text boring.
2. Break up text into many sections.
3. Make reader's task easy.

Report notes

NOTE Names of magazines, newspapers, books, or periodicals should be in *italics* or underlined.

The internet as well as libraries, whether company, university, or public, are usually the best source of information on a wide variety of subjects. Each library will have its own system for retrieval of publications and other materials that might be useful. If you encounter any difficulty, a librarian is usually available to provide assistance (see Unit 16, "Information/Reference Sources/Internet").

Once you locate the material you need, use an index card or a laptop computer to record each relevant piece of information. Be sure to record in full the bibliographical information for any sources that you might quote in your report, as detailed below.

For a book: Name(s) of author(s) and/or editor(s), book title and subtitle (if any), the name and location of the publisher, year of publication, and page number(s). Additional information might be required, such as edition or volume number.

For a magazine, journal, or newspaper article: Author (if known), name of article, name of publication, date of publication, page number. Volume numbers are also sometimes included.

The outline Once you have collected all the relevant data, prepare an outline for your report, similar to the following illustration.

NOTE Some software packages help in producing outlines. The software automatically assigns section designators (numbers, letters, etc.) and appropriate indents. If you decide to add or delete information, the program will renumber and reorganize the outline, together with accompanying text.

OUTLINE—THE BUSINESS REPORT

I. Locating Information
   A. Company sources
      1. The resource centre
      2. Online databases
   B. Internet
   C. University libraries
   D. Original research

II. Appearance
   A. Advantages and disadvantages of printer types
      1. Laser
      2. Dot matrix
      3. Ink jet
   B. Stationery choices
      1. Recycled
      2. Paper weights
      3. Colour
      4. Finish

III. Production and Distribution
   A. In-house facilities
   B. Outside print sources

A typical outline

Rough draft Build on the outline and add the appropriate substance to the report.

◆ First write an introduction stating the purpose of the report and indicating research methods, background information, and any other pertinent details.

◆ Enlarge on the points made in the introduction by giving details, comparisons, statistics, etc. Organize the body into sections and subsections and try to provide clear headings for each topic or paragraph.

◆ End with a conclusion that summarizes the report findings or research, and offer your recommendations for future action.

To be of greatest benefit to the reader, a report should be

◆ complete (any questions should be anticipated and answered)
◆ concise (this enables the reader to quickly understand the facts being presented)
◆ clearly written and easy to read (no confusion should be raised in the reader's mind)
◆ more objective than subjective
◆ developed in logical sequence
◆ accurate and contain only verified information
◆ supported by specific and precise evidence that reinforces your arguments

Final report Edit and polish the rough draft (several times if necessary) until you are satisfied that your words tell an accurate, understandable story.

Read the draft aloud to hear how it flows; ask yourself if every point has been clearly expressed; try to see your work from the reader's perspective. If you have time, put the report away for a couple of days and come back to it with fresh eyes before the final production occurs.

If you plan to mail the report, enclose a *letter of transmittal* that explains the purpose of the report and contains your recommendations.

Parts of the report

Depending on its length, a report usually consists of all or most of the following parts. See Unit 14, K42–66, for properly formatted examples.

Title page or cover sheet The title of the report, name and department or company of the originator, name of the recipient (unless intended for broad distribution), and the date are attractively keyed on this first page.

Table of contents Each heading and its page number are set up for easy reference on this sheet. When keying the contents page, use dot leaders for easy reference to page numbers. (See Unit 14, K45.) The contents page tells the reader what topics are covered in the report and where to find them quickly. Illustrations may also be listed in the table of contents.

TIP   Use the automatic table of contents feature in your word-processing software.

Preface or summary In long reports, a preface or summary enables the reader who does not have enough time to read the whole report to pick out the main points quickly.

Body of the report The main body of the report consists of an introduction, details of the topic under discussion, and a conclusion as described earlier under "Rough draft."

TIP   If you use the styles feature of your word-processing software, you can easily update formats and generate automatic tables of contents.

Footnotes, endnotes, and textnotes These are numbered references that provide additional information or identify specific sources used in the report. Footnotes appear at the bottom of each page; endnotes appear on a separate page at the end of the report; textnotes are recorded in the appropriate place in the report. (See Unit 14, K58.)

Bibliography The titles of books, periodicals, and other reference sources; their authors; and date, place, and name of publisher comprise this list of sources used in compiling the report. It is always arranged alphabetically by author or editor. (See Unit 14, K64.)

Appendix When a number of graphs, tables, special vocabulary lists, etc., are included in a report, they are compiled in an appendix. The appendix/appendices should be placed before the bibliography.

TIP Use all caps when keying in the word APPENDIX (e.g., APPENDIX A, APPENDIX B, and so on). You may also use the roman numeral designation (e.g., APPENDIX I, APPENDIX II).

NOTE Roman numerals should line up from right to left:

APPENDIX I
APPENDIX II
APPENDIX III

Number the pages using the same numbering format as the body of the report, and place the appendix pages behind the body of the report.

E30 ORAL EXPRESSION

Most people spend more time speaking (giving instructions, asking questions, selling, etc.) than they do writing. With the spoken word, tone, pitch, volume, rate, enunciation, pronunciation, and language skills are important considerations. Skilful use of the voice and clever choice of language will help you achieve the desired effect on your audience.

Tone: Indication of attitude and feelings; voice modulation.

Pitch: Degree of highness or lowness of the voice (variations in pitch add interest and indicate meanings).

Volume: Quality that enables you to be heard (volume is influenced by the size and acoustics of a room and use or non-use of a microphone).

Rate: Tempo of your speech (use a rate that ensures each word is intelligible).

Enunciation: The precision with which you express each word (let your audience hear your words: "What did you say?" not "Wojasay?").

Pronunciation: Correct expression of each word (correct pronunciation is the mark of an educated person: film not filum; maintenance not maintainance).

E31 PRESENTATIONS

▶E32 Introducing a speaker

Keep the introduction short and simple. Include the following:

◆ the speaker's name, printed or written, on the board or flip chart (if available, or if you feel it is necessary); this is helpful for the audience if the name is difficult to pronounce or to spell

◆ a warm, welcoming comment

◆ a statement of the speaker's topic

◆ a very brief summary of the speaker's background or special interests

◆ an introduction of the speaker by name (Do this *last*. The speaker knows that at this point he or she takes over.)

▶E33 Thanking a speaker

Again, say very little. Comment on the importance of the speech and then simply thank the speaker, expressing appreciation on behalf of everyone present.

▶E34 Making a speech or oral report

Getting started

Establish a purpose. Is your purpose to inform, persuade, or entertain (or a combination of these)?

Determine your topic and decide on the key ideas.

Consider your audience age, type, and number.

Collect and organize your reference materials.

Preparing an outline

Prepare an outline by building a "frame" that consists of an introduction (what your presentation is about), the body (which includes the details needed to satisfy the listeners' curiosity and keep them interested), and a conclusion (which reaffirms the opening statement).

Your outline will resemble the one shown for a written report in E29.

Writing the speech

Enlarge on your outline until you have produced a speech (either in point form or in full) that is the right length.

◆ Have a compelling opening. Use a startling question or a challenging statement, or recount an incident that will grab the audience's interest.

◆ Keep the main points you want to make to only three or four. Audiences won't remember if you say something once and just move on. Make the point. Say it again differently, illustrate it, and then say it again.

◆ Have a strong closing. Use a summary of the points you have made and the conclusions to be drawn, or make some type of appeal for action.

E

Producing your speaking notes

From the finished speech, produce your speaking notes. These may be in one of three forms:

◆ Cut back your speech to key words or phrases and write these boldly on small cue cards.

◆ Use the outline you prepared earlier, with the key points highlighted or underscored.

◆ Use your entire speech, with the key points highlighted or underscored. This is the least desirable option because you should not get up in front of your audience and *read* a speech. If you must use this method, then type the speech using only the top half of each sheet so that you will be glancing only at the top of the lectern and can keep your head up.

Practising

Even the most experienced speakers practise their presentations. Inexperienced speakers may find it helpful to practise the presentation aloud to a friend or in front of a mirror. Audio- or videotaping your speech and playing it back can also help you identify any problems.

◆ Time yourself, allowing time for laughter or audience participation if applicable.

◆ Practise your opening and your closing until you have memorized them. Do not, however, memorize the rest of the speech. This will restrict your delivery.

Delivering the speech

When it is time for you to speak, walk calmly to the appointed spot, look up, smile, and make your presentation, bearing in mind these tips:

◆ Do not bring a cell phone; if you do—turn it off.

◆ Make a good first impression. Look as good as you can. Have good posture and maintain this all the way through the presentation.

◆ Be well prepared. Preparation breeds confidence.

◆ Don't *read* your speech. It is preferable to use an outline or cue cards. If you insist on the comfort of a full script in front of you, don't turn the pages on the lectern. As you finish a page, slide it face up to your left so that your eyes move easily to the next sheet. If you do this, you will not look down as much.

◆ Speak slowly, clearly, and loudly enough to be heard by everyone. Keep your head up and be sure that people in the back row can hear you. Articulate carefully; do not drop *g*'s on words like *going, saying,* and *something* (not *goin* or *gonna, sayin,* or *somethin*).

Presentation tips

◆ Dress appropriately; business clothing is recommended if you are speaking to a group of businesspeople. Women: no bare midriffs; your hair should be clean and neatly coiffed (not hanging in your eyes).

I

- ◆ Speak with enthusiasm and vary the pitch of your voice. Vocal variety is vital.
- ◆ Try to be natural, spontaneous, and conversational in your delivery, but avoid using too many words like "uh," "like," "you know," etc.
- ◆ Feel your audience's reaction and respond to it.
- ◆ Establish a bond with each listener in the audience by making frequent eye contact.
- ◆ Body language is important. Use gestures, body movements, and facial expressions as valuable tools. However, avoid irritating mannerisms (too many hand movements, fiddling with buttons, playing with hair, or moving around too much).
- ◆ Maintain good posture throughout the presentation (avoid bouncing around or rolling back and forth on your heels and toes).
- ◆ Conceal any nervousness as well as you can. Use a lectern to hold on to, keep taking deep breaths, don't hold on to papers—they rustle!
- ◆ Make use of visuals if possible to present difficult concepts or statistical information. Make sure the audience can see them—don't get in the way!

WORDS OF WISDOM

To be a good speaker, be a good listener!

Closing

- ◆ Be aware of the time available and don't exceed it.
- ◆ Deliver your strong closing and turn the proceedings back to the chair or facilitator.

▶E35 Pointers for effective oral presentations

Physical setting

- ◆ Make sure everyone can hear and see easily.

Rate of speaking

- ◆ Speak slowly. This means at a relaxed rate, not unnaturally slowly. Don't overdo it.

Speech plan

- ◆ Try to create a "road map" to your presentation. Clearly state the purpose of your presentation and how many points you'll make. Try to say "First," "Second," "Next," etc., so that the audience has a sense of the progression as well as a set of expectations about where you're taking them.

Language

- Simplify your vocabulary and avoid ambiguities.
- Explain essential content vocabulary.
- Reduce the use of idioms.
- Use active voice and positive sentences where possible.
- Monitor sentence length.

Visual cues

- Use charts, maps, pictures, or photographs.
- Do not put too many items or points on a visual; there should only be six to eight items on a page or screen.
- Use a large-print font for easy reading.
- Take a course on how to use software packages for electronic presentations (e.g., PowerPoint, Photoshop, Presentations, Acrobat, or CorelDRAW).
  PowerPoint or Presentations will help you create the following:
  - charts and spreadsheets
  - handouts
  - outlines
  - slides
  - sounds and images
  - speaker's notes
  You can also establish links to websites you refer to in your presentation.
- Today's employees are expected to be knowledgeable in using presentation software.

NOTE Proofread very carefully; errors in visuals or handouts can damage the impact of the presentation.

Handouts

- Provide an outline of the presentation.
- Provide a list of the key terms used.
- Provide copies of important charts or other visuals.

TIP Decide whether you wish the audience to have the handouts *during* or *after* the presentation.

Give handouts *after* the presentation, if they are not needed for reference, to prevent the flipping of pages (which eliminates the noise factor and gets the undivided attention of your audience).

I

E36 DICTATION TECHNIQUES

Whether you dictate to a person or into a recording device, advance preparation is the key to success. For greater efficiency, plan to do all of your dictating in one session, if possible. If you travel on the job and are required to document details, you may be wise to dictate a report (or brief notes to be expanded later) after each call or contact, while the information is still fresh in your mind.

Preparation

◆ Assemble all the information you need—files, correspondence, calendar, address book.

◆ Organize your thoughts in advance and make notes of the points you want to include.

◆ When you want to reply to incoming correspondence, make notes in the margins.

◆ Set time aside to dictate your material.

◆ Close your office door or post a "DO NOT DISTURB—DICTATION IN PROGRESS" sign; if possible, give the time that you do not wish to be disturbed (e.g., "from 10 to 11 a.m.").

◆ To avoid interruptions, ask someone to take your phone calls during this scheduled time (ringing phones, including cell phones, are a distraction).

◆ Never dictate with a radio playing in the background.

NOTE If you bring dictation home with you, do not let children play with the equipment when you are not in the room (could be embarrassing).

Dictation instructions

◆ Identify the type of message (letter, memo, long or short report, fax, etc.).

◆ Indicate priority or rush work.

◆ Specify the number of copies to be made and to whom they should go.

◆ Give any special instructions regarding format (spacing, layout) or stationery to be used.

◆ If you are dictating into a recorder, identify yourself by name, title, and location. As well as following the points noted above, if your recorder has the capability, indicate where communications end and if there are any corrections.

Dictation

◆ Remain stationary and do not smoke, chew gum, eat, or play with keys or jewellery while dictating.

E

◆ If your job necessitates dictating from your car, roll up the car windows and park the car. *Never* dictate and drive. *Never* dictate during a flight unless you are travelling on a company executive jet and it is appropriate to do so.

◆ Hold the microphone or telephone receiver about 10 cm from your mouth.

◆ Use a natural, conversational voice level and speed.

◆ Give the name and address of the addressee.

◆ For memos, indicate the subject.

◆ Dictate numbers slowly and spell proper names not accessible to the transcriber.

◆ Spell out troublesome technical terms and other difficult words or names.

◆ Give as many punctuation and paragraphing instructions as possible.

◆ Place correspondence being replied to face down on the desk when dictation is finished so that the order of items on the tape is obvious to the transcriber.

◆ If necessary, stamp or write on correspondence being replied to, with date and name of person who took dictation (may be needed for future reference).

WORDS OF WISDOM

There is nothing more beautiful than to hear a language spoken properly.

3 INTERPERSONAL AND SOCIAL/SOFT SKILLS

II

SELECTED CONTENTS

IS1	**SOCIAL/SOFT SKILLS**
IS2	**INTERPERSONAL SKILLS**
IS3	Professional Image
IS4	Interpersonal Skills on the Job
IS5	Communicating
IS6	Communications
IS7	Listening Skills
IS8	Becoming a Better Listener
IS9	**FRONT-LINE RECEPTION, PUBLIC RELATIONS, AND CLIENT/CUSTOMER SERVICE EXCELLENCE**
IS10	Greeting Visitors
IS11	Dealing with Difficult Visitors
IS12	Introductions
IS13	Hints on Remembering Names
IS14	Ethics
IS15	Conflict Resolution
IS16	Gender Role Stereotyping and Discrimination
IS17	Gender Equity
IS18	Dressing for the Job
IS19	Dining Out
IS20	Smoking
IS21	The Bill
IS22	Tipping
IS23	Invitations
IS24	Acceptance
IS25	Regrets
IS26	**BUSINESS ETIQUETTE ABROAD**

IS1 SOCIAL/SOFT SKILLS

The social skills demanded of people in their business lives are essentially no different from those that apply in their private lives. *Tact* and *courtesy* in dealing with other people are the keys to successful relationships. Whether business is conducted at home or abroad, employees are required to possess social skills that will reflect well on their organizations. Knowing how to behave correctly in any situation leads to the comfort of all concerned and can play a significant part in job promotion. Social skills are so important in today's business world that agencies exist for the sole purpose of training personnel in the art of *good manners*.

Some companies (such as law firms, advertising agencies, government departments) schedule professional development days to update employees on social etiquette/protocol. Training courses/seminars may also be provided for employees who must interact with out-of-country personnel, such as training on social protocol during government functions.

Visit http://text.alis.gov.ab.ca/tips/archive.asp?EK = 3303 for more information on soft skills.

IS2 INTERPERSONAL SKILLS

In very simple terms, interpersonal skills are those needed to assist us in getting along with people. Human interaction is an integral part of any job because no job exists where contact with others does not occur. We are all team players.

The successful employee demonstrates many characteristics—all the technical skills needed to complete the job and the interpersonal skills such as thoughtfulness, insight, sensitivity, and concern for others—that permit him or her to be a successful and accepted part of the office team.

- ◆ Master the art of listening, to improve accuracy and save time (see IS7).
- ◆ Be co-operative. If something is not your responsibility, don't say, "That's not my job." You might suggest, "Joe looks after that. Would you like me to get him to do it for you?"
- ◆ Offer assistance if you are not too busy and a co-worker is obviously under pressure.
- ◆ Keep an open mind and show yourself to be receptive to new ideas and procedures.
- ◆ Look like a professional. Dress for success! First impressions are very important in the business world. A negative image reflects poor self-confidence and self-worth. Make a statement about yourself with colours, fabrics, clothes, hair, and personal hygiene. Keep your wardrobe neat, clean, in good repair, and varied.

    Fingernails should be clean, kept fairly short, and have a well-cared-for look. If you use polish, wear a subtle shade. Keep your hair well brushed and clean (if coloured, maintain roots on a regular basis)—no overstyled hairstyles. Avoid flashy, dangling, and noisy jewellery.

II

IS3   PROFESSIONAL IMAGE

A professional image involves more than dressing appropriately for the office. In order to advance or succeed in a career, you must combine a business-like appearance with essential hands-on skills, communication and listening skills, and a positive and professional attitude.

◆ Be careful about language. Profanities are never acceptable.

◆ Watch your body language. Your energy level tells a lot about you. Vitality is noticed, but don't overdo it. Check your posture and project a comfortable but confident image. Hunched shoulders or crossed arms and legs suggest a defensive attitude.

IS4   INTERPERSONAL SKILLS ON THE JOB

Professionalism in the office is very important in order to maintain a positive working environment. At work, relationships exist with co-workers, with employers, and with customers and visitors, and the successful office worker will know how to relate successfully to all three groups. The employee demonstrating good interpersonal skills usually follows these guidelines:

◆ *leaves personal troubles at home*

◆ *learns to accept the lifestyles and values of others* (beliefs, eating habits, housing, education, leisure activities, dress style), respecting the rights of others to choose how to live and behave

◆ *avoids making judgments* without having all the information

◆ *maintains a good appearance*
  • pays attention to health care and personal hygiene
  • knows that office workers represent their organizations to the outside world and have a responsibility to maintain good grooming and appropriate dress standards

◆ *displays a good and co-operative attitude*
  • demonstrates a willingness to work hard and carry his/her own weight
  • avoids getting involved in gossip
  • avoids being part of the problem; becomes part of the solution
  • gives an honest day's work and saves time and money where possible
  • shows adaptability by, for example, being willing to help out in "rush" situations
  • is anxious to learn and move ahead on the job
  • is courteous, respectful, and considerate of others and is generally cheerful and approachable
  • shows respect for more senior personnel; is sensitive to the level of company language informality and addresses senior staff formally until invited to use first names
  • respects co-workers' time by avoiding interrupting them
  • is an excellent listener

- is *tactful* and *sensitive* in dealing with others
- displays self-discipline, competence, loyalty, trustworthiness, honesty, and responsibility
- does not impose on others by abusing sick leave, taking long breaks, or coming in late and leaving early

◆ *observes rules*
  - knows and follows both the written and unwritten rules of the organization

IS

◆ *respects the work and personal space of colleagues*

◆ *develops tolerance*
  - is aware that some *mannerisms can be irritating* (loud laughter, bragging, complaining, gossiping, vulgar language), and recognizes the things that cannot be controlled or changed and learns to live with them

◆ *attempts to separate the behaviour from the person*
  - knows that although a person may have done something that was offensive, that person has not become totally offensive

◆ *gets ahead while maintaining good relations with co-workers* In seeking advancement, the person displaying good interpersonal skills is aware of the pitfalls to avoid:
  - does not become a winner by making others look like losers
  - knows that getting along with co-workers must always be a priority
  - accepts praise gracefully and resists bragging about it
  - shares credit where it is due
  - flatters only with sincerity
  - acknowledges thoughtfulness
  - is a good team player (let your reputation speak for itself)

WORDS OF WISDOM

Freedom of speech means we all have the right to our opinions, but it doesn't mean everyone has to agree with them.

WORDS OF WISDOM

The nice thing about teamwork is that you always have others on your side.

II

IS5 COMMUNICATING

The most important ingredient for success in developing interpersonal skills is the ability to communicate well. Communicating well means sharing a message or idea in such a way that there is a high level of understanding between the sender and the receiver of the message. Communication breakdowns can lead to misunderstanding, frustration, and even costly errors. Breakdowns in communications are often avoidable and usually occur because of the following:

◆ *poor language skills* (inappropriate and poorly chosen words)

◆ *poor listening skills* (not concentrating fully on what has been said)

◆ *poor reading skills* (do not understand written communication or information presented in business office manuals)

◆ *emotional involvement* (judging the speaker or writer rather than the words)

   All of the above barriers can be overcome with the right effort.

◆ Choose words with care and develop a vocabulary extensive enough to assist you in using words with precision.

◆ Learn to listen well (see IS7). As a listener, try to empathize with the feelings and ideas that a person is communicating. If the message is not clear, ask for clarification. As a speaker, be aware that you may be misinterpreted and seek confirmation that you have been understood.

◆ Be as objective as possible. Avoid letting personal biases and prejudices get in the way.

How to have an effective discussion

A discussion is not a conversation. A conversation can involve a variety of subjects, whereas a discussion should be focused on a specific topic or list of topics. A conversation generally has no specific purpose, but a discussion is aimed at a definite objective—it may be to solve a problem, to decide on a course of action, or to reconcile conflicting opinions. The people involved in a discussion are joined in a kind of partnership by working towards a conclusion acceptable to all sides. The success of some of our most important relationships, whether personal or business, will depend on the success of discussing things.

   The motto of an effective discussion should be "We can work it out":

◆ What is the objective? The aim is to reach an understanding with the involved parties.

◆ Be prepared. A discussion should embrace all points of view and all the facts should be disclosed; if important opinions or facts are left unspoken out of politeness or tact, the resolution of the question may never come to completion.

◆ Allow equal time for each speaker. People who view a discussion as a battle to be won often try to win it by attrition—they will make the same point over and over again in an attempt to wear down their opponents.

IS

◆ Keep the discussion from getting personal. Sarcasm or sharp criticism aimed at an individual can prompt retaliation, but incompatibility need not be an obstacle for a successful discussion. Take a break if the discussion is getting heated and personal.

◆ A little comic relief is welcome in serious discussions, but there is a fine line between a jest and a jeer.

◆ A discussion should not be taken as an occasion to show off one's wit or superior knowledge; the participants involved should not feel intimidated. For example, although W. S. Gilbert and Sir Arthur Sullivan loathed each other, they formed one of the most fruitful partnerships in the history of musical theatre.

◆ Try not to confuse assumptions with facts. A fact is something that is capable of verification by demonstration. Never pretend to know something you actually don't know. Facts should not be assumed, nor should they be twisted to fit one's opinions. No matter how objective we like to think we are, our convictions are bound to be subject to a degree of distortion arising out of various backgrounds and interests.

◆ Talk *to* the people involved, not *at* them. Whenever we talk *at* people, we turn what should have been dialogue into diatribe.

◆ A discussion is a matter of alternately speaking and listening. One important qualification for being a good discusser is to be a good listener.

◆ Improve your listening skills by asking questions whenever you are unclear about the meaning of a statement.

◆ Summarize your understanding of a statement to verify that you have heard it accurately.

◆ Be on guard against the tendency to hear what you want to hear; people are subject to a form of wishful thinking, changing the meaning of what is being said.

◆ Replace general language with specific language in order to refine the terms for all to understand.

WORDS OF WISDOM

Speaking kindly never hurt anyone.

IS6 COMMUNICATIONS

For guidance on situations requiring written communications, see Unit 2, E1; for guidance on oral communications, see Unit 2, E30.

In responding to written and other communications, bear these two guidelines in mind:

◆ Answer letters within 48 hours.

◆ Deal with telephone calls, email, and fax messages promptly.

IS7 LISTENING SKILLS

Studies show that the average person spends about 80 percent of his or her waking hours engaged in communication. This communication time is divided among four skills: listening, speaking, reading, and writing.

The average adult listens at no better than a 25 percent efficiency level. For example, after listening to a 10-minute oral presentation, the average person understands and remembers less than half of what was said. If a speaker talks for more than 10 minutes, as often happens in the classroom and in seminars, conferences, and business meetings, efficiency in listening might well be less than 25 percent.

Employees who do not listen effectively can cost organizations billions of dollars. Poor listening skills can account for letters, contracts, and reports that must be rekeyed and shipments that must be reshipped; they can lead to co-worker misunderstandings and the loss of valuable clients/customers.

REMEMBER Education brings knowledge, knowledge is power, and knowledgeable workers are a huge asset in the workforce.

Techniques of a good listener

Improve your attitude—you must realize the **importance** of good listening skills and develop them to become a better listener.

◆ Good listeners pay **attention** to whomever is speaking. They concentrate on what is being said, avoid distractions, and do not let the mind wander.

◆ Good listeners are **interested** in what is being said; poor listeners usually decide after hearing a few words from the speaker that they do not really like the topic and then lose interest, missing out on valuable information.

◆ Good listeners are **motivated** and want to gain knowledge; the more they know about the topic, the more they can contribute.

◆ Good listeners maintain eye contact with the speaker and try to listen and **learn** as much as they can about the subject.

◆ Good listeners do not interrupt or change the subject until the speaker indicates that he/she is **finished speaking** on the topic.

◆ Good listeners take notes and then ask questions in order to clarify information; they **listen attentively** rather than mentally rehearsing what they are going to say next (they think before they speak).

Good listening skills can assist with problem solving, making you a valued employee: "The chronic kicker, even the most violent critic, will frequently soften and be subdued in the presence of a patient, sympathetic listener—a listener who will be silent while the irate faultfinder dilates like a king cobra and spews the poison out of his system" (Dale Carnegie).

WORDS OF WISDOM

IS

Sometimes you have to be silent to be heard.

IS8   BECOMING A BETTER LISTENER

Employers often complain that many of their employees have poor listening skills. Do not allow yourself to be open to this criticism. More effective listening leads to greater understanding and, therefore, to greater personal efficiency. Force yourself to concentrate on what is being said, so that you comprehend the intended meaning. The process of listening requires an active mind.

The roadblocks to effective listening are that we can think much faster than a person can speak and so sometimes our minds wander or we are busy planning a reply rather than truly listening. At other times, our emotions get in the way and cloud our understanding. To overcome these roadblocks and improve your listening skills, do the following:

◆ Keep quiet and focus on what is being said.

◆ Review the speaker's statements in your mind as you listen.

◆ Use non-verbal actions (nods, smiles, frowns) to encourage the speaker. This also ensures that you must actively listen.

◆ Judge the words, not the speaker. Don't be affected by distractions.

◆ Have a notepad handy. Listen and then write down the main points. Don't trust your memory.

◆ Give the speaker your undivided attention. Try not to permit interruptions (e.g., telephone calls) while someone is speaking to you.

◆ If the speaker's message is not clear, ask for clarification or repetition.

◆ When asked a question, listen carefully, repeat it word for word in your mind, and then formulate an answer.

WORDS OF WISDOM

Listening is a compliment in action.

IS9 FRONT-LINE RECEPTION, PUBLIC RELATIONS, AND CLIENT/CUSTOMER SERVICE EXCELLENCE

All organizations are concerned about the image they present to outsiders and must provide clear guidelines for employees to follow. Be aware of and follow your organization's wishes in dealing with visitors. Some employers, for example, want to see *all* visitors; others, only after an interview has been arranged and the visitor has been announced.

Whatever approach is taken by your employer, be aware that goodwill, an invaluable business asset, is created by customer satisfaction. Goodwill is the friendly, honest, warm feeling that can be conveyed by employees and is as important as the good reputation of the product or service sold. The good reputation of a company can be fostered by employees who

◆ demonstrate a genuinely helpful attitude
◆ offer a pleasant, friendly smile and cheerful greeting
◆ remember and recognize customers
◆ show courtesy, understanding, and respect
◆ demonstrate competence

Remember: Every problem is an opportunity for success!

IS10 GREETING VISITORS

◆ Always dress professionally.
◆ Never chew gum or any other food items when greeting clients/visitors.
◆ Do not eat in the reception area or at your desk if you are greeting/receiving clients.
◆ Maintain a professional work area (e.g., a tidy desk with no food or drink on it).
◆ Never judge a visitor by appearance. Appearances can deceive!
◆ Never ignore a person who comes into the reception area for an appointment or requesting assistance.
◆ Deal with everyone with equal kindness, patience, and concern.
◆ If you are handling a phone call, ask the caller to hold momentarily in order for you to acknowledge the client/visitor.
◆ Give the visitor your complete attention; smile and make eye contact.
◆ Listen patiently and carefully to people who may have difficulty expressing themselves because of unfamiliarity with the language.
◆ Write down pertinent information, such as the visitor's name (ask for the spelling of the name if it is a long or difficult one to remember), name of company, etc.
◆ Make visitors feel at ease and comfortable. Introduce yourself. Hang up coats and offer refreshments and reading materials (if appropriate) if the visitor must wait.
◆ Arrange to have daily newspaper(s) available in the reception area.

◆ Ensure that the caller sees the person who can best help him or her.
◆ Make visitors feel important. Address them by name when speaking to them or advising them that Mr. or Mrs. *(whomever they have come to see)* will see them now.
◆ Make introductions properly and confidently (see IS12).

Client/visitor interaction

◆ It is not necessary to carry on a conversation with a client, but if he or she initiates a conversation, keep it light and be courteous and polite; the conversation should be on a very impersonal note.
◆ Never discuss personal or company business with a client, and do not get involved in conversations (including telephone conversations) about company employees or business with other co-workers when a client/visitor is present.

Greeting government officials or international visitors

◆ Use official titles when greeting provincial or federal government officials; e.g., Mr. Premier, Mr. Prime Minister, Councillor (last name), or Mayor (last name).
◆ The general rule for all international visitors is not to use first names. Use titles and last names.

NOTE   In China, the first name is the surname.

Handling complaints

◆ Deal with complaints yourself if possible. If not, find the right person to do so. Customers must never just be passed on to someone else and have to repeat their story more than once.
◆ Offer sincere apologies and be genuinely interested in solving the problem.
◆ Know your company policies, procedures, and products well so that you can provide accurate information in response to questions.

IS11 DEALING WITH DIFFICULT VISITORS

◆ Some visitors will be hard to handle and will require special treatment.
◆ Be *tactful* but firm. Ask visitors wishing not to announce themselves or state their business to write this information down so that it can be given in confidence to the appropriate person.
◆ Where the employer is unwilling to see visitors who have not made appointments, explain the company policy and tactfully suggest that the visitor might like to phone in to arrange an appointment.
◆ Be cautious with people who try to obtain information about the company or particular employees. If their inquiries seem to be legitimate and do not involve a breach of company confidentiality, respond to them politely.

◆ Try to be a good listener and *avoid arguing* with the visitor. Frequently, the anger will be exhausted if the person is given an opportunity to get the matter off his/her chest. The customer may not always be right, but the customer's viewpoint must always be considered.

◆ Don't take problems personally. The irate customer is not really mad at *you*. Maintain your poise and stay calm.

◆ If the visitor becomes hostile or threatening, call security (if security is not available, call the person designated to handle this type of situation).

See Unit 4, TT7, for hints on dealing with difficult telephone callers.

IS12 INTRODUCTIONS

Business presents constant opportunities for meeting new clients, employees, or supervisors. When someone is introduced to you, good etiquette demands that you stand as you greet the person. When you are called on to introduce a prospective employee, a friend or relative, or any one person to another, follow these general guidelines:

1. *Introduce the person holding the less important position to the person holding the more important one.* For example, the president of a company (Mr. Lin) is to be introduced to a new accounts receivable clerk: "Mr. Lin, I'd like you to meet Sandy Ross, who joined us on Monday." In reply to Mr. Lin's greeting, the new clerk would say, "How do you do?"

2. *Introduce the younger person to the older one.* For example, a person is about to introduce his or her mother to a colleague: "Mother, may I introduce Miss Gauthier (Ann)?" "Ann, this is my mother, Mrs. Duncan."

3. *Introduce the man to the woman.* For example, when two people of equally important positions are introduced: "Mrs. Hussain, may I introduce Mr. McIntyre?" However, if the male president of a company is meeting a female employee for the first time, the woman would be introduced to the man, "Mr. Ferris, I'd like you to meet our new staff member, Keetah Pimi."

4. *Introduce the new employee to the supervisor:* "Mrs. Oliver, I'd like you to meet our new receptionist, Ms. Natarajan."

5. *If spouses have different names, make this clear.*

NOTE   If you develop the habit of saying first the name of the older person or the name of the person holding the more important position, the rest follows automatically.

On being introduced

◆ If you did not hear the introduction clearly, ask to have it repeated.

◆ If you forget a name, admit it.

- Introduce yourself, using your first and last names.
- Stand when someone senior is being introduced.

Handshakes

- Take the initiative and extend your hand.
- Shake firmly, allowing genuine enthusiasm to show, but don't make it a bone crusher.
- Make confident, friendly eye contact at the same time as the hand-shake. It complements the process.
- If the handshake is rejected, don't be alarmed. It may be that health problems, such as arthritis, are the cause, or there may be a cultural reason involved.

IS

IS13 HINTS ON REMEMBERING NAMES

- Write down the name if possible.
- Make a determined effort to remember a name by listening carefully and paying attention as it is said and by asking for spelling or pronunciation, if needed.
- Say the name out loud.
- Watch for names on business cards, name tags, office doors, documents, etc.
- Use the name in greetings and partings.
- Maintain and update a card file or database regularly.

IS14 ETHICS

Ethics is concerned with morality—the right and wrong of a situation—and is different from legality. Photocopying copyrighted printed materials (such as sheet music) for resale is illegal, while photocopying a personal document would be unethical. Employees use unethical business practices when they do any of the following: they are frequently late or take prolonged breaks; they use office equipment and supplies for personal matters; they play computer games, send personal emails, or surf the internet on company time; they are disloyal to the organization in any way or they use company telephones for personal calls.

Not all office-related ethical or moral issues are clear-cut; some may require serious thought. For example, in the following situations, what would you do if you

- are asked to cover for the "boss" when you know he or she is in the office
- observe other employees violating company rules

If you cannot establish satisfactory solutions to such problems and your personal ethics are frequently in conflict with those of your organization, you may need to seek a new position.

II

IS15 CONFLICT RESOLUTION

Occasionally, a misunderstanding or error in communication can lead to hurt feelings, embarrassment, or loss of temper. See IS5 for ways to resolve conflict through discussion. A recommended process of resolving conflicts is outlined in Unit 7, "Human Resources Management," H34.

IS16 GENDER ROLE STEREOTYPING AND DISCRIMINATION

Sexual harassment is against the law. Most companies also have anti-harassment and fair-treatment policies and programs that stress the value of a diverse workforce. If your company does not have a stated policy, be very careful on the following issues:

◆ Know that females prefer to be addressed as "women" rather than as "ladies" or "girls."

◆ Avoid comments or behaviour that may be considered sexist, racist, or harassing. Think about how you might feel if such comments were directed towards you.

◆ Avoid jokes that may be construed as sexist or racist.

◆ Use gender-inclusive language (see Unit 1, T14).

◆ Be aware that ageism is a form of discrimination and must be avoided.

IS17 GENDER EQUITY

The rules of etiquette might change over time, but good manners based on courtesy are always in fashion. The following reflect current business practices:

◆ When leaving an elevator, equality prevails. A speedy exit is what counts, so either male or female may exit first.

◆ As far as opening doors is concerned, whoever is in the lead should open the door and hold it for others. Visitors should be allowed to go through the door first. Whoever opens the door should be thanked for the gesture.

◆ For greetings in public, a handshake is acceptable, but kissing is not.

◆ Men should not stand up to acknowledge the arrival of women at business meetings, except under the circumstances outlined in the "Introductions" section IS12.

◆ All staff should rise
  • if a visitor comes to the office or to a meeting
  • for a higher-ranking executive who is an infrequent visitor

◆ Men should not feel obliged to pay the meal bills for women, unless playing the role of host.

◆ Men are not required to help female co-workers with their chairs or with putting on their coats unless asked.

◆ No one should make comments about a person's physical appearance, nor should sexist jokes be told.

- Either a male or a female may hail a cab.
- Avoid office romances.

IS18 DRESSING FOR THE JOB

- Dress appropriately for the job. You should dress like a professional if you are in a business environment.
- Do not wear low-cut blouses or skirts that are too short.
- Do not wear tight-fitting clothing.
- Wear sensible shoes in the office; keep the spike heels for after hours (safety is the main consideration here).
- Avoid wearing too much jewellery; keep it simple and you will look more elegant.
- When "casual" days are scheduled, wear suitable attire; avoid wearing jeans that are too tight. If you do not look good in jeans, wear a nice pair of casual pants. No bare midriffs or low-cut blouses/sweaters.
- Check your image in a head-to-toe mirror before leaving for work.

IS19 DINING OUT

Eating out is often part of the working day. If you are called on to represent your employer at a club, restaurant, or social event, do not let inexperience deter you from enjoying the occasion.

- For business meetings, choose a quiet restaurant and make a reservation. Use a restaurant that you know offers good food and service and has the right atmosphere.
- If *you* are inviting people, let them choose the time. Ask if they have preferences as to type of food (vegetarian, seafood, a national favourite).
- Arrive before your guests and wait at your table, but do not order anything.
- Sit opposite your guests for best eye contact.
   Order a light meal at a business meeting, especially during the working day.

For information about Dining Etiquette, please visit the Text Enrichment Site for this text at *www.pearsoned.ca/text/campbell.*

▶ IS20 Smoking

Smoking is unacceptable while anyone is eating. It is a good idea to ask permission before you smoke, even after the meal has ended.

For information about Table Etiquette, please visit the Text Enrichment Site for this text at *www.pearsoned.ca/text/campbell.*

IS

WORDS OF WISDOM

*You can see how important manners are
by watching people who don't have any.*

▶IS21 The bill

It is customary for the person who issues the invitation to pay for the meal. If you are the host and anticipate a dispute about payment of the bill, arrange with the server before the end of the meal for you to take care of it. Payment by credit card usually assists in resolving this kind of situation. Check the bill carefully as errors can occur. When in a group, it is acceptable to request separate bills; do this before ordering.

▶IS22 Tipping

The customary tip for good service is 15 percent of the cost of the meal, not including tax. If you are dissatisfied with the meal or the service, the amount of the tip (if any at all) is your choice. If a group dinner has been arranged, it would be wise to check about tipping. On these occasions, service is often included in the total charge per person.

NOTE Tipping may vary from country to country.

▶IS23 Invitations

For such special occasions as weddings and formal dinners, formal invitations are often used. The invitation may be engraved, partially engraved, or handwritten. Keyed formal invitations are not considered good etiquette. Formal invitations should follow this format:

> Mr. and Mrs. Terence McPhail
> request the pleasure of
> Mr. and Mrs. James Meilleur's
> company at a dinner
> in honour of
> The Right Honourable Ramon Hnatyshyn
> on Friday, the seventh of September
> at half past eight o'clock
> Safari Room, Deerfield Lodge
> Charlottetown
>
> R.S.V.P.   Formal

Printed or engraved invitation

Invitations should be sent out three to five weeks ahead of the event (except for extremely prestigious dinners, which require at least eight weeks' notice).

Invitations should be answered within one week.

NOTE Responding to an invitation even though an R.S.V.P. is not requested is a thoughtful gesture.

IS

▶IS24 Acceptance

The acceptance should contain virtually the same words as the invitation. It should be handwritten in the third person, as the following illustration shows, on fine-quality, double-folded stationery.

> Mr. and Mrs. James Meilleur
> accept with pleasure
> the kind invitation
> of
> Mr. and Mrs. McPhail
> to attend a dinner
> on Friday, the seventh of September
> at half past eight o'clock.

Formal acceptance

▶IS25 Regrets

To decline an invitation, write a regrets note on good-quality paper. The wording follows the same pattern as the acceptance.

> Mr. and Mrs. Joseph Villeneauve
> regret that they will
> be unable to accept
> the very kind invitation
> of
> Mr. and Mrs. McPhail
> to attend a dinner
> on Friday, the seventh of September
> as they have already accepted
> an invitation for that evening.

Formal regret

II

IS26 BUSINESS ETIQUETTE ABROAD

As Canadian business becomes increasingly global, Canadians must become more aware of how business is conducted in other lands. Consulates and trade offices exist to help with advice on customs and practices in particular countries. Contact your local MPP's office for additional information as well. In general, the following should prove useful.

Doing business In some countries, it is not standard practice to get right down to business. Take time for the social niceties first, as custom dictates.

Business cards Handle business cards (and present your own) with respect. Never write on business cards. If you do much business in a particular country, have your cards printed bilingually, one language on each side.

Decision making In some cultures, this can take longer than in North America because team decisions are typical.

Punctuality Most nations favour punctuality, but its importance can vary. Research the attitude towards punctuality in any country you might visit.

Holidays (and holy days) Know what they are and avoid scheduling business on those days.

Name usage and greetings Ask the correct method of addressing your business counterpart. In China, for instance, the surname precedes the first name. Although handshakes are the most common form of business greeting, this is not always so. Some research will help.

Body language Hand or facial gestures, touching, even handshakes, have varying connotations. Do your homework *before* you leave home.

Eye contact Eye contact does not denote politeness or interest everywhere. This should be investigated.

Status North American informality is not the norm worldwide, so business travellers should be prepared for some of the following:

◆ Hierarchical lines of communication must be strictly observed, especially in correspondence.

◆ Educational and position titles are commonly used in addressing businesspeople abroad. Use these until invited to be less formal.

◆ Know that formal and informal language levels exist for addressing individuals in some cultures.

Language usage: Oral Communicate clearly. Avoid jargon, slang, colloquialisms, humour, proverbs, or clichés that might confuse your business counterpart. Speak at a rate that is not too fast but is also not slow and patronizing, and do not hesitate to repeat to clarify your point.

Language usage: Written Keep your correspondence simple and try to deal with one issue at a time. Be conscious of the time needed for translation and decision making.

Clothing and shoes Dress to suit your surroundings in the visited country. Be aware of shoe removal and specific dress customs.

Tipping Check the level of tipping that is customary. Overtipping is unacceptable everywhere. In some situations, little gifts could be useful alternatives.

Gift giving and receiving In many countries, gift giving is standard procedure, for varying reasons. Let the customs of the country guide you. You may be wise to carry uniquely Canadian items to give to your client(s) when this is appropriate.

Thank-you notes Don't delay thank-you notes until you're home—take personalized notepaper with you on your trip.

Being a good host When on foreign soil, visitors—especially from status- and group-oriented cultures—require careful attention. Make them comfortable and provide all the support they need to do their job here. Their dietary and religious habits should be respected and their style of entertainment researched to avoid possible embarrassment.

WORDS OF WISDOM

A smile is contagious; start an epidemic.

4 TELEPHONE TECHNIQUES AND SERVICES

II

SELECTED CONTENTS

TT1 TELEPHONE TECHNIQUES

TT2 Answering Calls
TT3 Identifying Yourself
TT4 Transferring Calls
TT5 Monitoring Calls
TT6 Taking Messages
TT7 Dealing with Difficult Callers
TT8 Being Tactful and Discreet
TT9 Making Calls
TT10 Leaving Messages
TT11 Returning Calls

TT12 TELEPHONE SERVICES

TT13 Area Code Overlays
TT14 Long-Distance Calls (North America)
TT17 Overseas Calls
TT20 Special Needs Service
TT21 Special Types of Calls
TT27 Telephone Directories
TT31 Internet Access Phone Directory

TT33 BUSINESS TELEPHONE SYSTEMS AND EQUIPMENT

TT34 Centralized Answering
TT35 Key Telephone Systems
TT36 Computer-Based Telephone Systems
TT37 Cell Phones
TT38 Cell Phone Etiquette
TT39 Videophone
TT40 Telemarketing Fraud
TT41 Voice-Mail Systems (Message Services)
TT42 Pagers
TT43 Telephone-Answering Services
TT44 Internet/Phone Line
TT45 Digital Subscriber Line (DSL)
TT46 Virtual Private Network (VPN)

Today's sophisticated telephone technology interconnects telephone lines, fibre optics, digital systems, microwaves, and satellites to transmit voice, text, data, and images across the world. The never-ending additions to the telephone service, as well as portable telephones and telephones in cars, planes, and trains, have reinforced the telephone as a key player in the business world. This unit provides details on the telephone, its many features, and the services available.

TT1 TELEPHONE TECHNIQUES

TT2 ANSWERING CALLS

Often the voice at the other end of the business telephone line is the introduction to a company. Sometimes it is the only impression a caller gets. A warm and enthusiastic greeting encourages client and vendor alike. Businesspeople can be good ambassadors for their organizations if they are knowledgeable about company operations, and if they employ good telephone techniques.

NOTE Usually a caller can detect the mood of the person answering the phone. A bored or disinterested voice shows indifference. A tired voice reflects a tired employee. A harried voice indicates confusion at the other end.

Be alert: Bosses have been known to call their companies to check on how employees are answering phone calls. *Never* use the company phone for personal calls unless it is an emergency. Companies can check phone bills for abuse of company phone lines. All calls can be traced back to the extension or user.

TT3 IDENTIFYING YOURSELF

Answer promptly—before the third ring—and identify yourself and your affiliation. Listen actively: concentrate on the caller's voice and remember to be helpful and tactful. Welcome callers courteously and professionally with "Good morning," "Good afternoon," etc., followed by the appropriate identification:

For a firm "Elliott Galleries. How can I help you?"

Your own telephone "Gilles Beaupré (or Mr. Beaupré). Can I help you?"

Department telephone "Credit Department. Rajan Sharma speaking."

Another's telephone "Mr. Lieberman's office. Rajan Sharma speaking. Can I help you?"

Make your callers comfortable by bearing these points in mind:

Voice, language, and tone
◆ Give all callers an attentive ear.
◆ Enunciate clearly:

- Speak distinctly; do not smoke, chew food or gum, or conduct other conversations at the same time.

◆ Be natural; keep your voice volume moderate.

◆ Train your emotions, voice, and vocabulary to be positive, even on a "down" day. For example, say, "Let me see if [name of person] can help," rather than "We can't help you." Or, "[Name of person] will be available at 10 tomorrow morning. May I have her call you?" rather than "Sorry, [name of person] has gone for the day."

◆ Stay away from the slang "OK" and "no problem"; use "certainly," "very well," "all right," instead.

NOTE   Do *not* have a radio on when you are answering a phone—the background noise is amplified on the receiving end and is not appreciated by callers.

◆ Did you know you are amplifying your voice when you cover the mouth section of the receiver or if you hold the phone to your chest?

◆ Did you know that most callers can tell when a person is not telling the truth?

TT4   TRANSFERRING CALLS

◆ Transfer only when it is essential and only if the caller agrees.

◆ Complete the transfer within 20 seconds.

◆ If you do not know who should handle the call, note the caller's name and number and have the appropriate person call back.

◆ If you *do* know who should handle the call, make sure that person is available and give a brief explanation of the call before you transfer it.

◆ If you must leave your desk, arrange for your telephone to be answered (e.g., use call forwarding).

TT5   MONITORING CALLS

◆ Avoid keeping callers on the line. Offer a choice such as, "That line is busy. Will you hold or shall [name of person] call you back?" Offer to call back if you need to obtain information for the caller. If you must leave the line, first ask the caller's permission and then provide progress reports every half-minute.

TT6   TAKING MESSAGES

◆ Keep a note or message pad and pen near the telephone.

◆ Take messages correctly: check doubtful spellings with the caller; note information accurately and repeat it if you are in doubt.

◆ Always note the number (including area code) to save time later.

◆ Make sure the company directory is current. Keep names, job titles, job transfers, changes in phone numbers or extensions, and new employee additions up to date. It is embarrassing if you cannot locate a person when a client calls.

◆ Do not say, "I have never heard of that person." Ask the caller/client to hold and make inquiries to verify the employee's name and extension number. For additional information, see Unit 3, IS9.

◆ Print the name of the person who received the phone message; this is important in case of a follow-up inquiry.

TT

```
         MESSAGE FOR

M S. Jean Won
          WHILE YOU WERE OUT

M r. Liboc

OF    Central Library

PHONE NO.    236-9102
```

TELEPHONED	✓	RETURNED YOUR CALL	
CALLED TO SEE YOU		PLEASE CALL	
WANTS TO SEE YOU		WILL CALL AGAIN	

```
MESSAGE:    The books you
            wanted are in.




DATE  July 6  TIME  2:30
RECEIVED BY          B H
```

Telephone message form

TT7   DEALING WITH DIFFICULT CALLERS

If an angry or aggressive person attacks your company or you in a tirade, calm the caller by saying the following:

◆ "I understand your irritation . . ." or

◆ "I apologize for the inconvenience . . ."

and always be loyal to colleagues and company.

When an irate caller says, "Why do you want to know who's calling?" you could reply "This will enable [name of person] to give you better service when he or she answers."

◆ Deal with complaints and aggressive calls by listening, offering a sympathetic voice, and suggesting a reasonable solution. See Unit 3, IS11.

TT8   BEING TACTFUL AND DISCREET

◆ Deal with wrong numbers efficiently and courteously.

◆ Don't tell callers that people being called are on holiday, at lunch or on a break, or sick. Give a return date or time and suggest that you transfer the call to someone else who can handle the inquiry.

◆ Encourage callers to come to the point quickly by politely questioning them as to their needs.

◆ Maintain and display a calm demeanour, especially when flooded with, or transferring, calls.

◆ Handle persistent callers by addressing them by name and cheerfully discouraging them.

◆ If you are required to screen calls, state that the person called is unavailable, or "[Name of person] is working on a report right now. May I tell her you called?"

TT9   MAKING CALLS

Use a cheerful and businesslike greeting, followed by an appropriate identification:

> *For a firm* "Laura Larney of Elliott Galleries here."
>
> *Your own telephone* "It's Yuying Hou calling."
>
> *Your department* "This is Winston Kennedy of the sales department."

◆ Keep an up-to-date directory of frequently called numbers (including area codes). Do this on your computer so that you can take advantage of automatic dialing if this feature is available to you, or program frequently called numbers into your telephone.

◆ Plan ahead: check the number, have questions ready, make notes if necessary, and/or have files available.

◆ Identify yourself and your affiliation.

◆ Use the most appropriate service and dial direct if possible.

◆ Consider time zones when making long-distance calls (see Appendix).

◆ Take advantage of any special rates or discounts (see the front section of your telephone directory).

◆ If you contact a wrong long-distance number, call the operator (0) to have the charge cancelled.

◆ Anticipate that you may be answered by a recording and have a brief message thought out (see TT10).

TT10 LEAVING MESSAGES

As a result of office automation, a caller is frequently connected to a recorded message instead of a person. Be prepared for this and have your message clearly thought out and complete before even making the call. Keep the message short—as little as 30 seconds might be allowed after the "beep."

◆ Speak clearly and slowly.

◆ Give your name, affiliation, number, and the date and time.

◆ State the reason for your call.

◆ Ask for a return call or say you will call back.

Use words to identify letters
Phonetic Alphabet

A as in Alpha	J as in Juliet	S as in Sierra
B as in Bravo	K as in Kilo	T as in Tango
C as in Charlie	L as in Lima	U as in Uniform
D as in Delta	M as in Mike	V as in Victor
E as in Echo	N as in November	W as in Weather
F as in Foxtrot	O as in Oscar	X as in Xray
G as in Golf	P as in Papa	Y as in Yankee
H as in Hotel	Q as in Quebec	Z as in Zula
I as in India	R as in Romeo	

TT11 RETURNING CALLS

◆ Do this within six hours if possible, for the sake of courtesy, even if only to acknowledge the call.

◆ When asking someone to return a long-distance call, suggest "collect" if company policy permits.

If the recorded message offers several alternatives, be patient, keep a pen handy, and listen carefully in order to obtain the information you want without delay and frustration.

Creating your own recorded message
Start with a warm, professional greeting (without gimmicks) identifying yourself and your company and asking the caller to leave a name, number, message, time, and date. Assure the caller of a quick response. Write out and practise the message before recording it.

> This is Heidi Schwartz of Cape Breton Fashions. Please leave your name, number, and a short message after the beep and I'll call you as soon as I can.

TT12 TELEPHONE SERVICES

A wide variety of types of calls and special services is available to telephone customers. Information about such calls and services, as well as information pertaining to calls in specific areas, is provided in the introductory pages of the telephone directory. Consult these pages before making a long-distance call.

Because telephone service is now open to competition, some organizations and individuals subscribe to companies offering alternative long-distance services to those provided by the telephone company in each province.

To use such services, the caller enters a system access number or a password on a Touch-Tone telephone before dialing the rest of the number as usual. Long-distance calls are then billed separately.

TT13 AREA CODE OVERLAYS

Local call dialing using 10-digit dialing was introduced in January 2001, and now it is a reality in most of Ontario and Quebec.

Reprogram any modems/internet dialers, fax machines, home security systems, options such as call forwarding, speed dialers and lists, and wireless phones.

For more information, access www.bell.ca/business or 1-800-668-6878.

TT14 LONG-DISTANCE CALLS (NORTH AMERICA)

Direct dialing (from one number to another) is the most economical way of phoning long distance. Whenever an operator is used, the cost of telephoning increases.

Rates

◆ Choose the right time and save, e.g., 60 percent savings from 6:00 p.m. to 8:00 a.m.
◆ Charges apply according to the rate that is in effect at the time of the connection.
◆ There is a minimum charge on all calls, regardless of the time period.
◆ Rates apply to each whole minute or portion thereof and are calculated on the total length of the call.
◆ "Other line" charges may apply for calls to locations in Télébec and Québec Téléphone territory.
◆ You can dial station-to-station calls directly from a residence or business phone.

Remember:

◆ There are time differences. See www.worldtimezones.com for the current time in major cities around the world.
◆ It may take up to 45 seconds for an overseas phone to ring.

◆ Overseas ringing and busy signals are often different from those in Canada.

NOTE Packages as well as discount plans are available for long-distance callers. Check with your phone service provider for special rates.

Long-distance inquiries For long-distance inquiries, dial 1 + area code + 555-1212 and give the operator the name and address of the person you are calling.

Time zones Check the phone directory for the time zone map showing area codes, or see the Appendix at the end of this book, for example

Time difference/TD

Pacific time	8:00 a.m.
Mountain time	9:00 a.m.
Central time	10:00 a.m.
Eastern time	11:00 a.m.
Atlantic time	12:00 noon
Newfoundland time	12:30 p.m.

▶ TT15 Dial direct

Station to station A direct call with operator intervention only for particulars of billing. The charge begins when the called telephone is picked up. To call within your own area or outside it, dial 1 (access code) + area code + the number.

From St. John's to Corner Brook, Newfoundland (same area code [709]):
Dial 1 + 709 + 721-8014

From Toronto to Miami Beach, Florida (different area code):
Dial 1 + 305 + 421-4353

Collect The person receiving the call agrees to accept the charge.

Dial 0 + area code + number. When the operator responds, say "collect" and give your name.

Bill to a third number A call made from one number but billed to another.

Dial 0 + area code + number. When the operator responds, say "bill to" and give the area code and number to which the call should be charged. If the call is made from a public telephone, the operator will confirm acceptance with someone at the third number before connecting the caller.

Calling card (credit card) Available from the telephone company, and very convenient for anyone who travels frequently and makes many calls. The person or company named on the card is billed monthly.

NOTE Calling cards can no longer be used for calls outside North America. Major credit cards can, however, be used from appropriately equipped telephones.

Dial 0 + area code + number. When the operator responds, say "credit card" and give the telephone credit card number.

TT

II

►TT16 Operator assisted

Person to person This service is useful when contact is required with a specific person or department. The charge begins when the specified contact is made. Person-to-person calls are more expensive than station-to-station calls.

> Dial 0 + area code + number. When the operator responds, give the name of the person you wish to reach. Collect, bill to third number, and calling card services may be requested with person-to-person calls.

TT17 OVERSEAS CALLS

The most economical overseas telephone call is made by dialing direct (e.g., 011 + country code + local number).

Overseas inquiries To obtain the telephone number of an overseas party, dial 0 and ask the operator for the number.

There is an access charge on all international/overseas directory assistance requests. There is no charge if the foreign directory service cannot be reached. Customers may request up to two listings per call if supplied by the same foreign directory operator at the same time.

►TT18 Dial direct (see telephone directory for listing of countries)

Station to station Cheapest type of overseas call.

> Dial 011 + country code (2 or 3 digits) + routing code (1 to 5 digits) + local number (2 to 9 digits). The country code and routing code are obtainable from the telephone directory.

Collect, calling card, bill to third number, and person to person May be requested at an additional charge.

> Dial 011 + country code + city code + local number. When the operator responds, identify the kind of call you want and give the information shown in "Dial Direct" (see TT15).

►TT19 Operator assisted

Where direct dialing is not possible, dial 0 and the overseas operator will make the call for you.

TT20 SPECIAL NEEDS SERVICE

Special equipment that makes phone use easier is available for hearing, speech, visual, or other physical disabilities. Disabled customers are entitled to some discounts.

TT21 SPECIAL TYPES OF CALLS

►TT22 Conference calls

This type of call is made when several people at different locations (domestic and/or international) all wish to confer at the same time. Plan the call in advance. Dial 0 and ask for the conference operator (see Unit 10, M25, on teleconferencing).

▶TT23 Marine and mobile calls

Used for communicating with boats, ships, and automobiles that are equipped with mobile telephones. Dial 0 and ask for the mobile operator.

NOTE In some countries, cellular telephones are called *mobiles*.

▶TT24 211 and 311 services

211 Service
This live service offers free community, government, social, and health information and referrals to the general public. Currently this service is available with Bell Canada in Ontario and Quebec, while Telus covers the rest of Canada.

311 Service
This new service, available by the end of 2006, will provide single-number access for residents in need of information and non-emergency services within their municipalities. This number will handle non-emergency police or fire department service calls as well as distribute information on road hazards, traffic and street light outages, noise complaints, animal disturbances, property taxes, garbage and recycling, building permits, water quality, and parking tickets.

▶TT25 900 and 976 services

Lines are available to sponsors of information programs. The content of these services is the responsibility of the companies that provide the information. The person who dials up the program is charged for the call.

▶TT26 WATS (Wide-Area Transmission Service)/Toll Free

Inwats (INcoming WATS—Code 800/Toll Free) This system is used by businesses and service companies to encourage customers to call long distance free of charge within a certain radius. Dial 1 + 800 + special Inwats number. For example, this service is used by hotels to accept reservations from out-of-town clients.

Outwats (OUTgoing WATS) This service is available to companies that make many wide-area calls. The charge is lower than for regular long-distance calls because customers usually pay on a flat-rate basis.

There are six WATS zones across Canada. The subscriber pays according to the zone coverage desired. In addition, a choice of rate structures based on hours of usage is possible.

TT27 TELEPHONE DIRECTORIES

The telephone company directory is divided in two parts: alphabetic (White Pages) and classified (Yellow Pages™ directories).

TT

▶TT28 Alphabetic directory (White Pages)

Names, addresses, and telephone numbers of individuals and organizations are listed alphabetically by name. Names of subscribers are automatically listed free of charge, but a monthly charge is levied against subscribers wanting unlisted numbers.

The introductory pages list worldwide area codes, the types and rates of calls, telephone services available, and other useful facts. For ease of reference, government department listings are placed together in a separate section of the phonebook.

▶TT29 Classified directory (Yellow Pages™ directories)

Organizations wishing to be listed alphabetically by service or product and to advertise their services or products subscribe to the Yellow Pages™ directories. A charge is made for each listing and each advertisement.

This directory also contains the Talking Yellow Pages™ for obtaining current information on, for example, business news, community events, investments, and weather forecasts. All calls are free.

NOTE In large metropolitan centres, the White and Yellow Pages™ directories may come in separate directories. The Yellow Pages™ directories may include sections with street and transit system maps and local and surrounding area postal codes.

In smaller communities, one telephone directory may be issued consisting of White and Yellow Pages™ directories.

Web Number™ service is a new user-friendly search tool that complements the Yellow Pages™ directories. Just type in a business phone number into your internet browser and add .yp.ca at the end of it.

For example, if you type 416-555-7890.yp.ca into your browser, you will see:

◆ a map showing the location of the business
◆ what else is in the area

▶TT30 Government Pages

This section of the telephone directory provides phone numbers for local municipal government services and federal government services.

Information on the Government of Canada: 1-800-O-Canada (622-6232)
Website: canada.gc.ca
TTY for the Deaf: 1-800-926-9105
Government of Ontario, Ministry of Government Services: www.mgs.gov.on.ca

▶TT31 Internet access phone directory

You can find Canada-wide online directory assistance at www.canada411.ca. This site accesses the Yellow Pages™ directories and White Pages so that you can search for a person, a business, toll-free numbers, and postal codes.

Canada 411™ The Phone Directory for Everyone™

Find a Business | Toll-Free Numbers | City Guides | YellowPages™.ca | Français

Our Partners
AOL.ca
Bell Mobility
Canada.com
Fido
globeandmail.com
NationalPost.com
Netscape.ca
Sympatico.ca
Telus Mobility
Toronto Transit
Commission

City Guides
CalgaryPlus.ca
EdmontonPlus.ca
MontrealPlus.ca
OttawaPlus.ca
QuebecPlus.ca
Toronto.com

Find a person

Step 1: Enter person's name
Hint: Use full or partial name. First name optional.
LAST: [   ]   FIRST: [   ]

Step 2: Enter person's location
Hint: Adding location will improve your search results
CITY/TOWN: [   ]   PROVINCE: [Search All ▾]
(optional)

Step 3: [Start Search]   FAQs   Search Tips

Use of the information in Canada411 for commercial or illegal purposes is strictly prohibited.
See terms of use.

5 DVDs for 49¢ each

PICK YOUR MOVIES

Screen capture, as found at http://www.canada411.ca/eng/person.html, published with the authorization of Yellow Pages Group Co.

▶TT32 Personal directory

Frequently used telephone numbers can be organized for quick reference in a personal directory. This may be a list, a card index file, an indexed container, or an electronic (computerized) directory. The list should be organized alphabetically and should show the area code, the number, and the extension, if appropriate.

If you are on a network or have a modem, your electronic directory can function as an auto-dialer also.

TT33   BUSINESS TELEPHONE SYSTEMS AND EQUIPMENT

Telephone lines are leased from telephone companies; telephone systems and equipment can be purchased, leased, or rented from and installed by telephone companies and numerous other suppliers.

TT34 CENTRALIZED ANSWERING

The type of central answering service an organization has will be determined by the number of trunk (in/out) lines, extension lines, and services it requires. All calls coming into an organization are dealt with through some type of switching equipment.

PBX (private branch exchange)

The *manual* PBX requires an operator to complete the connections for all incoming, outgoing, and interoffice calls. The switching system is usually located on the company premises.

The *electronic* PBX requires a switchboard operator—normally located on the company premises—to handle only incoming calls. Outgoing and interoffice calls are dealt with by employees directly.

A screen and keyboard can be added to this equipment that enables the operator to monitor constantly all extensions and thus deal with incoming calls more quickly and efficiently.

The *automatic* PBX not only switches all calls but can also keep a record of communications patterns and expenses. You can also program it for special functions such as transmitting data, providing an electronic directory, and acting as a message centre for telephone mail.

Centrex

This is a large switchboard in one location—usually not on the company premises—that has its own exchange number. Every telephone number in the system has the same first three digits, with the last four digits changing from telephone to telephone. Thus, each employee has an individual telephone number and can make and receive direct as well as interoffice calls. Extremely large corporations and governments use Centrex.

TT35 KEY TELEPHONE SYSTEMS

These are equipped with a number of buttons or keys that can be used in various ways. For example, a simple key telephone system comes with incoming (trunk) line buttons, an intercom button, and a hold button. Large versions of these desktop systems can accommodate up to 150 ports or lines with the number of trunk and local lines decided by the user. They can provide central answering services for a company or within a department. The operator handles only incoming calls.

How a basic key telephone system works

◆ A call is signalled when a bell or buzzer rings and a button light flashes on and off.

◆ When the lighted button is depressed and the receiver lifted, the light stays on but the flashing stops.

◆ The *hold* button is depressed if a caller is asked to wait.

◆ The *intercom* button is depressed when connection to an inside-company extension must be made.

Modularity (the addition of segments) permits the expansion of services on single- or multiple-line keyed telephone sets by simply adding on the required equipment. For example, to speed up the handling of incoming calls, a monitor with a "busy lamp field" can be connected to the "switchboard" to indicate to the attendant which individuals are actually using their telephones.

TT36 COMPUTER-BASED TELEPHONE SYSTEMS

Computerized telephone systems are available for any size of installation. These can provide all the services of PBX or Centrex, plus integrated voice and data communications as well as many features listed in "Additional Features" (see the Text Enrichment Site).

For example, voice mail can be integrated into these telephone systems. The caller, on being connected, says a number and is automatically transferred to the correct "mailbox" and offered a list of options. The caller then selects an option and receives a response or some desired information.

TT37 CELL PHONES

Technology has brought many changes to the cell phone, e.g., the combination of cell phones with PDAs (personal digital assistants). Features available are:

◆ audio capabilities to play music
◆ call waiting and call forwarding
◆ the ability to complete transactions initiated from the desktop browser
◆ corporate mail accounts and databases
◆ digital assistants to forward messages and manage how and when you can be reached
◆ handwriting recognition systems
◆ instant messaging (IM), email
◆ personal information management (PIM), including managing contacts
◆ phone, fax, and email messages delivered into a single mailbox accessible from the phone
◆ pictures and graphics
◆ speakerphone for hands-free calls
◆ speed-dial numbers
◆ text messaging (short messages of approximately 160 characters)
◆ voice recording
◆ Web browsing
◆ weather forecasts

TT38 CELL PHONE ETIQUETTE

◆ Do not talk on a cell phone while driving; pull over for safety reasons, and turn the radio down or off, if it was on.
◆ Avoid talking on your cell phone in restaurants or public places (since this can be annoying for other patrons).
◆ Turn off your cell phone when attending a religious gathering, funeral or wedding ceremonies, the library, the theatre, classroom lectures, or examinations/testing areas.
◆ Do not use your cell phone in restricted hospital areas/wards (for patients' safety).
◆ Avoid using your cell phone for personal use while in the workplace, i.e., incoming/outgoing calls. This is misuse of company time.
Above all, use your cell phone discreetly.

TT

II

TT39 VIDEOPHONE

This equipment comprises a telephone linked to a TV screen through a computer installed with a circuit board with a digital data unit and software, and a miniature video camera. It enables two or more people in different locations to converse, to see each other as though in person, and to exchange text and graphics on the screen at the same time. Check with computer manufacturers and large retailers for detailed information.

For information about Additional Features, please visit the Text Enrichment Site for the text at *www.pearsoned.ca/text/campbell*.

TT40 TELEMARKETING FRAUD

Most telemarketing fraud is conducted by cell phone. Beware of blocked phone numbers. Avoid becoming a victim of fraud by following the advice below:

◆ Hang up on callers asking for personal and financial information.
◆ Hang up on callers saying you've won a free prize, but must pay a fee to collect.
◆ Hang up on callers asking for investment money for real estate or bank programs.
◆ Hang up on unfamiliar long-distance calls and do not call back.
◆ Regularly check your phone bill. Report any unfamiliar numbers or charges to your phone company.
◆ Resist high-pressure sales tactics, guard your personal information, and do not believe promises that sound too good to be true.
◆ If you think you have been approached by a telemarketing scam artist, contact PhoneBusters, the Canadian anti-fraud call centre, at 1-888-495-8501 or www.phonebusters.com.

TT41 VOICE-MAIL SYSTEMS (MESSAGE SERVICES)

The Net

This service of Stentor Canadian Network Management (the group of telephone companies in Canada) permits voice-messaging by linking a company's telephone and data terminal to The Net system.

The caller uses a Touch-Tone telephone to enter the message, which is stored on computer, and the recipient hears the saved message on a similar telephone by touch of a button.

Pre-recorded messages and lists of questions (with time allotted for answers) are examples of how voice-mail systems can be used in taking orders and collecting information. (See Unit 5, "Electronic Mail," for more information.)

TT42 PAGERS

A pager is allocated a number. When this number is dialed, the type of pager determines how the call is handled.

♦ The receiving pager displays the calling number, which the recipient contacts.

♦ An operator receives the call, sends the message (which appears as a readout) to the recipient, who then contacts the caller.

♦ An operator receives the call and leaves a voice message on the recipient's pager. The message can be tuned in and may or may not require a response.

TT43 TELEPHONE-ANSWERING SERVICES

Organizations exist that will answer telephone calls on a subscriber's behalf, for a fee. Such services are available on a 24-hour basis if needed. The telephone can be answered in the name of an individual, the name of a company, or any other identification requested. Some organizations simply take messages; others offer paging services. Consult the Yellow Pages of your telephone directory for a list of the answering-service organizations in your area.

TT44 INTERNET/PHONE LINE

A dedicated phone line (cable) is recommended for frequent internet users; otherwise, callers will receive a busy signal if you are online. You could miss important incoming calls.

TT45 DIGITAL SUBSCRIBER LINE (DSL)

DSL service is similar to cable because it uses wires that run to an organization or a home. However, DSL is faster than cable. The majority of DSL users are businesses that already have telephone service in place. DSL service is available from several providers, not just the local telephone company. The faster the rate desired, the more expensive the service.

TT46 VIRTUAL PRIVATE NETWORK (VPN)

A VPN is authentication, encryption, and data-packaging technology that lets private network traffic travel over public networks. Used by companies such as banking and insurance, where the confidentiality of personal customer information is vital to the business, VPNs ensure the secure transfer of information.

WORDS OF WISDOM

Remind me to think before I speak,
rather than to regret what I have said.

5 ELECTRONIC MAIL

II

SELECTED CONTENTS

EM1	**COMPUTER-BASED MESSAGE SYSTEMS (IN-HOUSE/INTRANET)**
EM2	Email/Voice-Mail Planning
EM3	Email Etiquette/Netiquette
EM4	Malware
EM5	Spyware
EM6	Spam Mail
EM7	Communicating (Networked) Computers/Email
EM8	Internet/Email Messaging
EM9	Computer Teleconferencing
EM10	Facsimile Transmission
EM11	Types of Fax Machines
EM12	Fax Features
EM13	Costs of Fax Transmissions
EM14	Voice Mail
EM15	Incoming Messages
EM16	Outgoing Messages
EM17	**USING EMAIL SERVICES**
EM18	Managing Email
EM19	Asynchronous vs. Synchronous Communications
EM20	Voice Technology/Voice over Internet Protocol (VoIP)
EM21	Personal Digital Assistants (PDAs)
EM22	Internet Protocols/Servers

In today's fast-paced global business world, instant communication and high-speed information transfer are essential. Electronic mail (email) makes immediate intercommunication possible through telephone and computer link-ups, cables, microwaves, light beams, and transcontinental satellites. At one time, separate equipment was needed for the electronic transmission of data, text, graphics, voice, and video. Now, advances in technology permit the integration of such telecommunications.

♦ Many companies have their own private (in-house) networks (intranets) and can exchange electronic mail from person(s) to person(s) through the use of computers, cables, and modems.

◆ Smaller companies with some electronic equipment can send and receive electronic mail through their own systems linked to telecommunications services provided by various organizations.

◆ Companies or individuals without their own electronic mail facilities can use the email services offered by organizations such as Canada Post.

This unit briefly describes the scope of electronic mail systems. The unit opens with a chart that highlights the commonly used email services and then moves into a discussion of computer-based message systems (in-house electronic mail/intranet).

EM

System	For sending	Service	Delivery time
Computer-based message systems (LANs, WANs, and modems)	correspondence and documents of all types	in-house system (intranet), communications companies	instantaneous
Dialcom	correspondence, documents	Unitel Communications	same day
Fax	exact copies (contracts, plans)	telephone companies	within minutes
Internet	correspondence and documents of all types, e.g., web graphics	global communication	instantaneous

EM1   COMPUTER-BASED MESSAGE SYSTEMS (IN-HOUSE/INTRANET)

Workers are linked through the computer network and can receive, send, and manage correspondence with other users. Appointments can be scheduled and calendars kept up to date using the software. Most electronic mail passes to employees as brief messages, reports, and statistical data. Computer-based message systems save time. For example, instead of making several phone calls to arrange a meeting, the caller uses a terminal just once to transmit the details to all participants. Rather than send a report in hard copy to several colleagues for their comments, the author keys in the text and data, which are then displayed on the recipients' screens for reading and editing.

Although this communication tool is important in today's office, if it is not used properly productivity can be affected and the disadvantages can outweigh the advantages.

Advantages

◆ saves time by eliminating telephone tag
◆ sender can distribute one or more messages to several people

- ◆ sender can add attachments to messages
- ◆ receiver can read messages at his or her convenience
- ◆ receiver can print hard copy if needed
- ◆ messages can be circulated, deleted, stored
- ◆ messages can be sent/received on a 24-hour basis
- ◆ costs less than sending paper letters and faxes or than making long-distance telephone calls

NOTE Grammar/spelling/communication skills are apparent through email use; employers can use email as an evaluation tool when assessing an employee for career advancement.

Disadvantages

- ◆ time wasted if abused or used for personal interoffice messaging; do not send chain letters or graphic jokes (workplace time abuse)
- ◆ time lost if receiver does not access messages regularly or if receiver/sender is absent due to illness, leave of absence, etc.
- ◆ email is designed for short messages; if long reports are input, forwarded, or stored, these messages use memory and can clog the network
- ◆ outbox or trash must be emptied on a regular basis, otherwise more network memory needed
- ◆ deleting an email message doesn't guarantee it will be permanently erased because all email is tracked on the mail servers (be very careful of what you input and send)
- ◆ unethical users may try to intercept email; protect email by storing mail messages in a file that only you can access
- ◆ computer viruses can be transmitted over the internet via email

Important

- ◆ The user list should be updated on a regular basis. Add new employee names and delete names of employees no longer on the network.
- ◆ Passwords should be changed on a regular basis if you are handling high-priority or confidential files.
- ◆ Passwords should be left with superiors or assistants who may need access in case of your absence (check company policy).
- ◆ See Unit 16 for additional information on the internet.

EM2 EMAIL/VOICE-MAIL PLANNING

Communicating by email and voice mail is so easy that sometimes people are guilty of using these methods without planning properly. This can leave people and their messages open to all kinds of misinterpretation.

- ◆ Think through your message before you respond; jot down important points to remind you to give a complete response.

- Email may not be private. Many unfortunate rumours have been started this way.
- Use your email facility as a business communications tool only.
- Utilize MS Outlook to efficiently manage email communication.
- Follow the basic rules of writing when you use this medium; keep your messages short and businesslike, but not so brief that they can be construed as being abrupt and hostile.

EM3 EMAIL ETIQUETTE/NETIQUETTE

Give special attention to preparing messages, because voice intonation is lost with email. Choose words carefully and reread and rewrite the message if necessary. These points will be useful:

- Double-check email addresses before sending messages.
- Use one message for one subject.
- Make paragraphs concise.
- Remain professional.
- Key email text in lower- and uppercase, not all in capitals.
- Do not send chain letters, jokes, or material unrelated to your workplace; this is a form of workplace time-theft, and only clogs the network.
- Check time-zone differences and holidays in other countries.
- Follow the usual hierarchical lines of communication.
- Take care with the use of humour, sarcasm, etc.
- Keep your return address details to a maximum of four lines at the end of the message.
- Respond promptly to email messages received.
- Proofread carefully for grammar and spelling errors.
- Do not overload the network with large attachments, e.g., reports.
- Empty outboxes and trash on a daily or weekly basis.
- Advise co-workers or clients of availability, e.g., vacation dates or extended absences.

NOTE Do not open unfamiliar email messages, especially those with attachments, to avoid infection by unwanted viruses. Caution: Be careful about redirecting personal email messages received from others; they may contain viruses.

EM4 MALWARE

These software programs are designed to infiltrate or damage a computer system without the consent of the owner. Malware includes such computer viruses as Trojan horses, spyware, and adware.

EM

II

EM5 SPYWARE

Spyware programs are commercially produced for the purpose of gathering information about computer users. These programs will track a user's internet use and generate pop-up ads accordingly. Spyware also alters web-browser behaviour to financially benefit the spyware creator, i.e., it redirects search engine results to other full-page advertisements. Other programs overwrite affiliate marketing codes so that website revenue goes to the spyware creator rather than the legitimate website owner.

Signs of infection:

♦ Internet speed—the speed is drastically reduced (many malware programs, especially worms, are able use up your bandwidth).

♦ Pop-ups—pop-ups appear while you are not actively browsing the internet.

♦ Network light—your network activity light is rapidly blinking on the network card or on your router/cable or DSL modem while your computer is idle. (Those lights blink when data is being transferred and can be a good indicator that your computer is transferring data while you are not.)

♦ Startup times—the startup time has increased dramatically. Malware, like any program, needs to be running in order to work. The program will have to tell the operating system to run it on startup. This will slow down your startup time drastically if there is a severe infestation.

♦ Strange icons—strange icons appear on your desktop or in your browser Favourites.

♦ Virus scanner—your virus scanner has ceased functioning (fails to update its definitions, disappears when it is opened, disappears when you run a scan, doesn't open at startup). Often these programs will be disabled by malware to prevent detection.

Source: Adapted from www.lumrix.net

EM6 SPAM MAIL

Spam or junk mail has become epidemic and is causing many problems for business and home PC users. This nuisance mail affects productivity and, in some cases, implants unwanted viruses (worms/web bugs) that can cause additional costly workplace problems.

Senders of "spam" mail get into a system by exploiting holes in the intricacies of network settings.

How to avoid spam

♦ Do not purchase products from a spam message; deal with reputable companies only.

♦ Avoid the free products (nothing is free); do not fill in personal information forms.

♦ Do not open unknown attachments. The web is full of viruses and spyware that often travel via email. Email attachments with messages from people you do not know can download software onto your hard drive and report information back to spammers.

◆ Notify internet service providers (ISPs).

Prevention

◆ Purchase a mail-filtering program. When your email address has spread to spammers, anti-spam software can keep it usable. Programs like SpySweeper or AdAware can be customized to block pop-up ads and unwanted email.

◆ Purchase an anti-virus program to prevent costly virus intrusion, e.g., Norton Antivirus or McAfee Antivirus.

◆ Higher-priced packages are available that offer features such as:
  • disc management help tools (how to speed up the hard drive)
  • Windows error resolution (quick-fix tool for resolving problems)
  • registry cleaner (to remove old data/files)
  • compression tool (frees up space on hard drive)
  • antivirus software
  • personal firewall
  • blocking feature (for pop-up ads and unwanted emails)
  • data recovery (lost/deleted data)

EM

EM7 COMMUNICATING (NETWORKED) COMPUTERS/EMAIL

Electronically networked computers can send and/or receive messages instantaneously. This most popular electronic mail service operates within a department, a corporation, a country, or globally. Communicating computers have a built-in "mailbox" at each terminal.

◆ The sending operator keys in the receiver's number to make a connection and then keys in the message.

◆ The "send message" command puts the message into the recipient's mailbox.

◆ The receiver reads the mail on his or her monitor when convenient.

◆ The recipient can add to, then print or forward the message.

◆ The recipient can circulate an incoming message by using the "forward message" command.

◆ The "group" command permits message distribution to several boxes.

◆ The "store and forward" capability enables the sending computer to store the message for future delivery.

◆ A "timed message delivery" command can be used as a reminder to transmit.

◆ The receiving box can accept messages as they are transmitted or store them for retrieval on a 24-hour basis.

◆ Messages can be transferred to be combined with other electronic files for storage, or they can be deleted.

EM8 INTERNET/EMAIL MESSAGING

Email messaging is universal and is now one of the accepted methods for sending and receiving mail within and outside companies (intranet) and for global communication.

The letter "**e**" in front of mail means electronic. Just as your street address is where your everyday mail is sent, an email address identifies where your electronic mail should be sent, e.g., cam123@aol.com or cam123@netcom.ca.

NOTE Do not use spaces. Periods are called *dots* and they separate the elements of an address but are not placed at the end of the address.

An internet email address must have a Domain Name System (**DNS**), which consists of a name or identifier, followed by @ (the symbol for *at*), followed by the domain name.

Domain name Computers connect to each site using a series of numbers for identification; however, because it would be very difficult to remember numbers, most sites have a name that allows users to access a site without having to know the numerical address. Domain names always have two or more parts separated by dots.

Dot.com This term refers to business on the internet. Most commercial sites end with *.com* (which stands for "commercial"). Many Canadian businesses end in *.ca* (Canada) and other countries use their own endings/zone names. Examples:

.edu – education	mcgill.edu (McGill University)
.gov – government	gov.ab.ca (Alberta government)
.org – other organizations	isoc.org (the Internet Society)

Provincial sub-domains include *.ns* for Nova Scotia, *.ab* for Alberta, *.on* for Ontario, *.bc* for British Columbia.

Internet email format

The format of an email is similar to the simplified office memo with the following guide words:

Send to: Copy to: Subject: Sender:

The date and sender's name and email address are automatically inserted. Salutations and complimentary closings may be omitted.

If you are sending a message to more than one person, use a comma to separate the names, and add each recipient's email and address.

NOTE Some software programs display additional information, i.e., routing data to show all the relays/computer links required to forward an email message.

See illustration below.

Email format

EM9 COMPUTER TELECONFERENCING

Just as teleconferencing enables more than two people to conduct a meeting without face-to-face communication, computer teleconferencing permits immediate information exchange and discussion without the need for people to travel. Computer teleconferencing takes place as follows:

◆ The meeting is conducted through computer keyboards and monitors operated by the participants.

◆ The material to be discussed (which all members can access) has been entered and stored in a computer.

◆ Each member at a computer terminal can call up these documents, as well as exchange information by keying in text that other participants can share and react to immediately.

Some of the features of computer teleconferencing are as follows:

Personal notepad and file Electronic "desk" containing files of current memos, correspondence, and plans. These can be sent to other participants or to the "discussion" file.

Bulletin board The equivalent of the traditional bulletin board for policy changes, notices, job postings, etc.

Status and tracking functions An electronic means of catching up on how a project is proceeding.

Online search operations A reminder, if needed, of the names of conference members, points of discussion, and participants' personal notepads. See Unit 10 for information on Net meetings.

EM

EM10 FACSIMILE TRANSMISSION

Facsimile transmission (fax) is common for both large and small businesses. It is the virtually instant sending of a document over telephone lines to a remote location where it appears as an exact copy of the original (statistical information, graphics, photographs, or documents with signatures). The sender simply dials a number (as with a telephone call) and is connected to the receiver's fax machine.

Operation of a standard fax machine

A photocell or laser beam scans the document to be sent and converts the text, graphics, etc., into analog signals, which are received at another fax machine or computer. The receiving machine reconverts the signal and prints a replica of the transmitted document.

▶EM11 Types of fax machines

The following standard fax units are suitable for transmission of text, image, and data:

◆ simple fax attached to telephone

◆ fax with telephone and memory built in

◆ PC-fax: A microcomputer with a faxboard, modem, scanner, and printer enable a PC to double as a fax machine. This allows you to send and receive soft copy directly from the computer without the need for printing.

For transmission of text, image, data, and voice, as well as for video and audio conferencing, subscription to one of the public carriers is needed.

▶EM12 Fax features

Fax units come in desktop size or stand-alone models; as portable units for travel and home use; with colour-transmission capability; compatible with cellular phones; as a combination of fax, copier, personal computer, telephone, and answering machine; or as voice-to-fax, where the caller leaves a voice message that the machine converts into a printout. As well, numerous additions to fax machines are available to increase their capability.

Constantly evolving technology is bringing even greater variety for fax users. To make the best choice, check with vendors before purchasing a fax unit.

▶EM13 Costs of fax transmissions

Fax to fax Charge is based on the time taken to transmit. One fax page can be transmitted in as little as six seconds, depending on the speed capability of the sending unit.

Computer to fax Charge is for message only, on the basis of the number of characters per half page.

Courier to fax for courier or postal delivery Charge is for message only and is based on the number of characters in the message.

NOTE Fax service is also available through commercial outlets. The sender simply presents the hard copy to be transmitted and pays when the communication is sent.

When sending a fax, use a cover sheet. Make sure all pertinent information is given, i.e., sender's name, address (company or home if necessary), phone and fax numbers, receiver's name and phone and fax numbers, date, and number of pages being sent. See illustration below.

EM

Cosmo Corporation

Facsimile Cover Sheet

Date: January 8, 2008   Time: 3:21 PM

Total number of pages being sent (including this cover sheet)   6

If you have any questions concerning this transmission, contact:

Fax: **905-555-0001**

Phone: **905-555-0000** (Main Office)

Phone:

To: *(individual)*   **Carter Darling**

          (department)   **Human Resources**

          (company name) **P&P Data Systems**

          (fax number)   **416-665-0000**

From: *(sender)*   **Erika Campbell**

          (department)   **Transportation**

Contents/ Message: _____

Confidentiality Notice: Facsimile
The documents accompanying this facsimile transmission contain confidential information, intended only for the use of the individual(s) named above. If you are not the intended recipient, any disclosure, copying, or distribution of this material is prohibited. Please notify us immediately if you have received this facsimile in error.

P.O. Box 3034, Hamilton, ON L8N 3T2 (905) 555-0000

Fax cover sheet

EM14 VOICE MAIL

This is in fact a sophisticated telephone-answering service that combines telephone, computer, and recording devices. Organizations install voice-mail systems (which can be purchased or leased) to speed up the handling of incoming calls and routine inquiries. Telephone companies also offer voice-mail services to their subscribers. The caller leaves a message with a voice-storage device that converts the voice into digital format and stores it in the absent or busy recipient's mailbox (terminal equipped with necessary software) to be retrieved when convenient. Features of voice mail are as follows:

◆ operates in the same way as telephone-answering system

◆ is good for short messages

◆ is convenient, especially for evenings, weekends, and when an organization operates on shifts

▶EM15 Incoming messages

You can

◆ check the sender's number, date, time, and length of message

◆ play urgent messages first

◆ dial in from remote locations to collect your voice mail

◆ forward messages to other mailboxes

◆ designate how many days to archive your messages

▶EM16 Outgoing messages

You can

◆ identify messages as "private" to ensure confidentiality

◆ identify urgent messages

◆ send one message to several clients without dialing each number directly

◆ acknowledge receipt (or non-receipt within two days) of your message

◆ postdate several messages to different destinations and send them up to one month in advance

NOTE   Once you have sent a voice-mail message, you cannot recall it.

With the more advanced, completely automated voice-response telephone systems, a caller can simply push a button to

◆ switch to several extensions and leave messages or hear pre-recorded announcements of often-requested information

◆ choose between two languages

◆ contact pagers or mobile telephones

The same system offers fax-response capabilities:

◆ The caller hears a pre-recorded message, enters a fax number, and sends a fax, or enters a fax number and can receive a fax.

◆ Faxes are stored until accessed or can be forwarded to remote machines.

◆ Documents from a PC or fax can be entered into memory; the voice-response system tells callers which numbers to press on Touch-Tone telephones to receive any of those documents.

◆ The system provides an automated attendant function that works if the required extension is busy. A voice tells the caller this, the number of callers waiting, and offers these choices: wait, leave a message, or switch to another extension.

NOTE   Remember to change your voice message for incoming calls on a regular basis (e.g., when on vacation or not available—give dates).

TIP   Email and telephone answering devices/answering machines/voice mail are not always appropriate and should not substitute for personal contact. In many cases, people prefer to interact with co-workers, management, and especially clients.

EM17 USING EMAIL SERVICES

◆ Most of these services are now less expensive than telephone calls. Don't just reach for the phone—especially when expensive daytime rates prevail.

◆ Use the least expensive service possible. Some offer time advantages; some, speed.

◆ The ease of communicating using computer services makes it tempting to abuse the system with "conversations" that are not always necessary. Avoid this trap.

◆ Check your electronic mailbox several times a day—set a schedule and read the urgent messages first.

◆ File messages, remembering to give them document names for future access.

◆ Delete messages once handled to avoid unnecessary clutter.

EM18 MANAGING EMAIL

◆ Create two or more email addresses, e.g., one for business messaging, one for confidential/strict access messaging, and one for personal use.

◆ Create a list of frequently used email addresses; update on a regular basis.

◆ If possible, read messages daily, then reply, delete, or save them for future reference.

EM19 ASYNCHRONOUS VS. SYNCHRONOUS COMMUNICATIONS

The term *asynchronous* (not synchronized—not occurring at predetermined or regular intervals) is usually used to describe communications in which data can be transmitted intermittently rather than in a steady stream. For example, a telephone conversation is asynchronous because both parties can talk whenever they like. If the communication were *synchronous,* each party would be required to wait a specified interval before speaking.

The difficulty with asynchronous communications is that the receiver must have a way to distinguish between valid data and noise. In computer communications, this is usually accomplished through a special *start bit* and *stop bit* at the beginning and end of each piece of data. For this reason, asynchronous communication is sometimes called *start-stop transmission.*

Most communications between computers and devices are asynchronous. See illustration below.*

*Information from www.webopedia.com.

Asynchronous

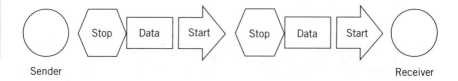

Sender   Receiver

Synchronous

Sender   Receiver

Asynchronous vs. synchronous communication

EM20 VOICE TECHNOLOGY/VOICE OVER INTERNET PROTOCOL (VOIP)

With the development of both wireless broadband and voice recognition technologies, we now have phone service technology available over the internet (also known as *IP Telephony*). This technology converts a person's voice into packets of data that are sent to various destinations via the internet.

VoIP refers to the process of transporting voice communication over internet protocol (IP) networks. Advanced technology permits the use of voice commands to search the internet for information.

EM21 PERSONAL DIGITAL ASSISTANTS (PDAs)

Personal digital assistants, such as BlackBerry or Palm handhelds, can be used almost anywhere to obtain information. Access to the following is possible by keypad or voice command: email, directions to meeting locations, stock quotations, weather forecasts, electronic calendars, and more.

EM22 INTERNET PROTOCOLS/SERVERS

Various protocols are used between clients/customers and servers to communicate within the internet mail system. Some of these are:

EM

- ◆ **FTP (File Transfer Protocol):** The internet protocol that permits you to copy files from one computer to another.
  - • **FTP client:** A program used to copy files to or from an FTP receiver.
  - • **FTP server:** A server to which or from which files can be copied using FTP.
- ◆ **HTTP (Hypertext Transfer Protocol):** The protocol used to transfer data/information between Web clients/customers (browsers) and Web servers.
- ◆ **IMAP (Internet Message Access Protocol):** A protocol used by a mail client/customer program to receive incoming messages from a mail server. Messages will remain on the server until they are deleted by the user.
- ◆ **IMAP server:** A server that a mail client/customer program can access to receive incoming mail via the IMAP protocol.
- ◆ **IP (Internet Protocol):** The protocol used with TCP to send data over the internet. The IP sends the data blocks.
- ◆ **POP (Post Office Protocol):** A protocol used by a mail client/customer program to receive incoming messages from a mail server. Messages are deleted from the server as soon as they are sent to the client/customer.
- ◆ **POP (Point of Presence):** An access point to the internet provided by an ISP; usually accessed by dialing a telephone number.
- ◆ **POP server:** A server that a mail client/customer program can connect to, to receive incoming mail via the POP protocol.
- ◆ **Private Communication Technology (PCT):** A protocol developed by Microsoft, used to provide secure connections over the internet.
- ◆ **SMTP (Simple Mail Transfer Protocol):** This protocol is used to send messages to a mail server.
- ◆ **TCP (Transmission Control Protocol):** This protocol, along with IP, sends data over the internet. IP sends the data blocks and TCP manages the data flow and ensures that the data arrive intact, without errors.
- ◆ **TCP/IP:** A family of protocols used to run the internet.

◆ **VoIP (Voice over Internet Protocol):** This technology transmits voice signals over high-bandwidth networks using internet protocol, the same standard that computers use to exchange data online.

◆ **WiFi (wireless fidelity):** A high-speed, broadband network that gives users wireless access to the Internet.

NOTE See Unit 16 for information on searching/surfing the internet.

WORDS OF WISDOM

Doing it right is so much better than doing it over!

6 PRODUCTIVITY/TIME MANAGEMENT SKILLS

PT

SELECTED CONTENTS

PT1	**TIME MANAGEMENT AND EFFICIENCY**
PT2	The Starting Point
PT3	Planning Your Day
PT4	Time-Saving Tips
PT5	Dealing with Correspondence
PT6	Maintaining an Appointment Schedule
PT7	Scheduling Appointments
PT8	Procedures Manuals
PT9	Decision Making
PT10	Office Technology
PT11	Reading Skills
PT12	Improving Your Reading Skills
PT13	**ERGONOMICS AND SPACE MANAGEMENT**
PT14	Ergonomics
PT15	Computer Considerations
PT16	*Monitors*
PT17	*Keyboards*
PT18	Lighting
PT19	Noise
PT20	Heating, Ventilation, and Air Conditioning (HVAC)
PT21	Chairs
PT22	Workstations
PT23	Colour
PT24	Space Management
PT25	Office Layout and Landscaping
PT26	Health in the Workplace
PT27	Stress Management
PT28	Workplace Safety
PT29	Substance Abuse
PT30	Violence in the Workplace
PT31	WHMIS—Workplace Hazardous Materials Information System

Accomplishing all that is required of you in a day—keeping your sanity, accepting the challenges of an increasingly technological workplace, and maintaining a high efficiency level—is a difficult juggling act. In this unit you will find ideas on how to become a successful "juggler"—how to manage time well, how to make good use of software and technology, how to avoid stress, and how to get more out of your day without the day taking too much out of you.

PT1 TIME MANAGEMENT AND EFFICIENCY

To make the best possible use of your time, you will need to plan carefully and use efficient methods.

PT2 THE STARTING POINT

◆ Find out what you are currently doing with your time by keeping a record of each day's activities over a period of several weeks.

◆ Analyse your findings and try to determine which time periods were most productive in a typical day and which were least productive.

◆ Rank all the types of jobs you must do in order of their importance and compare this with the actual time spent on each job.

◆ Make up a revised schedule showing how much time you should spend on each job, according to its importance.

◆ Keep a record of estimated time to complete a job versus the actual time to complete the job. Write this information on the file or hard copy or key in "document comments section" on disk.

◆ Now start to plan your days for the most efficient use of your time.

PT3 PLANNING YOUR DAY

THINGS TO DO

1. Call Marnie re Monday's meeting.

2. Order more disks.

3. Set up appointment with M. Nehru re phones.

4. Start collecting figures for August sales report for key-ing into spreadsheet.

5. Start on checklist for January sales conference.

Task list

- Make a daily work schedule for yourself—list exactly what you must accomplish that day.
- Assess each task, assign priorities (A, B, C), and establish deadlines.
- If possible, delegate all C jobs (and as many others as you can). For example, you could delegate the following:
  - opening and sorting mail, and faxing
  - photocopying
  - annotating magazine articles
- Do unwelcome jobs first, when you are freshest.
- Check each job off the list as you complete it (this is a positive act and very satisfying).
- Finish one job before you start another if the jobs are reasonably small.
- If you are faced with a large task that cannot be handled at one time, do it in small chunks. Work on the assignment by doing small parts of it in any 10- or 15-minute spare-time segments that occur during the day.
- Maintain a long-term calendar as well as a daily one, and note routine dates (regular meetings, report due dates, etc.) and other commitments for several months ahead.
- At the end of the day, analyse why each unchecked job was not completed. Incorporate these incomplete jobs into your "to do" list for the next day.
- Incorporate into your daily plan as many of the following time-saving tips as you can.

PT

PT4   TIME-SAVING TIPS

Office management

- Try to get everything done in the shortest time with the fewest wasted motions. Think out an activity and reduce it to a series of mechanical routines.
- Avoid interruptions. The stop-start approach to a job wastes time. Avoid an "open door" policy. Don't position your desk so that you appear to welcome casual socializers; sit with your back or side to the door.
- Surround yourself with useful reference sources (e.g., telephone directories for all provinces, fax directories, software manuals, office procedural manuals, an atlas, and an excellent office handbook).
- Pace yourself. Allow sufficient time to complete a job so that you are not under unnecessary stress (see PT27).
- Refer to notes on previous documents where you recorded the time it took to complete large tasks (e.g., monthly or annual reports), and then plan accordingly.
- Keep your desk tidy. You waste time trying to find documents buried under other paper. Set up a separate folder for each job.

- At times, working away from the office may be advantageous.
- Set firm and realistic deadlines.
- Learn to say no if you are overloaded.
- If you know you cannot accomplish everything, be realistic and request outside help, whether from another department or from a temporary employment agency.
- Set up a records management system that is easy to use and clean it out frequently (see Unit 8). Do not file records and forms that no one needs.
- Develop good reminder and follow-up systems.
- Don't file paper documents if filing electronically would do, but make sure you have a good computer backup system.
- Maintain an up-to-date database of customers and suppliers that you contact frequently so that you have available in one source all the information you will need for a number of purposes, such as fax numbers, invoices, form letters, invitations, announcements, greeting cards.
- Learn to compose at the keyboard. Keying is faster than writing.
- Guard against schedule disruptions due to the absenteeism of key personnel by training backup staff to fill in or by having detailed procedures manuals available (see PT8).

Computer software/email/telephone

Remember to empty computer trash or email messages regularly. Clean up your disk directories; delete information not needed and back up important documents.

NOTE Some database software packages have a communications feature that allows you to dial anyone on the list automatically.

- Create a database of factual information you may use again on your own or on a supervisor's behalf (e.g., equipment repair services, conference and accommodation facilities, restaurants).
- Read instruction manuals (e.g., fax, software, printer) to get the best use out of your equipment and software.
- Maintain equipment to maximum efficiency by scheduling annual maintenance checks.
- Guard against downtime on major equipment by
  - becoming fully familiar with manufacturers' instruction manuals, making sure the updates to equipment problems are placed in manuals on a regular basis
  - arranging for guaranteed fast and efficient service from vendors or other service organizations
  - arranging for emergency backup with another department or at vendors' offices
- Use professional consultants and/or services to help you maximize office potential (e.g., records management).

◆ Do not put everything into writing.

◆ Send notes to co-workers by email so that you don't interrupt them or run the risk of long conversations. (Make sure they are available so they can respond.)

◆ Do not send unnecessary emails if a quick phone call will do.

◆ Prepare and save form letters, form paragraphs, and frequently used formats.

◆ Create a frequently used email list for quick reference.

◆ Create a tip sheet on shortcuts for software functions that are not used by all employees on a regular basis (e.g., merge function, graphics, etc.).

◆ If necessary, post IMPORTANT INFORMATION regarding printing, printers, procedures, etc. Update on a regular basis.

◆ Create templates or macros for such things as frequently used headings, letter parts, or expressions peculiar to your organization.

◆ Manage your telephone time efficiently. Make all of your calls in a block of time set aside for this purpose. Have questions prepared in advance, with files, calendar, pen, and note pad handy (see Unit 4 for more hints).

◆ Block time to access your email and voice mail each day.

◆ Have an easy-to-read telephone number and record system that is well cross-referenced.

◆ If you are working on a difficult or rush project, activate your email or answering machine to avoid disrupting telephone calls. Store messages until you can deal with them.

◆ Obtain the telephone company services that will allow you to become more efficient (see Unit 4).

◆ Investigate personal call-management software. Thousands of names and numbers can be stored and then auto-dialed. Each entry allows for a notes section, maps, or photographs. It also identifies callers and their telephone numbers whenever the telephone rings and can prioritize incoming calls in order to alert you to the most urgent ones. Update regularly.

◆ If you must leave the office frequently, make yourself fully productive by acquiring equipment that will allow you to continue your work wherever you are (e.g., portable or cellular telephones, laptop or hand-held computers, portable fax machines, portable photocopiers).

◆ Or, consider renting or leasing computer equipment as well as collators, power staplers, paper shredders, postage machines, etc.

◆ Use outside print shops for large printing, collating, and binding jobs. If you produce pamphlets and other textual material, explore the possibilities of desktop publishing software (see Unit 15).

◆ Investigate a type of software known as groupware (see Unit 12). This allows people on a network to work together and speed up document processing and group communications such as meeting planning and multi-use calendars.

PT

- Time-management software (also known as electronic organizers) can be invaluable. Depending on the make purchased, these programs feature appointment scheduling (i.e., can be used to notify potential meeting participants and then confirm attendance; set up appointments and inquire into co-workers' availability without having to personally contact them), project and task management (i.e., an automated "to do" list), a database of basic reference material, expense tracking, note-making, and a database of telephone numbers that can be auto-dialed.

- Hand-held electronic organizers allow you to record appointments, store telephone numbers, record notes, and do calculations. Many can be linked to PCs, allowing notes to be edited and printed later.

PT5 DEALING WITH CORRESPONDENCE

- Schedule a specific time of day for dealing with correspondence and discourage all interruptions during this time.

- Don't write unless it's absolutely necessary. Use the telephone and email as much as possible. If it is easier, walk over and talk to people in the office.

- Use word-processing equipment. Changes are easily made and rekeying is avoided.

- Don't procrastinate. Handle each document only once and make decisions immediately, if possible. Often you will know nothing more about the subject three days later.

- Learn to dictate efficiently and avoid writing by hand material that can be keyed.

- Use a pocket-sized dictating machine for use when you are out of the office. Ensure that the recording medium is compatible with the transcribing units in the office.

- Use preprinted slips for repetitive information such as distribution lists. The stick-on type is best.

| For your information and disposal PS |
| RUSH | Please read and pass on PS |

Distribution
J. Ligtenberg ✓
T. Micone
G. Davis
W. Armstrong

Preprinted stickers/Routing slip

◆ For some routine requests, consider simply writing on incoming letters or memos, photocopying them for your file, and sending the original back to the writer.

◆ Follow up on unpaid bills by photocopying them and writing or keying a reminder on them.

◆ Use rubber stamps (see Unit 17, "Business Forms and Form Design").

PT6 MAINTAINING AN APPOINTMENT SCHEDULE

◆ Use a pencil to write in your diary or calendar all relevant information about appointments (names and telephone numbers) in case changes are needed.

◆ Keep all diaries and calendars used in the office up to date with each other.

◆ In particular, the assistant should maintain a diary or calendar that matches the supervisor's.

◆ Update your home calendar to facilitate personal appointments.

◆ Note appointments for the following year at the back of your calendar and enter next year's appointments in the new calendar as soon as you receive it.

◆ Use calendaring software efficiently.

PT7 SCHEDULING APPOINTMENTS

◆ Write down the name, company, and phone number of the client/visitor.

◆ Check that the information is correct; always spell the name and repeat the phone number for the client to ensure that all information is correct.

◆ Check your employer's appointment calendar at the end of each day in order to be better prepared for daily activities, i.e., write down names, company names, phone numbers, etc. (in case of a delay or for rescheduling in case of an emergency).

◆ Make sure your calendar is up to date with your employer's and with other office workers' for whom you are scheduling appointments.

◆ If you are using office scheduling software, make sure you key in information correctly, and keep the appointments and scheduler up to date.

◆ Make sure another employee is trained for backup and is aware of your scheduling procedures (in case of illness or vacation, leave of absence, etc.).

◆ Effectively use calendaring, scheduling, and contact management software (MS Outlook).

PT

II

PT8 PROCEDURES MANUALS

Manuals that outline the standard procedures of an organization are excellent guides for avoiding wasted time. They are efficient handbooks for new employees, eliminate the need for verbal instructions from one employee to another, and are invaluable reference sources. To be truly effective, they must be updated regularly.

Ideally, procedures manuals are keyed and maintained in a database that all employees can access. This eliminates the need for printing and binding, saves shelf and desk space, and makes updating a simple task. If a computer network is not available, the manuals should be keyed, saved, and issued in a loose-leaf format that can easily be updated. Examples of effective procedures manuals are

♦ a manual for your records management system that describes the types of equipment used; explains indexing, coding, cross-referencing, and charge-out procedures; and outlines your records retention policy

♦ job descriptions to aid takeovers when a person leaves

♦ job procedures for reports, etc., that are not done frequently or that are not done by one person all the time. The instructions must be clear enough that anyone can follow them and do the job

♦ a company style manual so that all employees follow the same writing style rules and have available an instant reference source

♦ a manual for form paragraphs or form letters appropriate for most routine situations

REMEMBER

♦ Keep procedures manuals up to date.

♦ Add new formats.

♦ Create instruction manuals for software applications and for training purposes.

Well-written procedures manuals contain easy-to-follow instructions and readily understood terminology, are liberally illustrated, and use many headings and subheadings to make items easy to find. (See also Unit 7, H15, for help with creating a staff manual.)

PT9 DECISION MAKING

Making responsible and reasonable decisions is an important part of efficiency. The office worker should understand the decision-making process and must never make a fast decision without considering the consequences. All decision making should involve common sense, logic, previous similar experience, and intuition or creativity. The following systematic approach will assist in decision making:

♦ Define the problem and write it down. Try to state the problem broadly and express it as a question.

♦ Gather the facts.

◆ Develop a list of alternative solutions to the problem.

◆ Examine the advantages and disadvantages of each possible solution.

◆ Select the best solution and review the possible consequences.

◆ Implement your decision.

◆ Evaluate the results.

PT10 OFFICE TECHNOLOGY

To work efficiently, staff members must have the best possible equipment. Today, that usually means electronic equipment, which is now quite affordable or can usually be rented or leased. For cost-effectiveness, of course, consideration must be given to the capability of the equipment and the best return possible on the investment. Constant updating and upgrading of office equipment is mandatory. For further information on electronic equipment and processes that can improve office efficiency, see Unit 5, "Electronic Mail" and Unit 13, "The Integrated Office/New Technologies."

PT

PT11 READING SKILLS

Reading skills are very important for understanding written instructions and information presented in letters, reports, and office manuals, etc.

◆ Reading is informative.

◆ Reading stirs the imagination and leads to creative and productive thinking.

◆ Reading teaches you new things; the more you read, the more you know.

◆ Reading is exciting and enhances research skills.

PT12 IMPROVING YOUR READING SKILLS

Research has shown that the faster you read, the more you concentrate and the more you retain what you have read. Most people read material of average difficulty at approximately 250 words per minute (wpm). The most efficient reader can get as high as 1000 wpm, with 500 wpm being attainable by most people after some effort.

Efficient readers do not read every word, pause, skip back, or silently mouth the words; they skim the pages while focusing on key words. To encourage efficient reading, find your present rate and then be determined to increase it.

Finding your reading rate

◆ Start a stopwatch.

◆ Read a two-page, non-fiction article.

◆ Stop the watch. Calculate the amount of time (in seconds) that it took you to read the two pages.

◆ Count the number of words in the article by adding up the number of words in one line and multiplying this by the total number of lines in the article.

◆ Divide the total number of words by the number of seconds that it took you to read the article.

◆ Now multiply the answer by 60 to obtain your score in minutes.

There is no such thing as a uniform reading rate; the difficulty of a passage will determine your rate. Your goal is to attain the fastest possible rate, adjusted to the purpose and nature of the material, without sacrificing comprehension.

Tips to increase your reading rate

◆ Always try to read as fast as you can.

◆ Increase the size of the image your eyes send to your mind. In other words, instead of reading one word at a time, stretch your vision to include three or four words at one time. Remember, you don't need to look at every letter of every word to absorb the sense of a group of words.

◆ Look for topic sentences (main ideas) and don't get bogged down with details.

◆ Don't worry about unfamiliar words. The meaning of these usually becomes clear as you continue to read, and rarely does the sense of a paragraph depend on them. Keep reading, so that you don't lose the main idea.

◆ Work at building a wider vocabulary.

◆ Skim to find particular pieces of information.

◆ For the best results, take a speed-reading course and practise faithfully in short, daily sessions, or buy a good self-instruction manual, master the techniques, and follow a consistent training schedule.

Tips to increase your reading efficiency

◆ Decide why you are reading before beginning to read a book or article in earnest. Ask yourself:
  • What do I want to find out?
  • What do I already know?
  • Is this new material?
  • Should I read all of this?

◆ Preview the material:
  • If it is a book, read any information on the jacket.
  • Review the table of contents.
  • Read the first paragraph or first sentence of several chapters to get a feel for the author's style and purpose.
  • Survey the subheadings and take a look at the illustrations and graphics.

- Determine what level of concentration will be needed.
- Ask yourself whether the article or book is worth reading at all.

PT13 ERGONOMICS AND SPACE MANAGEMENT

PT14 ERGONOMICS

Ergonomics is the study of the compatibility of people, equipment, and surroundings. This is a vitally important concept in efficiency because comfort and productivity are closely related. Poor terminal design, bad lighting, high noise levels, poor ventilation, uncomfortable chairs, improperly designed workstations, and unsuitable colour schemes all contribute to occupational stress.

Repetitive motion injuries, or repetitive strain injuries—painful disorders of muscles, tendons, and nerves, e.g., carpal tunnel syndrome, tendonitis, thoracic outlet syndrome, and tension neck syndrome—are caused by awkward postures resulting from badly designed work areas and work activities that are frequent and repetitive. Obviously these injuries must be guarded against.

Some authorities say that many work injury problems can be diminished or eliminated by changing tasks often to help alleviate the muscular stress that causes injuries. Take rest breaks to ease muscle aches, eyestrain, and stress. Stand up. Move around. Do stretching exercises, shoulder rolls, leg lifts.

◆ Change your *body position frequently* when working at a computer.
◆ Use a document holder to reduce the number, pattern, and extent of neck movements, thus reducing muscular strain to your neck, shoulders, and back.

Eyes

If you wear glasses or contact lenses, ask your optometrist for *your* focal length and adjust the screen and copyholder distances accordingly.

If your job involves a lot of keyboarding and you wear contact lenses, be aware that lenses can dry out in non-blinking situations such as staring at a computer screen.

If you wear bifocals, the variety of neck adjustments needed to read the different copy surfaces may cause strain. Have your eyes checked regularly.

The National Institute for Occupational Safety and Health (NIOSH) recommends that if your job involves many hours of keyboarding you should take a 15-minute break after two hours of continuous keyboarding. The Canadian Centre for Occupational Health and Safety recommends a five to ten-minute break for every hour at the keyboard. After two hours the eyes are fine, but the tense body takes longer to de-stress; therefore, when the job is stressful take a break after one hour.

PT

Reducing the risk

IFS — Information Fatigue Syndrome
CPI — Carpal Tunnel Syndrome
RSI — Repetitive Stress Injury

Keyboarders can reduce the risk of developing IFS/CPI/RSI by following some helpful guidelines.

Workstation

◆ Position the keyboard directly in front of the chair.
◆ Place the keyboard at elbow height.
◆ Situate the front edge of the keyboard even with the edge of the desk; wrists should not be restricted while keying.
◆ Place the monitor about 45 to 60 cm from your eyes; the top edge of the screen should be at eye level.
◆ Locate the mouse next to and at the same height as the keyboard.

Chair and sitting position

◆ Adjust your chair regularly.
◆ Keep your feet flat on the floor while keying.
◆ Sit erect and keep your shoulders back (do not slump).

Arm and wrist movement

◆ Keep your forearms parallel to the floor and level with the keyboard; your wrists should be in a flat, neutral position rather than flexed upward or downward.
◆ Keep your elbows in, near the side of your body, in a relaxed position.

Keyboarding techniques

◆ Keep your fingers curved and arched over the home-row keys.
◆ DO NOT rest your wrists on any surface while keying.
◆ Strike keys lightly; do not "pound" the keyboard.
◆ When using a keyboard or mouse, take short breaks.
◆ Exercise your neck, shoulders, arms, and fingers regularly.

▶PT15 Computer considerations

PT16 Monitors

◆ Ensure that characters on the monitor are sharply focused and flicker-free to reduce eyestrain while doing onscreen activities.
◆ Monitor stands should permit tilting and swivelling so that the screen position can be adjusted. The top of the screen should be at eye level and the monitor should be tilted backwards a little so that the centre of the screen can be viewed with a slight downward gaze.

◆ Adjust contrast and brightness controls to levels that alleviate eyestrain.

◆ Use a filter or anti-glare spray to eliminate glare.

◆ Clean the screen regularly.

◆ Have any flicker or screen noise problems attended to promptly.

◆ Look away from the monitor often to rest your eyes.

◆ Vary work tasks to include non-computer tasks as well as computer assignments.

◆ Use an adjustable document holder and alternate it from one side of the computer to the other to prevent neck muscle strain.

PT17 Keyboards

PT

◆ Ideally, the keyboard should be separate and adjustable to provide the greatest flexibility. The keys should be gently contoured to the fingers and matte-finished to prevent fingers from slipping on the keys.

◆ The type of keyboard selected should be geared to the needs of the user. The professional word processor should choose one that offers the most comfortable arrangement of alphabetic and function (or service) keys. The person using the keyboard for numeric applications such as spreadsheets and accounting should select one that provides an easy-to-use number pad and a separate cursor key pad in addition to the standard alphabetic keys.

◆ Forearm and upper arm should form an angle of 80° to 100°, with wrists relaxed, not bent. Raised wrist rest devices are available to help ease the strain on wrist muscles.

◆ Move the keyboard occasionally to change arm and shoulder positions.

Keyboards are available that are designed to put the wrist in a neutral position, level with the forearm and perpendicular to the upper arm. These include keyboards that

◆ are divided and support wrists while fingers rest in cups containing keys

◆ are split in half (see below), each hand resting at shoulder width to strike the keys

◆ incorporate wrist rests

◆ have a hinged pan that allows the keyboard to move up and down or be pushed out of the way when not in use

Internet keyboard	The enhanced keyboard provides ten "hot keys" that can be programmed for quick online access to frequently used programs or websites, such as email and favourite or frequently used programs (a Pentium computer is required for this keyboard).
Detachable palm rest	An ergonomically designed palm rest can be attached to the keyboard to reduce wrist strain.

II

For information about a split keyboard, please visit the Text Enrichment Site for this text at *www.pearsoned.ca/text/campbell*.

The mouse

The mouse should be contoured to fit the hand and support the palm. Ideally it should suit the size of the user's hand and have some type of wrist support.

▶ **PT18 Lighting**

Good lighting means a sufficient quantity of light, sufficient brightness, proper contrast, and minimal glare. Light fixtures should not emit noise of any type.

◆ Lighting should be uniform and suited to easy reading of handwritten and printed material.

◆ Ambient (deflected) and task lighting (e.g., a desk lamp) are better, more flexible sources than overhead (direct) lighting because they help eliminate problems of glare (light reflected from a desktop, wall, or screen directly into one's eyes). Hoods and anti-glare filters are available, however, to shield monitor screens from reflection.

◆ Lighting should be adjustable to permit change from computer tasks to paperwork jobs.

◆ Drapes, window blinds, and partitions should be used where glare is a problem.

◆ Grid or parabolic filters on fluorescent lights should be used to evenly disperse light.

◆ Anti-glare finishes and neutral colours should be used on walls, furniture, and equipment.

◆ Windows should be located at right angles to the screen.

▶ **PT19 Noise**

Sounds from office equipment bounce off walls, ceilings, and other surfaces and cause noise disturbance. Ceiling insulation, carpeting, drapes, and room-dividing panels are invaluable sound-absorbing materials. Some companies use non-distracting background sound ("white noise") to solve the problems created by unavoidable noise.

▶ **PT20 Heating, ventilation, and air-conditioning (HVAC)**

For greatest efficiency, people and equipment must perform in comfortable temperature and humidity ranges. Too much heat induces sleepiness, and equipment will not function well in high heat or low humidity. A humidity level of 50 percent and a temperature level of about 22°C is comfortable for most people.

▶PT21 Chairs

Lower back pain can reduce productivity. Improper seating is often the cause of such discomfort. A chair with adjustable backrest and height features and a stable base is best. A five-caster (star) design ensures stability.

The seat of an office chair should have a woven fabric that "breathes" and a contoured front edge. If chairs have arms, they must not interfere with use of the work surface or with keyboarding action.

◆ The highest point of the seat should be just below the kneecap.

◆ The seat must not press against the underside of thighs.

◆ The backrest of the chair should support the hollow in the lower back.

◆ Your chair and/or the height of your work surface should be readjusted throughout the day to vary body position. Adjust the chair, then adjust the work surface. The work surface should be regulated so that it is at elbow level when your arms are hanging straight down. When you are sitting at a keyboard, your elbows should be level with the middle row of keys.

◆ Don't share chairs. We are all unique.

◆ An adjustable footrest should be used if your feet do not rest flat on the floor.

PT

▶PT22 Workstations

Desks and work surfaces

Furniture-purchasing decisions should be based on what tasks users perform, what tools they use, amount and type of office space available, and how tasks are organized.

◆ The angles and heights of work surfaces and shelving in desks and tables should adjust to match placement of equipment to each worker's particular physical needs. This flexibility also means that changes can be made during a working day to permit a worker to avoid fatigue by changing posture.

◆ Colour is an important consideration in work surface choice. Light colours are easier on the eyes than are dark ones.

◆ Desks should allow the neat and safe installation of equipment cables.

Workstation design

For computer use, the standard office desk is not appropriate. The typical workstation in an electronic office should have provision for most of the following:

◆ computer

◆ file cabinet(s) and/or drawers and disk and stationery storage

◆ telephone

◆ reference materials

◆ space for secure storage of personal items

NOTE CPUs are available in tower systems that sit vertically—on a desktop or, more usually, on the floor—creating more desk space and keeping the system away from hazards such as coffee spills.

For information about a well-designed workstation, please visit the Text Enrichment Site for this text at *www.pearsoned.ca/text/campbell.*

Systems workstations have a number of advantages:

◆ They permit greater concentration because their acoustic panelling reduces noise levels.

◆ They produce enough room to work yet do not take up a great deal of floor space. This is achieved by means of cabinets and shelves suspended on the acoustic panels.

◆ They help to eliminate visual distractions because of the privacy they afford.

◆ They offer well-planned lighting, come in a variety of colours, and provide an attractive working environment.

▶PT23 Colour

The influence of colour in wall, floor, and window coverings on comfort, mood, and productivity is significant. The colours at the warm end of the spectrum (red, yellow, orange) are exciting, vital, and stimulating. Blue, green, and purple—the colours at the cool end of the spectrum—induce a muted, comfortable, soothing response. Office colour(s) should be geared to the nature of the business being conducted.

PT24 SPACE MANAGEMENT

▶PT25 Office layout and landscaping

Office layout has considerable influence on efficiency and productivity levels. Work areas must be set up with the performance of tasks in mind as well as with consideration for the individual's need for privacy, quiet, and security.

◆ Consider an open-plan office concept. Its flexibility means that 80 percent of available space can be used, whereas the conventional plan permits use of only 40 percent.

◆ Provide enough space for people to move around freely.

◆ Match the positioning of desks and workstations to the information flow. Paperwork must flow smoothly, with a minimum of interruptions and backtracking.

◆ Choose records storage cabinets or shelves to suit the amount of space available and the types of records to be stored (see Unit 8). Locate these near the people who will use them most.

◆ Position shared equipment (e.g., fax machines, copiers) so that the area does not serve as the office socializing spot.

- Locate people who have frequent outside visitors close to the office entrance.
- Group together employees using the same equipment or project records.
- Locate service sections (e.g., mailing departments) near the departments that use them most.
- Consider L-shaped desks, which provide 80 percent more workspace than conventional ones. Choose light or medium colours for desktops because they are less tiring on the eyes than dark colours.
- Consider systems or modular furniture, which create the most efficient workstations as far as space and employee productivity are concerned. Modular furniture consists of pre-wired movable panels of varying heights plus added components such as work surfaces, files, and individual lighting in whatever configuration is best suited to the tasks performed by the occupant.
- Use colour, wall coverings, art, plants, and music to help create a pleasant working atmosphere. Flowers and plants do more than provide eye appeal—they take in pollutants and stale air and produce oxygen.

PT26 HEALTH IN THE WORKPLACE

- Avoid eyestrain by taking frequent breaks from intense keyboarding tasks.
- Take assigned breaks for stress/work relief; occasional breaks are helpful when working on complicated or long assignments.
- Do not regularly skip breaks, lunch, or dinner because of work.
- Wash your hands regularly, especially after using the washroom.
- Report any unclean eating areas and washrooms to your office manager or supervisor.
- Clean your telephone on a regular basis, especially the mouthpiece if you share a telephone.
- Avoid using a co-worker's phone if he or she has a cold or the flu.
- Get flu shots before the flu season.
- Clean earphones regularly to avoid ear infections and germs.
- Clean coffee cups thoroughly; do not share cups or water glasses.
- Clean your work area once a week (desktops, keyboards, monitors, mouse, etc.).
- Eat healthfully; maintain a well-balanced diet.
- Exercise regularly.
- Use sick days when you are ill to avoid spreading germs to co-workers; a sick day can sometimes prevent a more prolonged illness.
- Dress appropriately for office/workplace temperatures (air conditioning in summer/dry heat in winter months).
- Avoid use of perfumes as this can adversely affect those with allergies or sensitivity to such products.

PT

◆ Avoid injury by bending, lifting, and shifting properly when moving boxes or office equipment.

◆ Schedule regular medical checkups.

HEALTH WARNING Use of a keyboard or mouse may be linked to serious injuries or disorders.

When using a computer, as with many activities, you may experience occasional discomfort in your hands, arms, shoulders, neck, or other parts of your body. However, if you experience symptoms such as persistent or recurring discomfort, throbbing pain, aching, tingling, numbness, burning sensation, or stiffness, DO NOT IGNORE THESE WARNING SIGNS. PROMPTLY SEE A QUALIFIED HEALTH PROFESSIONAL, even if these symptoms occur when you are not working at your computer. Symptoms such as these can be associated with painful and sometimes permanently disabling injuries or disorders of the nerves, muscles, tendons, or other parts of the body. These musculoskeletal disorders (MSD) include carpal tunnel syndrome, tendonitis, tenosynovitis, and other conditions.

While researchers are not yet able to answer many questions about MSDs, there is general agreement that many factors may be linked to their occurrence. These include medical and physical conditions, stress and how one copes with it, overall health, and how a person positions and uses the body during work and other activities (including the use of a keyboard or mouse). Some studies suggest that the amount of time a person uses a keyboard may also be a factor. If you have questions about how your own lifestyle, activities, or medical or physical condition may be related to MSDs, see a qualified health professional.

PT27 STRESS MANAGEMENT

Stress is often a result of poor time management. An inability to handle stressful situations well results in loss of efficiency. The main stress management tip is to pace yourself throughout the day so that you avoid periods of stress and fatigue. Other tips are

◆ Prepare for the morning the night before.

◆ Plan the toughest or least pleasant jobs or appointments for the start of the day.

◆ Don't cram too many activities into a short time span. Plan for breathing space between appointments and tasks.

◆ If you must leave the office or building, allow sufficient time to arrive at your destination without rushing.

◆ Allow for rest periods when planning long business trips. Jet lag is a serious stress problem.

◆ Delegate as many routine tasks as possible.

◆ Keep breaks short, but take them. A break will keep your energy level up.

◆ Don't rely on your memory. Record appointment times and other important details on work calendars as well as home/personal calendars if necessary.

◆ Avoid procrastination. Whatever you want to do tomorrow, do today if you can; whatever you want to do today, do it now.

◆ Ask questions. Taking a few moments to confirm directions or to restate what someone expects of you can save hours.

◆ Organize your work space so that you always know exactly where things are. Put things where they belong.

◆ Check your breathing throughout the day and before, during, and after high-pressure situations. If you find that your stomach muscles are tied in knots and your breathing is shallow, relax all your muscles and take several deep, slow breaths.

◆ Get up and stretch periodically if you have to sit for extended periods.

◆ Take a lunch break every day. Try to get away from your desk or work area in body and mind, even if it's just for 15 or 20 minutes. Avoid lunch and evening business appointments.

◆ Maintain a proper diet and exercise program. Non-rigorous exercise—stretching plus deep breathing—can be done in the office. Out of the office setting, rigorous, non-competitive exercise is excellent.

◆ Do not get into the habit of bringing work home.

◆ Consider how colour, art, plants, workstation layout, and chair contour all have an impact on stress control in the workplace (see PT13).

◆ Use your weekend time for a change of pace.

◆ Attend stress management seminars/workshops.

PT

PT28 WORKPLACE SAFETY

Unsafe practices are inefficient practices. Bear the following safety pointers in mind:

◆ Do not leave desk drawers and filing cabinets open.

◆ Do not stand on swivel chairs.

◆ Repair tears in carpeting immediately.

◆ Wipe up spills as soon as they happen.

◆ Be careful when lifting or moving equipment.

◆ Do not permit obstructions in aisles.

◆ Use separate power outlets for each machine.

◆ Avoid use of extension cords.

◆ Deal with defective cords, wires, and cables immediately.

◆ Do not trail cords, wires, or cables across walkways.

◆ Cover up loose wires and cables.

◆ Know where fire exits and extinguishers are located, and understand the procedures to follow in the event of an emergency.

- Display emergency numbers in a prominent place.
- Be able to locate the first-aid kit.
- Know where to obtain first-aid assistance.
- Know the rules for handling any dangerous substances that might be present in the workplace.

PT29 SUBSTANCE ABUSE

Substance abuse refers to the use of alcohol or drugs to the point where an individual is unable to perform workplace or personal tasks efficiently. The misuse of alcohol and drugs (prescription or otherwise) is becoming a leading cause of absenteeism in the workplace. Even small amounts of drugs in a person's system can cause deterioration of alertness, unclear thinking patterns, and reduced reaction speed.

Seek professional help if you are or if you suspect a workplace employee/employer is abusing alcohol or drugs.

PT30 VIOLENCE IN THE WORKPLACE

Workplace violence is a growing and complex problem. All workers deserve a safe, secure, and nurturing environment. The solution involves an active, collective commitment by employers and employees to prevention and intervention strategies.

Violence in the workplace is viewed as an occupational hazard that is unacceptable at any time. It is a learned behaviour, and there is a fundamental similarity between all forms of violence. It involves the exertion of power and control by one person over another person or group. Using intimidation or force over a person results in hurt, fear, or injury. This injury may be physical or non-physical (e.g., gossip, spreading hurtful rumours, or the social rejection of others).

It is the responsibility of the employer to establish a policy regarding the prevention of violence in the workplace. It is important that employers and employees clearly understand the accepted values and expectations of behaviour within the work environment.

PT31 WHMIS—WORKPLACE HAZARDOUS MATERIALS INFORMATION SYSTEM

This is a Canada-wide system that provides employers and employees with information about the hazardous materials they work with on the job. The system has three purposes:

1. to apply labelling and other information requirements of WHMIS to suppliers of hazardous materials and to establish rules for deciding what substances are considered "hazardous"
2. to allow manufacturers to protect their legitimate trade secrets without endangering employee health and safety

3. to apply WHMIS under the federal labour jurisdiction by amending the health and safety section of the *Canada Labour Code*

The *Occupational Health and Safety Act* (OHSA) requires employers to identify hazardous materials in the workplace.

Employers have the duty under the law to deliver WHMIS employee training. The *Health and Safety Act* directs employers to instruct employees and acquaint them with workplace hazards. With the addition of WHMIS, employers must instruct and train employees who are likely to be exposed to hazardous materials and/or hazardous physical agents.

NOTE Canadian Centre for Occupational Health and Safety: 1-800-263-8466, www.ccohs.ca.

PT

Environment Canada website: www.ec.gc.ca

For more information about the *Occupational Health and Safety Act*, please visit the Text Enrichment Site for this text at *www.pearsoned. ca/text/campbell*.

WORDS OF WISDOM

Challenge your mind—stretch and exercise it like any other part of your body.

UNIT

7 HUMAN RESOURCES MANAGEMENT

II

SELECTED CONTENTS

H1	**HUMAN RESOURCES PLANNING**
H2	**RECRUITMENT OF STAFF**
H3	Job Analysis
H4	Recruitment Procedure
H5	Sources of Applicants
H7	The Application Form
H8	Screening
H9	The Interview
H13	Orientation
H14	Training and Retraining
H15	Staff Procedural Manual
H16	**EMPLOYEE EVALUATION**
H17	Regular Performance Review
H19	Transfer Policy
H20	Promotion Policy
H21	Dismissal and Resignation
H24	Employee Records
H25	Payment Policy
H26	Minimum Wage in Canada
H29	**WORKING ENVIRONMENT (ERGONOMICS)**
H30	**SUPERVISING THE STAFF**
H31	Motivating
H32	Qualities of a Good Supervisor
H33	Taking a Team Approach
H34	Conflict Resolution
H35	**TEMPORARY HELP**
H36	Finding Temporary Help
H37	Making the Best Use of Temporary Help
H38	**WORKING IN A UNIONIZED ENVIRONMENT**
H39	**EMPLOYEE ASSISTANCE PLAN (EAP)**
H40	**THE *CANADIAN HUMAN RIGHTS ACT***
H41	**EMPLOYMENT STANDARDS LEGISLATION**

The success of any business organization depends on the effective management of its human resources (staff). Company policy must be fair and consistent in recruiting, training, motivating, paying, and caring for employees, and supervisors must have the skills and personal qualities to administer it. This unit looks at sound human resources management policies suitable for most firms, large or small, and outlines the supervisory techniques and qualities necessary for success.

Human resources management must be flexible, because it must meet the challenges of the changing workplace:

- changes in employment practices, with increases in contract work and employees working from home
- changes in the workforce in gender and ethnicity
- focus on self-management and teamwork rather than traditional hierarchical or authoritarian approaches
- breaking down of traditional roles and decreased emphasis on status
- integration of many activities due to technology

H1   HUMAN RESOURCES PLANNING

In human resources planning, these are the first questions to assess: What are the firm's needs for staff? How are these needs to be met? Most organizations favour the following systematic procedure to answer such questions:

1. Study existing use of staff to see if greater efficiency can be achieved.
2. Predict future volume of work, based on the firm's long-range plans.
3. Forecast future numbers and types of employees needed to deal with the anticipated volume and types of work.
4. Seek input from existing staff about how work is currently done and how it might be done in the future.
5. Consider the present human resources inventory so that the anticipated contribution of the present staff to future needs is known.
6. Decide if full-time or contract workers would be best.
7. Plan the recruitment of the right numbers of appropriately qualified staff.
8. If necessary, evaluate/test current staff for specific strengths and weaknesses.

H2   RECRUITMENT OF STAFF

H3   JOB ANALYSIS

People involved in recruiting must be properly prepared and know the details of any job to be filled. The position must be clearly defined (usually by a department manager or other executive) and a job description drawn up. A typical job description shows title, location, responsibilities, hours of work, equipment used, skills and other qualifications needed (including education and experience), salary, and opportunities for promotion.

Job descriptions are useful in other ways. They can be used in advertising for staff and for acquainting new employees with their responsibilities.

JOB DESCRIPTION

Title: Administrative Assistant

Department: Sales

Supervisor: Jason Hayward

Hours: 8:30–4:30   Salary: $27 000–$32 000

Skills and Training

The position demands excellent written and oral communication skills. Ability to compose responses to routine communications is essential. A knowledge of all basic business procedures is required. Exceptional interpersonal and public relations skills are mandatory. This tends to be a high-pressure job at times. Flexibility and the ability to prioritize tasks are needed. Skill in word processing and spreadsheet preparation is required. Excellent English language skills are essential. Promotion to sales staff is possible after one year.

Education and Experience

Must be post-secondary business graduate. Business experience desirable (preferably gained full-time but could have been acquired through co-op or part-time employment).

Responsibilities

1. Responding to routine sales inquiries.
2. Dealing with customer queries in writing, by telephone, and in person.
3. Maintaining department records management system.
4. Planning meetings and making travel arrangements for department executives.
5. Conducting research as needed.

Typical job description

H4   RECRUITMENT PROCEDURE

Human rights legislation (Section 15 of the *Canadian Charter of Rights and Freedoms*) affects the staff selection procedures (wording of advertisements, information required on application forms, and questions that can be asked during interviews) and precludes discrimination in hiring practices, levels of salary, and conditions of employment. This legislation varies with each province but, essentially, discrimination is not allowed on the basis of race, colour, national or ethnic origin, age, gender, religion, marital status, conviction for an offence that has been pardoned, and physical disability. Check the legislation that applies in your province.

Employment equity plans also exist in many organizations. Known also as affirmative action, employment equity involves taking note of past cases of possible discrimination and setting up procedures to ensure that such situations are remedied and that new ones do not occur. This could involve people with physical or intellectual disabilities, Native peoples, women, men, and people of all races and religions.

H5   SOURCES OF APPLICANTS

- ◆ personnel already employed (promotion from within or lateral transfers)
- ◆ advertisements placed in local or national newspapers or on the organization's webpage on the internet
- ◆ student services or placement offices of schools, colleges, and universities
- ◆ employment agencies and human resources consultants
- ◆ applications already on file
- ◆ recommendations of other employees
- ◆ walk-in applicants
- ◆ professional associations
- ◆ local Canada Employment Centres
- ◆ local union offices

H

►H6   Advertisements

The job description can serve as the advertisement for most of the sources of applications shown here. Advertisements placed in local or national newspapers or professional journals will require special treatment. A well-written advertisement gives a complete, clear description of the job and strikes a suitable balance between over- and underselling the position.

Hints for effective advertising

- ◆ Be specific. Avoid vague expressions such as "good wages," "pleasant working conditions," "good personality needed," "large," "progressive," "expanding," or "leading" company.
- ◆ Limit each advertisement to one job.
- ◆ Aim to attract the most suitable applicants for the job, not just to obtain a large response.
- ◆ Choose newspapers with care. Some are best for management positions, others for clerical positions.
- ◆ Advertise in newspapers towards the end of the week, as there is a larger readership then.
- ◆ Remember that mention of salary can be a natural screening device.
- ◆ Gear the size of the advertisement to the importance of the position.
- ◆ Follow the provisions of federal and provincial human rights codes.

◆ Be truthful. If the job has many routine aspects, say so. Applicants do not want to waste their time applying for the types of jobs they do not want, and employers do not want to screen unsuitable candidates.

II

JR. ADMIN. ASST.

Admin. asst. required for busy sales dept. to respond to sales inquiries. Excellent language skills essential. Other duties include making travel/meeting plans, maintaining records management system. Word processing, spreadsheet skills needed. Post-sec. business grad with some experience. Excellent promotion prospects. Salary range $26 000–$30 000. 3 weeks' annual vacation. Dental plan. Send written application with résumé to B & G Specialty Products Ltd., 1349 Portage Ave., Winnipeg, MB R8A 2N9 or fax to (204) 837-0191.

Concisely worded advertisement

H7   THE APPLICATION FORM

The application form must provide a detailed yet pertinent description of the candidate. Care must be paid to its design so that the form

◆ gathers sufficient relevant information
◆ provides enough writing space for full responses
◆ meets federal and provincial legislative requirements
◆ is clearly worded

The form should be divided into five sections: *personal, education, work experience, interests,* and space for any *additional information* the candidate may wish to provide. Since the form may be the only source of information on some applicants, provide enough space to write in starting and finishing dates with other employers so that gaps that may require explanation are apparent.

NOTE   Review the design and wording of the application form from time to time to make sure it is still effective. An electronic master will make updating easy.

TIP   Use colour-coded application forms for sorting efficiency.

H8   SCREENING

Screening is the process of narrowing down applicants so that only the most appropriate candidates are interviewed. Applications are sorted on the basis of how well applicants match the job specifications (close, possible, unsuitable). Interview appointments are made with suitable applicants and letters of regret (see Unit 2, E18) are sent to the others. If the organization intends to reply only to those selected for interview, state this in the advertisement as a courtesy.

`NOTE` Keep application forms of possible future candidates on file and reactivate them when job openings occur.

H9 THE INTERVIEW

The interview:

◆ Helps the employer assess details that are not apparent in the application form or résumé—appearance, attitudes, ambitions, skills.

◆ Gives the applicant a chance to discuss details not present in the advertisement—salary, working conditions, promotion possibilities, fringe benefits.

▶H10 How to conduct an interview

Be properly prepared

◆ Prepare a list of the desired applicant characteristics, such as qualifications and experience, personality and attitudes, general intelligence, special aptitudes, interests, and career goals.

◆ Be familiar with the details of the job being applied for and the special skills needed, as set out in the job description.

◆ Review the applicant information already on hand—covering letter, résumé, application form.

◆ Have questions ready. Be objective—ask the same carefully thought-out questions of all candidates. (In wording questions, consider the provisions of your provincial Human Rights Commission.) Questions should, of course, be designed so that they capture information appropriate to the job description.

◆ Create a chart that allows you to evaluate on a scale each candidate's response to set questions. This is especially useful when more than one company representative is involved in the interview.

◆ Where two or more people form an interview team, decide on the areas to be covered by each person and the procedure to be followed; take notes for reference later.

Make the applicant comfortable

◆ Do not keep the applicant waiting.

◆ Be the first to offer a handshake.

◆ Indicate clearly where the applicant is to sit.

◆ Provide a comfortable chair and be sure not to put the candidate at a disadvantage (e.g., ensure that the applicant's chair height is not lower than that of the interviewer's or that the sun is not shining in the applicant's eyes).

◆ If possible, sit on the same side of the desk as the candidate so that there are no artificial barriers between you.

H

◆ Applicants are likely to be nervous, so make them feel comfortable enough to present a fair picture. You must therefore lead the interview and the discussion at first.

◆ Use a language level appropriate to the candidate.

◆ Be warm and friendly and give your full attention to establish a good rapport.

◆ Avoid interruptions such as telephone calls.

◆ Avoid making long notes during an interview; take brief notes about each candidate.

Give the applicant an opportunity to respond

◆ Be a good listener.

◆ Word questions so that they encourage a full response, not just a "yes" or "no" answer.

◆ Allow sufficient response time so that you can determine each applicant's ability to think and to express him- or herself quickly and clearly. Time taken to respond will also indicate a great deal about the candidate's confidence and attitudes.

◆ Ask applicants to explain their specific interests and goals and why they feel suited to the position.

◆ Gently probe any vague answers, gaps, tendencies to change jobs, or personality conflicts.

◆ Invite questions.

Provide all details of the job

◆ Offer a full description of the position.

◆ Outline company policy, fringe benefits, promotion possibilities, etc.

Closure

◆ End on time.

◆ If a person is obviously unsuitable, try to indicate this gently at the interview. Giving false hope is not kind.

◆ If a person is a likely candidate, try to give a definite date by which you will be in touch again. He or she may be considering other jobs.

◆ Find out when the applicant could start if chosen for the job.

Record your reactions

◆ Before you go on to the next interview, write up a full impression of the applicant who has just left. It may be a few days before you refer to this application again and you might confuse candidates.

◆ Complete the interview chart if you prepared one.

▶H11   Tests

◆ Don't test for the sake of it. Tests are not necessarily good indicators of a candidate's probable performance on the job. An applicant's portfolio of job samples might serve just as well.

◆ Allow for nervousness.

◆ Provide a comfortable test setting and adequate equipment and supplies.

◆ Make your testing relevant (e.g., ask an administrative assistant to produce a finished letter from a rough draft rather than to take a five-minute speed test).

◆ Use testing material that does not contain unusual terms peculiar to your firm.

◆ If testing on equipment, make sure all equipment is in working order.

▶H12   Follow-up to the interview

◆ Create a short list of possible candidates, ensuring that those listed closely match the job description.

◆ Depending on the firm's policy:
  • check references
  • arrange for a medical examination
  • set up a second interview that involves the candidate's prospective supervisor

◆ Offer the position to the best candidate and confirm all details in writing.

◆ Contact the unsuccessful candidates as soon as possible.

◆ Keep on file the records of candidates who might be suitable for future job openings.

H13   ORIENTATION

A careful orientation and initial training program is necessary for all new employees. This can be a difficult time for them. As soon as they begin work—or shortly after—they should be properly informed about the company's products or services, facilities, policies, structure, and senior management. Acquaint them with their supervisors and with company work standards; explain their jobs and the roles their jobs play within the organization. Let staff know of the arrival of new employees, and ask one person to be responsible for a newcomer's orientation for at least the first few days. The supervisor should check periodically to identify problems early and deal with them quickly.

H14   TRAINING AND RETRAINING

New employees may require training if applicants without the necessary skills are hired (e.g., someone with word-processing knowledge but without experience on the particular software used).

H

II

Training of existing employees (retraining) may be required because of changes in office technology, a lack of trained personnel in certain fields, the need for trained backup staff for some specialized positions, or because of company restructuring.

Training programs are available from several sources, including the following.

Equipment manufacturers or vendors

Programs offered by equipment manufacturers or vendors are usually short and do not permit effective monitoring to ensure that each student has understood every step. Supervisors should not, therefore, expect total proficiency immediately. Follow-up sessions may be necessary.

In-house

If employees need in-house training on new equipment or software, manufacturers frequently offer self-instructional materials. These materials include audiotapes, videotapes, interactive video instruction (where the learner can see, hear, and do), or computer-aided instruction provided on computer software or CD-ROMs.

Allow time for the employee to complete the self-instructional program and then gradually to become involved in actual applications. A knowledgeable person (a trainer) should be available at all times or employees should have access to the problem "hotline" service provided by many manufacturers and vendors.

The person selected as a trainer must have the following:

◆ considerable knowledge of the equipment or process being taught
◆ the desire to do the training (the best qualified operator may not always be the best teacher)

Schools and colleges (public and private)

Public and private educational institutions provide adult training and retraining, and distance learning programs. Contact local boards of education and community colleges for details. Private colleges are listed in the Yellow Pages of the telephone book, as well as on the internet.

Seminars, workshops

Professional consultants offer training programs on a wide range of business procedures, philosophies, and systems.

H15 STAFF PROCEDURAL MANUAL

A well-prepared and well-maintained staff manual is invaluable. An up-to-date manual provides useful background information for new employees and for temporary and contract workers, and it facilitates job-sharing and flextime situations.

Ideally, the staff manual should be keyed on a computer and saved. If the company is served by a computer network, all employees can access parts of the manual as needed; there is no need to print it and it can be updated easily. Or, the manual should be prepared in loose-leaf format, so that only single pages will require revision. Keep the manual current so that it maintains its usefulness. The staff manual should contain all or most of the following:

◆ company history and current information
◆ mission statements detailing the company's goals
◆ general rules and procedures
◆ health and safety procedures
◆ organization chart of the company
◆ names and company positions of key personnel
◆ job descriptions
◆ telephone extension and electronic mailbox numbers

H

H16 EMPLOYEE EVALUATION

H17 REGULAR PERFORMANCE REVIEW

Job performance reviews are designed to identify dissatisfied employees; unsuitable employees; employees in need of assistance, another job elsewhere within the company, or transfer to another department or branch; employees ready for promotion; employees eligible for salary increases or bonuses. To keep the employee evaluation unbiased, use a carefully designed rating form.

The employee evaluation might be based on quality of work, productivity, initiative, interpersonal skills, attitude and co-operativeness, punctuality, and attendance. Two approaches that might be used in the evaluation process are as follows:

◆ The supervisor might complete a performance appraisal form, then discuss it with the employee and invite reaction.
◆ The employee might be invited to fill out the evaluation form for discussion with the supervisor.

The firm's human resources policy should provide for a follow-up interview with a new employee after the first few days and then for a regular review either at annual or semi-annual intervals, depending on the job.

PERFORMANCE APPRAISAL FORM

Name _____

Job _____

Department _____   Supervisor _____

Date of last review _____   Present salary _____

Each of the skills listed below is to be rated as follows:
A - Strength   B - Meets requirements   C - Needs improvement   D - Not applicable

KNOWS THE JOB		COMMUNICATIONS	
Understands job requirements, skills, and procedures		Listens and demonstrates understanding of information	
Keeps current in job-related knowledge		Writes clearly and convincingly	
Knows our industry and products		Speaks clearly and convincingly	
WORKS WITH OTHERS		**GETS THE JOB DONE**	
Works effectively as a member of a team		Follows up on all required aspects of jobs/projects	
Helps others with work-related problems		Meets deadlines	
Gains the co-operation of others		Produces quality work	
Keeps supervisor and others informed		Pays attention to accuracy and detail	
MANAGES THE WORK		Produces required quantity of work	
Identifies and analyses problems and recommends solutions		Exercises good judgment	
Sets demanding but realistic goals		Finds innovative approaches	
Establishes sound priorities		**ADDITIONAL SKILLS**	
Keeps on top of all jobs/projects			
Monitors and operates within budget			
Manages time effectively			

Supervisor's comments and recommendations _____

_____

_____

_____

_____
SIGNATURE

Employee's comments _____

_____

_____

Date of review _____

_____
SIGNATURE

Employee rating form

▶H18 How to conduct a review

The supervisor should do the following:

◆ use an employee rating form

◆ evaluate frequently and regularly so that the appraisal contains no surprises

◆ allow sufficient time for a full discussion with the employee

◆ be familiar with the job being evaluated (reviewing the job description ahead of time is useful)

◆ listen carefully

- be as objective as possible
- avoid personal discussion
- give credit where it is due and not permit the review to be for negative criticism only
- establish reasonable objectives with the employee so that a campaign for improvement can be set up
- criticize the work, not the person

H19   TRANSFER POLICY

Transfer means to move from one job to another in the organization, usually without a change in responsibilities or salary (known also as a *lateral move*). Not all employees want to change jobs; some are content to stay put and will decline transfer or promotion possibilities. Employees may initiate transfer requests or management may seek them when

- an employee is unsuited to his or her present job
- a staff member has personality conflicts with colleagues
- changes in technology and company restructuring have caused changes in the nature of the work
- work in a particular department has decreased
- change is necessary because of unpleasant or routine jobs
- there is concern for older or disabled workers
- an employee's interests and skills change
- the company is downsizing

When management initiates the transfer, the employee should be informed of the reason for the move. An unexplained transfer can cause concern not only to the employee but also to colleagues.

When the employee initiates the request, he or she should give a reason and the request should be carefully considered. Flimsy or "heat of the moment" reasons should never be the basis for a transfer request.

H20   PROMOTION POLICY

Promotion means advancement of an employee to a more responsible and better-paid job. A firm's promotion policy should be to promote someone already on staff (promotion from within) and might be based on *equality of opportunity* (any suitably qualified employee is invited to apply); *merit* (the ability to do a job well); and *seniority* (length of service). Separately, merit or seniority as the only basis for promotion has definite disadvantages:

- Merit alone may unfavourably affect the morale of very experienced senior but less able employees.
- Seniority alone, although impartial, could prevent the best candidate from getting the job and could be discouraging to new, ambitious, and able staff members.

A fair promotion policy, therefore, mixes merit and seniority.

H

H21 DISMISSAL AND RESIGNATION

▶H22 Dismissal

The dismissal of an employee may be unavoidable because of loss of business or company reorganization, takeover, merger, or closure. It may also arise because of employee incompetence, personality conflicts, dishonesty, or failure to comply with company policy. Whatever the cause, dismissal is a very serious matter and should be the subject of a clearly defined policy.

◆ All dismissals should be based on careful documentation. Employees should first be warned and given an opportunity to change.

◆ Care should be taken not to influence negatively a person's chances for employment elsewhere.

Except in rare cases (e.g., being discovered in a criminal act), notice of dismissal must be given in writing. The length of notice will depend on the nature of the job, the length of employment, and the contractual agreement with the company. Check with your provincial department of labour to clarify the legal requirements in your province.

In a legal sense, there are two ways to dismiss or terminate an employee: "with cause" and "without cause." In Ontario, the onus is on the employer to prove cause for dismissal, rather than for the employee to prove there is no cause for dismissal; i.e., the employee is presumed innocent until proven guilty. Economic downturns, corporate restructurings, angry disagreements, and the like do not constitute "cause" in a legal sense. If the employer decides that an employee must be terminated and the employer knows or is advised by a lawyer that there is no cause, an agreement will have to be reached with the employee. A list of what should be considered when determining cause follows.

Rules to prove cause for termination

1. Give the employee written warning.
2. Advise the employee of the standard of competence required.
3. Inform the employee that her or his job is in jeopardy.
4. Tell the employee *exactly* what must be done to improve job performance.
5. Give a reasonable time or opportunity to improve job performance.
6. If possible, show the employee how her or his job performance compares to others in the same job category.
7. Demonstrate that the employee has had reasonable opportunity to learn the requirements of the position.
8. Show access to adequate training.
9. Prove that what the employee did, or did not do, damaged the organization.
10. Advise the employee at the time of termination that it was a result of incompetence.

11. Show that the company did not contribute materially to the employee's incompetence.
12. Show that the incompetence is not due to temporary factors.
13. Do not give positive evaluation/letters, salary increases, or merit bonuses prior to termination.
14. Ensure that incompetence is balanced against previous evaluations, years of service, and pressures of age, long service, and change.

For more information, obtain a copy of the *Employment Standards Act* for the province or territory involved. See additional information regarding the *Canadian Human Rights Act* at the end of this unit.

▶H23   Resignation

Treat resignations with the greatest seriousness. Obtain a reason for every resignation so that you might

◆ encourage a valued employee to stay
◆ resolve the underlying problem

H24   EMPLOYEE RECORDS

Keep a file or computer record on each employee in a system that ensures confidentiality. The file might contain

◆ application form and correspondence (including references from previous employers, if appropriate)
◆ current personal particulars
◆ periodic evaluation reports
◆ attendance record
◆ salary record
◆ courses and additional training taken
◆ job description of the position currently held
◆ an indication of career potential and interests

Consult the file or computer record for promotion opportunities. Therefore, in the employee's best interests, records must be complete and up to date.

H25   PAYMENT POLICY

A firm's payment policy will be based on

◆ legal minimum rates
◆ the need to attract and keep the right kind of employee
◆ the need to keep employees motivated and satisfied

A payment policy must be competitive with that of other firms in the area and in similar businesses, and provide for regular pay increases to cover

- increases in cost of living
- rewards for length of service
- merit

When a labour union is involved, payments will also be influenced by the union contract.

▶H26 Minimum wage in Canada

Province	General Wage	More Information
Alberta	$7.00	Alberta Human Resources and Employment
BC	$8.00	B.C. Ministry of Labour
Manitoba	$7.60	Manitoba Labour
New Brunswick	$6.70	Training and Employment Development
Newfoundland and Labrador	$6.75	Labour Relations Agency
NWT	$8.25	
Nova Scotia	$7.15	Environment and Labour
Nunavut	$8.50	
Ontario	$7.75	Ministry of Labour
PEI	$7.15	Community and Cultural Affairs
Quebec	$7.75	Commission des normes du travail
Saskatchewan	$7.55	Saskatchewan Labour
Yukon	$8.25	

Websites for Employment/Labour Standards in Canada:
Federal: www.hrsdc.gc.ca/en/gateways/topics/lxn-gxr.shtml
Canada Business Service Centre: 1-800-567-2345
Provincial Enquiry Centre: www.cbsc.org/ontario
The homepage lists all provincial contacts or phone numbers, or call 1-800-267-8097

Source: Adapted from various provincial labour documents.

▶H27 Establishing pay scales

The decision as to how much to pay one employee in relation to another is best determined by an accurate and fair evaluation of each job. This might be achieved by classifying jobs in order of importance or difficulty and establishing a pay scale for each category.

▶H28 Fringe benefits

Fringe benefits are supplements to income. They are designed to encourage more and better work and to keep employees content. Benefits vary with the size and success of the business. Paid annual vacations and some insurance benefit payments are required by law (see Unit 19, MF85 and MF86). Other benefits might include paid sick leave, profit-sharing plans, bonuses, flexible working hours, supplementary pension plans, supplementary health insurance and dental plans, group life insurance, staff discounts, payment of education fees, subsidized recreational facilities, seasonal gifts, subsidized meals, child care facilities, and other employee assistance services.

NOTE   Fringe benefits are not usually available to temporary or contract workers.

H29 WORKING ENVIRONMENT (ERGONOMICS)

Ergonomics is the term used to describe the compatibility of workers with their machines and surroundings. Supervisory staff should be concerned that the physical and psychological needs of employees are met in their working environment. Office design, lighting, acoustics, heating and ventilation, colour, office landscaping, furniture, and safety are critical factors to an employee's well-being and productivity. More detailed information on ergonomics is provided in Unit 6.

H30 SUPERVISING THE STAFF

H31   MOTIVATING

High employee morale leads to greater productivity. Lateness, absenteeism, poor work, and carelessness are minimized when employees are satisfied with their working conditions. Although outside influences over which the firm has no control may affect employee morale, supervisors can regulate the following on-the-job factors.

Nature of the work The job should be interesting and worthwhile, with clearly defined objectives, responsibilities, and lines of authority. Recognition for a job well done should be given, and promotion should be a possibility.

Working conditions These should be safe, pleasant, ergonomically sound, and should include rest and eating areas.

Pay and fringe benefits These should be competitive with those paid in the same locality and/or industry for similar skills, education, and experience. Regular review is required.

Treatment by others Employees must understand that their opinions and their problems will be considered.

Security Employees need to be in an atmosphere where they feel that they are important to the organization and that the organization has genuine concern for their well-being, safety, and future.

Communications Employees need to have a sense that they know what is going on. Keeping people informed fosters self-esteem and is an important motivator.

H32   QUALITIES OF A GOOD SUPERVISOR

Different management techniques can be used, depending on the culture, administrative structure, and management philosophy of the organization. Most companies today favour a team approach: Managers and supervisors do not make decisions in isolation—they encourage employee input in the form of ideas and concerns, and use this information in final decision making. Today's supervisors need to provide motivation to win worker commitment, not to try for absolute control.

Good supervisors support management in achieving the firm's objectives, know how to recruit the best people, and strive to help employees realize their full potential. The following suggestions will help you be a good supervisor:

- Be an excellent role model.
- Demonstrate effective interpersonal and public relations skills.
- Look for better and cheaper ways of performing tasks.
- Set achievable guidelines and objectives as to quantity and quality of work expected.
- Provide clear instructions and easy-to-follow procedures.
- Create a motivating atmosphere (see H31).
- Foster team spirit.
- Let people know they matter and that their jobs are important.
- Resolve conflicts.
- Give recognition when due.
- Listen to people and encourage them to share ideas and views.
- Know when training, retraining, change, and job enrichment are needed.
- Be concerned about continuing professional growth and development of yourself and your staff.
- Delegate responsibilities to enable employees to develop skills.
- Be a creative problem solver and a capable decision maker.
- Welcome change and be prepared to lead the way.
- Encourage protection of the environment, for example, through recycling of paper, coffee cups, bottles, etc.
- Know how to deal with emergencies:
  - Fire: Know where the firefighting equipment is kept and know the escape routes.
  - Accidents: Know where the first-aid supplies are kept and who on staff has first-aid training.
- Be conscious of the need for safe practices in the office and in handling and transporting dangerous substances.

H33 TAKING A TEAM APPROACH

Many of today's companies are downsizing and reorganizing due to economic pressures, increased competition, and advancing technology. A team approach is necessary within and among company departments and divisions. Effective teams have a common purpose that the group understands and pursues. A team approach has these advantages:

- It encourages equity and efficiency.
- It creates energy as the team works towards a common goal.
- It has a flexible structure but an orderly organization.
- It permits staff to develop multiple skills.
- It allows staff to set up the most appropriate local system.
- It makes the best sense in a computer environment.
- It encourages innovation.
- It fosters team spirit.
- It creates a sense of belonging and trust.
- It encourages learning, as teams pursue new ideas together and engage in joint problem solving.
- It ensures that team players understand the objective and have a sense of direction.
- It encourages team members to focus on the objective and communicate well with each other.

H34 CONFLICT RESOLUTION

Conflict resolution is an important leadership skill. Conflict need not be thought of as totally negative. Properly managed, it may bring about creative solutions that can improve the workplace atmosphere and result in increased productivity. Reaching towards a situation in which both sides become winners—a win-win approach—is the most desirable. In handling conflicts

- Give both sides a hearing.
- Persuade each side to state the problem from its viewpoint.
- Persuade each side to see the problem from the other's point of view.
- Encourage each side to work with the other to find a solution that both can live with and that allows the self-esteem of each to remain intact.

Negative feedback and counselling

Positive feedback that is sincere and appropriate helps to create a productive and contented workforce. However, there are times when negative feedback is required, such as for unnecessary absenteeism, poor punctuality, or other forms of cheating. The supervisor must deal with these issues promptly so that the behaviour can be turned around. The following are useful guidelines:

NOTE Some problems may not be work-related, but due to home difficulties, illness, drugs, or alcohol.

- Stay calm.
- Arrange a private interview.
- Give very specific details of the behaviour being discussed, stating days, times, etc. Criticize actions or behaviour, not the person.
- Explain the effect of this behaviour on other team members.

- ◆ Ask the employee to explain the behaviour.
- ◆ Listen carefully and encourage a full account.
- ◆ Encourage the employee to suggest how to change the behaviour.
- ◆ Agree on a plan that includes timelines for change. Be positive and supportive; do not threaten.
- ◆ Arrange for or suggest professional counselling if necessary.
- ◆ Arrange a follow-up or series of follow-ups to monitor improvement.
- ◆ Resolve a conflict as soon as possible; positive resolutions contribute to a healthy workforce and workplace.
- ◆ Identify the following workplace irritants: the office gossip, negativity in the office, jealousy among employees, and the "martyr (poor me) syndrome." If an employee identifies with any of these, meet with him or her to discuss the situation and the importance of a positive work ethic.

NOTE Arrange the interview for early in the day so that there is time later to speak to that person in a friendly way.

H35 TEMPORARY HELP

H36 FINDING TEMPORARY HELP

If you need additional help for short periods of time (to cover vacations, inventory-taking, etc.), temporary workers are available from a number of sources:

- ◆ agencies that specialize in providing skilled help of all kinds; the employer pays the agency and the agency pays the temporary employee. Investigate more than one agency (check the Yellow Pages for a list of local agencies). Find out how each agency operates:
  - • Are employees bonded (insured as to their honesty)?
  - • Have employees been tested?
  - • Does the agency handle all payment details?
  - • Is satisfaction or a fast replacement guaranteed?
  - • Can the agency handle requests at short notice?
- ◆ advertisements
- ◆ Canada Employment Centres
- ◆ former employees

H37 MAKING THE BEST USE OF TEMPORARY HELP

To obtain the best value for your temporary-help dollar, organize the temporary helper's work in advance and

- ◆ Provide a properly equipped work space.
- ◆ Have all necessary supplies available.
- ◆ Supply as many written instructions as possible (e.g., a style manual or job models).

◆ Have reasonable expectations.

◆ Be available to answer questions.

NOTE See Unit 14, K106, for hints on using temporary document processing help.

H38 WORKING IN A UNIONIZED ENVIRONMENT

Many companies in Canada are unionized, and employees perform their daily tasks through job description guides, workplace conditions, and for wages that have been agreed upon by management and the union.

A union consists of members (employees/workers) in a company or organization. Elected representatives, known as a union committee or the local executive board, represent the workers and meet with management at regularly scheduled meetings (usually monthly) to discuss benefits, wages, and working conditions.

Union members pay dues, usually monthly through payroll deductions, to support union activities (day-to-day expenses, strike fund, etc.).

Issues that are not resolved at the local level are handled through a grievance procedure. A grievance report is filed and both sides address the issues outlined in the grievance. If agreement cannot be reached in a designated period, the grievance proceeds to arbitration. At this level all issues are resolved.

Members vote on contracts by secret ballot. Contracts are finalized when the majority of workers approve the acceptance of the agreement. Working contracts must be signed by both parties before they are implemented in the workplace. Union dues are tax-deductible.

H39 EMPLOYEE ASSISTANCE PLAN (EAP)

Many companies have employee assistance plans to help employees in times of need, e.g., addiction to alcohol/drugs/gambling, bereavement (loss of a loved one), financial difficulties, and other personal problems. These help plans are usually offered at off-premise locations to protect the individual's privacy. Contact the human resources department regarding this type of workplace plan. If your company or organization does not have an EAP, contact your family physician.

H40 THE CANADIAN HUMAN RIGHTS ACT

The *Canadian Human Rights Act* sets out clear guidelines regarding discrimination, and these must be considered in human resources management: "Every individual should have an equal opportunity with other individuals to make for himself or herself the life that he or she is able and wishes to have, consistent with his or her duties and obligations as a member of society."

The *Canadian Human Rights Act* (Section 2): **Discrimination**
Discrimination means treating people differently, negatively, or adversely
without a good reason. As used in human rights laws, discrimination
means making a distinction between certain individuals or groups based
on a prohibited ground.

Under the *Canadian Human Rights Act*, it is against the law for any
employer or provider of service that falls within federal jurisdiction to
make unlawful distinctions based on the following prohibited grounds:

◆ race

◆ national or ethnic origin

◆ colour

◆ religion

◆ age

◆ sex (including pregnancy and childbirth)

◆ marital status

◆ family status

◆ pardoned conviction

◆ physical or mental disability (including dependence on alcohol or drugs)

◆ sexual orientation

Everyone is protected by the *Canadian Human Rights Act* in dealings
with the following employers and service providers:

◆ federal departments, agencies, and Crown corporations

◆ Canada Post

◆ chartered banks

◆ national airlines

◆ interprovincial communications and telephone companies

◆ interprovincial transportation companies

◆ other federally regulated industries, such as certain mining operations

All provinces and territories have similar laws forbidding discrimination
in their areas of jurisdiction. The *Canadian Human Rights Act* deals with discriminatory behaviour in its various forms:

◆ differential treatment of an individual or a group of individuals based
on a prohibited ground

◆ all forms of harassment

◆ systemic discrimination—a seemingly neutral policy or practice that
in fact is discriminatory

Employment A person cannot be denied a job because of a disability that
does not affect job performance or that can be reasonably accommodated.

Employment applications and advertisements Federally regulated employees
cannot include requirements that are not clearly related to the job, such
as previous Canadian experience.

Equal pay A job performed mostly by women cannot be paid less than a job of equal value done mostly by men. Examples of jobs that might be of equal value are nursing assistants and electricians or secretaries and maintenance staff.

Employee organizations Because of provisions in certain collective agreements, some unions enjoy a monopoly on referring job applications to employers. It is discriminatory for such unions to exclude designated group candidates as referrals.

Provision of goods and services A bank cannot ask a married woman for her spouse's signature when applying for a loan.

Reasonable accommodation An individual unable to work certain days for religious reasons may not be denied employment if reasonable accommodation is possible.

Discriminatory notices A poster that encourages discrimination is illegal.

Hate messages Pre-recorded telephone hate messages are forbidden.

Harassment Making demeaning comments because of the person's colour, ethnic origin, age, disability, sex, or any of the grounds in an employment or service situation is prohibited under the act.

Harassment
Harassment includes, but is not limited to, the following:

◆ inappropriate or insulting remarks, gestures, jokes, innuendoes, or taunts about a person's race, ancestry, place of origin, colour, ethnicity, citizenship, creed, sex (gender), sexual orientation, handicap (disability), age, or record of offences

◆ unwanted questions or comments about an employee's private life

◆ posting or display of materials, articles, or graffiti, etc., which may cause humiliation, offence, or embarrassment on Code-prohibited grounds.

Sexual harassment
Sexual harassment is one or a series of comments or conduct of a gender-related or sexual nature that is known or ought reasonably be known to be unwelcome or unwanted, offensive, intimidating, hostile, or inappropriate.
Employees and students have the right to be free from

◆ sexual solicitation or advances made by a person in a position to confer, grant, or deny a benefit or advancement

◆ reprisal or threat of reprisal for the rejection of a sexual solicitation or advance where the reprisal is made by a person in a position to grant, confer, or deny a benefit or advancement
Sexual harassment includes, but is not limited to, the following:

◆ unwelcome remarks, jokes, innuendoes, or taunts about a person's body, attire, gender, or sexual orientation

◆ unwanted and inappropriate physical contact, such as touching, kissing, patting, hugging, or pinching

- unwelcome inquiries or comments about a person's sex life or sexual preference
- leering, whistling, or other suggestive or insulting sounds
- inappropriate comments about clothing, physical characteristics, or activities
- posting, keeping, or displaying materials, articles, or graffiti, etc., that are sexually oriented, including electronic publishing of same
- requests or demands for sexual favours that include, or strongly imply, promises of rewards for complying (e.g., job advancement or job opportunities, improved academic grades) and/or threats of punishment for refusal (e.g., denial of job advancement or job opportunities, diminished academic grades)

All or part of these grounds for harassment may create a negative environment for individuals or groups and may "poison" the work environment. This includes conduct or comment that creates and maintains an offensive, hostile, or intimidating climate. See Unit 6, PT30 for information on violence in the workplace.

Exceptions
The act provides for exceptions such as

Bona fide occupational requirement A job may be refused to a person who cannot perform it safely, efficiently, and reliably.

Bona fide justification A service may be refused to a person when it cannot be offered without undue costs.

Equal pay guidelines A difference in wages between men and women performing work of equal value in an establishment may be justified by different performance ratings, seniority, red-circling,* training and rehabilitation assignments, internal labour shortages and surpluses, and regional wage rates.

Maternity and child care An employer can grant workers special leave or benefits in connection with pregnancy or childbirth, or for the care of their children.

Mandatory retirement A worker can be retired at the age that is "normal" for the kind of work involved.

Age guidelines Lower transportation fares are permitted for children and senior citizens.

The Canadian Human Rights Commission
The Canadian Human Rights Commission administers the *Canadian Human Rights Act* and ensures that the principles of equal opportunity and

---

*A method of protecting the current pay of employees whose jobs are found to have been over-valued prior to the job evaluation in order that there is no loss in pay.

non-discrimination are followed in all areas of federal jurisdiction. The commission, comprising two full-time and up to six part-time commissioners, meets regularly to decide on individual complaints and to approve commission policies.

Complaints

When the Canadian Human Rights Commission receives a complaint, it follows the following process:

- It determines if the commission is the right agency to handle the complaint. If yes, the complaint is accepted for investigation. If no, it is referred to another agency that might help.
- An investigation begins; sometimes it results in an early settlement to which both parties agree.
- If the complaint cannot be settled, a report is prepared for commission review.
- The commission may dismiss the complaint, appoint a conciliator, or send the complaint to a Human Rights Tribunal.
- The conciliator tries to settle the complaint by reaching an agreement acceptable to the two parties. If conciliation does not result in a settlement, the case is returned to the commission for a decision. The case may either be dismissed or sent to a tribunal.
- At the tribunal, a hearing takes place where a written decision is given. Unless appealed, tribunal decisions are binding on the parties.

H

Appeals

Tribunal decisions can be appealed to a review tribunal or to the courts, by the complainant, the respondent, or the commission, depending on the circumstances. Review tribunal decisions can be appealed to the Federal Court or in some cases to the Supreme Court of Canada.

Right to protection

The *Canadian Human Rights Act* provides for fines up to $50 000 for threatening, intimidating, or discriminating against an individual who has filed a complaint, or for hampering the investigating process.

- For more information, contact the Canadian Human Rights Commission:

National Office of the Canadian Human Rights Commission

Telephone: (613) 995-1151
Fax: (613) 996-9661
TTY: 1-888-643-3304 (Deaf and Hearing Impaired)
Email: info.com@chrc-ccdp.ca or
Head office: call 1-888-214-1090

Provincial regional offices: call 1-800-999-6899
Website: www.chrc-ccdp.ca

H41 EMPLOYMENT STANDARDS LEGISLATION

Employment legislation in Canada covers the following:

◆ benefit plans
◆ compassionate care leave
◆ equal pay for equal work
◆ hours of work
◆ maternity leave
◆ minimum wages
◆ overtime
◆ parental leave
◆ public holidays (religious holidays)
◆ vacation pay

Website: investincanada.gc.ca

WORDS OF WISDOM

*Freedom of speech means we all have the right
to our opinions, but it doesn't mean everyone
has to agree with them.*

WORDS OF WISDOM

*Leadership is the power to evoke
the right response in other people.*

8 RECORDS AND INFORMATION MANAGEMENT (RIM)

R

SELECTED CONTENTS

R1	**THE ALPHABET IN RECORDS MANAGEMENT**
R2	**INDEXING**
R3	**ALPHABETIC SEQUENCING**
R4	Names of Individuals
R5	Names of Companies
R6	Titles and Degrees
R7	Initials and Acronyms
R8	Abbreviations
R9	Prefixes
R10	Punctuation
R11	Hyphenated Names
R12	Symbols
R13	Geographic Names
R14	Compass Points in Names
R15	Numbers
R16	Associations, Societies, etc.
R17	Boards, Committees, Estates, Trustees
R18	Governments and Their Divisions
R19	Identical Names
R20	Telephone Directory Alphabetic Sequencing
R21	**BASIC DOCUMENT RECORDS ORGANIZATION AND SUPPLIES**
R22	Parts of a Typical Alphabetic Document File
R26	**RECORDS MANAGEMENT SYSTEMS**
R27	Alphabetic Filing
R28	Geographic Filing
R29	Subject Filing
R31	Numeric Filing
R32	The Records Cycle
R33	**MANAGING DOCUMENT RECORDS**
R39	Document Filing Tips
R40	**ELECTRONIC RECORDS**
R42	**RECORDS RETENTION**
R43	Transfer Methods
R44	Destruction
R45	Shredders

R46	**RECORDS STORAGE EQUIPMENT**
R51	Special Filing Equipment
R52	**AUTOMATED FILING EQUIPMENT**
R53	**IMAGE TECHNOLOGY**
R54	Image Processing
R55	Optical Disk Storage
R56	**DOCUMENT-BASED MANAGEMENT SYSTEMS (DBMS)**
R57	**OTHER ELECTRONIC RECORDS SYSTEMS**
R59	Databases
R61	**LEGAL ADMISSIBILITY OF MICROGRAPHIC AND ELECTRONIC RECORDS**
R62	**RECORDS AND INFORMATION MANAGEMENT (RIM)**
R63	Records Management Program
R64	Key Functions
R65	Elements of a Records Management Program
R66	Advantages of Good Records Management

II

Records management involves the safe and orderly storage of records, using a system that ensures fast and easy retrieval of required information. An organization's information might be stored in the form of paper documents or might be stored using magnetic, electronic, or optical media. Today's office worker, therefore, must be familiar with the techniques for successfully managing records of a great many types and complexities. This unit will provide the information you need to meet the challenge, regardless of whether the system is manual or electronic. You will be guided through the management and control of storing documents, magnetic media, microfilm, and optical disks; you will be introduced to various types of storage equipment; you will find out about computer-based systems; and you will learn the terms used in the records management process.

R1   THE ALPHABET IN RECORDS MANAGEMENT

Because the alphabet is the basis of many records management systems, one uniform set of rules for placing file captions (names, places, subjects) in alphabetic order must be followed by everyone who uses the records in the system. The rules that follow are based on those developed by ARMA International, the Association for Information Management Professionals, for standardizing alphabetic filing. These rules also take into account the needs of electronic systems and should be adopted so that there is consistency between both manual and electronic sorting methods.

Additional reference material on information management is available on the ARMA International website www.arma.org (www.armacanada.org) or by calling 1-800-422-2762.

R2   INDEXING

Before file captions (names, places, subjects) can be arranged in alphabetic order, they must be indexed. *Indexing* means determining the most important part of a caption and then putting that word or set of words first, if necessary. The indexed version of the caption should be placed on the file folder, record card, or record container.

If you index for an electronic sorting system (for database records, for example), you must take special care because, while the software can sort with amazing speed, it cannot make indexing decisions.

Normal order	Indexed order
Laura L. Fleming	Fleming, Laura L.
The Sharp Electronics Company	Sharp Electronics Company, The

NOTE   Commas are used to indicate that parts of a caption have been rearranged.

If a database is used for automatically preparing envelopes or labels, depending on the software, you may need to use several fields: one for producing alphabetic lists and one for mailing purposes, as the following illustrates:

Field 1:	Mailing label name:	Miss Elaine Cheng
Field 2:	Family name:	Cheng
Field 3:	Given name:	Elaine

Field 1 will be used for labels and envelopes; fields 2 and 3 will be used for alphabetic lists.

The easiest way to handle the indexing process if you have doubts is to set up the information in unit order as illustrated below:

Unit 1	Unit 2	Unit 3	Unit 4
Jack	Bird	Plumbing	Co.
Fleming	Laura	L.	
Sharp	Electronics	Company	The

R3   ALPHABETIC SEQUENCING

Consider each part of the caption as a separate unit, working from left to right until a comparison point is reached. For correct filing order, always follow the rule *Nothing comes before something*.

Unit 1	Unit 2	Unit 3
Bird	J.	
Bird	Jack	
Bird	Shop	The
Birde	J.	John

◆ Use all units, including articles, prepositions, and conjunctions. If words such as *the, a, an* come first, treat them as the last unit.

R4 NAMES OF INDIVIDUALS

◆ Consider family names first, given names or initials second, middle names or initials third.

◆ A family name standing alone precedes a family name with initials.

◆ A family name with initials precedes a family name with a full given name:

> Johnson
> Johnson, N.
> Johnson, Nadia

NOTE The name of a married woman may be alphabetically sequenced as given and cross-referenced to her husband's name, depending on how the woman prefers to be known:

> Jones, Sara (Mrs.)
> Cross-reference: Jones, Robert (Mrs.) <u>see</u>
>   Jones, Sara (Mrs.)
>
> Jones, Sarah (Mrs.)
> Cross-reference: Jones, Allan (Mrs.) <u>see</u>
>   Jones, Sarah (Mrs.)

Non-English names

When it is difficult to distinguish the family name from the first name, index the name as it appears. Cross-reference when there is doubt:

As written	Unit 1	Unit 2	Unit 3
* Leung Hung Pok	Leung	Hung	Pok
Daniel To	To	Daniel	

> * <u>See</u> Pok, Leung Hung

R5 NAMES OF COMPANIES

Company names are usually filed as written:

> Ford Motor Company, The
> Pourquoi Pas Restaurants Ltd.
> Sara Lee Kitchens
> Spruce Springs Antiques

NOTE In cases in which a company is named after a person and is generally referred to by the family name, cross-referencing might be considered to avoid confusion. For example, "Terence Singh Electronics Ltd." might be referred to generally as "Singh's." In this case, it would be filed as written to follow ARMA rules and could be cross-referenced under "Singh, Terence, Electronics" to avoid possible confusion.

R6 TITLES AND DEGREES

Disregard these for alphabetic sequencing purposes (unless required to distinguish between identical names) but key on to the caption after the name:

Normal order	Caption order
Mrs. Jane Alexander, B.A.	Alexander, Jane (B.A.) (Mrs.)
Dr. Alan H. Draper	Draper, Alan H. (Dr.)
Captain James Morgan	Morgan, James (Captain)

If a title is part of a person's given name or a business name, file it as written:

Normal order	Caption order
Lord Simcoe Hotel	Lord Simcoe Hotel
Sir Nicholas Restaurant	Sir Nicholas Restaurant
Sister Gabriella	Sister Gabriella

Social or courtesy titles are used for indexing only when two or more names are identical:

Pearson	Terry	Miss
Pearson	Terry	Mr.
Pearson	Terry	Mrs.
Pearson	Terry	Ms.

R7 INITIALS AND ACRONYMS

When initials or acronyms form all or part of the name of an organization, treat them as one filing unit. Also treat TV and radio call letters as one unit:

	Unit 1	Unit 2
CAC Realty	CAC	Realty
CFMT Television	CFMT	Television

When the meaning of the initials or acronym is known, cross-reference to avoid confusion (e.g., IBM Canada Ltd.; cross-reference: <u>Use for</u> International Business Machines Canada Ltd.). This allows you to file under the common abbreviation while acknowledging the full title. See R36 for information on cross-referencing.

R8 ABBREVIATIONS

Treat as they are written and indexed alphabetically. Note that *Saint, St.,* or *Ste.* when used as a title is considered a separate unit. When *Saint, St.,* or *Ste.* is a prefix to a personal name, it is considered part of the name.

As written	First unit	Second unit
Saint Patrick's Church	Saint	Patrick's
St. John's Bookstore	St.	John's
Jacques Ste. Marie	Ste. Marie	Jacques
James Brown	Brown	James
Jane Brown	Brown	Jane
Jas. Brown	Brown	Jas.

R9 PREFIXES

In names that contain a prefix, such as *D', Da, De, De la, Des, Di, El, Fitz, L', La, Las, Mac, Mc, O', St., Ste., Ten, Van,* and *Von,* the prefix is considered to be part of the name (i.e., prefix plus name equals one word). In other words, ignore spacing, punctuation, and capitalization in alphabetic sequencing in such names:

P. D'Ambrosia	D'Ambrosia, P. (considered as if spelled <u>Dambrosia</u>)
O. De Kleine	De Kleine, O. (considered as if spelled <u>Dekleine</u>)
P. St. Clair	St. Clair, P. (considered as if spelled <u>Stclair</u>)
D. von der Heidt	von der Heidt, D. (considered as if spelled <u>vonderheidt</u>)

El Matador (considered as if spelled <u>Elmatador</u>)

La Scala Dining Room (considered as if spelled <u>Lascala</u>)

Le Chien Élégant (considered as if spelled <u>Lechien</u>)

R10 PUNCTUATION

Ignore all punctuation in alphabetic sequencing, no matter where it occurs, but key it into the caption:

LeLarge Inc.

Lela's Hairstyling

Lelas, T.

L'Élégant Beauty Salon

L'Élégant Ltd.

R11 HYPHENATED NAMES

Treat hyphenated names as one filing unit; disregard the hyphen while establishing filing order but key it into the caption:

	Unit 1	Unit 2	Unit 3
Canadian-American Pen Co.	Canadian-American	Pen	Co.
James William Curtis	Curtis	James	William
Ellen Curtis-Brown	Curtis-Brown	Ellen	
Winston Curtis-Jones	Curtis-Jones	Winston	
Nu-Style Beauty Salon	Nu-Style	Beauty	Salon

R12 SYMBOLS

Treat these as though they are spelled out, and each is considered to be a separate unit:

	Unit 1	Unit 2	Unit 3	Unit 4
Chui & Kwak Ltd. (*treat as*)	Chui	and	Kwak	Ltd.
Easy $ Car Rental (*treat as*)	Easy	Dollar	Car	Rental

R13 GEOGRAPHIC NAMES

Treat these as though each word is a separate unit (i.e., they are filed as written). However, treat geographic names starting with non-English articles or prefixes as one unit:

	Unit 1	Unit 2	Unit 3
Lake Huron Fisheries	Lake	Huron	Fisheries
Las Olas Importers	Las Olas	Importers	
Mount Vernon Antiques	Mount	Vernon	Antiques

R14 COMPASS POINTS IN NAMES

When names include compass points, consider the compass points as they are written (i.e., each word will be a separate unit):

Unit 1	Unit 2	Unit 3
North	Atlantic	Fisheries
North	West	Airlines
North-West	Sportswear	
Northwestern	Auto	Service

R15 NUMBERS

Several rules apply in relation to captions that include numbers:

1. Place captions beginning with *arabic numerals* in numeric order and list these before all alphabetic files.

   <u>747 Travel Agency</u> before <u>Able 2 Taxi Service</u>

2. Place captions starting with *roman numerals* after those starting with arabic numerals.

   <u>747 Travel Agency</u> before <u>III Star Club</u>

3. File names beginning with *spelled-out numbers* in appropriate alphabetical sequence.

   <u>Four Seas Fashions</u> after <u>Able 2 Taxi Service</u>

4. When numbers come *within a name,* consider these as spelled out.

   <u>Able 2 Taxi Service</u> = <u>Able Two Taxi Service</u>

   747 Travel Agency
   III Star Club
   Able 2 Taxi Service
   Able II Taxi Service
   Four Seas Fashions

R16 ASSOCIATIONS, SOCIETIES, ORGANIZATIONS, BANKS, RELIGIOUS INSTITUTIONS, COLLEGES, SCHOOLS, UNIVERSITIES

These remain unchanged for filing purposes:

Normal order	Indexed order
Bank of Montreal	Bank of Montreal
Church of the Redeemer	Church of the Redeemer
L'Amoreaux Collegiate	L'Amoreaux Collegiate
R.H. King Academy	R.H. King Academy
Stephen Leacock College	Stephen Leacock College
University of Manitoba	University of Manitoba

Cross-reference, if necessary, to avoid confusion (e.g., Montreal, Bank of).

R 1 7   BOARDS, COMMITTEES, ESTATES, TRUSTEES

Rearrange names of boards, etc., to bring the most important word to the front:

Normal order	Indexed order
Board of Governors	Governors, Board of
Estate of D. Chung	Chung, D., Estate of

Cross-reference to the normal order of the words, if necessary, to avoid confusion.

R 1 8   GOVERNMENTS AND THEIR DIVISIONS

File these under the name of the particular level of government (federal, provincial, municipal), with further subdivisions where necessary:

Normal order	Indexed order
Government of Canada	Canada, Government of
Ministry of Agriculture	Agriculture, Ministry of
Saskatchewan Ministry of Health	Saskatchewan, Province of, Health, Ministry of
Windsor Board of Education	Windsor, Education, Board of

Foreign government names

File these in the order of the country, department, bureau, or other subdivisions:

Normal order	Indexed order
Ministry of Trade, Korea	Korea, Trade, Ministry of

R 1 9   IDENTICAL NAMES

If two or more names are identical, distinguish among them by proceeding through the following steps until a point of comparison is found:

1. personal/professional, courtesy title
2. geographic location
3. address

Barbara Brogly, B.A.	Brogly, Barbara (B.A.)
Dr. Barbara Brogly	Brogly, Barbara (Dr.)
Ms. Barbara Brogly	Brogly, Barbara (Ms.)
Prof. Barbara Brogly	Brogly, Barbara (Prof.)

If no titles of any type are given for identical personal names or if identical company names occur, file alphabetically by location (i.e., the province/state/country is compared first; then town/city; then street name; then street number, numerically):

Brogly, Barbara, <u>Nova Scotia</u>
Brogly, Barbara, <u>Saskatchewan</u>
General Goods Co., Main Street, Edmonton, <u>Alberta</u>

General Goods Co., 73 <u>Fifth</u> Street, Charlottetown, <u>Prince Edward Island</u>
General Goods Co., 49 <u>Third</u> Avenue, Charlottetown, <u>Prince Edward Island</u>
General Goods Co., <u>150</u> Third Avenue, Charlottetown, <u>Prince Edward Island</u>

R20 TELEPHONE DIRECTORY ALPHABETIC SEQUENCING

Telephone directories do not follow all ARMA rules. If you are looking for information in a telephone directory, note the following possible variations in alphabetic sequencing:

◆ Company names that include individuals' first and last names may be listed under the family name.

◆ Some abbreviations are treated as though spelled out (e.g., Assoc., Insce.). Ampersands (&) are disregarded.

◆ Numbers are treated as though spelled out (e.g., "7-Eleven Stores" after "Sevcenko, E.").

◆ Hyphenated names are sometimes treated as separate units and sometimes as one (e.g., "Servo-Clean" after "Servite Inc.").

◆ Government organizations are listed within the government body (i.e., federal, provincial, and municipal) and appear separately after the residential listings in the telephone directory.

R21 BASIC DOCUMENT RECORDS ORGANIZATION AND SUPPLIES

Despite the increased use of such records management technology as magnetic disks, optical disks, and EDI (electronic data interchange), vast quantities of document records are still kept by both large and small organizations.

R22 PARTS OF A TYPICAL ALPHABETIC DOCUMENT FILE

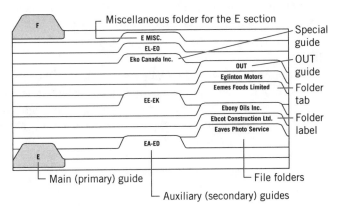

Parts of a typical document file

▶**R23   Guides**

Use *main* (primary) and *auxiliary* (secondary) guides (folder-sized cardboard with metal or plastic tabs) to separate file folders into divisions and subdivisions to facilitate filing and retrieval. Use *special* guides when files for particular subjects or correspondents are frequently referred to and must be speedily located.

▶**R24   Folders (legal- or letter-size)**

Individual Prepared for each person, organization, or subject; placed in alphabetic order behind the relevant guide.

Miscellaneous Prepared for documents concerning a new correspondent or subject; placed at the back of the proper subdivision until at least five documents have accumulated. An individual folder is then prepared and moved to the appropriate position.

▶**R25   Suspension folders**

So that file folders do not slide around in file drawers, place them inside suspension folders that hang from a special framework inserted in the file drawer.

Folder tabs
Folders are available in a variety of *cuts* that leave a tab visible in the file drawer or on the file shelf.

For information about folder tabs with top cuts, please visit the Text Enrichment Site for this text at *www.pearsoned.ca/text/campbell*.

You can use the same cut for all folders in a system, or cuts may be varied to stagger folders so that one folder tab is not obscured behind another. Cuts may be top tab or side tab. Use side tab folders for lateral filing cabinets and shelf filing systems. See R47 and R48.

Folder labels
Folder captions are usually keyed on labels available in roll or sheet form and in various colours. Key captions neatly in a consistent style and position the labels carefully so that the captions can be easily seen. You can use colour to indicate particular years, particular departments, etc. Plastic tabs are provided with suspension folders to readily identify the file folders they house.

R26 RECORDS MANAGEMENT SYSTEMS

Records may be arranged alphabetically, by geographic location, by subject, by number, or by a combination of letters and numbers.

Below is a description of how these systems accommodate document records. The principles of alphabetic, numeric, geographic, subject, and chronological records management can also be applied to electronic, optical, and micrographic media.

R27 ALPHABETIC FILING

◆ Names and subjects are filed in simple alphabetic order (see R3).

◆ Main guides indicate each letter of the alphabet.

◆ Auxiliary guides break down each letter of the alphabet into sections. Folders are arranged alphabetically by name behind these guides. The user merely looks for the first two or three letters on the auxiliary guide and then looks behind for the desired folder.

◆ This system is simple, easy to operate, but difficult to expand.

◆ Alphabetic filing is used in small organizations where specialized breakdown by subject or location is not needed.

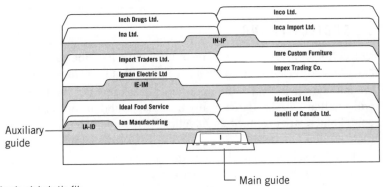

Simple alphabetic file

R28 GEOGRAPHIC FILING

◆ Files are grouped by geographic location from the largest geographic division to the smallest (e.g., from province to town).

◆ The largest divisions (provinces) appear on the main guides, and the cities or towns on the auxiliary guides. File folders for correspondents in each city or town are placed alphabetically behind these guides.

◆ This system is useful for firms or departments whose main interest is territorial data (e.g., sales records); however, it should be noted that the successful operation of a geographic system demands sound geographic knowledge.

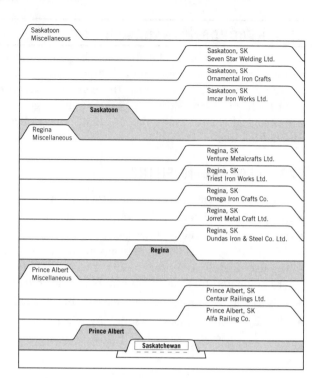

Typical geographic file

R29 SUBJECT FILING

◆ Subject filing means organizing records by topic (i.e., the content of the material) and then arranging the files alphabetically by those topics.

◆ The main guide indicates the main topic breakdown in the filing system. Auxiliary guides indicate any necessary subdivisions of the topic. Folders are arranged alphabetically by topic behind the appropriate guide.

◆ Establishing subject classifications demands care and considerable knowledge of the organization's activities.

◆ To facilitate retrieval, an alphabetic master list or card index is needed that shows all the main subject divisions, auxiliary divisions, and individual folder categories.

◆ Many cross-references are likely to be required.

◆ This filing system is used when subject matter is more important than correspondents' names.

▶R30   Use of letters and numbers in subject filing

Subject files may also be identified by letters and numbers used in combination or sometimes by numbers alone. Such systems are particularly useful in large, centralized document filing systems because they can overcome the restrictions generally imposed by simple alphabetic subject systems. These variations offer flexibility, diminish misfiling possibilities, and ease expansion difficulties.

Alpha-numeric

A combination of letters and numbers is used. Main topics are given letters and related subtopics are assigned numbers:

A	ADMINISTRATION
A1	**Human Resources**
A1–1	Company Policies
A1–1–1	Absenteeism
A1–2	Employee Records
A2	**Physical Plant**
A2–1	Electrical Wiring
A2–1–1	Alarm System
A2–2	Fixtures
B	CUSTOMER SERVICE

Decimal

This system is based on the concept that all materials can be grouped into ten or fewer main categories. Each of the ten major subjects may be sub-divided into ten more parts and so on indefinitely:

100	ADMINISTRATION
110	**Human Resources**
111	Company Policies
111.1	Absenteeism
112	Employee Records
120	**Physical Plant**
121	Electrical Wiring
121.1	Alarm System
122	Fixtures
200	CUSTOMER SERVICE

Duplex-numeric

A combination of numbers is used. Each primary topic is given a consec-utive number, and secondary and tertiary (third subdivision) topics are subdivided down from that number:

1	ADMINISTRATION
1–1	**Human Resources**
1–1–1	Company Policies
1–1–1–1	Absenteeism
1–1–2	Employee Records
1–2	**Physical Plant**
1–2–1	Electrical Wiring
1–2–1–1	Alarm System
1–2–2	Fixtures
2	CUSTOMER SERVICE

R

Subject-numeric

Subject groups are assigned alphabetic codes (usually of three letters) and secondary and other categories are represented by numerals:

ADM.OO	ADMINISTRATION
ADM.01	**Human Resources**
ADM.01-0	Company Policies
ADM.01-0-1	Absenteeism
ADM.01-1	Employee Records
ADM.02	**Physical Plant**
ADM.02-0	Electrical Wiring
ADM.02-0-1	Alarm System
ADM.02-1	Fixtures
CST.OO	CUSTOMER SERVICE

R31 NUMERIC FILING

Numeric filing offers accuracy, confidentiality, and unrestricted possibilities for expansion.

Sequential numeric system

In sequential numeric systems, one number is used to cover all the records of a client, case, or account:

- As new folders are required, new numbers are added in sequence.
- Main guides are used to indicate round numbers.
- Auxiliary guides are used to break down the round numbers into smaller categories.
- When a file is opened, a number is allocated and an alphabetic record (computerized list or index card) is made up.
- The number to be used for a new file is determined by consulting the *access register,* a record of file numbers already allocated. The next unused number is allocated to the new file.
- The system *must* have a complementary alphabetic system that shows the client's name, address, assigned number, and any other pertinent information. If the file number is unknown, consult the alphabetic system and the file number is easily located.

Alphabetic record system that complements the numeric filing system

NOTE Some companies use both a name and a number on the file folder, but where confidentiality is required, only a number is used.

Numeric file

R

Terminal digit filing

◆ In this type of numeric filing system, you read numbers from right to left in equal groups of numbers (i.e., the first two numbers at the right are *primary,* the next two are *secondary,* and the rest are *tertiary*). For example, file number 091832 is read as 32 18 09.

◆ To file or retrieve, you first look under section 32 of the file, then under section 18, and finally under section 09. In such a system, 32 could be the cabinet number, 18 the drawer number, and 09 the client number within the folder. Spaces, hyphens, and periods can be used to separate numbers.

◆ Users of this system include insurance companies and hospitals.

◆ The main reason for using this system is to avoid the concentration of new files in one file drawer or shelf.

◆ The system speeds retrieval.

For more information on management and control of records, please visit the Text Enrichment Site for this text at *www.pearsoned.ca/text/campbell.*

R32 THE RECORDS CYCLE

The management of records by an organization is most easily viewed as having four stages. This is generally referred to as the records cycle.

Creation A record is prepared by an organization or received by it.

Maintenance and use The record is stored efficiently and accurately so that it can be retrieved quickly.

Transfer The record is moved from active to inactive storage (known as archives), which may be on- or off-site.

Destruction The record is finally removed from the system.

R33 MANAGING DOCUMENT RECORDS

In some organizations, records are kept in a *centralized* storage area under the direction of a records manager; in other departments, records are retained in individual departments (i.e., they are *decentralized*). Regardless of the size or sophistication of the system, a consistent and careful routine is necessary for efficient records management.

You must routinely check all documents to ensure proper *releasing* for filing; then they should be *coded* and, if necessary, marked for *cross-reference* and *follow-up*. In addition, efficient *charge-out* and transfer procedures must be used.

R34 RELEASING

◆ No document should be filed until somebody has released it (i.e., indicated that all necessary action has been taken).

◆ Initials, a rubber stamp, or a copy of a reply attached to the original document are generally used as filing releases.

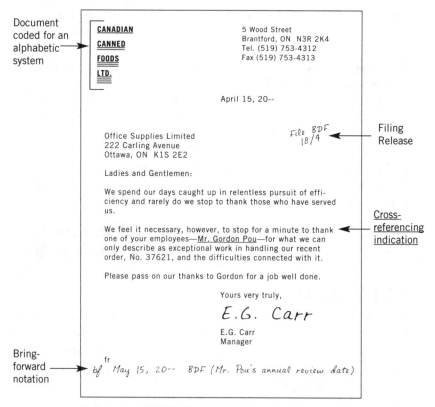

Document coded for an alphabetic system

Filing Release

Cross-referencing indication

Bring-forward notation

Example of a letter coded for alphabetic filing, showing typical release, cross-reference, and bring-forward (follow-up) notations

R35 CODING

Coding means identifying on the record where it is to be filed.

◆ Underscore or circle the word(s) under which the document is to be filed, or write the appropriate caption on the document.

◆ The filing units may be indicated quite simply by the use of one or more underscores:

Unit 1	Unit 2	Unit 3	Unit 4
Canadian	Canned	Foods	Ltd.

◆ In the case of a numeric system, the appropriate number is underscored, circled, or written on the document.

NOTE Coding makes refiling easier if documents taken from the system must be replaced.

R36 CROSS-REFERENCING

R

Cross-referencing means indicating in one or more places where a record is located. File records under the most important classification and cross-reference them under the other(s).

CROSS-REFERENCE

NAME OR
SUBJECT _Dixon Pencil Co. Ltd._   Folder No. _____

Address _531 Davis Drive_

Newmarket, ON   L3Y 2P1

REFER TO
Folder No. _Eberhard Faber (Canada) Ltd._ _____

531 Davis Drive

Newmarket, ON   L3Y 2P1

(Division of Dixon Pencil Co.)

Date of letter or paper: _November 8_ 20 _--_

Remarks: _Inquiry about automated_

storage systems

Cross-reference sheet

SEE ALSO
Folder No. _____   _____

File this cross-reference under the name or subject written at the top of this page.

Use cross-references when a document refers to more than one subject or when a file might be looked for under more than one heading. For example:

♦ when names contain several important words:

Vancouver Board of Education

♦ for names that sound alike but have different spellings:

Noel/Nowell

♦ for companies referred to by initials when the meaning of the initials is known:

CBC/Canadian Broadcasting Corporation

Three cross-referencing devices are as follows:

Cross-referencing sheets Specially designed letter-size sheets that can be filed inside the cross-referenced folder as though they were correspondence. These direct the searcher to the correct folder.

Cross-referencing folders Tabbed half-folders placed in the file drawer or shelf in the cross-referenced position as though they were actual folders. These half-folders are labelled to indicate the position of the actual correspondence folder.

Cross-referencing computerized lists or small index cards Used in a large system in which many cross-references occur. Keep lists in folders or binders; keep cards in a separate drawer.

Dixon Pencil Co. Ltd.

See: Eberhard Faber
(Canada) Ltd.

Cross-reference shown on the tab of a half-folder

DIXON PENCIL CO. LTD.
531 Davis Drive
Newmarket, ON L3Y 2P1

See: Eberhard Faber (Canada) Ltd.
      531 Davis Drive
      Newmarket, ON L3Y 2P1

Note: Eberhard Faber is a division of Dixon
       Pencil Co.

Cross-reference card

R37 FOLLOW-UP OR REMINDER (TICKLER) SYSTEMS

A good follow-up system ensures that documents that will require attention in the future are brought forward at the proper time. Any document that has a "bring forward" notation on it should have the request recorded in one of the following devices before you place the document in the files.

Desk calendar

On the appropriate day, note the reminder request and the location of the material.

Follow-up or chronological file

◆ Label 31 folders (one for each day of the month) and 12 folders (one for each month).

◆ Place the folders in a file drawer.

◆ File a follow-up request for the current month in the appropriate *day* folder. If the follow-up is for a future month, place it in the appropriate *month* folder.

◆ Deal with material in each day's folder on the appropriate day then move the empty folder to the back of the *day* folders.

◆ At the beginning of each month, move the previous month's empty folder to the back and transfer papers from the current month's folders into the daily folders.

◆ Do not use dates of weekends or holidays for bringing forward documents unless business is usually conducted on those days.

◆ For a very large system, set up daily folders for a *year*.

NOTE The material in the folder may be the original, a copy, or simply a note to serve as the follow-up reminder.

Tickler file

This system is identical to the follow-up file except that it is in card form and is housed in a small index card container. You can make reminder notes on separate cards and insert them behind the appropriate day or month guides.

Electronic reminder systems

The follow-up reminder is keyed onto an electronic calendar and is seen on the appropriate day. See Unit 12, "Computers: Hardware and Software," for information on electronic calendar software.

R38 CHARGE-OUT PROCEDURES (BORROWING STORED MATERIALS)

Every records management system should have an efficient charge-out procedure for establishing the whereabouts of a record or a file while it is out on loan.

◆ Keep careful records of all documents and files out on loan in case they are needed by someone else. Simple ways of achieving this are by means of a completed requisition form; small index cards that show the name of the borrower, date of borrowing, description of the record or title of the file; or a computer record that can be easily updated.

II

◆ While the record is out on loan, use an OUT guide or an OUT folder to replace it. OUT guides are satisfactory for single documents. OUT folders are best for replacing complete folders because new records can be safely stored in them while the folders are out on loan.

◆ Ensure strict follow-up of overdue material to make sure that borrowed material is returned. Use a bring-forward tickler system, a desk diary, or electronic calendar for this purpose.

◆ If the record is given by the borrower to another person (rerouted), the borrower should inform the records department and you should change the OUT guide and follow-up record to show the new borrower's name.

◆ Two ways of guarding against the non-return of material are
• demanding written requests, or (but more costly)
• copying what has been lent

For information about OUT guides, please visit the Text Enrichment Site for this text at *www.pearsoned.ca/text/campbell*.

Machine-readable labels (barcoding)

This system for charging out files requires a dedicated microprocessor. Labels on file folders contain bar codes that can be read by a photo-electric wand.

◆ When a file is requested, it is removed from shelf storage and the operator passes the wand over the bar code.

◆ The file is then taken out of inventory and the information stored in the wand is entered into the records centre database.

◆ This action records the location of the file in the computer, and thus overdue items are automatically indicated.

◆ Records for archival storage can be easily identified in this system.

R39 DOCUMENT FILING TIPS

◆ For faster filing, sort papers into large groupings that follow the arrangement used in the cabinets or shelves (e.g., A–G, H–L, M–S, T–Z). Sorters are available in desktop models or large portable-tub types.

◆ Place documents in file folders with the left edge against the crease in the folder.

◆ Arrange documents in chronological order, with the most recent date on the top.

◆ Keep a "Miscellaneous" folder at the back of each alphabetic or numeric division to hold documents that are not designated to a specific file. When five documents have accumulated for a client or subject, make up an individual folder.

- Place a maximum of 100 sheets in a folder. Do not exceed the space provided by the creases. Use an expansion folder for heavy correspondence.

- Consider using suspension folders in cabinets, as they keep materials neater and make files easier to handle.

- Consider using boxed suspension folders, as they are useful when a folder and other bulky records must be kept together.

- Do not crowd file drawers or shelves. Allow 10 cm (4″) of unused space.

- Use coloured labels. Colour speeds retrieval and prevents misfiles because the interruption that a misfile makes in the bands of colour is quickly identified.

- Colour can also be used effectively to indicate time periods and therefore can make the job of transferring old files easier.

- File every day if possible.

- Develop a filing manual outlining all the procedures you use so that someone else can take over if necessary.

R

For information about a desktop sorter, please visit the Text Enrichment Site for this text at *www.pearsoned.ca/text/campbell*.

R40 ELECTRONIC RECORDS

Electronic records are those kept in digital form on tape or on disk. The system may be centralized, decentralized, or a combination of both. In a centralized system, information is saved centrally in word-processing, database, or spreadsheet files. Network users can retrieve information onto their own screens from remote locations. Files may be open to all users or may require the use of a password or code for access. If a system is decentralized, users have stand-alone computers and their own disks.

The terms used in electronic record-keeping tend to be similar to those used in non-electronic systems. Depending on the software used, reference will be made to directories, files, folders, cabinets, etc.

R41   MANAGING ELECTRONIC RECORDS

The management of centralized electronic records systems tends to be a specialized field under the control of trained records management experts. For managing a smaller, decentralized system, the following information will be useful.

Storage

- A systematic approach similar to that described for documents is needed (see R46).

◆ Records produced can include disks, cassettes, cartridges, DVDs, and printouts. These may be stored in standard file cabinets, but specialized equipment is available that provides for safety and ease of access, including the following:
  • three-ring binders with heavy-gauge vinyl pockets
  • boxes, racks, and rotary stands
  • shelves
  • binders that fit on suspension racks

◆ Disks and tapes are vulnerable to climatic conditions and should be maintained at constant acceptable temperature and humidity levels.

◆ For the sake of safety, do not store disks or tapes and hard copies (printouts) together.

> For information about storage devices for electronic records, please visit the Text Enrichment Site for this text at *www.pearsoned.ca/text/campbell*.

Record identification

The value of an expensive electronic facility is seriously diminished if the operator is unable to locate records quickly. Identify clearly disks, cassettes, CD-ROMS, etc., through a standard alphabetic, alpha-numeric, or subject system that is understandable by others. This applies both to the storage device and to the records stored in it.

◆ Decide on what disk and under what directory folder the file should be located and follow a consistent procedure for naming files. Clear identification is essential.

◆ Label each disk with a general classification and date.

◆ Print a directory, which can be folded and placed in the disk jacket or kept separately.

◆ If one disk is full, use the same general classification and add "1," "2," etc., to successive disks.

Coding

◆ On the record, key a descriptive file name and the initials of the author (e.g., Saleslet3.DM). See Unit 14, Part 2, for file-naming ideas. If a hard copy of the record is also filed, the file name recorded on the document permits fast and easy retrieval of the disk.

Control

◆ Make backup copies of important storage disks and all software and store them with care.

◆ Control borrowing (charge-out) carefully.

◆ Create a procedures manual that contains a complete description of your storage system and procedures to assist users if you are absent.

◆ If confidentiality is required for records stored on disk or tape, use passwords or codes so that the directory or index is meaningless in the wrong hands.

◆ Regularly purge your system of old files.

◆ Regularly update databases.

R42 RECORDS RETENTION

Periodically clean out and purge hard-copy records and purge material on disks to dispose of outdated or unnecessary material. Routine correspondence may be destroyed but legal considerations control the retention of some materials. Seek the advice of legal counsel or an auditor as to which records must legally be retained by each type of business.

The paper pollution problem can be eased by a careful assessment of which records might be kept on film, tape, or disk, and which—because of legal requirements—must be retained in the original form.

A records retention schedule (a timetable for the life of a record) is essential. The schedule should show the types of records and the time periods for which they should be kept; it should contain instructions for their eventual disposal or destruction (e.g., transfer from active to inactive storage, microfilmed, stored on disk, or authorized destruction). The records retention schedule is usually drawn up by management, the records manager, and the company's legal counsel and, perhaps, auditor.

R

R43 TRANSFER METHODS

Inactive files, containing records that are old and not in use but that should be kept for some reason, should be removed (transferred) from the active files and stored elsewhere so that there is no unnecessary crowding of the active files. The transfer method to be used will be determined by the nature of the business and will be either perpetual or periodic.

Perpetual transfer When a particular piece of work (e.g., a legal case) is finished, the file is transferred into storage.

Periodic transfer After a certain period (e.g., on a particular date each year), all the files are transferred.

R44 DESTRUCTION

A few records can be disposed of by simply placing them in the garbage or arranging for recycling. However, most require special treatment because of the need for confidentiality. Shred records of this type.

R45 SHREDDERS

Organizations usually purchase their own equipment for paper disposal, or contract with outside companies to pick up and dispose of large quantities of paper.

Shredders must be able to handle the types and volumes of documents needed to be shredded.

Shredder Needs Survey

1. What types of materials need to be shredded?

    (a) correspondence
    (b) printouts
    (c) complete files
    (d) other

2. Volume of paper?

    (a) individual/department/organization assessment
    (b) what is the volume now, future, etc.?

3. Shred type:

    (a) strip cut
    (b) cross cut
    (c) top security cut (meets security requirements, i.e., codes, etc.)
    (d) particle cut

4. Size of shredder:

    (a) small personal units that fit under desks
    (b) full-size office models that can handle continuous shredding from multiple feeds

5. Location:

    (a) who will use? individual, department, or whole organization?

6. Installation:

    (a) warranty work, maintenance, and other repairs (can they be handled locally?)
    (b) ease of use
    (c) is training provided?

7. Cost:

    (a) budget for maintenance
    (b) training

R46 RECORDS STORAGE EQUIPMENT

R47 FILE CABINETS

Lateral file cabinets have the length of the file against the wall and offer a considerable saving in time and space requirements over the once-popular vertical file cabinets.

◆ Lateral cabinets have up to five pull-out drawers or shelves and are available in letter and legal size.

◆ The drawers may be fitted with a cradle over which hanging (suspension) folders may be hooked, either to serve as file folders or to house other, smaller folders.

R48 SHELVES

◆ Shelves, which may be open or closed, are advantageous where large quantities of files are maintained. Shelves save space and offer a plentiful storage area. Most systems use boxes or suspension units that attach to the shelves to house materials.

◆ Shelves offer great flexibility and can, for example, be adapted to house computer printouts and magnetic tape reels.

◆ If floor space is limited, shelves can provide maximum filing capacity.

For information about shelves, please visit the Text Enrichment Site for this text at *www.pearsoned.ca/text/campbell*.

R49 MOBILE CARRIAGE FILING SYSTEMS

Also known as *laterally rolling modular filing systems,* these space-saving systems may have movable rows or stationary back rows and laterally rolling middle and front rows. Depending on the make, the rows may be moved manually, mechanically, electrically, or electronically. This system allows easy access to any file in any row. Built-in safety features ensure that staff members cannot be caught between moving shelves.

◆ Some systems offer microprocessor electronic controls that permit keyboard commands and computer control.

For information about types of mobile carriage filing systems, please visit the Text Enrichment Site for this text at *www.pearsoned.ca/text/campbell*.

R50 ROTARY (CIRCULAR) FILES

These are available in several versions, including an electronically driven one. They *bring* files to the operator.

R51 SPECIAL FILING EQUIPMENT

Special equipment—plan files, card record systems, binding cases, magnetic disks and tape containers, optical disk "juke box" storage devices, etc.—is available from office supply companies. Alternatively, manufacturers will build special equipment and provide expert consultation services if necessary.

R

R52 AUTOMATED FILING EQUIPMENT

Automated storage means that the location and replacement of a particular record (file, tape, reel, card, cheque, etc.) is handled by push-button command.

◆ The system is controlled by an operator who sits at a simple keyboard.

◆ The operator keys in the record identification and gives the *Start* command.

◆ A mechanism then moves to the appropriate location, couples itself to the requested file container, and transports the container to the workstation.

◆ After the file has been dealt with, the operator gives a *Re-Store* command and the mechanism automatically returns the file container to its proper position.

◆ The system can be interfaced with a computer.

R53 IMAGE TECHNOLOGY

This is today's term for records management systems based on *micrographics* or *optical disks* (usually referred to as *image processing*). Micrographics systems are *analog;* image processing systems are *digital*.

For information about micrographic material, please visit the Text Enrichment Site for this text at *www.pearsoned.ca/text/campbell*.

R54 IMAGE PROCESSING

Image processing is a digital technology that is being used increasingly in records management. Documents are scanned or read in and the computer stores them on optical disks. The strength of the system lies in its ability to capture, store, process, and retrieve documents for information, printing, and distribution, regardless of format or content.

Image processing is heavily used in insurance claims processing, banking, health care, business, and government.

▶R55   Optical disk storage

◆ A scanner captures data and a laser records it onto high-density 5.25″ or 3.5″ optical disks. Storage of text, graphics, photographs, and sound is possible.

◆ Optical disk technology offers quick access, sophisticated indexing capabilities, and extensive cross-reference possibilities.

◆ Made from aluminum, sturdy, and long-lasting, optical media are particularly attractive because they are impervious to damage by magnetic or electrical spikes or surges.

◆ Data can be accessed by several users at the same time.

NOTE   For full details of the kinds of optical disks available, see Unit 12, "Computers: Hardware and Software," C38.

R56 DOCUMENT-BASED MANAGEMENT SYSTEMS (DBMS)

DBMS are the core of image processing systems and applications. They allow for complete integration of a company's document records and can be used for storage of active or inactive files.

◆ The system uses optical disks as the storage medium.

◆ Imaging guarantees absolute accuracy, as opposed to keying. Document files are scanned in; files stored on disk or tape are read in.

◆ Users do not have to wait. Information on disk can be accessed quickly and easily and in many ways because of cross-referencing.

◆ Files are always accounted for because they are not removed from the system.

◆ Information can be customized to each company's preferences.

◆ In some systems, a change in one record can be registered automatically in other relevant documents.

◆ Correspondence and responses can be matched in files.

◆ Responses to queries can be handled immediately because there is less dependence on other people to provide information.

In an accounts receivable application, for example, a complete customer file can be maintained electronically. An electronic invoice is generated from the mainframe computer, a signed bill of lading indicating proof of delivery is scanned in, and a "notes" function is available to allow details such as telephone calls to be recorded. The system can be email- or fax-enabled for instant transmission of information.

R57 OTHER ELECTRONIC RECORDS SYSTEMS

R58   COMPUTER OUTPUT TO LASER DISK (COLD)

Computer output to laser (optical) disk is widely used in mainframe data centres to replace COM (computer output to microfilm), computer-generated printouts, and magnetic tape storage.

R59   DATABASES

Some records may simply be facts—names, telephone numbers, addresses, inventory stock items, policy numbers, information on customer buying habits, client credit ratings, etc. Records of this type are frequently kept in an electronic database, a computerized system that permits highly organized storage of such data. The information is cross-referenced in several ways so that it can be searched for under many categories. (See Unit 12, "Computers: Hardware and Software," C17.)

R60   ELECTRONIC DATA INTERCHANGE

Electronic data interchange (EDI; see Unit 13, "The Integrated Office: New Technologies," IO4 and IO5) will bring an end to most paper records in many organizations and an increased focus on electronic records.

R61 LEGAL ADMISSIBILITY OF MICROGRAPHIC AND ELECTRONIC RECORDS

In Canada, microfilm is accepted as being legal if the following guidelines are followed:

◆ *MICROFILM AND ELECTRONIC RECORDS AS DOCUMENTARY EVIDENCE* (CAN/CGSB-72.11.93)

◆ *Canada Evidence Act* (Publication #YXC35)

◆ *Ontario Evidence Act* (Publication #110559) or equivalent legislation for your province

Where records are kept on tape or disk, a lawyer should be consulted before the decision is made to eliminate the hard copy versions.

R62 RECORDS AND INFORMATION MANAGEMENT (RIM)

Records and information management is the systematic control of all records in an organization, regardless of media, from creation to distribution, filing, retention, version control, storage, and disposal. The records management program implemented must meet legal requirements as well as efficiently serve the operational needs of the business or organization.

R63   RECORDS MANAGEMENT PROGRAM

For organizations to operate efficiently, they should set up records information management programs. How the organization manages information and its corporate records can directly affect its ability to compete, comply with regulations, and recover from disaster.

▶ R64   Key functions

Key records management functions include the following:

◆ guidelines for records centre operations

◆ vital records programs—identifying, managing, and recovering business-critical records

◆ requirements for managing electronic messages as records

◆ retention management for records and information

◆ establishing alphabetic, numeric, and subject filing systems

▶ R65   Elements of a records management program

◆ Decide what records should be created and stored in each area of business, e.g., accounting, company/personnel contracts, payroll, etc.

◆ Determine the form and structure of how records are to be created and what technologies will be used in the process.

◆ Determine the method for retrieving, using, and transmitting records between business processes and other users.

◆ Decide how long records need to be kept based on organizational and legal requirements (retention program).

◆ Determine how records will be stored in a safe and secure environment.

◆ Decide how to organize records for efficient access.

◆ Determine the risks involved if records are not available.

◆ Decide on the process for handling electronic records (e-records).

◆ Determine what information is to be stored and how the records are to be created.

◆ Decide on an audit schedule.

◆ Decide how records are to be destroyed and how the destruction will be documented.

▶ R66   Advantages of good records management

◆ Improved job performance: employee/management stress is reduced if information can be accessed easily and efficiently.

◆ Reduced costs: time and money are saved when records are found quickly.

◆ Enhanced support to the legal department: If a record is needed in a court of law, good records management ensures easy access to the appropriate version of a record.

◆ Reduced training time and costs: When an established records management program is in place, less time is needed for training employees to use the program.

R67   PRIVACY

Consumers and clients want to be assured that their sensitive information is collected, stored, and used safely.

R68   OUTSOURCING DATA

The outsourcing of computer services and data processing (e.g., financial services, medical data, and tax information) is a rapidly growing global trend in large and small businesses. It is important that basic privacy safeguards be established for the transferral of this data.

UNIT

9 COPYING PROCESSES

SELECTED CONTENTS

CP1	IMAGING TECHNOLOGIES
CP2	MAKING THE RIGHT CHOICE
CP3	PHOTOCOPYING
CP4	Types of Photocopying Equipment
CP5	Convenience Photocopiers
CP6	Photocopier Features
CP7	Producing Quality Copies
CP8	Using Your Copier Economically
CP9	Monitoring Copier Use
CP10	Key Operators
CP11	CENTRALIZED COPYING SERVICES
CP12	Phototypesetting
CP13	Using a Centralized Service
CP14	SPECIALIZED COPIERS
CP15	Intelligent Copiers
CP16	DIGITAL CAMERAS/PHOTOGRAPHY
CP17	Digital Duplicators
CP18	Offset Duplicating
CP19	COMMERCIAL COPYING SERVICES
CP20	COPYRIGHT CONCERNS
CP21	FINISHING EQUIPMENT
CP22	CHOOSING COPYING EQUIPMENT

Copying or duplicating processes are an important part of the office worker's world. Those using copying processes are responsible for choosing the best and cheapest one for each task and knowing how to use that system wisely.

In this unit, you will be introduced to the equipment and processes available to you, shown how to use the equipment or process to best advantage, made aware of copyright restrictions, and helped in choosing the most appropriate equipment for your office, should this be required of you.

CP1 IMAGING TECHNOLOGIES

There are two basic technologies in image processing: analog and digital. An understanding of both provides a guide to their applications.

Analog

Analog is the technology of the most common photocopying process now used. In this process, light is reflected through mirrors and lenses to a drum, creating a latent image. The drum is applied to paper, where it leaves a pattern created by static electricity. Toner, a black powder, sticks to the statically charged places and a copy is created. Originals are scanned by the equipment each time a copy is made.

Digital

The digital copying process uses the binary technology of the computer. The original is scanned once, a digital film master is made, and printing is done from the master. If necessary, the user can manipulate and edit the digital signals before the film master is made.

CP

CP2 MAKING THE RIGHT CHOICE

You have three options for handling your copying and duplicating requirements:

♦ **Do the work yourself.** This is convenient and fast but may not offer the range of services provided by more specialized services.

♦ **Use a centralized, in-house (within the company) service** if one exists. This can provide a more professional-looking product but may not offer the speed required.

♦ **Send the work out.** You will usually get both speed and quality from commercial houses, but this is economical only if you need a large number of copies.

When choosing a copying service, consider the number of copies needed, the quality of reproduction required, the intended use of the finished product, speed, and cost.

CP3 PHOTOCOPYING

CP4 TYPES OF PHOTOCOPYING EQUIPMENT

Photocopying equipment tends to fall into three major categories:

1. Low-volume (convenience): For a requirement of fewer than 20 000 copies each month. Speed: Up to 65 copies a minute.

2. Mid-volume: For from 20 000 to 85 000 copies each month. Speed: From 20 to 145 copies a minute.

3. High-volume: For 85 000 copies or higher each month. Speed: 50 to 200 copies a minute.

CP5 CONVENIENCE PHOTOCOPIERS

Usually several convenience photocopiers are used in larger organizations, located in places where the greatest need arises. They may be situated within one department or shared among several.

They are

◆ small, relatively inexpensive, desktop or console (floor) models

◆ simple to operate and require no special training

◆ able to use plain paper—they do not need specially treated stationery

◆ useful for volumes of less than 20 000 copies a month

◆ available in speeds ranging from 3 to 65 copies a minute, with the low-speed type being suited only to very low-volume, light usage

For light business or home use, small, portable personal copiers are available. These versatile little machines even permit colour copying if needed.

CP6 PHOTOCOPIER FEATURES

The trend in photocopying is to high productivity. New machines provide unattended copying, as they offer automatic handling of originals and sorting and finishing of copies. These machines feature paper trays and hoppers that can carry hundreds of sheets and can automatically switch from one tray to another so that there is no risk of running out of paper. Technology is facilitating even greater efficiencies. For example, job settings can be stored in memory or on small plastic insertable cards and maintenance problems can be resolved automatically over telephone lines.

The basic photocopier comes with an automatic counting device, exposure control, and the ability to handle letter- and legal-sized paper.

CP7 PRODUCING QUALITY COPIES

The image should be sharp, the background should be white, and the copy should be spot- and streak-free.

◆ If copy quality is unsatisfactory, check your toner and developer levels, ensure that the glass plate is clean, and then request a service call if the problem has not been eliminated.

◆ Use pen instead of pencil for sharp reproduction.

◆ Carefully made corrections will not show—use cover-up liquids and tapes.

◆ Use cut-and-paste techniques to create documents that are as good as originals if your photocopier does not have image editing capability.

- Keep your original properly positioned if you do not have the automatic feed feature. It is wasteful to run off a large number of copies and then discover that the top heading is missing, for example, or that the type is going uphill!
- Make any needed exposure adjustments when you are working with a coloured original.
- If you are working with punched paper, be sure the holes will come out on the correct side before you start the print run.
- Take care when loading feeder trays that the paper is right side up.
- Fan paper to reduce paper jams.

CP8   USING YOUR COPIER ECONOMICALLY

Avoid costly and wasteful practices such as the following:

- producing copies for distribution to staff members when circulation of the original document would do
- using a photocopier when a cheaper process would serve
- making more copies than you actually need

NOTE   If you accidentally make too many copies, use the blank sides for notepads or printing drafts on your laser printer.

Make the best use of your copier:

- Save your copying until you have several items: avoid frequent walks to and from the machine.
- Use the right size of paper for the job.
- Make the exact number of copies needed.
- Use two-sided copying (duplexing) as much as possible.
- Make use of the collating feature if one is available.
- Label a separate bin in which employees can place spoiled or unneeded copies (with the exception of confidential materials, which should be properly disposed of). Use these copies for other office uses, such as notepads.

CP9   MONITORING COPIER USE

Some organizations control copier use. This serves several purposes: costs may have to be billed to customers, usage by departments may need to be monitored, or copier abuse (such as overcopying and personal copying) may need to be prevented. Copy management systems may take the following form:

- a log showing date, number of copies, department, and name of person making the copies
- a full-time operator who works only from a requisition form approved by a supervisor

CP

- a key, cartridge, or plastic card provided by the machine vendor that may be issued to only a few people. Some of these devices have counters built into them

- codes allocated as passwords for individuals and/or departments

CP10 KEY OPERATORS

Key operators are specially appointed people in an organization who are responsible for maintaining the copying equipment. The name(s) of the key operator(s) should be clearly indicated on the equipment.

If you are the key operator, be sure you:

- familiarize yourself with the equipment by requesting a vendor demonstration

- understand how to read the self-diagnostic indicators

- know how to use the hotline service if one exists, and to follow instructions given

- know how to clear routine jams

- know when and how to add toner/developer

II

NOTE   Using office copiers for personal use is a form of theft from the workplace.

CP11 CENTRALIZED COPYING SERVICES

A centralized in-house copying service can reduce costs, control equipment use, and permit direct charging of costs against users or jobs. A full-time, trained staff is on hand and high-powered, sophisticated equipment is available. Some centres—also known as graphic arts centres or print shops—are large and sophisticated enough that they can often provide a full range of services, including artwork and binding.

The creation of desktop publishing masters (see Unit 15, "Desktop Publishing") as originals for copying or duplicating has led to an increase in in-house printing and the use of large copier-duplicators. Some print shops also offer phototypesetting among their services (see next section).

CP12 PHOTOTYPESETTING

For in-house phototypesetting (or photocomposition), text is entered directly into a special phototypesetting unit (much like a word processor) or through word-processing equipment or an OCR (Optical Character Reader) unit linked to it. The result is professional typesetting, offering proportional spacing, justified text, and a variety of fonts and spacing. Where in-house phototypesetting is not available, some specialized commercial printers can convert text stored on disk into phototypesetting.

CP13 USING A CENTRALIZED SERVICE

Complete a copy centre request form indicating your specific requirements. Careful completion is essential as this form is used to prioritize requests and will be rigidly followed by the operator.

COPY CENTRE WORK REQUISITION

Name _____ Date _____

Department _____ Required Date _____

Telephone _____ Required Time _____

Charge to Account No. _____

Copy Centre Use: Job No. _____

Cost _____

Time Received: _____ Time Completed: _____

No. of Originals _____ No. of Copies Each _____

Job Description _____

Delivery Method: To be picked up ❑
                 To be delivered ❑

Instructions: | Cost:

❑ print one-sided   ❑ two-sided

❑ 3-hole punched paper   ❑ unpunched paper

❑ coloured paper   colour:

❑ other size paper   size:

❑ collate

❑ staple

❑ bind   type:

❑ special instructions

Copies to: Copy Centre, Billing Dept., Requester

Copy centre request form

CP14 SPECIALIZED COPIERS

CP15 INTELLIGENT COPIERS

The intelligent copier is a sophisticated, computer-based piece of equipment. It combines the technology of the microprocessor, laser printer, and photocopier and has certain features of both printers and copiers. It can accept text, graphics, and instructions from computers, word processors, or magnetic media, and it can be programmed to form paragraphs,

CP

locate information from memory, image edit, and copy at high speed directly from the digitized information it receives. It can then distribute information to other compatible equipment in the network. The intelligent copier offers many of the features of convenience copiers and can be operated as a convenience copier when required.

As more businesses integrate office practices, the current trend is to increased digital applications, because these allow for the creation, manufacture, management, and delivery of a document in one process. Current digital copiers comprise scanners and printers that will network with faxes, printers, and computers. Advanced models will combine into one unit a copier, fax, scanner, telephone, printer, and computer.

CP16 Digital Cameras/Photography

Digital photography options allow you to store, delete, or print images in record mode before they are stored on memory cards.

The memory card is an electronic storage device that stores each picture until it is uploaded to the computer; you can use these stored images for internal pages, presentations, printed publications, and other applications.

Digital cameras offer high-quality image enhancement technology and are instantly ready to print out. You can send the images through email, or view them on television using a video cable.

CP17 Digital Duplicators

Digital duplicators scan originals once, make a digital film master of the image, and print directly from the master. (Regular photocopiers scan originals once for every image made.) Cost per copy decreases as more copies are printed.

CP18 Offset Duplicating

Offset duplicating is a lithographic process that can produce thousands of high-quality copies that closely resemble commercial printing. Specially trained operators must run the duplicating machine, but preparation of the offset master requires only keyboarding skills. Because of the special skill needed to operate the equipment, most office workers will not become directly involved with offset duplicating but should be aware of the existence of the process and its capabilities. Offset duplicators are usually a feature of the centralized printing service described earlier. Two new trends in offset duplicating are

◆ a direct link between desktop publishing systems and offset presses that automates the production of printing plates and eliminates the necessity to make film

◆ automation and mechanical improvement of the presses to speed production, making presses easier to use and enhancing quality, particularly when using colour

CP19 COMMERCIAL COPYING SERVICES

When a copying job is too big or is needed more quickly than your in-house facility can accommodate, consider a commercial copying or printing service. Consult the Yellow Pages of your telephone book for local companies and compare their services based on rate, quality, and speed. Be sure to provide full details of the job, and request quotations.

CP20 COPYRIGHT CONCERNS

The illegal use of copyrighted materials is an issue of serious concern to authors and publishers, who justifiably view such use as theft of their property. The *Copyright Act* provides severe penalties for the unauthorized copying and use of copyrighted printed and published materials and software. Anyone copying and/or using photocopied material should be aware that written permission is usually required before copyrighted materials may be reproduced and distributed. Among materials that may not be copied are bank notes, birth certificates, books, periodicals, and computer software.

CP

NOTE   Copyright symbol: ©

Example: Cover images copyright © 2007 PhotoDisc, Inc.

CP21 FINISHING EQUIPMENT

Among the array of finishing equipment that allows documents to be presented attractively are the following. Consult the catalogues of office equipment suppliers and stationers for more details.

◆ collators

◆ specialized staplers (power, long, heavy-duty)

◆ binding machines

◆ folding, inserting, sealing, addressing, and meter-stamping equipment

◆ headliners (typesetting devices that produce print in various sizes and fonts)

Additional information on finishing is provided in Unit 15, "Desktop Publishing."

CP22 CHOOSING COPYING EQUIPMENT

If you are involved in selecting copying equipment for your office, bear the following in mind. For the greatest efficiency at the lowest cost, choose the right equipment for the job. Several basic considerations should be kept in mind:

◆ Cost: Which is best—buying, leasing, or renting?

◆ Speed: How important is speed? Is the extra cost involved in obtaining faster copying justified for your needs?

- Space: How large a space do you have available in an area that is accessible yet removed enough that noise is not a problem?

- Monthly needs: How much copying do you need? The system should be the right size: not so powerful that its capability is wasted; not so small that overuse poses a problem of frequent breakdown.

- Quality of copy produced: Will the copy quality meet all of the firm's requirements?

- Type of material to be copied: Is the system capable of handling all your needs for both in-house and outside use?

- Needs for the future: Will the system fit in with future expansion possibilities? Are you moving towards desktop publishing, for example?

- Service agreement that includes routine maintenance calls, as well as on-call emergency service.

Comparative details

Considerable care must go into the selection of the office copier because many types and makes are available. Compare copiers on at least the following basic points:

- trade-in value of present machine
- warranty details
- lease to purchase option
- cost of service contract
- noise level
- speed
- service response time
- ease of restocking the machine with paper, developer, and toner
- movability
- special wiring or power supply needed
- "instant on" or warm-up period
- control devices available so that machine use can be measured and/or restricted
- additional features available (see CP6)

WORDS OF WISDOM

*A guide to building self-esteem:
praise loudly, blame softly.*

UNIT

10 MEETINGS, NET MEETINGS, AND EVENT PLANNING

SELECTED CONTENTS

M1	**PLANNING A MEETING**
M2	Announcing a Meeting
M3	The Agenda
M4	Last-Minute Preparations
M5	**CONDUCTING A MEETING**
M6	Parliamentary Procedure
M9	**PROXIES**
M10	**RECORDING A MEETING**
M11	Meeting Minutes
M12	Taking Notes for the Minutes
M13	Tape-Recording the Minutes
M14	Production and Approval of the Minutes
M15	**MEETING FOLLOW-UP**
M16	**CONFERENCES AND CONVENTIONS**
M25	**TELECONFERENCES/VIRTUAL MEETINGS**
M28	Video Conferencing
M30	**COMPUTER CONFERENCING**
M31	**DIRECT BROADCAST VIDEO**
M32	**NET MEETINGS**
M33	**TERMS**

M

Meetings, conferences, and teleconferences are a regular and important part of business activities. *Meeting* usually refers to a small gathering of people; *conference* or *convention/trade show* is applied to a much larger one; and *teleconference* or *net meeting* refers to electronic communication when a face-to-face meeting is not necessary or possible. Meetings may be quite informal sessions, designed to permit participants to exchange ideas and information in a relaxed atmosphere. For example, staff meetings are held regularly to discuss and solve problems, project team meetings may be held at various stages during a project, and committee meetings are called when one particular objective is the focus. Formal meetings, on the other hand, are conducted strictly according to the organization's constitution and bylaws (the official meeting rules of conduct). For example, annual general meetings (AGMs) are the official gatherings of shareholders and are conducted under strict parliamentary procedure (see M6).

Conferences are frequently held over several days in hotels, convention centres, or resorts and may include both business and social activities.

Teleconferences are invaluable when it is impossible or unnecessary to physically bring together all participants.

Although meetings and conferences vary in purpose, size, length, and degree of formality, the planning, announcing, conducting, and recording procedures are very similar. Advance plans must be well laid, the sessions must be conducted efficiently, and points raised and decisions made must be recorded accurately. This unit will help you successfully organize any type of meeting or conference.

M1 PLANNING A MEETING

Before taking any action, clarify these points:

◆ purpose of the meeting
◆ type of accommodation needed, and whether breakout rooms (additional seminar rooms) will be required
◆ number of participants
◆ desired location
◆ most suitable time
◆ budget allocation
◆ specialized equipment needed
◆ whether a meeting/convention planning agency or consultant should be used

Whether the meeting is to be held on the company's premises, in a hotel, or in other accommodation, book and confirm the space and services well in advance. List what needs to be done before the date set and do each job early enough to guard against problems. Make calendar entries to remind you when each arrangement is to be checked and confirmed. (For help with conferences and conventions see M16; for help with teleconferences, see M25.)

◆ Once the meeting date has been set, reserve the meeting room and double-check the booking later. Ensure that the room will accommodate the number of attendees expected.
◆ Notify all potential attendees of the confirmed meeting date and location.
◆ Plan, order, and confirm refreshments and/or meals, glasses, and water.
◆ Invite speaker(s) or special guest(s) well in advance.
◆ Make and confirm hotel bookings for out-of-town participants.
◆ Be sure that any required sound equipment is ordered.
◆ Ensure that blackout curtains are available if needed.
◆ Check that lecterns, podiums, tables, etc., are available.

- Check on the number of electrical outlets available for computers, projectors, etc.
- Arrange for pencils, pads, copies of agendas, committee reports, and other required materials.
- Plan the seating so that everyone can see and participate equally well.

Room layout Depending on the type of meeting and the size of the group, choose from the following standard set-ups:

- Boardroom style: Formal setting, small groups.
- Classroom style: Long, narrow room, good for speaker focus and note-taking.
- Round-table style: Informal, small groups and discussion groups.
- Theatre style: Lecture presentation from a stage, large audiences.
- U-shaped set-up: Medium-sized group, interaction desired.

Meetings involving meals Take special care when food is to be served at or during a meeting, i.e., allergies, vegetarian, etc.

- Reserve a table in a reputable restaurant. Provide a contact name, telephone and fax numbers, the number in the party, the time of arrival, and the method of bill payment.
- For an elaborate mealtime meeting, you may be asked to arrange a cocktail hour, select the menu, make a seating plan, and organize after-dinner entertainment. Hotels and restaurants frequently employ specialists who assist with such details.

M

M2   ANNOUNCING A MEETING

Meetings may be announced verbally (and then confirmed), in writing, or via communicating computers and electronic calendars. To identify a convenient date for all (or most) participants:

- Offer three possible dates and notify all attendees of the one chosen by most.
- When you use electronic calendars, check the participants' schedules, "book" the meeting date, time, etc., and ask them to confirm their attendance by email.

NOTE   If you plan regularly scheduled meetings, create and save a "Notice of Meeting" form (see examples on the next page) on your computer or word processor and simply fill in the blanks for each meeting.

When you invite participants to a meeting, note the following:

- Include the time, date, location, purpose, and if possible, the length of the meeting.
- Send out the notice far enough in advance so that people can fit the meeting into their plans but not so early that it can be forgotten.
- For formal meetings, send out the announcement in writing far enough in advance to allow the necessary length of time specified in the constitution or bylaws.

◆ With a formal meeting, send out the notice of the upcoming meeting with a copy of the agenda and the minutes of the previous meeting.

ELLIOTT GALLERIES
82 Charlotte Drive
Victoria, BC V9B 4N6

Telephone No. (250) 987-2424
Fax No. (250) 987-2447

To: Members of the Board   20-- 11 20

NOTICE OF MEETING

A meeting of the Board of Directors will be held at 10:00 a.m. on Wednesday, December 12, 20--, in the Confederation Room of the High Ridge Hotel at 24 Marine Drive, Victoria. The agenda is attached.

S. Dominelli
Executive Secretary
Elliott Galleries

Formal notice of meeting

INTEROFFICE MEMO

To: Sales Representatives

From: D. Sanderson, Sales Manager

Subject: Quarterly Sales Meeting

Date: February 26, 20--

Please be sure to attend the sales meeting for the second quarter of this year on March 20, 20--, at 10:30 a.m. in the conference room. The items to be covered are:

Sales to date by area
(I will provide this data and comment on performance to date)

Public relations and promotion suggestions
(each of you will be expected to contribute your thoughts in this area—10 minutes or so)

Quotas for the second quarter
(Mary, our budget officer, will provide details)

Discussion
(this will provide an opportunity to share mutual concerns)

I have arranged lunch at the Board of Trade for all of us at 1:00 p.m. If we haven't covered all items on the agenda by then, we can continue the meeting over lunch.

PHE   D.S.

Informal notice of meeting

M3   THE AGENDA

The agenda is the *plan* for the meeting. It lists the purpose, place, date, and time of the meeting, as well as the items of business to be discussed and the order in which they are to be dealt with. No fixed format needs to be followed in preparing agendas. An interoffice memo indicating the discussion topics serves well for small, informal meetings. A detailed agenda indicating discussion topics and length of discussion times may be useful for larger gatherings with much to cover. Send the agenda out in advance of the meeting so that participants can be properly prepared. Otherwise, a copy should be put at each attendee's place at the meeting or handed out prior to the meeting.

NOTE   For regular meetings conducted under an identical format, consider creating and saving a template, filling in the blanks each time.

NOTE   Send out important motions and items requiring special consideration, such as reports, with the agenda at least four days prior to the meeting.

M

Elliott Galleries **Board of Directors Meeting** **20-- 12 12** **High Ridge Hotel** **Agenda** 1. Call to order 2. Reading and approval of minutes 3. Reports from officers 4. Matters arising from the minutes 5. New business 6. Next meeting 7. Adjournment	**Procedure** 1. Chairperson starts the meeting, conveys apologies sent by absent members. • Secretary takes attendance. • Secretary announces whether a quorum (minimum number of members) is present for voting purposes. 2. Secretary reads minutes of last meeting. Chairperson asks for corrections. Group votes on changes, if any; if not, minutes are approved as read. 3. Reports from officers are read; copies are given to attending members. 4. Unfinished business from the last meeting is taken up. 5. New items are discussed. For example, nominations of new officers and elections could take place. 6. Date of next meeting is decided. 7. Chairperson closes the meeting.

Agenda and procedure for formal meeting

> ELLIOTT GALLERIES
> Quarterly Sales Meeting
> Conference Room
> 20-- 03 20
> 10:30 a.m.
>
>
> A G E N D A
>
> 10:30 Welcome and introductions
>
> 10:40 Reports:
>
> Sales update by area: D. Sanderson
>
> Public relations and promotion suggestions: sales
> representatives by area
>
> Quotas for second quarter: M. Misener
>
> 12:00 Discussion
>
> 12:30 Lunch (at the Board of Trade)

Informal meeting agenda

M4   LAST-MINUTE PREPARATIONS

◆ Conduct a last-minute check of all details.

◆ Try out any special equipment (e.g., DVD/VCR, CD player, projector, or computer) to see that it works properly. Check that overhead pens, etc., are available if needed.

◆ Have extra bulbs available for the overhead projector.

◆ Check the room temperature and furniture arrangement so that a comfortable working atmosphere exists. (See "Room Layout," M1.)

◆ Have available where appropriate:
   • name tags if participants do not know one another
   • a list of names and affiliations of those attending
   • extra agendas
   • extra copies of the minutes of the last meeting
   • the minute book or file
   • copies of the constitution and bylaws
   • any previously submitted motions
   • copies of reports to be presented

M5   CONDUCTING A MEETING

Meetings are conducted by a chairperson. With informal meetings, the chairperson's role is simply to maintain order, ensure that the meeting follows the agenda, and facilitate the proper communication of ideas and dissemination of information.

In some formal meetings, parliamentary procedure (formal rules of order) may be used, and it is the chairperson's task to see that these rules are followed. Although the rules of order might seem cumbersome, they do give everyone an equal right to be heard, to have all points of view considered, and to vote. In particular, the chairperson

- ensures there is a quorum present. A quorum—the minimum number of members that must be present—is required before a formal meeting can proceed. Unless a quorum is present, the business conducted at the meeting cannot be considered legal or binding. The size of the quorum is established in the constitution of the organization
- calls the meeting to order (i.e., makes sure that it starts on time)
- maintains order
- explains and decides all questions of procedure
- announces and clarifies all business under consideration
- states motions (formal proposals) and resolutions (expressions of opinion) on which a vote is to be taken
- suggests a time limit for discussion on any particular topic or motion
- when necessary, keeps track of those wishing to speak to a motion and calls on them in order
- formally calls an end to the discussion before voting is to begin
- conducts voting
- announces voting results

M

M6 PARLIAMENTARY PROCEDURE

▶ M7 Presenting a motion

Parliamentary procedure requires that certain formal rules of order be followed when initiating discussion on a topic. When a proposal is made at a formal meeting, it is referred to as a *motion* and must have the support of another person, who is referred to as the *seconder*. Chairpersons do not require seconders for motions they propose.

The participant making the motion should rise and be recognized by the chairperson. After the motion has been made and seconded, the mover speaks on behalf of it. Next follows a debate during which supporters and opponents of the motion speak. The mover makes the final comment and the chairperson then puts the motion to the vote.

> A typical motion begins, "I move that . . ."
> A typical motion support begins, "I second the motion . . ."
> Discussion and, perhaps, amendment of the motion follow.

NOTE Although motions to amend a motion may be made, only one main motion at a time can be handled. Motions to amend must be discussed and voted on so that the main motion is properly amended before it is finally discussed and a vote taken. For example:

Main motion
I move that the staff receive a bonus this year.
Seconded by J. Persaud.

Amendment

I move to amend the motion that the staff receive a bonus this year only if the company earns a profit in excess of 10 percent.
Seconded by S. Boquist.
Discussion
Vote carried.

Amended main motion

I move that the staff receive a bonus this year, provided that the company earns a profit in excess of 10 percent.

The chairperson finally conducts the voting (by ballot or show of hands) on the motion as amended and announces the result of the vote. If more than half of the voters are in favour, the motion is adopted (carried). If there is a tie or less than half are in favour, the motion is defeated. If a motion is not voted on, the procedure for disposing of it is to *lay it on the table*, or, as this is more commonly expressed, to *table it*. A tabled motion can be revived, debated, and voted on at a subsequent meeting.

►**M8   Point of order**

If a meeting member feels that a debating rule has been broken, that member can interrupt the person speaking and address the chairperson directly, without waiting for recognition, by saying, "Mr. (or Madam) Chairperson, I rise to a point of order." An example of a broken debating rule that might initiate a point of order would be the introduction of a topic totally unrelated to the motion under discussion.

Points of order must be made immediately after the alleged violation. They are not debatable, and the member who was interrupted must yield until the matter is clarified.

NOTE   Only a brief outline of parliamentary debating procedure has been included here. Full details appear in *Robert's Rules of Order*, available in paperback or hardbound editions. Anyone who is required to conduct or take notes at an important formal meeting should become familiar with Robert's Rules.

M9 PROXIES

The constitution and bylaws of most organizations permit a person who cannot attend important meetings to be represented by proxy. A proxy can be either

◆ another person who can attend the meeting with authority to vote and make decisions on behalf of the absent person

◆ a ballot (voting card) that has been sent out before the meeting and has been completed and returned by the absent person (see example)

Name of recipient
Address
City, Province
Postal code

FORM OF PROXY

I, the undersigned (whose name appears above), a policyholder of (Name of Company), hereby appoint the Director named by the Board of Directors, or instead _____ as proxyholder to attend, vote, and act on my behalf at the Special Meeting of the Company to be held on December 15, 20--, and any adjournment thereof.

Without limiting the general authorization and power hereby given, the above designated proxyholder is specifically directed to vote as indicated herein in respect of the resolution set forth in the Management Proxy Circular:

Vote   For ❑   or   Against ❑

The Special Resolution, with or without amendment, approving the amalgamation pursuant to the proposed Amalgamation Agreement between [Name of Company] and [Name of Company], approving the proposed bylaws scheduled thereto and approving the form of Amalgamation Agreement, copies of which are contained in the Management Proxy Circular that accompanies this form of proxy.

I authorize the proxyholder to act and vote as the proxyholder sees fit in respect of any other matters which may come before the meeting and to vote in favour of the item above in the absence of specific direction.

DATED _____, 20--   Signature _____

Example of a proxy

M

M10 RECORDING A MEETING

M11 MEETING MINUTES

Minutes are a permanent document designed to record, first, that a meeting was held and, second, the decisions made at the meeting. In addition, some minutes record proposals made and rejected as well as a summary of the discussion. Minutes must provide sufficient information for those not present to have a clear picture of what took place. Most companies keep a minute book in which copies of minutes are filed.

Minutes are legal documents, so it is important that they are accurate. Properly prepared minutes

- clearly state the name, purpose, time, date, and place of the meeting
- record who was present (and sometimes who was absent)
- are accurate, concise, impersonal, and unbiased
- provide a summary of the results, not a complete description of the proceedings
- contain exact statements of motions, movers, and seconders
- state the terms of any resolutions adopted
- indicate the method of voting used and the outcome of the voting
- note appointments made
- make mention of the adjournment, including the time at which the meeting ended
- give notice of when the next meeting will be held
- contain the secretary's and chairperson's signatures

M12 TAKING NOTES FOR THE MINUTES

- Sit close enough to the chairperson so that you can get his or her attention if you miss a detail. Make sure you are comfortable.
- Study the agenda in advance and read over any specified papers prior to the meeting so that you are familiar with names and terms.
- Go over the minutes of the previous meeting to familiarize yourself with previous discussion topics.
- Prepare in advance a list of people who should attend so that only a checkmark is needed to designate their absence or attendance.
- Make a seating plan and assign a number to each person present. Identify each person by some feature that will help you to recall names.
- Set up your note pad so that you have room for names and discussion topics. Organize your notes so that all discussion on any one subject is kept together. Note the name of each person introducing a topic. (You might consider preparing a template, an outline that you can use at every meeting, on which information can be quickly inserted.)
- Take more notes than necessary; they can be edited later.
- For formal meetings, consider using a preprinted note-making sheet. It is especially helpful for motions because they must be recorded verbatim (word for word). Record whether a motion was adopted, defeated, referred to a committee, or tabled. Record also the names of those involved.
- Note anything that demands action after the meeting.
- Do not hesitate to interrupt discreetly to ask for restatement of a motion, clarification of a point, or identification of a speaker; or perhaps arrange a signal with the chairperson, who will then stop the meeting and have the point clarified.

◆ Be prepared to read back a motion at the chairperson's request before the vote is called.

NOTE If possible, take a laptop or notebook computer into the meeting. This will simplify final preparation of the minutes.

M13 TAPE-RECORDING THE MINUTES

It is often helpful to use tape-recording as a backup reference to your own written meeting notes. Before using a tape recorder, remember these disadvantages:

◆ Some people may object to being taped.

◆ It may be technically difficult to set up so that the voices of all members are audible.

◆ Playing back and transcribing may be time-consuming.

◆ Speakers' voices may be difficult to identify.
  If you do use a tape recorder, keep in mind the following:

◆ Change tapes during pauses in meetings or use two recorders and start recording on the second tape as the previous one is ending.

◆ Number and identify each tape.

M

M14 PRODUCTION AND APPROVAL OF THE MINUTES

◆ Prepare a rough draft while the information is still fresh in your mind (preferably on a computer or word processor and saved so that if changes are needed you can avoid complete rekeying).

◆ Follow the sequence of topics used in the agenda.

◆ Refer to previous minutes and use the same style and format.

◆ Make motions and resolutions stand out in some way (e.g., use capitals).

◆ Use concise and impersonal language. Do not use contractions (Unit 1, T38), interjections (T35), or direct quotations (T44).

◆ Be objective—do not include personal opinions.

◆ Record whether a motion was adopted, defeated, referred to a committee, or tabled.

◆ Reports, depending on their importance, can be
  • summarized and the summary attached to the minutes
  • attached in their entirety
  • referred to in the body of the minutes

◆ Submit the final draft to the chairperson of the meeting for approval—within 24 hours is advisable. When possible, use communicating computers to permit shared editing of the draft.

◆ Produce enough copies for participants, others on the distribution list, and for the file (or official minute book), as well as extras for the next meeting.

◆ Members must approve minutes at the next meeting. If changes or additions are necessary, they can be written into the next minutes in the case of small or informal meetings. Where formal meetings are concerned, the minutes represent a legal document, and changes and/or additions are inked into the original and initialled by the chairperson. Once the minutes have been officially approved, no further changes are allowed.

NOTE   An example of minutes from a formal meeting follows.

Elliott Galleries
Board of Directors Meeting
20-- 12 12
High Ridge Hotel

M I N U T E S

Attendance	Present: J. Elliott, N. McCune, J. Ackroyd, S. Dominelli, R. Wilson, D. Darrigo, V. Vanlaarhove, W. Chan, G. Kotzell. Regrets: J. Revell, M. Toren, P. Lutz
Call to Order	Jayne Elliott, the President, chaired the meeting and called it to order at 10:00 a.m. by wishing all directors the compliments of the season and a successful new year.
Approval of Minutes	The minutes of the August 10 meeting were read. Norman McCune moved that the minutes be approved and David Darrigo seconded the motion.
Matters Arising from the Minutes	Since there were no matters arising from the previous minutes, the Chairperson proceeded with the business at hand.
In-House Desktop Publishing	Joachim Ackroyd informed the meeting that after extensive research by his department it seemed advisable, in view of present economic times, for the organization to invest in an in-house desktop publishing program. The cost- and time-saving benefits would be apparent in the first year, he felt. Copies of the report were distributed and the recommendation was discussed.
Motion	BE IT RESOLVED that the purchase of an in-house desktop publishing system be approved, and that Mr. Ackroyd provide quarterly reports on the operation of the program. Moved by J. Vanlaarhove, seconded by R. Wilson. The motion was carried unanimously.
Announcement	The next Board of Directors meeting will be held on 20-- 03 07.
Adjournment	The Chairperson adjourned the meeting at 12:40 p.m.

Chairperson _____

Date _____   Secretary   _____

Minutes of formal meeting

M15 MEETING FOLLOW-UP

◆ Distribute the minutes soon after the meeting.

◆ Deal with any requests that may have arisen at the meeting (e.g., for additional information).

◆ Send reminders, if necessary, about action to be taken. (Send copies of the committee's conclusions to those responsible for their implementation.)

◆ If feasible, circulate minutes of the previous meeting with the notice and agenda of the next meeting, so that participants can check items in advance for accuracy, and absent members can be kept informed.

◆ Send out appropriate thank-you notes.

◆ Note required items for the next meeting on your calendar.

◆ Note the date of the next meeting on your own and any other calendar for which you may be responsible.

M16 CONFERENCES AND CONVENTIONS

Conferences and conventions are large (sometimes massive) meetings of people with a common bond—such as members of a nationwide organization, association, or profession—gathering to exchange information and ideas, to make decisions, and to socialize. Many are annual events. Because conferences and conventions often involve a stay of several days in one centre and may include people from many locations, a considerable amount of highly detailed planning is required well in advance of the event.

M17 PROGRAM

◆ Obtain speakers and/or panellists and confirm their attendance in writing early (even as much as a year in advance, in some cases).

◆ Contact potential sponsors early and obtain commitment.

◆ Invite and confirm possible exhibitors (companies/people who display their products).

◆ Where workshops, seminars, or study sessions are included, allow time for study and reflection.

◆ Provide time for relaxation, exercise, or simply for enjoying the hotel or resort facilities.

◆ Include activities for family members accompanying delegates, if appropriate.

M18 PUBLICITY

Promotion of the event may be handled in several ways, such as by

◆ announcements placed in magazines and journals

◆ a mailing to each member that includes a description of the program, details of date, times, and location, and a registration form

Whichever method is used, early promotion is desirable.

M19 CONFERENCE OR CONVENTION SITE

In establishing the conference or convention site, the planner will be required to compare costs and facilities offered by the various possible locations. The information needed to obtain cost comparisons includes the number of delegates, the type of meeting, dates, arrival and departure times, accommodation required, number of hospitality suites required, and preregistration and registration procedures anticipated.

Be aware that sites capable of accommodating very large conventions are limited and may have to be booked as much as five years in advance.

The following are key points for comparison of various possible sites: cost per delegate, convenience of location, type of accommodation offered, number and size of meeting rooms, banquet facilities, services offered, and recreation facilities available.

Most major hotels, resorts, and convention centres employ specialists in conference planning. These people will assist with such tasks as registration of delegates, name tags, meeting room layouts, arrangement of facilities required by speakers, and organization of social activities. They should be relied on; they are experts.

Once you have chosen the venue, confirm the booking in writing and insist on written confirmation. It is a good idea to send along a checklist of your requirements so that there is no doubt as to what has been agreed.

M20 PREPARATION OF MATERIALS

Arrangements must be made for the following:

◆ printing of announcements and programs, and for such other items as name cards, tickets for special events, and flyers describing local events and other activities

◆ preparation of information packages for each delegate, containing details of sessions and locations, local attractions, hotel services, meal tickets, etc.

NOTE Use your computer to good effect. Your word-processing merge feature will minimize repetitious tasks in your preparation of notices, letters, and programs; a database will be invaluable in record-keeping and follow-up; and an electronic spreadsheet will simplify budgeting and financial management.

M21 EQUIPMENT NEEDS

◆ Prepare a list of all audio-visual aids, flip charts, bulletin boards, computers, overhead projectors, and sound and other equipment that may be required for each of the separate meetings or sessions. Make sure all equipment is working properly.

M22 PREREGISTRATION AND REGISTRATION

◆ Make arrangements with the conference or convention location staff for dealing with those who register early or at the start of the event.

◆ Set up a registration desk where delegate materials, such as information packages and name tags, can be distributed.

M23 REPORT OF THE PROCEEDINGS

◆ When the conference or convention is over, a report of the proceedings is frequently required. Some organizations keep a summary only; others prefer to keep a verbatim report, which may include copies of papers presented by speakers.

◆ Some organizations distribute the report of the proceedings free; others charge a fee.

M24 CONFERENCE OR CONVENTION WRAP-UP

◆ Send thank-you letters to speakers and others.

◆ Follow up on and then file comments and ideas suggested by participants and organizers for the next conference.

M

M25 TELECONFERENCES/VIRTUAL MEETINGS

Teleconferencing is a viable alternative to traditional face-to-face meetings. It allows people to communicate across distances without leaving their offices. Through the medium of telecommunications, teleconferencing offers the benefits of voice-to-voice communication or voice-and-visual communication. Although expensive, teleconferencing can save an organization money and time if used properly. Plan conferences well in advance so that relevant materials can be distributed and studied by the scheduled participants.

In its simplest form, a teleconference can take place among three people, each at his/her own telephone. In more complex forms, it can take place among several individuals on their own telephones in various locations, communicating with one person or a group of people at company headquarters. It can also be an audio and visual communication among several people in one centre and their colleagues in one remote location, or among groups in various locations, hearing and seeing each other as if they were in one room.

The three categories of teleconference service are audio conferencing, audio-plus conferencing, and video conferencing.

M26 AUDIO CONFERENCING

Audio conferencing is a simple telephone hookup among several people in different locations. Speakerphones or audio terminals permit discussion by all participants.

The chairperson can direct-dial to connect all members, or each participant can call in to a prespecified number, or the telephone company operator can arrange to set up the conference.

M27 AUDIO-PLUS CONFERENCING

Audio-plus conferencing is useful in situations where people need to share documents or graphics. Speakerphones or audio terminals transmit speech exchanges and a terminal screen and/or console allows document transmission via facsimile, electronic messaging, or an electronic blackboard (the blackboard can be seen by the other participants). In planning such conferences, note the following:

◆ Arrange the seating plan so that all participants can see the graphics monitor or screen and each other.

◆ Check the lighting to ensure comfortable viewing.

◆ Provide light pens or other equipment for members to use.

◆ If microphones (small clip-on models are effective) are necessary, position the sound speakers carefully.

The telephone company operator is required to set up an audio-plus conference.

M28 VIDEO CONFERENCING

Video conferencing via a screen, console, and audio equipment is available where face-to-face communication is essential but a physical meeting is not feasible. The features of audio conferencing are also included in this service. A video conference can be held in two ways:

◆ *Point-to-point:* Participants in two locations are involved in an exchange and discussion.

◆ *Point-to-multipoint:* Participants in one location can address people in several locations, but no discussion can take place.

The high costs associated with video conferencing limit its use to large organizations. High-end video cameras must be set up at the participating locations. The cameras are wired to a large black box called a *codec.* Just as *modem* means modulation/demodulation, *codec* stands for compression/decompression. The codec compresses the video signal into manageable chunks of data and transmits the data stream along to an integrated services data network (ISDN) modem set up next to the codec.

ISDN is a technology used to carry large volumes of data over telephone wires at very high speeds. The modems can transmit the data to the telephone lines and on to the receiving location where a modem and codec decompress the signal, relaying the data to a screen projector and then onto a screen for viewing.

Some large organizations and hotels provide video conferencing facilities for other businesses. It is more common, however, to use the facilities of telephone companies that handle the planning and set-up.

When planning a video conference in this way, make reservations at least six weeks in advance.

M29 PREPARATION FOR A TELECONFERENCE

Since teleconferences are charged based on time, participants must arrive early and be thoroughly prepared. Participants must know well in advance that a teleconference rather than a regular meeting is being arranged in order to avoid costly delays.

M30 COMPUTER CONFERENCING

Computer conferencing enables people to conduct meetings via linked computers. Participants can communicate simultaneously or call up stored messages at their convenience.

M

M31 DIRECT BROADCAST VIDEO

Direct Broadcast Video (DBV), also known as *one-way video*, is the video transmission from one location combined with a telephone response from each of the receiver locations. DBV is used by marketing people and corporate people for introducing new products and for making corporate announcements.

Meeting Wizard website: www.meetingwizard.com
Meetings Industry Megasite: www.mimegasite.com

M32 NET MEETINGS

Net meetings are very popular for product presentations through a network. These meetings are prearranged for up to approximately 20–60 people at different locations. All participants receive a participation code in advance, and on the date and time of the meeting/presentation, they log in and become active participants through their LAN (local area network) mobile phones (through activation of their speaker phones). The person who hosts this event is able to mute (turn off) all phones while the screen presentation is taking place (to block out background noises and interruptions). Upon completion of the presentation, all phones are de-muted (opened up) to allow discussion.

M33 TERMS

Ad hoc committee: A committee created to deal with a specific issue

Agenda: A list of items to be handled at a meeting

Amendment: A change to a motion that has been presented

Motion: A proposal requiring a proposer and a seconder

Parliamentary procedure: Rules governing the proper conduct of formal meetings

Point of order: A question about the validity of meeting procedures

Proxy: A person delegated to vote for an absent meeting member or a voting ballot sent in prior to the meeting

Quorum: The minimum number of members that must be present before a meeting can take place

Resolution: A formal decision approved at a meeting

Tabled: Postponement of a motion or discussion until a later date

WORDS OF WISDOM

Most of us would get along very well if we used the advice we give to others!

II

SELECTED CONTENTS

TA1	**USING A TRAVEL AGENT**
TA2	**AIR TRAVEL**
TA3	Airfares
TA4	**Discounted Fares**
TA5	Types of Flights
TA6	Confirmation and Cancellation
TA7	Baggage
TA8	Check-in Considerations
TA9	Getting to and from the Airport/Ground Transportation
TA10	Chartered Planes
TA11	**TRAIN TRAVEL**
TA12	Rail Fares
TA13	Classes of Accommodation
TA14	Cancellations
TA15	Baggage
TA16	Auto Transport
TA17	**RENTAL CARS**
TA18	**HOTEL/MOTEL ACCOMMODATION**
TA19	Hotel and Restaurant Terms
TA20	**THE ITINERARY**
TA21	**TRAVELLERS' ELECTRONIC BUSINESS KIT**
TA22	**SUPPORT STAFF RESPONSIBILITIES**
TA23	**TRAVEL FUNDS**
TA24	Foreign Currency
TA25	**EXPENSE REPORTS**
TA26	**TRAVEL INSURANCE**
TA27	**INTERNATIONAL TRAVEL**
TA28	Travel Documents
TA29	**Passport**
TA34	**Visa**
TA35	**Health Requirements**
TA36	Customs
TA37	Making Travel Arrangements
TA38	**GLOBAL POSITIONING SYSTEMS (GPS)**

TA

Planning a trip for business or pleasure involves making travel reservations, booking accommodation and rental cars, arranging for the necessary travel documentation, buying foreign currency, and organizing a host of other details. Large corporations may have their own travel departments with direct computer access to carriers, hotels, etc., but more often office workers will use the services of a travel agent or do the work themselves.

Corporate travel includes businesspeople travelling from one city, province, or state to other countries around the globe. These travellers are usually attending business meetings, seminars, conferences, or international conventions.

TA1 USING A TRAVEL AGENT

Travel agents are paid by transportation companies (carriers) and hotels; there is no charge to the user. These travel counsellors can reduce the travel arrangement workload because they have instant access to all travel-related data. Travel agencies can offer excellent advice on accommodation, package tours, travel documents, car rentals, overseas travel, etc. In addition, they can be helpful about exchange rates, suitable clothing, climatic conditions, customs arrangements, special events, and places of interest. However, an incompetent or unscrupulous agent can be a costly one, so before you employ an agency, check its reputation with the Better Business Bureau or the local chamber of commerce.

NOTE For those who prefer not to use the services of a travel agent, the *Official Airline Guide (OAG)*, a detailed listing of flights and services, may prove useful. The Official Airline Guide is also available for a fee in online electronic database form for those with computers that have access capability. Also, direct booking with carriers is available on the internet for no fee.

Canadian Tourism Commission website: www.canadatourism.com

TA2 AIR TRAVEL

You can make reservations by telephone or in person at the airport, at an airline ticket office, at a travel agency, or online via the internet. Tickets are prepared when payment has been made or credit has been established. Some companies maintain monthly accounts with travel agencies or airlines; other organizations provide key employees with credit cards for charging their travel bookings. You can also pay via bank, airline, hotel, and oil company credit cards. The reservation information needed includes the following:

- name(s) of traveller(s)
- date(s) and preferred times of travel
- departure and arrival airports

- class of service
- method of payment
- frequent-flyer number
- contact telephone number(s) of the traveller(s)

Frequent-flyer plans/air miles

Some organizations award bonus air miles to people who fly frequently on a particular airline or who use certain credit cards, hotels, and car rental agencies. These plans allow you to accumulate air miles through business or personal travel, car rentals, and credit card purchases.

- Be prepared to be flexible when you apply to use your "free" air miles.
- Do your own research regarding these plans—travel agents are too busy.
- Know all the details of the frequent-flyer plans you choose.
- Check your company's policy on frequent-flyer points for personal use.
- Remember to provide individual air mile plan numbers at the time of booking hotels, air travel, car rentals, and vacation packages (where applicable).

Client statements are usually mailed out monthly or after the completion of air travel, vacations, etc. Check each statement to make sure that the earned air miles have been properly credited to the client's account. Also check expiry dates for use of accumulated points.

TA

TA3 AIRFARES

The National Transportation Agency of Canada evaluates airline flight tariffs and monitors competitive economy fares between Canadian destinations. International fares are regulated by the International Air Transportation Association (IATA) based on bilateral agreements between international carriers.

First class This most expensive fare provides passengers with special check-in privileges: a VIP airport lounge, spacious and more comfortable seating, and greater personalized service than other classes receive.

Business or executive class Passengers in this category are entitled to a special check-in counter, first choice of meals and literature, and a more comfortable seat than economy-class travellers.

Economy class This service is the cheapest of those available in the regular-fare category.

▶TA4 Discounted fares

Discounted fares are individual round-trip fares that sell for less than two one-way tickets. Airlines provide a limited number of seats in economy-class cabins for these special bargain fares, which are offered on some flights.

APEX (Advance Purchase EXcursion)

APEX purchasers must travel during specific time limits, they must make bookings well in advance of the journey and pay shortly after booking, and they must adhere to prearranged departure and return dates. A charge is made for cancellation or any change in the reservation.

Super APEX

This extra-special discount fare is lower than regular APEX and usually requires a deposit within one week of booking. The same limitations apply to Super APEX as to APEX fares. Check with the airline or your travel agent.

Seat saver

This extra-special discounted fare applies to specific domestic destinations.

Group fare

Group-fare purchasers travel economy class as members of groups on scheduled flights and usually must purchase a land arrangement such as a hotel or rental car.

TA5   TYPES OF FLIGHTS

Scheduled flight   The regular flight established by an airline that departs regardless of the number of seats sold.

Nonstop flight   No stops are made until the aircraft reaches its destination.

Direct flight   A stop or stops along the way will be made, but there will be no need to change aircraft.

Connecting flight   Passengers must get off one aircraft along the route and board another. Some airlines routinely route all traffic through their hubs (home bases). This usually means a change of aircraft though not necessarily of airline.

Charter flight   An aircraft booked exclusively for group travel. This is among the cheaper forms of air travel but passengers should anticipate full planes, a penalty for cancelling, inflexibility in changing dates, and a possible weight restriction on baggage.

NOTE

◆ Complimentary meals/snacks are included on most flights, and complimentary bar service is provided for first- and executive-class passengers.

◆ Passengers can make calls from aircraft by using telephone company credit cards.

TA6   CONFIRMATION AND CANCELLATION

It is important to confirm and/or cancel flights within the time period established by the airline. If your travel plans change, call the airline and cancel your reservations. Failure to do so may result in penalties.

Remember, of course, that with certain fares, cancellations result in loss of the total cost.

TA7 BAGGAGE

Although international carriers sometimes base their free baggage allowance on mass, the usual practice is as follows: Each adult is permitted two articles to be checked (maximum dimensions of the first piece are 1.6 m [5.25'] in length, height, and width; of the second piece, 1.35 m [4.25'] in length, height, and width); and cabin luggage (maximum dimensions 1.2 m [4'] in length, height, and width if it will fit under the seat). No single piece of luggage may exceed 31.8 kg (70 lbs.). Airlines provide packaging for unusual or fragile items as well as special handling for these articles. Luggage allowance for charter passengers varies with the carrier. Check with the airline if in doubt.

Airline liability for lost or damaged baggage is limited in accordance with its current tariffs. Verify these at any ticket office. The airline accepts no liability for loss or damage to fragile or perishable items, money, jewellery, or negotiable securities.

TA8 CHECK-IN CONSIDERATIONS

Airline passengers should make sure they allow adequate time before actual departure to

- check in (at least 90 minutes before a domestic flight and 3 hours before an international flight)
- deal with current stringent security regulations
- contend with special or excess baggage arrangements
- pay airport improvement fees
- handle last-minute details such as duty-free purchases and perhaps foreign currency exchange

NOTE Because adverse weather conditions or other problems can cause delays, it is wise to confirm that your flight is on time before leaving for the airport.

TA9 GETTING TO AND FROM THE AIRPORT/GROUND TRANSPORTATION

Taxis and limousines are the usual means of transportation to and from airports. Airport buses operate from major hotels and local transit stations on a regular schedule; many hotels transport their clients by minibus. Helicopter services may also be available. Compare costs and time involved. Consult the Yellow Pages.

The distance and direction of the airport, travel time needed, types of ground transportation available, and approximate costs are listed in the *Official Airline Guide* for all destination cities.

TA

TA10 CHARTERED PLANES

If all commercial flights are fully booked, consider arranging a specially chartered flight. Check with airports in the vicinity or private airline companies.

TA11 TRAIN TRAVEL

There are many ways to make train reservations and purchase tickets: in person, by telephone, online, at a self-service kiosk, or through a travel agent. Reservations are required for most types of train accommodation. Reservation information needed includes the following:

◆ destination

◆ departure and return dates and times

◆ type of accommodation required

TA12 RAIL FARES

Although regular fares are available year-round, a wide range of discounted fares is also available. Special excursion fares with discounts of 25 to 40 percent are available for journeys of one day, two to five days, and one to ten days on short runs. Special fare reductions are offered for groups, children up to 11 years of age, students, and passengers over 60. A Canrail Pass provides unlimited travel in Canada for a specified period of time. Consult your VIA Rail office or a travel agent, and book early.

TA13 CLASSES OF ACCOMMODATION

Coach Reclining seat with footrest; snack and beverage included in cost of fare; bar service available at seat.

First class Reclining seat with footrest; fare includes a hot meal and complimentary glass of wine.

Upper or lower berth The upper berth is folded down from the side of the car to become a bed. During the day, with the upper berth in its folded position, passengers use the lower berth as seating accommodation.

*Roomette** Private compartment with washroom facilities. It sleeps one person.

*Bedroom** Private compartment with washroom facilities. It sleeps two people. Chairs are provided during the day.

*Ensuite** Two bedrooms separated by a collapsible wall. It sleeps up to four people.

*Drawing room** Three adjoining bedrooms.

*Passengers in these types of accommodation have priority for dining car service.

A snack bar with lounge facilities (often attached to the bar car) is available for all passengers and operates on trains between most major centres. The Transcontinental (the cross-Canada train) is equipped with a dome car, lounges, a bar, a café, and a dining car with a chef for full meal service.

TA14 CANCELLATIONS

Train ticket cancellations must be made quickly. Refunds are made on regular fares, but cancellation of excursion or high-season fares normally involves a penalty. Consult your booking agent.

TA15 BAGGAGE

Up to 70 kg (155 lbs.) per passenger is carried free in the baggage car (two suitcases is the maximum suggested for luggage in the passenger car). Arrangements can be made to transport animals in the baggage car only. Feeding, etc., is the responsibility of the owner.

TA16 AUTO TRANSPORT

Some companies will arrange to send your car by rail for you. These operate in all major centres. Consult the local telephone directory.

For more information about sea travel, please visit the Text Enrichment Site for this text at *www.pearsoned.ca/text/campbell*.

TA17 RENTAL CARS

TA

Travellers wanting to rent cars can do so online, at airports, bus and train stations, hotels; through travel agents or airlines; or directly from the car rental companies. Advance reservations are essential and comparison shopping is recommended. Some companies quote unlimited distance rates and others a flat fee plus a charge per kilometre. Obtain written information on what is included in the daily or weekly rental fee, then ask about additional charges (e.g., daily road tax; gas; provincial, county, or state tax).

Carefully check all details of the insurance coverage offered by the rental company and be certain to purchase enough insurance to provide adequate but not excessive protection. Find out the amount of your liability (deductible amount) in the event of an accident or theft, and find out the amount to be paid if you drop off the car at another location.

TA18 HOTEL/MOTEL ACCOMMODATION

There are many ways of reserving hotel or motel accommodation:

◆ Large hotel chains provide websites or toll-free telephone numbers for travellers across the continent. They might also have computer, fax, or telephone tieline hookups with their branches.

◆ Independent hotels are accessible online, by telephone, computer, fax, or letter.

◆ A travel agent could arrange reservations.

◆ An airline company might arrange discounted accommodation at designated hotels if you travel with that airline.

In requesting accommodation, state the type and size of room required, if non-smoking accommodation is required, the length of occupancy, and the arrival and departure dates. Rates are based on double occupancy of the room per night; a small additional charge is made for accommodating more people.

Hotels consisting of suites only might be considered for team and/or lengthy out-of-town visits. Be sure to take advantage of any special guest rates, convention group rates, or corporate discounts available to members of the Canadian Professional Sales Association or other registered associations and to others who give hotels regular business. Room rates do not include meals and taxes, although a continental breakfast is sometimes provided. In some hotels, parking may appear as a daily charge on your room bill, and there may be a charge for every local call that you make.

Check availability of fax, wireless connections, modem, and other communications equipment.

In-room amenities sometimes include make-up mirrors, hair dryers, and special clothes hangers. As well, for the security of clients, many hotels have installed more secure room door-locking systems, brighter lighting in halls and other public areas, surveillance cameras, and easily identifiable alarm systems in underground garages for assistance in emergencies.

NOTE Private bathrooms are a standard feature in North American hotels but not necessarily in hotels in other parts of the world.

Guaranteed bookings

Hotels do not generally hold a reservation beyond 6 p.m. unless a guaranteed booking is requested. A guaranteed booking means that the room is held indefinitely and a bill will be sent even if the room is not used. Cancellation before 6 p.m. is permissible without penalty. Use a credit card to guarantee a booking.

NOTE *The Official Hotel and Resort Guide,* an annual publication that provides information on North American hotels, motels, resorts, and meeting facilities, or the internet may be useful reference sources if you have to make many bookings.

TA19 HOTEL AND RESTAURANT TERMS

If you are considering a package travel plan, the following definitions may be helpful:

- single: room occupied by one person
- double: room with one large bed or two twin or double beds for two persons
- twin: room with two beds for two persons
- suite: a living or sitting room connected to one or more bedrooms
- European Plan (EP): no meals included
- American Plan (AP): room and meals

◆ Modified American Plan (MAP): room, breakfast, and dinner

◆ Continental Plan: room and breakfast

◆ table d'hôte: fixed charge for the meal

◆ prix fixe: fixed charge for the meal

◆ à la carte: each dish on the menu is charged separately

TA20   THE ITINERARY

An itinerary is a detailed list of travel arrangements, accommodation, appointments to be kept, and essential reminders. If you are making arrangements through a travel agent, the agent will provide a travel itinerary as part of the service.

In drawing up a workable itinerary, allow sufficient time for checking in at airports, ensure that the traveller knows that arrival and departure times are local times, remind the traveller to reconfirm return international flights, and allow sufficient travel recovery time before meetings are scheduled. See the next page for an example.

TA21   TRAVELLERS' ELECTRONIC BUSINESS KIT

TA

Electronic communications equipment may be part of your luggage. To make sure your kit is complete, compile a list of each piece of equipment, its serial number, and ancillary items required, as shown below.

Equipment	Serial no.	Ancillary item
cellular phone	ES-37201	batteries (2)
portable fax	91-3247019	paper, spare ink cartridge, cables
dictation equipment	17-0933	batteries (3), tapes (2)
laptop or notebook computer	VZ-78517	USB key, power card

Use the list to check off each item before and after the trip, and remember to register the equipment with Customs before you leave Canada. Check with the nearest Canada Customs office to find out how this is done.

TA22   SUPPORT STAFF RESPONSIBILITIES

If as a member of the support staff you are responsible for keeping the office running smoothly during the absence of another staff member, these points may help:

◆ In the absence of the senior executive:
  • deal with telephone calls and incoming mail by
    – forwarding or referring them for action
    – answering them yourself

	ITINERARY, RESERVATIONS, and APPOINTMENTS for James Viegas April 15–18, 20--	
Date	**Appointments/Departure Information**	**Locations/Reservations**
Sunday, April 15		
2:00 p.m. (14:00)	Air Transit Pickup 423 Oak Crescent	To Pearson International Airport, Terminal 1
5:00 p.m. (17:00)	Leave Toronto Air Canada Flight 129	To Montreal Montréal-Trudeau Airport
6:30 p.m. (18:30)	Arrive in Montreal	Cab to Four Seasons Hotel Reservation #V36054 Confirmation #312 (attach) Late Check-in
Monday, April 16		
9:00 a.m.–11:30 a.m.	Meeting with Managers of Communications Division Contact: Laura Elliott Ph. 514-671-4887	Four Seasons Hotel Conference Rm. West 3A
12 noon–1:30p.m. (13:30)	Luncheon Meeting with John Wilson, CEO	Mr. Wilson will meet you in hotel lobby at 12 noon
2:00 p.m.–4:30 p.m. (14:00–16:30)	Meet with Eileen Jacques of Laurier Products	1791 Sherbrooke West Ph. 514-673-4550
7:00 p.m. (19:00)	Leave Montreal Air Canada Flight 222	To Quebec City
8:30 p.m. (20:30)	Arrive in Quebec City	Cab to Laurentian Hotel Reservation #5608 Confirmation #756 (attach)
Tuesday, April 17		
8:30 a.m.–10:30 a.m.	Breakfast meeting with Mme. Danielle Coté of Office Systems Inc.	Laurentian Hotel Willows Dining Room
12 noon–1:30 p.m. (13:30)	Meeting and Lunch with William Dubois and Support Staff of Caspar Electronics	Caspar Electronics 198 Rue St. Laurent Ph. 514-396-7122 *Note:* Take laptop computer to this meeting
4:00 p.m. (16:00)	Leave for Airport	Cab to Airport
5:30 p.m. (17:30)	Air Canada Flight 172	To Ottawa
7:00 p.m. (19:00)	Arrive in Ottawa Uplands Airport	Cab to Radisson Hotel Sparks Street Reservation #4450 Confirmation #2119 (attach)
Wednesday, April 18		
9:00 a.m. – Noon	Meeting with Minister of Finance, Mr. James M. Flaherty	House of Commons Langevin Bldg. Proposals in briefcase (two extra copies enclosed)
4:00 p.m. (16:00)	Leave Ottawa for Toronto Air Canada Flight #176	Cab from Hotel to Airport
5:00 p.m. (17:00)	Arrive at Pearson International Airport	Terminal 1
	Ground Transportation	To home

Itinerary prepared by: Gladys Jones, Ext. 450

Sample business itinerary

- keep a record of your actions (a daily log is efficient)
- open a file for all the messages, correspondence, and data. Prioritize the documents for action

◆ On the executive's return:
  - allow a day or so for catching up (do not schedule demanding meetings)
  - present the action file
  - follow up on tasks activated by the trip
  - assist with thank-you letters
  - update computer files; distribute new information
  - help prepare the expense report

TA23   TRAVEL FUNDS

To avoid the need to carry large sums of cash, take funds in one of these forms:

Credit cards Credit cards such as Visa and American Express are acceptable for most purchases in and outside Canada.

Traveller's cheques (See Unit 19, MF81.) These are easily replaced if lost or stolen and are widely accepted. They are available in varying denominations. It is usually a good idea to obtain traveller's cheques in the currency of the country to be visited.

Letters of credit (See Unit 19, MF71.) These permit the holder to obtain amounts of cash up to a set limit in any branch of the bank that issued the letters.

`NOTE`   Most countries now have ATMs (automated teller machines) from which cash can be withdrawn as required.

TA24 FOREIGN CURRENCY

Travellers should carry at least a small amount of the host country's currency for transportation costs from airport to hotel, tips, refreshments, etc. Most financial institutions carry U.S. dollars, but order other foreign funds well in advance of the departure date to ensure their arrival in time. Other sources of foreign funds are foreign currency exchange services, such as the Bank of America Currency Exchange, which can exchange your Canadian dollars for the required currency. Rates of exchange offered can vary, so compare rates if time permits. You can purchase foreign currency at airports, but the rate of exchange may be higher than the norm.

Outside North America, you can exchange money at banks and frequently at major hotels. The customer may be required to present a passport as proof of identity.

If the need for an emergency supply of money arises, money can be telegraphed to the traveller.

TA

TA25 EXPENSE REPORTS

Because expense reports must be accurately completed, the traveller should make notes and keep all receipts for business expenses incurred. Use a company form, such as the one illustrated on page 283, or take advantage of a computer spreadsheet program to build a template for an expense worksheet. You can enter data frequently and the computer will automatically update totals, or you can record all the figures once a month and then print out the hard copy for approval and submission to the accounting department.

TA26 TRAVEL INSURANCE

Health, life, and baggage insurance additional to that provided by carriers is obtainable from travel agents or insurance company booths at airports and railway stations.

Travellers to international destinations can take the precaution of buying medical insurance in case of accident or injury while they are away from Canada. They can also purchase trip cancellation insurance on charter flights. This insurance is effective only in case of cancellation of the booking on medical grounds.

TA27 INTERNATIONAL TRAVEL

Making arrangements for international travel is similar to that required for domestic bookings. You may prefer, however, to rely more on a travel agent's specialized knowledge. Remember these points:

◆ Allow for jet-lag recovery time.
◆ Be aware of the host country's customs and national holidays (see Unit 3, IS26).
◆ Know international time differences. (see Appendix, page 563 for world time zones)
◆ Be familiar with airport names and cities.

Should you need assistance or travel advice while abroad, a list of Canadian missions is contained in the booklet *Bon Voyage, But* . . . published by the federal Department of Foreign Affairs and International Trade.

See Canada's Department of Foreign Affairs and International Trade (DFAIT) website for information for Canadians who travel abroad to work, voyage.dfait-maeci.gc.ca. This website includes a link to Canadian government offices abroad, as well as travel updates on conditions of foreign destinations, political unrest, any threatening security or health conditions, entry requirements, and consular contact numbers. The addresses of foreign consulates in Canada may also be obtained at the DFAIT website.

TA28 TRAVEL DOCUMENTS

NOTE As of January 1, 2004, citizens who were not born in Canada but have been permanent residents of Canada for several years must obtain a Canadian Permanent Resident Card in order to re-enter Canada.

▶TA29 Passport

A passport is required for travel to all overseas destinations. It is available from the Passport Office, Foreign Affairs and International Trade, Ottawa, or from regional offices in all major centres in Canada, and is valid for five years. The application form must be accompanied by a birth certificate, citizenship certificate, or an expired passport, as well as two recent photographs, the signature of a professional person who has known the applicant for at least two years, and the appropriate fee. A passport can be processed within three days in a major centre or it may take up to two months if application is made from a remote area.

A passport application form may be obtained online at www.pptc.gc.ca.

NOTE As of January 23, 2007, Canadians who enter the United States by air need a passport or another accepted document that establishes the bearer's identity and nationality. While an exact date of implementation has not been set, the requirement will be extended to land and sea crossings as early as January 1, 2008.

The new land-border document proposed by the U.S. would be approximately the size of a credit card and contain a biometric scan of the holder's face, or possibly a fingerprint.

TA

▶TA30 Digitized photos

Canada has recently introduced biometerics (the branch of biology that deals with living things by measurements and statistics) in the use of passports with the help of digitized photographs. The passport contains a chip that holds a picture of the person and personal information such as name and date of birth.

This technology is being used at border crossings with electronic readers that are able to read the chip in the cards and verify the information present in the card and on the passport. This method allows for increased efficiency and accuracy when identifying people at border crossings.

▶TA31 Canpass

CANPASS is a method of identification developed by Canada Customs. Frequent travellers to major centres can be identified by a digital picture of their eye. This technology is becoming more popular; it helps increase security and travellers with a CANPASS experience shorter wait times at customs.

▶TA32 Nexus

NEXUS is a joint customs and immigration program for frequent travellers implemented by Canadian and American governments. Since NEXUS identifies low-risk frequent travellers, a NEXUS member will be able to use dedicated lanes at various border crossings, and may not be regularly subjected to the usual customs and immigration questioning.

▶TA33 Security measures

Due to heightened security measures in airports all over the world, check with the Canadian Air Transport Security Authority (CATSA) for current air travel restrictions before you fly. CATSA will have a list of what is permitted in carry-on baggage.

For additional information:

Phone:	1-888-294-2202
Website:	www.catsa.gc.ca
Transport Canada website:	www.tc.gc.ca

Travellers should build extra time into their itinerary to allow for carry-on baggage inspection.

▶TA34 Visa

A visa is a special permit required for visits to certain countries. Travel agents have information on these countries, the documents required when travelling to them, and the visa fee. Allow plenty of time for obtaining visas.

▶TA35 Health requirements

The International Health Regulations adopted by the World Health Organization (WHO) advise that certain vaccinations and immunizations are required for entry to some countries. Travel agents or local health officers can provide full details about the requirements and the documentation needed. Do not leave this until the last minute because certain vaccinations consist of a series of injections given over several weeks.

ALERT During your travels, you may be exposed to an infectious disease. Symptoms can start several days to months after exposure. While the risk from most of these diseases is low, some may be life threatening. If, after your travels, you become sick or get a fever, Health Canada recommends you contact a physician and cite your travel history. If you have travelled to an area where malaria occurs, request a blood test to rule out malaria.

TA36 CUSTOMS

Travellers are allowed to bring duty-free purchases back into Canada under the following circumstances. See next page.

Included in the last two allowances are liquor (1.14 L of alcohol [40 oz.], 1.5 L of wine or 24 355-mL [12-oz] bottles or cans of beer) and tobacco (200 cigarettes, or 50 cigars, or 200 grams of manufactured tobacco). Travellers may, of course, bring back additional items, provided they are

Absence	Goods to a value of
Less than 24 hours	$ 50 (liquor and tobacco not permitted)
More than 48 hours (on an unlimited number of trips)	$200
After 7 days	$750

prepared to pay the duty. The importation into Canada of some types of items is restricted or prohibited. Some items, such as certain food and plants, may not be brought into Canada. Check with your local Canada Customs office if you are in doubt about a planned purchase.

It is wise also to check Customs restrictions—especially regarding antiques, jewellery, art, animals, or agricultural products—before departing from Canada. Register any valuables (e.g., camera, jewellery) being taken out of the country with the Customs office prior to leaving so that no problems are encountered in bringing them back into Canada.

NOTE For more information, see the Canada Border Services Agency website: www.cbsa-asfc.gc.ca.

TA37 MAKING TRAVEL ARRANGEMENTS

If your company does not have someone to look after travel arrangements, you could be asked to handle this for individual travellers.

Preparation guidelines

◆ Open a file for each business person for whom you are making travel arrangements.
◆ Prepare a travel arrangements worksheet.

For information about a travel arrangements worksheet, please visit the Text Enrichment Site for this text at *www.pearsoned.ca/text/campbell.*

◆ Have up-to-date lists of airlines and hotels available for quick reference.
◆ Have an atlas available for reference and other information, such as populations of cities/countries, climate, customs, etc.
◆ Have a contact person at a local bank whom you can call to get daily currency exchange rates.
◆ If one is not available, create a procedural manual for the company's travel policies, travel advance forms, expense claim forms, names of airports in Canada and the United States, etc. (Use this book as a reference.)
◆ When preparing itineraries, include the airline, flight numbers, and the terminal where passengers are departing and arriving. Include the names of hotels, and give confirmation and reservation numbers of hotels and car rentals. Provide names of individuals to meet with, phone numbers, meeting times, and meeting locations/addresses.

TA

- Pay attention to details, and make your traveller aware of any changes that could affect his or her commitments at the destination points.
- Never assume that you are making the correct decision regarding changes; always check with the person for whom you are making the travel arrangements.
- Be aware of special needs for the traveller, for example, special diet, wheelchair assistance, smoking or non-smoking hotel rooms, etc.
- Confirm all airline flight numbers, departure and arrival times, hotel accommodations, confirmation numbers, and arrival times one week before and the day before the traveller is departing.
- Key or update the final itinerary the day before travel, and arrange a convenient time for you and the traveller to go over all the details of the trip.

Booking online

Airline and hotel reservations may be booked directly online by accessing specific websites.

- for airlines, major hotel chains, car rental companies, and particular destinations:

    Excite, Yahoo!, Webcrawler, Lycos, or Expedia.ca

- for hotel and flight information for business travellers:

    www.cheaptickets.com

- for locating the lowest airfares:

    www.travelocity.ca   www.expedia.ca

Online fare finders assist you in finding the lowest published airfares between two cities; information is updated daily.

- for access to more than 17 000 hotels around the world:

    www.travelweb.com   www.expedia.ca
    www.airlineticketsdirect.com   tickets.priceline.com
    www.travelaxe.com

- For information on city convention and visitors' bureaus and state tourism offices see the Travel directory, then "Travel Guides" at www.yahoo.ca.

NOTE Many major hotels have their own websites, for example:

    Radisson Hotels Worldwide www.radisson.com

Business traveller information online

Executive travellers can access world travel information at the following websites:

    www.btonline.com   www.cheaptickets.com
    www.yahoo.ca   www.travelweb.com

www.excite.com

www.webcrawler.com

www.airlineticketsdirect.com

tickets.priceline.com

www.expedia.ca

www.lycos.ca

◆ For common phrase language translations (e.g., French, Italian, etc.):

www.fodors.com/language

◆ For weather:

www.accuweather.com

TA

TRAVEL EXPENSE REPORT

Name _____

Title _____   Department _____

Date(s) of Trip _July 19, 20--_   To _____July 21, 20--_____

Purpose _____

			Transportation						
					Auto		Other		
Date	From	To	km*	Own Car	Rental	Prkg.	Travel Method	Payment Method	Cost
July 19	home	airport	43	✓					19.35
	airport	S.W. city					air	cr. card	234.00
July 19-21	airport	in city			(3d) ✓				162.00
" 21	airport	home	43	✓		cash 25.00			44.35
	Totals		86			25.00			459.70
	Total All Transportation Costs								459.70

*Claim 45¢/km

	Accommodation, Meals, and Other Expenses						
Date	Hotel Name	Amt.	Brkft.	Lunch	Dinner	Other (Explain)	Amt.
July 19	Delta Suites	95.00		7.50	21.50		124.00
20	Red Dragon Inn	73.00	4.50	6.75	13.00	(tip) 1.00	98.25
21			4.50	6.75			11.25
	Totals	168.00	9.00	21.00	34.50	1.00	233.50
	Total All Costs of Accommodation, etc.						233.50
	Total All Expenses						693.20

Signature _____   Date _____

Attach all receipts to this form

Company expense report

TA38 GLOBAL POSITIONING SYSTEM (GPS)

A GPS is a hand-held device that is useful for people on the move. These devices provide the following features:

◆ lightweight and waterproof

◆ user-friendly interface

◆ primary controls on the same side of the unit to allow easy one-handed operation

◆ automated stopwatch (specifically designed for jogging and walking workouts)

◆ mapping database that shows major cities, highways, roads, waterways, and marine navigation

◆ automatic route generation

◆ sunlight-readable display

◆ off-route recalculation and turn-by-turn directions with alert tones

◆ an icon-driven menu to help find points of interest

◆ preloaded with a 16MB base map of North America (optional maps available through MapSend software)

◆ high-speed USB data port allows the transfer of map data from a PC to other electronic equipment

◆ three-axis electronic compass (gives accurate readings no matter how it is held)

WORDS OF WISDOM

*You can't make a hit if you
don't have an aim in life!*

UNIT

12 COMPUTERS: HARDWARE AND SOFTWARE

SELECTED CONTENTS

C1	COMPUTER TYPES
C2	PORTABLE COMPUTERS
C3	COMPUTER OPERATING SYSTEMS
C4	COMPUTER COMPONENTS
C5	Central Processing Units (CPUs)
C9	Monitors
C10	Input Devices
C11	Keyboards
C12	Non-Keyboard Input Devices and Methods
C13	CHOOSING A COMPUTER SYSTEM
C14	SOFTWARE (PROGRAMS)
C15	Business-Related Software
C32	Choosing Software
C33	STORAGE AND RETRIEVAL
C39	PRINTERS AND PLOTTERS
C40	Printer Types
C41	Plotters
C42	COMMUNICATIONS
C49	COMPUTER (PC) MAINTENANCE
C50	INFORMATION SECURITY
C51	COMPUTER LITERACY
C52	COMPUTER TERMS

C

Computer technology is changing at a mind-boggling rate. The almost daily changes make it impossible to keep up. The basics of the computer should, however, be understood by all office personnel—the processes, the uses, the software, and the terms—and that general information is provided in this unit.

Because the topic is so massive, the role of the computer in an integrated environment is dealt with separately in "The Integrated Office/New Technologies" (Unit 13), and the place of the computer in desktop publishing (DTP) is provided in "Desktop Publishing" (Unit 15). Where needed, cross-references are given.

C1   COMPUTER TYPES

Three main computer types are used in business. The essential differences among them are their storage capacity (memory), processing speed, and cost.

Mainframes These powerful computers are used only by large organizations for their centralized data-processing needs and are generally operated only by experts.

Minicomputers Minicomputers can perform many of the functions of mainframes but are significantly smaller. They can perform a variety of business functions and can also have applications in such fields as science, engineering, and production.

Microcomputers (commonly called personal computers or PCs) These small, desktop computers are now so powerful that in many businesses they have replaced mainframes and minis. They may be used as stand-alones or linked to a network.

Desktop computers come with varying capabilities—from simple data entry and editing to the ability to create multi-dimensional presentations in real time (live video, graphics, and text with stereo sound accompaniment).

C2   PORTABLE COMPUTERS

Several types of portable computers are available that can do virtually everything a desktop model can do.

Laptops/notebooks/palmtops These are small (laptops weigh approximately 3–7 pounds for ease of carrying) and extremely convenient.

◆ They can be used with a desktop computer with a specially designed docking station and provide a wide range of computing power.

◆ They can be used with the monitor and printer of a compatible desktop computer or coupled to a full keyboard.

◆ The removable hard drive can be plugged into a desktop computer.

◆ They have their own inbuilt connections for a printer/fax.

◆ Smart cards containing microprocessor chips can be inserted that can expand the range of their functions.

Personal digital assistant (PDA) A hand-held device that combines computing, email, telephone, internet, and networking features. A typical PDA can function as a cellular phone, email client, Web browser, and personal organizer. Unlike portable computers, most PDAs began as pen-based, using a stylus rather than a keyboard for input; they also incorporate handwriting recognition features. Some PDAs can also react to voice recognition technologies. At this writing, PDAs are available in either a stylus or keyboard version.

PDAs are also called palmtops, hand-held computers, and pocket computers, i.e., the BlackBerry and the Palm Tree.

C3 COMPUTER OPERATING SYSTEMS

An operating system is software that manages the basic functions of a computer, such as controlling the application software, copying disks, and storing files. Most computers are sold with the operating system software already installed.

The key operating system is Microsoft Windows, which merges NT (new technology) and an easy navigational graphical user interface (GUI), an operational system that is a must for ever-changing online security flaws. The most common Windows operating systems are Windows XP and Windows Vista.

Graphical user interface (GUI)

To interface in computer language means to communicate. A GUI (pronounced "gooey") refers to the way in which icons (small pictures) are used on the screen to represent desktop tools such as file folders. Instead of keying words, the user simply clicks a mouse onto an icon to carry out an operation. Examples of such operations are opening and closing applications and files and moving items around the screen.

C4 COMPUTER COMPONENTS

C5 CENTRAL PROCESSING UNITS (CPUs)

The CPU, also referred to as the microprocessor, is a silicon chip consisting of thousands of electronic circuits and transistors. This is the "brain" of the computer.

A computer follows the instructions it receives from a program. The program is fed into the computer memory, as is the data to be processed. The program and data are accessed (located and read) by the CPU, and whatever action is required is carried out. The CPU has three parts:

Primary storage unit (memory) This unit provides for the temporary storage of data. All data and instructions must be received here before the computer can start its work. All calculations performed are also stored here until further processing or output is required.

Arithmetic/logic unit This unit processes the data. It can do calculations and take logical action (compare possible courses of action and decide between alternatives). It might, for example, compare two figures, decide which is the larger, and put them in order.

Control unit This unit maintains order and controls the entire system (input, output, and CPU), ensuring that everything is working in accordance with the program it has received.

CPUs vary as to processing power, memory, and storage space and are constantly being enlarged/upgraded.

Pentium III or P4 Expanded upgradeable central processing units. Pentium III, P4, and Celeron CPUs are modular and plug into a slot on the motherboard.

Bus speed From 533 MHz to today's 3.73 GHz, the bus speed on a processor determines its bandwidth or throughput; the higher the bus speed, the more productive the system will be.

▶ C6   Processing power

Processing power is a major consideration in computer choice. It is determined by the kind of CPU installed. The benefits of higher-powered machines are faster opening and saving of files, deleting blocks, running spell checks, or, say, processing changes in calculations in a spreadsheet.

▶ C7   Memory

Although lower memory is less expensive, you should consider future needs and the quantity of memory needed for each program you may want to run. A computer has two types of internal memory:

Random access memory (RAM)

◆ Also known as *working memory,* it stores data and programs and can be accessed or altered by the user.

◆ Memory measurements normally refer to RAM. The size of the program and amount of data with which you are working are limited by the amount of RAM installed in your computer.

Read-only memory (ROM)

◆ It is used by the manufacturer to store preprogrammed instructions.

◆ It can be read and used by the user but not accessed or altered.

◆ It is used when you turn on your microcomputer:
  • It checks RAM and loads the operating system.
  • When the computer is turned off, anything in RAM is lost if not already saved. ROM contents are kept.

▶ C8   Storage space

RAM is where the CPU does its work. With more storage space (larger RAM), the computer can work faster and handle more complex tasks.

Many programs require a great deal of memory. Current versions of Windows, for example, require at least 512 megabytes (MB) of RAM; however, 1 gigabyte (GB) is recommended for basic Windows operations. Newer versions still to be released will require even more.

The hard drive is the device used most frequently to store software and data. Again, because programs require considerable disk space, the larger the capacity the better. At the time of writing, 80 to 250 gigabytes (GB) would be the minimum and 500 GB would provide flexibility for future expansion capabilities. (Currently, the average is 160 to 500 GB.)

For additional data storage devices, see C33.

C9   MONITORS

Monitors are rated on their ability to use dots (pixels) to create patterns— the more pixels, the better looking the picture. The quality of display is referred to as *resolution*.

Colour is an important consideration. Quality, however, is not necessarily associated with colour.

Monitors vary in size, shape, type, and quality of resolution and the amount of text or data they can display. They come in 15-, 17-, 19-, and 21-inch liquid crystal display (LCD) sizes, and 17-, 19-, and 21-inch cathode ray tubes (CRTs).

Resolution and cost are factors in size of screen, and the refresh rate determines the use of CRT or LCD; LCD is good for small-desk office use and offers smoother-quality images and animations due to the way it refreshes, and CRT is good for CAD (computer-aided design) and computer games, as the refresh rate on CRT can vary for smoother picture and quality of animation. For today's use, 17-inch is the minimum with a 1024×768 resolution preferred; 1280×1024 will fit more information onscreen and will speed up production.

C10   INPUT DEVICES

Before data can be read (loaded) into the computer, it must be changed into a format acceptable to the computer (i.e., it must be digitized). By far the most commonly used direct input device is the keyboard.

▶ C11   Keyboards

When a key is pressed, an electrical pulse is emitted that is converted into a digital code. Most keyboards contain some or all of the following:

Function keys These programmable keys perform whole functions such as save, print, delete.

Cursor control keys These position the marker (cursor) that indicates the working point on the screen. They are usually labelled with arrows.

Designated-purpose keys (ctrl, alt, etc.) The use of these keys is determined by the software used.

Some keyboards provide a *numeric keypad* and some a *trackball* that functions like a mouse.

See Unit 6, pages 177–178, for information on newer, ergonomically designed keyboards.

Radio frequency (RF) wireless keyboards

These keyboards transmit keystrokes to the computer via radio signals that are beamed to a receiver.

The advantage of a wireless keyboard is the elimination of the cord. There are disadvantages: local weather conditions or unshielded power cables have the ability to amplify or increase the range of radio signals, and there is also the danger of someone, with the right equipment, picking up your radio signals and receiving whatever you type.

The more sophisticated wireless keyboards that operate with beams of infrared light are practically immune to this kind of accidental transmission.

▶C12 Non-keyboard input devices and methods

Bar code The computer reads information contained in specially imprinted codes. The universal product code (UPC) used in retail stores is a major example of the use of this system. Other uses are in inventory control and records.

Digital camera Digital cameras offer high-quality image enhancement technology: Images can be instantly printed out, sent through email, or viewed on TV with a video cable. You can choose which pictures to print and/or store. You can use software to organize and record pictures, and to correct colour-casts and contrast problems. You can choose to share or delete the images in record mode before storing them on the memory card.

Digital writing system This system is a fast and effective mobile solution for turning handwritten information into digital documents. It allows for integration with applications like email and Microsoft Word to increase productivity.

Electronic signature A paperless way to sign a document using an electronic symbol or process attached to or associated with the document.

Graphics tablet This allows the user to draw anything—images, graphics, schematics—onscreen. It is popular in DTP, CAD, and presentation graphics applications. The user employs a graphics pen to draw on a special pad attached to the computer.

Handwriting recognition This is a device that records handwriting electronically for processing.

Light pen The light pen enables the user to write or draw directly onto the screen (monitor).

Magnetic disk or tape For large processing tasks such as payroll or accounting, it is faster to encode data onto a magnetic disk or tape and then feed it into the computer.

Magnetic ink character recognition (MICR) A special ink containing a trace of iron is used to imprint the MICR code on documents. The iron is magnetized, and the computer senses it and interprets the data it contains. This method is used by financial institutions for processing cheques.

Memory card This electronic device stores each picture until it is loaded to the computer. You can use these images for presentations, printed publications, internet pages, and other applications.

Mouse This is an electronic pointing device used to move the cursor around the screen and to help in making selections. The type of mouse used will vary with the operating system of the computer. Most have two buttons and some have three. They are available in mechanical, optical, cordless radio, or high-resolution versions.

An optical mouse has no trackball and uses an optical sense called IntelliEye. It scans the surface under the mouse 1500 times a second to track the smallest motion, and a mouse pad is not required.

NOTE   Other pointing devices are joysticks and trackballs.

Optical mark reading (OMR) In this system, marks on cards or sheets are scanned and interpreted by the computer. Market research surveys are examples of the use of OMR.

Point-of-sale terminals These are used, for example, in stores to track inventory and pricing when goods are sold.

Scanner Images of all kinds (text, numbers, graphics) can be scanned and converted by the computer into digital information for processing (known as *image processing*). The images can be manipulated into new shapes and sizes. This is particularly useful in page composition and page layout, for example in desktop publishing.

You can also use scanners to convert a black-and-white or colour printer into a copying machine or fax, and/or to scan images into installed email applications. There are two types of scanners for general use: the *flatbed,* which looks like a photocopier; and the *sheet-fed,* which can accept single sheets or paper documents. The *photo scanner,* a small sheet-fed machine, is used for photographs. *Hand-held* scanners have a span of 2" to 5".

All scanners work in essentially the same way: a light-sensitive device called a CCD (charged-coupled device), similar to what a camcorder uses to "see" images, converts light reflected from the original into an electronic signal. The signal is then digitized and stored on the computer's hard drive.

The *flatbed* scanner moves its CCD past the original, which sits on a fixed, transparent surface; *sheet-fed* and *photo scanners* use rollers to move the original past a fixed CCD.

Scanners typically come with three basic types of software: one to control the scanning, one to adjust an image's appearance after it has been scanned, and one to recognize text.

Touch-sensitive screen The touch of a finger will cause the computer to respond. Menu selection is the most frequent use of touch technology.

Video input Images can be captured from a video camera, stored electronically, and processed by the computer for incorporation into any type of document.

Voice recognition This system is based on the unique quality of each person's voice and permits direct input by means of the spoken word. A microphone attached to the computer records the voice electronically, processes it as text, and provides a soft copy onscreen for editing. The voice can also be used to activate certain computer commands, as in forms completion (see Unit 5, EM20).

C13 CHOOSING A COMPUTER SYSTEM

Usage	Processor	Memory	Hard Drive
Basic home applications	Intel® Celeron® processor at 2.4 GHz to Intel® Pentium® 4 Processor at 3.73 GHz	256 MB to 512 MB	40 GB to 80 GB
Advanced performance	Intel® Pentium® 4 Processor at 3.0 GHz	512 MB to 1024 MB	120 GB to 200 GB
Ultimate capability	Intel® Pentium® 4D Processor with HT Technology at 3.4 GHz	1 GB to 2 GB	250 GB to 500 GB SATA (serial bus)

Source: Adapted from www.dell.ca.

For product reviews on the top ten PCs, CD-RW drives, monitors, printers, and digital cameras, see the following websites: www.pcworld.com, www.pcmag.com.

C14 SOFTWARE (PROGRAMS)

The computer must be told how to solve a problem or carry out a task by means of a *program,* a series of instructions written in computer language that guides the computer step by step through a process. Programs are written by computer manufacturers, by software marketing companies (vendors), or by an organization's own programmers.

Popular software today consists of office suites made up of word processing, spreadsheet, database, presentation, personal information manager, email client, and web browser programs.

C15 BUSINESS-RELATED SOFTWARE

Because there is such an immense variety and diversity of software available, most businesses purchase software packages rather than write their own. These packages are updated regularly and updates can usually be bought for a reasonable price. The most popular software types (known as *applications software*) for business use follow.

►C16   Accounting and financial management software

Many programs are available covering report-generating, job-costing, order-processing, accounts receivable and payable, general ledger, collections, inventory control, cheque-writing, and payroll. Some packages offer most or all of these functions; some handle just one task.

►C17   Communications software

These programs allow you to connect computers so that they can "talk" to each other. You can transfer files or send messages across the room or across the country. As well, they allow you to take advantage of online information services and connect with electronic bulletin boards.

Communication among computers is possible because of communications software and modems (see C43).

Many integrated software packages feature communications as part of the package. Most incorporate a telephone book feature that allows you to store and automatically dial frequently called numbers.

►C18   Databases

These electronic records management programs are designed to help organize, record, track, access, and analyse information. You can input millions of records (customers' names and inventory records, for example), sort them in any order, quickly select any information, and display and print your needs.

◆ After data is entered, you can access it easily. You can sort, search, and arrange the data in any way you wish without any rekeying.

◆ Sorts can be alphabetic or numeric, in ascending or descending order.

◆ Printing can be in many forms: reports, lists, labels, envelopes, for example.

◆ Searches can be as specific as you wish.

Databases are created on electronic forms that you design to meet your own needs. Each form consists of *fields* (as many as you need), which are separate information items such as name, address, telephone number. A separate form is keyed for each client (or whatever). The completed form is known as a *record*. A set of records is referred to as a *file*.

Databases are of two types—flat and relational:

Flat Stores, organizes, and retrieves data from one file at a time. Each record contains all the data related to a particular topic.

Relational Allows linking between databases so that, for example, an inventory database could be linked to a database of manufacturers; as stock gets low you could contact the manufacturer to reorder.

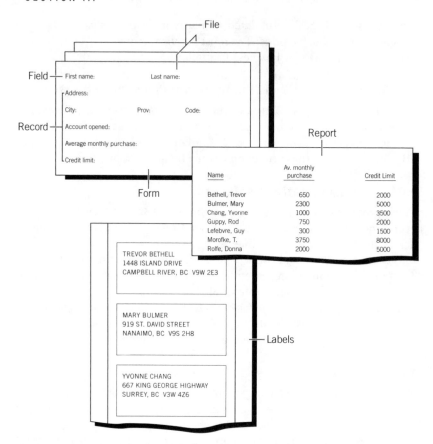

Databases can be printed as lists (reports) or as labels.

Additional features of databases

◆ They permit integration with word processing so that merging can occur (e.g., name and address information can be combined with text to generate business letters, envelopes, or labels).

◆ Some permit the user to change font, size, style, and colour.

▶ C19 Desktop accessory packages

These combine some or all of word processing (notepad), appointment calendar, electronic filing (database), email, and a calculator. Some provide an alarm clock to remind you of the time and events in your calendar.

▶ C20 Desktop publishing software

Complete details are provided in Unit 15.

▶ C21 Forms software

This type of software is available to assist in the design of requisitions, invoices, telephone messages, timesheets, etc. These programs

♦ include logos and graphics, text and database functions, and design tools

♦ contain a library of sample forms

♦ permit automatic calculations

♦ provide indexing and sorting capabilities

See Unit 17, "Business Forms and Form Design," for more details.

►C22   Graphics software

There are essentially five types:

♦ Paint programs	♦ Presentation graphics
♦ Draw programs	♦ CAD programs
♦ Photo-editing software	

Paint programs provide access to a variety of tools, colours, and patterns that allow the user to "paint" the screen. They can be used to create colourful pictures and images for documents, brochures, and newsletters.

Draw programs are used by designers, engineers, and architects to create sophisticated graphic art illustrations.

Presentation graphics software, in its simplest form, allows for the attractive display of information—charts, graphs, etc. In its most complex form, it refers to highly sophisticated multi-media presentations that include live video, graphics, animation, text, and stereo sound.

CAD programs are computer-aided design programs created to replace the drafting table and drafting tools. They are used for sophisticated engineering and architectural work. One drawing can be presented from several perspectives, and on-screen objects can be rotated.

C

►C23   Groupware

This is software designed for use in a network. The software programs used are basically the same as those used for any computer application. It is their ability to be shared that makes them different.

♦ Some are for small groups only, e.g., as few as five on a local area network (LAN). Others can accommodate up to 100 000 on a wide area network (WAN) through gateways. WANs have evolved into multiple-linked networks now known as the *internet*. See Unit 13 for more information on networks.

♦ They can handle all internal business operations and communications electronically (meetings, appointments, tasks, paperwork), with automatic reminders of upcoming events.

♦ Participants can accept, reject, or delegate meeting requests. Personal calendars across any number of networks—even in dissimilar operating systems—can be checked for conflicts.

♦ They can control how information reaches staff, where it is filed, and where it is routed.

- ◆ Incoming mail can be automatically sorted and forwarded to others in a user's absence or it can be handled from a laptop or other device at a remote location (see Unit 5, "Electronic Mail").
- ◆ Users can check the status of any message or project as well as retract and rethink any unopened message.

▶C24 Integrated software

This software combines programs such as word processing, spreadsheet, database, and communications. Some packages also include graphics, electronic scheduler, calculator, telephone dialer, and utilities programs. While not always quite as sophisticated as programs that are available separately, integrated software offers these advantages:

- ◆ data is easily merged between applications (e.g., a spreadsheet can be integrated into a memo)
- ◆ easy to learn—some commands can be used for several applications
- ◆ less time spent on loading and in opening and closing files
- ◆ most allow data to be exchanged among other programs
- ◆ cheaper than buying the separate applications
- ◆ takes up less disk space and is therefore ideal for notebook computers and less powerful machines

NOTE Office suites are sets of software sold as a package that permit easy integration of data via importing, exporting, and linking. Content varies, and the choice is usually determined by the word-processing package included. Such packages are less expensive than separate components. Office suites can be loaded with standard, custom, or laptop configurations.

Middleware A form of software that gathers information from a variety of databases currently in use and repackages it for display on hand-held computers. For example, store clerks can check to see if an item is in stock, on order, or if a customer is waiting for that item.

▶C25 Shareware

These are programs that can be distributed and copied at little or no cost without breaking copyright laws. They are distributed through the internet, electronic bulletin boards, online information services, user groups, and mail-order services.

NOTE See Unit 16 for more information on freeware and shareware.

▶C26 Spreadsheets

These are electronic worksheets designed to assist those involved in calculations and financial analysis (number-crunching) of any kind—from balancing a chequebook to running a large organization.

The worksheet resembles accounting paper and consists of multiple columns and rows, the number depending on the program purchased. The intersection of each row and column is known as a *cell,* into which you enter data (values or labels) and formulas. Complex calculations can be performed instantly and the results presented in a clear, organized format. If you change one value or formula, the effect is reflected immediately and automatically throughout the entire spreadsheet. As well, spreadsheets

◆ allow formulas to be saved

◆ permit sorting and moving columns and rows with formulas intact

◆ can copy existing values (replicate) or can increase or decrease incrementally by a specified value

◆ can be printed in a variety of formats

◆ provide "what-if" scenarios (i.e., testing of important decisions)

◆ permit the user to control the way numbers are displayed (dollar signs, decimal places, negative numbers, etc.)

◆ allow users to start with a result and work backwards in some cases

◆ offer macros that perform repetitive functions

C27   Spreadsheet formulas

While extensive mathematical skill is not needed to operate a spreadsheet, an understanding of the basics of formula creation and symbols is needed. Formulas tell software how to calculate the value in a cell, using the following symbols:

+	addition	/	division
−	subtraction	^ or **	exponentiation
*	multiplication	=	equal to

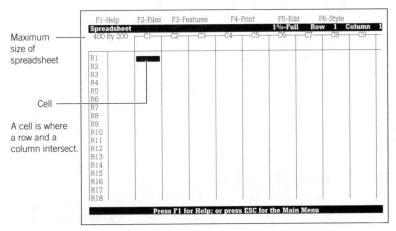

Typical spreadsheet screen

	F1-Help	F2-Files	F3-Features	F4-Print	P5-Edit	P6-Style	

Spreadsheet — 1%-Full — Row 1 — Column 1
400 By 200 — C3 — C4 — C5 — C6 — C7

R1	No. of Passengers	264	150		100	
R2	Expenses/Passenger	$128.00	$128.00	$128.00	$128.00	
R3						
R4	Expenses	$31,600.00	$18,000.00	$31,600.00	$31,600.00	
R5						
R6	Operating Expenses	$14,520.00	$8,250.00	$14,520.00	$14,520.00	
R7	General & Admin.	$6,500.00	$6,500.00	$6,500.00	$6,500.00	
R8	Permit Fees	$1,250.00	$1,250.00	$1,250.00	$1,250.00	
R9						
R10	Total Expenses	$22,275.00	$16000.00	$17,375.00	$22,275.00	
R11						
R12	Monthly Profit	$9,415.00	$2,500.00	$3,625.00	$9,415.00	
R13						
R14						
R15						
R16						
R17						
R18						

Press F1 for Help; or press ESC for the Main Menu

Spreadsheets can be printed as reports or graphics.

	October	November	December	January
	180	192	170	135
	$120.00	$120.00	$120.00	$120.00
	$21,600.00	$23,040.00	$20,400.00	$16,200.00
	$8,900.00	$10,560.00	$9,350.00	$7,425.00
	$6,500.00	$6,500.00	$6,500.00	$6,500.00
	$1,250.00	$1,250.00	$1,250.00	$1,250.00
Total Expenses	$17,650.00	$18,310.00	$17,100.00	$15,175.00
Monthly Profit	$3,950.00	$4,730.00	$3,300.00	$1,250.00

Each software program has its own method of building a formula; however, common starting symbols are = and @.

Operations are performed in a specific order. That order is ^; – (when used for a negative number, not a minus sign); + (positive); * and / (evaluated from left to right if both appear); + and – (evaluated from left to right if both appear). You can change the order of calculation by using parentheses. If you enclose a calculation in parentheses, the software does the calculation within the parentheses first. The following examples show how parentheses change the order of calculations:

◆ 5 + (5 * 3) – 12
The answer will be 8.
(Multiply 5 by 3, then add 5, then subtract 12.)

◆ (5 + 5) * 3 – 12
The answer will be 18.
(Add 5 and 5, then multiply by 3, then subtract 12.)

◆ (5 + 5) * (3 – 12)
The answer will be –90.
(Add 5 and 5, then subtract 12 from 3, then multiply the results.)

To save time, spreadsheet software provides many inbuilt mathematical, trigonometric, and statistical formulas for use in calculations. Consult your manual for a full listing. The most-used business formulas generally provided include average, round to, total, depreciation allowance, and interest.

C28 Spreadsheet graphics

Spreadsheet information can be presented automatically in graphs and charts of various kinds. The user chooses the type of graphic, indicates the titles, labels, and legends to be shown, and the software does the rest.

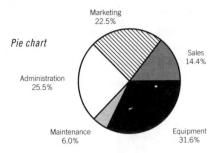

Pie chart

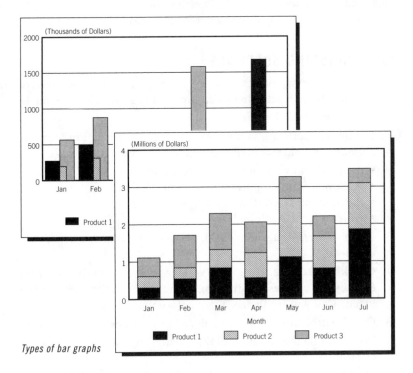

Types of bar graphs

▶C29   Utilities

These are useful packages designed to assist with disk management. They help organize files and will come to the rescue when things go wrong (e.g., if data are lost).

▶C30   Virus protection

This software will help prevent virus problems (i.e., disks or files that have been contaminated).

Important (for students)

◆ Always keep backup disk copies of your work.
◆ Use a mobile storage device (e.g., CD, memory stick) for the lab you are working in, and keep another for open access or home use.

◆ Do not keep bad/unusable storage devices.

◆ If virus protection is not on your system/network, report any virus message to the instructor or monitor in the lab you are working in—write down the screen message regarding the virus.

◆ Anti-virus programs should be upgraded regularly. See Unit 5, "Electronic Mail."

▶ **C31   Word processing**

Additional information on word-processing software is provided in Unit 14, "Keying and Formatting Documents for Processing."

C32   CHOOSING SOFTWARE

Observe the following points if you are buying software for business or private use (for help in selecting word-processing software, see Unit 14):

1. Carefully establish your needs first.
2. Be sure the software is compatible with your system in terms of memory and hardware. For example, is it compatible with
    • the kind and version of operating system you have?
    • the kind of monitor and video adapter available?
    • the amount of RAM available?
    • your particular printer?
3. Make sure reference manuals (documentation) and instructions are clear.
4. Check into service. Does your vendor represent a reliable, well-established business? Is training offered? Is a hotline service provided? Can you try the software before you buy it?
5. Can the program be custom-tailored to your needs if necessary?
6. What will be the situation in the event of updates or the discovery of errors?
7. Must the program be compatible with other programs you already own?
8. Consider the skill level of the people who are likely to use the program. How difficult will it be to learn?
9. Consider the future. Will this package be appropriate for some time? Don't risk outgrowing the software in a few months.

C33 STORAGE AND RETRIEVAL

The CPU stores data for processing and instructions as well as data that has been processed. However, since the amount of internal memory is limited, external (or auxiliary) storage is needed when processed data is to be stored for future use. Depending on the equipment used, storage may be on any of the following media.

C34 HARD DISKS

Hard disks are rigid, random-access, high-capacity magnetic storage devices, and are much faster and more convenient than floppies. Hard drives may be internal or external. All computers today come with hard drives built right into the system.

Today, capacities range from about 40 GB up to 500 GB.

C35 MEMORY STICKS

Memory sticks are commonly used portable memory devices that plug into a USB port, e.g., the Lexar Jump Drive. Memory sticks hold from 16 MG to 8 GB of data, and the price is based on the memory capacity.

Memory sticks are not infallible. They last for approximately two years, depending on usage; the more they are used, the more quickly they can become unusable. Make sure you back up the data to a permanent type of storage, i.e., recordable DVD.

NOTE: For additional information regarding the products mentioned in this unit, please access the product website.

C36 MAGNETIC TAPE

Magnetic tape may be in reel, cassette, or cartridge format that holds large amounts of data. Magnetic tape, a very inexpensive medium, tends to be used only in very large systems; however, tape backup is a viable option on PCs.

C37 MICROFILM DEVICES (MICROFORMS)

These devices are used to microfilm information directly from the computer. The process is known as COM (computer output microfilm) and is described in Unit 8, "Records and Information Management (RIM)."

C38 OPTICAL DISKS

For archival and backup purposes, the trend is towards cost-effective optically stored data. One 700-MB CD-ROM optical disk can replace 250 000 sheets of paper, for example. Optical disks offer these advantages:

◆ They are not affected by the same problems as magnetic disks.

◆ The software does the filing and retrieval so there are no misplaced files.

◆ They allow data to be accessed by several users at the same time.

◆ They enable images to be retrieved to a screen or to be printed.

◆ They are particularly attractive because of their non-volatile nature (they retain data with or without power, like a hard disk) and long shelf life (30 years or more).

◆ They are impervious to damage by magnetic or electrical spikes or surges.

Optical mass storage is available in these general forms:

◆ CD-ROM (compact disk, read-only memory); this means that it cannot be resaved or erased by the user. However, data can be edited and saved by another name.

◆ M-O (magneto-optical), which come in two versions:
  • WORM (write once, read many)
  • rewriteable (known also as erasable)

CD-ROM These are 4.75″ optical disks that look like the compact discs used in the music industry. These are useful for storing archival data.

◆ CD-ROMs are available in read-only or rewriteable formats (CD-RW).

◆ CD-ROM drives can be internal or external. A CD-ROM drive uses a laser that projects a tiny beam of light onto the disk to read the data.

This technology offers wide, multi-functional capabilities, including the ability to store text, graphics, video, and sound on the same disk.

Massive volumes of information are now available on CD-ROM, including encyclopedias, huge medical databases, manufacturers' parts lists and manuals, applications software packages, computer operating system manuals, multi-media training courses on everything from the Japanese language to electronic publishing, libraries of clip art, and digitized images of photos.

A CD-ROM disk is created using a laser beam, which alters the surface of the disk creating bumpy and flat "pit" areas on the bottom of the disk. These areas represent data.

WORM (write once, read many) WORM disks are more flexible than CD-ROM because data can be added. Data cannot be changed, however.

◆ WORM disks come as blank disks on which an organization can etch its own data for storage.

◆ They are capable of storing images and sound as well as text.

Rewriteable (erasable) These disks are rewriteable, allowing the user to write data, erase data, and write over it again.

CD-RWs (compact disk read/write) These disks should be used for backup of information stored on the hard drive; also known as *burning a CD*.

How to choose a device for storage capacity needs
There is a different device for every storage need. The nature of the task will determine the device needed:

Computer-based storage capacities

Storage device	Capacity	Approximate no. of standard text pages
3.5 inch diskette	1.44 MB	400
Memory stick	2 GB	varies
ZIP diskette	100 MB	27 000
	250 MB	67 000
CD-ROM/CD-R (writeable)	475 MB	131 500
	650 MB	180 000
Hard disk drive	3 GB	832 000
	17 GB	4 700 000
Portable USB drives	120 GB	varies
Note: 10–15% of the capacity of each storage medium is used for directory and page-formatting features.		

For working at home You will need a secure digital card device. Computers with an SD slot allow extension of capacity as needed via flash media, or, if speed is a factor, a USB (universal serial bus) flash memory drive.

To perform incremental data backups You will need an external hard drive. This allows backup of large-volume hard disks. Alternatively, rewriteable DVD drives/DVD burners are a bit more expensive and slower than external hard drives, but the media are cheaper in the long run.

To archive audio files, data, and images A rewriteable DVD is available, but a CD-RW drive is the cheaper option.

For sharing data and multimedia purposes You will need a CD-RW or rewriteable DVD drive; these are highly compatible and can accommodate various projects. The newer DVD burners can rapidly copy several gigabytes of information.

To expand system storage capacity Use a portable USB. This is the least expensive way to get more space.

C39 PRINTERS AND PLOTTERS

C40 PRINTER TYPES

Printers may be impact or non-impact. For information on printer types, see the chart on the following page. In selecting the appropriate printer, consider production speed and the print quality desired. If space is limited, consider a laser *bookshelf printer*. These are not much taller than a hardcover book and produce high-quality work.

In a networked environment, costly printers may be shared. This is possible also in a non-networked environment through switch boxes, which are available for shared printers.

A *photo printer* prints top-quality photos directly from a digital camera. See Unit 9, "Copying Processes," for more about digital cameras.

Type	Characteristics	Used for
Impact		
Dot matrix	• hammer-driven pins create a character by building up a composite of dots • several fonts possible from one head • near-letter quality is produced when head is passed several times over same line • top-line model has 24 pins and produces good quality. This does not need a second pass • can print graphics and in condensed mode	• where print volume and speed needed • rough draft, graphics, and near-letter-quality work • colour work
Non-Impact		
Bubble jet Ink jet*	• inexpensive • controlled jet of quick-drying ink forms dot patterns on page • faster and noiseless	• home/personal use • high-quality reproduction superior to dot matrix • draft and letter-quality work • colour work and graphics
Laser/Colour laser	• printing is by laser beam • quiet and fast • flexible font/typeface selection • enables users to scale fonts	• photographic or offset reproduction • high-quality, high-resolution work • colour work and graphics
PostScript laser	• all the features of lasers • provides a wide range of scalable fonts	• high-resolution graphics • desktop publishing
Thermal transfer	• melts wax-based ink off the printer ribbon and onto paper • higher quality than dot matrix • low noise	• very high quality text • high-quality colour work

*Ink jet printers require either black or colour cartridges or both. High-resolution print cartridges are expensive; therefore, set print for draft copy if possible.

Note: A printer warranty may become void if you use recycled print cartridges (cartridges that are refilled).

C41   PLOTTERS

These output devices are used for producing graphics. A movable arm holds coloured pens that draw images on a page. They are used in engineering, architecture, and construction, and are good for printing blueprints and electrical diagrams.

C42   COMMUNICATIONS

Computers and some peripherals do not need to be in the same room or even in the same geographic area. They can be connected in a network. Networks are described in detail in Unit 13, "The Integrated Office/New Technologies."

Stand-alone computers not connected to any other computer can also have data communications capability through the use of a modem.

C43   MODEM

A modem (MOdulator-DEModulator) sends and receives information between computers over telephone lines. The modem converts the analog (wavelike) signals of telephone lines into the digital (on/off) signals needed by computers.

C44   HIGH-SPEED HOOKUPS/TRANSMISSION

High-speed hookups are used for high-speed internet data and voice transmission through a cable hookup for a fee.

C45   ROUTER

Routers allow data to be delivered by a high-performance wireless network in your home or office. As well, routers restrict internet access to groups or individuals based on specific services, URL (uniform resource locator), or time and date. Wireless routers are also available.

C46   FAX

Faxes can be sent directly from some PCs. A mix of hardware and software permits the computer to function as a fax and allows you to send and receive files directly without the need for a separate fax machine (see Unit 5, "Electronic Mail").

C47   VIDEO CONFERENCING

This capability can be added to a desktop computer (see Unit 10, "Meetings, Net Meetings, and Event Planning"). A video camera, a board to fit in a desktop computer and software, and network communications enable people at considerable distances to see each other while holding a telephone conversation. Screen-sharing is permitted so that users can jointly edit documents.

C48 VOICE MESSAGING

Today's computers can be used to provide all the functions of a regular answering machine. It can take messages, retrieve messages, forward messages, prioritize messages, send messages, and play greetings from a Touch-Tone telephone. See Unit 5, "Electronic Mail."

C49 COMPUTER (PC) MAINTENANCE

A number of periodic tuneups are recommended for computer (PC) maintenance:

Daily

Virus scanning To keep your PC system free of unwanted viruses, always download the latest virus definitions of your anti-virus program, e.g., McAfee VirusScan (www.mcafee.com), or Symantec Norton AntiVirus (www.symantec.com). Anti-virus program upgrades are critical to stopping viral threats. The application runs in the background to screen incoming/outgoing traffic and any infections.

Backup A USB memory stick is ideal for daily automatic backups and allows a large storage capacity.

Weekly

Automatic hard-drive virus scanning Activate your real-time anti-virus protection and allow your program to check for virus signature updates as often as possible. Schedule a virus scan once a week to catch any viruses that may have slipped through. There are programs available that will assist you in setting up a schedule, e.g., when your PC is not in use. It will scan your PC and recommend updated drivers, system files, security, and other updates.

Monthly/bi-monthly

Disk cleanup This Windows utility removes temporary internet files, clears the Recycle Bin, and removes other unwanted disk contents.

Scheduled tasks With this Windows tool, you can automate housekeeping chores such as Backup and Disk Cleanup.

Dusting Open the side panel once every two months and use compressed air to keep dust out of the fans and system.

Task review Once a month, review your Scheduled Tasks to see if they are still active, e.g., do not schedule Disk Cleanup for the first of the month at 8:00 a.m. if your PC is turned off at that time.

Yearly
PC cleaning Carefully remove dust from inside your PC; use a soft brush attachment on a home vacuum or a mini-vacuum. Use canned compressed air (with the straw) to clear dust in tight spots. Do not blast air into floppy, CD-ROM, or other removable-media drives; the heads and other internal components can be easily damaged. Cleaning will prolong fan life and greatly reduce the risks of overheating your PC. Use reputable products, e.g., Discwasher, for cleaning optical drives.

Other
◆ Disks used elsewhere should be scanned for viruses.
◆ Keep your monitor dust-free (cover when not in use).
◆ Cover keyboard when not in use; do not put anything heavy on top of the keyboard.
◆ Never have food or drink around your computer workstation.

When should you turn off your PC?
You should turn off your computer at the end of the workday. While switching a computer on/off causes some degree of wear and tear which over many years could lead to a malfunction, turning it off enables the monitor's energy-saving feature and allows the screen to power down when not in use, thus saving money and benefiting the environment.

Removing all personal/sensitive data from a hard drive
You need to write over existing data to totally erase all data on a hard drive. Simply deleting files or reformatting the drive will not do it. There are many free and inexpensive wipe programs (also known as *shredders*) that can cover the existing data with zeros or random patterns, making the data unreadable by data-restoration software, e.g., LSoft Technologies' Active@KillDisk and Active@KillDisk Professional.

C50 INFORMATION SECURITY

Information is a valuable commodity, and keeping information confidential is a major issue in the business world. Most organizations implement a program that uses some or all of the following:
◆ user identification such as an access password, fingerprint, or retina scan
◆ activity logs
◆ anti-theft software
◆ appointment of a security official to
  • investigate violations
  • audit activity logs
  • monitor hard copies to guard against equipment misuse
  • supervise secure storage of sensitive data

C51 COMPUTER LITERACY

It is essential for every office worker to have an understanding of basic computer operations. If you are not already "computer literate," try the following:

◆ Take a keyboarding course. Keyboarding skills are invaluable for computer use; it is recommended that you achieve a minimum of 30 wpm.

◆ Take a computer course—many short, introductory ones are available. One-day workshops are useful for an overview of a particular software package.

◆ Don't be afraid of computers. A simple word-processing package would get you started easily.

◆ Watch and talk to computer users; ask as many questions as you can.

◆ Read as much as you can.

◆ Check TV guides for regular computer updates or program tutorials.

◆ Subscribe to computer magazines. Some magazines focus on particular hardware and software applications and upgrades.

◆ Join a user group or local association. Groups consist of keen users who favour particular hardware, software, and industry trends. They can be contacted through telephone directories, vendors, bulletin board services, and the internet.

◆ Attend business expos and seminars for new product and software information.

◆ Hire a tutor for more in-depth or reinforcement training.

◆ Access the internet to keep abreast of industry changes and technological advances.

For the latest Windows downloads and help articles, see: www. office.microsoft.com.

C52 COMPUTER TERMS

Access: The operation of seeking, reading, or writing data on a storage unit.

AGP: Accelerated graphics port; the latest in technology for high-end graphics card support.

Artificial intelligence: Software that will permit a computer to perform such human-like functions as reasoning and learning.

ASCII: American Standard Code for Information Interchange; pronounced "askee"; an 8-bit code developed to ensure compatibility among equipment produced by different manufacturers.

Binary: Something made up of or based on two things or parts such as a binary star or a binary numbering system.

BIOS: Basic Input/Output System. The BIOS is built-in software that determines what a computer can do without accessing programs from a disk. On PCs, the BIOS contains all the code required to control the keyboard, display screen, disk drives, serial communications, and a number of miscellaneous functions.

Bit: The smallest measurement of data; taken from the term *binary digit,* a bit is an electrical representation that is either 0 or 1.

Bit streams: Processors (32 bits to 64 bits) with the capability of processing information at extremely high speeds.

Bitmap: Graphics that consist of an arrangement of small dots.

Blade servers: A set of compact motherboards with a common power supply and a common cooling system.

Boards: Used to house computer chips. The *motherboard* holds the microprocessor chip of the computer.

Boot process: The process of starting the computer, either by turning on the power, pressing the reset switch, or pressing the special keys simultaneously.

Buffer: A storage device used to compensate for a difference in rate of data flow when transmitting from one device to another. It is a temporary location for the transmitted data to occupy.

Bug: An error in a computer program. *Debugging:* A procedure to identify and correct any mistakes found during the testing of a program.

Byte: A measurement of computer memory or disk space. It represents roughly one character or eight bits.

Cache: High-speed memory for temporary information storage, usually used between a slow storage device (e.g., a disk) and a fast central processing unit.

CAD/CAM: Indicates the relationship between computers and manufacturing. CAD is computer-aided design. CAM is computer-aided manufacturing. CAD increases the productivity of draftspeople, designers, and engineers. Onscreen designs can be translated into tapes that are then fed into a computer that operates the equipment.

Cascade: A window arrangement that layers open windows and fully displays the active window and the title bars of all other open windows behind it.

Click: The process of using the mouse pointer to select an icon or menu item.

Client-server: Mainframe use is gradually diminishing in favour of more economical and efficient client-server networks, in which computing tasks are split up and distributed among various desktop computers and servers.

Clipboard: A memory area that temporarily stores or translates information to be copied or moved within files and applications.

Compatibility: This term describes the ability of some hardware and/or software to work harmoniously with other hardware and/or software.

Configuration: Description of a computer hardware set-up, such as amount of memory and number and types of accessible drives.

Crash: Refers to a failure of a computer's hardware or software, which prevents the system from functioning.

CRT: Cathode ray tube/monitor/display screen.

DDE: Dynamic data exchange—a process that allows the linking of information between applications.

Dialog box: A window that provides information needed to complete a command.

Downloading: Capturing information from the internet, bulletin boards, or online services and importing to a software package for processing. (Downloading can also mean write to a CD. See C38, page 301.)

Downtime: Time that is lost due to computer breakdown.

Dump: To copy the contents of all or part of a storage device, usually from a central processing unit, into an external storage unit.

DVD: Digital versatile disc.

Electronic data interchange (EDI): A technology developed to allow interbusiness communication without the use of paper.

Embedded object: An object that is stored in the destination document and can be edited using the server application.

Expansion slot: A connector on the system motherboard into which an adapter card can be inserted, i.e., ISA and AGP slots.

Expert systems: Systems programmed to organize knowledge according to given rules, conditions, or situations. They can call up information relevant to a problem and determine which data to select in certain circumstances. Expert systems are based on *artificial intelligence* (see above).

Explorer: A Windows application that helps organize or view files on disk.

Field: A unit of information on a database record.

File: A collection of information (records) stored in a database.

File server: See *Client server*.

Gigabyte (GB): Approximately one billion bytes of information.

Graphical user interface (GUI): The capability to communicate with a computer by selecting graphic objects on the screen.

Hard copy: A printed copy.

Hierarchy: A tree-like representation of the organization of files and folders on disk.

Icon: A graphic object that represents elements of Windows (e.g., a document that can be opened or a program that can be run).

Interactive processing (online or real time): Terminals can access the computer and get results immediately. Banks, airlines, and hotels use interactive processing constantly.

Interface: The connection between the system board and a peripheral.

ISA: Industry standard architecture; a type of expansion slot that operates at 8.33 MHz bus speed.

Kilobyte (KB): 1024 bytes of information.

LCD: Liquid crystal display (flat panel monitor).

Megabyte (MB): Approximately one million bytes of information.

Megahertz (MHz): Millions of cycles per second; the measurement used in the speed of processing data.

Motherboard: Main circuit board inside your computer with most or all of the RAM and the microprocessor.

Multi-tasking: Running more than one application program at a time (e.g., sort an accounts receivable file, print out some word processing, and work on a spreadsheet). Operator can move from one program to the other without interrupting them.

Multi-user: Several terminals connected to a single computer with different users working simultaneously, or several computers connected to each other, actively sharing programs and information.

OLE: Object linking and embedding—a process that allows the creation of an embedded object.

Online: Terminals hooked up to the computer using its processing capabilities in real time.

Open database connectivity (ODBC): A subsystem to Windows that allows the user to open or connect to databases created by different database programs.

Operating system: Controls all input to and from the disk drives, keyboard, display, printer, and other peripherals, and the running of other programs.

Parallel port: Also called *printer port*, or LPT 1; the parallel port is used to attach a printer or other peripheral using a Centronics parallel cable.

Peripherals: Equipment such as printers, screens, etc., that can be externally connected to a computer.

Personal digital assistant (PDA): Also called *palmtops or hand-held/pocket computers*.

Printer ports: The ways in which a printer transmits data to and from the system unit. They are either *serial* or *parallel*. (Be sure you know which one is appropriate for your printer.)

Properties: The attributes and settings associated with all items on the screen.

Protocols: Sets of rules governing the way in which devices communicate; *protocol converters* exist to help compatibility problems.

RAID: Redundant array of independent discs.

RISC (reduced instruction set computing): RISC computers are able to run any software under any operating system, with no hardware or software additions.

Robots: Computer-controlled arms or manipulators used in the manufacturing industry.

Scroll arrows: The arrows on the scroll bar that move information in the direction of the arrows and that allow new information to be viewed onscreen.

Scroll bar: A bar window located on the bottom or right window border that displays text not currently visible in the window; it contains scroll arrows and a scroll box.

Scroll box: A box on the scroll bar that indicates the position within the area of available information; this box can be moved to a general location within the area of information by dragging it up/down the scroll bar.

Serial port: A communication port used by the computer to communicate with the outside world, i.e., mouse, modems, serial printers, plotters, and other serial devices.

Shading/fill: A feature that changes background from black and white to various shades or densities of black.

Sleep mode: A "hot key" on the newer keyboards, such as Internet keyboards, which suspends the PC and lets you resume work later (an energy saver).

III

Soft copy (readout): The processed information displayed on a screen. Printers can be linked with computer terminals if a permanent record of the readout is required.

Source file: The document where an object was created.

Status bar: At the bottom of a window; displays information about current program settings (e.g., tasks being performed).

Subfolder: A folder that is created within another folder.

Taskbar: A Windows desktop element that contains the start button, buttons that represent active applications, the clock, and other indicators.

Toolbar: A bar of icons displayed below the menu bar and used for shortcuts for many of the common menu commands.

Toolbox: A toolbar of icons provided for the most common drawing commands; used with Paint.

Tooltip: A description or help message displayed when pointing at the taskbar or toolbar icons.

Turnaround time: Time between submission of a job to the computer centre and the return of the results.

Uptime: Time that is spent on the computer or time when the computer is running.

USB: Universal serial bus; a new standard for attaching peripherals to PCs.

User-friendly: A system designed for ease of operation.

Windowing: Several documents can be displayed on the screen side by side or overlaid.

Wiping: A term used when erasing data from a hard drive.

NOTE Online dictionary and search engine for computer and internet technology/terminology: webopedia.internet.com *or* www.whatis.com

WORDS OF WISDOM

Knowledge can never be lost or stolen!

C

....**UNIT**....

13 THE INTEGRATED OFFICE/NEW TECHNOLOGIES

SELECTED CONTENTS

I01	INFORMATION PROCESSING
I02	Information Processing Technologies
I03	TYPICAL INTEGRATED OFFICE APPLICATIONS
I04	ELECTRONIC BUSINESS
I06	ADVANTAGES OF THE INTEGRATED OFFICE/NEW TECHNOLOGIES
I07	NETWORKING AND COMMUNICATIONS
I08	Networks
I09	LANs and WANs
I010	Network Configurations
I011	THE INTEGRATED OFFICE
I012	WORKPLACE MANAGEMENT
I013	RETURN ON INVESTMENT (ROI)
I014	IMPACT OF INTEGRATION AND NEW TECHNOLOGIES ON PEOPLE
I015	NEW TECHNOLOGIES
I016	ELECTRONIC SURVEILLANCE

III

In the past, information was processed in a one-step-at-a-time fashion. Now, information processing is increasingly automated and performed as a single operation.

The extent to which organizations are using office automation technologies varies with size and need. This unit will introduce the separate components and build towards the ultimate—electronic business, where integrated technologies in one organization are meshed with the integrated technologies of trading partners so that entire trading operations can occur with very little human intervention.

This unit describes the excitement and challenges of the integrated office and new technologies.

I01 INFORMATION PROCESSING

Information processing is the term used to describe the manipulation of all forms of knowledge expressed in words, numbers, graphics, and images, and by the human voice.

Information processing in the automated office is achieved through the integration of people, systems, procedures, and technology. For example, under one linkage, data and word processing, financial management, electronic mail/messaging, database management, document distribution, and information storage and retrieval can be achieved and communicated in a highly efficient and cost-effective way.

In today's world, information is needed fast. Technology is constantly being redesigned and improved to meet this need. More and more, the business world is taking advantage of the time savings and cost-efficiencies that technology makes possible in information processing functions and tasks.

102   INFORMATION PROCESSING TECHNOLOGIES

The following table shows the types of information that might be processed, kinds of information processing systems, and the communications links available for transmitting processed information to those who need it.

Information Processing Systems and Communications Links		
Types of information to be processed	**Information processing systems**	**Communications links**
words	word processing	email
data (numbers and symbols)	data processing	facsimile
	reprographics	linked computers
graphics (drawings and illustrations)	records management	local-area networks
voice (the spoken word)	voice processing	modems
	image processing	teleconferencing
images (e.g., photographs, videos, microforms)		wide-area networks
		the internet

Word processing describes the equipment, people, and methods used in the production of a document.

Data processing means changing raw facts (letters, numbers, symbols) into usable information.

Copying processing covers methods of reproducing or duplicating information.

Records management describes the control of a firm's records. With some procedures, some records never appear on paper.

Voice processing means that the human voice originates and/or edits information.

Image processing means converting images into a digital form acceptable to a computer. Material for imaging can even include photos and handwritten notes, typed invoices or preprinted forms, and newspaper clippings.

Communications links are the electronic means of moving information over a distance.

Bar-coding Bar codes are a pattern of stripes that contain a wealth of data. Light and dark areas are read by a laser scanner and translated into data.

Some can be read in two dimensions—width and height. One quick pass with a laser gun replaces several manual procedures. Bar-coding is useful in integrated systems:

♦ for indexing purposes

♦ to replace some paper documents

♦ for labelling with detailed warnings or histories

In some organizations, these information processing technologies are operated independently as their own departments (e.g., word processing, records management). In others a co-ordinated plan links the technologies and creates an integrated automated office.

103 TYPICAL INTEGRATED OFFICE APPLICATIONS

Many tasks can benefit from the integrated office, ranging from the relatively straightforward production of a document for a mass mailing or a report produced collaboratively (as described in the following examples) to the highly complex electronic data interchange (EDI) described in the next section.

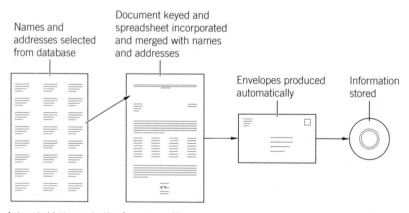

Automated letter production for mass mailing

Examples of integrated activities

1. An administrative assistant keys in a letter to all shareholders and incorporates a spreadsheet report produced in the accounting department. The letter is automatically merged with names and addresses selected from a database that contains all of the company's contacts.

2. A report is to be produced for distribution to members of the board and to department heads at remote locations. Several staff members are involved. During production, the network allows them all to work on the report at the same time and send it back and forth via email instantly for editing and polishing. When completed, the

report can be printed by laser as camera-ready copy. Advanced copying processes mean the copier used to produce the report can automatically collate, insert dividers, staple, bind, and provide a cover. Soft copies of the report can be distributed to the staff at remote locations through the network for printing and binding there if needed.

3. Where an organization has taken advantage of image processing technology, dealing with a customer's inquiries is very straightforward and speedy, as the following example illustrates.

   • All the records related to a particular customer are scanned and saved electronically on optical disk. An employee dealing with a customer inquiry can instantly call up on a computer screen every document related to that customer (relevant correspondence, records of telephone conversations, etc.) and satisfy the client without delay. When image processing is not used, each of these records would be kept in a separate records management system and several time-consuming searches would be needed to assemble all the relevant information.

4. Communication software packages permit travelling businesspeople, newscasters, sportscasters, and others to keep in touch with the home office. These integrated communication packages (also referred to as *groupware*) are used for

   • checking calendars and scheduling appointments, meetings, etc.
   • decision making through information transfer
   • electronic messaging: retrieving and sending email
   • image and graphic transfer
   • information sharing with corporate databases (e.g., spreadsheet updates, etc.)

For information about automated production and distribution of a business report, please visit the Text Enrichment Site for this text at *www.pearsoned.ca/text/campbell.*

104 ELECTRONIC BUSINESS

Electronic business (ebusiness) is the online buying and selling of products or services. The sale may be consumer to consumer or business to business, and should involve internet protocols beyond mere voice transmission (voice over internet protocol). The information processing technologies used in one company are meshed with technologies in others so that computers exchange documents with minimal human intervention. It means that employees can be freed from the grind of data re-entry and assume more creative roles in *exception processing* (dealing with orders that are in some way unusual). Electronic data interchange (EDI) is one type of electronic business that demonstrates the workings of this process.

105 EXAMPLE OF EDI IN OPERATION

A retailing giant (*A*) in dealing with a major supplier (*B*) does not place orders. *A* connects its point-of-sale terminals (cash registers) directly to *B*'s computers. Bar codes on the products let *A*'s computers know how many of which *B* products are sold and this information moves to *B* by a secure internet connection. That, in turn, activates a re-supply command for the number of items required to keep *A* in stock. *A* pays when the goods leave the shelves—but not by cheque: funds are deposited electronically in *B*'s account and arrive with enough information to make clear the reason for the remittance. No purchase order, no shipping notice, no invoice, no cheques are involved. This reduces inventory-control problems, increases profits, decreases paper use, and virtually eliminates keying errors.

Governments and banks are already substantial users and will become bigger users, and transportation companies are turning increasingly to EDI.

Security of information is not a problem because of the security protocols built into the process.

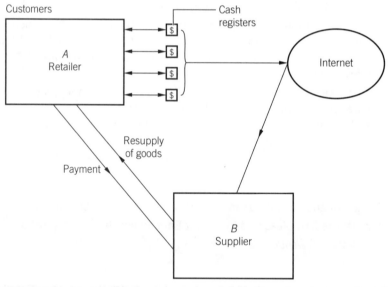

Typical electronic data interchange process

106 ADVANTAGES OF THE INTEGRATED OFFICE/NEW TECHNOLOGIES

Increases productivity and efficiency

◆ It eliminates many tedious tasks.

◆ All users on a network can access and share data and processing capability.

◆ Letters, reports, and other communications can be composed, edited, formatted, distributed, stored, and printed in one process.

- It forces rethinking of outmoded methods (e.g., the need for certain forms).
- Standardization is promoted because the same software can be used throughout an organization.
- People can better understand the operation of the entire organization.
- It practically eliminates human error.
- Access to outside (subscriber) databases and the internet (see Unit 16, "Information/Reference Sources/Internet") can provide a wealth of information on any subject to any terminal.

Speeds up information interchange

- Information can be electronically communicated instantly within the same building, across the country, or across the world in an immediately usable form.
- Voice and other messages can be stored and forwarded to reduce telephone interruptions and "telephone tag."

Maximizes equipment use

- One person can perform a variety of complex tasks working at a single PC.
- Expensive equipment such as laser printers can be shared.

Minimizes software costs

- A licence for using expensive software in a network can be cheaper than buying separate pieces of software for stand-alone workstations.

Improves competitiveness

- Because of fast communications, customer service can be improved.
- Twenty-four-hour global communication is readily available.
- Interbranch information exchange—credit checks, approval of copy for advertisements, confirmation of large orders, agreement of contract terms—can be instant.
- Electronic commerce is made possible (see IO4).

Decreases duplication of effort

- Duplication of effort among departments is lessened because communication and sharing are possible.

Increases storage and retrieval speed

- Information stored electronically on magnetic disk or tape, on file servers, on optical disk, or on microfilm can be rapidly retrieved by many users.
- Databases make possible storage and retrieval of many kinds of information that can be cross-referenced and retrieved by several users in various formats.

Improves management effectiveness

◆ Administration, management, professional, and technical personnel can deal with information and ideas still being worked on. For example, spreadsheets allow instant calculation and recalculation; communications links permit transmission of this data for others' reactions.

◆ Rapid receipt of information and faster decision making increase efficiency and competitiveness.

◆ Managers responsible for productivity can monitor staff performance through computers.

◆ Those involved in writing tasks have access to word-processing capability, can draw on information sources instantly, and can rapidly produce statistical information in attractive formats with ease.

◆ Staff is provided with an easy way to schedule and co-ordinate appointments and meetings through software and the communications network.

I07 NETWORKING AND COMMUNICATIONS

I08 NETWORKS

A computer network links expensive hardware, software, and peripherals in the same building or building complex, and often worldwide, by telecommunications. Computers within a networked system can share files and send messages and documents back and forth. Terminals can access software and information from a central source, process information in a variety of ways, use peripherals in the network, and communicate with other workstations.

Networking may be achieved in a number of ways. The two basic methods are as follows:

Shared-logic system Several dumb terminals (ones without processing ability) and peripherals share the storage and processing power of one central, or host, computer.

Shared-resource system Intelligent terminals (ones with their own processing power) are linked so that they share printers, servers, and other peripherals.

▶I09 LANs and WANs

Networking may be over a local area (LAN) or a wide area (WAN). Connection is by transmission lines that can be of several types.

LANs are privately owned. They connect small groups in a small area— a building or group of buildings.

◆ Usually, they connect PCs to one another.

◆ They can connect server computers to a PC.

◆ Most systems are multi-tasking, allowing several users access to large amounts of data at the same time. They can also handle numerous transactions from multiple users at the same time.

When communication is required over a larger geographic area than that provided by LANs, a communications server (a gateway or bridge) can link LANs and non-networked devices into WANs for long-distance interaction (across the country or around the world).

WANs are publicly owned and use satellites, fibre-optic lines, telephone lines, microwaves, and dedicated communications channels to transfer data.

◆ They can connect to mainframes, minicomputers, and PCs.

◆ Online information services are available through WANs.

◆ WANs can provide access to remote banking, home shopping, and electronic home bulletin boards.

NOTE Many portable computers are network ready, needing only a telephone jack to access data from an office computer or to send messages to anyone on the office network.

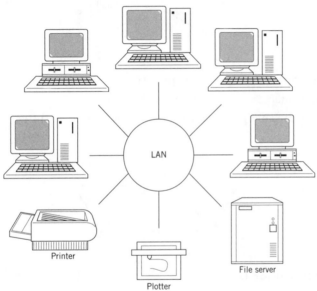

Typical LAN

►I010 Network configurations

In networks, equipment may be linked in various patterns (topologies or network configurations). The most frequently used are shown here.

Ring

◆ Information is communicated by being relayed around the circle in sequence through each device.

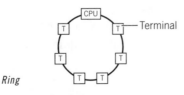

Ring

Peer to peer

◆ This type is like the ring, except that every desktop in this network has equal prominence, which is made possible by software known as *groupware* (see Unit 12, "Computers: Hardware and Software").

Star

◆ Each device has direct contact with the central controller. Terminals (nodes) do not depend on the operations of each other.

◆ All communications pass through the central computer. Terminals cannot talk directly to each other.

◆ The file server is usually dedicated.

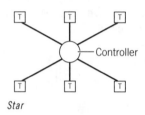

Star

Totally connected (point to point)

◆ Direct contact is made between each node.

◆ Because of cabling difficulties, only a few devices can be accommodated.

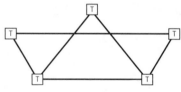

Totally connected

Hierarchical (or tree)

◆ This type is useful when all information does not have to be shared with the entire network on a regular basis.

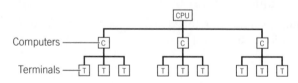

Hierarchical

Bus

◆ This type offers an open communications channel.

◆ It can move around the organization, joining equipment as needed.

◆ No central computer is necessary.

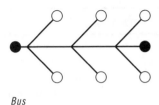

Bus

NOTE LANs may also be *wireless* (i.e., they allow computers within small areas to communicate with one another without the need for cables).

1011 THE INTEGRATED OFFICE

Today, more than ever, workers are faced with information overload; the amount of information available is growing through the use of internets/intranets and the increased range and connectivity of communication media. It is essential that the data available be organized, analysed, interpreted, and turned into useful information.

Some organizations move gradually into integrated office automation in stages. As their needs change, they increase the degree of sophistication. However, the results of simply layering technology on top of current work practices may prove disappointing, because this may produce only localized, individual task-level improvements.

A productive environment comes through careful management of people, productivity, and time, and working towards clearly identified goals. Achieving this goal may lead to the redesign of entire processes, not just automating some of them. This redesign is known as *business process re-engineering*. There are four stages involved in re-engineering:

♦ recognizing that change is necessary

♦ analysing the present processes and environment and understanding the shortcomings

♦ designing a new and harmonious work environment that ensures optimum productivity

♦ implementing (i.e., making the transition from the old to the new)

To achieve a successful and effective re-engineering, certain criteria must be established:

♦ Equipment and software must be fully compatible and networkable. Purchases must be carefully controlled so that both immediate and future needs are considered.

♦ Staff must be accepting of, and involved in, the change-over process; they must be provided with suitable training or retraining and they must receive support as they make the adjustment to new procedures and equipment.

10

I012   WORKPLACE MANAGEMENT

Improving performance is a major challenge for every organization. At the executive level, supervisors must identify what knowledge is needed, which employees can handle specific tasks, and how this knowledge can be used to improve products, services, and client/customer relationships. Most importantly, employees must be part of an ongoing cross-training process, and feel secure in the new technologies as they are introduced in the workplace.

Workplace management ensures that *all* participants in the work process have *all* the information needed to do the job, and access to the required knowledge to complete the job successfully.

There are three basic principles of successful workplace management:

◆ *Performance*—the effective application of technologies to contribute to the design and performance of business objectives

◆ *Potential*—work management technologies that complement and maximize existing basic business technologies

◆ *Productivity*—a business/organization is more efficient when its processes are specifically designed to produce a desired result

I013   RETURN ON INVESTMENT (ROI)

Businesses are always looking at the bottom line or a good **return on investment.** This can be achieved through the following:

◆ customer response time—keep up-to-date information about the customer and product to reduce call-backs and unnecessary paperwork

◆ inventory control—maintain an up-to-date filing system to avoid lost and misplaced documents

◆ reduction in errors—provide proper training to eliminate the need to redo a job due to lack of training or outdated technologies

I014   IMPACT OF INTEGRATION AND NEW TECHNOLOGIES ON PEOPLE

The impact of integration and new technologies on office organization structures, on personnel, on job qualifications required, on procedures, on training, and even on job locations is significant.

◆ More fulfilling jobs are emerging and more routine ones are being eliminated as technology automates routine activities.

◆ All office staff must be computer literate (understand computer capabilities and the terms involved) and all office workers should have keyboarding skills.

◆ As staff spend increased hours at computers, ergonomic and work environment concerns are important (see Unit 6, "Productivity/Time Management Skills").

◆ New skills and attitudes are needed. Employees will require strong interpersonal skills and will need to view themselves as team players.

◆ People must be flexible and accepting of change. As technology and software advance and improve, we will need to welcome it and reap its benefits.

◆ Office staffs must appreciate that new skills will be needed continually and be ready to accept retraining as required.

NOTE　See Section V, "Job Search," for information on careers in information processing.

1015　NEW TECHNOLOGIES

Information processing is a field of enormous growth and never-ending advancement. Just a few of the important emerging technologies include the following.

Internet phones/internet telephony　Internet phones are regular phones that can be plugged into a special box called an analog telephone adapter. One side of the box plugs into the router that controls the user's broadband connection (either DSL or cable modem); a regular phone plugs into the other side.

For a monthly fee, you have unlimited calling to anywhere in Canada and the U.S., plus reasonable global rates.

Smart cards　A large memory on a small chip makes the smart card ideal for portable storage of constantly changing data. Smart cards look like credit cards but they are entire microprocessors with embedded memory chips. They can:

◆ be used to pay highway tolls without the driver needing to stop

◆ be used for building or individual office entry, cafeteria lunch payment, or vending machine purchases

◆ permit access to computers or other equipment

◆ carry complete medical records

◆ contain pictures, fingerprints, or retinal scans for user identification

Data warehouse　Traditional operational systems involve the keying of information into a database. This information must be analysed and managed efficiently and safely. Today, many companies are establishing decision-support systems built around a data warehouse.

The process of "data warehousing" is the means of getting information from business transactions, storing it, making it accessible for designated employees, and providing users with the tools to analyse the data and make better business decisions. The data warehouse also consolidates data from a wide variety of existing analytical systems in organizations.

An effective data warehouse system:

◆ provides accurate, high-quality data pertinent to the decision-making process

10

- offers an ongoing and integrated view of data
- enables easy access to data
- provides timely access to data through efficient automated data gathering and delivery processes
- offers effective access to interface technologies
- affords flexibility to grow and adapt to changing business requirements

Educational technologies Learning management software is available, such as WebCT and WebCT Vista, that provides storage for teachers' notes, video and audio clips, discussion rooms for students, and virtual office hours for professors and teachers. Students may call up multi-media material and lecture notes at their convenience. This feature extends the classroom environment to an online space for discussion.

WebCT also provides support for people with various learning styles and special needs.

Many new technologies support increased student/teacher interaction. For example, instant polling devices that look like a television remote allow a large group of students to respond to instructor queries in class. The software then translates the answers into a bar chart, giving the teacher immediate feedback on student comprehension.

Online courses are available and can be delivered by video streaming. The teacher can teach physically in one class and have the same content delivered in a number of other classrooms by video.

Online learning is rapidly becoming one of the preferred ways for professionals to upgrade their skills.

Distant learning/e-learning With internet-based, real-time synchronous activities, a student with a dial-up or high-speed internet connection can share a common screen and application with other students at various locations and at different times.

NOTE See Unit 5, EM19, Asynchronous vs. Synchronous Communications.

Five-language talking translators This hand-held device translates more than 100 000 words and 11 500 popular phrases in English, French, Spanish, German, and Italian. World time can be accessed in 200 cities, local time in 12- and 24-hour format. These devices have an alarm feature as well as eight useful currency and metric conversions. A 32K databank with a password feature allows the storing of appointments, telephone numbers, addresses, and memos in one convenient place.

Mobile managers A hand-held device that enables you to store and access office documents, emails, photos, songs, video, voice mails, and contacts and appointments on a high-resolution colour screen.

Palm-held/Smartphones These hand-helds enable users to combine business and personal tasks in one compact, full-featured quad-band phone with email, a Palm OS organizer, an MP3 player, messaging and Web browsing capability, and a digital camera.

Power station A portable charging station with plug-in ports for cell phones, PDAs, and MP3 players.

Microsoft Media Center Media Center software now comes preloaded on many higher-priced desktop, laptop, and home PCs. A computer equipped with Media Center can perform as a computer, television, and personal video recorder (PVR).

1016 ELECTRONIC SURVEILLANCE

According to an American Management Association survey, more than three-quarters of major companies record and review employee communications and on-the-job activities. Monitoring tactics include hiring a third party to keep an eye on employee activity, hiring investigators to catch workers' compensation fraud or other abuses, and using camera and audio monitoring in the workplace. Current technology records keystrokes, email, online conversations, and instant messaging.

WORDS OF WISDOM

Minds are like parachutes;
they only function when open.

10

14 KEYING AND FORMATTING DOCUMENTS FOR PROCESSING

SELECTED CONTENTS

PART 1 KEYING AND FORMATTING

K1	**PAGE PLACEMENT INFORMATION**
K2	Paper Sizes
K3	Default Settings
K4	Fonts and Point Sizes
K5	**FORMATTING TECHNIQUES**
K6	Envelope Addressing
K17	Letters
K18	Basic Letter and Punctuation Styles
K19	Additional Letter and Punctuation Styles
K20	Letterhead
K21	Letter Placement
K38	Displayed Information
K39	Form Letters
K40	Letters on Small Stationery
K41	Memorandums
K42	Reports, Essays, Manuscripts
K43	Title Page
K44	Preface
K45	Contents Page
K46	Body of the Report
K47	*Placement Guide*
K48	*Starting Lines*
K49	*Spacing and Indents*
K50	*Headings*
K51	*Numbering Systems*
K52	*Ending the Pages*
K54	*Displayed Information*
K55	*Graphics*
K56	*Special Effects*
K57	*Quoted Material*
K58	*Footnotes, Endnotes, and Textnotes*

III

K63	*Constructing References*
K64	**Bibliography and References**
K65	**Glossary**
K66	**Index**
K67	Tables (Tabulation)
K72	Metric Expressions
K78	**Spacing Rules for Punctuation Marks**
K79	**EDITING AND PROOFREADING**
K80	Proofreading Marks
K81	Productivity Tips
K82	Making Documents Attractive
K83	Document Style Manuals

PART 2 DOCUMENT PROCESSING

K84	**DOCUMENT-PROCESSING CYCLE**
K85	Inputting
K86	**WORD-PROCESSING SOFTWARE**
K87	Software Features
K88	Integrated Software Packages
K89	**GETTING THE MOST FROM YOUR SOFTWARE**
K90	Using the System to Its Full Potential
K91	**STORAGE**
K92	Disk Care
K93	Disk Backup
K94	Disk Management
K97	**PRINTERS**
K98	Paper-Handling Devices
K99	**METHODS OF ORIGINATING TEXT FOR DOCUMENT PROCESSING**
K100	Machine Dictation Equipment
K101	Centralized Recording Units
K102	Transcription Units
K103	Machine/Microtranscription
K104	**ORGANIZATION OF DOCUMENT-PROCESSING ACTIVITIES**
K105	**SERVICE BUREAUS AND CONSULTANTS**
K106	**TEMPORARY DOCUMENT-PROCESSING HELP**
K107	**CHANGING TECHNOLOGY IN DOCUMENT PROCESSING**
K108	**DOCUMENT-PROCESSING TERMS**

K

Part 1 of this unit will focus on the production of business communications. Regardless of the equipment used, this section will answer many of your keying and formatting questions. The information is presented in five major categories:

Page Placement Information covers paper sizes, default settings, type sizes, starting lines, and margin settings.

Formatting Techniques provides the detailed information needed to help you key accurate, attractive, and effective business documents.

Style Practices covers the keying of punctuation, metric expressions, and special symbols.

Editing and Proofreading contains proofreading symbols.

Formats and Language Style covers formatting and document style practices.

 **PART 1** • • • • • • • • • • • • • •

KEYING AND FORMATTING

K1 PAGE PLACEMENT INFORMATION

K2 PAPER SIZES

Standard (letter-size) paper dimensions

- ◆ $8^{1}/_{2}$" × 11" (21.5 cm × 28 cm)
- ◆ available in sheets or continuous form for computer use on dot matrix printers. After printing, pages are detached and edges stripped off to give the appearance of cut sheets

Legal-size paper dimensions

- ◆ $8^{1}/_{2}$" × 14" (21.5 cm × 35.5 cm)
- ◆ available in sheets and continuous form

NOTE Monarch and Baronial (small-size stationery) are described in K40.

K3 DEFAULT SETTINGS

All word-processing software comes with default (preset) format settings. Usually these are:

MS Word

1"	top margin
54	text lines
1"	bottom margin
6"	line length
1.25"	left margin
1.25"	right margin
10 pt.	point
single	spacing
half-inch interval tabs	

While these dimensions can be changed, they are convenient for most documents. Work with these default settings as much as possible to speed up your document production time.

K4 FONTS AND POINT SIZES

Software allows for various fonts and point sizes. All offer 10, 12, and more. As well, printers offer various choices.

Point size refers to the vertical height of an upper case character, measured from the baseline to the top of the character. For example, if 36 point is chosen, the height from the baseline to the top of the upper case character would be $^1/_2$ inch. This is also discussed in Unit 15, "Desktop Publishing."

This is 14 point.

This is 12 point.

K5 FORMATTING TECHNIQUES

Format means the set-up of a document and refers to the margins, spacing, page length, etc., that should be used. Contained in this unit are examples of most business documents. For properly formatted examples of the following business communications, consult the units indicated:

- ◆ agenda: Unit 10, "Meetings, Net Meetings, and Event Planning"
- ◆ application letter (personal business style): Unit 20, "Job Search Skills/Career Planning"
- ◆ forms: Unit 17, "Business Forms and Form Design"
- ◆ itinerary: Unit 11, "Travel Arrangements"
- ◆ meeting announcements: Unit 10, "Meetings, Net Meetings, and Event Planning"
- ◆ minutes: Unit 10
- ◆ press release: Unit 2, "The Expression of Language"

K6 ENVELOPE ADDRESSING

Canada Post has issued guidelines for a *preferred style* of addressing envelopes that is strongly recommended to ensure maximum efficiency in sorting and delivery, especially for mass mailings. However, the traditional style of envelope addressing is still acceptable, because Canada Post recognizes that some businesses have large mailing databases that were prepared this way.

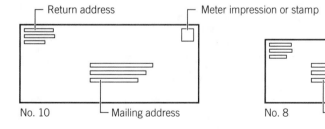

4 1/8" x 9 1/2" (105 mm x 241 mm)	3 5/8" x 6 1/2" (92 mm x 165 mm)

The two most frequently used business envelopes

General guidelines

- Key carefully and accurately.
- Single-space throughout.
- Include a return address in the top left corner.
- Align the address so that each line starts at the same point.
- Use a maximum of six lines.
- Always include a postal code. Obtain this from letterheads, return addresses on envelopes, or from *Canada's Postal Code Directory,* available from Canada Post (see Unit 18).

K7   Canada Post preferred style

- Key the entire return and mailing addresses in upper case, and single-space.
- Do not use punctuation of any kind (e.g., Vancouver BC V6B 4P4).
- Place attention lines or special mailing notations ("Confidential") above the name and address of the company.
- Use the two-letter province or territory abbreviations that are provided in K9.
- Use Canada Post abbreviations, as shown in K8.
- Start keying on line 15 on a No. 10 envelope, and line 13 on a No. 8 envelope, five spaces to the left of centre, so that the postal code appears within the optical character recognition (OCR) area. If necessary, start higher for each additional line needed (e.g., "Attention," "Confidential").
- Use standard fonts, avoiding script, italic, etc.
- Show suite or apartment number on the same line as the street address, before the street name.
- Separate the postal code from the province abbreviation by two spaces.

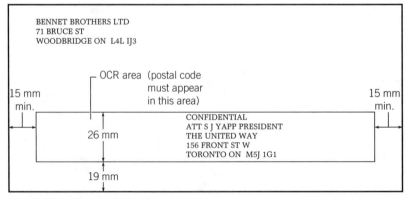

Canada Post preferred style for addressing envelopes

NOTE   Postal codes online: www.canadapost.ca

NOTE   If envelopes or labels are generated from the inside addresses of letters, appropriate changes in the inside addresses of the letters will be needed (see K24 for an example).

►K8   Canada Post abbreviations

	Preferred style		Preferred style
Apartment	APT	Heights	HTS
Avenue	AVE	Lane	LANE
Boulevard	BLVD	Mountain	MTN
Building	BLDG	Parkway	PKY
Centre	CTR	Place	PL
Circle	CIR	Road	RD
Court	CRT	Route	Rte
Crescent	CRES	Rural Route	RR
Drive	DR	Street	ST
Estates	EST	Trail	TRAIL

►K9   Places

Canadian provinces and territories

Provinces and territories	Abbreviations
Alberta	AB
British Columbia	BC
Manitoba	MB
New Brunswick	NB
Newfoundland and Labrador	NL
Northwest Territories	NT
Nova Scotia	NS
Nunavut	NU
Ontario	ON
Prince Edward Island	PE
Quebec*	QC
Saskatchewan	SK
Yukon Territory	YT

K

*QC is the official two-letter abbreviation for Quebec introduced in 1992 by Canada Post for optical character reader machines. However, envelopes marked with a PQ or a Que. will be delivered to their addresses in that province.

U.S. states, districts, and territories

The two-letter U.S. Postal Service State abbreviations, districts, and territories must appear on all envelope addresses.

States, districts, and territories	Abbreviations	States, districts, and territories	Abbreviations
Alabama	AL	Montana	MT
Alaska	AK	Nebraska	NE
Arizona	AZ	Nevada	NV
Arkansas	AR	New Hampshire	NH
California	CA	New Jersey	NJ
Colorado	CO	New Mexico	NM
Connecticut	CT	New York	NY
Delaware	DE	North Carolina	NC
District of Columbia	DC	North Dakota	ND
Florida	FL	Ohio	OH
Georgia	GA	Oklahoma	OK
Guam	GU	Oregon	OR
Hawaii	HI	Pennsylvania	PA
Idaho	ID	Puerto Rico	PR
Illinois	IL	Rhode Island	RI
Indiana	IN	South Carolina	SC
Iowa	IA	South Dakota	SD
Kansas	KS	Tennessee	TN
Kentucky	KY	Texas	TX
Louisiana	LA	Utah	UT
Maine	ME	Vermont	VT
Maryland	MD	Virgin Islands	VI
Massachusetts	MA	Virginia	VA
Michigan	MI	Washington	WA
Minnesota	MN	West Virginia	WV
Mississippi	MS	Wisconsin	WI
Missouri	MO	Wyoming	WY

▶K10 Envelopes with international addresses

For international addresses, follow the preceding rules. If the traditional style of address is used, show both the place name and country in upper case. Include zip codes, postal codes, zone numbers, or postal districts before the country name.

Canada Post preferred style	Traditional style
LAWRENCE T HAMILTON 8632 ALASKA AVE N APT 107 CHICAGO IL 60652 -1187 USA	Mr. Lawrence T. Hamilton 8632 Alaska Avenue North Apartment 107 CHICAGO, ILLINOIS 60652 -1187 U.S.A.
MISS S HOOSHOLLEY ELLIOTT GALLERIES LTD 51 LUTON RD HARPENDEN HERTS AL5 2UB ENGLAND	Miss S. Hoosholley Elliott Galleries Ltd. 51 Luton Road HARPENDEN, HERTS. AL5 2UB ENGLAND

▶K11 Production hints

Use word-processing software to automatically produce envelopes or self-adhesive labels. These can be printed from source lists (e.g., selected clients from a database) when producing form letters or, with some software, from inside addresses of letters. Capitalize the city or town name in the inside address as you key in the letters.

►K12 Folding and inserting correspondence

Enclosures should fit envelopes as closely as possible.

Small envelope (No. 8)

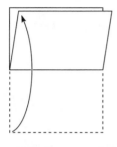

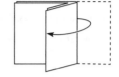

1. Place letter *face up* on desk. Fold in half.

2. Fold right third to left, making the fold slightly less than one-third of the way over.

3. Fold left third so that it extends 0.5 cm beyond the other two-thirds.

4. Insert last folded edge first.

Large envelope (No. 10)

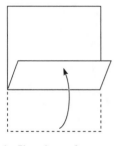

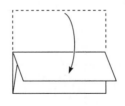

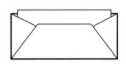

1. Place letter *face up* on desk. Fold slightly less than one-third up towards top.

2. Fold down top of letterhead.

3. Insert so that second fold goes in first.

►K13 Window envelopes

When window envelopes are used, be sure the enclosure fits the envelope snugly so that the address (including the postal code) cannot shift out of the window area.

Standard size specifications (with acceptable window positions) are available from Canada Post.

►K14   Speedy envelope sealing and stamping by hand

Sealing

◆ Use a damp sponge or other moistener.

◆ Assemble 10 envelopes one behind the other with flaps open and glued side up.

◆ Run the sponge over the first two or three envelopes. Seal them.

◆ Continue until all envelopes are sealed.

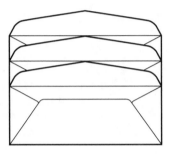

Envelopes assembled for speedy sealing by hand

NOTE   Adhesive-strip flaps are available at a higher cost than traditional-seal envelopes.

Stamping

If a franking machine (postage meter) is not available, do this:

◆ Assemble 10 envelopes so that the stamp area is visible.

◆ Moisten a horizontal row of 10 stamps.

◆ Quickly attach a stamp to each envelope.

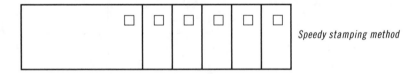

Speedy stamping method

►K15   Standard-sized envelopes

◆ The largest envelope for Canada Post delivery is 245 mm × 150 mm (10″ × 6″) and the smallest is 140 mm × 90 mm ($5^1/_2$″ × $3^1/_2$″). Courier services will handle any size.

◆ Insert the return address in the top left corner.

◆ Position the mailing address so that it appears in a band 15 mm in from the sides and 19 mm up from the bottom. Key the address on the envelope itself or use a label.

NOTE   Canada Post will deliver non-standard-sized mail for a higher fee.

▶K16   Labels

Because of the time-saving feature of labels, businesses use them for regular mail as well as for large envelopes and parcels. They may be prepared on electronic labellers or with word processing software. Be sure the address is positioned in the centre of the label and affixed to an envelope so that Canada Post rules are followed. When a dark envelope is used, light-coloured labels are particularly useful.

K17 LETTERS

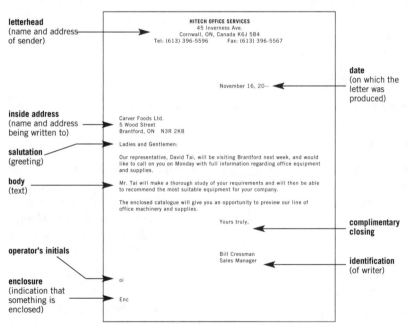

Basic letter parts

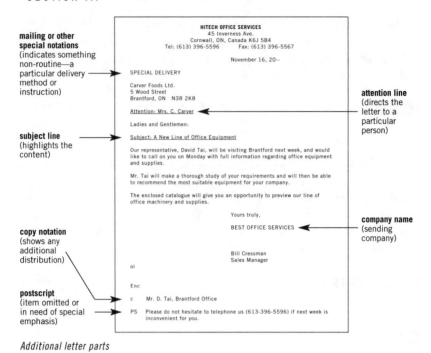

mailing or other special notations
(indicates something non-routine—a particular delivery method or instruction)

attention line
(directs the letter to a particular person)

subject line
(highlights the content)

copy notation
(shows any additional distribution)

company name
(sending company)

postscript
(item omitted or in need of special emphasis)

Additional letter parts

▶K18 Basic letter and punctuation styles

Most business letters are formatted in one of two basic styles.

Basic letter styles

Basic punctuation styles

Full block style

◆ all lines start at the left margin

Open punctuation

◆ punctuation is *not* used after the date, inside address, salutation, complimentary closing, or identification unless these end with an abbreviation

Modified block style

◆ date and complimentary closing start at the centre

◆ all other lines start flush with the left margin

Mixed (two-point or standard) punctuation

◆ a colon follows the salutation

◆ a comma follows the closing

◆ punctuation is *not* used after the date, inside address, company name, or person's name unless these end with an abbreviation

NOTE

◆ Full block style and open punctuation is the most time-saving style.

◆ Attention lines, subject lines, mailing notations, enclosures, reference initials, and copy notations have ending punctuation *only* if they end with an abbreviation.

◆ Time-saving tips for formatting letters appear in K81.

Basic letter and punctuation styles

August 24, 20--

Mr. William Johnstone
Box 24
Allan, SK S0K 0C0

Dear Mr. Johnstone

Yours truly

L. Bitz

Full block style, open punctuation

August 24, 20--

Mr. William Johnstone
Box 24
Allan, SK S0K 0C0

Dear Mr. Johnstone:

Yours truly,

L. Bitz

Modified block style, mixed punctuation

206 Emerald Terrace
Saskatoon, SK S7J 4J1

August 24, 20--

Mr. William Johnstone
Box 24
Allan, SK S0K 0C0

Dear William:

Would you be available for a brief meeting on September 17?

I am coming your way during that week and would very much like to talk to you about some new milking equipment I bought this year that is just great. Milking time is really reduced, and this leaves a few more hours each week for all those other chores that we farmers constantly face.

Give me a call or drop me a note if September 17 suits you.

Please give my best to your family. Look forward to seeing you soon.

Kindest regards,

Lyle Bitz

Personal business letter: Block style, mixed punctuation

K

▶ K19 Additional letter and punctuation styles

November 20, 20--

Mrs. Sheila Billings
Nursing Co-ordinator
North York General Hospital
2005 Sheppard Avenue East
Willowdale, ON M2J 1E1

SIMPLIFIED LETTER STYLE

You might select this letter, Mrs. Billings, for use in your office if you are looking for a way of cutting letter production time to a minimum. Notice that letters in the simplified style have neither a salutation nor a complimentary closing. Note also that a subject line is always included.

This letter is very similar to the full block style, and should be formatted in the same way. The only major change to make is to the subject line. This can be located a double space below the inside address and a double space above the body.

Craig Hkoury
Manager

oi

Simplified style, open punctuation

November 6, 20--

Dear Mr. Carella:

The letter style favoured by most government departments, civil service offices, and senior executives for their personal correspondence is known as the official style.

The official style is essentially a regular letter that has the inside address as the _last_ item. The letter may have blocked or indented paragraphs and may be produced in any one of the three punctuation styles.

If the letter includes a postscript, enclosure, or copy notation, these are placed in their usual positions.

Yours sincerely,

F. Benjamin

oi

Mr. S. Carella
247 Barrington Street
Halifax, NS B3H 2P8

Official style, mixed punctuation

November 16, 20--

Mr. J. Villeneauve
Fleming and Sons
372 Pender Street West
Vancouver, BC V6B 1T4

Dear Mr. Villeneauve:

Have you been searching for a letter guaranteed to catch the attention of your customers through its eye appeal? Look no further! The hanging indented (or suspended) style will do the job for you.

Paragraphs in this letter style start normally, but the second and all succeeding lines are indented. The indentation may be five or ten spaces, depending on just how eye-catching you want your letter to be.

For the remaining details, simply follow the formatting procedure for the block style letter.

Yours sincerely,

Maya Eby
Circulation Manager

oi

Hanging indented (suspended) style, mixed punctuation
Used mainly for advertising/marketing purposes.

November 16, 20--

MRS SHEILA BILLINGS
NURSING CO-ORDINATOR
NORTH YORK GENERAL HOSPITAL
2005 SHEPPARD AVE E
WILLOWDALE ON M2J 1E1

Dear Mrs. Billings

You might select this letter style because of its simple, uncomplicated format.

Please note that the inside address is in capitals, with no punctuation, to follow the Canada Post guidelines.

Sincerely yours

George Lacey
Manager

oi

Full block letter showing Canada Post preferred style for inside address. Use this when envelopes and labels are produced automatically

▶K20 Letterhead

◆ Most organizations have preprinted letterhead.

◆ Create an elegant letterhead for your personal business letters if you have appropriate software.

Mobile Software Consultants

2430 Tecumseh Rd. Windsor, ON N9E 1X8
Phone (519) 246-9870 Fax (519) 246-9873

▶K21 Letter placement

Letters should be positioned on the page so that they are attractively framed by a balanced amount of white space.

◆ Word-processing software has a default (automatic) setting of a 6″ line, which is appropriate for most letters.

◆ Insert the date approximately 1 1/2″–2″ below the printed letterhead. For a short letter, leave eight to ten lines between the date and inside address; for a longer letter, leave only four lines.

◆ Allow four to six lines for the signature block.

◆ Preview your letter, if possible, and adjust the spacing to achieve a balanced look before printing. This adjustment can be done by reducing or increasing the space between the date and inside address and in the signature area.

`NOTE` If an organization's letterhead is not standard (e.g., demands a wide left margin), create a default document and save it. Avoid changing margins. Leave a bottom margin of at least one inch for continuation pages. We provide guidelines for dealing with continuation pages in this unit at K37.

K22 Date

As mentioned, position the date a double space below the letterhead or approximately 1 1/2″–2″ either at the margin or the centre, depending on the letter style being used. Either of these styles is acceptable:

◆ Numeric: 20— 07 29 (year, month, day)

◆ Standard: July 29, 20—
  Insert the date from the computer system to save keyboarding time.

K23 Mailing or other special notations

◆ Show mailing notations at the left margin, midway between the date and inside address.

◆ Use these only when a special mail service, such as registered mail, is used.

- Use this position also for special notations such as "Confidential," "Personal," etc.
- In the rare situation where you might have both a mailing and a special notation, position them one above the other.
- Use uppercase, or initial caps and underscore, or boldface and no underscore.

> PERSONAL   – or –   Personal – or – **Personal**

K24 Inside address

Canada Post preferred style

Canada Post has a preferred style for envelopes. When you use the inside address of your letter to generate envelopes or labels, you will need to use this style in your letters (see K6). If you key envelopes as a separate step, follow the traditional style for keying inside addresses.

Canada Post preferred envelope style	*Traditional style*
MS JENNY McCARTNEY	Ms. Jenny McCartney
ELLIOTT GALLERIES LTD	Elliott Galleries Ltd.
1257 SALT SPRING RD	1257 Salt Spring Road
VANCOUVER BC V1R 6R7	Vancouver, BC V1R 6R7

Traditional style

- Use at least three lines for the address.
- Keep line lengths approximately equal.
- Avoid abbreviations as much as possible. For acceptable street abbreviations, see K8; for provincial and state abbreviations, see K9.
- Indent any continuation lines by two spaces.
- Include a social title—Mr., Mrs., Miss, Ms., Messrs. (plural male), Mesdames or Mmes (plural female). In cases where gender is unknown (e.g., Chris Fisher), omit social title.
- Do not abbreviate professional titles and special titles such as Professor, Reverend, etc. You may abbreviate Doctor (Dr.).
- Do not show titles *and* degrees—use one or the other, but not both (B. Turcotte, Ph.D. or Dr. B. Turcotte).
- Check the proper form of address if you are writing to a prominent person in public life, politics, the clergy, or the military (see Unit 2, "The Expression of Language").
- A person's position in an organization may be shown in these ways (note the use of the comma):

Mr. F. Sharman, President
Buttonville Golf Club

Mrs. Jane Tobias
Director of Services
Collingwood Consultants Ltd.

Mr. F. Ciampaglia
President, BIB Inc.

◆ Key names of organizations so that they match those on letterheads for spelling, capitalization, and abbreviations.

◆ When street names are numbers, use words for one to ten and use numbers for over ten:

160 Seventh Street   32 South 13th Street   43 - 13 Street

◆ Separate the town from the province with a comma.

◆ Use initial caps only for city or town names. Do not use all capitals.

◆ Show province names in full or in the abbreviated form (see K9).

◆ Show the postal code as the *last* item, immediately after the province and separated from it by two spaces, or on its own line.

◆ For addresses in the United States, include the zip code two spaces after the name of the state and USA as the last line.

◆ Place routing codes for overseas addresses *before* the country name:

Mme D. Dupont
5, rue des College
F-61760 Barr
FRANCE

NOTE French addresses take a comma after the street number.

◆ See K6 for envelope addressing illustrations.

K25   Attention line

◆ Place the attention line two lines below the inside address, centred or starting from the left margin (preferred). The following are acceptable styles:

ATTENTION MR. J. DUNN
Attention: Mr. J. Dunn

◆ To produce envelopes or labels from the inside address of a letter or if using window envelopes, incorporate the attention line into the inside address:

Attention: Mr. John James
Aoko Golf Wearhouse
137 Bishop Crescent
MARKHAM, ON L3P 4N5

K26   Salutation

◆ Place the salutation two lines below the address (or attention line if there is one and it is shown below the address).

◆ Capitalize the first word and all nouns:

Dear Mr. Waugh   Ladies and Gentlemen
Dear Chris Fisher (gender unknown)   Dear Ms. Patel
Dear G. O'Keefe (first name and gender unknown)

◆ See Unit 2, "The Expression of Language," for help in selecting the appropriate salutation.

K27 Subject line

◆ Place the subject line two lines below the salutation, starting from the left margin. The following are acceptable styles:

ANNUAL SALES CONVENTION
Annual Sales Convention

K28 Body (message part of the letter)

◆ Begin the body two lines below the salutation or subject line.

◆ Single-space; double-space between paragraphs. In the case of an extremely short letter, the entire body may be double-spaced.

◆ Paragraph indents will be determined by the letter style used.

K29 Complimentary closing

◆ Place the complimentary closing a double space below the body, starting at either the left margin or the centre, depending on the letter style used.

◆ Capitalize the first word only:

Yours truly   Very sincerely yours

◆ See Unit 2, "The Expression of Language," for help in selecting the appropriate complimentary closing.

K30 Company name in closing

◆ If the company name is used in the closing, key the company name in all capitals a double space below the complimentary closing:

Yours truly

GRANATO GRAIN CO.

◆ When the company name is long, it may be centred under the complimentary closing. In this case, be consistent and centre the identification line(s) also:

Yours truly

GRANATO CANADIAN GRAIN COMPANY

(4–6 lines)

Rosalie Granato

K31 Identification line (author's name and position)

◆ Place the identification line anywhere from four to six lines below the closing or company name.

◆ Use it as a balancing line. For example, if there is only a small amount of space left at the lower edge of the page, leave four lines, but stretch this to six lines if there is surplus space to be used.

◆ Show the name of the author and/or the position held:

Yours truly
↓2
PARANI, WONG & COMPANY

↓4–6

Jason D. Wong
Sales Director

Yours sincerely

4–6

Vikki Cranfield, Ph.D.
Chair, History Department

◆ A man does not usually indicate his courtesy title in the closing; a woman has choices:

Grant Parker, President	Ms. M. Chantrell
Mary Chantrell	Miss M. Chantrell, Principal
M. Chantrell	Mrs. M. Chantrell

◆ When the courtesy title is not shown, include it in parentheses:

Yours sincerely

Mary Chantrell

(Miss) M. Chantrell

Yours sincerely

Miss M. Chantrell

Mary Chantrell (Miss)

◆ Use one or two lines, but do not let the identification extend beyond the margins.

◆ If you are authorized to sign a letter in the author/signer's absence, use one of these forms:

Barb Davison
per
Charmaine Reynolds

Charmaine Reynolds
for
Barb Davison

(The author is Barb Davison; the signer is Charmaine Reynolds.)

K32 Reference initials

◆ Insert reference initials at the left margin. Use the same line as the identification line or two lines below it.

◆ If the author's name is keyed in the identification, it is not necessary to show his or her initials. If both author's and operator's initials are used, show the author's initials first, and the operator's initials second. Choose from these styles:

PHE:OI	– *or* –	PHE:oi
OI	– *or* –	oi (only operator's initials shown)

K

K33 Enclosure/attachment notation

◆ Use this notation when something is to be included with the letter.

◆ Show the notation one or two spaces below the reference initials. Choose from any of these styles:

enc:	Enclosure	Enc Cheque $453.95	
Encl	Enc (2)	Enc 3	Encls
Attach	Attachment	Attach (Report)	Attachments

NOTE Attachment notation indicates that the material is held together by a paper clip or is stapled.

K34 Copy notation

◆ Use this notation when one or more people are receiving copies of the letter.

◆ Insert the notation one or two spaces below the enclosure notation (or whatever comes last in the letter), at the left margin. The following are acceptable styles:

c Mrs. M. Daniel	Copy to	Mr. F. Rocca
cc Mr. D. Ling	Copies to	Mr. W. Roswell
courtesy copy		Ms. F. Fiore
Fax Mrs. G. Rollins *–or–* fc (fax copy)		Mrs. G. Rollins

◆ When the distribution of the copies is not to be shown on the original, a blind copy notation should be used on the copies only:

bc Mr. D. Roswell

◆ Some organizations prefer the use of *pc* (photocopy) in place of *c* or *cc:*

pc Mr. D. Ling

K35 Postscript

◆ Use the postscript (PS) to add emphasis or to include something omitted from the body.

◆ Place it a double space below the last item, and set up in either style shown:

PS   Thank you so much for your lunch invitation. I'm sorry I can't make it this time.

PS   Thank you so much for your lunch invitation. I'm sorry I can't make it this time.

▶ K36 Filing notation/path and filename

This is a coded notation that indicates where the document is stored or saved on disk. Most software packages have an automatic filename insert feature.

◆ Use a small font size (8- or 9-point) for the filing notation and include the path and file name.

◆ Key the filing notation on the left as a footer or a double space below the reference initials, the enclosure notation, or the copy notation, whichever is last.

> oi
> A:\unit12.doc

NOTE *oi* means operator's initials.

▶K37 Multi-page letters

◆ When letters take up more than one page, insert a header on successive pages showing the addressee, the page number, and the date.

◆ Use the same quality stationery as used for page 1, but use a plain sheet (unless your firm has printed continuation-page stationery).

◆ The header should be placed one inch from the top of the page.

Example:

Cooper Lumber Co.   2   20-- 08 12

↓ 2

cheque will be received from you within the next few days. If this cheque is not received, the matter will be . . .

Example:

Newfoundland Lumber Supply Company
Page 2
20-- 08 12

↓ 2

cheque will be received from you within the . . .

◆ Use the addressee's name as it appears on the first line of the inside address on page 1.

◆ Do *not* have fewer than two lines of a paragraph at the foot of one page or at the top of the continuation page.

◆ Do not isolate the signature block. Have at least two lines of the body on the page with it.

◆ Use the header feature and the widow/orphan protect feature for very long letters.

▶K38 Displayed information

Numbered sentences or items in a list

◆ Leave a line space above and below each numbered item.

◆ Single-space each numbered item and double-space between them.

◆ Either line up the numbers with the existing margin or indent one-half inch from the left margin.

◆ Use the automatic indent feature.

K

April 19, 20--

Ms. A. R. Mendes, President
Astrolite Limited
380 Georgia Street West
Vancouver, BC V6B 4P4

Dear Ms. Mendes:

Because of the increasing number of contacts being made from this office, it might be advisable to consider enlarging the staff here. May I suggest the following:

1. The appointment of someone as assistant to the vice-president. This person's major duties would be to take care of office administration.

2. The appointment of a sales representative. His or her duties would be to follow up contacts and act as a technical consultant to potential customers.

Creation of these positions will release time to the vice-president so that additional attention can be given to the mounting number of contacts in the central and northern regions.

Sincerely yours,

L. C. Horton, Vice-President

oi

Numbered sentences

Quoted or inset information

◆ Leave a line space above and below any information that has been quoted or that must be set off from the rest of the body.

◆ Indent one-half inch from the left and right margins.

◆ Single-space the quoted or inset text.

Tabulated information

The preferred style would be to use the table feature of your software package; remove all grid lines.

Dear Mrs. Bourne:

Please send us a quotation on each of the following items:

5 cm steel casing	SC4	5 sections
1.5 cm Logan pump	LP1	4 sections
3 cm twist steel cable	TS7	400 m

Please show f.o.b. to Prince George, British Columbia.

Tabulated information

April 19, 20--

The Toronto Star
One Yonge Street
Toronto, ON M5E 1E5

Gentlemen:

Please insert the following advertisement in the classified
advertising section of your paper in category 710, General
Help Wanted.

> Automotive parts manufacturing firm requires
> person to perform packaging and warehouse
> duties in the Toronto distribution centre. We
> offer a full benefits program, 5-day week, and
> good starting salary. Phone (416) 232-3198.

Please make the advertisement a small one and arrange
for it to appear on Thursday and Friday, July 10 and 11.

> Yours truly,

> M. Walesa
> Human Resources Manager

oi

Quoted or inset information

Special effects

A particularly eye-catching letter or insert can be created as needed by:

◆ using different fonts and point sizes

◆ highlighting sections in boldface

◆ justifying inset or quoted blocks

◆ using the table feature or border lines

▶K39   Form letters

Form letters contain basic information that will be sent to a number of people, yet each letter must appear to be individually produced. Use the mail merge feature of your software to achieve this.

◆ Create and save the form letter.

◆ Create and save the data source list of variables (names, addresses, dates, amounts).

◆ Use the merge option to produce the finished letters.

NOTE   Envelopes or labels can automatically be produced from a data source list. Check the software instruction manual.

K

April 19, 20--

«Title» «Initial» «Last Name»
«Address 1»
«City», «Province» «Postal Code»

Dear «Title» «Last Name»:

Thank you for applying for a charge account with us.
Enclosed is your credit card as approval of your
application. We are pleased to inform you that your
credit limit has been set at «Amount of Credit» and
that your account balance will be calculated on the
«Date of Account Balance» day of each month.

We appreciate the opportunity to be of service to you
and welcome you as a Lockwood charge account
holder.

Yours very sincerely,

D. Kappelhoff
Credit Manager

oi

Encl

Merged main document using MS Word

April 19, 20--

Mr. G. Grevenitis
556 Wynford Place
Acton, ON L7J 2L5

Dear Mr. Grevenitis:

Thank you for applying for a charge account with us.
Enclosed is your credit card as approval of your
application. We are pleased to inform you that your
credit limit has been set at $2000 and that your
account balance will be calculated on the 19th day
of each month.

We appreciate the opportunity to be of service to you
and welcome you as a Lockwood charge account
holder.

Yours very sincerely,

D. Kappelhoff
Credit Manager

oi

Encl

Merged letter using MS Word

Title	Initial	Last Name	Address1	City	Province	Postal Code	Amount of Credit	Date of Account Balance
Mr.	G.	Grevenitis	556 Wynford Place	Acton	ON	L7J 2L5	$2000	19th
Mr.	P.	Deragon	95 Kingsgate Court	Dundas	ON	L9H 3Z6	$1500	19th
Mr.	B.	Hennick	15 Wildewood Avenue	Hamilton	ON	L8T 1X4	$2200	19th

Merged data source using MS Word

III

▶K40   Letters on small stationery

◆ The names given to stationery that is smaller than standard are
   Monarch and Baronial.

◆ Senior business executives may use them to add distinction to their
   letters or when it is necessary to catch a reader's attention.

◆ Set margins of one inch (2.5 cm) from each side and follow the standard formatting rules for letters.

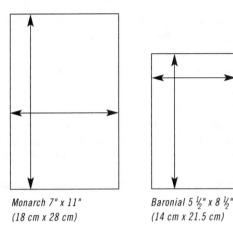

Monarch 7" x 11"
(18 cm x 28 cm)

Baronial 5 ½" x 8 ½"
(14 cm x 21.5 cm)

K41 MEMORANDUMS

Use interoffice memorandums (memos) or email when written communication between company employees is necessary.

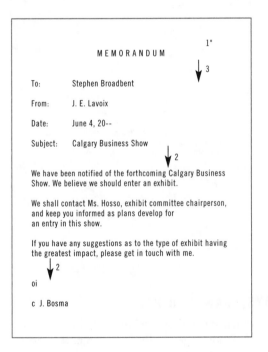

Interoffice memorandum

You may also use the following format:

◆ Omit MEMORANDUM in the top line.

◆ Do not use the inside address, salutation, and complimentary closing.

◆ Use the default margin settings.

◆ Use block style (i.e., do not indent paragraphs).

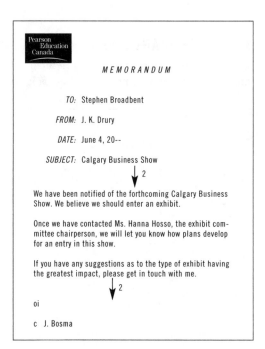

◆ Do not repeat the author's name in the signature area if it is given at the top. Typist's initials should, however, be shown at the left side, a double space below the body.

◆ Job titles are optional in the *To* and *From* sections.

◆ Apply the same format details for enclosure and copy notations, postscripts, and multiple pages as for letters (see K33–K37).

◆ If preprinted stationery is not used, place *Memo To* or *To, From, Date,* and *Subject* one under the other as illustrated. With printed stationery, insert the relevant information to suit the stationery.

NOTE The copy (copies) notation may also be keyed at the top of the memo as in the example on the left.

Memorandum

To: Erika Darling, Director

Copies to: L. Bognar, J. Bosma

From: Carter Campbell, Manager

Date: March 4, 20--

Subject: Environmental Issues

Interoffice memorandum
on preprinted stationery

Pearson Education Canada

M E M O R A N D U M

TO: Stephen Broadbent

FROM: J. K. Drury

DATE: June 4, 20--

SUBJECT: Calgary Business Show
↓ 2

We have been notified of the forthcoming Calgary Business Show. We believe we should enter an exhibit.

Once we have contacted Ms. Hanna Hosso, the exhibit committee chairperson, we will let you know how plans develop for an entry in this show.

If you have any suggestions as to the type of exhibit having the greatest impact, please get in touch with me.
↓ 2

oi

c J. Bosma

K42 REPORTS, ESSAYS, MANUSCRIPTS

Reports may be formal or informal. When they are informal, the memo format described in the previous section is generally acceptable. If a formal report is required, the following will be helpful:

◆ Reports, essays, and manuscripts are enough alike that the instructions here apply to reports used in business, to formal academic essays, and to material being prepared for publication.

◆ Reports, essays, and manuscripts usually consist of a title page, contents page, body, and bibliography. Some may also contain a preface, appendices, a glossary, and an index.

- Use the many automatic functions of word-processing software as you produce reports. These features are discussed here because some parts of reports can be generated automatically.
- Use good-quality, plain white, letter-size paper, unpunched.
- Always save a copy on disk or make a photocopy of the document.

▶K43 Title page

The title page (also known as the cover page) shows the name of the company, organization, or institution; document title (topic); name of author; name of person and/or company to whom submitted; and the submission date.

- Format the page so that it is attractive and easy to follow.

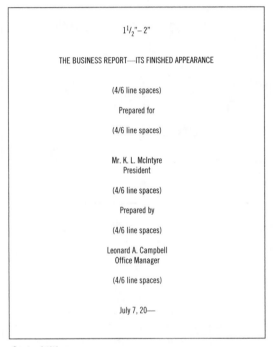

$1\frac{1}{2}" - 2"$

THE BUSINESS REPORT—ITS FINISHED APPEARANCE

(4/6 line spaces)

Prepared for

(4/6 line spaces)

Mr. K. L. McIntyre
President

(4/6 line spaces)

Prepared by

(4/6 line spaces)

Leonard A. Campbell
Office Manager

(4/6 line spaces)

July 7, 20—

Centred title page

- Use the software to good advantage (lines, bold, italics, different fonts) but don't overdo it—a simple, conservative style is best.
- Use the page centring feature of the word-processing software.
- The paper used can be heavier than that used for the body.

▶K44 Preface

The preface (also known as the introduction, abstract, foreword, synopsis, summary, or digest) outlines the purpose of the work, its scope and limitations, the methods of research employed, the major ideas, the name of the person who authorized it, and any special observations or acknowledgments.

THE MARITIME PAPER COMPANY
Head Office

THE BUSINESS REPORT: ITS FINISHED APPEARANCE

Prepared for
Mr. K. L. McIntyre, President

by
Leonard A. Campbell, Office Manager

20-- 07 15

Blocked title page

1½"–2" Top margin

PREFACE
↓ 2

    The results of research into the importance of the visual effect of reports indicates that their appearance is indeed a significant factor in their impact.

    It is hoped that this report will have the effect of making report writers in the company aware of the need to devote sufficient time and energy to illustrations, reproduction means, and binding methods.

↓ 2

<u>Acknowledgments</u>

↓ 2

    In presenting this report, we wish to acknowledge the assistance and co-operation received from the print shop staff and the desktop publishing personnel.

◆ Key the preface as a separate page.

◆ When a contents page is used, the preface will precede it. When there is no contents page, the preface will go between the title page and the body.

◆ Use the same margins, placement, and spacing as for page one of the body but leave the page unnumbered.

▶K45   Contents page

The contents page lists each major section (and sometimes subsections) of the document, as well as page numbers. It is needed only in longer reports (ten or more pages) and should be prepared *after* the rest of the report has been finished so that accurate page numbers can be included.

The contents page can be produced automatically with most software. Check the manual and use this feature.

◆ Use the same margin settings as the body.

◆ Use a 2″ top margin on the contents page.

◆ If the contents list is a short one, use the same margins, placement, and spacing as for page one of the body but leave the page unnumbered.

◆ If the contents list is a long one and likely to take up more than one page, insert the heading $1^1/_2$″ to 2″ from the top of the page and finish 1″ from the bottom edge line. Start the continuation page 1″ from the top of the page. Use roman numerals to number these contents pages; place the roman numerals at the bottom centre of contents pages.

◆ The contents page should follow the heading pattern and/or numbering system used in the report, essay, or manuscript itself.

◆ Use dot leaders (tab leaders), leaving one space before and after the dots.

NOTE   An informal report usually does not include a glossary or an index.

K

$1^1/_2$″ – 2″

TABLE OF CONTENTS

Introduction	1
Current Software	2
Who Uses Desktop Publishing (DTP)?	3
Skills Needed in DTP	4
Advantages and Disadvantages of DTP	6
DTP Hardware	7
DTP Software	8
Producing a Document	10
Plan the Publication	10
Prepare Preliminary Page Design	10
Prepare Text	11
Prepare Artwork and Graphics	12
Finalize Page Layout	12
Print Final Version	12
Language of Typography	13
Principles of Design	13
Samples of DTP	14
Conclusion	17
Appendices	18

▶K46   Body of the report

K47   Placement guide

Starting line *(top margin)*	Page 1 Page 2, etc. (If the document is presented in chapters or separate units, start these $1^1/_2$" or 2" from top of pages.)	$1\frac{1}{2}$" or 2" 1"*
Line length *(side margins)*	6" 1" left/right margins	
Last line *(bottom margin)*	1"	

NOTE   Increase the left margin by $^1/_2$" for a bound report containing paper printed on one side only. Increase both margins by $^1/_2$" if paper is printed on both sides. The printer menu of some software provides a binding feature. If you use this, you will not have to change margins from the default settings.

NOTE   Use double spacing throughout the report for productivity (e.g., after the date, before and after side headings and paragraph headings).

1"

Page 2

Keeping the reader on track and making the reading task easier are particularly important when you have to persuade your reader. Breaking the text into short units with suitable headings will help.

Reproduction (Initial Caps and Bold)

The type of report and its functions will influence the kind of reproduction method used. Photocopies may be appropriate for internal copies, but reports to shareholders, for example, should be reproduced by a process that will produce good-quality copies. Some small printing houses offer very good prices and will do a fast job. Be sure to obtain comparative quotes.

Binding (Bold)

The binding will depend on the size and purpose of the job.

Long Reports. (Bold)   If the report is more than ten pages long, there are a number of economical ways you can use to dress it up. You might purchase binders or you might consider coloured plastic ring binding.

1¹/₂" or 2"

(14pt., bold)

THE BUSINESS REPORT: ITS FINISHED APPEARANCE

↓ 2

An effective business report requires research, organization, and writing skill. The final layout and appearance must also be carefully considered if the report is to achieve its desired effect.

↓ 2

Illustrations (12 pt., bold)

↓ 2

Pictures, graphs, or illustrations will help you get an idea across quickly or emphasize a particular point. Remember:

↓ 2

• Graphs and charts have more impact than tables.

• Each graph, chart, or picture should make only one point.

• Keep the graph or picture as close to the related text as possible.

↓ 2

Headings (12 pt., bold)

↓ 2

"Headings and subheadings pinpoint and summarize ideas for easy absorption by the reader."[1] If you want your message to be acted upon, make it as easy to read and understand as possible.

---

[1] Farmiloe, Dorothy, *Creative Communication for Business Students*, Holt, Rinehart & Winston, Toronto, 1991, p. 186.

K

NOTE Single-space bulleted items but double-space between bullets if space permits.

K48 Starting lines

For page one of the body and major units or chapters, key the heading 1¹/₂" or 2" from the top. For continuation pages, start 1" from the top.

K49 Spacing and indents

◆ Use double spacing and a ¹/₂" first line paragraph indent. For business reports, economic and/or environmental-concern considerations might call for single or 1¹/₂" spacing. The first rough draft should, however, be double-spaced.

◆ Use single spacing for displayed information (e.g., long quotations, numbered lists, tables).

K50 Headings

◆ Use headings and subheadings to organize the material, to show relationships, and to indicate the relative importance of the separate sections of the report.

◆ Decide what the heading pattern will be and stick to it.

◆ Use of a full header is an option on page two and succeeding pages of a report and can be keyed in Initial Caps or ALL CAPS: e.g., THE BUSINESS REPORT Page 2. Right align Page 2 and use a border line to separate the header from the text.

◆ Suggested styles that will permit five levels of headings as shown below are:

1. Capitals, bold and centred (if the heading is long, use two lines and centre both)
2. Capitals, side or initial caps in bold
3. Initial capitals, side, underscored or boldfaced
4. Initial capitals, indented $1/_2$", underscored or boldfaced
5. Initial capitals, indented $1/_2$", underscored or boldfaced, known as a paragraph heading

◆ To speed up keying, if working from a draft, decide on heading categories *before* keying and then code each heading in the job (e.g., number them from one to five). Follow the code sheet as you proceed.

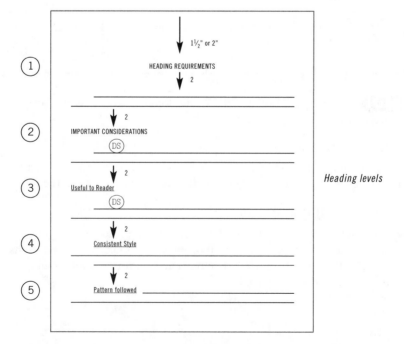

Heading levels

NOTE Use style features of word-processing software for headings and body text.

♦ Because mixing double and triple spacing on a computer can be both a nuisance and time-consuming, use double spacing throughout the report. Always tab for new paragraphs when using double spacing.

K51   Numbering systems

If information will be presented in sections and subsections, use a consistent pattern of numbers, letters, and indents so that the reader can easily identify the relative importance of the material. The following system works well.

    I. A major topic.
        A. A section of the major topic.
            1. The next subsection.
                a. Part of 1, above.
                    (1) A subsection of a.
                    (2) A second subsection of a.
                b. Another part of 1, above.
            2. A second subsection.
        B. Another section of the major topic.

    II. The next major topic.
        A. A section of this major topic.

NOTE The five-space or $^1/_2$" tabs preset on your software are useful here.

K52   Ending the pages

Each page should have a bottom margin of 1". *Exception*: You can adjust the bottom margin by $^1/_2$" to accommodate one lone line.

    The software will page automatically, but follow these rules and make adjustments if necessary:

♦ Keep at least two lines of a paragraph at the foot of one page and always show at least two lines at the top of the next page to avoid widows and orphans.

Orphan The first line of a paragraph appears by itself on the last line of a page.

Widow The last line of a paragraph appears by itself as the first line of a page. Most software has automatic widow/orphan control.

♦ With three-line paragraphs, fit all three lines at the foot of one page or carry all three over to the top of the next. Use the *"Keep Lines Together"* feature to accomplish this.

♦ Do *not* key a heading on one page and the body on the next so that the heading is isolated. Use *"Keep Lines Together."*

♦ Do *not* break tables unless they are very long and have natural breaking points in them. Use *"Keep Lines Together."*

K

K53 Numbering the pages

Introduction (table of contents, preface)

◆ Leave these unnumbered unless many pages are involved.

◆ Use roman numerals or letters of the alphabet if several pages are involved with each section, and place these at the foot, centred. Count the title page as *i* (1), but do not show the number.

Body

◆ Word-processing software can automatically insert *headers* and *footers* on subsequent pages (page titles and page numbers). At your choice, the information will remain the same; the page number will increase automatically.

◆ Leave the first page unnumbered.

◆ Number the second and succeeding pages either 1″ from the top line or 1″ from the bottom edge of the page, at the centre or on the right side.

◆ Discontinue the headers on the endnotes or notes pages, but keep the page numbers on these pages.

Ending (appendices, bibliography, index)

◆ Number these as part of the report or as separate sections.

◆ Use roman numerals, arabic numerals in parentheses, or letters of the alphabet if several pages are involved within each section, and place these at the foot.

◆ Use a numbering system that has not already been used in the introductory pages.

K54 Displayed information

Numbered or bulleted lists

◆ Align with the margins or indent $^1/_2$″. Using automatic indent is the fastest method.

> NOTE Use the automatic-numbering features of word-processing software.

◆ Single-space each numbered item but double-space between them.

1. Enumerations occur frequently in reports and deserve special treatment.

2. Display these by means of spacing and indents.

Tabulated material

If the material has already been keyed in a spreadsheet or other document, import it into the new document if possible so that rekeying is avoided. If keying is needed:

◆ See K67–69.

◆ Do *not* let tables extend beyond the margins of the body text.

◆ Use single spacing.

◆ Consider using a different font. A new font could be used to highlight material or so that the table takes less space.

◆ Leave a blank line above and below the table.

◆ Insert a footnote for a table directly below it, rather than at the foot of the page.

K55 Graphics

Graphics—pie charts, line graphs, bar graphs—can be used effectively in reports to replace text and present complex information in a simple format.

◆ If using integrated software, prepare graphics separately and then incorporate them into the text. Graphics from spreadsheets created on non-integrated software can be imported into most word-processing software.

◆ If a list of illustrations is required, insert this as a separate sheet after the body of the report and before the bibliography.

K56 Special effects

Change point sizes and fonts for variety. Justify the right margin to add a professional look. Use lines and shading effectively. Keep pages simple and uncluttered. Don't overdo it, though. These text enhancers lose their value if they are overused.

White space is a very important tool to use with page design. White space is empty space—margins, spacing between lines, etc. Use this space to set off the design of the page and to give the page a look of balance, clarity, simplicity, and organization. Again, don't overdo it (see K82).

K57 Quoted material

Short quotations

Quotations of three lines or fewer should appear in the body of the report within quotation marks. End each with a raised numeral indicating a footnote or endnote reference. If the software cannot produce raised numbers (superscript), show the numerals in brackets [1] or parentheses (1).

Quoting complete sentences

Use quotation marks, begin the quotation with a capital, and end it with a period:

> Writers should be aware that "Quotations of just a few lines are double-spaced and placed within quotation marks."[2]

Quoting parts of sentences

Use the ellipsis (. . .) to indicate that not all of the sentence from which the quotation is taken has been used:

Writers should be aware that quotations and paraphrases ". . . of just a few lines are double-spaced."[1]

Writers should be aware that quotations ". . . of just a few lines . . ."[1] are double-spaced and may be introduced and ended by the ellipsis.

NOTE If the closing ellipsis comes at the end of the sentence, add a period (i.e., ...).

Long quotations
For quotations longer than three lines
◆ Leave a line of space above and below the quoted material.
◆ Single-space the quoted material.
◆ Indent $1/_2$" on each side of the margins.
◆ Do *not* use quotation marks.
◆ Indent the first line an additional $1/_2$" if quoting from the beginning of a paragraph:

> Dorothy Farmiloe says on this subject:
>
> > An appendix is the place to put supplementary material not essential to the report but which may aid the reader's understanding of it in some way.[2]

◆ If the quotation opens partway through a sentence, use an ellipsis to begin the quotation.
◆ If the quotation closes with an incomplete sentence, use the ellipsis *plus* a period at the end.

K58 Footnotes, endnotes, and textnotes
◆ Footnotes appear on the page on which the referenced material appears.
◆ Endnotes provide the same information as footnotes but are keyed on one separate sheet headed "Notes" or "Endnotes" at the end of the section, chapter, or report.
◆ Textnotes provide a third choice for showing references. Here, the writer records the information source in parentheses at the appropriate point in the document. Textnotes are not numbered. Usually a short version is used and full information is provided in a bibliography.

> Bartering involved the exchange of goods or services for other goods or services; no money changed hands. (Bedford et al., *The Canadian Office*, p. 2)

For academic situations, follow the style stipulated by the institution. Endnotes and textnotes are increasingly being used in other situations as well because they are so easy to produce. Footnotes, endnotes, and textnotes are also used as follows:

◆ to provide additional useful information on a particular topic to that noted in the body of the report

6.   For more detailed information on Canada's population, consult the statistical data published regularly by Statistics Canada.

◆ to identify the source of information quoted exactly or paraphrased

11.   H. Ramsey Fowler et al., The Little, Brown Handbook, 2nd Canadian ed. (Don Mills, ON: Addison-Wesley, 1998), p. 117.

K59   Numbering notes

Textnotes are not numbered. Sophisticated software offers automatic footnoting or endnoting and is very easy to use. If this feature is not available, do the following:

◆ Use arabic numerals and number each quotation or reference consecutively. Use asterisks when only a few references are needed.

◆ In the body, insert the reference numbers a half line above the regular keying line at the *end* of the quotation or reference, outside any punctuation, and without space before it. If your software does not offer superscript, number as in example 2 below.

1.   ... spacing is as you would expect."[2]
2.   ... spacing is as you would expect."[2]

In the footnote or endnote itself, the numeral may or may not be raised. When using the automatic footnoting feature, this decision will be made by the software used.

K60   Keying footnotes

Footnotes must be inserted on the page on which the reference appears. Software with automatic footnoting does most of the work for you. You simply key in the appropriate reference information when you key in the quotation, and the software positions the reference correctly.

◆ Single-space footnote references and leave a single space between them.

◆ If the text is short on the last page, still insert footnotes at the *foot* of the page.

◆ Follow the style of either example shown below. They will suit most applications. However, academic institutions may have specific requirements and these must, of course, be followed.

◆ Follow the order and punctuation shown in K62, which vary with the type of publication being cited.

1.   Jonathon Whelan, *E-Mail @ Work: Get Moving with Digital Communications* (Toronto: Pearson Education Canada, 2000), p. 204.

NOTE   Italicize or underline names of books, magazines, newspapers, and periodicals.

K61   Keying endnotes

Sophisticated software numbers endnotes automatically. Follow these guidelines:

- Use a separate sheet.
- Start $1^1/_2$" or 2" from top margin.
- Use the heading "Notes" and centre it.
- Single-space each reference and double-space after each one.
- If continuation pages are required, start 1" from top margin and use a page numbering system that has not already been used (e.g., lower-case roman numerals).
- The finished page(s) appear after the body of the document and in front of the bibliography.

NOTES

1. Aspasia Kaplaneris, "Earthbound . . . for Now," *Between Worlds: A Reader, Rhetoric, and Handbook*, 1st Canadian ed., ed. Susan Bachmann, Melinda Barth, and Karen Golets Pancer (Don Mills, ON: Addison-Wesley, 1998), p. 139.

2. Chris Howard, "Performance Appraisals: Appraise This!" *Canadian Business*, 29 May 1998, p. 24.

K62   Keying textnotes

- If a work is short and no bibliography is to be provided, include a full reference the first time it is used and a short one thereafter:

    Jonathon Whelan, *E-Mail @ Work: Get Moving with Digital Communications* (Toronto: Pearson Education Canada, 2000), p. 204.

- If a bibliography is provided, short references are appropriate throughout the document:

    Whelan, *E-Mail @ Work*, p. 204.

K63   Constructing references

Provided here are standard, acceptable methods. Some academic institutions and publishers have set rules in this regard and their preferences should be followed. Simplicity is the keynote in the style suggested here.

Anthologies and collections

In references to a selection from the collected works of one author, state the author and the work, the title (in italics or underscored), the name(s) of the editor(s), the place of publication, the publisher, the year of publication, and the page number:

1. W. B. Yeats, "The Lake Isle of Innisfree," <u>W. B. Yeats Selected Poems</u> (New York: Gramercy Books, 1992), p. 57.

If a reference is made to a work in an anthology, follow this pattern:

1. Alice Walker, "Even as I Hold You," *Poetry: A Longman Pocket Anthology*, 2nd ed., ed. R. S. Gwynn (New York: Addison-Wesley Educational Publishers Inc., 1998), p. 313.

Books

Full footnote The standard footnote includes the footnote number, the author(s) and/or editor(s), the book title, the place of publication, the publisher, the year of publication, and the page number(s):

> 5. H. Ramsey Fowler, et al., <u>The Little, Brown Handbook</u>, 2nd Canadian ed. (Don Mills, ON: Addison-Wesley, 1998), p. 117.

◆ For two authors, list their names in the order used on the title page of the book:

> 6. T. Palmer and V. D'Amico, <u>Accounting for Canadian Colleges</u>, 2nd ed. (Toronto: Addison Wesley, 2001), p. 206.

◆ For more than two authors, state the first author and then add *et al.* (and others):

> 7. Burnett et al., <u>Introduction to Integrated Marketing Communications</u> (Toronto, ON: Prentice Hall Inc., 2001), p. 25.

Non-print sources

For CD-ROMs, recordings, tapes, interviews, speeches, videos, and performances, provide sufficient information for the reader to identify and locate the source if necessary:

> 17. Personal interview with Mr. Alan Nelson, Manager, Mentor Guaranty Ltd., Red Deer, Alberta, December 21, 2003.

> 18. Ramsden, Peter G. "Iroquois," in *The 1997 Canadian World Encyclopedia* (CD-ROM), Toronto: McClelland and Stewart, 1997.

The Internet

When referencing information from the internet, give the website name, location, etc.:

◆ to calculate the worth of the Canadian dollar in other currencies

> www.bloomberg.com/invest/calculators/currency.html

◆ Canadian Human Rights Commission

> www.chrc-ccdp.ca

◆ to gain access to Canadian postal codes

> www.canadapost.ca

◆ resource for investors; provides investors with research on public companies traded on most North American stock exchanges

> www.stockgroupmedia.com

Magazines and newspapers

State the author's name, the article title (in quotation marks), the magazine or newspaper name (italicized or underscored), the month and year of publication, and the page numbers if possible:

> 11. Brian Bergman, "Software on Demand," *Maclean's*, 25 May 1998, p. 48.

> 12. Lisa Wright, "Selling Yourself the Write Way: How to Sharpen Your Résumé," <u>Toronto Star</u>, June 3, 1998, E1.

K

Other

For referencing sources other than printed material, you might divide them into sections, for example, Section A, Interviews; Section B, Radio/television programs; Section C, Movies; Section D, Musical performances or compositions; and Section E, Videotapes, etc.:

Section A—Interviews

> Interview with Jenny McCartney, Professor, Mohawk College, Hamilton, ON. March 23, 2006
> Interview with Dennis Heming, DHT Travel, Owner, Hamilton, ON. February 16, 2006.

Section B—Radio/television programs

> *The Money Market,* prod. John Sourdough, CBC Special, February 13, 2006.
> *Investing for the Future,* prod. Carmen Bisson, NBC Special, June 2006.

Section C—Movies

> *Titanic,* dir. James Cameron, Leonardo DiCaprio and Kate Winslet, Paramount and 20th Century Fox, 1998.

Section D—Musical performances

> George Frideric Handel, *Messiah,* ed. Watkins Shaw, Novello Handel Edition (Sevenoaks, Eng.: Novello, n.d.).

NOTE *n.d.* means no date.

Section E—Videotapes

> *Serenade,* chor. George Balanchine. Perf. San Francisco Ballet. Dir. Hilary Bean. 1981. Videocassette. PBS Video, 1987.

Shortened and recurring references

After a work has been cited in full once or is to be shown in the bibliography, shortened references may be used following any of these styles:

♦ the *short form* (author, title, page number)

♦ et al. (*et alii,* meaning "and other people"): this refers to three or more authors; list only the first author's name followed by et al.

♦ ibid. (short form of *ibidem,* meaning "in the same place"): this refers the reader back to the immediately preceding footnote

♦ op. cit. (*opere citato,* meaning "in the work cited"): this refers the reader back to a previously cited work but a different page number

♦ loc. cit. (*loco citato,* "in the place cited"): this refers the reader back to the previously cited work, same page number

> 11. Palmer and D'Amico, Accounting for Canadian Colleges, p. 283.
> 12. Ibid., p. 304.
> 13. Sharman, The Business Bible, p. 147.
> 14. Reid, op. cit., p. 326.
> 15. Sharman, loc. cit.

NOTE Of these methods, the short form is preferred in business reports and academic papers. The other references are rarely used now.

►K64 Bibliography and references

The bibliography is an alphabetical list of all the source material consulted by the author in the preparation of the report. Usually shown in each entry are the author(s) and/or editor(s), title, place of publication, publisher, and date of publication.

If using the footnoting feature of the software, automatically generate a bibliography with no need to rekey. If you must, you can create one yourself:

- Key the bibliography on a separate page (or pages).
- Use the same margins as for the body. Start the first page $1^{1}/_{2}"$ or $2"$ from the top edge of the paper and succeeding pages $1"$ from the top.
- Number pages as part of the report, or use roman numerals but leave the first page unnumbered.
- Centre and capitalize the main heading.
- Start the first line at the margin and indent the second and succeeding continuation lines $^{1}/_{2}"$ from the margin (hanging indent style).
- Single-space each reference and leave a line space between them.
- Do not number bibliographic references.
- Follow the punctuation shown in the illustration.
- Note that the first author is listed by family name first.
- When the work does not have either an author or editor or the person's name is not known, position the work in alphabetical order by the first word in the title, ignoring *A, An,* or *The.*

K

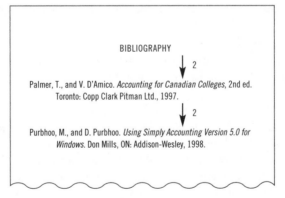

BIBLIOGRAPHY

↓ 2

Palmer, T., and V. D'Amico. *Accounting for Canadian Colleges,* 2nd ed. Toronto: Copp Clark Pitman Ltd., 1997.

↓ 2

Purbhoo, M., and D. Purbhoo. *Using Simply Accounting Version 5.0 for Windows.* Don Mills, ON: Addison-Wesley, 1998.

TYPICAL BIBLIOGRAPHY ENTRIES

One author	Rock, Michael E. *Ethics: To Live By, to Work By.* Toronto: Holt, Rinehart, 1992.
Two authors	Cox, Michael, and Michael Rock. *The Seven Pillars of Visionary Leadership.* Toronto: Dryden, 1997.
Three or more authors	Bedford, Jennie M. et al. *The Canadian Office: Systems and Procedures.* Toronto: Copp Clark Pitman Ltd., 1995.
Second book by same author(s)	——. *The Canadian Office: Systems and Procedures, Instructor's Manual.* Toronto: Copp Clark Pitman Ltd., 1995.
Editor(s) as authors	Hattersley, M., and L. McJanet (eds.). *Management Communication: Principles and Practice.* Boston: McGraw-Hill, 1997.
Magazine article	Howard, Chris, "Performance Appraisals: Appraise This!" *Canadian Business*, 29 May 1998, p. 24.
Newspaper	Wright, Lisa, "Selling Yourself the Write Way: How to Sharpen Your Résumé." *Toronto Star*, 3 June, 1998, E1.
Institution as author and publisher	Certified General Accountant's Association of Canada. *International Financial Management*, ed. Jim Storrey. Vancouver: Certified General Accountant's Association of Canada, 1997.
Government publication	Canada. *Career Handbook.* Ottawa: Human Resources Development Canada, 1996.
Non-print sources	Cockburn, Bruce. *The Charity of Night.* Toronto: True North, 1997.

NOTE You can also use the term "References" (same as Bibliography) to indicate sources of information in the report. If the report is short, place the References a double-space below the body of the report. If there are several references, use the traditional format and place on a separate page.

▶K65   Glossary

The glossary is a list of difficult or special technical terms used in a report, thesis, or book. It is usually included in formal or lengthy reports.

▶K66   Index

An index is an alphabetical listing of all topics and their page numbers. It is often provided with very lengthy reports and academic papers.

Indexes will vary considerably with the nature of the material. However, use the same margins and starting and finishing lines as the rest of the document. Plan your work so that the information is easy to follow.

Some software permits the automatic generation of an index if the required references are indicated as the document is keyed.

K67   TABLES (TABULATION)

To tabulate means to set up information in columns so that it is easy to read and attractive in format.

Spreadsheet software does *all* the work for you. Word-processing software offers features such as tables and decimal tabs that simplify the keying of tabulations. However, you must position margins and tab stops.

Before you get into time-consuming calculations, take advantage of the many shortcuts the software offers, such as the following:

◆ Use the pre-set (default) tabs and estimate how the tabulation will look on the page. Insert or delete space or move blocks later.

◆ Use the table feature.

◆ Save the format for frequently used tabulations (e.g., in monthly reports).

SCOTT NEHLAWI ENTERPRISES
Sales by Area: May 20--

Area	Dealer	Amount
N. Ontario	Maria Kim	$92 468
Manitoba	Raj Kumar	90 650
Quebec	Daniel Keith	87 943

▶ **K68   Positioning tables in documents**

If the table is to be keyed on one page, it should be centred on the page by using the page-centring feature.

◆ Try to keep tables to one page.

◆ If the table is part of a document, it should be designed to fit within the margins of the rest of the document.

◆ Avoid breaking a table. Note the following possibilities for dealing with this situation:

  • Carry the whole table to the next page and leave extra space on the previous page.

  • Position the table in an appropriate location where it will fit and not disrupt the flow of the reading.

NOTE   Use the header row and row break features available in the table feature.

▶ **K69   Keying tabulations**

Note the following points.

Abbreviations

To save space in tables, abbreviations are permitted. However, use these sparingly and consult Unit 1, T96, for help with standard ones.

Numbers

Whole numbers Align these from the right (units, tens, hundreds, etc.):

```
127
 32
159
```

Separate digits into groups of three by using commas; this prevents fraudulent alterations.

```
1 205              12,141
        – but –
1 630               1,630
```

> **NOTE** The metric system in Canada uses spaces rather than commas to separate digits into groups of three for numbers greater than 9999. The major accounting associations consulted do not have a set policy on comma usage. Most accounting firms use the comma, as do law firms (the comma is the natural connector for keeping numbers together and prevents fraud).

Decimals Align the decimal point using a consistent style. Use the decimal tab feature as a great time-saver here, bearing in mind that tabs must be set for the decimal point, not the start of the column.

```
9.00              9.0        0.93               0.93
        – but –                      – not –
15.51             15.51      2.91               2.91
```

Dollar signs Position these to accommodate the longest line, but insert at the beginning of columns and in subtotals and totals only:

```
  $ 37
  1,021
 $1,058
```

Percentage signs Place these after the figure. Use after the first entry and on totals or subtotals only.

```
50%
```

Times Align the hours and minutes at the colon:

```
 9:15 a.m.
10:36 p.m.
```

Totals Follow the spacing shown below.

```
127
 32
159
```

References

Source references used with tabulations are normally positioned *under* the table rather than in a footnote or endnote.

JANUARY TOTALS*

N. Ontario	Manitoba	Quebec
72 468	100 650	67 943
9 005	20 725	6 319
37 291	5 432	18 250
118 764	126 807	92 512

*Statistics Canada, May 20--

K70 FINANCIAL STATEMENTS

Financial statements are reports prepared regularly for management that show the worth of the company, the operating results, the cash flow, and a host of other information used for decision making.

The two main financial statements are the balance sheet and the income statement. A properly keyed balance sheet is shown in Unit 19, "Math and Financial Management."

Accounting software packages, such as AccPac or Simply Accounting, will generate or produce financial statements.

K71 LEGAL DOCUMENTS

Preparing legal documents is straightforward. Simply apply the usual rules of style and, with some modifications, the rules of report keying (see K42).

◆ If you are employed by a legal firm, follow the style guide of your office.

◆ If you do not work in a legal office and are required to complete legal documents, consult a specialized reference source.

K72 METRIC EXPRESSIONS

The style to be used in keying common metric terms, units of measure, and their symbols is as follows.

▶K73 Symbols

◆ Use only the symbols specified in the SI Metric System (see "Metric System" in the Appendix).

◆ Use symbols rather than terms with numbers:

30 m   – *not* –   30 metres   – *but* –   thirty metres

◆ Use lowercase, except when the symbol is derived from the name of an individual:

mm *for* millimetre   *Exception:* Use capital *L* for litre:
N *for* Newton   3 mL   2 L
C *for* Celsius

♦ Leave a space between quantity and symbols:

2.75 m

The degree sign occupies the space in temperature expressions:

32°C

♦ Do not start a sentence with a symbol:

Distance is expressed in metres.

– *not* –

m is used to express distance.

♦ Do not pluralize metric symbols—the singular and plural forms are the same:

1 kg   75 kg

♦ Symbols are not abbreviations. Use a period only if the symbol occurs at the end of a sentence:

He bought 0.75 kg of cherries.

He bought 0.75 kg.

♦ Show square and cubic symbols by means of exponents (numerals keyed a half-line higher). Use superscript on your word-processing equipment or a half-line on a typewriter.

16 m^2 32 cm^3

♦ Use the solidus (/) or right oblique to represent *per:*

He drove at 60 km/h.

▶ K74   Numbers

♦ Express fractions as decimals:

2.75 kg   – *not* – $2^3/_4$ kg

♦ Use a zero in front of the decimal point when no whole number is shown:

0.75 kg

♦ Use hard spaces/non-breaking spaces to group figures into blocks of three for numbers over 9999. This applies to grouping on both sides of the decimal point. The space may be omitted in four-digit numbers unless these numbers are listed in a column with other numbers of five digits or more.

17[ ]243.57 m   1467 m

▶ K75   Numeric times and dates

Numeric times and dates are not metric expressions but are related because they are methods of measurement.

♦ Bring the date in from the network for productivity purposes, e.g., year, month, day; year (four digits, space, month (two digits), space, day (two digits):

20-- 04 12 (meaning April 12, 20--)

◆ When times are based on the 12-hour clock, use four digits and separate hours and minutes with a colon:

12:00 p.m.   11:42 a.m.

◆ When times are based on the 24-hour clock, no punctuation is used between the hours and the minutes:

0430   1622

K76 SPACING RULES

▶ K77 Spacing rules for symbols

Symbol	Spacing	Example
Addition	one on each side	$3 + 2 = 5$
Ampersand (&)	one before and one after*	Smith & Wesson
At (@) (each costing)	one on each side	2 @ $15 = $30
Cent sign	one after	He paid 75¢ for it.
Decimal	no space	1.05
Degree symbol	no space	30°C
Division	one on each side	$6 \div 2 = 3$
Dollar sign	one before	She paid $15.
Equality	one on each side	$6 \times 2 = 12$
Feet	no space before, one after	He was 6' tall.
Inches	no space before, one after	He was 6' 2" tall.
Multiplication	one on each side	6×2
Number (#)	one before, none after	17 Avenue Rd., #3
Oblique or right slash	no space	3 3/5; and/or; 31 km/h
Percentage (%)	none before, one after	5% plus 10%
Subtraction	one on each side	$6 - 2 = 4$

*But not in all-cap abbreviations: R&D

▶ K78 Spacing rules for punctuation marks

See the chart on punctuation marks and spacing on the next page.

NOTE **Proportional spacing** Each letter of a proportional typeface takes up a different amount of space (e.g., "i" uses less space than "m"). Times New Roman is an example of a proportional typeface. Non-proportional typefaces, like Courier New, assign the same amount of space to every letter. See the examples below:

The quick brown fox jumped over the lazy dog. [Times New Roman font]
```
The quick brown fox jumped over the lazy dog. [Courier New font]
```

NOTE See Unit 1, T131, for spacing in metric expressions.

K79 EDITING AND PROOFREADING

Editing and proofreading are often thought to mean the same thing. In fact, they don't.

K

Editing means checking and revising content and style, asking questions such as: Is it accurate? Is it clear? Does it say what I want? Have I made the best selection of words? Does it develop logically? If you are editing someone else's work and have questions about the content, check with the originator.

Punctuation mark	Spacing	Example
Apostrophe		
as possessive	no space	The manager's office
as omission sign	no space	Aren't you coming?
Colon		
as punctuation	proportional type: one after non-proportional: two	He bought: disks, He bought: disks,
as time	none before or after	10:30 p.m.
as ratio	none before or after	3:6 is 1:2
Comma	one after	a desk, a chair, a phone
Dash	two hyphens without spaces	He can--he said.
Exclamation mark	proportional: one after non-proportional: two	Good grief! What Good grief! What
Hyphen	no space	editor-in-chief
Parentheses	one before the opening, one after the closing	Can you (as a friend) do this?
Period		
◆ at sentence end	proportional: one space non-proportional: two	Go home. It's time. Go home. It's time.
◆ after abbreviations with:		
◆ one abbreviation in caps	one space	Mr. J. Chong
◆ two abbreviations or more in caps	no space	S.C.I.B.
◆ any abbreviations in lowercase	no space	f.o.b.
Question mark	proportional: one after non-proportional: two	Can you? Will you? Can you? Will you?
Quotation marks	one before opening quotation and one or two after completing quotation (if a punctuation mark ends the closing quotation, use the spacing required by that punctuation mark)	"Is the letter ready?" Mr. Winters asked.
Semicolon	one after	She went east; he went west.

Proofreading means checking against the original to ensure there are no errors or omissions; checking for the mechanics of language such as grammar, punctuation, and spelling; and checking that the format details are correct.

The better job you do of onscreen proofing and editing, the more productive, efficient, and cost-effective you will be. This is an area where care is needed because onscreen proofing is more difficult than proofing from hard copy.

- Use the spell-check feature to find obvious errors. Do not rely solely on the spell-check feature as there may be many errors that it cannot check. Spell checkers do not recognize homonyms (words that sound alike but are spelled differently). They do not know what words or sections have been omitted and cannot indicate inaccuracies in figures, for example. Fortunately for keyboarders, some software packages offer a feature that will automatically correct common spelling errors as you key, such as transposed characters—*adn* will be corrected to *and, recieve* corrected to *receive,* etc.

- Use the thesaurus if you keep running into the same word. It will quickly provide you with choices so that the writing is varied.

- Grammar- and style-check features of your software program are also useful in this area; however, use them with discretion. You do not have to accept every suggestion for improvement that they make.

- Redlining, Review, and Tracking features are useful for group proofing and editing. Changes made are not final.

- Check that you have been consistent in your word treatments (e.g., did you use "email" or "e-mail" throughout the report?). Find and replace is valuable here.

- Move the cursor from line to line as you read.

- Ask someone else to proofread the screen as you read aloud from the original.

- For complex tasks—tabulations, for example—isolate the section by putting it into a second document and edit it there.

The editing of documents that word-processing software permits can cause its own problems:

- Be sure that if a paragraph is replaced, the old one has been deleted.

- Be sure that if text has been moved, it is in the right place.

- Be sure that moved text does not appear twice.

- Be sure that new, added, or imported material is consistent in format with the rest.

Frequently recurring errors to watch for include the following:

- errors in headings

- repeats of words at the beginnings and ends of lines

- keying *you* for *your, now* for *not*

- transposing numbers, such as phone numbers, money amounts, street addresses, e.g., *1081* for *1801,* etc.

K

◆ errors in titles, e.g., *Ms.* instead of *Mrs.*

◆ errors in spacing

◆ format inconsistencies, e.g, indenting paragraphs

When lists of items are keyed, count them to make sure nothing has been missed.

Proofread the hard copy as well when you have printed it out.

K80 PROOFREADING MARKS

These symbols are generally used in correcting communications produced as rough drafts. The list includes those needed for desktop publishing applications as well as those used in routine document production.

Meaning	Symbol	Edited	Correction
Align horizontally	=	Lakshmi By	By Lakshmi
Align vertically	||	Bluffers Park Guildwood	Bluffers Park Guildwood
Because	b/c		
Change hyphen to dash	– –	ready-made to	ready—made to
Change punctuation to a period	⊙	Stay there	Stay there.
Change word	—	manufacture We produce	We manufacture
Close up	⌒	per cent	percent
Delete and close up	⌒/	per/cent	percent
Delete letter	℮	better writings	better writing
Delete underscore	ℓ——ℓ	very long day	very long day
Delete word	～℮	offer you quality	offer quality
Double space	ds⌈	ds⌈That should be ⌊the way to work.	That should be the way to work.
Drop below the line	∧	H2O	H_2O
Indent 1 em space	⊡	⊡Tea's ready!	Tea's ready!
Insert 1 en dash	$\frac{1}{N}$	1997$\frac{1}{N}$1998	1997–1998
Insert 1 em dash	$\frac{1}{M}$	the desk$\frac{1}{M}$ not used	the desk—not used
Insert a hyphen	$\overline{\overline{\wedge}}$	ready made	ready-made

(continued . . .)

Meaning	Symbol	Edited	Correction
Insert letter or word	∧	pr͡ze and ͡was	prize and it was
Insert punctuation mark(s)	ᵛᵛ∧ ∧ᵛ ⌄ ∨ᵛ	ᵛᵛHome∧James∧ don't spare the horses∨	"Home, James; don't spare the horses."
Insert space	# ∧ {	withit for͡he	with it for the
Leave in, do not omit (stet)	_ _ _ _	This ~~service~~ will	This service will
Make all capitals	≡	B̲e̲n̲j̲a̲m̲i̲n̲	BENJAMIN
Make capital letter small (lc)	/	at this ₵ompany	at this company
Make italic	——	P̲.̲O̲.̲H̲.̲	*P.O.H.*
Make a small letter capital (uc)	≡	w̲hen she arrives	When she arrives
Move as shown	♂	is available ⟨to you⟩	is available
Move number of spaces in direction shown	5]	5]By the time	By the time
	[5	[5By the time	By the time
New paragraph	¶	¶ During the last	During the last
Raise above this line	∨	according to Jones∨	according to Jones[1]
Single space	SS⌐ ss	⌐payroll preparation ⌐various employees	payroll preparation various employees
Spell out, do not abbreviate	○	Bring ④ books. Third ⟨Ave.⟩	Bring four books. Third Avenue
Transpose letters or words	∿ ∿	rec͡i͡eve receipts⟨cheques and⟩	receive receipts and cheques
Others Bottom margin	*bm*		
Top margin	*tm*		
Hard page break/ forced page break	*Hpg*		Break the page here.
Soft page break	*Spg*		Natural page break.
Without	*w/o*		
Wrong font	*wf*	*wf* Be bold.	Be bold.

K

K81   PRODUCTIVITY TIPS

Whether preparing transcripts from notes, a recorded tape, a handwritten or keyed draft, or an in-person dictation, aim for productivity in the workplace. Prepare in advance by using the following guidelines:

- ◆ Gather any special supplies and reference sources (e.g., articles, books, magazines, or file folders) with pertinent information that may be needed.

- ◆ Look up information *before* keying the documents (e.g., proper spelling of names, addresses, etc.).

- ◆ Keep a reference section on file or on disk (for speedy access).

- ◆ Keep the information updated for future use.

- ◆ Set aside time for large keying jobs so that you can make progress and save time.

- ◆ Proofread all work carefully; have someone else look it over before sending to print if there is going to be a mass mailing or printing of the material (saves time and money).

- ◆ Bookmark frequently referenced internet webpages (e.g., special features, grammar rules, etc.).

- ◆ For letters, use the full block or simplified style and open punctuation.

- ◆ Eliminate periods after initials.

- ◆ Because mixing double and triple spacing in some software can be a problem, double spacing after main headings, before side headings, and under page numbers in headings is quite acceptable.

- ◆ With proportional type, use only one space after periods, question marks, exclamation marks, and colons.

Keying from written notes

- ◆ Check for urgent items and deal with them first (prioritize your work).

- ◆ Read each item through before keying and check on special instructions to make sure you understand what must be done.

- ◆ Keep special notes or instructions in a notepad, and draw a diagonal line through each item as it is completed.

Keying from recorded tapes

See K103 for in-depth information on machine/microtranscription.

K82   MAKING DOCUMENTS ATTRACTIVE

Today's software permits better-looking documents, close to what is achieved with desktop publishing (DTP). Some offer a variety of fonts and some basic drawing and charting tools. You can create multiple newspaper-style columns. You can also include bulleted lists and graphics from the package or from supplementary clip-art packages.

Use some creativity and make your work visually stunning but also businesslike. Business documents do not have to look dull. Some suggestions are as follows:

- ◆ Use an appropriate graphic on the cover page of a report.
- ◆ Use borders around information that should be emphasized.
- ◆ Use the vast array of fonts available to add some sparkle. Use the fonts with knowledge, however. A serif font, such as Times Roman, is good for most applications because the serifs (small "feet" attached to the letters) make the work easier to read. A sans serif font (without serifs) like Arial is harder to read but is excellent for headings.
- ◆ Change the spacing if you wish. Most software will allow, for example, spacing that is a little wider than single spacing but not as great as double, or a little more than double, and so on. This can add interesting variety to an otherwise dull-looking document.
- ◆ Some software provides character sets to enhance document appearance (dashes, bullets, fractions, multinational symbols, box drawing, borders, icons, and math and science symbols). Use these to good effect.

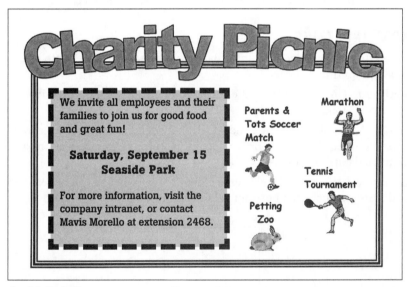

Special effects ideas

K83   DOCUMENT STYLE MANUALS

The style manual can take many forms. It might be a simple binder containing samples of properly formatted and keyed documents. In its most sophisticated form, it might be a professionally produced document containing examples of communications, inputting procedures, records management procedures, and language and style instructions. Ideally, the pages that make up the manual will be saved on disk and updated and reissued as needed. On a networked system, a hard copy is not really necessary provided a proper backup system is in place. Users can simply access relevant parts from a shared database as required. Make sure updated information is made available to all support staff who will benefit from the information.

WORDS OF WISDOM

People know you for what you have done,
not for what you plan to do.

PART 2

DOCUMENT PROCESSING

K84 DOCUMENT-PROCESSING CYCLE

The stages through which a document passes from the original idea to its final destination are usually referred to as the *document processing cycle*.

K85 INPUTTING

When the original ideas and information have been combined into a document, inputting is needed.

Keyboard This is currently the most frequently used input device for word processing.

Mouse A graphical user interface (GUI) between user and screen allows a user to select menu options from icons (pictures of the applications and commands) using a mouse.

Scanner Keyed, printed, and even handwritten information can be scanned and stored without the need for rekeying.

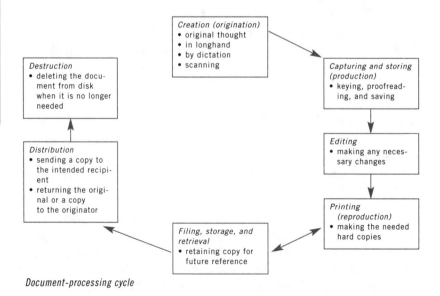

Document-processing cycle

Voice recognition The operator simply speaks through voice recognition equipment. This technology already has many applications. See Unit 12.

K86 WORD-PROCESSING SOFTWARE

Word-processing software packages range from extremely simple to extremely sophisticated and from cheap to expensive. They can vary from creating simple "words on paper" to creating documents that can support sound and video. All software provides basic editing and formatting; the more sophisticated packages contain a great number of additional features.

K87 SOFTWARE FEATURES

**Basic editing and formatting standard
to all word-processing software**

- ◆ Text may be edited (changed) by inserting, deleting, or striking over, and text may be moved to other locations.
- ◆ All software has default (inbuilt) settings for margins, starting line, line lengths, lines per page, and tabs appropriate for routine documents. These settings can be customized as needed.
- ◆ Centring, indenting, justifying (an even right-hand margin), underlining, boldfacing, and decimal tab are standard.
- ◆ Word-wrap and page breaks are routine, and spacing, font, and point variations are easily achieved.
- ◆ Storage and retrieval of text is routine, as is the ability to print in a variety of typefaces.

Additional possible software features

Calculating ability This feature allows you to calculate numbers you enter into columns of your document—subtotals, totals, and grand totals.

Conversion Some software can convert documents produced on another manufacturer's software.

Customizing You can customize your software in several ways. These include measurements (decimal or imperial) of lines and cursor positions, screen colours, symbols, and printer types.

Find and replace The software can be instructed to find expressions or words and insert others in their place.

Fonts Fonts are type styles. Most software allows you to change font styles and sizes at any point in the document.

Grammar check This permits the automatic checking of specific grammar, punctuation, and style points.

Graphics Some programs include their own graphics (clip art) collections and/or allow for the importation of others.

Headers and footers Pages may be automatically identified with a caption and with incremental page numbering either at the top or the bottom.

K

Hyphenation This feature tidies up the right margin by dividing words where needed. "Manual" lets you decide. "Auto" automatically hyphenates according to rules set in the software.

Line drawing This feature allows you to draw lines and create boxes. Lines can be horizontal or vertical, and both thickness and density can be varied.

Line numbering This is useful for documents to be discussed line by line.

Logical operators Logical operators are used in formulas and functions where numbers are compared in two or more cells. The comparison will be either true or false, i.e., the conditions are met or they are not met.

Macros These allow short, frequently used expressions to be keyed, saved, and recalled with a single keystroke as desired.

Merge Form letters can be combined with a mailing list stored on disk to produce what appear to be original letters.

Newspaper-style columns These are particularly useful for desktop publishing applications, can be used for reports, and can speed up some tabulation tasks.

Redlining Where several people are working on a document, you can indicate parts to be added, deleted, or amended.

Sorting Some software will allow you to sort information alphabetically, and some alphabetically or numerically.

Spell checker Spell checkers "read" the text and identify misspelled words for correcting.

Split screen Two parts of a document can be viewed on the screen at the same time.

Syntax checker This is a support feature that checks capitalization, grammar, phrasing, and other types of syntax errors.

Thesaurus This provides alternatives to words used and is a useful feature for writers.

Windowing Some software can display many screens (or "windows") at one time. You can work on a different file in each window, switching easily, without having to continually open and close files.

WYSIWYG (What You See Is What You Get) This feature allows you to view the document onscreen before printing, so that positioning can be checked.

K88 INTEGRATED SOFTWARE PACKAGES

Integrated software packages and suites are available for microcomputers that combine some or all of word processing, desktop publishing, database management, spreadsheet, graphics, and communications. These packages are invaluable for home or business use. See Unit 12 for more details on integrated software and suites.

K89 GETTING THE MOST FROM YOUR SOFTWARE

The advantages of document processing are so obvious, it seems impossible that there could be a negative side. However, there is one; you must avoid problems such as the following to maintain cost-effectiveness.

Perfectionism The ease with which changes can be made can lead to unnecessary waste. Instead of one draft and a finished job, for example, some people produce multiple drafts.

Excessive paper use Printers are fast and powerful but more printing than is needed can occur if the paper is not aligned correctly, if the printer is not set up properly, or if only a casual onscreen proofreading was done.

Unnecessary records storage You will need increased storage if both disks and hard copies are kept on file when both may not really be necessary; delete/purge unnecessary data/files on a regular basis.

Eyestrain and fatigue These problems can occur if you sit at a terminal for too long without a break or if the workstation or equipment is not ergonomically sound (see Unit 6 for information).

Duplication of effort Document processing is not exclusively the domain of support staff. Supervisors and managers should take advantage of its time- and cost-saving benefits by keying rather than handwriting.

Not using the system and the software to its full potential Learn all the automatic features of your software.

K90   USING THE SYSTEM TO ITS FULL POTENTIAL

Study the manual carefully to see what the software can do for you. Tutorials on disk and training workshops on videos will help.

Moving around the screen

◆ Use the cursor properly. Don't make manual moves around the screen. Learn the command that will take you to the beginning of a document or the beginning of a line in one move, for example.

◆ Use the delete/select keys properly (e.g., character, word, line, select all). Don't delete one character at a time.

Use the automatic features

◆ Use the automatic date feature where appropriate. This saves many keystrokes.

◆ Use the automatic indent for numbered sentences and hanging indents. Don't space over.

NOTE You must, of course, use automatic indent with justified text. If you space over in this situation, your text will not align at the left.

Use the printer properly

◆ Preview or view the document onscreen before printing to make sure it is displayed on the page as you want it (e.g., not too high and not too low).

◆ Use draft mode for rapid printing of something that is not required in finished form.

◆ Print only the pages you want. Identify particular pages. Don't print the whole document.

◆ When printing multi-page documents, know how to cancel a print job if an error is discovered (saves paper waste and time).

Take advantage of the default settings

◆ Unless your organization's stationery is oddly shaped, work with the default settings provided. Key all documents on a 6.5" line and insert lines of space (white space) as needed to provide balance. Change margins only in rare and exceptional conditions (e.g., for a widowed line).

◆ Use the default tab stops as much as possible.

Create new default settings and templates to suit your particular needs

◆ If your firm's stationery is different in size from the software default, create a new default template. Don't make changes every time.

◆ Create templates of frequently produced jobs and save for future use (financial statements, for example). Templates can include a header and footer, call for a specific printer, print in a specific font, have a specified paragraph format, and have tab stops where desired.

Speed up your letter production

◆ Save and reuse as many form paragraphs as possible.

◆ Don't type envelopes. Use mailing labels or print envelopes from the inside address using the automatic envelope/label feature. The procedure for doing this will vary with software. Your software manual will usually show the way.

◆ Create macros for letter endings (see below).

Use the spell checker properly

◆ Create a personal dictionary in your spell checker by adding abbreviations, specialized terms used in your work, names of people, code names, brand names, and company names that you use frequently.

Be productive with reports

Many features speed up the production of reports and manuscripts:

◆ Use the automatic table of contents or outline feature.

◆ Use the binder feature to automatically move text over.

◆ Use the keep with text feature to stop breaks in tables, quotations, etc.

◆ Use automatic page number and automatic headers and footers.

◆ Import tables from spreadsheets; don't redo them.

◆ Use widow/orphan protection.

◆ Decide on hyphenation on/off feature.

Use macros

Macros are amazing time-savers. Use them to automatically

◆ provide the ending to your letters

◆ insert memo headings when you don't have preprinted stationery

- key headings that are used frequently (e.g., agendas, minutes)
- insert your name and address at the top of each personal letter you compose

NOTE Some macros can repeat themselves, can pause for a specified time, or can pause to allow you to key in needed information.

K91 STORAGE

The storage method and media you use will vary with the operating system and type of computer. Storage can be on 3.5″ high-density formatted disks, CD-ROMs, an internal or external hard drive, or USB memory stick.
  In-depth information on disk types can be found in Unit 12.

K92 DISK CARE

Note the following points in protecting your precious software and storage disks:

- Do not expose the disk to any magnetic sources, such as telephones.
- Avoid extreme heat and cold.
- Print or write clearly on labels, and then attach them to disks.
- Invest in a disk file (see Unit 8, "Records and Information Management," for assistance) to protect from dust, dirt, smoke, or spills.
- Protect disks against virus contamination (see Unit 12).
- Write-protect your disks (see below).
- Keep valuable disks in a safe, secure place.
- Create a software inventory. This will
  - help take advantage of updates when they become available from the manufacturer
  - assist if security or copyright problems occur
- Make backup copies (see K93).
- Become familiar with disk management techniques provided in the instruction manual or tutorial for your software.
- Get to know the operating system for your hardware. Operating systems vary considerably in the ways in which they format, copy, erase, rename, and display disk contents.
- Eliminate (purge) unnecessary files regularly.
- Learn to use a utility program to help organize files. These can also recover damaged or lost information, delete files, and copy files.

CD care

- Handle the disk only by the outer edge to prevent fingerprints and smears on the surface.
- Store the disk in the protective case.
- Do not leave the disk in direct sunlight or in a hot, humid environment.

K

◆ Do not stick adhesive labels on disks; use only a felt-tip permanent pen when labelling. Write only on the printed area or on the clear inner diameter of the disk.

Cleaning the disk

◆ Use a soft, lint-free cloth to remove spots, dust, or fingerprints. Always wipe from the centre to the outside edge and never wipe in a circular motion.

Write-protecting disks

Write-protecting the disk preserves the data on the disk and keeps any other data from being written on it. For a 3.5″ disk, slide the write-protect shutter.

K93   DISK BACKUP

The term *backup* is used in two ways. It means copying entire disks and it means saving parts of your work on disk at regular intervals as you proceed.

Because of the danger of power supply difficulties, human error, or disk problems, make backup copies. Remember that copying commercial software without permission is an infringement of the *Copyright Act*.

Most software provides automatic timed backup of work at regular intervals. If yours does not permit this, back up regularly every 15 or 20 minutes. As well, make regular backup disk copies of what is on the hard drive—preferably on a daily basis.

You may wish to invest in a rewriteable DVD drive or a second hard disk; it will let you back up data quickly.

III K94   DISK MANAGEMENT

Regardless of the computer type you use, you need a method of organizing files (the documents on your disks).

▶ K95   Naming files

Word-processing software provides an index that acts as a table of contents for the files saved. Some systems permit many characters to be used in the file name (up to 255 characters). When work is saved, it is essential that the file name provide a reasonably clear indication of the content. A suitable code system must therefore be established.

The second of a series of sales letters sent to customers concerning chairs in February 2006 might be shown as:

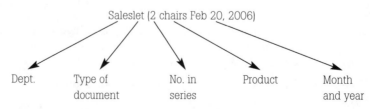

Saleslet (2 chairs Feb 20, 2006)

| Dept. | Type of document | No. in series | Product | Month and year |

◆ If keying the file name onto a document, create a useful cross-reference between document and disk.

◆ Identify files by date and time. Record them when creating and modifying files, and they can be useful in tracking changes and in finding particular versions of files.

◆ Save all data files for a particular program on one disk. If working with a spreadsheet and a word processor, for example, keep them separate.

◆ Keep all files related to a particular project on one disk.

◆ Label the disks clearly in order to avoid overwriting valuable files.

▶K96 Working with folders

Files can be organized by placing them in folders and subfolders. The main folder on the hard drive is known as the *root* directory. All other folders have to be created by the user. A tree structure, such as the one illustrated, works well in the Windows environment. You can open folders for each application software you use and then open subfolders for the different kinds of documents you create with each piece of software. This makes finding information much easier and keeps related files together. Any Windows manual will show you the steps to follow.

Windows enables you to create folders with the *File Manager* program or folders with *Windows Explorer*.

Macintosh allows you to keep everything in order through the use of *folders*. As with Windows, you work with icons.

As a general rule, folders are created on hard drives, CD-ROMs, and other storage devices with large capacities. You can, however, create folders on smaller-capacity disks, e.g., a 3.5″ high-density disk.

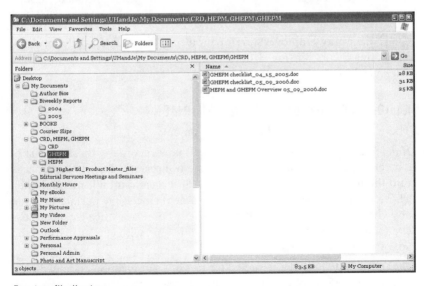

Tree-type file directory

K97 PRINTERS

Printers for keyed documents range from low-resolution dot matrix to high-quality, near-typeset laser printer. The quality of the output required will determine the one you use. Consult the chart on printers in Unit 12 for full details.

K98 PAPER-HANDLING DEVICES

When working on very large word-processing printing jobs (such as many individualized letters), avoid paper-handling problems with the following:

Paper feeders These feed and align cut sheets into the printer automatically. On completion of printing, sheets are ejected into a hopper and automatically stacked.

Envelope feeders These are similar to paper feeders but with provision for the added thickness of an envelope.

NOTE Purchase low- to high-cost paper shredders to eliminate wasted paper, or contract independent firms for weekly/monthly on-the-spot recycling of paper waste in the office.

K99 METHODS OF ORIGINATING TEXT FOR DOCUMENT PROCESSING

A number of choices are possible as methods of originating material for document processing, including original thought, handwriting, and in-person dictation. The most cost-effective choice is machine (audio) dictation. Because dictation can take place at any time, it also offers the advantage of flexibility.

NOTE Many employers prefer inputting their material themselves. When this occurs, the main function of the word-processing operator is to "clean up" the material.

K100 MACHINE DICTATION EQUIPMENT

There are three types of dictation equipment:

Hand-held portable units Similar to small tape recorders, these consist of a recorder, a microphone, and a separate transcriber. The dictator speaks into the microphone (or the entire unit if it has an inbuilt microphone). These small units are particularly convenient since they permit dictation anywhere—in the office, a car, a plane, etc. Some are voice-activated, use cue tones to indicate document starts, and come with clocks, alarms, and appointment reminders.

Desktop units These are designed for use in a workstation and need electricity. They offer controls on the microphone with such features as playback, interrupt, fast-forward, and end of letter. Some are voice-activated and offer cue tones to indicate end of document or special instructions. Many permit conference recording (i.e., recording conversations). Some provide a clock, alarm, and appointment reminders and can double as answering machines.

Centralized recording and transcribing units with a telephone hookup These systems permit dictation to a central location where transcription service is provided.

▶K101 Centralized recording units

Centralized recording systems allow for multiple recording, can be either analog or digital, and can permit productivity tracking.

Analog This older system uses magnetic audiotapes. Documents are retrieved by fast-forwarding through everything on the tape.

Digital This translates the spoken word into binary language to interface with a computer. It can store more in less space, offers random access, and permits more efficient editing.

Automatic changer (also known as discrete media recorder) This type of equipment permits continuous central recording without the need for someone to insert a new cassette when one becomes full, because the recording medium is changed automatically. Long periods of dictation are possible and transcription can be under way while dictation continues.

Endless loop The recording tape is sealed into a tank and is not removed or touched. Such a system offers automatic, unattended use 24 hours a day. A supervisory console (or monitoring panel) enables dictation to be directed automatically to the person who can transcribe it most rapidly. With this system, transcription can occur just a short time after the dictation.

Telephone hookup Telephone hookup to a central recording device may be made through a private telephone system or through the regular telephone service. The telephone receiver is used for recording in both systems.

◆ *Private systems (purchased or rented):* These are not supplied by the public telephone service. Three types are available:
 • *non-selector:* Equipment is connected to one recorder only (if the recorder is in use, the dictator must wait)
 • *manual selector:* Dictator can select a vacant recorder
 • *automatic selector:* Dictator is automatically connected to the first free recorder

◆ *Telephone company system:* Equipment provided by local telephone service is connected with the centralized recording equipment. Access to the recording device is gained by dialing particular numbers, and dictation is possible from any extension telephone or from any outside telephone.

NOTE Advice on efficient dictation techniques is provided in Unit 2, E36.

▶ K102 Transcription units

Transcription units are used by the document-processing operator to transcribe the dictated material. These units consist of a headset, a foot pedal, and the playback unit in which the recording medium is placed.

▶ K103 Machine/Microtranscription

Microtranscription is a valuable marketable skill in the workplace. This is a communication area where an employee's comprehension, grammar, proofreading, and spelling skills will surface. A good transcriptionist must also be a good listener. See Unit 3, IS7 and IS8, for more information on becoming a good listener.

Productivity techniques

◆ Make sure the equipment is working properly.

◆ Plan work in advance; for example, determine how many items are on the tape, the approximate length of each item, and how long it will take to transcribe each item.

◆ Schedule time for transcription work (e.g., if possible, uninterrupted intervals of at least one hour).

◆ If the dictator is unfamiliar, listen through each tape to get an idea of what to expect.

◆ If the dictator has a strong accent, listen through the tape a couple of times in order to become familiar with the voice.

◆ Listen and adjust the controls for suitable tone, volume, and speed.

◆ Listen carefully, and if after a few times you are unsure of what a word is or what has been dictated, then ask someone else to listen as well (if it is not strictly confidential material). If that person cannot decipher the word(s), then ask the dictator.

◆ Check the indicator (if one is provided by the dictator) for instructions and corrections.

◆ Listen to a complete phrase or thought, stop the machine, and key the phrase (keep a list of repetitious phrases or terminology for quick reference).

◆ Proofread the transcription carefully; run your spell checker for errors.

◆ Always check for enclosures or attachments (e.g., letters or memos); make sure they are included with the document before presenting it to your boss for a signature.

NOTE Some equipment will scan electronically to find errors, corrections, and special instructions.

K104 ORGANIZATION OF DOCUMENT-PROCESSING ACTIVITIES

The size and needs of the firm will determine the way in which organizations set up their document-processing facility. This may range from a large, self-contained, fully equipped department (centralized) to a single, independent unit used by one operator (decentralized).

DOCUMENT-PROCESSING DAILY WORK OUTPUT

OPERATOR _____   DATE _____

JOB NO.	TYPE OF WORK	ORIGINATOR	NUMBER OF LINES/PAGES	TIME USED HOURS	MINUTES

Operator's daily log

DOCUMENT-PROCESSING JOB REQUEST

DATE _____

JOB NO. _____

SECTION 1

ORIGINATOR	DEPT.
WHEN NEEDED	SUBJECT OR REPORT TITLE
PAPER ❑ INTEROFFICE ❑ CO. LETTERHEAD ❑ BOND ❑ OTHER _____	
ORIGINAL AND ____ COPIES	SPACING ❑ SINGLE ❑ DOUBLE ❑ ONE AND ONE-HALF

NOTE: TEXT WILL BE RETAINED ON TAPE FOR THREE WORKDAYS UNLESS REQUESTED OTHERWISE.

SPECIAL INSTRUCTIONS

❑ SPECIAL RETENTION ___/___/___
DATE

ATTACHED IS YOUR JOB PRODUCED IN ACCORDANCE WITH YOUR INSTRUCTIONS. PLEASE ATTACH THIS FORM TO THE JOB IF REVISION IS REQUIRED.

ASSIGNED TO	INPUT METHOD	
1. ORIGINAL	❑ MACHINE DICTATION TAPE NO. _____	
2. REVISION	❑ LONGHAND	
	❑ HARD COPY	
	❑ EDITED COPY	

PRODUCTION DATA	LINE COUNT _____	PAGE COUNT _____

REMARKS

PRODUCTION TIME

HARD COPY	DATE/TIME	MACHINE DICTATION	DATE/TIME
WORK SUBMITTED	____	WORK SUBMITTED	____
PROOFING COMPLETED	____	PROOFING COMPLETED	____
JOB DELIVERED	____	JOB DELIVERED	____
TURNAROUND TIME	____	TURNAROUND TIME	____

SECTION 2

COPY 1 ORIGINATOR'S COPY   COPY 2 SUPERVISOR'S COPY   COPY 3 PRODUCTION COPY

Job request form

K

Centralized departments are separate departments that have their own budgets and report directly to management. Two forms typical of those used in a centralized document-processing department to control the flow of work are illustrated on page 391.

Decentralized departments (mini-centres) are small document-processing centres set up to serve individual departments under the direction of each department manager.

Satellite centres are set up like mini-centres but exist only in firms that also have centralized document processing. The document-processing department handles the bulk of the company's output; satellite centres deal with any special requirements of a department (e.g., confidential or rush jobs).

Single units are used in traditional manager/assistant relationships.

K105 SERVICE BUREAUS AND CONSULTANTS

Document-processing service bureaus—which provide mail service, convert word-processing text to typesetting, and supply telecommunications, printing, and personnel—can be of use to organizations that do not have their own facility, as well as those that do. They are useful for

◆ handling overload situations

◆ meeting tight deadlines—some will offer after-hours service

◆ projects requiring special knowledge or technology not available in-house

◆ conversions from other systems

◆ advice on document-processing applications
  Consult the Yellow Pages for local bureaus.

K106 TEMPORARY DOCUMENT-PROCESSING HELP

If your document-processing demands are high or you need short-term assistance, consider using the services of a temporary agency. Make best use of their services and ensure you obtain the most appropriate temporary help:

◆ Specify the make and type of equipment and type of software you use.

◆ Describe the type of application (letters, reports, statements).

◆ Name the kind of input (print, longhand, shorthand, audio).

◆ State the degree of proficiency and experience needed.

◆ Identify the length of time of the assignment.

K107 CHANGING TECHNOLOGY IN DOCUMENT PROCESSING

Programs are available that incorporate audio, animated graphics, and video into an electronic letter. They will take office communications beyond paper and into electronics in a way that will not only speed the flow of information but also add to the scope of what can be conveyed.

K108 DOCUMENT-PROCESSING TERMS

Bug: A defect in a program that causes a malfunction in the computer.

Command-driven software program: Instructions are given to the word-processing equipment by means of keystrokes (commands) that must be learned.

Continuous loop: See endless loop recorders (K101).

CD–R: A CD that is recordable but not rewriteable (can be used only once for storage).

CD–RW: A CD that is rewriteable (up to 1000 times).

Cpi: A term that means characters per inch.

Cps: A term that means characters per second.

DDE: A term that means dynamic data exchange; the means by which a linked object is created.

Downtime: Time when equipment is not operating correctly because of some malfunction.

Dumb terminal: A text-editing terminal of a computer-based system that relies on a mainframe or mini-computer for its intelligence.

Electronic mail (email): The use of electronic means (telephone lines, private networks, or satellite networks) to transmit information.

Embedded object: An object created by using OLE in which the embedded data is stored in the destination document.

Footer: Document identification used at the foot of a page.

Formatting: Setting margins, indents, etc., for various business communications (e.g., letters and reports).

Global find and replace: The capability of word-processing software to locate a particular word or expression in stored information and replace it automatically with another word or expression.

Hanging indent: The first line of a paragraph begins at the left margin and the following lines are indented one-half inch.

Hard copy: A typed or printed document on paper.

Header: Page identification used at the top of a page.

Letter quality (LQ): The ability of a printer to produce high-quality print impressions.

Linked object: An object created using DDE in which the linked data is stored in the source document.

K

Menu-driven software: The program user instructs the word-processing equipment by selecting choices from a list of options (menu) shown on the screen.

Merged text: A term used to describe what appear to be individually keyed communications but are in fact letters or documents created from standard paragraphs.

Modem: A communications device (see Unit 12).

Near-letter quality (NLQ): Print impressions produced by a dot matrix printer when the print head has passed several times over the paper.

Network: A series of terminals and devices connected by communications channels.

OLE: A term that means *object linking and embedding;* the means by which an embedded object is established.

Optical character recognition (OCR): Scanners, using OCR software, scan and enter keyed materials directly into the word-processing system without the need for rekeying.

Output: The completed document.

Peripherals: Items of equipment that may be attached to the system (e.g., printers, plotters, scanners).

PPM: Pages per minute.

Purge: To delete obsolete files/folders.

Smart (intelligent) terminal: Terminal that has its own computer power but shares the printing and/or storage facilities.

Template: A feature with fixed settings, such as fonts, layout, and special formatting, used for creating special documents like faxes or memos.

Text: Printed or written matter.

Text editing: Revising recorded information.

Transcribing unit: Playback component of a dictation machine.

Turnaround time: The time taken between the beginning and the completion of a job once it has been given to the word-processing operator.

Wizards: A feature that asks questions and uses your responses to automatically create a format layout for your document.

WORDS OF WISDOM

The best angle to approach any problem is the try-angle.

UNIT

15 DESKTOP PUBLISHING

SELECTED CONTENTS

DP1	**WHO USES DTP?**
DP2	**ADVANTAGES AND DISADVANTAGES OF DTP**
DP3	**SKILLS NEEDED IN DTP**
DP4	**DTP HARDWARE**
DP5	**DTP SOFTWARE**
DP6	**PRODUCING A DOCUMENT**
DP7	Planning the Publication
DP8	Preparing Preliminary Page Designs
DP9	Preparing the Text
DP18	Preparing the Artwork and Graphics
DP20	Web Graphics
DP23	Finalizing the Design and Page Layout
DP30	Printing and Finishing the Final Version
DP35	Portable Document Format (PDF)
DP36	**A FINAL WORD**
DP37	**DTP TERMS**

DP

The term *electronic publishing* covers two important activities—desktop publishing and multi-media document production.

In desktop publishing (DTP), most or all of the business-related documents (brochures, catalogues, advertisements, forms) within the organization are produced on a desktop computer. The skilled desktop publisher can electronically blend text and graphics (drawings, photographs, etc.) into a professional-looking printed product, thus combining the specialized skills of designers, copywriters, artists, typographers, and printers in one operation.

In multi-media document production, computer-generated slide or overhead presentations and electronic documents that combine elements of sound, video, animation, text, and graphics are created. For example, entire catalogues might be created and distributed on disk that allow the customer to see a product, perhaps even to see the product in use, and to hear that product being described.

This unit will focus on DTP, the print form of electronic publishing.

DP1 WHO USES DTP?

◆ Many organizations and businesses use DTP for document production. Such documents might be in-house or external reports, announcements, advertisements, newsletters, brochures, office stationery, catalogues, forms, manuals, or flyers.

◆ In the printing industry, DTP is used for magazine and newspaper layouts and for advertising layout and design.

◆ Advertising and marketing firms use it extensively to produce high-quality communications of all kinds.

◆ Educational institutions use it for announcements, instructional materials, calendars, and yearbooks.

◆ Community organizations such as religious organizations and service clubs use it for newsletters, bulletins, etc.

DP2 ADVANTAGES AND DISADVANTAGES OF DTP

Advantages

Cost Production and printing times are shortened and operator costs are lessened.

Flexibility Changes can be made easily and at any stage at a lower cost.

Control Each phase of the process can be easily overseen.

Time Production and printing time is saved when there is no need to wait for the outside production of copy and graphics.

Security and confidentiality Because all or most phases of production stay within the organization, outsiders do not see the document.

Professionalism DTP allows even small businesses to create professional-looking forms, stationery, etc.

Disadvantages

◆ Documents that show lack of design knowledge, lack of writing expertise, or lack of skill with typography.

◆ Too many people having access to DTP and producing documents that are not unified (i.e., that can damage a firm's image).

◆ Too many unco-ordinated mailings and promotions.

DP3 SKILLS NEEDED IN DTP

Some companies install their own DTP shop and employ specialists. Many companies assume that because an office worker already has keying and word-processing skills, DTP is a natural extension of those skills. In organizations like these, *anyone* may be expected to do it. However, because

DTP combines the skills of many specialists, considerable knowledge is needed. This knowledge includes the following:

◆ expertise with the software used

◆ knowledge of design and layout principles

◆ skill with typography

◆ awareness of the publishing process

◆ familiarity with the vocabulary of DTP

This unit will provide a summary of that essential knowledge.

DP4 DTP HARDWARE

The following hardware and peripherals are needed, regardless of the type of computer used:

◆ A powerful microprocessor, or central processing unit (CPU), that can handle the work efficiently is essential. At least an 80 GB hard drive is recommended for professional-looking documents. Graphics require a considerable amount of storage space, as do completed pages of text and graphics.

◆ A networked system is not essential but is valuable if files are to be shared.

◆ Laser printers are now the printers of choice.

◆ A mouse or wireless mouse is essential. The keyboard is used for many operations but cannot be used on its own.

◆ A scanner (image digitizer) allows for text, illustrations of all types, and handwriting to be digitized (i.e., changed to a form a computer can store) and manipulated (i.e., edited, moved, rotated) so that they can be included in your document.

◆ Digital cameras allow for easy photo integration.

DP

DP5 DTP SOFTWARE

A wide range of DTP software is available. High-end, professional software offers the features needed for producing sophisticated documents. Low-end packages are appropriate for less sophisticated documents and for home and community use.

◆ All DTP software allows the user to integrate graphics and text on a page and to design, lay out, and produce attractive, effective documents.

◆ DTP packages all have text-editing capability, but this is usually appropriate only for short passages and headings. Lengthy text is normally produced with word-processing software and then copied (imported) into the DTP application.

◆ DTP packages usually offer simple graphics-creation ability such as lines, circles, and boxes. When more complex graphics are needed, they are usually produced in a separate graphics program or digitized by a scanner and imported.

Word-processing software

Any word-processing software capable of being saved in ASCII can be used for DTP. Some word-processing software packages allow limited DTP on their own. For example, they allow columns, permit type size and style changes, contain their own clip art, and permit line drawing. Clip art can also be downloaded from the internet.

Illustration software

This software allows users to create original drawings, or work with the many clip-art images and fonts provided, or edit scanned images. The high-quality results can then be imported into DTP applications.

Some illustration software packages permit the user to work with photographs—cropping, rotating, resizing, or creating special effects—and some provide animation possibilities.

DP6 PRODUCING A DOCUMENT

To produce an effective document, use a systematic approach such as the following:

1. Plan the publication.
2. Prepare preliminary page designs.
3. Prepare the text.
4. Prepare the artwork and graphics.
5. Finalize the design and page layout.
6. Print and finish (collate, bind) the final version.

DP7 PLANNING THE PUBLICATION

To effectively plan the publication, you might try answering the following questions:

What is the purpose? To inform? To persuade? To amuse? To obtain a reaction?

Who is the audience? What age group? To what social and cultural group do they belong? How much are they likely to know already about the subject matter?

What image should be projected? Contemporary, classic, dynamic? Solid, dependable, well informed? Creative, aggressive, avant-garde? Scholarly, reliable, authoritative? Exciting, adventurous, entrepreneurial?

How long should it be?

How much money is available?

How is the document to be produced? In-house printing or not?

When is it needed?

Who will do what? Who in-house will be involved? Will freelance personnel be needed? Who will do the writing? Who will do the designing? What tasks can be performed simultaneously?

How will it be distributed? Mailed? Self-mailer?

DP8   PREPARING PRELIMINARY PAGE DESIGNS

Thumbnail sketches are usually produced to indicate page layout and design. Text is represented with solid lines and graphic areas with the shape of the graphic. Stock (paper) (see DP33) and colours to be used (see DP22) are often determined at this stage and samples included with the thumbnail sketches.

Thumbnail sketch

DP9   PREPARING THE TEXT

▶ DP10 Body text

This refers to the main copy (paragraphs, etc.) of a publication.

DP11 Text content

The amount of text and the approach taken will vary with each document. The following considerations, however, apply to any publication:

- Write clearly and concisely.
- Avoid biased language related to gender, race, age, ethnic background, religion, physical ability.

DP

♦ Check spelling, grammar, and punctuation.

♦ Proofread and use the spell-check and grammar-check features of the software.

♦ Use consistent style.

♦ Ensure that content is accurate.

DP12 Body text format

Text can be produced in four formats: flush left, ragged right; justified; ragged left, flush right; or centred. Each may be used to add to the appearance of your document. Some formats, however, are harder to read than others. Justified is better for longer publications; ragged right is better for short documents.

Paragraphs may be indented or blocked. Most DTP software provides a *style sheet*. The user can decide, for example, on the indents and heading styles to be used. The style sheet will automatically make them consistent throughout the document.

DP13 Display text

This refers to headings and is normally created in the DTP package. Keep headings short and in capitals or have just the first letter of the first word capitalized. The latter is preferred.

DP14 Working with typefaces (fonts) and type styles

DTP allows you to work with many different typefaces (fonts) and styles. The software provides many fonts, laser printers provide additional ones, and you can buy even more as cartridges or on disk if you need more variety.

DP15 The language of typography

Font A typeface in one specific size and style and all the characters and symbols available in that typeface (e.g., 10-point Times Roman is a font). People involved in DTP tend to use *typeface* and *font* as interchangeable terms.

Font style The choices available of roman (upright), italic (slanted), outline, bold, shadow, reverse, etc., that exist within the typeface (or font) selected.

Kerning The amount of space between adjacent letters on a page; usually affects only type of 12 points or more. In some cases, the space between characters may appear to be too large. By using the kerning feature you can remove some of this space and create a consistent spacing that improves appearance and readability. All DTP software provides a kerning feature. The high-end type allows for automatic kerning.

Leading The spacing in points, measured from the baseline of one line to the baseline of the next, between horizontal lines of type. Leading adds to the readability of text. The body text of this book is printed in 9.5-point type with 12-point leading, which would be described as "9.5/12" and read as "nine-point-five on twelve." The page would have looked crowded and would have been difficult to read if 9.5/9.5 had been used.

III

◆ DTP usually has a default leading of two points, which is fine for most publications:
- Extra leading increases readability.
- Type set on its own body size without additional spacing (leading) is "set solid."

Points Point size is measured by the vertical height of an uppercase character, i.e., from the baseline to the top of the capital letter—72 points equal one inch. Most letters, memos, newsletters, and reports are created in 12 point. Point size is used with proportional spacing, i.e., an uppercase W takes more space than a lowercase i. Typefaces of the same point size can have different horizontal measurements. Consider this if space is an issue. For advertisements, flyers, and headings, larger point sizes are needed.

Sans-serif A typeface without short lines, or feet, attached to the bottoms of characters. Characters are perfectly plain, with lines of uniform thickness. Sans-serif type is generally used only for headings and very short blocks of text because it is harder to read than serif type. The main heads in this book are in a sans-serif typeface.

Serif A typeface with short, light lines or feet projecting from the top or bottom of the main stroke of the character. Serif type is generally used for body text. The body of this book is in a serif typeface.

Typeface A particular style of type. Typefaces come in three general classes: serif, sans-serif, and script (which resembles handwriting).

DP16 Commonly used typefaces

Font style	Fonts	
Decorative type font	*Script*	**Brush Script**
Serif font	Times New Roman	Garamond
	Century Schoolbook	Nueva
Sans-serif font	Arial	Futura
	Univers	Modern

Typeface examples

DP

DP17 Type selection

Remember these points as you choose typefaces and styles for your document:

◆ Try to use only two fonts in a document but make them different enough that the difference shows. Also, take advantage of the many styles (italic, bold, outline) that exist in those particular fonts.

◆ Some typefaces are more appropriate for some situations and audiences than others. Try to match your choice to the job (e.g., an informal invitation might be attractive in Script whereas a business form would be better in Times Roman).

- Use uppercase (capitals) for single words and very short headings, but not otherwise. Too much emphasis kills the purpose!
- Ornate typefaces are hard to read; use a large point size (18 point or larger) so that the text is easily read.
- Consider your audience. Young and old like large type. Busy people like to quickly scan; therefore, something easy to read is helpful to them.
- Do not use text lines that are too long for the eye to follow.
- Consider reading distance (e.g., billboard posters).

DP18 PREPARING THE ARTWORK AND GRAPHICS

Artwork may be drawings, sketches, photographs, or anything that has not been produced on a computer. *Graphics* are illustrations of any kind produced on a computer.

Artwork can be added to a document in a number of ways. For example:

- Original line drawings can be pasted into the final layout.
- Photographs can be professionally converted into film and stripped into film of the layout.
- Any artwork can be scanned and imported into the DTP file.

▶ DP19 Creating graphics

The following methods are possible:

- scanning and digitizing artwork and then importing it into your DTP file; the result can be sized and cropped (wing dings) to the desired shape
- creating graphic images using a graphics software program
- using commercially prepared graphics known as *clip art*. These are available in a great variety and are easy to use. You can also edit and change parts
  - Some DTP packages contain their own clip art; others can be purchased.
  - Clip art is copyright-free.
- using the symbol and ornamental typefaces (dingbats) available in DTP software (some word-processing packages refer to these as *character sets*)
- creating line graphs, bar graphs, and pie charts in the DTP program, in charting software, or in a spreadsheet, and then importing them

▶ DP20 Web graphics

Web graphics is the process of creating pictures to use on a website by using a software graphics package, which allows you to optimize pictures for print or online use using the default or customize settings.

Most graphics files are either GIF or JPEG. These picture file formats can be used for printing, but if you are manually saving Web graphics, you can choose the appropriate format as discussed below.

GIF—Graphics interchange/internet format

The GIF format is a picture format commonly used on the internet to store non-photo pictures, such as drawings, cartoons, and icons, and can display a maximum of 256 colours. It is best used for black-and-white line drawings, colour clip art, and pictures that use large blocks of solid colours, such as cartoon characters.

Unlike pictures saved in JPEG, pictures saved in GIF format will not degrade in quality, even though the file is compressed.

NOTE To reduce download time, an animated GIF should contain only a few frames.

JPEG—Joint photographic experts group

The JPEG format contains thousands or even millions of colours and can be used to display high-quality photographs, scanned pictures, photographs from a digital camera, or smooth colour gradations.

JPEG format was designed as an image storage format; therefore, it can efficiently compress large, high-quality photos into compact file sizes. The more reduction of the picture's file size, the more image information is omitted, decreasing the quality of the picture.

TIP Keep backup copies of all pictures to revert to the originals if necessary.

JPEG does not support *transparency* or *animation*. When a picture is saved in a .jpg file, the transparent areas in the picture are converted to the nearest solid colour.

▶DP21 Hints for using artwork and graphics

◆ Use them to help explain text and to support instructions.
◆ Use them only if they add to the message.
◆ Keep them with the relevant text.
◆ Mix them with text; don't isolate them.
◆ Keep them simple.
◆ Use captions to explain them unless they are merely decorative.
◆ Change shapes and sizes to add interest to the layout.
◆ Hard-hitting charts and graphs are attention-grabbers, but using too many can reduce their impact.
◆ Refer to the source of the artwork and graphics in the caption.

▶DP22 Colour

Colour is an important aspect of document production.
◆ Colour can be used to add emphasis, as a background tint, and as decoration. Functionally, it
  • helps get ideas across
  • speeds comprehension

DP

- clarifies relationships
- creates moods (dark colours, for example, are prestigious)
- focuses attention

Consider the colour scheme in advance of production and be aware of the printing process capabilities. Colour separations can be expensive!

DP23 FINALIZING THE DESIGN AND PAGE LAYOUT

Graphic design is the process of selecting the individual elements (text, illustrations, and headings) that will make up the finished page. The selection includes choices of typefaces, styles, and point sizes, as well as margins and column widths. *Layout* refers to positioning the various elements on a page.

▶ DP24 The DTP layout screen

The screen displayed by DTP software resembles a designer's layout page. This is the working screen on which text and graphics are manipulated and arranged. Menu commands and tools needed to create the publication are shown on the screen.

- ◆ The user creates a master page (a grid or skeleton of a finished page) for each document, showing top, bottom, and side margins, column widths, and paper size. This helps to determine graphics sizes. Once designed, the page can be saved as a template for future use.
- ◆ A single page or two facing pages may be displayed at any one time.

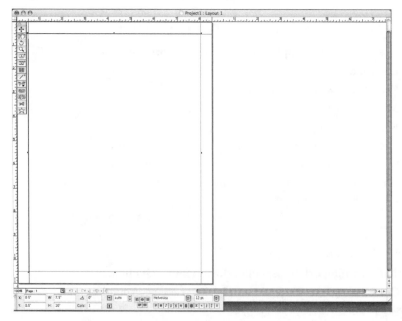

A DTP layout screen

III

◆ DTP elements can be placed temporarily on the pasteboard while page layout is under way.

◆ Horizontal and vertical rulers help with positioning the elements.

◆ The tools permit text and graphics to be displayed in a variety of ways. Typically, they allow you to draw squares and rectangles with and without corners, circles and ovals, straight lines at any angle, horizontal and vertical lines and lines at 45° angles, and to crop (trim) the edges of graphics.

▶ DP25 Graphic lines

Use graphic lines to

◆ separate information on the page

◆ divide a heading from the body of a page

◆ break up a page into columns

◆ design customized forms

◆ create borders and unify page elements

Lines can be enhanced by a number of DTP features, including the following:

◆ shading (also known as *fill*), or screening, which permits blocks of shading or fill from 10 percent to 100 percent to be inserted over ruled sections

◆ patterns that permit backgrounds of various types (such as cross-hatching) to be shown in graphic shapes

◆ layering, which permits shapes to overlap each other

◆ drop shadows, which create a three-dimensional effect by layering two identical shapes

For information about lines and layering, please visit the Text Enrichment Site for this text at *www.pearsoned.ca/text/campbell*.

DP

▶ DP26 The principles of design

The principles of design—proportion, balance, contrast, rhythm, and unity—should be followed to achieve an effective page layout.

Proportion The golden rule of proportion states that rectangles with a ratio of approximately 1.6:1 (e.g., a long side of 3.2 cm and a short side of 2 cm) are the most pleasing to the reader. "Golden rectangles" (placed vertically or horizontally), comfortable margins, and appropriate white space create proportion.

Balance This is achieved through an appropriate symmetry of elements, white space, and the weighting of text and graphics on the page. If a page is in balance, everything above, below, to the left, and to the right of the optical centre will be symmetrical.

Balance aids in sending a formal, conservative, and precise message. An informal, asymmetrical design sends the opposite message—a less formal, more energetic one.

Contrast This attracts and keeps the reader's attention. Contrast is achieved by the use of boldface, reverse type, or graphics, for example.

Rhythm This is created by arranging elements so that the flow is smooth. Repeated elements such as horizontal, vertical, or diagonal units help create a sense of rhythm.

Unity This means that the design elements blend with each other and complement one another. Rules should match line drawings, typefaces should be weighted to rules, etc.

▶DP27 Design hints

There are no absolute rules in this area, but the following hints will be useful in achieving good design:

◆ Consider the eye movement of your reader and be aware that, typically, the reader is attracted to a point close to the centre of the page (the optical centre) and will scan in a Z-pattern, with the eyes coming to rest towards the bottom right-hand corner.

◆ The optical centre and the Z-pattern both help to grab your reader's attention with the careful positioning of headings and text.

◆ Avoid too much balance; such a design can be bland.

◆ Unify, co-ordinate, and organize each page around a single, dominant, visual element.

▶DP28 Placement of text

Working with columns:

◆ Vary column widths to attract the reader's eye.

◆ Don't leave too much space between columns. Two/three spaces is standard.

◆ Try to keep columns the same length.

◆ Avoid widows and orphans.

▶DP29 Placement of graphics

One-column format Place graphics that are less than a third of a page deep at the top of a page. Those more than a third of a page deep should go at the bottom.

Two-column format Place graphics within a column, overlapping columns, or at the top or bottom, bearing in mind the size of the graphic, placement of the text to which it relates, and the design principles described earlier.

Text can be wrapped around a graphic for increased eye appeal if desired.

DP30 PRINTING AND FINISHING THE FINAL VERSION

The considerations here will vary with the size of the job. Very small jobs may be printed and finished in-house, some may best be handled by a service bureau (check the Yellow Pages), and larger and more complex ones may be completed by a commercial printer.

▶DP31 Working with commercial printers

The following hints can prevent costly errors:

- ◆ Write out your printing specifications very clearly.
- ◆ Obtain written quotations from several printers and be sure these match your specifications before you make your selection.
- ◆ Inform the selected printer of the production schedule.
- ◆ Stay in touch with your printer through all the production stages.
- ◆ Ensure that your printer orders the required paper stock early enough.
- ◆ Make sure that your camera-ready art or disk(s) is acceptable.
- ◆ If colour is involved, try to arrange to approve a press proof. If possible, go to the printing plant to approve the colour on site.

▶DP32 In-house printing

Printing will generally be by laser, photocopier, or offset printer and will depend on the size and sophistication of the job and the equipment available within the organization. New developments in in-house printing include the following:

Intelligent printer/copiers that combine the technology of the microprocessor, laser, and photocopier and have features of both printers and copiers. They can accept text, graphics, and instructions from computers or magnetic media. They produce hard copy directly from the digitized information received.

Colour printers that work on regular paper provide colour close to that on the computer screen, can be shared on a network, and can accept input from different types of computers.

Direct imaging that merges the high quality of offset printing with the speed and convenience of a photocopier. The page layout (image data) is converted to high-resolution digital masters that can be sent directly from the computer to the printing press without the typical intermediary film and plate stages. The entire document production process—printing, folding, cutting, collating, stitching, binding, stacking, etc.—can be done in-house in minutes. The masters can also be archived digitally for repeats.

See Unit 12, page 291, for information on scanners.

DP

▶DP33 Stock (paper)

The type of paper selected and its finish will contribute to the effectiveness of your document. Therefore make your choice carefully, based on

- ◆ budget available
- ◆ purpose of the document and image to be projected to the reader
- ◆ printing process to be used (in-house photocopier or commercial printer)
- ◆ size and number of pages

Standard paper sizes exist to save waste. To save money, create a dummy of your document and make it fit one of the standard sizes.

Paper types

Groundwood (newsprint) Inexpensive and useful for documents with a short life span such as flyers, newspapers, and inexpensive catalogues.

Bond A high-quality paper used for most office-related documents.

Book (also known as offset) Used mainly for book and magazine production.

Cover Heavyweight stock used, as the name implies, for covers of pamphlets and journals.

Paper finishes

The decision will be related to the image you wish to create. Select from among gloss, dull, matte, vellum, textured, smooth, linen, and rippled finishes.

▶ DP34 Finishing

Finishing refers essentially to collating and binding. Commercial printers will arrange this as part of their service. In-house possibilities include easy-to-use mechanical binders that connect pages of documents such as reports by means of plastic strips, or binders that may be purchased from a stationery store and customized with your own cover page.

DP35 PORTABLE DOCUMENT FORMAT (PDF)

Portable document format is a file format created by Adobe Systems. It uses the PostScript printer description language and is highly portable across computer platforms. PDF documents have a .pdf file extension, i.e., filename.pdf.

PDFs are used to

◆ share files with others who do not have the same software

◆ share files with others who use a different computer platform, e.g., Linux, Mac, or Windows

◆ share files that can be protected from copying, editing, printing, or unauthorized viewing

◆ publish electronic documents such as ebooks (electronic books)

◆ create files that will print on many different types of printers

◆ create files with annotations, bookmarks, and hyperlinks that can be shared via email and on the Web

◆ create interactive forms that can be shared via email and the Web

◆ create files that are more efficient than PostScript or original file formats typically used in commercial printing

Some desktop publishing programs can create PDF files from within the program, usually with the assistance of helper programs such as Adobe Acrobat or deskPDF Professional.

Many designers email their layouts to clients in PDF form for approval. Clients can approve designs onscreen without the appropriate fonts and software installed on their computers. All they need is Adobe Acrobat Reader, a free downloadable program, to view the PDF.

Source: © Jacci Howard Bear (http://desktoppub.about.com/od/electronicpublishing/g/pdf.htm). Used with permission of About.com, Inc., which can be found online at www.about.com. All rights reserved.

DP36 A FINAL WORD

If you are new to DTP, consider these ideas:

◆ Seek the help of experts when a difficult job is involved.

◆ Keep a file of ideas available or preferred.

◆ Look at all the junk mail that arrives and consider it for ideas, "how-to's," and "how-not-to's."

◆ Study the DTP manual. The software can do amazing things.

◆ Keep abreast of new technology and software by subscribing to current magazines.

◆ Focus on the design element in everything you read. Many aspects of design can be learned, but it is experience that really helps.

◆ Register for a course.

◆ Observe, and ask questions of, experts.

See www.desktoppublishing.com for more DTP ideas.

DP37 DTP TERMS

Ascender: The proportion of the lowercase letter that rises above the x-height, as in the letters *b, d, f, h, k, l,* and *t.*

Banners: Large headlines or titles extending the width of the page.

Crop: To choose a section of a graphic, illustration, or photograph and size it to fill a specific area on a page.

Descender: The part of a lowercase letter that drops below the x-height, as in the letters, *g, j, p, q,* and *y.*

Display type: Type larger than 14-point; commonly used for headlines and advertising copy.

DPI (dots per inch): Describes the resolution of a printer. Over 1000 DPI is considered to be typesetting quality; about 300 DPI is desktop laser quality.

Drop capital: A capital that hangs below the top line and takes the vertical space of more than one line at the beginning of a paragraph.

Em dash (—): A long dash used to indicate a sudden break in thought. Originally, the length of an em dash was the portion of a line occupied by the letter *m.* Now it refers to the square of any size of type.

DP

Em space: A square of a given point size. A 12-point em space would be a square of 12×12 points.

En dash (–): Half the length of an em dash but longer than a hyphen. Used mainly to indicate continuing or inclusive numbers (e.g., 2004–12; pages 56–99).

En space: Half the width of an em space. Most commonly it is the width of the character *0* (zero).

Halftone: The process by which a continuous tone is simulated by a pattern of dots of varying size. This is used, for example, when photographs must be changed to a format of dots so that a printer can reproduce them. Specify lines per inch (lpi) for the printer. All halftones in one document must be the same lpi screen.

Mastheads: Similar to banners but located at the top of the first page or cover and usually containing the name of the bulletin, newsletter, or company.

Process colour separation: To reproduce full-colour documents using offset lithography, colour pages must be broken down into the four-process separation plates—cyan, magenta, yellow, and black.

Resolution: The accuracy of reproduction and distinctness of visual elements. For printer output and computer screens, resolution is defined in dots per inch. The more dots per inch, the better the output quality.

Run-around/wraparound: A feature that automatically causes text to flow around a box, picture, or line.

Scale: To reduce or enlarge text or pictures according to a fixed ratio.

Style sheet: Allows user to save character styles, tabs, and margins. Once created, style-sheet format information can be applied to any paragraph.

Template: An electronic prototype of a document that provides the layout grid and style sheet for similar publications. DTP operators can create and save their templates.

Text wrap: Lets you specify the relationship of text to graphic; can go around, through, or over a graphic.

TIFF files (tagged image file format): An electronic format for storing and transmitting scanned images between applications.

WYSIWYG (what you see is what you get): The representation on a computer screen of text and graphic elements as they will look on the printed page.

x-height: The size of the lowercase *x* in a typeface; considered the main element of the character, excluding ascenders and descenders.

WORDS OF WISDOM

Every job you do is a portrait of you.

UNIT

16 INFORMATION/ REFERENCE SOURCES/INTERNET

SELECTED CONTENTS

IR1	**ELECTRONIC INFORMATION SOURCES**
IR2	Electronic Reference Sources
IR3	Databases
IR4	Commercial Databases
IR5	Major Database Services
IR6	Using Commercial Database Services
IR7	Cost
IR8	Advantages
IR9	**USING LIBRARIES**
IR10	Book Retrieval
IR11	Non-Print Media Retrieval
IR12	Electronic Information Retrieval (Databases)
IR13	Virtual Books
IR14	**THE INTERNET**
IR15	Home/Small Business Use
IR16	Internet Service Providers (ISPs)
IR17	How to Choose an Internet Provider
IR18	Website Addresses (Internet URLs)
IR19	Search Engines
IR20	Tips for Searching the Net or Web Browsing
IR21	Common File Extensions Used on the Web
IR22	Downloading from the Internet
IR23	FTP (File Transfer Protocol) Sites/Space
IR24	Freeware/Shareware
IR25	Downloading Files from the Internet
IR26	Firewalls
IR27	Usenet/Netnews and Usenet/Netnews Search Engines
IR28	Webpage Creation
IR29	Suggestions for Effective Webpage Design
IR30	Intranets
IR31	Advantages of Using the Internet
IR32	Disadvantages of Using the Internet
IR33	Best of the Web
IR34	Blogs

IR

IR35	Internet Terms
IR36	Copyright
IR37	**PRINT INFORMATION SOURCES**
IR38	Biographical References
IR39	Dictionaries
IR40	Directories
IR41	**Business**
IR42	**City**
IR43	Encyclopedias
IR44	English Language Usage and Style
IR45	Financial References
IR46	Government References
IR47	Office Handbooks
IR48	Postal Information
IR49	Telephone Directories
IR50	**FACTS ABOUT CANADA**
IR51	The Government of Canada
IR52	Government Services

The volume of business-related information available is staggering and ever increasing. To keep pace with it all is impossible for the human mind. Therefore, the secret to success in this area is not *knowing everything* but *knowing where and how to find information*. This unit will provide useful guidelines to help in your search.

First, we will review comprehensive coverage of electronic information retrieval, today's computer-based way of obtaining information and doing research. Next, we will outline the many services provided by libraries and the internet. Finally, we will examine the most authoritative printed sources of information as consulted most often by businesspeople and in the categories they use most frequently.

IR1 ELECTRONIC INFORMATION SOURCES

IR2 ELECTRONIC REFERENCE SOURCES

◆ Most word-processing software includes a dictionary to assist with spelling and many include thesauruses to provide alternatives to words.

NOTE You can add new words or terms to existing spell-check packages (e.g., medical or legal terms).

◆ Grammar and style checkers are also available in software to assist in the writing process.
◆ Dictionaries may also be purchased in electronic (small notebook) form.
◆ Some electronic translators contain two to five languages.

IR3 DATABASES

A database is a large volume of information stored in electronic format. Organizations may maintain databases of information relevant to their own organizations or they may use commercial ones.

▶IR4   Commercial databases

Many hundreds of commercial databases cover most fields of knowledge. Some provide fast-changing (time-sensitive) information such as stock and commodity prices. Others provide information on business activities, the professions, education, industry, science, technology, political activities, issues, people, places, international news, airline schedules, weather, and sports. Most of the world's newspapers are available online, as are some books, reports, research documents, scholarly papers, encyclopedias, and periodicals. In fact, almost all information imaginable is available through a commercial database of some type. Most databases now use the internet as a delivery mechanism.

Online databases are critical in obtaining the most up-to-date information on any given subject. For research purposes, two types of online text (or searching) services are available.

Bibliographic Searches in this type of online text database lead you to documents but do not provide the documents themselves (i.e., you obtain a *list* of published reference sources on the topic being researched).

Full text This type of service provides *all* of the article or paper being sought. This is the preferred option because it allows the user to access the article immediately.

In the past few years, magazine publishers have become more comfortable with the concept of electronic access to the full text (often including images) of their articles. Many are licensing this data to electronic publishers for inclusion in reference databases. An advantage of a full-text database is the capability to perform a key-word search on the full text of an article, which can significantly increase the chances of retrieving information on a hard-to-find topic.

IR

▶IR5   Major database services

Listed below are the websites for some of the major database services. These websites provide information from current newspapers, magazines, and journals, and have archives of these materials from previous years. There are fees charged for using these services.

ProQuest: www.proquest.co.uk

Dialog: www.dialog.com

EbscoHost*: ejournals.ebsco.com/Login.asp

*EbscoHost is made available free of charge via many public library websites (user must have a library card to obtain access).

▶ IR6   Using commercial database services

Depending on the database being accessed, computer search requests can be made by author, title, subject, or key word(s). In searching, the computer looks for a match between words selected to describe the subject of the search and words used by the database service to index its collection of references. You "log on" (are connected) to the database by keying in a user number or password. Next, using specific commands or key words, define the parameters (framework) of the information sought (e.g., in researching women in Canadian business, you might indicate the time period from 1975 to today and specify the advertising industry). Searching commercial databases is similar to searching on the internet. Knowing advanced search techniques will greatly improve search results.

NOTE   See http://searchenginewatch.com/facts/article.php/2156021 for a great explanation on how to improve online searching.

▶ IR7   Cost

Charges for database use vary. Some are available on a flat fee subscription basis; others are charged on a pay-per-use basis. Although commercial database use may be expensive, users find the cost is generally offset by savings in time. In addition, some databases are an economical alternative to buying magazines and books.

▶ IR8   Advantages

While database services may be costly, the advantages are considerable:

- Obtaining the most current information can be critical for many businesses and medical/legal practices.
- In-depth searches can be made quickly.
- The user is an active participant and can amend requests by interacting with the computer, if necessary, as searches progress.
- Re-searching using new key words or topics is possible. Manual searches would be too time-consuming to permit such re-searching.
- A far wider range of information sources is available than is possible through local library sources.
- The indexing provided by the database service offers more access to information than the indexing normally available for print media.
- Note-taking is unnecessary; results may be printed, downloaded, and even sent to an email address.
- Costs of searching are specific and can be directly allocated to a project. Manual searches are indirect and difficult to cost.

IR9 USING LIBRARIES

IR10 BOOK RETRIEVAL

All libraries, regardless of size or specialization, provide catalogues of the books and other materials they own. A *library catalogue* is a database of books and non-book items housed in the library. Many online library catalogues are now available via the internet. Even national libraries can be accessed. These websites can be a great resource tool for any researcher. You can search online library catalogues in a number of ways, including by author, key word, and format.

Classification systems

All libraries use a classification system to catalogue their holdings. The two most widely used are the Dewey decimal and the Library of Congress systems. The Dewey decimal system is generally used in school libraries and public libraries. This system provides 10 major categories that are further divided into subcategories. The major Dewey decimal categories are:

000–099	General
100–199	Philosophy
200–299	Religion
300–399*	Social Sciences
400–499	Language
500–599	Science and Mathematics
600–699*	Applied Sciences and Industries
700–799	Fine Arts and Recreation
800–899	Literature
900–999	History, Travel, and Biography

*Most business information is contained in these sections.

The Library of Congress system is generally used in college and university libraries. This system provides 21 major categories, based on the alphabet, to classify the principal areas of knowledge.

IR

IR11 NON-PRINT MEDIA RETRIEVAL

Non-print media, such as films, records, and tapes, may also be sources of information and are available in or through most libraries. Although these may be stored separately from the books and periodicals, the cataloguing system is the same as that described for books.

```
24 NOV 2008              MARKHAM COMMUNITY BRANCH              02:22 pm
                              CIRCULATION MODULE

Call Number    ADULT NON-FICTION COLLECTION         Status : CHECKED IN
               651.30202 CAM 2008

   AUTHOR      Campbell, Joan I.

    TITLE      Pitman Office Handbook /

  EDITION      7th ed.

PUBLISHER      Don Mills, ON. : Pearson Education Canada / 2008

  DESCRIP      vi, 608 p. : ill.

SUBJECT(S)     1) Office practice -- Handbooks, manuals, etc.

                              - - - - More on Next Screen - - - -

Press «Return» to see next screen:
Commands: SO = Start Over, B = Back, RW = Related Works, C = Copy status S = Select, «Return» = Next Screen, ? = Help
```

Computer library reference

IR12 ELECTRONIC INFORMATION RETRIEVAL (DATABASES)

Most libraries offer free access to a wide selection of online services that would be very expensive if purchased by the individual. Online magazine and newspaper articles and encyclopedias are usually available simply by accessing the public library webpage. The information available could be at least one month out of date; therefore, if you need more current information, accessing a fee-for-service database would be the best option. A public library may offer this service, but if not, you may need to use a private company. The service fees are high, but it would be far more expensive to acquire your own search account and do your own searching because you will be paying hourly fees. The longer you take to search, the higher the fees. Professional online searchers would do the same search in a fraction of the time, and pass the savings on to their clients.

Many public libraries, even in very small communities, provide access to electronic journal services. Listed here are just a few. If you have a library card for any of the following libraries (you usually have to live in the vicinity of the library to obtain a card), you can use their electronic journal services free of charge.

> www.myhamilton.ca/myhamilton/LibraryServices
> www.tpl.toronto.on.ca
> www.vpl.vancouver.bc.ca
> www.halifaxpubliclibraries.ca

IR13 VIRTUAL BOOKS

Virtual books, also known as e-audio books, are free through your local library and can be downloaded onto a computer or an MP3 player. Classic literature and language learning books, e.g., learning Spanish, are the most popular kinds of virtual books. These files expire after two weeks, so patrons are not charged a late fee.

IR14 THE INTERNET

The internet (the Net) was developed by the U.S. Department of Defense in the 1960s and was made available to the general public in 1984. The internet is a communications network where a registered user can sign on to a huge worldwide "network of networks" to obtain information in a multimedia format that includes animation, graphics, text, video clips, and sound.

NOTE No one owns the internet.

The World Wide Web (WWW or the Web) is a user-friendly mechanism of the internet. Anyone can publish information, then list it by subject matter, and users can easily gain access to this information. The Web is very popular for business, academic, and home use. Messages can be sent at any time of the day or night to connected users anywhere in the world.

IR15 HOME/SMALL BUSINESS USE

You will need a computer running Windows, with at least 512 MB to 1 GB of RAM. To get the most out of the internet, your PC should have a fast processor, a V.90 56K modem, speakers, and a microphone.

♦ Internet access—you must purchase internet time from an internet service provider (ISP) and arrange to connect your computer to the ISP's host computer.

IR16 INTERNET SERVICE PROVIDERS (ISPs)

The ISP maintains the host computer, provides a gateway or entrance to the internet, and sets up electronic "mail boxes" with facilities for receiving and sending email. The ISP charges a fee for access to the internet and email services. Each time you want to access the Net, you must log on. You will have to arrange to connect your PC to the ISP. There are four choices for the home computer:

IR

Ways to connect to an ISP		
Name	**Speed**	**Connection**
Dial-up	Slow	Regular telephone line*
ISDN (Integrated Services Integrated Network)	Medium	ISDN telephone line*
DSL (Digital Subscriber Line)	Fast	Regular telephone line*
Cable	Fast	TV cable

*The telephone is inaccessible only when using the dial-up method. There is an additional monthly charge for cable service to avoid this problem.

Obtain the fastest internet connection you can afford. DSL and cable are better than ISDN, and ISDN is better than a regular dial-up connection.

IR17 HOW TO CHOOSE AN INTERNET PROVIDER

◆ Reputation (word of mouth)—ask people who are connected; are they pleased with the service? Is online help available?

◆ Charges—get a flat monthly rate that is suitable for your needs, such as 10 hours or unlimited access for a higher rate. Some ISPs will offer the first month or two free. Use this free time to chart your use to enable you to select a suitable billing plan.

◆ Email sharing—will others (such as family members or roommates) be using the connection? If so, set up different email addresses to avoid sorting mail. This is also recommended for a home-run business (keeps personal mail separate from business mail). Find out how many mail addresses are provided by the ISP.

◆ Technical support—is help available? 24-hour assistance? Is there a 1-800 number that can be called if needed? Do they provide help on their website?

◆ Local phone access—whenever you use the Net, your modem must dial the phone number of the ISP and connect to a modem at the other end of the line. Do you have local access phone numbers?

◆ Waiting time for access—ask about the number of phone lines. You don't want to be kept waiting for long periods.

◆ Does the ISP provide software to new customers? Do you download the software yourself from the internet? Is the software provided on disk? Do you need an internet browser, such as Internet Explorer or Netscape, as well as email and setup software?

◆ Does the ISP charge a fee to set up a personal webpage? (Most ISPs do not.)

◆ Does the ISP anticipate making any infrastructure repairs or improvements that could interrupt service?

◆ Are refunds available for customers who cancel the contract?

◆ How long has the company been in business?

IR18 WEBSITE ADDRESSES (INTERNET URLs)

A URL (uniform resource locator) is the website address. It refers to the location of a specific webpage. For instance, the Government of Canada is located at canada.gc.ca.

URLs often end in a *.ca* or *.com* suffix. If the webpage cannot be located, simply changing the suffix from *.com* to *.ca* or vice versa can sometimes fix the problem.

Searching the Net is a learned skill that is valuable for researching information, and when used properly, it can save time and money and increase productivity in the workplace. This skill is also important for personal use, such as when researching topics for presentations, reports, etc.

Today's knowledge worker should be proficient in surfing the Net for accurate and up-to-date information.

See Unit 5 for more detailed information on electronic mail.

TIP Remember to keep an updated reference index of frequently used email addresses/websites. When using Internet Explorer (Microsoft), the index icon is called *Favorites*. When using Netscape, the index icon is called *Bookmarks*.

IR19 SEARCH ENGINES

With the creation of Web browsers several years ago, computer users now spend hours surfing the Net. Remember that you are not searching the entire Web; you are only searching the database of webpages that a search engine or search directory has previously sought out and stored.

A **search engine** is a program that can search a huge database for specific information, i.e., it allows users to search for sites that contain the key word(s) entered by the user.

IR20 TIPS FOR SEARCHING THE NET OR WEB BROWSING

◆ Become familiar with the different search engines and tools on the Web, and their characteristics and strengths, in order to locate exactly what you are searching for. Examples of internet search engines:

> www.altavista.com
> www.google.ca
> www.lycos.ca
> www.webcrawler.com
> www.yahoo.ca
> www.alltheweb.com

◆ Insert quotation marks around words that must be together (e.g., a name, "Joan Campbell") because when quotation marks are used around a search phrase, the search engine will look for an exact match.

◆ Save your favourite websites (using either Favorites or Bookmarks, depending on your browser).

◆ Delete dead websites from your Favorites/Bookmarks file which are no longer accessible.

◆ If your search does not provide the desired results, try again using different search terms, and perhaps a different search engine.

◆ Remember to use the advanced searching options and access online tutorials to improve your searching abilities. The more you search, the greater your skills, but these skills can be enhanced only by increasing your understanding of how information can be located. For greater searching capabilities, use the advanced features provided

IR

by most search engines. The following website addresses can be used for advanced searches.

www.google.ca/advanced_search?hl=en
search.yahoo.com/search/options?fr=fp-top&p=
search.lycos.com/adv.asp

◆ Use wild-card searches: To find a phrase or quote, you don't have to know all the words. Wrap a portion of the quote that you know in quotation marks; for the best result, add related words, e.g., the speaker's name.

IR21 COMMON FILE EXTENSIONS USED ON THE WEB

Extension	Meaning
asp	Webpage generated in a specific way
exe	Executable program
gif	Image/picture stored in GIF format
jpg	Image/picture stored in JPEG format
htm	Webpage
html	Webpage
txt	Plain text
wav	Music/sound file
zip	Compressed collection of files

IR22 DOWNLOADING FROM THE INTERNET

The internet is not just used for searching. Another available feature is uploading and downloading files.

IR23 FTP (FILE TRANSFER PROTOCOL) SITES/SPACE

All computers/servers that allow the file transfer protocol are also called FTP sites. Using FTP allows you to both download and upload files from FTP sites on the internet. These files can consist of software, text, and graphics.

FTPSpace is internet-accessible disk space, or what is known on the internet as a server or storage space for webpages and other files that may be shared with the internet. For example, your internet service provider will often supply its members with space on the Web. The cost of this service is included in your monthly fee.

FTPSpace also contains a list of Web publishing tools that you can download and use to create webpages. Some of these tools are free and others (such as shareware) are not.

IR24 FREEWARE/SHAREWARE

As defined in Unit 12, shareware is copyrighted software that the programmer makes available to others for personal use.

Many websites offer free software. Most of the programs will be either freeware (no charge) or shareware (try it and then pay for it if you decide to keep using it).

Examples of freeware/shareware sites:

www.tucows.com

www.pilottheshareware.com

NOTE   When you copy a file/webpage from the internet to the hard drive (usually C: or D:) on your own computer, this is known as a download. When you copy a file/webpage from your computer hard drive to the internet (as you would when creating a webpage), this is known as an upload.

NOTE   Files uploaded to your FTPSpace are available to anyone on the internet, unless they are uploaded to a private directory; this directory is automatically created. Other people can upload files to the directory by creating an incoming directory.

IR25 DOWNLOADING FILES FROM THE INTERNET

Most programs consist of multiple files, and all files are needed to use the program. To avoid downloading each file separately, gather the required files together and put them in a larger file called an archive. No matter how many files the program requires, only a single file, the Archive file, needs to be downloaded.

These files are compressed and therefore take less room, so it is faster to download the archive than it is to download the files separately. *Compressed format* means that the file has been altered to reduce its original size.

To download and install a program from the internet

◆ Locate the program you want.

◆ Download the archive for the program.

◆ Unpack the archive.

◆ Install the program.

After the archive file is downloaded, the compressed files need to be decompressed and restored to the normal/original size (also called "unpacking" or "unzipping").

To search an archive, use a Usenet/Netnews search engine. These search engines access articles that have been posted to newsgroups around the world.

When a file is downloaded from the internet, you can use two different systems:

1. HTTP—the protocol used to transfer information between Web servers and Web client/customers.

2. Anonymous FTP—free software available on the internet that permits reliable, worldwide distribution of software and other data.

IR26 FIREWALLS

A firewall is a combination of hardware and software that protects computer networks from unwanted intrusions. Private networks/intranets erect firewalls to prevent access to sensitive company data except by authorized personnel.

IR

Public internet sites also have firewalls to prevent unscrupulous people from accessing areas that store private information, e.g., credit card numbers, customer lists, etc.

There are precautions you can take when giving out credit card information over the internet. Before doing so, ensure that you are using a secure server.

Two ways you can ensure the server is secure:

1. The http in the URL includes an "s", i.e., https.

   http://www.chapters.indigo.ca   (unlocked—do not give credit card information)

   https://shop.chapters.indigo.ca   (locked—it is safe to give credit card information)

2. You will see a "lock icon" in the lower left-hand corner. The lock should be in the locked position, not open.

See Unit 19, "Math and Financial Management," for information on identity theft prevention.

IR27 USENET/NETNEWS AND USENET/NETNEWS SEARCH ENGINES

UseNet/Netnews is a global system of thousands of different discussion groups/newsgroups; these newsgroups send in articles and topics on current events nationwide.

UseNet/Netnews search engines allow you to access hundreds of articles that have been posted to all the newsgroups around the world. These search engines are free; they are run by companies that sell advertising for revenue.

IR28 WEBPAGE CREATION

Ebusiness (electronic business) or B2B (business to business) has created thousands of websites where the buying and selling of products takes place. To attract potential clients or customers, entrepreneurs create their own webpages. The Web provides a means of exposing their business or product to a wide audience.

Webpages use a text-based code called HTML (Hypertext Markup Language), which is used to connect related text, webpages, and graphics. Webpages can only be accessed through (hosted by) an ISP or a free Web hosting provider, such as Yahoo!, AltaVista, etc. Webpages are stored as files on a Web server.

Steps for creating webpages

◆ Create a webpage using code, e.g., use a text-based code (HTML) to connect related text, pages, and graphics; small instructions called "tags" are used to format a graphics-based webpage.

◆ Create a webpage using web design software; most ISPs provide software for webpage design. Many office software packages also include webpage design formats.

◆ For a professional appearance, hire a webpage designer to create a webpage, or take a webpage design course to create your own webpages.

IR29 SUGGESTIONS FOR EFFECTIVE WEBPAGE DESIGN

◆ Create a homepage that acts as an entry to the whole website.

◆ Ensure that the site is easy to read, pleasant to view, and well organized.

◆ Use a larger font or attractive graphic (one or two preferred) to draw the attention of the reader.

◆ Avoid using too much information.

◆ Keep in mind that the more graphics used, the longer it takes the reader to access the webpage.

◆ Avoid linking webpages. If necessary, ensure that users can easily navigate from the homepage to secondary/linked pages.

◆ Do not use bright or busy background pages.

◆ Do not use music; if you must, set it up so that the reader must press a button to hear the music.

◆ Remember to proofread for grammar and spelling.

Sitekits

Sitekits are prepackaged website templates available in one downloadable, compressed file. These files are straightforward and complete; only text needs to be added. The images are in jpeg format and are optimized for minimum file sizes, and the templates are free for non-commercial use.

IR30 INTRANETS

An *intranet* is an internal webpage system that uses the same technology as the internet but operates only within the confines of a business. An intranet can be used to navigate between objects, documents, webpages, and other destinations using hyperlinks.

A company intranet offers organizations a number of groupware capabilities in a networked environment, e.g., annual reports, contact information, committees, clubs, departments, divisions, email and phone directories, news and events, policies, search, training, technical support, and useful weblinks. It is designed for sharing company information and for creating custom applications for access via web browsers. (See Unit 12, C23 for more information on groupware.)

IR31 ADVANTAGES OF USING THE INTERNET

Although the internet is an excellent source of information, there are advantages and disadvantages to consider when using this technology. Some advantages are as follows:

IR

- in business, for marketing and access to financial information, bonds, mutual funds, and stocks
- in government, for linking agencies and sharing information, databases, etc.
- in education, for academic research, to prepare assignments, reports, and term papers
- in health care and facilities where up-to-date information is accessed quickly
- in small businesses that are run from the home (e.g., desktop publishing, etc.)
- in creating a reference list of websites that are accessed on a regular basis, for example:
  - www1.paramountparks.com/canadaswonderland
  - www.cbc.ca
  - www.thesaurus.com
  - www.library.nyu.edu/research/journal (Bobst Library—Journalism and Mass Communication Resources)
  - www.vacation-properties.com
  - www.theweathernetwork.com
  - www.stockgroupmedia.com
  - www.canadianbusiness.com
- for saving time through instant messaging/communication

IR32 DISADVANTAGES OF USING THE INTERNET

Some of the disadvantages of using the internet are as follows:

- Anyone can create a webpage on any subject; therefore, much of the information on the internet is not from a reputable source. Always check the source of the webpage content before using the information. For instance, health information should be obtained from a website created by a well-known hospital, such as The Hospital for Sick Children or the Mayo Clinic. Current news should be taken from daily newspaper sites, such as those of *The Globe and Mail* or the *Wall Street Journal*.
- Delays in getting online access—The internet is used by people all over the world; therefore, sending messages or files can be time-consuming.
- Quantity/volume of information available—There is so much data that searching to find the correct information can be intimidating.
- The environment changes daily, with new host computers being added and other sites dropped or no longer maintained.
- Validity of information—Critical business/research data must be confirmed before using, as well as the copyright status of the information; make sure you access the official website for a person, company, or organization.
- Privacy—There is a lack of security for email and file transmission; information can be intercepted, altered, or copied.

◆ Pop-up/message advertising—You will see nuisance or pop-up advertising while you are in the middle of accessing/sending information on the internet. You can purchase reasonably priced programs that will block all pop-up/message advertisements.

◆ Cost.

◆ Planted viruses.

IR33 BEST OF THE WEB

Business and finance information

www.edgar-online.com (Guide to Canadian Company Information)

www.sedar.com

www.edgar-online.com (U.S. Companies)

www.Vertmarket.com

www.fuld.com (Guide to Competitive Intelligence)

Education

www.aucc.ca (Guide to Canadian Universities and Colleges)

Encyclopedias

www.britannica.com (Encyclopaedia Britannica)

Environmental issues

www.ene.gov.on.ca (Ontario Ministry of the Environment)

www.pollutionwatch.org/home.jsp (An environmental information service provided through a partnership of several government agencies and associations. Identifies polluters and details the chemical toxins released in communities across Canada.)

www.earthwatch.org (An international non-profit organization that supports scientific field research worldwide through its volunteers and scientists working together to improve our understanding of the planet.)

www.environmentaldefense.org/home.cfm (A worldwide resource featuring a free newsletter, news releases, global reports, and an interactive set of pages. Among numerous sections on many topics, there is an interesting feature on global warming.)

Health and medical information

hsl.mcmaster.ca (Medical and health care information from the McMaster Health Sciences Library)

www.sickkids.on.ca (A health care, teaching, and research facility dedicated exclusively to children; affiliated with the University of Toronto)

www.mayo.edu (The Mayo Clinic)

Government

www.canada.gc.ca (Government of Canada)

www.firstgov.gov (Government of the United States)

www.statcan.ca (Statistics Canada)

europa.eu (European Union)

IR

National libraries

www.nlc-bnc.ca/index-e.html (Library and Archives Canada)

www.loc.gov (Library of Congress—national library for the United States)

Newspapers

www.theglobeandmail.com (The Globe and Mail)

online.wsj.com/public/us (The Wall Street Journal)

www.nytimes.com (The New York Times)

www.timesonline.co.uk (The London Times, U.K.)

Other

www.webopedia.com (Online encyclopedia dedicated to computer technology)

www.amazon.ca (shopping/e-tailers)

IR34 BLOGS

A weblog (blog) is a type of website where entries are made by an individual in reverse chronological order (most recent entry first). Blogs often provide commentary or news and information on various topics. Most blogs are primarily textual, although some may focus on photos, videos, or audio (podcasting). They are part of a wider network of social media interaction.

IR35 INTERNET TERMS

ADSL: Asynchronous digital subscriber line; internet service at a very fast speed.

Browser: A type of software used to browse sites on the internet, e.g., Internet Explorer or Netscape.

Common gateway interface (CGI): A system used to pass data between a web server and a program designed to process the data.

Cookie: When a user visits a website, a cookie/indicator lets the webmaster know that the user has been surfing. Cookies do not read hard drives; however, they do indicate when a user makes a return visit.

Cyberspace: Internet space.

Cyberworld: Internet world.

Dial-up modem: A device that downloads data from a distant computer (e.g., at 56.6 kilobits per second or faster).

Dial-up phone number: A number users can dial to access an online bulletin board system.

Domain: A string of words or letters that identifies a particular website.

Domain name system (DNS): The DNS translates hostnames into IP (internet provider) addresses.

Download: The process of copying a file from another computer to your computer.

CAUTION   Make sure you download from a reputable site to avoid unwanted bugs and viruses.

External networks: Large, commercial networks (e.g., America Online, CompuServe, Prodigy, the Microsoft Network, and UseNet).

Extranet: Business-to-business communication using the internet.

FAQ: Frequently asked questions—answers to the most common questions asked on a specific topic.

File transfer protocol (FTP): A communication standard that allows users to access and send files over the internet.

Flame/s: Personal criticisms/verbal attacks on other internet users via email, UseNet, or mailing lists.

Global domain: The last letters of a domain name that indicate the category to which a website belongs (e.g., .com indicates that the website is part of a commercial enterprise and .edu indicates that it is part of an educational domain).

Homepage: The introductory page of a website

Hostname: The unique name given to an internet computer.

Hypertext Markup Language (HTML): A special programming language for creating webpages.

Hypertext Transfer Protocol (http): The communication standard established for the World Wide Web.

Icon: A symbol used to represent a command.

Internet email address: Used to send mail electronically, it consists of the user name, the @ symbol, and the domain name of the host (mail server).

Internet service provider (ISP): A company that provides access to the internet for a fee.

Intranet: A network within an organization that can be connected to World Wide Web servers for the distribution of information within the company.

Intranet services: Uses the same communication technology as the internet but access is restricted to members of a particular group or organization.

Local dial-up phone number: A number customers can dial to log on to their internet account.

Modem: A communications device.

Multi-tasking: Many tasks performed at the same time.

NC: Network computer.

Netiquette: How to act on the Net—remember there is a person at the computer on the other end.

Platform for internet content selections (PICS): A set of standards developed for creating rating systems for internet resources.

Point of presence: A local dial-up phone number.

Portable document format (PDF): High-quality printable documents.

Query string: Use of key words to find information.

Rich text: Text written in HTML that contains regular text and elements such as boldface, italics, various typefaces, pictures, and links to websites.

Search engine: A web tool that uses words or strings of words to search for information on the World Wide Web (e.g., AltaVista, Excite, Google, Lycos, The Electric Library, Yahoo!).

IR

Snail mail: Regular post office mail.

Spam: Advertisements or unsolicited mail/messages sent by email.

Surfing the Net: Looking for websites for information.

Tags: Files stored on a web server contain information that will be on the page, along with special instructions called *tags*. These tags are written according to a set of specifications using HTML and indicate what components are to be used and how they should be displayed on the page.

Uniform resource locator (URL): A unique string of characters used to identify and navigate a specific address/webpage on the internet, e.g., www.pearsoned.ca.

Upload: To copy a file from your computer to another computer.

Visual reality modelling language (VRML): A program language used to create a three-dimensional environment on the web.

Web browser: A computer program that allows users to view and interact with websites.

WebCrawler: Lists the number of pieces of information available on a topic (e.g., television AND news AND mass communication).

Webpage: A page of a website; webpages are created with HTML.

Web server/website: A computer where files/webpages are stored; these pages can contain text, graphics, audio or video, and links to other pages where information is stored.

IR36 COPYRIGHT

Concerns about copyright protection for original creative works transmitted via the internet will likely produce a comprehensive revisitation of copyright law; most authors will probably not want to have their works freely pirated without their consent. If information is transmitted via the internet, however, it should be assumed that it could become public knowledge.

> **NOTE** Information taken from the internet should be referenced by website (e.g., author, title, etc.). For example:
>
> Morrissy, John. "Tracking New Brunswick's Economic Revolution." *The Best in the Business* Oct. 1997: 21 pars. Online. New Brunswick Publishing Co. Available: http://www.nbpub.nbca/bizbest/editor.htm. 10 Dec. 1997.

IR37 PRINT INFORMATION SOURCES

For information about almanacs, yearbooks, and atlases, please visit the Text Enrichment Site for this text at *www.pearsoned.ca/text/campbell*.

IR38 BIOGRAPHICAL REFERENCES

These supply data about famous people in the present and past. Biographical dictionaries such as *The Macmillan Dictionary of Canadian Biography, Who's*

Who in Canada, and *Canadian Who's Who* provide information about individuals in a dictionary format, i.e., individuals are listed alphabetically by surnames. The information is concise and factual, somewhat like a résumé, without analysis or commentary on the data. Each entry includes such elements as family information, date of birth, education, marital status, business background, important positions held, achievements, and any honours received.

◆ *Canadian Who's Who*. Toronto: University of Toronto Press.

◆ *Current Biography*. New York: H. W. Wilson.

◆ *Who's Who in Canada*. Toronto: Global Press.

◆ *Who's Who in Canadian Business*. Toronto: University of Toronto Press.

◆ *International Who's Who*. London, England: Europa Publications.

◆ *Who's Who in America*. Chicago: Marquis Who's Who Inc.

◆ *Who's Who in the World*. Chicago: Marquis Who's Who Inc.

NOTE For information about notable people no longer alive, refer to encyclopedias or to the *Dictionary of National Biography* of the relevant countries.

IR39 DICTIONARIES

Dictionaries contain words that are listed alphabetically, usually with the following information:

◆ *definitions*

◆ *preferred form of spelling* if more than one is acceptable

◆ *syllabic division* shown by a heavy accent, light accent, centred period, or hyphen

◆ *correct pronunciation* indicated by accent marks—a heavy one ($\bar{e}$) shows special emphasis; a lighter mark ($\breve{e}$) denotes less stress

◆ *part of speech:* if more than one is indicated, any change in pronunciation will also be shown

◆ *derivations of words* (their origins) in square brackets at the end of an entry

◆ *synonyms and antonyms* indicated by *syn* and *ant* at the end of an entry

◆ *usage examples* in phrases and clauses to complement the common definition and clarify usage

◆ *prefixes and suffixes,* with their definitions

Consult the front of the dictionary for detailed information on etymology (word origins), pronunciation, and abbreviations used in the dictionary. The alphabetical list of words is sometimes followed by an addendum of words not listed in the body of the dictionary and further senses and constructions of words already treated, plus a section on abbreviations and foreign words and phrases. Some dictionaries also supply information on international currencies, scientific and technical terms, titles of address, and weights and measures.

IR

- *Gage Canadian Dictionary*. Toronto: Gage Publishing Ltd.
- *The Concise Oxford Dictionary of Current English*. Oxford University Press.
- *Merriam-Webster's Collegiate Dictionary*. Springfield, MA: Merriam-Webster Inc.

Specialized dictionaries are available for most professions as well as for scientific, technical, and trade specializations. For example:

- *Terminology for Accountants*. Toronto: Canadian Institute of Chartered Accountants.
- *Dictionary of Business*. Oxford University Press.
- *Dictionary of Computing*. New York: Oxford University Press.
- *Black's Law Dictionary*. St. Paul's, MN: West Publishing Co.
- *Black's Medical Dictionary*. London: A. & C. Black.
- *Blakiston's Gould Medical Dictionary*. New York: McGraw-Hill.
- *Dictionary of Scientific and Technical Terms*. New York: McGraw-Hill.

IR40 DIRECTORIES

▶ IR41 Business

This section identifies several business, trade, and professional sources that list names and addresses of organizations, corporations, and chief executive officers, as well as products, services, and brand names.

Directories are lists of persons or organizations, arranged in some logical order, usually alphabetical. The telephone book is, of course, the directory format with which we are most familiar. Specialized directories provide information for a defined clientele, and are valuable tools for reference in the workplace.

- *Associations Canada: An Encyclopedic Directory*. Toronto: Canadian Almanac & Directory Publishing Co. Ltd.

  Annual publication that contains a list of Canadian and international associations in Canada, plus dates and locations of major conferences, shows, and meetings scheduled for the current year.
- *Blue Book of Canadian Business*. Toronto: Canadian Newspaper Services International.

  Information on and business rankings of major Canadian corporations.
- *Canadian Advertising Rates and Data*. Ed. Wayne Ibsen. Toronto: Maclean Hunter.
- *Canadian Key Business Directory/Répertoire des principales entreprises canadiennes*. Toronto: Dun & Bradstreet Canada Ltd.

  Names and addresses of more than 20 000 companies by geographical location and type of business, plus names of key executives.
- *Canadian Trade Index*. Toronto: Canadian Manufacturers' Association.

  Alphabetical list of manufacturers, plus classified list of products.

III

♦ *Directory of Associations in Canada*. Ed. Lynn Fraser. Toronto: University of Toronto Press.

♦ *Fraser's Canadian Trade Directory*. Toronto: Maclean Hunter. Alphabetical list of manufacturers, plus a list of products by trade names and their manufacturers.

♦ *KWIC Index to Services*. Toronto: Ontario Ministry of Government Services.

♦ *National List of Advertisers*. Toronto: Maclean Hunter.

♦ *Scott's Directories, Ontario Manufacturers*. Ed. Cynthia D. Gardiner. Oakville, ON: Scott's Directories.

♦ *Standard and Poor's Register of Corporations, Directors and Executives*. New York: Standard and Poor's Corp.

♦ *The Financial Post Directory of Directors*. Toronto: The Financial Post.

♦ *The Fortune Directory*. Chicago: Fortune Magazine. Information on and rankings of the 500 largest industrial companies in the United States.

▶IR42 City

City directories provide information on local residents and companies. They usually contain the following sections:

Classified business directory Similar to the Yellow Pages of the telephone directory, with companies and services listed alphabetically.

Alphabetical directory Shows adult residents, their addresses, occupations, and marital status. Also included are business and professional organizations with the address, type of business, and official personnel of each.

Postal code directory Provides postal codes in alphabetical street order.

Street directory Lists each street alphabetically and indicates where inter-sections occur. The numbers of the residences and business organizations are arranged numerically under each street, and the names of household-ers and companies and their telephone numbers are placed opposite them.

Telephone number directory Contains a numerical listing with names and addresses of the subscribers beside each number.

Publishers of such directories include the following:

Halifax:	Might Directories
Toronto:	Bowers Metropolitan Cross Reference Directory Limited
Southern Ontario:	Vernon's Directory*
Vancouver:	Henderson, Division of Polk Canada Limited

*Vernon Directories are published by the city of Vernon, i.e., each city has its own directory of miscellaneous information concerning street names, businesses, maps, etc.

IR

IR43 ENCYCLOPEDIAS

For historical facts and general information across all disciplines, people, and places of note, these sources are among the most common:

◆ *The Canadian Encyclopedia*. Edmonton: Hurtig Publishers.
◆ *Columbia Encyclopedia*. New York: Columbia University Press.
◆ *Encyclopedia America*. Danbury, CT: Grolier Inc.
◆ *New Encyclopedia Britannica*. Chicago: Encyclopedia Britannica Inc.
◆ *Encyclopedia Canadiana*. Toronto: Grolier of Canada.

IR44 ENGLISH LANGUAGE USAGE AND STYLE

The following selections contain information on the fundamental rules of grammar, punctuation, style, famous quotations, and synonyms and antonyms:

◆ *The Canadian Style: A Guide to Writing and Editing*. Toronto: The Department of the Secretary of State of Canada.
◆ *The Canadian Writer's Handbook*. Toronto: Prentice-Hall, Inc.
◆ *A Dictionary of Modern English Usage* (H. W. Fowler). Oxford: Clarendon Press.
◆ *Bartlett's Familiar Quotations*. Toronto: Little, Brown & Co.
◆ *Colombo's Canadian Quotations*. Edmonton: Hurtig Publishers.
◆ *Roget's Thesaurus of English Words and Phrases*. London, England: Longman.
◆ *The New Roget's Thesaurus in Dictionary Form*. New York: G. P. Putnam's Sons.

IR45 FINANCIAL REFERENCES

Two of the publications issued by the major financial reporting organizations are

◆ *Financial Reporting in Canada*. Toronto: Canadian Institute of Chartered Accountants.
◆ *Dun & Bradstreet Reference Book*. Toronto: Dun & Bradstreet Canada Ltd. Dun & Bradstreet will provide credit information and individual credit reports to subscribers.

Members may also contact the local credit bureau for credit information.

IR46 GOVERNMENT REFERENCES

Federal
The publisher for the federal government:
Canada Communication Group–Publishing, Ottawa, ON K1A 0S9
www.fedpubs.com

This group is responsible for co-ordinating, publishing, distributing, and marketing federal publications, each of which is either produced or sponsored by a government department or agency.

◆ Topics include aeronautics, agriculture, art, communications, education, energy and natural resources, environment, fauna, fisheries, forestry, geography, geology, government and legislation, health and nutrition, history and archeology, labour, linguistics, marine, science and technology, sociology, trade, transportation, and weather.

◆ Priced publications may be ordered direct or through local booksellers.

◆ An annual catalogue of several hundred publications is available.

◆ Free publications are available from the departments that produce and publish them.

Statistics Canada, a federal government agency, is responsible for the publication of all statistical reporting.

The *Statistics Canada Catalogue* contains a list of publications that provide data on primary industries, manufacturing, transportation, travel, commerce, education, health and welfare, and many other subjects.

NOTE Contact your local federal member of Parliament for up-to-date information on federal government issues.

Provincial

Provincial government publications on a variety of subjects are available from government bookstores. Each provincial government department produces its own publications. Contact local elected provincial representatives for government information as well.

Publications Ontario website: pubont.stores.gov.on.ca/pool/english

IR47 OFFICE HANDBOOKS

For guidance on document formatting, business practices and etiquette, and English language conventions, refer to this handbook or to others that are available, including the following:

◆ *The Canadian Office Management Manual.* Vancouver: Self-Counsel Press.

◆ *The Gregg Reference Manual.* Westerville, OH: Macmillan, McGraw-Hill School of Publishing.

◆ *Robert's Rules of Order* (revised). Glenview, IL: Scott, Foresman and Company.

◆ *Emily Post's Etiquette.* New York: Harper & Row.

NOTE Maintain and update the following:

◆ reference manuals on the hardware and equipment used in your office

IR

♦ reference manuals on the software used in your office (most of these are now available on CD-ROM)

♦ reference manuals related specifically to your organization (e.g., company policies and procedures)

IR48 POSTAL INFORMATION

Canada's Postal Code Directory provides a postal code for every address in Canada. Use the appropriate provincial section to ensure correct addressing of envelopes and faster mail delivery. Copies of this directory are usually available at post offices and postal outlets or can be ordered at the address shown below.

The *Canada Postal Guide* provides complete information on Canada Post services. For complex or unusual mailing situations, consult this guide or contact a Canada Post representative.

Copies of the directory and the guide can be obtained by writing to

> National Philatelic Centre
> Canada Post
> 75 St. Ninian St.
> Antigonish NS B2G 2R8

For more information:

> Canada Post Corporation (in the White Pages)
> Customer Service Information   1-800-565-4362
> www.canadapost.ca

IR49 TELEPHONE DIRECTORIES

These are issued by the telephone company. The Customer Guide in the introductory pages at the front of the directory lists the services provided:

♦ The White Pages list individuals, businesses, and organizations alphabetically.

♦ The Blue Pages/blue-bordered pages list the three levels of government alphabetically and by department, i.e., federal, provincial, and municipal governments.

♦ The Quick Finder Index is helpful for locating a specific product or service.

♦ The Subject Index is a reference section of general categories to help find a product or service.

♦ The Yellow Pages include an alphabetic and subject index of goods and services and, in many cases, give the website address of the company.

♦ The Advertiser Guide is helpful for businesses that wish to advertise in the Yellow Pages. This section includes local and surrounding area guide maps.

For more information:

> Bell Customer Service   1-800-668-6878 or
> www.bell.ca

> See Unit 4 for telephone techniques and services.

IR50 FACTS ABOUT CANADA

Origin of the name

The first use of "Canada" as an official name came in 1791 when the Province of Quebec was divided into the colonies of Upper and Lower Canada. In 1841, the two Canadas were again united under one name, The Province of Canada. At the time of Confederation, the new country assumed the title "The Dominion of Canada." While the name of the country is Canada, its official title is The Dominion of Canada, reaffirmed by the *Constitution Act,* 1982, which patriated the Canadian Constitution.

History

Ten provinces and three territories make up Canada today. However, in 1867 when the *British North America Act* was proclaimed, creating the new Dominion of Canada, there were only four provinces: Ontario, Quebec, Nova Scotia, and New Brunswick.

The newly acquired regions, Rupert's Land and the North-Western Territory, were combined to form the Northwest Territories. The *Manitoba Act,* 1870, created the province of Manitoba from a small part of this area.

In 1871, the colony of British Columbia joined the union with the promise of a railway to link it with the rest of the country.

In 1873, Prince Edward Island became the country's seventh province.

Yukon, which had been a district of the Northwest Territories since 1895, became a separate territory in 1898.

Meanwhile, Canada was opening up its west, just as its neighbour to the south had done before, and immigrants from eastern Canada and Europe began to fill the prairies, which were still part of the Northwest Territories. Then, in 1905, the provinces of Saskatchewan and Alberta were created, completing the map of western Canada.

After great debate and two referenda, Newfoundlanders voted to join Confederation, creating the Dominion's tenth province on March 31, 1949. In 2001, an amendment to the Constitution officially renamed it Newfoundland and Labrador.

Through the *Nunavut Act,* 1993, the Eastern Arctic was severed from the Northwest Territories to become Nunavut Territory in 1999.

IR51 THE GOVERNMENT OF CANADA

The people of Canada are governed by elected officials at the federal, provincial, and local levels of government.

There are six government parties:

The Conservative Party (also called the Tories)
The Liberal Party (also called the Grits)
The New Democractic Party (NDP)
The Bloc Québécois (known as the Bloc)
The Green Party
Other (made up of several independents)

IR

The federal government is made up of 308 ridings (seats in Parliament) across the country. When candidates are elected, they are sworn in and form Parliament (the national law-making body of Canada), consisting of the Senate (appointed officials) and the House of Commons (elected officials). Parliament sits in the city of Ottawa, the capital of Canada.

The party who has the most votes in a federal election is the leading party in the House of Commons. The leader of that party usually becomes the prime minister of Canada for the duration of the term in Ottawa (usually four years, but that can change if the opposing parties call and get a majority vote for the dissolution of Parliament).

The prime minister is appointed by the governor general and stays in power until he or she resigns or is dismissed by the governor general.

The governor general is also entitled to choose the next prime minister, and she/he must decide which party has the best chance of winning the confidence of the House of Commons.

The provincial government is made up of elected candidates at the provincial level. These elected officials form the provincial government, look after issues concerning the province, and report to the federal government on all provincial matters.

The premier of each province is also elected by the voting public.

Local government is made up of elected local officials (councillors and a mayor) who look after community/municipality issues, e.g., maintenance of roads, garbage pickup/disposal, building permits, etc.)

IR52 GOVERNMENT SERVICES

The Government of Canada provides services designed to meet the changing needs of Canadian citizens. The following websites can be accessed for up-to-date information on various topics:

Canada Business Service Centres www.cbsc.org

Canadian Tourism Commission www.travelcanada.ca

Contracts Canada www.contractscanada.gc.ca

Culture and Heritage www.canadianheritage.gc.ca

Job Bank (network of job postings) www.jobbank.gc.ca

Canadian Health Network www.canadian-health-network.ca

Citizenship and Immigration Canada www.cic.gc.ca

Natural Resources Canada www.nrcan.gc.ca

Social Development Canada (information on income security programs) www.sdc.gc.ca

Public Service Commission of Canada www.psc-cfp.gc.ca

Canada Revenue Agency www.cra.gc.ca

Canada Border Services Agency www.cbsa-asfc.gc.ca

Canadian Weather www.weatheroffice.ec.gc.ca

Youth Path www.youth.gc.ca

Service Canada

Service Canada was introduced by the government of Canada to provide Canadians with access to benefits and services through the channel of their choice, i.e., by phone, in person, or via the internet.

At this writing, Service Canada is building partnerships and new ways of working with provinces and territories, non-governmental organizations, and the private sector.

Website: www.servicecanada.gc.ca

For additional information on Government of Canada Services, call 1-800-O-Canada (1-800-622-6232).

The Maple Leaf Flag

The flag was adopted by resolutions of Parliament on December 15, 1964 (House of Commons) and December 17, 1964 (Senate), and was proclaimed by Queen Elizabeth II to take effect on February 15, 1965, when the Maple Leaf Flag was first raised over Parliament Hill.

The Prime Ministers of Canada

Sir John A. Macdonald	(Conservative)	1867–73
Alexander Mackenzie	(Liberal)	1873–78
Sir John A. Macdonald	(Conservative)	1878–91
Sir John J. C. Abbott	(Conservative)	1891–92
Sir John Sparrow Thompson	(Conservative)	1892–94
Sir Mackenzie Bowell	(Conservative)	1894–96
Sir Charles Tupper	(Conservative)	1896
Sir Wilfrid Laurier	(Liberal)	1896–1911
Sir Robert Laird Borden	(Conservative)	1911–17
Sir Robert Laird Borden	(Union)*	1917–20
Arthur Meighen	(Conservative)	1920–21
W. L. Mackenzie King	(Liberal)	1921–26
Arthur Meighen	(Conservative)	1926
W. L. Mackenzie King	(Liberal)	1926–30
Richard Bedford Bennett	(Conservative)	1930–35
W. L. Mackenzie King	(Liberal)	1935–48
Louis St. Laurent	(Liberal)	1948–57
John George Diefenbaker	(Conservative)	1957–63
Lester Bowles Pearson	(Liberal)	1963–68
Pierre Elliott Trudeau	(Liberal)	1968–79
Charles Joseph Clark	(Conservative)	1979–80
Pierre Elliott Trudeau	(Liberal)	1980–84
John Napier Turner	(Liberal)	1984
Martin Brian Mulroney	(Conservative)	1984–93
Avril Kim Campbell	(Conservative)	1993
Joseph-Jacques Jean Chrétien	(Liberal)	1993–2003
Paul Edgar Philippe Martin	(Liberal)	2003–2006
Stephen Joseph Harper	(Conservative)	2006–

* Union Government

The National Anthem

O Canada!
Our home and native land!
True patriot love in all thy sons command.

With glowing hearts we see thee rise,
The True North strong and free!

From far and wide,
O Canada, we stand on guard for thee.

God keep our land glorious and free!
O Canada, we stand on guard for thee.

O Canada, we stand on guard for thee.

WORDS OF WISDOM

Knowledge becomes wisdom only after
it has been put to practical use.

III

SELECTED CONTENTS

B1	**WHAT ARE FORMS?**	
B2	**FORMS USED IN BASIC BUSINESS ACTIVITIES**	
B3	Purchasing	
B6	Receiving	
B8	Inventory Control	
B11	Producing	
B13	Selling	
B15	Shipping	
B18	Billing	
B21	Collecting	
B23	Disbursing	
B24	**PREPRINTED BASIC BUSINESS FORMS**	
B25	Rubber Stamps, Die Stamps, and Preprinted Stickers	
B26	**DESIGNING BUSINESS FORMS**	
B27	**ELECTRONIC FORMS SOFTWARE**	
B30	**OTHER FORMS-RELATED TECHNOLOGIES**	
B31	**FORMS CONTROL**	
B32	**GOVERNMENT FORMS**	

B

Regardless of size, nature of business, or type of ownership, organizations tend to operate along similar lines because they must all deal efficiently with certain basic activities. These activities are purchasing, receiving, inventory control, producing, selling, shipping, billing, and keeping records of money received and paid out. These interdependent activities are linked by means of forms, each designed for a particular purpose.

More and more, activities related to forms are being automated. However, the basic activities do not change. Familiarity with an organization's activities helps office workers understand the business, the roles people play in it, and the best way of serving customers.

The illustrations on pages 440 and 441 describe the flow of activity around purchasing and sales, the two systems that constitute the lifeblood of any business organization. The illustrations show the interdependence of the departments involved and identify the types of forms used at each stage of activity.

B1 WHAT ARE FORMS?

Forms are used to record the details of business transactions. A form can be used to create or cancel a transaction, request action, confirm a request, give instructions, report facts, summarize information, and serve as a base for workflow.

Forms can be in hard copy (i.e., to be completed by computer input or by longhand), or by soft copy (electronic forms) to be displayed on a computer screen and filled in by keying in the information. Some must be completed entirely; with others, considerable amounts of information can be inserted automatically, simply by, say, inserting an account or telephone number.

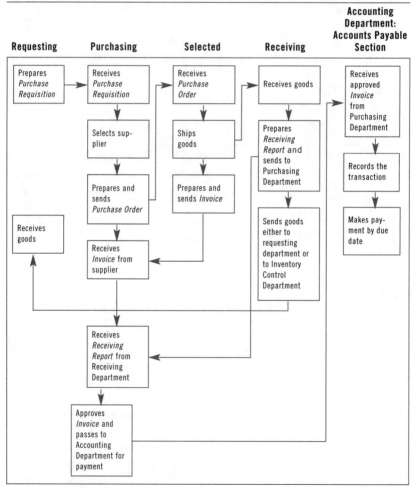

The flow of activities in a typical purchasing system

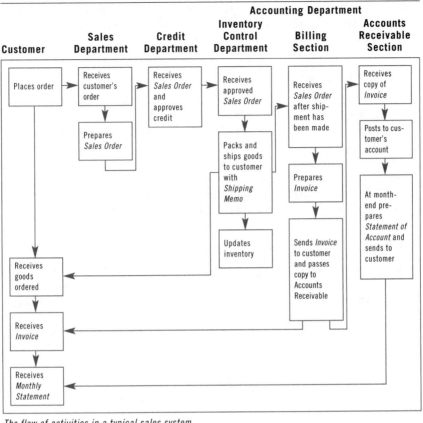

The flow of activities in a typical sales system

Regardless of their type or appearance, forms always serve the same purpose—to ease the flow of information.

B2   FORMS USED IN BASIC BUSINESS ACTIVITIES

In some small organizations, hard-copy forms are used exclusively to implement the various business activities, with each department creating forms that meet its particular needs. To carry out the procedures illustrated in the preceding diagrams, the appropriate form would be sent from one department to another in the order shown.

In electronic systems, however, the supplier (in the case of a purchase) and the customer (in the case of a sale) might be the only people in the chain who receive a hard-copy form. All the intercompany departments are linked electronically, so that as each department completes its required action, the information is fed into a database that informs the next department of the action required of it, until the procedure has been completed. Electronic systems vary depending on the type of programs used.

In the following sections, each of the common activities carried out regularly by most companies is discussed and the usual required number of hard copies of each form is indicated. In the case of an electronic system, of course, the information is automatically transmitted to the appropriate departments and the necessary action is taken.

B3   PURCHASING

Purchasing means buying everything an organization needs in its operation, from paper clips to delivery trucks. In a small company, buying may be done quite informally (by email, fax, letter, or telephone, for example), but a large company needs forms to control and record purchasing functions. In most organizations, buying is handled by a purchasing department, which acts only on receipt of an approved purchase requisition.

Today, many small and large companies are using online buying of goods and services, also known as *e-business* (electronic business) or *e-commerce*.

▶ B4   Purchase requisition

- ◆ issued by a company department and, if approved by a designated person in that department, sent to the purchasing department for action
- ◆ usually, only one copy for the purchasing department and one for the requesting department

REQUISITION (NOT A PURCHASE ORDER)			007266	
TO *Purchasing Dept.*		DATE *Aug. 20* 20 --		
ADDRESS		FOR		
SHIP TO *Production Dept.*		DATE REQ'D. *Sept. 17*		
QUANTITY	PLEASE SUPPLY		PRICE	AMOUNT
1 50	*oak frames, 50 cm x 35 cm*			
2 25	*mahogany frames, 70 cm x 60 cm*			
3 50	*panes non-glare glass, 50 cm x 35 cm*			
4 25	*panes non-glare glass, 70 cm x 60 cm*			
5 3	*rolls canvas, 80 cm wide*			
6				
7				
8				
9				
JOB NO. *1602*	SALES TAX (CHARGEABLE) NOT CHARGEABLE	ORDERED BY *W. Stanley*	APPROVED BY *E. Chin*	

Purchase requisition

▶ **B5 Purchase order**

◆ prepared by the purchasing department from the information provided in the purchase requisition and sent to the vendor (supplier) who offers the best price and delivery terms

◆ copies for the supplier, receiving department, and purchasing department

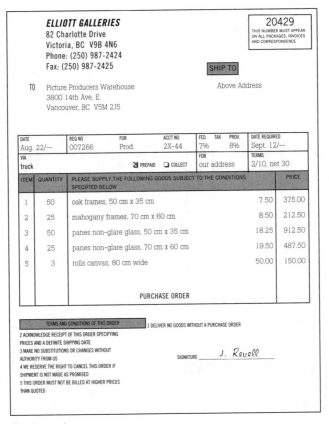

Purchase order

B6 RECEIVING

Goods received must be matched against the original purchase order for accuracy in quantity and type. The goods must also be checked for condition. The receiving department is responsible for checking the goods and completing a receiving report.

▶B7   Receiving report

◆ prepared after incoming goods have been checked against the purchase order

◆ copies for accounts payable, purchasing, inventory control, and receiving

ITEM NO.	QUANTITY	WEIGHT	ACCEPTED	REJECTED	DESCRIPTION
1	25		✓		oak frames, 50 cm x 35 cm
2	25		✓		oak frames, 50 cm x 35 cm
3	25		✓		mahogany frames, 70 cm x 60 cm
4	25		✓		panes non-glare glass, 50 cm x 35 cm
5	10		✓		panes non-glare glass, 50 cm x 35 cm
6	25		✓		panes non-glare glass, 70 cm x 60 cm
7	1		✓		roll canvas, 80 cm wide
8	1		✓		roll canvas, 80 cm wide
9	1		✓		roll canvas, 80 cm wide

RECEIVED FROM Picture Producers Warehouse
DATE Sept. 11 / --
3800 19th Ave. E. Vancouver BC V5M 2J5
PPD ✓ COLL AMOUNT
FREIGHT | EXPRESS | TRANS. | MAIL | VIA truck
PRO BILL NO. BY 4720 NO. OF PKGS. 9
FOR Production Dept.
PURCHASE ORDER NO. 20429

RECEIVING REPORT

15354

PARTIAL ✓ | COMPLETE | POSTED BY | RECEIVED BY AM | INSPECTED BY AM | STORES LOCATION

Receiving report

B8   INVENTORY CONTROL

Inventory control is responsible for the storage, care, and distribution of supplies and raw materials required for operations, and of finished goods to be sold.

▶B9   Inventory record

An inventory record can vary in format, but the following is one example.

◆ kept for each product; shows quantity received and distributed either within the company or to customers, and the amount of each item currently on hand

◆ only one copy usually required for inventory control

NOTE   In many businesses, inventory control is automated. Additions and deletions to inventory are handled automatically as customer invoices

ELLIOTT GALLERIES						PERPETUAL INVENTORY CARD	
ITEM: Oak frames, 50 cm x 35 cm				Maximum:		200	
CODE: S342			STOCK NO.	PR89		Minimum: 20	
Date	Mdse. on order		STOCK				
			Received		Issued		
20--	Purchase req. #	Amt.	Purchase order #	In	Stock req. #	Out	Balance
June 6							130
July 7					347	10	120
July 13					703	35	85
July 27					912	50	35
Sept. 11	7266	50	20429	50			85

Inventory record

are issued and supplier invoices are paid. Periodic computer printouts provide a hard-copy inventory record, if required.

▶B10 Stock requisition

◆ sent to the purchasing department by the inventory control department when it is necessary to replenish supplies that have reached minimum-quantity levels

◆ purchasing department handles a stock requisition in the same manner as it does a purchase requisition from the other company departments

◆ one copy usually needed for the purchasing department and one for inventory control

NOTE In some automated systems, the computer is programmed to notify inventory control when minimum quantities of supplies or raw materials have been reached and more must be ordered.

B11 PRODUCING

In manufacturing firms or in some service businesses (such as garages or equipment repairers), an authorization form known as a *production order* or *work order* is required before the actual production of goods or servicing of equipment can begin.

▶B12 Production order (work order)

◆ given to the person, division, or section within the production department that will do the job

◆ usually one copy for the worker, division, or section doing the job and one for the requesting department

ELLIOTT GALLERIES
82 Charlotte Drive
Victoria, BC V9B 4N6
Phone: (250) 987-2424
Fax: (250) 987-2425

PRODUCTION WORK ORDER	
Work Order No.	F276
Customer P.O. No.	AE49
Date -- 09 16	
Job done by	

Customer
Scotts Art Stores
739 Appian Way
Coquitlam, BC   V3J 2J9

Ship to:
same address

Billing Instructions
Prepaid ❏   Collect ❏
        Invoice ☑

Date Required   -- 09 30

Shipping Instructions
Phone when ready.
Customer will pick up.

Job Description	Unit Price	Total Cost
30 B.C. Scenic prints No. 10-160 to be framed in oak frames with non-glare glass. 50 cm x 35 cm	50.00	1500.00

Date Completed_____
Inspected by_____
Date Shipped _____

Production order

B13 SELLING

A customer who wants to buy goods or services places an order with a firm, activating the sales procedure.

▶ B14 Sales order

◆ made up by a sales representative after taking an order in person, by telephone, through the mail, by fax, or by email, for example

◆ copies usually required by the credit department, customer, and the inventory control, shipping, accounts receivable, and sales departments

NOTE In retail sales, a sales slip is issued at the time of a sale and given to the customer with the goods purchased.

◆ copies usually required for the customer, the accounts receivable section (when the sale is on credit), and the sales department

Picture Producers Warehouse   0179

3800 14th Avenue E.
Vancouver, BC V5M 2J5
Phone: (604) 521-6307
Fax: (604) 521-6322

SOLD TO	Elliott Galleries	S H I P T O	same
	82 Charlotte Drive		
	Victoria, BC V9B 4N6		

DATE	SHIP VIA	CUSTOMER ORDER NO.	SALES REP.
Sept. 8/--	truck	20429	Kenneth Ramsey

QUANTITY ORDERED	DESCRIPTION	UNIT PRICE
50	oak frames, 50 cm x 35 cm	7.50
25	mahogany frames, 70 cm x 60 cm	8.50
50	panes non-glare glass, 50 cm x 35 cm	18.25
25	panes non-glare glass, 70 cm x 60 cm	19.50
3	rolls canvas, 80 cm wide	50.00

Sales order

B15 SHIPPING

When goods are shipped, acknowledgment of their receipt by the addressee is often necessary. Many companies use a specially prepared shipping memo.

                     040573

FROM	Picture Producers Warehouse	DATE	Sept. 11/--
TO	Elliott Galleries	YOUR ORDER	20429
ADDRESS	82 Charlotte Drive	CITY	Victoria

PACKAGES	RECEIVED IN APPARENT GOOD ORDER	WEIGHT
9	Contents - frames	
	- glass	
	- canvas rolls	

RECEIVED BY		TOTAL PACKAGES	9	TOTAL WEIGHT	
A. McLaughlin		C.O.D. CHARGE		DELIVERY CHARGE	

Shipping memo or delivery receipt

B

▶B16 Shipping memo (delivery receipt)

◆ signed by the customer and returned to the carrier on receipt of merchandise

◆ two signed copies usually required: one for the customer, and one for the shipper or electronic signature upon delivery

▶B17 Bill of lading

◆ the standard shipping document that serves as a contract between the consignor (the supplier) and the carrier of the goods

◆ used for all forms of transportation (rail, water, air, or road transportation) (see Unit 18, P55)

B18 BILLING

After the supplier has shipped the articles ordered or provided the service requested, the customer is billed. This is done by sending the top copy of the invoice described below.

▶B19 Invoice

◆ sent by the billing section of the accounting department to the customer

◆ shows details of the goods ordered or services provided, cost, shipping charges, terms of payment, discount applicable, taxes, and total amount due

◆ three copies usually required: one for the customer, one for accounts receivable, and one for the billing section

◆ additional copies of the invoice may also be required by the credit, accounts receivable, sales (to acknowledge an order or to indicate that shipment was made), inventory control, and shipping (as a packing slip to accompany the goods) departments

    If the total order cannot be shipped, the invoice will show that fact. For example, if a quantity of 100 were ordered and only 80 were available for shipment, 20 would be entered in the "Back Ordered" column and 80 in the "Quantity" column. The outstanding 20 would be shipped and invoiced at a later date.

    When electronic invoices are issued, automatic updating of inventory, accounts receivable, and general ledger accounts occurs.

III

Picture Producers Warehouse   101001

3800 14th Avenue E.
Vancouver, BC V5M 2J5
Phone: (604) 521-6307
Fax: (604) 521-6322

SOLD TO	Elliott Galleries	SHIP TO	SAME
	82 Charlotte Dr.		
	Victoria, BC V9B 4N6		

DATE	SHIPPED VIA	FED. LICENCE NO.	PROV. LICENCE NO.	YOUR ORDER NO.	PROV. SALES TAX	TERMS	SALES REP.
Sept. 8/--	our truck	Z276	BC0490	20429	316592	2/10 n30	

BACK ORDERED	QTY. ORDERED	DESCRIPTION	QTY. SHIPPED	UNIT PRICE	AMOUNT
	50	oak frames, 50 cm x 35 cm	50	7.50	375.00
	25	mahogany frames, 70 cm x 60 cm	25	8.50	212.50
15	50	panes non-glare glass, 50 cm x 35 cm	35	18.25	638.75
	25	panes non-glare glass, 70 cm x 60 cm	25	19.50	487.50
	3	rolls canvas, 80 cm wide	3	50.00	150.00
					1863.75
		Trade discount 20%			372.75
		Sales Tax Exempt			1491.00
		6% GST			89.46
		TOTAL			1580.46

INVOICE	DATE SHIPPED	B/O FROM	B/O TO
	Sept. 8/--		

Invoice

▶B20   Credit invoice

◆ issued by the billing section of the accounting department in cases of returned or damaged goods or an overcharge

◆ informs the customer that his or her account is reduced (credited) by the amount shown

◆ copies usually needed: one each for the customer, accounts receivable, and billing

B21   COLLECTING

Customers who do not pay for each order as it is invoiced are sent a monthly statement.

▶B22   Statement of account

◆ sent by accounts receivable section of the accounting department to the customer

◆ itemizes purchases, returns, payments made, and any interest charges for the month, and shows total balance due

◆ three copies are usually necessary—for the customer, accounting, and accounts receivable

B

Picture Producers Warehouse
3800 14th Avenue E.
Vancouver, BC V5M 2J5
Phone: (604) 521-6307
Fax: (604) 521-6322

TO ▶ Elliott Galleries
82 Charlotte Dr.
Victoria, BC V9B 4N6

MONTH OF September 20--	CUSTOMER ACCOUNT 2X-44	AMOUNT OF REMITTANCE

PLEASE RETURN THIS PART WITH YOUR REMITTANCE   DETACH HERE ▼

Picture Producers Warehouse
3800 14th Avenue E.
IN ACCOUNT   Vancouver, BC V5M 2J5
WITH   Phone: (604) 521-6307   Fax: (604) 521-6322
KEEP THIS PART

STATEMENT DATE: Sept. 31/20--   ACCOUNT NO.:   2X-44   AMOUNT PAID:

DATE		PARTICULARS	DEBIT		CREDIT		BALANCE	
		PREVIOUS BALANCE FORWARD					735	28
Sept.	5	Payment received			735	28	nil	
Sept.	8	Invoice No. 101001	1580	46			1580	46
Sept.	21	Invoice No. 101036	46	33			1626	79

STATEMENT   Please pay last amount...   ▲ IN THIS COLUMN

Monthly statement of account

B23   DISBURSING

Payment of a company's costs and expenses is most frequently made by cheque by the accounts payable section of the accounting department. Salaries and wages are handled by the payroll section (see Unit 19, "Math and Financial Management").

III

B24 PREPRINTED BASIC BUSINESS FORMS

If a business is small and the expense of custom-printed forms is not felt to be justified, preprinted forms may be purchased at stationery or office supply stores or created in-house. These forms may then be keyed or rubber-stamped with the company name and a form identification number if necessary. Preprinted forms include:

billing forms	purchase orders
customer statements	receipts
expense accounts	requisitions
invoices	sales representatives' order books
ledger sheets, accounting paper	shipping memos
petty cash vouchers	time and payroll forms

Preprinted or electronic business forms are also available for specialized business purposes, such as the following:

◆ Legal forms for mortgages, leases, wills, etc., are available from major stationery and office supply houses.

◆ Tax forms are available through the Canada Revenue Agency.

◆ Banking forms of various types can be obtained from financial institutions.

B25 RUBBER STAMPS, DIE STAMPS, AND PREPRINTED STICKERS

In some situations, rubber stamps can replace forms. You can stamp information directly onto documents to indicate date of receipt, date of shipment, priority in handling, department routing of documents, filing information, etc.

In addition, rubber stamps can be imprinted with an organization's name and address or any other required information. These are useful with preprinted forms.

Self-inking die plate stamps may also be purchased. You can use these to show such variables as time, date, and year, and they are also available as self-inking sequential numbering devices.

Carefully worded stickers may do the job of forms in certain circumstances. For example, routing of documents, message taking, and payment reminders can be dealt with in this way.

For information about stickers, please visit the Text Enrichment Site for this text at *www.pearsoned.ca/text/campbell*.

B26 DESIGNING BUSINESS FORMS

Forms must be well designed so that they are effective working tools, economical to produce, and a favourable reflection of the company image. Business forms should be designed with the primary goal of speeding the flow of information. Poorly designed forms that are difficult to understand will waste employees' time.

B27 ELECTRONIC FORMS SOFTWARE

There are many excellent forms software packages available to meet the needs of every size and type of organization. These software packages facilitate the design and automation of all forms typically used in the business world.

B28 FORMS DESIGNED FOR COMPUTER USE

Many business forms are produced for computer use. Such forms may be designed specifically for an organization or may be standard ones personalized with an organization's identification. Forms for computer use must be compatible with the software used so that lines, boxes, etc., are in the right place for the printed output.

These types of forms are available in multi-copy sets, carbon paper interleaved, or carbonless, and in various colours. Parts of the form may be blocked out if desired. For example, the last part of an invoice might have the price column blocked out so that it could be used as a shipping memo (delivery receipt).

B29 MAILING SETS

Suppliers also offer a one-part, self-contained mailer (mailing set) in continuous form for key business activities. This speeds mailing by presealing one or more inserts (including even a return envelope) into one outgoing mailing piece. Folding, stuffing, sealing, and postal metering are eliminated. Most self-contained mailers are for impact printers, but some are available for laser printers.

In the case of the monthly statement mailing set shown here, the external part of the mailing set provides a file copy. The mailer set is the envelope, a statement (which may include a remittance stub if desired), and a return envelope for payment.

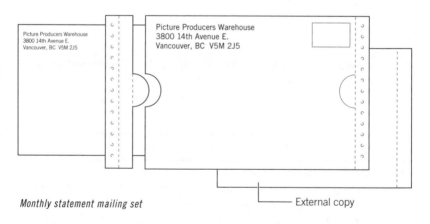

Monthly statement mailing set   External copy

III

B30 OTHER FORMS-RELATED TECHNOLOGIES

Bar codes

A quick pass with a portable laser gun can replace several manual procedures. For example, it can replace a bulky invoice pack to show the contents of a shipment, what has to be done with it, where it has come from, where it has to go next, and when.

Electronic data interchange

It takes time and costs money to manually generate a paper form, duplicate it, process it, store it, and eventually destroy it. Therefore, completing business transactions electronically is recommended to save both time and money (see Unit 13).

Imaging and forms

Scanners with optical character recognition (OCR) software can automatically translate information from forms into data and store the image in a readily retrievable manner. Any type or size of form can be handled.

The system scans and converts forms as they are fed in. It produces an electronic image of the form, strips away all the rules, lines, and preprinted information, and converts the remainder into computer data. Images of zones that cannot be read (e.g., handwritten information) are displayed onscreen so that an operator can enter and verify manually.

The image of each form can be held in optical storage and indexed so that fast retrieval is possible in the event of queries. Hard copies can be made as needed.

Pen-based computers

These small, hand-held computers allow the user to print directly onto a screen with an electronic pen. The form is displayed onscreen and the operator fills in information as checkmarks, letters, and numbers. The computer translates this into data to process immediately and transfers it to a larger computer for further processing. A customer signature can be captured onscreen for authorization of the transaction.

Voice-activated forms

A slow, well-modulated voice, speaking directly to a microphone, can be used to complete forms without the need for keying. For example, a lawyer can fill in a standard legal form (e.g., a will) by calling the standard form onto the screen and speaking the details out loud.

Voice macros can be created to fill in known information. For example, a code word could result in the completion of name, address, telephone number, and account number.

B31 FORMS CONTROL

Forms control is the planned and orderly management of all phases of a form—its authorship, design, specifications, ordering and reordering, storage and distribution, numerical control, and function.

All of these phases must be managed to guarantee that the business form will perform the function for which it was intended within the business system. The goals of an efficient forms control program are to

◆ maintain aesthetic design technique standards

◆ eliminate forms that perform the same functions

◆ ensure that forms are designed for economy, whether purchased from a supplier or produced internally

◆ provide well-designed forms that are effective working tools

◆ eliminate unauthorized forms

◆ review all forms to determine their usefulness and efficiency

B32 GOVERNMENT FORMS

Government forms are always needed in the workplace for various government/workplace situations, e.g., applications for tax deductions, child tax benefits, claims for moving expenses, etc.

Frequently requested forms fall into two categories: customs forms and tax forms. You can access these forms at the following websites:

www.cra-arc.gc.ca   www.cbsa-asfc.gc.ca

WORDS OF WISDOM

Few burdens are heavy when everyone lifts!

18 POSTAL AND SHIPPING SERVICES

SELECTED CONTENTS

PART 1 POSTAL SERVICES

P1	**MAIL-HANDLING TECHNIQUES**
P2	Incoming Mail
P3	Outgoing Mail
P4	Mail-Handling Equipment
P5	**CANADIAN POSTAL SERVICES**
P6	Postal Service within Canada
P7	Lettermail
P8	Publications
P9	Unaddressed Mail
P10	Parcel Services
P11	Special Canada Post Services
P29	Canada Post Service to the United States
P35	Canada Post Service to International Destinations
P43	**ALTERNATIVES TO CANADA POST SERVICES**
P44	Airlines
P45	Bus Parcel Express (BPX)
P46	Couriers
P50	Taxis

PART 2 SHIPPING SERVICES

P51	**SHIPPING SERVICES**
P52	**CHOOSING A TRANSPORTATION MODE**
P53	**FREIGHT FORWARDERS**
P54	**SHIPPER'S RESPONSIBILITIES**
P55	**DOCUMENTATION**
P56	**PRO BILL**
P57	**EDI**
P58	**INTERNATIONAL SHIPPING**

P

PART 1

POSTAL SERVICES

Technology has made possible the instant exchange of many types of information among businesses. However, the traditional method of delivering documents still has a major role to play. It offers the best service for some circumstances, and it offers the most economical services for some types of businesses. Knowledge of the wide range of postal services available and how to use them most efficiently is, therefore, important to all office workers.

Part 1 of this unit outlines suggestions for dealing with incoming and outgoing mail, a presentation of the key services offered by Canada Post, and a discussion of some alternative delivery methods. Part 2 provides information about shipping procedures and documentation requirements.

NOTE   Electronic mail is discussed in Unit 5.

P1   MAIL-HANDLING TECHNIQUES

Processing mail efficiently is important in the successful operation of any business, regardless of size. Knowledge of mail-handling equipment and procedures is a useful asset.

P2   INCOMING MAIL

In a small firm, one person is expected to open and process all incoming mail. In a large organization, a mail department with specialized procedures and trained staff is responsible for dealing with it.

If you are designated to handle incoming mail, you may be required to do some or all of the following:

◆ **Sort** the incoming mail into categories:
  • priority (letters, invoices, interoffice memos, or any items requiring prompt attention)
  • newspapers and periodicals
  • advertising materials

◆ **Open and date-stamp** all but *personal and confidential* correspondence. Use letter-opening equipment if it is available.

◆ **Read and annotate** the mail. If this is part of your duties, after reading each document, highlight or underline the important passages and make marginal notes to help the recipient formulate a reply. You can also use stick-on notes. Scan the tables of contents of magazines and journals and identify any articles that might be of interest to colleagues or your supervisor.

♦ **Distribute** the mail to the appropriate people by placing it on their desks or in their mail slots or in-trays. Use a routing slip (see Unit 6, PT5) for periodicals or non-urgent material.

Business etiquette calls for prompt responses to mail. This is also important if you are expected to reply to incoming mail in someone's absence.

Once incoming mail has been responded to, it should be marked for follow-up (see Unit 8, R37), filed, or disposed of.

P3   OUTGOING MAIL

Efficient mail procedures speed up the communications process. The following tips, based on established postal standards, will help to ensure prompt delivery of your mail by Canada Post.

♦ **Address mail carefully.** Refer to Unit 14, K6, for guidance in correctly keying addresses for domestic and international mail. Include postal codes for countries that use them.

Because of automated mail-sorting equipment, machine-printed or keyed mail can be sorted faster than handwritten mail. Mail that has no postal code may take longer to reach its destination. If a postal code is unknown, look it up on Canada Post's website at www.canadapost.ca or in the *Postal Code Directory*. This directory can be obtained at a reasonable cost at some post offices and postal outlets in Canada or can be ordered online, or from the

National Philatelic Centre
Canada Post
75 St. Ninian St.
Antigonish, NS B2G 2R8

NEW BRUNSWICK/NOUVEAU BRUNSWICK

Street	from	to	Postal CODE	Street	from	to	Postal CODE
LEGION DR				Even/Pair	98	104	E3A 1V4
Odd/Impair	101	105	E3A 2K9		200	228	E3A 1V6
	107	–	E3A 2L1	**MACKENZIE RD**			
Even/Pair	100	122	E3A 2K8	Odd/Impair	15	–	E3B 6B5
LEICESTER ST					55	65	E3B 6B6
Odd/Impair	7	23	E3B 4N3	Even/Pair	30	–	E3B 6B7
	63	75	E3B 4N5	**MACLAREN AVE**			
Even/Pair	4	–	E3B 4N2	Odd/Impair	537	603	E3A 3K9
	22	70	E3B 4N4		623	639	E3A 3L1
LESLIE ST					713	767	E3A 3L4
Even/Pair	52	–	E3B 5B2		771	777	E3A 3L6
LEVERMAN ST					781	807	E3A 3L8
Odd/Impair	9	–	E3A 4H7	Even/Pair	528	–	E3A 3K7
LILAC CRES					542	614	E3A 3K8
Odd/Impair	3	27	E3A 2G7		626	668	E3A 3L2
	29	65	E3A 2G8		672	686	E3A 3L3
Even/Pair	2	24	E3A 2G6		732	758	E3A 3L5

Courtesy of Canada Post.
Canada's Postal Code Directory page

Courtesy of Canada Post.

Online Postal Code Look-up screen

If you need a postal code immediately and do not have a directory, you can find postal code information in the telephone book under the Canada Post Corporation listing.

Within the section for each province, towns and cities are arranged alphabetically, with rural route and lock box number lists appearing at the end of each. To find the postal code in the directory, locate the town or city, the street (arranged in alphabetical order), and then the street number.

NOTE Standard-sized, meter-stamped mail without a postal code is more expensive than coded mail. Uncoded business mail may be returned to sender for the application of additional postage. The extra amount is collected by Canada Post when the organization replenishes its postage.

◆ **Use a return address.** In case of non-delivery, a return address enables Canada Post to return the item. Non-delivery of mail is usually caused by an incorrect address. Mail that cannot be delivered and has no return address is kept by Canada Post for a reasonable time, then opened and the contents sold at an annual public auction.

◆ **Use the correct Canada Post service and affix sufficient postage.** If there is a deficiency in the amount of postage paid, the item is returned to the sender. There is a fee for Return to Sender service.

◆ **Use standard-sized envelopes.** Envelopes that are larger or smaller than the limits set by Canada Post must be sorted manually. As a result, they require more postage.

NOTE If you are mailing a disk, enclose a covering letter that identifies the contents of the disk and mark the disk clearly. Encase the disk in cardboard or heavy plastic wrap and use a padded envelope or box for mailing.

◆ **Wrap parcels carefully.** Packages must be carefully wrapped to avoid damage, breakage, leakage of contents, or injury to postal handlers. Prohibited articles include animals, perishables, plants, liquor, drug samples, explosives, and other articles listed in the *Canada Postal Guide*.

◆ **Mail early.** Mailing departments of large corporations generally have their own deadlines (usually mid-afternoon).

P4 MAIL-HANDLING EQUIPMENT

Your company's size will determine the sophistication of the equipment used to process mail. The following are examples of some of the mail-handling equipment available.

Folders

If you must mail large quantities of documents often, machines that fold letters, reports, etc., for mailing are helpful. Some models can also perforate, score, or slit documents as well as fold them. Other models can fold and insert documents as well as seal envelopes.

Mail openers

These automatic machines are designed to open large volumes of mail quickly.

Postage scales

These weigh scales are used to ensure that correct postage is affixed. Items must be placed one at a time on the scale, so these scales are useful only for companies that have small volumes of mail.

Mail-handling systems

Several types of systems are available that provide combinations of mail-handling processes. There are three basic types: manual, automatic, and electronic (computerized).

◆ *Manual systems* accept hand-fed mail and seal and stamp it.

◆ *Automatic systems* accept mail from a stack and automatically seal it, postmark it, meter-stamp it, count the pieces of mail, and restack it.

You can rent or buy manual and automatic meter/mail-handling machines from postage meter manufacturing companies. They are available in two types. One type must be taken to the post office, where a bulk amount of postage credit is purchased and entered into it. When that amount has been used up, a further amount can be purchased. The other type, which is attached to a special base, can be replenished by simply telephoning the post office.

◆ *Electronic systems* (which are used by many companies with high volumes of mail) comprise several pieces of linked equipment. These machines can

  • handle single sheets or continuous business forms (e.g., invoices) that are automatically fed through a burster to be separated
  • feed documents into a folder and inserter, where they are folded, combined with any required inserts (e.g., return envelopes), and stuffed into mailing envelopes
  • move the envelopes on a conveyor belt through a postage meter to be automatically sealed, weighed, categorized, and stamped

  Electronic mail-handling systems can also provide reports such as
  • breakdown of costs by department or other desired category
  • daily total cost of mail
  • daily cost of mail by postal-service category
  • batch totals
  • cost of postage per batch

Electronic mail-handling systems can be custom-designed to take documents of varying dimensions through the stages of inserting, sealing, addressing, weighing, and stamping. These expensive systems are useful for mass mailings.

III

NOTE Computer software is available to assist in parcel handling. A weigh scale is connected to a microcomputer; after placing a parcel on the scale, the operator keys in such information as parcel identification number, destination, and the number of the invoice enclosed. The computer calculates the postage rate and can print out address labels if desired. An automatic report of daily parcel shipment activities can also be provided.

P5 CANADIAN POSTAL SERVICES

The amount of postage payable depends on the type of service used, the mass of the item, the destination, and any additional services required. Because postal rates change from time to time, it is wise to keep current postal information in your office. The *Canada Postal Guide* is available on Canada Post's website at www.canadapost.ca or it can be purchased from Canada Post at the National Philatelic Centre address provided in P3. Canada Post rate-information leaflets are available free at any post office.

P6 POSTAL SERVICE WITHIN CANADA

For Canada Postal service to the United States and overseas, see P29 to P41. *The Canada Postal Guide* is also available online at www.canadapost. ca/postalguide.

▶P7 Lettermail

Mail in this category consists of letters, business documents, greeting cards, and postcards that weigh up to 500 g. Items in envelopes larger or smaller than the limits specified by Canada Post are more costly to mail.

▶P8 Publications

A service is available only to companies that ship large quantities of printed matter (e.g., magazines). Contact a Canada Post commercial sales representative for information regarding this service.

▶P9 Unaddressed mail

Items addressed simply to "Householder" or "Occupant" or bearing no address at all can be sent by this service. It is the most economical postal service for distributing catalogues, samples, promotional leaflets, etc. The company sending out the mailing specifies to the post office the district to be covered and the letter carrier then distributes one mailing piece to every householder or occupant in that district. The charge is a fee per item, plus a sum per kilogram.

Exception: Those who have indicated "NO ADMAIL HERE" on their mailbox or receptacle. A similar service is available for addressed admail.

▶ P10 Parcel services

For parcels weighing up to a maximum of 30 kg, four services are available:

◆ **Regular Parcel:** Most economical service. Delivery confirmation and signature options are available for an additional fee.

◆ **Expedited Parcel:** A fast ground service is available to commercial customers only. Local is service next day, regional service is one to three days, and national destinations can take up to seven days (between major centres).

◆ **Xpresspost:** A service that offers the advantages of speed and economy, with local delivery the next business day, delivery between major centres within two days, and regional one to two days' delivery; this service includes delivery confirmation, an on-time delivery guarantee, and coverage up to $100.

Package size	Cost
◆ up to 1 m in length, width, or depth	◆ basic rate is charged
◆ any dimension exceeding 1 m	◆ surcharge is levied
◆ over 3 m length plus girth or any dimension over 2 m	◆ not accepted by Canada Post

◆ **Priority Courier:** The fastest and most costly Canada Post parcel delivery service. It provides next-day a.m. delivery of envelopes and packages (maximum 30 kg) between most major centres in Canada, computer tracking of items, signature on delivery option, and indemnity up to a specific level.

For information about how to calculate parcel size, please visit the Text Enrichment Site for this text at *www.pearsoned.ca/text/campbell*.

▶ P11 Special Canada Post services

P12   Aerogrammes (air letters)

An aerogramme is a self-contained, pre-stamped letter/envelope for airmail correspondence.

P13   Business reply cards and envelopes (prepaid—Canada only)

These are used by companies to encourage inquiries in response to advertisements, completion of consumer survey questionnaires, etc. The initiating organization is charged a fee per card or envelope plus the postage on each one returned.

P14   COD (Canada only)

Collect on delivery is a service available to organizations that mail items requiring payment on delivery. The amount to be collected (maximum of $1000, when the amount is to be collected in cash, and a maximum of $25 000 if the amount is in the form of a cheque payable to the sender) is paid to the letter carrier on delivery, and a receipt is given as proof of payment. Items in excess of $500 must be picked up at the post office unless they are payable by cheque. The sender pays a small fee for the service and receives payment for the goods mailed by means of a money order. If the goods are lost or damaged, the post office will reimburse the sender their declared value.

P15   Change of address cards (Canada)

A kit containing change of address cards can be purchased from the post office. The cards, which the sender completes and mails to correspondents, require letter or airmail postage.

NOTE   For an additional charge, the post office will, for four months, hold mail for you or redirect it, e.g., to the United States.

P16   Volume electronic mail

This service is available for large volumes (5000 letters or more each year). Canada Post receives text, and a mailing list is provided in an electronic format. The material is electronically transmitted to regional production centres and converted to hard copy for delivery.

P17   Electronic Shipping Tools

Electronic Shipping Tools (EST) is a free program provided by Canada Post to prepare statements of mailing. This program is available in both online and desktop versions, and is designed to eliminate manual paperwork and save time for those using Canada Post shipping and mailing services.

P18   Postal code products

For customers wishing to prepare their own mailings, postal code data are available for use in a company's database, for a fee, on CD-ROM, 6250 BPI or 1600 BPI Magnetic tapes, and IBM 3480 cartridge. While the initial fee is quite costly ($800 to $2000, depending on requirements), customers receive monthly updates.

P19   Coverage for loss or damage

For a fee, plus postage, compensation to a maximum of $5000 in Canada, and $1000 in the United States or designated countries, is provided for damage, loss, or rifling of mail. (Some exceptions apply.) Check the *Canada Postal Guide* for a list of acceptable/insurable items.

P

P20 Lock boxes

These are the equivalent of postal office boxes (see P23) located at retail outlets for customer convenience.

P21 Members of Parliament mailing privileges (franked mail)

Mail to or from the prime minister, governor general, senators, and parliamentary members of the federal government, either in Ottawa or in their constituencies, may be sent free of charge except during election periods.

P22 Money orders

Postal money orders permit the safe sending of money almost anywhere in the world. They can be purchased at post offices for a small fee and can be cashed at the recipient's post office at no cost.

Because they are numbered and the sale recorded, money orders can be replaced if lost.

NOTE You can purchase money orders at banks and some other financial institutions.

P23 Post office boxes (lock boxes and bags)

Lock boxes and bags are rented by businesses and individuals not wishing to use a full address and by those who want to pick up their mail at the post office or when letter carrier service is not available. The renter pays an annual fee, is allocated a box or bag number, and is given a key. He or she has sole access to the contents. Lock boxes are available in five sizes.

P24 Priority Courier

This service exists to provide next-day a.m. delivery of envelopes or packages (maximum 30 kg) between most major centres in Canada. A contract arrangement is possible when packages are sent frequently from one address to another (e.g., head office to branch office). Pickup and delivery service is available. Individual customers can also use this service by taking the item to a post office and purchasing a prepaid Priority Courier envelope. Consult the Canada Post sales department for details of designated areas and contract terms.

P25 Scheduled pickup for a fee

Account customers may use the scheduled pickup service. The weekly fee is dependent on the total volume of mail shipped for the week.

P26 On-demand pickup

On-demand pickup is available for Priority Courier only. This service is available to account customers for a fee.

P27 Registered mail

This proof-of-mailing and delivery service is useful when an important document or small item is to be mailed. The item to be registered must be taken to the post office. On payment of lettermail postage to Canadian destinations, plus a registration fee, the sender is given a numbered receipt. When the item is delivered, the addressee or authorized representative must sign for it. If a registered item does not arrive at its destination, the registration number facilitates tracing the package.

P28 Copy of signature

For a small fee, the sender of a registered item, or of any parcel item bearing a tracking bar code, can request a hard-copy signature of the person who accepted the item.

NOTE Canada Post provides many other services, such as the sale of traveller's cheques and the latest Canadian stamp releases. Refer to the *Canada Postal Guide* or the website for complete information on these and other services.

P29 CANADA POST SERVICE TO THE UNITED STATES

▶ P30 Letter-post

Letter-post travels by air to the United States and costs a little more than mail delivered in Canada. It includes materials up to 500 g and is required to comply with Canada Post standards. The rate and weight structure is quite specific:

◆ cheapest rate: standard-sized letters and cards up to 50 g

◆ most expensive rate: oversized (within Canada Post limits) items up to 500 g

▶ P31 Small packet

A small packet is a package usually containing goods. The maximum weight is up to 1 kg and can be sent by surface or air. Insurance coverage up to $100 is included, and a customs label must be accurately completed and affixed to the item.

▶ P32 Xpresspost-USA

Xpresspost-USA provides fast, guaranteed delivery of documents and parcels to the U.S. (from three to five days between major urban contres). The service offers on-time guarantee, delivery confirmation, and coverage for loss or damage up to $100. Customers may also purchase additonal coverage. Scheduled pickup is available for contract customers only.

CATEGORY		LENGTH	WIDTH	HEIGHT	WEIGHT
Documents and Parcels	max.	No dimension may exceed 2 m Length plus girth must not exceed 2.74 m			30 kg
	min.	210 mm	140 mm	1 mm	–
Prepaid Envelopes					
Standard	max.	260 mm	152 mm	–	350 g
Letter	max.	318 mm	241 mm	–	500 g

NOTE

1. An oversize charge applies if an item exceeds 1 m in any dimension (length, width, or height).
2. If weight is not indicated, a default weight of 5 kg applies.

These rules also apply to Xpresspost-International (see P39).

▶**P33   Expedited parcel service**

Mail from 1 kg to 30 kg with the same size restrictions as airmail packages but of a less urgent nature may be sent for a much lower price by expedited parcel service.

▶**P34   Special Canada Post services to the United States**

The following special services are available for mail delivery to the United States (see previous sections of this unit): coverage for loss or damage, money orders, international reply coupons, registered mail, and Purolator delivery.

P35   CANADA POST SERVICE TO INTERNATIONAL DESTINATIONS

▶**P36   Letters, cards, or postcards**

Letters of a business or personal nature and cards or postcards to a maximum of 500 g travel by air only.

▶**P37   Small packets**

A small packet is a package usually containing goods. The maximum weight is 1 kg, and 2 kg to international destinations.

International small packet prices are available for items that meet the correct size and weight requirements. Small packets must be posted in Canada for delivery in a foreign country, and must bear a Canadian return address.

CATEGORY		LENGTH	WIDTH	HEIGHT	WEIGHT
Small Packets	max.	Length + width + height = 90 cm Any dimension = 60 cm			1 kg (U.S.) 2 kg (International)
	min.	140 mm	90 mm	1 mm	–

▶**P38   International parcels service**

You may send parcels weighing more than 1 kg and less than 20 kg to most countries, and less than 30 kg to more than 100 countries by air or surface mail. International parcels service is an economical means of shipping packages of goods, merchandise, and other articles by air or surface, from Canada to international destinations, excluding the U.S.

International air parcels service is available only to countries not served by Xpresspost-International service. To determine the availability of the service to the country of destination, see the country listing in the *Canada Postal Guide*.

International parcels must meet the size and weight requirements for this service, be properly prepared and packaged, and not contain prohibited or dangerous goods.

CATEGORY		LENGTH	WIDTH	HEIGHT
All countries	min.	210 mm	140 mm	1 mm
Countries accepting oversize*	max.	1.5 m (length) 3 m (length plus girth)		
Countries not accepting oversize	max.	1 m (length) 2 m (length plus girth)		

*See the country listing in the *Canada Postal Guide* to find which countries accept oversize or parcels over 20 kg.

▶P39 Xpresspost-International

Xpresspost-International provides fast, cost-effective delivery for less than the cost of an international courier. The service offers an on-time guarantee, delivery confirmation, and coverage for loss or damage up to $100 (you can purchase additional coverage). Account customers can schedule pickup.

Prepaid envelopes are flat-rated and available for documents only. The coverage for loss or damage option does not apply.

CATEGORY		LENGTH	WIDTH	HEIGHT	WEIGHT
Documents and Parcels	min.	210 mm	140 mm	1 mm	–
Countries accepting oversize*	max.	No dimension may exceed 1.5 m Length plus girth: 3 m			20 to 30 kg*
Countries not accepting oversize	max.	No dimension may exceed 1 m Length plus girth must not exceed 2 m			20 to 30 kg*
Prepaid Letter	max.	380 mm	240 mm	–	500 g

*See the country listing in the *Canada Postal Guide* to find which countries accept oversize or parcels over 20 kg.

▶P40 Special Canada Post services to overseas destinations

The following special services are available for mail to many countries (see previous sections in this unit for descriptions): insurance, international reply coupons, money orders, registered mail, Xpresspost-International, and Purolator. Consult the *Canada Postal Guide* or your post office or postal outlet for a list of those countries to which these services apply.

▶P41 Customs declaration

Customs regulations demand that the contents, their value, and the name and address of sender be declared on every package leaving Canada. Forms are available at the post office or postal outlets. Xpresspost-U.S.A. and Expedited Parcel-U.S.A. shipping labels include customs declarations.

▶ **P42   Duty-free and tax-exempt importations by mail**

The Canada Border Services Agency can examine any items that come into Canada by mail. You can be charged duty as well as any goods and services tax (GST) or harmonized sales tax (HST) on a mail item you receive. This is determined by the item's value in Canadian dollars, and whether it is a gift.

Individuals may receive a gift valued at $60 or less (excluding alcohol and tobacco). Gifts valued at more than $60 are subject to customs duties and tax on the portion that exceeds $60.

NOTE   Alcoholic beverages, books, magazines, periodicals, tobacco, and goods ordered through a Canadian post office box or intermediary *do not* qualify for the $60 exemption.

TIP   To obtain delivery status information on Priority Courier, Xpresspost, Purolator International, and Delivery Confirmation/Registered items, call Canada Post customer service: 1-888-550-6333.

NOTE   Canada Post provides many other services, such as the sale of traveller's cheques, and is constantly adding services to the list. Refer to the *Canada Postal Guide,* your local post office, or www.canadapost.ca for complete information on these and other services.

P43 ALTERNATIVES TO CANADA POST SERVICE

P44   AIRLINES

Several airline companies offer fast, economical air delivery of letters and packages to destinations in North America and overseas. Refer to the Yellow Pages under "Airlines" or "Courier Service" or contact an airline company (see also Part 2 of this unit).

P45   BUS PARCEL EXPRESS (BPX)

A bus will transport letters or packages of a personal or business nature from one destination to another in Canada and the United States.

- ◆ The sender can take the package to the bus terminal and have it picked up at the arrival terminal.
- ◆ Door-to-door pickup and delivery service is available for an additional fee.
- ◆ Same-day delivery is possible, depending on the locations of sender and addressee.
- ◆ Maximum weight allowance is 35 kg.

P46   COURIERS

A number of courier organizations offer delivery services within cities, between provinces and states, and around the world. Charges are based on package weight (limit: 35 kg/package), destination, and the time period requested for delivery. Services normally operate on a five-day-week basis, although some urban areas offer seven-day-week services. A signature is usually required on delivery. For example, FedEx Ground is a small-package ground delivery company, serving business and residential customers throughout North America (www.fedex.ca).

▶ P47 Standard services

◆ same-day delivery (depending on destination, more expensive than next-day service)

◆ pickup and delivery

◆ specialized letter service for overseas next-day delivery

▶ P48 Additional possible services

◆ drop boxes similar to mailboxes, with specific pickup times

◆ shipments up to 2.25 tonnes (5000 lb.)

◆ acceptance of some dangerous commodities (provided the package and bill of lading clearly identify the contents)

◆ electronic tracking

◆ weekend service for an additional fee

◆ radio-dispatched vehicles for rapid pickup

◆ linked services with the receiving country's postal system

Check the Yellow Pages under "Courier Service" or "Delivery Service."

▶ P49 Using courier services wisely

If possible:

◆ Use computer-aided shipping, if offered. This saves paperwork, links you with courier agents, and permits tracking of parcels.

◆ Take advantage of volume discounts—use one courier rather than several and set up an account.

◆ Use deferred delivery—overnight or next-day service is cheaper than same-day delivery.

◆ Consolidate shipments—send all packages to one city in one bag once a day.

◆ Use courier drop boxes when possible to save pickup charges.

◆ Compare rates when insurance is needed and use the cheaper—your own insurer's rate or the courier's.

◆ Negotiate prices for non-routine arrangements and inquire also about package deals.

◆ Be a smart consumer—comparison-shop for the courier that offers the services that best meet your needs at the lowest cost.

P

P50 TAXIS

If a courier is unavailable for same-day delivery, consider using a taxi for an urgent local delivery.

PART 2

SHIPPING SERVICES

Vast quantities of raw materials and manufactured products are shipped daily across Canada and the U.S. This unit provides basic information about the types of shipping services that are available.

P51 SHIPPING SERVICES

Before choosing a particular type of transportation for shipping commercial goods in Canada, consider the factors outlined below.

Charges for transportation services are based on the following:

◆ the nature of goods being carried

◆ their destination

◆ their mass or volume, whichever is greater and can be paid in one of the following ways:

◆ prepaid by the shipper (consignor) in cash

◆ charged to the shipper's account

◆ COD, paid by the recipient (consignee)

P52 CHOOSING A TRANSPORTATION MODE

Whether you choose air, rail, or truck, consider these factors:

◆ Air:
  • is fastest but usually most expensive
  • may have mass or volume restrictions
  • may have restrictions on certain goods

◆ Rail and truck:
  • are best for heavy or high-volume goods
  • can be interchanged (e.g., piggyback), but transfer from one mode to another costs more

If you are shipping hazardous goods, contact Transport Canada for full instructions regarding packaging, marking, and documentation. The transportation of these materials is the combined responsibility of consignor and carrier.

Because costs and types of services vary, and because all carriers do not offer all services, you should comparison-shop to find the most suitable and economical carrier for your shipment.

P53 FREIGHT FORWARDERS

These agents offer a useful service for companies that ship merchandise requiring less than a full load. The freight forwarder leases a full load and uses the space to ship several small (part) loads from various consignors. In spite of the fee charged, the advantages to the shipper are as follows:

◆ *cost-saving* because of the full-load rate

◆ *time-saving* because the agent is familiar with carriers, routes, and rates; can monitor the shipment during transit; and serves as intermediary between shipper and carrier

P54 SHIPPER'S RESPONSIBILITIES

The shipper usually pays the freight charges. If a shipment is being sent COD, however, the shipper should obtain a written or electronic commitment from the consignee that payment will be made to the carrier on delivery of the goods.

A company shipping goods should check the maximum liability for merchandise lost or damaged by the carrier and perhaps consider additional insurance coverage.

P55 DOCUMENTATION

Prepare a *bill of lading* (often called a *waybill*) for each shipment. Blank forms are provided by the carrier but must be completed by the shipper. When the carrier picks up the shipment, the driver signs the bill of lading, acknowledging the carrier's contract to deliver the goods to the given destination. The bill of lading, which is a contract, also

◆ acts as the shipper's receipt from the carrier, acknowledging that the shipment is in good condition and that the number of packages in the shipment is correct

◆ provides the carrier with all relevant information on the destination of the goods

◆ can sometimes be used as a supporting document for loss, damage, or shortage claims by the shipper

A bill of lading must therefore be carefully prepared and its accuracy confirmed before a shipment is loaded.

The carrier supplies multiple-copy bills of lading. The consignor and the consignee each receive at least one copy and the carrier keeps the rest.

P56 PRO BILL

A *pro bill* form, which contains details pertinent to the carrier only, must also accompany a shipment. If a pro bill is not available, a *pro sticker* is completed from information taken from the shaded areas of the bill of lading.

P57 EDI

Currently, in many cases, shippers transmit all the necessary information by electronic data exchange (EDI; see Unit 13). For example, some parts of shipping processes are completed by the use of bar code labels on packages that can be read by hand-held scanners carried by transportation company drivers. In some cases, however, paper documents are still required for the actual shipping process because of the need for the signatures of the carrier and the consignee (in special cases, proof of identification is also required).

P58 INTERNATIONAL SHIPPING

The importing and exporting of goods involves preparation of many customs documents and adherence to a strict set of procedures. Companies that conduct international trade usually either have customs experts on staff or use the services of customs brokers or consultants. If you are ever required to handle any aspect of importation or exportation and do not have an in-house expert, consult a representative at the Canada Border Services Agency or a customs broker or consultant.

WORDS OF WISDOM

Give to the world the best you have, and the best will come back to you.

UNIT

19
MATH AND FINANCIAL MANAGEMENT

SELECTED CONTENTS

PART 1   MATH

MF1	**USING A CALCULATOR**
MF2	Touch Fingering
MF3	**DECIMALS, FRACTIONS, PERCENTAGES**
MF4	Decimals
MF6	Fractions
MF8	Percentages
MF10	Common Equivalents
MF11	**TYPICAL BUSINESS MATH APPLICATIONS**
MF12	Billing (Invoicing)
MF13	Commissions
MF14	Comparisons
MF15	Discounts
MF16	Foreign Currency Exchange
MF17	Interest
MF18	Pricing Goods for Sale
MF19	Sales Taxes
MF20	Statistical Data
MF24	Spreadsheets

PART 2   FINANCIAL MANAGEMENT

MF25	**ACCOUNTING**
MF26	Accounting Records
MF33	Financial Statements
MF37	Accounting Systems
MF38	Computer Accounting Systems
MF39	Accounting Software
MF40	Budgets
MF41	**BANKING**
MF42	Financial Institutions

MF

MF43	Types of Accounts
MF50	Making Deposits
MF51	Making Withdrawals
MF52	Preparing Cheques
MF54	Endorsing Cheques
MF55	Special Types of Cheques
MF56	Service Charges
MF57	Reconciling the Account Statement
MF58	Other Key Banking Services
MF82	**PAYROLL**
MF83	Calculation of Gross Earnings
MF84	Preparing the Payroll
MF85	Payroll Deductions
MF86	Vacation Pay
MF87	Severance Pay
MF88	Making Payroll Payment
MF89	Employer's Legal Financial Obligations
MF90	**PETTY CASH**
MF91	**AN OVERVIEW OF THE FINANCIAL MARKETPLACE**
MF99	**IDENTITY THEFT**
MF100	Workplace Identity Theft
MF102	Prevention Tips for the Workplace
MF103	Personal Identity Theft Prevention
MF104	**INVESTMENT TERMS**

PART 1

MATH

The computer makes the calculating task easy and has taken the drudgery out of many office-related calculating jobs. However, basic numeracy skills are essential for every office worker because some computer applications (e.g., spreadsheets) need mathematical expertise. Also, knowing how to use an electronic calculator is mandatory for small, everyday tasks. With this in mind, Part 1 of this unit focuses on basic math skills.

IV

MF1 USING A CALCULATOR

MF2 TOUCH FINGERING

Become an efficient calculator operator by using touch fingering, as shown in the illustration. The right index finger strikes the 1, 4, and 7 keys; the middle finger the 2, 5, and 8 keys; and the fourth finger the 3, 6, and 9 keys. The thumb strikes the zero and the right little finger strikes the + − ÷ = and total keys.

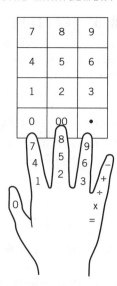

7	8	9
4	5	6
1	2	3
0	00	•

NOTE Keyboards are now available with left-hand numeric keypads.

MF3 DECIMALS, FRACTIONS, PERCENTAGES

This section is concerned with part quantities—decimals, fractions, and percentages—and the different ways of expressing them and calculating with them.

MF4 DECIMALS

Calculators and computers can work only with whole numbers and decimals. For example, a calculator cannot multiply by $12^{1}/_{4}$. You must change $12^{1}/_{4}$ to its decimal equivalent.

The decimal equivalent of $^{1}/_{4}$ is 0.25 (see the table of equivalents in MF10, or convert according to the instructions provided in MF7). The problem then becomes simply a matter of keying in the numbers and operations keys and reading the result. To multiply $12^{1}/_{4}$ by 4, key in as follows:

12.25 $\boxed{\times}$ 4 $\boxed{=}$ 49

NOTE In written work, always precede a decimal value of less than one with a zero: 0.25, not .25.

▶ MF5 Decimal places

For most business situations, working to two decimal places is sufficient (i.e., two figures after the decimal place). If your calculator does not allow you to set specific decimal places, round off as follows. Take 5 and over up one; leave 4 and below at the second decimal number:

427.6**75** to two decimal places = 427.6**8**
427.6**73** to two decimal places = 427.6**7**

Where a greater number of decimal places is required, follow the same basic rule:

427.6763 to three decimal places is 427.676
427.676678 to five decimal places is 427.67668

MF6 FRACTIONS

Fractions are parts of whole numbers and can be expressed as decimal fractions (0.25) or common fractions ($^1/_4$). Common fractions must be converted into their decimal equivalents before a calculator or computer can accept them for processing.

▶MF7 Converting fractions into decimals

To convert fractions into their decimal equivalents
Divide the numerator by the denominator:

$\dfrac{3}{5}$ (numerator)
(denominator)

3 ÷ 5 = 0.6

The decimal equivalent of $^3/_5$ is 0.6.

To change whole numbers and fractions into decimals
Change the fraction to its decimal equivalent by dividing the numerator by the denominator, and then write the result after the whole number:

$^5/_8$ as a decimal is 5 ÷ 8 = 0.625

The decimal equivalent of $6^5/_8$ is therefore 6.625.

For overtime, employees earn $1^1/_2$ times their normal pay rate. An employee's hourly pay is $12.10. If the employee worked one hour overtime, what was the overtime pay? The calculation is as follows:

$1^1/_2$ × 12.10

Convert $1^1/_2$ to decimal = 1.5

Key in 1.5 × 12.10 = readout 18.15 (to two decimal places)

The employee's overtime pay was $18.15.

MF8 PERCENTAGES

A percentage of a number is a one-hundredth part of that number. For example, 5 percent of a number is 5 one-hundredths of that number and can be expressed as follows:

$^5/_{100}$ or 0.05 or 5%

Percentage key
Use your calculator % key for routine percentage calculations, as follows:

Calculate 35% of 15:

15 × 35 %

Display shows 5.25 (i.e., 35% of 15 = 5.25).

When no % key is available, multiply the two figures and divide by 100 (which is the same as moving the decimal two places to the left):

Calculate 35% of 15:

$$\frac{35}{100} \times 15 = \frac{525}{100} = 5.25 \quad -or- \quad 0.35 \boxed{\times} \ 15 \ \boxed{=} \ 5.25$$

To change a fraction to a percentage

Divide the numerator by the denominator and multiply the result (quotient) by 100 (which is the same as moving the decimal two places to the right):

┌── (numerator)
↓
$\frac{4}{5} \times 100$
↑
└── (denominator)

$= 0.80 \times 100 = 80\%$

$^4/_5$ expressed as a percentage is 80%.

To change a percentage to a decimal

Divide the percentage figure by 100; that is, move the decimal point two places to the left, and remove the % sign:

$^1/_2\%$ expressed as a decimal is 0.005.

35% expressed as a decimal is 0.35.

189% expressed as a decimal is 1.89.

To change a decimal to a percentage

Multiply the decimal by 100; that is, move the decimal point two places to the right, and add the percentage sign:

1.34 expressed as a percentage is $1.34 \times 100 = 134\%$.

0.75 expressed as a percentage is $0.75 \times 100 = 75\%$.

0.025 expressed as a percentage is $0.025 \times 100 = 2.5\%$.

To find what percentage one number is of another

Divide the base number into the other number (the amount) and multiply by 100 (the base number will usually follow "of"):

What percentage of 25 is 5?

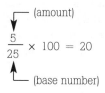

┌── (amount)
↓
$\frac{5}{25} \times 100 = 20$
↑
└── (base number)

5 is 20% of 25.

MF

Of $750 worth of total footwear sales, $150 was in socks. What percentage of total sales was in socks (or, more simply, what percentage is 150 of 750)?

$$\overset{\text{(sock sales) (amount)}}{\frac{150}{750}} \times\ 100$$

(total sales) (base number)

$\boxed{=}$ readout 20

Socks made up 20% of the total sales.

To find the full number of which a percentage is known
Divide the known number by the known percentage and multiply by 100:

If 10 is 20% of the total number, what is the total?

$$\overset{\text{(known number)}}{\frac{10}{20}} \times\ 100\ =\ 50$$

(known percentage)

10 is 20% of 50 (the total).

▶ MF9 Percentage increases and decreases
Routine percentage increases and decreases can be done on the calculator by simply depressing the $\boxed{+}$ or $\boxed{-}$ key after the $\boxed{\%}$ key, as illustrated in these two examples:

What will be the new selling price if the price of an item costing $15 is increased by 35%?

Key in 15 $\boxed{\times}$ 35 $\boxed{\%}$ $\boxed{+}$ $\boxed{=}$

Display shows 20.25 (i.e., the new selling price is $20.25).

What will be the selling price if the price of an item costing $15 is decreased by 35%?

Key in 15 $\boxed{\times}$ 35 $\boxed{\%}$ $\boxed{-}$ $\boxed{=}$

Display shows 9.75 (i.e., the new price will be $9.75).

To plan budgets and projections, organizations need to analyse figures and make comparisons. If you assist in these tasks and do not use a spreadsheet, it is useful to know how to calculate percentage increases and decreases and to understand the process involved. The following examples will assist you.

To find the percentage increase of one number over another
Subtract the base number from the increased number to find the *amount* of the increase. Divide the *base number* into the amount of the increase and multiply by 100.

If 25 increases to 30, what is the percentage increase?
30 (increased number) − 25 (base number) = 5 (amount of increase)

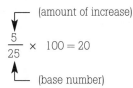

The rate of increase of 30 over 25 is 20%.

If sales rose from $4000 (base number) to $5000 (increased number), what was the percentage increase?

5000 $\boxed{-}$ 4000 $\boxed{=}$ 1000

1000 $\boxed{\div}$ 4000 $\boxed{\times}$ 100 $\boxed{=}$ 25

Sales increased by 25%.

To find the amount of increase when the base number and percentage increase are known
Add the rate of increase to 100, divide this total by 100, and multiply by the base number:

If 60 is increased by 15%, what will be the new amount?

15 (rate of increase) + 100

$$\frac{115}{100} \times \ 60 \ \text{(base number)}$$

(% rate of increase added to 100)

$$= 69$$

60 increased by 15% is 69.

If sales of $4000 must be increased by 25%, to what amount must sales increase?

$$\frac{25 + 100}{100} = 1.25$$

$$1.25 \times 4000 = 5000$$

Sales must increase to $5000.

MF

To find the amount of decrease when the base number and percentage decrease are known

Subtract the rate of decrease from 100, divide the result by 100, and multiply by the base figure:

If 60 is decreased by 15%, what will be the new amount?

$$\frac{85}{100} \times 60 \text{ (base figure)}$$

┌─ (100 − decrease of 15)

$$= 51$$

60 decreased by 15% is 51.

If sales of $4000 decreased by 25%, to what amount did sales decrease?

$$\frac{100 - 25}{100} = 0.75$$

$$0.75 \times 4000 = 3000$$

Sales of $4000 decreased by 25% equal $3000.

MF10 COMMON EQUIVALENTS

Percent (%)	Decimal fraction	Common fraction	Percent (%)	Decimal fraction	Common fraction
1	0.01	$\frac{1}{100}$	$37\frac{1}{2}$	0.375	$\frac{3}{8}$
5	0.05	$\frac{1}{20}$	40	0.40	$\frac{2}{5}$
$6\frac{1}{4}$	0.0625	$\frac{1}{16}$	50	0.50	$\frac{1}{2}$
$8\frac{1}{3}$	0.083	$\frac{1}{12}$	60	0.60	$\frac{3}{5}$
10	0.10	$\frac{1}{10}$	$62\frac{1}{2}$	0.625	$\frac{5}{8}$
$12\frac{1}{2}$	0.125	$\frac{1}{8}$	$66\frac{2}{3}$	0.666	$\frac{2}{3}$
$16\frac{2}{3}$	0.1666	$\frac{1}{6}$	70	0.70	$\frac{7}{10}$
20	0.20	$\frac{1}{5}$	75	0.75	$\frac{3}{4}$
25	0.25	$\frac{1}{4}$	80	0.80	$\frac{4}{5}$
30	0.30	$\frac{3}{10}$	$87\frac{1}{2}$	0.875	$\frac{7}{8}$
$33\frac{1}{3}$	0.333	$\frac{1}{3}$	90	0.90	$\frac{9}{10}$
			100	1.00	

Table of common equivalents

Certain percentages and their decimal and fractional equivalents are used so frequently that knowing them can save a great deal of calculation time.

MF11 TYPICAL BUSINESS MATH APPLICATIONS

In addition to the typical business mathematics examples that follow, see Part 2, "Financial Management," for account reconciliations, financial statements, payroll, and petty cash.

To help develop accuracy in your calculations, it is a good idea to esti-mate as well as verify answers and, when a printout is available, to proof-read carefully.

Estimating answers

Although calculators make mathematical calculations easy, try always to "guesstimate" an answer first.

> Multiply 596.86 by 21.63

> Round the figures up or down to the nearest whole numbers that are easy to work with: 600 × 20

> The "guesstimate" answer can be quickly calculated mentally as 12 000

> The actual answer when 596.86 is multiplied by 21.63 is 12 910.08

Note how the "guesstimate" answer helps to ensure the correct placement of the decimal point in the actual answer—a frequent problem where large numbers are involved.

Verifying answers

The skilled calculator user will routinely check answers and carefully proof-read printouts. The following are two suggestions for verifying answers.

Once you have completed a calculation such as

> What is 20% of 120?

> (Enter 120 $\boxed{\times}$ 20 $\boxed{\%}$ readout 24),

double-check by doing the calculation again or working the problem backwards:

> Enter 24 $\boxed{\times}$ 100 $\boxed{=}$ readout 2400.

> Divide by 20 = readout 120.

Verify a column of figures by working once from top to bottom and then from bottom to top.

MF

MF12 BILLING (INVOICING)

Billing is the process of completing an invoice—a record of a customer's purchases. This will show the unit cost, extensions, and some or all of discounts, taxes, and shipping charges. Note the sequence in which cal-culations must be made, as indicated by the following example.

20 packages computer paper @ 19.95/pkg.	399.00
4 boxes 3.5" disks @ 7.00/box	28.00
	427.00
Less 15% trade discount	64.05
	362.95*
Plus 6% GST	21.78
	384.73
Plus 8% PST	29.04
	413.77
Plus shipping charge	5.00
TOTAL	418.77

NOTE   See MF19. In some provinces, PST (provincial sales tax) is calculated on the basic invoice amount; in others it is calculated on the invoice amount plus the GST (goods and services tax).

MF13 COMMISSIONS

Commission is a percentage of the total amount of sales made by a sales representative that is payable to that representative. To calculate commissions payable, multiply amount of sales by rate of commission:

If the commission rate is $1^1/_4$%, what commission is payable on sales of $1784.50?

Convert $1^1/_4$% to a decimal: 1.25%

Key in 1784.50 $\boxed{\times}$ 1.25 $\boxed{\%}$ readout 22.31

Alternatively, key in as $\dfrac{125}{100}$ $\boxed{\times}$ 1784.50

Commission payable is $22.31.

If a real estate agent sells a house for $195 000 and the total commission is 6% (3% of which is payable to the agent and 3% to the real estate broker), what will the agent earn?

Key in 195 000 $\boxed{\times}$ 6 $\boxed{\%}$ readout 11 700.00

Since one-half is payable to the broker and one-half to the agent, divide the total by 2. The agent therefore earns $5850 on the sale ($11 700 $\boxed{\div}$ 2).

This can also be keyed in as follows:

$\dfrac{6}{100}$ × 195 000   (6 $\boxed{\times}$ 195 000 $\boxed{\div}$ 100)

MF14 COMPARISONS

Businesses frequently compare costs, percentages, etc., to make forecasts or prepare budgets. An example of such a calculation follows:

Sales in year 1 were $270 963, with expenses of $7852. In year 2, sales were $279 061 and expenses were $6981. Compare the relationship of expenses to sales in each year.

Year 1: $\dfrac{7852}{270\ 963} \times 100$

Key in 785 200 $\boxed{\div}$ 270 963 readout 2.8978

Expenses are 2.9% of sales.

Year 2: $\dfrac{6981}{279\ 061} \times 100$

Key in 698 100 $\boxed{\div}$ 279 061 readout 2.5016

Expenses are 2.5% of sales.

Financial statements provide useful opportunities for comparing operating results. See Part 2 for examples of comparative balance sheets and income statements.

MF15 DISCOUNTS

A discount is a percentage deduction off a selling price and may be offered as an inducement to buy for a number of reasons. Discounts are granted by wholesalers to retailers as short-term promotional gimmicks or for prompt payment of invoices, for example.

Trade and special discounts
To calculate the discount, change the percentage rate of the discount to its decimal equivalent (as described in MF8) and multiply by the total price:

A special summer discount of 5% is allowed on sales of tropical plants:

Total price (gross amount) for 5 plants at $6.20 each	=	$31.00
Discount of 5% is 0.05 (decimal equivalent of 5%) × 31	=	1.55
Amount payable (net amount) is total − discount	=	$29.45

NOTE Discounts of this type are deducted *before* sales taxes are calculated.

Cash discounts
Cash discounts are frequently offered to encourage prompt payment of a bill. For example, if the payment terms quoted are 2/10, N/30, this means

that a 2% discount can be deducted if the invoice is paid within 10 days of the invoice date. If the discount is not claimed, full payment must be made within 30 days.

> What discount can be claimed on an invoice for $140 with terms of 2/10, N/30?
>
> Convert 2% to its decimal equivalent = 0.02
>
> Multiply by $140 (140 × 0.02) = $2.80
>
> Subtract the discount amount of $2.80 from the invoice amount of $140. The amount payable is ($140 − $2.80) $137.20.

Chain discounts

When a series of discounts is granted (e.g., for quantity buying, as a special promotion, to particular industries or types of buyers), this is known as a *chain discount*.

   The first discount is taken off the list price. The second discount is taken off the remainder, and so on. Successive discounts cannot be added together.

$1000		• list (basic) price
−200	• 20% trade discount	• decimal equivalent of 20% (0.20) × 1000
800		
− 80	• 10% large-quantity discount	• decimal equivalent of 10% (0.10) × 800
720		
− 36	• 5% special summer promotional discount	• decimal equivalent of 5% (0.05) × 720
$ 684		• amount payable

Total discount allowed is as follows:
List (basic) price ($1000) − amount payable before taxes ($684) = $316.

MF16 FOREIGN CURRENCY EXCHANGE

The foreign currency exchange rate is the rate at which one country's currency can be exchanged for that of another's at a financial institution. Newspapers frequently publish lists of exchange rates, but the exchange rate quoted by institutions may vary from these because of the constant fluctuations caused by economic and political factors. Most currencies are now expressed as decimals and conversions are simple.

> Change $25 U.S. to Canadian dollars where:
>
> $1.00 U.S.   = $ 1.1886 Canadian (March 13, 2006 quote)
> 25 × $1.1886   = $32.54 Canadian
>
> Therefore, $25 U.S. equals $29.72 Canadian.

To change Canadian currency to U.S. currency at the same rate
(i. e., $1.1886 Canadian = $1.00 U.S.), the calculation is as follows:

$$\frac{1}{\$1.1886} = \$0.8413$$

Therefore, $1.00 Canadian = $0.8413 U.S.

Change $25 Canadian to U.S. dollars where:

$1.00 Canadian	=	$ 0.8413 U.S.
25 × $0.8413	=	$21.03 U.S.

In other words, it will cost you $25 Canadian to buy $21.03 worth of U.S. currency.

MF17 INTEREST

Interest may be earned or paid—earned on bank accounts, term deposits,
or promissory notes; or it may be paid on bank loans or mortgages.
Essentially there are two types of interest: simple and compound.

Simple Where interest is calculated only on the original principal, the
simple interest formula is $I = Prt$ (I = interest, P = principal, r = annual
rate, and t = time in years), but may also be expressed as follows:

$$P=\frac{1}{rt} \quad or \quad T=\frac{1}{Pr} \quad or \quad r=\frac{1}{Pt}$$

NOTE   Where the time involved is less than one year, express it as a fraction of a year. For example, express 60 days as $^{60}/_{365}$; 6 months as $^{6}/_{12}$. If
time is 1 year, show as 1.

What is the principal amount (P) when interest (I) is $18, rate ($r$) is 9%,
and time (t) is 2 years?

$$P=\frac{1}{rt}$$

$$P=\frac{18}{0.09 \times 2} \quad \text{(0.09 is the decimal equivalent of 9%)}$$

$$P=\$100$$

Compound Where interest is calculated periodically and added to the
principal so that for succeeding periods interest is calculated on the original principal plus the accumulated interest, the formula is as follows:

$$A=P(1+i)^n$$

A = amount that the principal (P) will accumulate to at i rate of interest per interest period for n interest periods.

Interest tables that do the compound interest calculations for you are
available in book form, as supplements to mathematics texts, and through
financial institutions.

MF

Two other interest-related formulas that may be useful are *effective interest rate* and *amortization*.

Effective interest rate

$$r = \frac{2Nc}{A(n+1)}$$

r = annual interest rate

N = number of payments in one year

c = cost of borrowing

A = amount borrowed

n = number of payments to pay loan in full

Assume that a person wants to buy a used car offered at $6000 with a $400 down payment. The arrangement offered is 36 equal payments of $170 with a cost of borrowing of $520, or 5.9%. The effective interest rate calculation will be as follows:

$$r = \frac{2 \times 12 \times 520}{5600 \times 37} \quad \text{(5600 is the basic cost minus the down payment)}$$

$$r = \frac{12\ 480}{207\ 200}$$

$$r = 0.0602$$

Expressed as a percentage, the true interest rate is 6.02% (i.e., the decimal point was moved two places to the right).

NOTE   When you work with algebraic expressions on a calculator, be careful about the sequence used to carry out the operations.

Amortization formula (mortgage payments)

◆ Repayment of a mortgage is a long-term process that may take 25 or 30 years. The time it takes to completely repay a mortgage, which is established when the mortgage is first negotiated, is called the *amortization period*.

◆ Most mortgages are arranged for six months to five years. This is known as the *mortgage term*.

◆ The formula for calculating the amount to be paid against a mortgage is as follows:

$$p = \frac{Pi(1+i)^n}{A(1+i)^n - 1}$$

p = amount to be paid per payment period

P = principal

i = interest rate per time period

n = total number of payment periods

◆ Books and software are available that provide the calculated information in table form. (Mortgage lenders, real estate agents, and libraries can also help.) These sources show amounts of interest payable under each option and consequences of paying the loan off faster, and should be consulted if this type of information is needed.

Calculating mortgage payments

The table below provides a rapid calculation of mortgage payments. Multiply the principal amount of the mortgage (in thousands) by the monthly payment factor shown in the appropriate amortization period opposite the current interest rate in the following table.

For example, for a principal mortgage amount of $95 000 amortized over 25 years at an interest rate of 8.00%, the monthly payment would be 95 × 7.63 = $724.85.

Interest rate (%)	Monthly payment factors		
	15 Yrs.	20 Yrs.	25 Yrs.
6.00	8.40	7.13	6.40
6.25	8.54	7.27	6.55
6.50	8.67	7.41	6.70
6.75	8.80	7.55	6.86
7.00	8.94	7.70	7.01
7.25	9.07	7.84	7.16
7.50	9.21	7.99	7.32
7.75	9.34	8.13	7.47
8.00	9.48	8.28	7.63
8.25	9.62	8.43	7.79
8.50	9.76	8.59	7.95
8.75	9.90	8.74	8.12
9.00	10.05	8.89	8.28
9.25	10.19	9.05	8.44
9.50	10.33	9.20	8.61
9.75	10.48	9.36	8.78
10.00	10.63	9.52	8.95

MF18 PRICING GOODS FOR SALE

Pricing means to establish the price at which goods can be sold, taking into consideration discounts or other allowances to be given, transportation costs, pricing legislation, demand, the type of business, competition, and the profit margin (i.e., percentage return on sales or investment).

Markup and margin

Most retail and wholesale prices are established by using markups. A markup is a percentage added to the cost price of the goods to cover operating expenses and to provide a reasonable net profit.

MF

If the owner of a business seeks a net profit of, for example, 12% of sales and the operating expenses of the business are expected to be 27% of sales, the selling price must produce a gross profit (margin) of 39%. The cost price of each article should, therefore, be 61% of its selling price.

sales (100%) − cost price (61%) = gross profit (margin) (39%)

gross profit (39%) − expenses (27%) = net profit (12%)

If cost price = $56, then 61% of the selling price is $56

The selling price = $56 \times \dfrac{100}{61} = \$91.80$

Therefore, markup = $91.80 − $56.00 = $35.80

Residential Mortgage Rates* As of September 16, 2006	
Fixed Rate	
Term	**Rate**
6-month open	6.4–8.4%
1-year open	7.7–8.65%
1-year closed	5.4–6.55%
2-year closed	5.4–6.65%
3-year closed	5.34–6.75%
4-year closed	5.35–6.75%
5-year closed	5.4–6.95%
7-year closed	6.13–7.25%
10-year closed	6.42–7.50%
Variable Rate	
Term	**Rate**
1-year open	8.55%
2-year open	6.40%
3-year open	6.50%
5-year open	6.0%

* These rates are subject to change at any time. Please contact a mortgage specialist at your banking institution for more information.

Example of a bank's mortgage rates, as the information might appear online

NOTE Most financial institutions have online access for mortgage calculation, where you can enter a mortgage amount, an interest rate, and an amortization period. Some sites also have tools to help you figure out how much you can afford by considering your income, debt, and monthly expenses.

NOTE Margin and markup are the same in amount but different in percentage because margin is related to selling price and markup is related to cost price.

If the selling price is known to be $91.80, then the margin is $35.80, or 39% of the selling price; if the cost price is known to be $56, then the markup is $35.80, or 61%.

Markdown

A markdown is often called a discount. It means a reduction in the regular price and is usually offered by the seller to attract customers and increase sales.

Break-even point

For a business to be worthwhile, income must exceed expenses. The point at which income and expense intersect is known as the break-even point (BEP). (Above the BEP, profit; below the BEP, loss!) The break-even point is calculated to determine the minimum output or sales necessary for income to cover costs. Break-even point analysis is particularly useful for comparing pricing alternatives:

$$BEP = \frac{\text{total fixed costs (costs that cannot be changed)}}{\text{suggested selling price per unit} - \text{variable costs (costs that can be changed) per unit}}$$

Total fixed costs for publishing a book are $90 000, variable costs per unit amount to $5.50, and the suggested selling price is $10.50:

$$BEP = \frac{90\ 000}{10.5 - 5.50} = \frac{90\ 000}{5} = 18\ 000 \text{ units}$$

Therefore, 18 000 copies of the book must be sold before a profit is achieved. To improve this position, the selling price might be raised or some way of cutting variable costs (e.g., using less expensive paper) might be sought.

MF19 SALES TAXES

Federal and provincial taxes are charged on most sales. Calculate sales tax as a percentage of the total value of the purchase, and both numbers add together.

The federal goods and services tax is 6 percent of the invoice amount. This 6 percent is charged on most goods and services, unlike provincial sales taxes, which tend to apply to merchandise transactions only. Provincial sales tax rates and the way in which provincial sales tax is charged vary from province to province. In some provinces, the provincial sales tax is charged on the base invoice amount. In others, the provincial sales tax is charged on the invoice price plus the GST. Examples of the two methods follow.

◆ Tax calculation showing taxes based on invoice price (PST charged on base invoice price):

Invoice amount	$250.00
Plus 6% GST	15.00
	265.00
Plus 8% PST	20.00
Amount payable	$285.00

◆ Tax calculation showing tax charged on invoice amount plus tax (PST charged on invoice price plus GST):

Invoice amount	$250.00
Plus 6% GST	15.00
	265.00
Plus 8% PST	21.20
Amount payable	$286.20

Check your provincial rules to ascertain the method to use in your province. More information on GST is available from Canada Revenue Agency (CRA) in Ottawa or CRA Excise GST offices in major centres throughout the country, which can be contacted toll-free in Canada. Procedures for accounting for GST are explained in Part 2, "Financial Management."

NOTE Merchandise that is purchased to manufacture items for retail sale (e.g., paper for making greeting cards) is taxed only when it is in its final form. A sales tax licence number on an invoice is used to indicate that the material is exempt from sales tax because this is not the final (end) sale of the paper.

Notes on tax calculations

◆ Calculate taxes payable before adding shipping charges.
◆ Deduct all discounts before calculating taxes.
◆ Use the memory or constant feature of your calculator when many similar tax calculations must be made.

IV MF20 STATISTICAL DATA

Frequently, business information is presented in the form of averages and ratios to indicate comparisons and trends.

▶ MF21 Averages

Mean

An average or mean is a single number that represents a central tendency in a group of numbers. Averages (means) may be simple or weighted.

Simple average Find a simple average by dividing the sum of a series of numbers by the total number of members of the series:

T-shirts sold for $10.95 in the spring sale, for $12.00 at the regular price, and for $11.50 in the fall sale. The simple average selling price was as follows:

$$\frac{\$10.95 + \$12.00 + \$11.50}{3} = \frac{\$34.45}{3} = \$11.48$$

Weighted average The *simple* average is based on only one unit of each number being added and then divided by the sum of the units. A *weighted* average is calculated when there is more than one unit in each item. A weighted average is calculated when a more accurate figure than that provided by a simple average is needed. To find a weighted average, multiply each quantity by its unit value, add the products, and then divide by the sum of the quantities:

120 T-shirts were sold at $10.95 in the spring sale, 230 at the regular price of $12, and 90 at $11.50 in the fall sale. The average (weighted) selling price was:

$$\frac{(\$10.95 \times 120) + (\$12.00 \times 230) + (\$11.50 \times 90)}{120 + 230 + 90} =$$

$$\frac{\$1314 + \$2760 + \$1035}{440} =$$

$$\frac{\$5109}{440} = \$11.61$$

Compare this weighted average with $11.48, the simple average calculated above.

Mode

Mode is the figure occurring most frequently in a list of numbers:

6, 7, 9, 6, 7, 8, 7, 8

The mode in this example is 7 since it occurs three times.

This type of statistical information is most interesting to a shoe retailer, for example, who wishes to know the most common selling shoe size.

Median

The median (middle value) in a series of numbers arranged in numerical order is the quantity that appears at the mid-point of the list. One-half of the quantities have a higher value and one-half have a lower value.

Find the median figure by arranging the series of numbers in order of size or value and then selecting the middle one.

Seven students earned these marks: 24, 76, 10, 73, 74, 70, 66.

Arrange in order: 10, 24, 66, 70, 73, 74, 76.

The median mark is 70. There are three numbers higher than 70 and three lower. When the number of items is even, the median is the simple average of the two middle numbers.

MF

▶ MF22   Ratio

The ratio of two numbers is the comparison of the size or value of one number with the size or value of another number.

There are 5 management staff and 20 support staff in the office. The ratio of management staff to support staff is 5:20 or 1:4 (reduced to its simplest form).

▶ MF23   Proportion

The term *proportion* is used to indicate that two ratios are equal: 1:4 is proportional to 2:8. When two ratios are equal, their cross products are also equal:

$$\frac{1}{4} \diagup\!\!\!\!\!\diagdown \frac{2}{8}$$

If three terms in a proportion are known, the fourth is easily found:

y:16 is proportional to 3:12

$$\frac{y}{16} \diagup\!\!\!\!\!\diagdown \frac{3}{12} \qquad \begin{aligned} 12y &= 48 \\ y &= \frac{48}{12} \\ y &= 4 \end{aligned}$$

4:16 is proportional to 3:12.

A firm has a policy of taking co-op students in proportion to its full-time staff. If the established ratio is 5 co-op students to every 100 full-time employees, what number of co-op students will there be if the present full-time staff numbers 360?

$$\frac{5}{100} \diagup\!\!\!\!\!\diagdown \frac{y}{360} \qquad \begin{aligned} 100y &= 1800 \\ y &= 18 \end{aligned}$$

Therefore, there will be 18 co-op students for a staff of 360 because 5:100 is proportional to 18:360.

MF24   SPREADSHEETS

Most businesses make considerable use of computer spreadsheet software to increase productivity and to provide a great deal of useful financial and numerical data. While extensive mathematical skill is not needed to operate a spreadsheet program, an understanding of the basics of formula creation and the use of mathematical symbols is needed. The information in Unit 12, "Computers: Hardware and Software," C26, will provide the necessary understanding.

If you have access to computer spreadsheet software, use it as much as possible for applications in which repeat calculations are required. Such programs are fast and accurate and will recalculate everything instantly if there is a need for any change. Unit 12 also provides information on possible spreadsheet uses.

IV

WORDS OF WISDOM

May your life be like arithmetic—
friends added, enemies subtracted,
joys multiplied and troubles divided.

FINANCIAL MANAGEMENT

All organizations, regardless of size—from local corner stores to giant corporations—must keep financial records. Most office workers are involved to some degree in financial record-keeping, depending on the size of the organization and the degree of automation used.

The efficient office worker must be able to carry out, or at least understand, the routine tasks associated with money management. The valuable employee understands the work of the organization's accounting department; can read and understand financial statements; knows how to use the business services provided by financial institutions; understands payroll procedures and, if required, can prepare a simple one; can use and operate a petty-cash fund; and is familiar with terms and processes related to money and banking.

MF25 ACCOUNTING

Accounting involves the recording of all financial transactions (purchases, sales, returns, money received, and money paid out), summarizing the recorded data into meaningful reports that indicate the firm's operating position, and interpreting the data to help management in the decision-making process. Although the accounting function in most large organizations is automated and is the concern of specialists in the field, every office worker should at least be familiar with the terms and processes involved.

MF26 ACCOUNTING RECORDS

▶ MF27 Source documents (forms)

The accounting process (cycle) starts with a basic business record or form known as a *source document,* which establishes that a transaction has taken place. Invoices, credit invoices, cheques, purchase orders, cash register tapes, and time cards are all examples of source documents. If an automated accounting system is used, the source document information must be

MF

translated onto a medium that can be used by the system (e.g., magnetic tape or disk). It may be keyed into a computer or it may be electronically scanned.

▶MF28 Journals

Information from a source document is recorded in a journal (a daily record of transactions). For very small manual or mechanical accounting systems, journals may be in loose-leaf, book, or card form. On computer-based systems, a printout may be produced. The journal entry shows the accounts affected by the transaction and provides a brief explanation. Very small businesses may use only one (general) journal; larger ones may use some or all of the following special journals:

Cash receipts journal Used to record cash received in currency, cheques, money orders, or other cash substitutes.

Cash payments (or disbursements) journal Used to record payments made by cash or cheque (other than payroll).

Purchases journal Used to record purchases made on account.

Sales journal Used to record sales made on account.

General journal Used to record transactions not already recorded in one of the other journals.

Payroll journal (See MF84.)

Some very small businesses integrate these journals into one multi-column combination journal.

▶MF29 Ledger accounts

General journal

| GENERAL JOURNAL | | | | | |
					Page 12
Date 20--		Description	Post Ref.	Debit	Credit
June	5	Cash	100	14 980	
		Service Fee Revenues			14 000
		GST Payable	201		840
		To record services performed for cash			
	10	Office Equipment	157	62 000	
		Cash	100		22 000
		Notes Payable	263		40 000
		Purchased equipment for cash and issued short-term note			

| Account – Cash | | | | | Account No. 100 |
Date 20--	Item	Post Ref.	Debit	Credit	Balance
June 1		J1	60 000		60 000
2		J1		12 000	48 000
3		J1		960	47 040
5		J12	14 840		61 880
6		J1		120	61 760

Ledger account

The information recorded in a journal is posted to (transferred to or recorded in) separate, individual accounts. An account is set up for each of the company's individual assets, liabilities, owners' equity items, revenues, and expenses. These are used for recording the effects of changes (transactions).

Each account has three columns—debit, credit, and balance—and a system known as *double entry* is used. This means that for every debit recorded, there must be a matching credit. Increases in assets, expenses, and purchases of merchandise for resale are recorded in the debit column; decreases are recorded in the credit column. Increases in liability, revenue, and owners' equity accounts are recorded in the credit column; decreases are recorded in the debit column. The difference between the total debits and total credits is known as the *account balance*. (In a computerized system, posting takes place automatically once the journalizing has been completed.)

►MF30 A ledger

A group of related accounts is referred to as a *ledger*. In a small organization, all the accounts may be referred to as "the ledger."

When accounts that *could* be part of a general ledger are grouped together for ease of handling, these are referred to as *subsidiary ledgers*. For example, you might have a subsidiary ledger for accounts receivable, another for accounts payable, and others for large numbers of similar accounts.

►MF31 Statement of account

Monthly statements of account are sent to customers as a record of the transactions that have taken place and a reminder of the balance owing. The statement shows the opening balance, purchases, returns, payments, and the closing balance for the month (see Unit 17, F22, for an illustration). The statement of account is, in fact, a copy of the relevant part of the customer's ledger account. In computerized accounting systems, statements are generated automatically; in manual ones, they must be specially prepared.

►MF32 Trial balance

A trial balance is prepared regularly to check on the mathematical accuracy of the ledger. The trial balance lists balances of all the separate accounts under the debit or credit headings. The totals of the two columns must be identical. The information provided in the trial balance is used to prepare the financial statements.

MF33 FINANCIAL STATEMENTS

The operating results and financial standing of a business are reported to shareholders, investors, management, and others by means of financial statements. The two key statements are the income statement and the balance sheet.

▶MF34 The income statement

This is a summary of the revenue, expenses, and net profit or net loss over a given period.

For a merchandising business (one that buys at one price and sells at another) or manufacturing business, the typical income statement will have three sections: income, cost of goods sold, and expenses.

Gross sales is the total amount of sales made.

Net sales represents gross sales minus any returns or discounts given.

Cost of goods sold is arrived at by adding the beginning inventory and purchases made during the period and then deducting the ending inventory.

Gross profit is found by deducting cost of goods sold from net sales. The figure should be large enough to cover the expenses of the business and provide a reasonable profit. If gross profit is not large enough to cover expenses, an overall loss will result.

Expenses are the costs incurred in operating the business (e.g., salaries, heat, light, telephone, etc.).

Net income is the gross profit less the expenses.

In comparative income statements, comparisons are usually related to net sales. Net sales are established at 100 percent and all other items are expressed as a percentage of that figure.

		Current Year	Previous Year
J. Savage Services			
Income Statement			
For the Month Ended December 31, 20--			
Income			
Gross Sales............................	$963 000		
Less Returns	13 000		
Net Sales		$950 000 (100%)	$750 000 (100%)
Cost of Goods Sold			
Opening Inventory, Dec. 1	$100 000		
Purchases.............................	450 000		
Cost of Goods for Sale	550 000		
Less Ending Inv., Dec. 31...	50 000		
Cost of Goods Sold.................		500 000	
Gross Profit		450 000 (47.36%)	$300 750 (40.1%)
Expenses			
Salaries Expense	$200 000		
Advertising Expense	35 000		
Depreciation Expense	20 000		
Miscellaneous Expense	15 000		
Total Operating Expenses....		270 000	
Net Income...........................		$180 000 (18.94%)	$105 750 (14.1%)

Comparative income statement

▶MF35 The balance sheet

The balance sheet provides information about how much a business is worth at a specific time. It summarizes the assets (owned items of value), liabilities (amounts owed by the business), and the owner's equity (capital),

```
                          J. Savage Services
                           Balance Sheet
                        as at December 31, 20--

                              ASSETS

Current Assets
Cash.....................................................  $    25 000
Accounts Receivable ...............................        95 000
Notes Receivable...................................        10 000
Inventory..............................................    50 000
                                                                        $   180 000

Fixed Assets
Land ...................................................  $1 450 000
Buildings ........................................ $500 000
   Less Depreciation ......................   50 000
                                                           450 000
                                                                          1 900 000

Total Assets...........................................                 $2 080 000


                            LIABILITIES

Current Liabilities
Accounts Payable .................................        $   152 000

Long-Term Liabilities
Mortgage Payable .................................        200 000
Total Liabilities.......................................                 $   352 000


                         OWNER'S EQUITY

J. Savage, Capital.................................       $1 548 000
Net Income ..........................................       180 000
                                                                          1 728 000

Total Liabilities and Owner's Equity.................                   $2 080 000
```

Balance sheet

which is the owner's claim against the assets. The "balance" in the title of the statement means that the total of the assets must balance with (equal) the total of the liabilities plus the owner's equity:

assets = liabilities + owner's equity

This formula is the underlying foundation of any accounting system, and is referred to as the *fundamental accounting equation*.

Current assets are assets likely to be sold, used up, or converted into cash within one year.

Accounts receivable is the amount owed to the company by customers supplied with goods or services on credit.

Notes receivable are outstanding promissory notes, which are written promises to repay a debt.

Fixed assets are the virtually permanent assets of the firm.

Current liabilities are debts that will normally be paid within one year.

Accounts payable refers to the amount of money to be paid by the business to its creditors.

Long-term liabilities are debts that are not likely to be paid off within one year.

Owner's equity (or shareholders' equity) represents the claim of the owner(s) or shareholder(s) on the assets.

▶ MF36 Financial statement analysis

Information in financial statements can be converted into percentages, ratios, and averages to provide information for business owners and managers, investors, creditors, and others, on which well-informed business decisions can be based. Such information can also be used to provide comparisons with company performance in previous years, to highlight trends, and to provide comparison with the performance of similar businesses.

Percentages, ratios, and averages provide clues only. They are useful indicators but do not give a full picture. The key ratios and relationships include those that show liquidity, performance, and profitability. A few examples are provided below.

Liquidity

Liquidity tests indicate a firm's ability to pay its debts and can be determined by examining the current ratio, working capital available, and the acid-test ratio.

The *current ratio* is a measure of a firm's short-term debt-paying ability. It is calculated by dividing total current assets by total current liabilities. To have meaning, the resulting figures must be compared with the company's ratio on previous dates or with the current-ratio average that exists for the industry to which the company belongs. The type of business must also be considered. A ratio of two to one is usually thought to be satisfactory.

Working capital is represented by the amount by which current assets exceed current liabilities, the amount that would be left free and clear if all current debts were paid off. This amount shows in monetary terms the company's debt-paying ability that is represented by the current ratio.

The *acid-test ratio* (or *quick ratio*) is found by dividing the total of cash and accounts receivable (liquid assets) by total current liabilities. A one-to-one ratio is considered satisfactory.

Performance

The *inventory turnover* ratio shows how much sales revenue is being earned with a given amount of capital invested in stock (i.e., how fast the inventory is being turned over). This is a useful device for comparing present performance with past performance or for assessing the efficiency of firms in the same type of business.

Profitability

Gross profit margin shows how much profit exists after the cost of goods has been deducted:

$$\text{gross profit margin} = \frac{\text{total sales} - \text{cost of goods sold}}{\text{sales}}$$

This is expressed as a percentage.

Net profit margin shows the profit remaining after all expenses have been paid. The formula is:

$$\frac{\text{net profit after taxes}}{\text{sales}}$$

It is important to remember that each ratio is meaningless on its own. Ratios, etc., should be used to measure the firm's performance in relation to its own past activities, the firm's close competition, and the firm's performance within that particular industry.

MF37 ACCOUNTING SYSTEMS

Accounting systems vary with the size of the company. Only very small organizations now keep records by hand. Such organizations often use a *one-write system*, in which several records are created as entries made on forms attached to a specially designed board. Computerized forms of one-write systems are now available. They are much more simplified than most accounting systems. In most organizations, a computer is used for all record-keeping and financial statement preparation.

▶MF38 Computer accounting systems

Computer accounting systems range from those used by individuals to produce cheques and reconcile bank accounts, to multi-user systems that take the data input by many operators and process it through all the required steps to produce financial statements.

MF39 Accounting software

Software packages are available that parallel the traditional manual systems and use the same language, or programs may be written especially for an organization. Such software can range from relatively simple types to highly sophisticated, integrated ones. The simpler programs provide modules covering all or some of the fundamental operations of journalizing, posting, trial balance, financial statement generation, payroll, job costing, inventory control, and sales order entry. The more sophisticated ones offer total integration of all the key aspects of an organization's finances—sales, inventory control, purchasing, billing, accounts receivable, accounts payable, payroll, budget control, and financial reporting.

Accounting experts analyse the data contained in source documents and data-entry staff input it into the accounting databases. Once transactions have been input, software automatically produces journals, updates ledgers, prepares trial balances and financial statements, and can manipulate data in other ways. Some, for example, can produce aged accounts receivable reports that show which accounts are 30, 60, and 90 days overdue. For security, administrators can allow or deny access to various accounting modules and functions within any or all of the accounting modules.

A spreadsheet also has wide applications in accounting. Spreadsheets can be used for totalling and balancing journals, calculating sales taxes and

MF

discounts, creating bad-debts schedules, and estimating profits and prices, for example. For more information see Unit 12, C27.

NOTE For more information on the accounting process, see Unit 17, where billing and purchasing are fully described in the context of the forms used in the processes.

MF40 BUDGETS

The preparation of budgets is an accounting-related activity. A budget is a financial plan for a period—usually a year—that projects expected income and expenditures. There are several types, but the two key types are

◆ operating budgets, related to such activities as sales, advertising, salaries, production, maintenance, etc.

◆ capital expense budgets, which project long-range expenditures on major items (new equipment, replacements, etc.)

The company-wide budgets determine division and departmental budgets and contain both capital and operating items. Budget information must be constantly updated so that those responsible for control of finances can track actual performance and make appropriate changes to ensure that budget requirements are met. Budgets may also be drawn up for projects. In this case, records of all costs associated with that project must be kept.

Spreadsheets are the best tool to facilitate budget record-keeping because

◆ calculations are done automatically (less room for error)

◆ changes can be reflected without the need for recalculating

◆ graphs and charts needed for reports can easily be produced

Expense reports

These may be a feature of the operating expense budget (see Unit 11, "Travel Arrangements," for information). Some software allows the two to be combined so that an expense report update automatically adjusts the budget.

MF41 BANKING

The banking transactions most commonly handled by general office workers include making deposits and withdrawals, preparing cheques, endorsing cheques, and reconciling the account balance with the chequebook balance. However, office workers should also be aware of the special services offered by financial institutions because this information may be useful for handling their personal finances and those of their employers, if necessary.

MF42 FINANCIAL INSTITUTIONS*

Legally, only chartered banks operating under the *Bank Act* can call themselves "banks." However, other financial institutions such as credit unions, trust companies, provincial savings banks, and caisses populaires offer services similar to those provided by banks. The information that follows is relevant to all types of financial institutions.

▶ MF43 Types of accounts

The accounts described here are available at most financial institutions; their names and terms might vary somewhat.

MF44 Business chequing account

This account is used by businesses for making deposits and payments:

◆ Interest paid is based on a tiered structure depending on account balance/s.

◆ An unlimited number of cheques may be written (based on a fee structure).

◆ Regular account statements, that include debit or credit memorandums (explanations of special transactions), are returned to the account holder.

◆ Monthly service charges vary based on services provided.

MF45 Personal chequing account

This account is used by individuals for making deposits and payments:

◆ A minimal interest rate is paid based on the daily balance maintained.

◆ Monthly fees depend on the number of cheques written. Some institutions waive fees if a specified monthly balance is maintained or if a significant amount of business is given to that institution, e.g., mortgage, savings, etc.

◆ Account statements are provided monthly.

> NOTE Some financial institutions offer a daily interest chequing account, a personal chequing account on which a low interest rate is paid.

MF46 Daily interest savings account

Generally, this type of account is used by individuals who want to earn interest on their savings. Interest is tiered based on the amount on deposit, and is paid monthly.

◆ Usually a charge is made for withdrawals if the daily balance falls below a minimum figure.

◆ A passbook is issued in which all transactions are recorded, but as of this date, financial institutions are starting to phase out passbooks; copies of statements are always available.

MF

*To register any concerns or complaints in the banking industry, call the Canadian Ombudsman for Banking Services and Investment at www.obsi.can, 1-888-451-4519, fax 1-888-422-2865, email ombudsman@obsi.ca, or write to P.O. Box 896, Station Adelaide, Toronto, ON M5C 2K3.

MF47 Investment account

Investment accounts are available through financial institutions, e.g., Financial Advisor.

MF48 U.S. dollar account

A selection of accounts is available to clients who want to keep funds in U.S. dollars. Inquire at your financial institution for details.

MF49 Joint account

A joint account is one that is shared by two or more people. Any type of account can be made into a joint account. Each person may use the account on his or her own signature, unless arrangements with the financial institution specify that two or more signatures are necessary for each transaction.

▶MF50 Making deposits

NOTE   This section on making deposits and the following one on making withdrawals do not apply to transactions carried out at an automated banking machine (ABM), which is discussed in MF60.

Deposit slips for all accounts are similar in format and are designed to indicate to the financial institution which account should be credited, the date of deposit, who is making the deposit, the amount of the deposit, and if some of the money is to be retained by the depositor. If a deposit is to be made to a savings account, provide the teller with the account passbook.

Current account deposit slips come in book form and consist of deposit slips with copy paper behind each one. When a deposit is made, the financial institution retains the original and stamps the copy, which remains in the book as the customer's record.

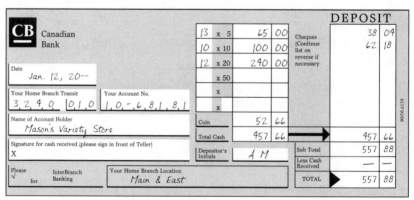

Completed current account deposit slip

To speed up the processing of your deposit:

◆ Fill out the deposit slip carefully.
◆ Arrange bills with the smallest denomination on top and place a rubber band around them.

◆ If there are enough of each coin denomination, roll them in coin wrappers.

◆ Endorse each cheque properly (see MF54).

►MF51   Making withdrawals

Where withdrawals are to be made from, for example, a chequing savings account, use the withdrawal slip provided by the financial institution. Where withdrawals are to be made from current or personal chequing accounts, a cheque or the withdrawal slip may be used.

►MF52   Preparing cheques

Cheques can be written for any amount up to the amount on deposit in the account. They can be prepared by hand, cheque protector machine, or computer.

◆ Complete the cheque stub or account record book first.

◆ Use ink if you prepare the cheque by hand.

◆ Insert the correct date.

◆ Correctly spell the full name of the payee. Titles such as Mr., Ms., Dr., Rev. are unnecessary. Fill in any unused part with a line so that no other name can be added.

◆ Write the amount in figures close enough to the printed $ sign so that the amount cannot be altered.

◆ Write the amount in words, making sure it is the same amount as the figures indicate. (Express cents as fractions of a dollar.) Begin at the extreme left and fill in any unused part with a line so that there is no space for changes.

◆ Do not erase or use liquid paper. Either prepare a new cheque or properly correct and initial the correction on the original cheque. Do not destroy an unused business cheque: write "Void" in large letters across the face of it and the stub, and keep the cheque in the files.

◆ Ensure that the cheque is properly signed in ink.

Completed personal cheque

Voucher cheques, which are commonly used in business, consist of a cheque portion and a voucher (stub) portion that contains the document number relating to the amount of the cheque and other explanatory details.

MF

Pearson Education Canada
P.O. Box 580 – 26 Prince Andrew Place
Don Mills, Ontario
M3C 2T8

Pearson Education

VENDOR No.	VENDOR NAME	CHEQUE NUMBER	CHEQUE DATE
0083	SPEEDY PRINTING	15353	10/08/20--

PEARSON EDUCATION CANADA
P.O. BOX 580 - 26 PRINCE ANDREW PLACE
DON MILLS, ONTARIO, M3C 2T8

THE ROYAL BANK OF CANADA
33 CITY DRIVE BRANCH
MISSISSAUGA, ONT. L5B 2N6

15352
CHEQUE NUMBER

Pay $ Four hundred & fifty dollars   450.36

to the order of : Speedy Printing

I· 03l32   III   003·I   I03III 802III 5II

Voucher cheque

MF53 Cheque clearing

Once a cheque has been cashed or deposited, the payee's financial institution submits the document to a clearing house to receive payment from
the drawer's institution. Technology now enables this process to be completed electronically on the day of the transaction. The issuer of a cheque
must ensure that sufficient funds are in the account to cover the cheque
being written.

▶MF54 Endorsing cheques

Before a cheque can be cashed or deposited, it must be properly endorsed.
This means that the payee signs his or her name on the back of the cheque
or, in the case of a company, uses a rubber stamp. The endorsement does
three things:

◆ relieves the financial institution of responsibility should the cheque
  be dishonoured

◆ acts as a receipt for the cash

◆ serves as identification of the payee

There are three types of endorsements:

Blank endorsement

This is used if the payee cashes or deposits a cheque:

◆ Endorse the cheque exactly as the name appears on the face of the
  cheque.

◆ Endorse the cheque only at the financial institution, just before cash-
  ing or depositing it, because the blank endorsement enables anyone
  presenting the cheque to cash it.

NOTE   If the payee's name is incorrectly spelled on the face of the
cheque, endorse the cheque twice—once as shown on the cheque and
then correctly. This is called a *double endorsement*.

Full endorsement

This is used if the payee wants to transfer ownership of the cheque to
another person. Endorse the cheque with the wording "Pay to the order of

[new payee]" and sign it as shown on the face. The new payee may then cash, deposit, or transfer ownership of the cheque again.

Restrictive endorsement

This limits what can be done with the cheque. For example, if the words "For deposit only to the account of . . ." are written on the back of the cheque, it is not possible for even the payee to cash it. It must be deposited. This provides protection against loss or theft of a cheque. The endorsement may either be written or rubber-stamped in the manner shown in the illustrations below.

Blank endorsement	Full endorsement	Restrictive endorsement
Mike Belza	*Pay to the order of A. Frendinette Mike Belza*	*For deposit only to Ac. 04-0167 for Mike Belza Mike Belza*
Double endorsement *Mike Belsa Mike Belza*		

Endorsement styles

▶MF55 Special types of cheques

Certified cheques

These are used when a personal cheque is not acceptable:

◆ Prepare a cheque in the regular way and present it to the teller for certification.

◆ The teller will stamp "Certified" on the face of the cheque and return it to you.

◆ The amount of the cheque will be deducted from your account by the financial institution and transferred to a special account to ensure payment when the cheque is presented.

Stopped cheques

For a fee, cheques can be stopped by a financial institution when for some reason—theft, loss, error in preparation—you do not want the institution to make payment on a cheque you have issued:

◆ Phone the financial institution immediately and ask for stop payment of the cheque, giving complete details of the cheque.

◆ Send a confirming fax or letter to the institution or go in person and fill in a stop-payment form.

◆ Do not issue a replacement cheque until the financial institution confirms that payment has been stopped on the first one.

Post-dated cheques

These are issued for a date in the future. Financial institutions recommend that they not be used because the issuer can easily forget them

MF

and the money may not be available in the account when they are actually presented.

Stale-dated cheques

In the eyes of financial institutions, cheques have a life span of six months. Stale-dated cheques are over six months old and will not be accepted.

NSF cheques

NSF means not sufficient funds. Cheques stamped with these letters are returned to the payee when the maker's account lacks enough money to meet the amount. It is up to the payee, not the financial institution, to follow up on the problem.

Cancelled cheques

These are cheques on which all transactions have been completed. With certain types of accounts, they are returned to the maker with the regular statement.

Dishonoured (irregular) cheques

This term is used when a cheque is not accepted by the financial institution for some reason (e.g., amounts in words and figures do not agree; the cheque is undated and/or unsigned).

▶MF56 Service charges

Several types of accounts are eligible for operating service charges. Charges are made for almost all services provided by financial institutions, but special packages that remove service charges are available. For example, for a monthly fee, some financial institutions will allow an unlimited number of free cheques.

▶MF57 Reconciling the account statement

The balance on the monthly statement sent to you by your financial institution will usually differ from the balance shown in your records. There may be several reasons for this difference:

◆ All the deposits you have made may not have been recorded.

◆ All cheques issued have not yet been cleared for payment (outstanding cheques).

◆ Interest or other credits (credit memos) may have been added.

◆ Service charges (debit memos) or NSF cheques may have been deducted.

◆ An error has been made.

Reconciliation procedure

Follow these steps to reconcile the discrepancy between the statement balance and yours:

IV

◆ Compare the amounts on cancelled cheques and other documents with the amounts shown on the statement and in your records. Call the financial institution immediately if there are any statement discrepancies.

◆ List the numbers and amounts of all outstanding cheques. Include any from previous reconciliation statements that still have not been cleared.

◆ Compare the deposits shown on the statement against those in your records.

◆ List any deposits not shown on the statement (late deposits).

◆ Write down the statement balance, then add the total of late deposits and subtract the total of the outstanding cheques. This balance will be the *adjusted statement balance.*

◆ Write down the balance in your cheque record book (or cash account) for the end of the month.
  • *Add* any credit memos shown on the statement.
  • *Subtract* the bank service charge and any debit memos or NSF cheques shown on the statement. The balance will be the adjusted amount of your records (*adjusted chequebook balance*).
The adjusted statement balance and the adjusted chequebook balance should now be the same. If they differ, repeat the above steps. If they still differ, contact your financial institution.

◆ Finally, produce for your permanent records a formal account reconciliation statement as illustrated here.

J. Young Landscaping Company
Account Reconciliation Statement
October 31, 20--

Account Statement Balance		$2542.00
Plus Late Deposit		350.00
		2892.00
Less Outstanding Cheques		
Cheque 102	$ 51.00	
Cheque 107	214.00	
Cheque 110	110.46	
Cheque 116	151.07	
		526.53
Adjusted Account Balance		$2365.47
Chequebook Balance		$2116.22
Plus Credit Memo—Bond Interest		47.00
		2163.22
Less Outstanding Charges		
NSF Cheque—Daley Co.	$132.50	
Service Charges	13.75	
Loan Interest	56.00	
		202.25
Adjusted Chequebook Balance		$2365.47

MF

Account reconciliation statement

NOTE   You may need to amend your chequebook balance or cash account to include the new information reported to you on the statement. Interest earned and service charges represent amounts that you often do not know until you receive the statement. Remember to record all bank service charges, debit memos, and credit memos in your accounting system.

▶MF58   Other key banking services

MF59   Accounting

Various types of accounting services are provided by some financial institutions, including payroll preparation and account statement reconciliation for customers who issue a large number of cheques. Large-volume customers can also receive daily updates of their accounts, if required.

MF60   Automated banking machines

An automated banking machine (ABM), sometimes called an automated teller machine (ATM), allows 24-hour access to a wide range of banking services such as deposits, cash withdrawals, automatic updating of accounts, payment of bills, or transfer of funds. Users receive a special card and a confidential code number (PIN: personal identification number).

The ABM network allows people to use their banking machine cards to withdraw cash from ABMs at any participating financial institution. A service charge is applied. Other banking transactions must still be carried out at an ABM operated by a customer's own financial institution.

The three main shared ABM networks in Canada are currently Interac, Cirrus, and Plus, of which the Canadian system, Interac, is the largest. Many Interac member institutions are also linked with Cirrus and Plus, international ABM networks that allow cardholders to withdraw cash both in and outside Canada.

NOTE   Be careful of exposing your PIN or of abnormal devices when using an ABM.

Electronic funds transfer at point of sale (debit cards)
Currently, only Interac offers debit card service in Canada. Called Interac Direct Payment, it allows cardholders to use their current ABM cards to pay retailers directly from their accounts.

Service charges vary among financial institutions. Additional charges may also apply when using banking machines provided by some retailers, such as at gas stations or convenience stores. These machines will inform you of any extra charges, and you can choose to cancel the transaction. Out-of-country service charges are higher for banking machine transactions.

MF61   Automatic bill payment

Many financial institutions now permit bill payments across Canada and in certain states via a computer connection or the telephone. When customers apply for this "link" service, they register with the bank a list of the companies they wish to pay.

To avoid late fees on bill payments, be aware that due date cutoff time is usually 6 p.m. Monday to Friday, excluding national holidays. Bills cannot be paid in real time; allow two to three business days to process payment to your account, e.g., if a bill is due on a Friday, pay by Tuesday before 6 p.m.

The types of bills that can be paid on a monthly basis are as follows:

- automobile club memberships
- cable
- car payments
- college/university tuition
- insurance (car, home, and life)
- mortgage
- subscriptions
- taxes (business/property)
- utilities (hydro, telephone, and gas)

`IMPORTANT` Make sure you notify companies where you hold credit card accounts if you change credit card companies or type of card. This is important when paying bills using the automatic billing feature with your financial institution.

You can also choose to have weekly/monthly payroll deductions for bonds and RRSPs (if offered) at your place of work.

MF62 Banking by telephone and online

Many financial institutions offer telephone and online services through which customers can carry out routine transactions such as paying bills, transferring funds, buying and selling mutual funds, and obtaining account and loan balances and information on interest rates and foreign exchange rates. These services vary from institution to institution, but many offer virtually worldwide 24-hour-a-day service through toll-free numbers in North America and paid calls from elsewhere and through the bank's website.

MF63 Credit cards

Participating financial institutions issue credit cards such as Visa and MasterCard to approved customers. These cards can be used to purchase goods and services, to withdraw cash, or to obtain cash advances.

Accounts can be paid in full or in part each month. If only partial payment is made, the unpaid balance is automatically carried to the next statement and interest is charged.

Interest If payment in full is not received by the payment due date, interest charges are assessed from the date when purchases are posted to the account. Interest is calculated and accrued daily (compounded); therefore, it is advisable to pay off balances in full to avoid high interest charges (17.9%–21.0%). Interest rates for cash advances are higher than for purchases (18.75%–22.0%).

Foreign transactions Transactions made outside Canada are converted to U.S. currency and then to Canadian currency, both at the exchange rates

MF

in effect at the time of posting. These rates may differ from the rates in effect on the date of the transaction.

Cheques for these credit card accounts are also available to holders for use in cases where the credit card is not accepted. These cheques are treated as cash advances. All cash advances are treated as loans on which daily interest is charged.

Cardholders usually pay a flat annual service fee.

MF64 Credit card protection

To protect your credit card and yourself, note the following:

◆ Never fill out forms in email messages that ask for personal financial information, and always ensure that you are using a secure website when submitting credit card or other sensitive information through your browser.

◆ Destroy unwanted cards immediately.

◆ Do not provide your MasterCard/Visa or any credit card number over the phone unless you have initiated the contact and you know the company is reputable.

◆ Memorize your PIN for your credit card/s; do not write it down or disclose it to anyone, and never leave it in your wallet with your card.

◆ When selecting your PIN, do not pick obvious number combinations such as your birth date, SIN, or phone number.

◆ Keep your credit card receipts and check them against your monthly statement to make sure no one else is using your card.

◆ Report lost or stolen cards immediately. Most fraudulent use of credit cards occurs within hours of the card being lost or stolen.

◆ Report unauthorized transactions or discrepancies to your financial institution immediately.

◆ Shred personal information such as bills, bank statements, and credit card offers before you recycle them.

NOTE Check your credit report frequently so that you are aware of any changes or unusual activity. Credit information can be obtained once a year at no charge from Equifax Canada at www.equifax.ca or 1-800-465-7166, or TransUnion Canada at www.tuc.ca or 1-800-663-9980.

NOTE *Bank cards* are issued to customers by financial institutions for withdrawing cash, transferring funds, or paying bills at ATMs. They can also be used for point-of-sale services.

MF65 Drafts

These are documents issued by one financial institution that instruct another to pay a specified sum to the person or company named on the draft.

Commercial drafts Once the buyer and seller have come to a financial agreement, the creditor originates a commercial draft, indicating that presentation of the draft will be made on a particular date. On that date, collection is made from the debtor's financial institution by the creditor's and the amount (less collection charges) is added to the creditor's account.

Domestic drafts For use in Canada only and can be obtained for unlimited amounts.

International draft For use outside Canada and can be obtained in domestic or foreign currency.

MF66 Electronic funds transfer (online banking)

This service permits the transfer of funds directly rather than by cash, cheque, or other means. For example, an account holder can instruct the financial institution to electronically credit a supplier's account and debit his or her own account in payment of a bill. The transfer is immediate. Instruction to the bank to transfer funds in this way can be by computer and modem, by telephone, or by personal visit. For security reasons, pre-arranged identification is needed before transactions are completed. The service is international in scope and enables funds to be moved between countries and cleared in a few days.

MF67 The Mondex Smart Card

This is a new product currently being introduced to the financial marketplace. The card's purpose is to eliminate the need to carry coins. The Smart Card is designed for use in parking meters, payphones, and vending machines, etc. When the limit is depleted, the card can be replenished by using any Interac machine.

These cards are also useful for college and university students for identification and access to services such as library, parking, cafeteria, transportation, and bookstore purchases.

MF68 Financial advice

Officers of financial institutions offer advice on savings and investment programs, pension and annuity plans, home ownership plans, trust fund arrangements, etc.

MF69 Foreign currency

This may be bought and sold at most branches of any financial institution. Some, however, deal only in U.S. dollars. Call your financial institution to order special currencies.

MF70 Investments

Customers can use a financial institution's services to invest in foreign exchange, foreign and domestic export trading, gold and silver bullion, bonds, and money market securities.

MF71 Letters of credit

A letter of credit gives instructions from one financial institution to another to pay up to a specified amount of money to the holder.

Satisfactory identification is needed. Letters of credit may be used in Canada and internationally.

MF72 Loans

These are available for many business and personal purposes. The contractual agreement to repay the loan is a *promissory note* (loan agreement), which shows the date of the agreement, amount borrowed, the interest rate charged, any other loan terms, and the due date.

MF73 Money orders

Domestic money orders are issued in Canadian dollars for amounts up to $1000. These may be purchased and redeemed at any Canadian financial institution.

International money orders are issued in U.S. funds up to $1000, pounds sterling to any amount, and unlimited Canadian dollars, for transmission to overseas destinations.

MF74 Mortgages

Approved clients may obtain mortgages for real estate purchases.

MF75 Overdraft protection

Businesses and individuals requiring protection against being overdrawn may apply for overdraft protection on certain types of accounts (e.g., current account, personal chequing account).

MF76 Package services

These are designed for people who use a variety of banking services frequently. For one fixed service charge each month, the customer is provided with personalized cheques; has free, unlimited chequing privileges; buys drafts, money orders, and traveller's cheques without a service charge; receives a discount on a safety deposit box rental if that facility is available; and often is provided with other services.

MF77 Payroll servicing

Some financial institutions will calculate, distribute, and record payroll transactions for an organization. The client provides the institution (frequently through a computer link-up) with the necessary information. The institution then produces a payroll register, payroll cheques, statement of earnings showing tax calculation, unemployment insurance payment, etc. It then deposits the appropriate salary in each employee's account, no matter what other financial institutions are involved. In addition, the institution will make up T4 slips, cost analyses, and any other payroll-related information the company requires. At month-end, the institution simply debits that company's account for the amount of payroll and charges.

MF78 Retirement savings plans

Some financial institutions will open and administer retirement accounts and retirement income funds. (For more information, see MF91.)

IV

MF79   Safety deposit boxes

These are available for rental by customers on the premises of some financial institutions for the safekeeping of valuables.

MF80   Term deposits

A term deposit is a savings plan that can be used when a sum is left on deposit for a preset period of time. Such deposits will earn a higher interest rate than in an account that can be accessed at the customer's convenience.

MF81   Traveller's cheques

Traveller's cheques are a safe method of carrying money for vacations or business trips, and are available in many currencies. If they are lost or stolen, your money will be replaced. The purchaser signs each traveller's cheque at the time of purchase and countersigns it when the cheque is used.

The fee for buying traveller's cheques is one percent of their value, unless the purchaser has an account that includes this service.

NOTE   Bank cards are the preferred method of many overseas travellers.

MF82 PAYROLL

Every business has a payroll—a listing of all employees being paid and the amounts they are to be paid. In larger organizations, the payroll is usually an automated function handled by a specialized department. In a smaller firm, the work may be performed as part of an office worker's other duties. As well, many companies use commercial payroll service organizations or their financial institution payroll service (see MF77).

Regardless of the number of employees and the extent of automation, the fundamentals of successful payroll operation are the same:

◆ Every employee should be paid on time.
◆ Payment must be accompanied by a statement explaining gross earnings, deductions, and net payment.
◆ Federal and provincial laws concerning payroll records and payment of collected funds to the appropriate government agency must be followed.
◆ All payroll information must be kept confidential.

It should be noted that all provinces have employment standards legislation that covers minimum wages, hours of work, statutory holidays, vacation pay, overtime, and other employment practices that must be followed.

MF83 CALCULATION OF GROSS EARNINGS

Earnings are usually calculated in one of the following ways:

Commissions Paid as a percentage of the dollar amount of sales. Employees may receive straight commission or a combination of salary and commission.

Piecework rates Earnings based on the number of units produced.

Salaries Incomes quoted for a specific period of time (weekly, biweekly, monthly, or yearly) with equal payments being made each pay period.

Wages Earnings based on an hourly rate.

In an hourly wage system, employers are required by law to keep a record of the hours worked by employees. In most cases, this work attendance record is some form of time card or time sheet. This provides a record of the employee's arrival and departure times, or the time spent on a particular job. The employee's gross earnings are based on the total hours shown on the time card. Overtime rates may be established by company policy, government regulations, or union contracts. In addition, most companies have a lateness policy and impose a penalty. Lateness is usually counted in 15-minute segments, as the time card illustration shows.

Time Card

Week Ended   September 14   20--
             Social Insurance No. 603 456 667
Name   Burns, Joseph

Day	Morning In	Morning Out	Afternoon In	Afternoon Out	Extra In	Extra Out	Total Hours
M	7:58	12:01	12:59	5:01			8
T	7:56	12:01	12:58	5:02			8
W	8:03	12:00	12:58	5:01			7 3/4
T	7:58	12:01	12:59	5:01			8
F	7:59	12:01	12:57	5:00	5:57	7:02	8/1
S	7:59	12:02					/4
S							

	Hours	Rate	Earnings
Regular Time	39 3/4	13.00	516.75
Overtime	5	19.75	98.75
Gross Pay			615.50

Time card

MF84   PREPARING THE PAYROLL

The payroll journal (summary or register) is kept as a permanent record of all employees' gross earnings, deductions, and net earnings. This journal must be complete for each pay period. In the payroll journal:

◆ The sum of the regular plus overtime earnings columns must equal the sum of the gross earnings column (i.e., the time card totals will match this column).

◆ The sum of the total deductions column must equal the total of all the separate deductions columns.

◆ The sum of the net earnings column must equal the sum of the gross earnings column minus the total deductions column.

EMP. NO.	NAME OF EMPLOYEE	NET CLAIM CODE	GROSS EARNINGS	NONTAXABLES RPP	UNION DUES	TAXABLE EARNINGS	INCOME TAX	CPP	EI	HEALTH INS.	GROUP INS.	TOTAL DEDUC- TIONS	NET EARN- INGS
1618	Brown, W.	7	900.00			900.00	201.85	20.86	22.35			245.06	654.94
1619	Hughes, M.	2	600.00			600.00	118.50	13.41	18.00			149.91	450.09
1620	Lumis, M.	1	600.00			600.00	122.60	13.41	18.00			154.01	445.99
1621	Kahn, S.	1	400.00			400.00	68.35	8.41	12.00			88.76	311.24
1622	Manga, K.	7	450.00			450.00	36.60	9.66	13.50			59.76	390.24
1623	Rinka, P.	8	500.00			500.00	41.15	10.91	15.00			67.06	432.94
			3450.00			3450.00	589.05	76.66	98.85			764.56	2685.44

PAYROLL JOURNAL   PAGE 19

COMPANY NAME _____
PAY PERIOD ENDING _____

Proof

Gross Earnings	$3450.00
Less: Total Deductions	764.56
Net Earnings	$2685.44

Payroll journal (summary or register) page

An employee earnings record must also be kept for each employee. This is a cumulative record of the employee's earnings and deductions for the whole year.

EMPLOYEE EARNINGS RECORD FOR THE YEAR 20--

NAME Lumis, M.
ADDRESS 29 Queens Street
Halifax, NS B3P 2L5
TELEPHONE 829-6712

DEPARTMENT Word Processing
POSITION Operator
SOCIAL INS. NO. 425-839-925
SALARY $600/week

DATE EMPLOYED 09/03/--
TERMINATION DATE
NO. OF DEPENDANTS 00
NET CLAIM CODE 1

EMP. NO.	REGULAR	OVERTIME	GROSS EARNINGS	CPP	EI	INC. TAX	HEALTH INS.	GR. INS.	OTHER	TOTAL DEDUC- TIONS	NET EARNINGS	TOTAL CPP TO DATE	CH. NO.	PAY PERIOD ENDING
1620	8400.00		8400.00	187.74	252.00	1716.40				2156.14	6243.86	187.74		Jan./Apr. 2
	600.00		600.00	13.41	18.00	122.60				154.01	445.99	201.15		Apr. 9
	600.00		600.00	13.41	18.00	122.60				154.01	445.99	214.56		Apr. 16
	600.00		600.00	13.41	18.00	122.60				154.01	445.99	227.97		Apr. 23
	600.00		600.00	13.41	18.00	122.60				154.01	445.99	241.38		Apr. 30
	600.00		600.00	13.41	18.00	122.60				154.01	445.99	254.79		May 7

Employee earnings record

MF85 PAYROLL DEDUCTIONS

The employer withholds a portion of an employee's pay because of compulsory government and union regulations and for fringe benefit schemes.

Compulsory deductions

Government pension Employees between ages 18 and 60 in all provinces except Quebec must contribute to the Canada Pension Plan. Employees may elect for early retirement at age 60 and receive a reduced pension, they may work and continue to contribute until retirement at 65 on full pension, or they may work and contribute until 70, at which time they receive an increased pension. Quebec employees must contribute to the Quebec Pension Plan, which is administered by that province. The amount of the Canada Pension Plan or Quebec Pension Plan contribution is shown in tables available from the Canada Revenue Agency (CRA). See www.cra-arc.gc.ca.

Employment insurance Deductions for employment insurance are compulsory for employees under 65 who are employed for more than a prescribed number of hours or paid a specific weekly sum. (The currently prescribed number of hours or weekly sum may be obtained by contacting the Employment Insurance Commission.) Deductions are made according to a schedule issued annually by CRA. The employer records payments made, weeks worked, and employment insurance contributions.

Income tax Deductions for income tax must be made for all employees except those whose yearly taxable income falls below the minimum taxable income. These deductions must be made in accordance with tables issued annually for each province by CRA. New employees must complete an Employee's Tax Deduction Declaration (TD1), a claim for personal exemptions that provides the employer with a net claim code for the employee.

Provincial health insurance In some provinces, it is compulsory for employers to deduct health insurance premiums. Sometimes the employer pays part or all of the premium as a taxable fringe benefit.

Voluntary deductions
The following is a list of other deductions that might be made. Such deductions may be made only with the employee's permission:

Private pension plan contributions	Professional association fees or union dues	Bond purchases
Extended health care plan contributions	Group life insurance premiums	Charitable contributions
Dental plan contributions		Stock purchases

These amounts are collected and then remitted by the company to the agency concerned.

MF86 VACATION PAY

In most provinces, it is mandatory for certain classes of workers to receive vacation pay. This is usually handled by issuing the regular paycheque for the vacation period on the payday before the holiday commences. The employee is paid for the most recent pay period worked as well as for the earned holiday period.

If an employee who has not earned the full year's vacation entitlement leaves a job without having taken the earned holiday time, that employee is entitled to vacation pay for a percentage of the annual salary. Provincial legislation determines the percentage.

MF87 SEVERANCE PAY

If an employee is to be discharged, the employer should give prior notice in writing. The discharged person may be entitled to receive severance pay according to his or her length of service. The severance pay entitlement is dictated by the employment standards legislation of each province.

MF88 MAKING PAYROLL PAYMENT

If payroll payment is not handled by a financial institution, employers pay employees by cheque, by transferring the funds to the employee's financial institution, or by cash.

Payment by cheque or transfer of funds eliminates handling large sums of cash and cuts down on the danger of theft. Payroll cheques are usually issued on a separate account. To transfer funds to this account, a regular cheque for the amount of the total payroll is issued and deposited in the special payroll account. This account is easy to reconcile because when all the cheques are cashed, the balance will be zero.

Attached to each employee's cheque is a voucher (earnings statement) that shows gross earnings, deductions, and net earnings. If funds are transferred to the employee's account, a statement showing the same information is forwarded to the employee.

STATEMENT OF EMPLOYEE EARNINGS AND PAYROLL DEDUCTIONS													
1620	600.00		600.00	13.41	18.00	122.60				154.01	445.99	187.74	3821	May 7, 20--
	REGULAR	OVERTIME	TOTAL GROSS	CPP	EI	INC. TAX	HLTH	GR. INS.	OTHER	TOTAL DEDUC-	NET	TOTAL CPP	CH.	PAY PERIOD
EMP. NO.	GROSS EARNINGS		EARN.			DEDUCTIONS				TIONS	EARNINGS	TO DATE	NO.	ENDING

Earnings statement

MF89 EMPLOYER'S LEGAL FINANCIAL OBLIGATIONS

Remittance of collected funds to Canada Revenue Agency
Each month, a remittance must be made to the Receiver General that includes the combined employee deductions for income tax, Canada or Quebec Pension Plan, and employment insurance, as well as the company's share of Canada or Quebec Pension Plan and employment insurance payments.

Workers' compensation
All provinces require employers to contribute to a workers' compensation fund. The amount is based on the annual payroll amount, the type of industry, and the company's safety record. Details of amounts payable and payment dates may be obtained from the Workers' Compensation Board.

T4 (withholding statement)
By February 28 of each year, employers must provide each employee with a T4 form, which shows the employee's gross earnings and the value of any taxable benefits (such as an employer-provided automobile) for the preceding year, and contributions withheld for Canada or Quebec Pension Plan, employment insurance, income tax, and any other deductions (such as union dues and charitable donations). One copy of the form must be sent to CRA as part of the annual T4-T4A employer's summary and two copies to the employee.

MF

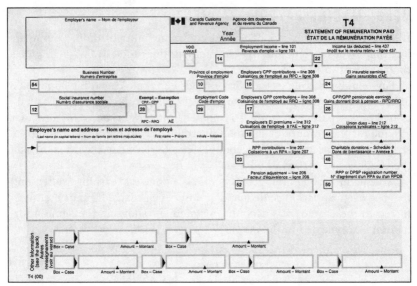

T4 form

Separation certificate

An employee leaving employment must be given a separation certificate (record of employment form). The person named must present this document to the local Canada Employment Centre in order to collect unemployment insurance benefits.

MF90 PETTY CASH

Petty cash is the amount of cash kept in the office to pay for small purchases or expenses such as taxi fares, stationery items, and mailing costs. The following are basic guidelines for administering a petty cash fund:

◆ Decide on a starting sum for the fund (usually enough to cover miscellaneous expenses for approximately one month).

◆ Give one person responsibility for operating the fund.

◆ Keep the cash and supporting records in a locked cash box or drawer during the day and in the vault or safe overnight.

◆ Fill out a petty cash voucher (showing amount paid, date, purpose of expenditure, and signature of spender) for each amount paid out of the fund. Obtain receipts (invoices, sales slips) whenever possible and attach them to the voucher.

◆ Record each transaction. Use a spreadsheet, petty cash book, or sheets of two- or three-column accounting paper kept in a binder.

◆ Replenish your fund before it becomes too low. (The amount required to restore the fund to its original amount should be the sum of the vouchers.)

◆ Prepare a petty cash replenishment request that summarizes by account name the information contained in the petty cash book, and pass this to the accounts department.

◆ Record the cash received in the petty cash book.
◆ The cash box should always contain cash and/or vouchers totalling the exact amount of the fund.

PETTY CASH VOUCHER

Date: _March 16, 20--_

Amount: _$5.12_

Account to be charged: _Postage Expense_ Acct. No. _170_

Paid to: _Drew Young_

For: _Mailing a registered letter_

Received payment: _D. Young_
(signature)

Petty cash voucher

Petty cash book page

Petty Cash Book for March, 20--			
Date		Receipts	Payments
March 1	Balance	100.00	
March 2	Postage		9.00
March 5	Taxi Fare		6.50
March 6	Owner's Drawings		25.00
March 8	Meals		15.85
March 16	Postage		5.12
March 21	Stationery		5.00
March 27	Donations		10.00
		100.00	76.47
Apr. 1	Cash on hand	23.53	
Apr. 1	Cheque No. 171	76.47	

LAURA LARNEY COSMETICS
Petty Cash Replenishment Request

Petty cash summary
Period March 1 through March 31, 20--

Postage	14.12
L. Larney, Drawings	25.00
Meals	15.85
Donations	10.00
Misc. expenses	11.50
Total disbursements	76.47
Cash on hand	23.53
Amount of petty cash fund	100.00

B. Farrar
Petty Cash Clerk

Petty cash replenishment request

MF

MF91 AN OVERVIEW OF THE FINANCIAL MARKETPLACE

Some basic products and services are available for investment purposes in the financial marketplace:

◆ short- and long-term deposits/Guaranteed Investment Certificates (GICs)
◆ Registered Education Savings Plans (RESPs)

◆ RRSPs (Registered Retirement Savings Plans)
◆ RRIFs (Registered Retirement Income Funds)
◆ mutual funds
◆ stocks and bonds

MF92 SHORT- AND LONG-TERM DEPOSITS/GUARANTEED INVESTMENT CERTIFICATES (GICs)

These deposit plans are good for people who have extra income for saving or investment purposes.

◆ Deposits can be short term (30 to 364 days) or long term (1 to 5 years).
◆ The primary objective is to improve investment income.
◆ The minimum/maximum deposit requirements vary within financial institutions.
◆ They are a higher-interest alternative to keeping funds in a savings or chequing account.
◆ They provide various interest incentives for larger deposits.

MF93 REGISTERED EDUCATION SAVINGS PLANS (RESPs)

These are contracts between an individual (subscriber) and a financial institution where contributions are made to a plan for educational assistance in later years, such as when the student enrolls in college or university.

◆ RESPs are tax-sheltered investments (savings are exempt from taxation until the student withdraws funds from the plan).
◆ The contribution limit is $4000 per year, for a lifetime maximum of $42 000.
◆ The student assumes the taxes of the RESP while attending college or university and therefore is taxed at a lower rate because of his or her income bracket.

MF94 REGISTERED RETIREMENT SAVINGS PLANS (RRSPs)

These are federal government–approved plans that encourage people to save money during their income-earning years to provide a source of income during their retirement years.

◆ They are tax-sheltered investments (i.e., savings are exempt from taxation until funds are withdrawn from the plans).
◆ Contributions to the plans are tax deductible and can be made at any time during the year; contributions made within the first 60 days of the current calendar year can be used as contributions for the current or previous tax year.
◆ A holder can have any number of different plans providing the total yearly contributions do not exceed the maximum amount allotted for that person's income range as defined in the *Income Tax Act*.

♦ RRSPs can be purchased from credit unions, banks, trust companies, life insurance companies, investment dealers, and mutual fund companies, or can be self-directed.

♦ RRSPs can be used to participate in the RRSP Home Buyer's Plan.

MF95 RRSP HOME BUYER'S PLAN

The Home Buyer's Plan could originally be used only by first-time home buyers. As of 1999, individuals are permitted to utilize the plan again if they have repaid all previous amounts received. A total of $20 000 can be withdrawn from an RRSP for the purchase of a residence located in Canada, without immediate deduction of withholding tax. The plan holder must repay (to any RRSP) the amount that was withdrawn, without interest and in equal payments, over a 15-year period commencing in the first calendar year following the year of the withdrawal. All withdrawals must be made within the same calendar year.

MF96 REGISTERED RETIREMENT INCOME FUNDS (RRIFs)

These funds are RRSP termination options that allow the investor to retain the same investments as were held in the RRSPs. RRIFs are designed to provide a source of income during retirement years.

♦ The present RRIF age is 69 (i.e., the plan holder must convert an RRSP plan to an RRIF plan by age 69).

♦ The funds are registered with CRA.

♦ The funds are designed to provide payments to the holder (subject to an annual minimum amount).

♦ RRIFs can be purchased from credit unions, banks, trust companies, life insurance companies, investment dealers, and mutual fund companies.

MF97 MUTUAL FUNDS

A mutual fund is an investment where a group of people pool their money in order to have greater investment flexibility with the potential for higher rates of return.

♦ Mutual funds offer improved potential returns (the firms selling the funds hire investment managers who research the funds carefully).

♦ There is reduced volatility because investments are diversified over many types of securities, countries, industries, and issuers.

♦ There is access to top-quality investments in markets anywhere in the world.

♦ Costs are lower and service is better because of simple administration and information.

Mutual funds are designed for investors who have a diverse range of investment amounts, time frames, and experience; for example, a program

MF

can be started for as little as $500. As well, mutual funds are well suited for experienced investors with substantial portfolios.

The risk factor The value of any mutual fund fluctuates day by day. Generally, the higher the opportunity for growth—such as funds invested in the stock market—the greater the fluctuation in price. Investors can lower potential risk, however, through diversification among various funds in the same family.

Mutual funds can be sold only by a licensed representative and are available through banks, trust companies, credit unions, life insurance companies, and independent brokers.

NOTE Mutual fund investments are not insured or guaranteed.

MF98 STOCKS AND BONDS

Stocks and bonds are other alternatives for investment planning.

Stocks (common shares versus preferred shares)

Common stocks Common shares represent residual ownership in the issuing company and entitle the holder to vote at shareholder meetings. Common shares are issued by corporations that need capital for long-term purposes. Interest is paid to investors through dividends and capital gains.

Preferred stocks Preferred shares are issued by corporations to raise capital for investment projects, and they represent a less important source of financing than either bonds or common shares. Preferred shareholders receive dividends before common shareholders, at the discretion of the corporation's management.

Stocks must be purchased through licensed stockbrokers.

*Share	A share in an investment that gives you part ownership or a share in a company.
How to Buy Shares	Shares are bought through an investment dealer registered with the Ontario Securities Commission. Prices depend on supply and demand of the shares being bought or sold.

*Source: Investor Education Fund www.investored.ca

Bonds

IV

Bonds are fixed income securities and are like loans that investors make to governments and corporations. The borrower agrees to pay interest regularly and to pay back the principal or par value at maturity. There are various types of bonds available, for example, government bonds (Treasury bills), corporate bonds, etc.

Bonds can be purchased through financial institutions or independent brokers.

MF99 IDENTITY THEFT

Identity theft is a crime in which an impostor obtains key pieces of information, such as a social insurance number (SIN) or driver's licence number, to obtain credit, merchandise, and services in the name of the victim. The impostor may even use the victim's good name for criminal activities.

The victim is left with a ruined credit history and the time-consuming and complicated task of regaining financial stability.

MF100 WORKPLACE IDENTITY THEFT

Identity theft affects consumers and businesses in a multitude of ways. Not only do businesses suffer direct loss due to this crime, but inadequate security and poor business practices may open a company up to liability suits, fines, and loss of clientele.

MF101 HOW TO MINIMIZE THE RISK FACTORS IN HANDLING CONFIDENTIAL INFORMATION

◆ *Access* Personal identifying information should be made available only to limited staff. Is database access audited and are passwords controlled?

◆ *Disposal* Ensure that electronic/paper documents and databases containing personal information are rendered unreadable prior to disposal; shred paper documents properly. What is in the workplace Dumpster?

◆ *Distribution* Personnel should be trained in the proper procedures regarding information disclosure.

◆ *Information acquisition* Gather information in a safe manner (cannot be overheard or seen by others, e.g., phone conversations, photocopying, etc.).

◆ *Personnel* Conduct background checks on all employees with access to identifying information, e.g., mailroom staff, cleaning crews, temporary workers, and computer or hotline service technicians.

◆ *Storage* Set up computer security measures around the systems storing confidential and personal data. Is the data considered highly classified and not common access?

MF102 PREVENTION TIPS FOR THE WORKPLACE

◆ Identify risk areas and their vulnerabilities.

◆ Schedule regular meetings to inform key staff members of updated security measures, e.g., monthly/quarterly meetings.

◆ Establish adequate controls and then communicate and implement the controls; review the controls on a regular basis.

◆ Remind employees to log off the company's network at the end of the workday.

MF

◆ Report any usual security incidents to superiors.

◆ Do not discuss workplace security outside the workplace, e.g., on cell phones, public phones.

◆ Do not leave laptop computers or PDAs with sensitive information lying around, e.g., exposed in your car.

◆ Make information security an integral part of competence and performance.

MF103 PERSONAL IDENTITY THEFT PREVENTION

◆ Do not keep your SIN card or passport in your purse or wallet; store them in a safety deposit box at the bank or a secure place at home until needed.

◆ Destroy or shred papers that have personal information on them, including promotional offers for new credit cards that you receive in the mail.

◆ Do not give out your credit card number by phone or email unless you are sure you know the identity of the caller.

◆ Pay attention to your billing cycle of credit card statements. If statements or utility bills do not arrive, contact the companies to ensure that they haven't been illicitly redirected.

◆ Check your credit report at least once a year to ensure it is accurate and doesn't include debts that you are not aware of.

◆ Change account passwords on a regular basis (two/three times per year). Do not use family names or birthdates; pick something obscure.

◆ Do not reply to suspicious email requests.

◆ Notify the local police if you suspect you have become an identity theft victim.

NOTE See Unit 2, E8 (How to Cancel a Contract).

MF104 INVESTMENT TERMS

Actively managed funds: Mutual funds in the investment portfolio, in which the manager can use his or her discretion to buy, sell, or hold. Most funds are actively managed.

B2B funds: "Business-to-business" funds are a specialized form of technology sector funds that seek internet companies investing in business-to-business solutions.

Balanced funds: Sometimes called "hybrid" funds, balanced portfolios are a type of mutual fund that invests in a combination of stocks and bonds.

Blue chips: A name given to large established companies.

Canadian Venture Exchange (CDNX): Market for Canadian small capitalization stocks.

Certified Financial Planner (CFP): A person licensed to advise and handle funds for investment purposes for clients.

Deferred sales charge (DSC): A commission paid to a financial advisor or institution.

Diversified funds: Mutual funds that invest in a wide variety of different types of stocks in the Dow Jones Industrial Average.

Dividend: A share of profit distributed among shareholders.

Equity-income funds: Conservative stock funds that seek dividend income as well as capital appreciation.

Growth funds: Stock mutual funds that seek out shares of companies with rapidly expanding earnings and/or revenue.

Index fund: Passively managed portfolios that track an existing market benchmark, e.g., Standard & Poor's 500 Index of blue-chip stocks.

Initial public offering (IPO): The first sale of shares by a company to the general public.

Management expense ratio (MER): Expenses incurred for the managing and marketing of a mutual fund portfolio.

NASDAQ (National Association of Securities Dealers Automated Quotations): Over-the-counter market where smaller capitalization stocks are bought and sold.

New York Stock Exchange (NYSE): The location where U.S. stocks are bought and sold.

Pre-authorized contribution plan (PAC): Authorized permission to deduct monies from a bank account for various plan contributions, such as RRSPs.

Toronto Stock Exchange (TSX): A financial facility where stocks of Canadian companies are bought, sold, and traded daily. The price of the stock is reported as the high, low, and closing price, as well as the number of shares traded for each day.

World Equity Benchmark Shares (WEBS): Stock exchange–traded index funds that reflect the stock market of a single country.

WORDS OF WISDOM

*No one knows about your honesty or
integrity unless you give them examples of it.*

MF

UNIT

20 JOB SEARCH SKILLS/CAREER PLANNING

SELECTED CONTENTS

J1	JOB SEARCH PREPARATION
J2	HELPFUL TIPS FOR FINDING A JOB
J3	THE SEARCH
J4	Personal Contacts
J5	Newspapers
J6	Agencies and Career Counselling Services
J7	Schools, Colleges, Universities
J8	Direct Company Contact
J9	Local Canada Employment Centres
J10	Professional Associations and Unions
J11	The Internet
J12	Posting a Résumé on the Internet
J13	THE APPLICATION
J14	The Application Letter
J15	The Résumé
J16	The Application Form
J17	Electronic/Online Application
J18	The Interview
J19	Serial/Team Interviews
J20	Video Interviews
J21	Interview Follow-Up
J22	SUCCESS ON THE JOB
J23	Job Search/Training Websites
J24	Top Ten Jobs
J25	Women in the Workplace

V

Applying for a job in a highly competitive market requires considerable thought and effort. The process demands a knowledge of yourself, thorough research of the job market, careful preparation, and perseverance. This unit provides ideas on how to search for the position you want, how to present yourself to best advantage in a written application, how to prepare a résumé, how to promote yourself effectively at the interview, and how to follow up afterward.

J1 JOB SEARCH PREPARATION

Be well prepared before you start your search. In today's fast-changing marketplace, the job seeker must give serious thought to career planning—to establishing a short-term objective and to setting long-term goals. If you know who you are and where you want to go, your preparation and confidence will show during the interview. The job applicant with a clear vision of the future will approach the working world with a knowledgeable and positive outlook.

With the current popularity of contract hiring (employment for only a fixed period of time), you may want to consider this style of employment as opposed to a full-time, permanent position, which may be more difficult to find.

J2 HELPFUL TIPS FOR FINDING A JOB

- ◆ Assess your skills, talents, and interests and match them to the local job market.
- ◆ Prepare a résumé.
- ◆ Customize résumés for each applied job.
- ◆ Volunteer in the community to develop new skills and contacts.
- ◆ Ask for an information meeting with companies and organizations where you think you would like to work.
- ◆ Let family and friends know that you are seeking employment.
- ◆ Read the want ads online and in newspapers/trade magazines.
- ◆ Visit employment centres on a regular basis (weekly) and check their bulletin boards.
- ◆ Go to job interviews fully prepared. Do some research on the company. Think about questions and your answers before the interview.
- ◆ Stay positive and determined.

J3 THE SEARCH

The wise job seeker carefully researches all available sources to find the most satisfying position. Explore the following avenues to help lead you to the best job for you.

J4 PERSONAL CONTACTS

Friends or relatives already employed by companies or organizations you would like to join may be able to tell you of available positions. Since many jobs are never advertised, it is a good idea to investigate companies on your own. Use the telephone to network with friends, former colleagues, relatives, and acquaintances—their recommendations can be invaluable door openers.

J5 NEWSPAPERS

Advertisers do not always word their advertisements as you might expect. Do not read the headings or titles *only;* they may be misleading. Read *all* of the advertisement. You may find you have the qualifications and that the job would interest you. Or, you may not be interested in or qualified for a job that attracted you by the heading or title only. Do not be discouraged if you do not have precisely the qualifications listed. Advertisers seeking "college plus two years' experience" may well consider someone with a college diploma, enthusiasm, and determination. Go ahead and apply. At this point, your goal is to obtain an *interview*.

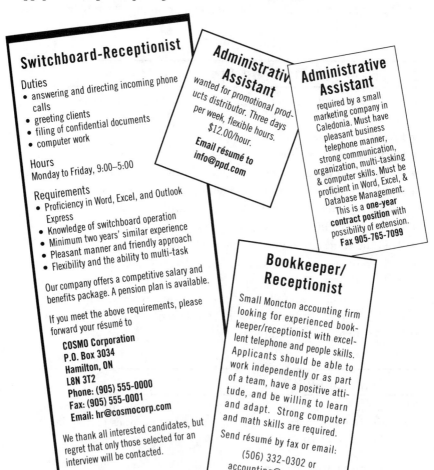

Switchboard-Receptionist

Duties
- answering and directing incoming phone calls
- greeting clients
- filing of confidential documents
- computer work

Hours
Monday to Friday, 9:00–5:00

Requirements
- Proficiency in Word, Excel, and Outlook Express
- Knowledge of switchboard operation
- Minimum two years' similar experience
- Pleasant manner and friendly approach
- Flexibility and the ability to multi-task

Our company offers a competitive salary and benefits package. A pension plan is available.

If you meet the above requirements, please forward your résumé to

COSMO Corporation
P.O. Box 3034
Hamilton, ON
L8N 3T2
Phone: (905) 555-0000
Fax: (905) 555-0001
Email: hr@cosmocorp.com

We thank all interested candidates, but regret that only those selected for an interview will be contacted.

Administrative Assistant

wanted for promotional products distributor. Three days per week, flexible hours. $12.00/hour.

Email résumé to info@ppd.com

Administrative Assistant

required by a small marketing company in Caledonia. Must have pleasant business telephone manner, strong communication, organization, multi-tasking & computer skills. Must be proficient in Word, Excel, & Database Management. This is a **one-year contract position** with possibility of extension.
Fax 905-765-7099

Bookkeeper/ Receptionist

Small Moncton accounting firm looking for experienced bookkeeper/receptionist with excellent telephone and people skills. Applicants should be able to work independently or as part of a team, have a positive attitude, and be willing to learn and adapt. Strong computer and math skills are required.

Send résumé by fax or email:
(506) 332-0302 or
accounting@acctco.com

Newspaper job advertisements

J6   AGENCIES AND CAREER COUNSELLING SERVICES

Many companies use the services of employment agencies in filling their vacancies. For job seekers, there are advantages to dealing with an agency:

◆ You are not charged any fee.

◆ The agency has a "bank" of jobs, so you do not have to spend time searching.

◆ The agency conducts skills tests and sends you only to job interviews for which you are suited.

◆ The agency will offer constructive criticism about your attitude and dress.

In addition to employment agencies, a number of career counselling organizations will guide job seekers in choosing a career path—by preparing them for interviews (e.g., role-playing, watching instructional videos, working with computer programs designed to help with career selection through aptitude testing) and by directing them to the most appropriate job agencies or professional contacts. Universities and colleges offer these services, as do private firms and federal and provincial governments. Some of these organizations charge for their services, some do not. Clarify this before you commit yourself to one of them.

J7   SCHOOLS, COLLEGES, UNIVERSITIES

Refer to bulletin boards and career counsellors in student service departments at schools or placement offices at colleges or universities.

J8   DIRECT COMPANY CONTACT

Contact the human resources manager of a firm or organization that interests you. Write an inquiry letter and follow it up with a personal visit. There may be an opening now or in the near future.

Dear [obtain the name of the appropriate person]:

The high regard in which a friend of mine (who is employed by you) holds your organization has prompted me to apply to you for a position of administrative assistant.

With four years of business experience, preceded by a college diploma in business studies, I can offer you computer proficiency (Microsoft Word, WordPerfect for Windows, Excel, Outlook), strong verbal and written communication skills, and accuracy and expertise in accounting. I am a good organizer, welcome new challenges and responsibilities, and enjoy being a team player in a professional environment. The enclosed résumé will provide you with the full details of my qualifications.

I will telephone you on Tuesday, November 21. I would appreciate the opportunity to meet with you to discuss my qualifications and determine how they might suit the needs of your organization.

Sincerely,

Letter of inquiry (suggested wording)

J

J9   LOCAL CANADA EMPLOYMENT CENTRES

Canada Employment Centres maintain lists of jobs available in various fields, both locally and across Canada.

J10   PROFESSIONAL ASSOCIATIONS AND UNIONS

Make inquiries, by telephone, mail, or in person, of professional associations and unions that represent the field in which you would like to work.

J11   THE INTERNET

The internet is becoming a very useful tool for job searching to gain access to online career centres, matching services, job centres, job banks, indexes and search engines, chat rooms, electronic networking, and email on the World Wide Web.

Employment is available through the internet, and you can fax or email applications for job opportunities. You can also develop a personal website and establish ongoing communications with human resources personnel around the country. Keep a file of or bookmark popular internet sites for ongoing use.

For samples of online résumés, visit recruitment websites such as these:

www.monster.ca	www.actijob.com
www.careerbuilder.ca	working.canada.com
www.workopolis.com	campus.workopolis.com

J12   POSTING A RÉSUMÉ ON THE INTERNET

Posting a résumé on the internet is an option as a job search tool. Some sites allow you to cut and paste the hard copy into the online form; others prompt you through each screen process (also known as résumé builder).

You can submit your résumé in English or French. It can be edited, viewed on screen, and either stored in a database where only you have access to it (inactive) or be activated at any time.

When your résumé is activated, interested employers will contact you via email, and your résumé is automatically redirected from the database of the website where it was posted. Employers will only see an email address if you respond to an inquiry.

NOTE   You can also find out how often your résumé has been viewed.

Sample résumé format

Title:	Specific job title, e.g., administrative assistant
Objective:	Supply information on employment objective (2000-character limit/approx. two-thirds of a page)
Target locations:	Willing to relocate? If yes, select location
Work experience:	In chronological order, with dates, e.g., Oct. 2004 to Present

Work description:	Describe responsibilities/tasks for each stint of employment (2000-character limit)
Education:	List names of colleges or universities and the time frame attended
Affiliations:	Professional associations, e.g., business organizations
Professional skills:	Specific skills, e.g., computer skills/knowledge, presentation skills, public speaking, writing, etc.
Additional information:	Additional information that may be helpful (3000-character limit/one page)
References:	Provide at least two/three references with area codes and phone numbers
Salary expected:	A figure must be selected

In some cases, the résumé can be stored with confidentiality, e.g., the references and current employers are hidden.

`NOTE` All required information must be provided to complete the résumé format.

Using the internet as a job search tool has both advantages and disadvantages, as discussed below.

Advantages:

◆ You can learn about new career opportunities and job titles.

◆ You can post your résumé free of charge.

◆ Your résumé becomes part of a database where employers search for qualified candidates.

◆ You can store your résumé in a database until you choose to activate it.

◆ You can easily research prospective employers and companies.

Disadvantages:

◆ You may not be contacted.

◆ Information is freely shared; confidentiality may be an issue.

◆ You may need to check the company's reputation.

◆ You must check email daily once your résumé is activated.

`NOTE` *Curriculum Vitae* (CV) is another term for a detailed résumé. It is a summary of one's academic history, professional history, and job qualifications for a prospective employer.

J13 THE APPLICATION

Once you hear of a job that interests you or see an appealing advertisement, you must convince someone to interview you. You do this by sending an application letter and a résumé that "sells" you.

J14 THE APPLICATION LETTER

Your letter of application must be carefully worded so that it

◆ sells you as the right person for this job

◆ summarizes why you are applying and why you are qualified

◆ provides all the facts asked of you

◆ is concise, specific, and to the point

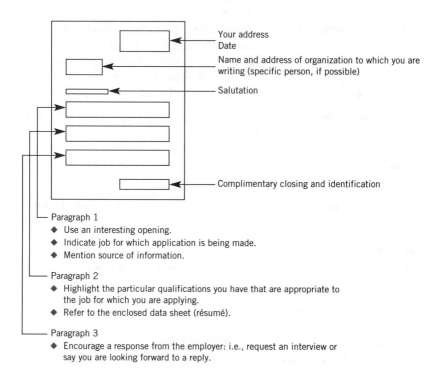

Paragraph 1
◆ Use an interesting opening.
◆ Indicate job for which application is being made.
◆ Mention source of information.

Paragraph 2
◆ Highlight the particular qualifications you have that are appropriate to the job for which you are applying.
◆ Refer to the enclosed data sheet (résumé).

Paragraph 3
◆ Encourage a response from the employer: i.e., request an interview or say you are looking forward to a reply.

Outline of an application letter

In preparing your letter of application (see Unit 14, K18, for format details):

◆ Use good-quality, businesslike stationery (plain white or buff-coloured, unlined).

◆ Use a computer or word-processing equipment. Although using the same letter for every application is not possible, you can save a master letter and tailor it to each application. This will permit you to create a fresh letter for each application with a minimum of effort.

◆ Include a reference to the source of your information about the job.

◆ Ask for some action (e.g., a telephone call or written reply) leading to an interview.

◆ Keep the letter to one page if you possibly can.

◆ Carefully check any doubtful spelling or grammar.

◆ Key your name beneath the signature.

◆ Address your envelope correctly (see Unit 14, K6).

---

441 College Avenue
Brandon, MB R7A 1E8
January 20, 20--

Mr. Jack Wallace, Manager
Human Resources Department
East/West Enterprises Ltd.
3419 McDonald Avenue
Brandon, MB R7B 0B5

Dear Mr. Wallace:

I believe I have the skills and personal qualities called for in your advertisement for an administrative assistant in last night's <u>Free Press</u>. Please consider this letter as my application for the job.

As you will see from the enclosed résumé, I have a three-year diploma from Sheridan Park Community College. This program included training in English language skills, computer applications, accounting, human relations, and business administration. After a year of experience at Creative Solutions, my present employer, I appreciate the importance of attending to details, accuracy under pressure, and meeting deadlines. Report writing and organizing meetings are among the challenges I enjoy. I have learned to deal successfully with members of the public, to establish good relationships with co-workers, and to be a contributing team player.

It is my hope that experience as an administrative assistant will add to my qualifications and prepare me for a management position with your company.

I feel I have much to offer to East/West Enterprises Ltd. and would welcome the opportunity of discussing your needs and my capabilities in person. Please telephone me at 489-2672, or email me at mbell124@hotmail.com so that we can arrange an appointment.

Yours very truly,

Marnie Bell

Marnie Bell

Encl

Typical application letter

◆ Always submit an original letter of application, never a photocopy, but do keep a copy for your own records and for follow-up.

◆ Don't forget to sign the letter.

103 Cranberry Court
Hamilton, ON   L8E 3R8
May 25, 20--

Mrs. Debbie Bruce
Human Resources Department
Cosmo Corporation
P. O. Box 2034
Hamilton, ON   L8N 3T2

Dear Mrs. Bruce

I wish to apply for the position of Administrative Assistant as advertised in [name of newspaper], on [date of issue].

As a recent graduate from [name of college/university] in the [name of program], I have acquired excellent computer skills as well as effective interpersonal relations skills and believe that I could be a valuable employee with your firm.

Enclosed is a copy of my résumé, which outlines my qualifications in various skill areas, as well as references.

I would be pleased to meet with you, at your convenience, to discuss your requirements and my suitability for the position.

Please call me at [phone number where you can be contacted during the day, as well as after working hours], or email me at [address].

Yours truly,

[Your Name]

Encl

Sample application letter

J15   THE RÉSUMÉ

The résumé (also known as the *data sheet* or *Curriculum Vitae*) is rarely read thoroughly by recipients. It must be short, easy to read, and organized so that it will draw attention to your most significant achievements and skills. The résumé helps the interviewer screen applicants and derive a short list.

Ideally, of course, a new résumé should be created to precisely match each job for which you apply. If your résumé is saved on disk, you can easily make minor changes to your basic résumé. However, if saving on disk is not possible, one well-thought-out résumé can be used for most applications, and your covering application letter can be designed to zero in on the specific job for which you are applying.

V

NOTE Never drop off or send a résumé without an accompanying letter of application or letter of introduction.

Getting started

Résumé writing is much easier if you begin by listing all the information you need to include. As step one, then, create a personal inventory (a list) of all your skills, aptitudes, preferences, experiences, and achievements. Make your list as complete as possible. Examples of the type of information you might list are shown below. In addition, the sample résumé presented in this chapter might give you some ideas.

- your abilities (speaking in front of a group, language fluencies, interpersonal skills, leadership traits)
- your skills (keying speed, accounting skill, software expertise)
- your priorities (being active on the job, new challenges, being given responsibility)
- your personal qualities (sense of humour, friendliness, punctuality)
- valuable work experiences (handled cash, made bank deposits, opened and closed the store, wrote company manual for XYZ software program)

Indicate part-time or full-time employment and give approximate dates (e.g., May 2006–June 2007).

- List volunteer work (e.g., volunteer at local food bank).
- Do not list political, religious, or fraternal affiliations; however, you can state that you were an election campaign volunteer.

This self-analysis will encourage you to focus on your strengths and will help you enormously in building your résumé.

Résumé presentation

A résumé is judged initially on its appearance; good presentation is essential. Follow these pointers for success:

- Use good-quality, businesslike paper.
- Use a computer (eye-appealing fonts and a laser printer provide a professional look).
- Make the format neat, attractive, and easy to read. Avoid ornate typefaces.
- Highlight headings and key words.
- Ensure that your résumé is error-free.
- Restrict the résumé length to no more than two pages—employers are busy people.

NOTE The number of pages will depend on your age, employment experience, etc. Do not omit important information by trying to cut down on length. Change the format—reduce white space in set-up; adjust font size (do not make too small).

◆ Place the résumé inside a colourful folder to add a touch of importance. A résumé with flair will be noticed and may open the door to that interview.

◆ Do not enclose or attach a photograph to the résumé.

Types of résumés

A *functional résumé* stresses an applicant's career achievements and responsibilities. It is often used by experienced workers and provides information under the following headings:

◆ personal information (name, address, telephone and/or fax number, email address)

◆ accomplishments (e.g., brief descriptions of leadership roles played, notable organizational accomplishments, writing achievements, conference planning)

◆ business experience

◆ education

◆ references (optional)

A *chronological résumé* (the preferred style) is a listing of employment history in reverse chronological order (last job first). It is used by both experienced and inexperienced workers and is appropriate for beginning workers who do not have much information to include. The chronological résumé is usually presented under the following headings:

◆ personal information (name, address, telephone and/or fax number, email address)

◆ career goals or objectives

◆ education (name of college, high school, date attended—summarize information)

◆ business experience—full-time and part-time

◆ other part-time employment/summer jobs

◆ interests

◆ references

If your education does not quite fit the job, give your work experience first. A section entitled "Additional Important Information" (as shown in the illustration of a chronological résumé in this section) works well because it helps to provide a complete picture of you.

Regardless of the type used, remember:

◆ Let the résumé reflect YOU and your capabilities.

◆ List all your achievements—do not be too modest.

V

- Be specific and positive—avoid vague statements.
- Tailor the résumé to suit the job posting and the nature of the business to which you are applying.

Key words to describe personal qualities for use in résumés:

ambitious	disciplined	loyal
analytical	discreet	reliable
conscientious	efficient	resourceful
constructive	enthusiastic	sincere
creative	hard working	tactful
dependable	imaginative	willing to travel/relocate

- Relate everything in the résumé to the employer's viewpoint.
- Read your résumé carefully before mailing—it may be the key to your future!

Personal information

- State your name, address, telephone number, email address (and fax number if you have one).
- Any other personal information you provide is voluntary. The law prohibits discrimination on the basis of gender, race, religion, marital status, age, or nationality. Such information is not relevant to any job.

Accomplishments

This section is used in a functional résumé only.

- State your language fluencies.
- Include any writings, workshops, or presentations you have done.
- List any initiatives you have taken (e.g., time-saving suggestions for tasks, cost-saving measures).
- Mention personal or sports awards or championships.

Marketable skills

List if you have experience in any of the following:

- creative writing (if you have been involved in writing for the school newspaper or local newspaper, etc.)
- planning or organization (if you have been involved in community, religious groups, or school committees)
- presentation (if you have experience using presentation skills; speaking to a group/s)
- budgeting/finance (if you have handled a budget for an association/local group)

J

NOTE Websites will ask you to fill in boxes that are designed to provide an employer with the same information that you would provide if you were submitting a hard copy résumé. For example, the website will ask you to fill in one box with your name, another with your address, another with your last employer, and so on.

NOTE To view an online résumé builder, try linking up to one of the job search websites we have listed in this unit. (Career goals can be included, omitted, or replaced with the heading "Special Skills/Skill Area.")

◆ leadership (if you have been a crew/section/group leader or class representative)
◆ problem solving (if you have experience in this area)
◆ proofreading (if you are an excellent proofreader; this is a highly marketable skill, especially in the publishing business)
◆ tutoring/training (if you have been a volunteer subject tutor or trainer)
◆ reception (if you have good telephone/reception skills)
◆ research (if you are proficient in researching topics and know where to find information quickly)
◆ meeting deadlines (if you work well under pressure)
◆ minute-taking or shorthand/speedwriting (if you have worked on committees)

In a chronological résumé, the above items could be listed under "Additional Important Information" or as part of the description of responsibilities in the "Business Experience" section, if appropriate.

Business experience
◆ List your previous jobs, starting with the most recent.
◆ Give approximate starting and ending dates of each job.
◆ Indicate your responsibilities (skills, equipment, and software used) in previous jobs—do not simply list the titles of those positions.
◆ Mention any promotions or increases in job responsibility. This shows the prospective employer that you developed skills on the job.
◆ Do not mention salary.
◆ If you have no work experience, demonstrate that you have developed organizational, leadership, and interpersonal skills by providing details of part-time or summer jobs, volunteer work, or co-operative education programs.

V

Education

◆ Do not include letters of commendation/reference.

◆ List certificates, degrees, or diplomas earned; mention your major study areas, lengths of programs, and honours, scholarships, or special awards. Names and addresses of institutions may be shown but this is not required.

◆ Note any work-related training—evening courses, professional workshops, special training courses.

◆ Do not include elementary school information.

Interests

◆ Include this section when such information would be beneficial, such as in the case of a person new to the workforce or where such interests have some connection to the job for which the résumé is being submitted.

◆ Give data that would provide useful insights for employers (e.g., volunteer work can demonstrate valuable administrative and/or teamwork experience; work with youth groups shows leadership qualities).

◆ Include specific sports interests, hobbies, intramural activities, and involvement in social organizations. Active people are more productive employees.

NOTE Employers are impressed with people who are involved in volunteer work. If this interests you, check the Volunteer Opportunities Exchange (VOE). You can provide a profile of your skills and interests, and agencies fill out a similar form, outlining their volunteer positions. The VOE then matches skills and needs. Privacy measures ensure the confidentiality of this information.

Volunteer Opportunities Exchange website: www.volunteer.ca/voe/

References

◆ Ask permission from people you identify as references *before* you use their names.

◆ Indicate that references are available on request, but go to the interview prepared with names, positions, addresses, and telephone numbers.

◆ Give a copy of your résumé to the person(s) you use as a reference (in case they are called for information regarding data).

◆ Good references are previous or present employers, teachers, religious leaders, doctors, lawyers, businesspeople, and politicians.

◆ Do not use relatives as references.

J15A SAMPLE OF CHRONOLOGICAL RÉSUMÉ (PREFERRED STYLE)

YOUR NAME (14 pt. Font)   Phone No./Fax No.

Address (12 pt. Font)   email address
City, Province PC

Career Goal: To obtain an entry-level position with your firm where I can utilize my skills and work my way up the career ladder.

EDUCATION

Mohawk College of Applied Arts & Technology, Hamilton, ON
Two-Year Office Administration (Executive) Diploma Program
Graduated in May, 2006

MARKETABLE SKILLS

- Excellent communication skills (speaking, writing, and spelling)
- Proficient in MS Word, Excel, PowerPoint, and Outlook Express
- Excellent organizational, planning, and presentation skills
- Keyboarding: 50–60 wpm with excellent accuracy
- Accounting and database management
- Internet research skills/Graphics and webpage design
- Front-line reception/Telephone experience/Multi-tasking
- Travel preparation

EMPLOYMENT EXPERIENCE

January/06–present   Part-time receptionist at ABC Real Estate
July–August, 2004/05   YMCA Camp Counsellor (14–16-year-olds)

ACHIEVEMENTS – Dean's Honour Roll, Campbell CSP Award
(Communication, Spelling, and Punctuation)

REFERENCES: Available upon request

J16 THE APPLICATION FORM

Although you have provided a comprehensive résumé, most organizations will still require you to complete an application form. You are judged on how carefully and accurately—not how quickly—you complete the form. Your attention to it tells the prospective employer whether you can follow instructions well, whether you are organized, and whether you care.

- Complete the form neatly and accurately. This might be the only handwritten document the interviewer has on which to judge your writing skills.
- Have your own copy of your résumé available to remind you of dates of previous jobs, education, etc.
- Be truthful but not unnecessarily modest.

◆ Do not leave any blank spaces; if the question does not apply to you, write in "N/A" (not applicable).

◆ If you make a mistake, erase it completely or put a neat line through the incorrect answer and neatly write/print correct information (do not scratch out).

NOTE If you left a job under circumstances that were unpleasant (e.g., you were dismissed, for personal reasons, etc.), write in "To be discussed" (this gives you the opportunity to discuss the situation in person).

J17 ELECTRONIC/ONLINE APPLICATION

Many companies now accept online/electronic résumés. Two types of electronic résumés are:

◆ Converted hard copy (faxed or scanned documents)

◆ Online via email (actual computer copy of résumé in ASCII or .txt format)

See the homepage of the specific company or organization to see if they offer/accept résumé submissions online.

J18 THE INTERVIEW

The interview is designed to inform both the employer and the applicant. Most interviews follow a pattern, and being aware of this pattern will make you a more confident interviewee.

You can expect a few minutes of introductory small talk during which the interviewer will try to make you feel comfortable. Next, the interviewer will ask you questions about your education and experience. Details of the position will then be given, and you will be invited to ask questions. Information about the company, its activities, and its products will probably be mentioned. Finally, you will be asked if, after hearing about the job first-hand, you are still interested.

The following are some important points to note in successfully presenting yourself at an interview.

Before the interview

Be prepared! If you are well prepared and feel comfortable, you will appear confident. Consider some or all of the following.

Personal preparation The actual day of your interview will go smoothly if you follow these tips:

◆ Plan your wardrobe the night before the interview so that you look your best and are comfortable—dress "up" but dress appropriately. See Unit 3, IS18.

◆ Make sure you are well rested.

◆ Have a positive attitude.

◆ Go alone. Leave family and friends at home.

- Arrive in plenty of time. Make the trip a day or two before to calculate the travelling time.
- Be polite to all staff you meet—you may have to work with them.
- Allow up to one hour for the actual interview.

Company research Try to do some or all of the following:

- Visit the organization ahead of your interview to gain background information, such as literature that details products sold, sales figures and types of sales, number of employees and branches, company history, name of the president, etc.
- Research the vendors/users of the product to learn about its quality and that of the company's service.
- Find out your interviewer's name and supervisory role.

Use this information to develop questions that will show your interest in and knowledge of the company you wish to join. Such preparation will make you stand out in a positive way.

Job research Try to obtain a job description and base your presentation on it. This might be available from

- the interviewer (telephone and ask)
- the employment agency, if that was your job referral source

If this is not possible, create your own job description by, for example,

- asking pertinent questions of the receptionist at the organization or some other employee
- carefully analysing the job ad and building on it

Interview "kit" Go to the interview with the following:

- pen and pad or paper to write down pertinent information
- a file folder that includes
  - a copy of your application letter, résumé, and any letters of recommendation
  - a copy of the want ad (if you are applying for a job from a newspaper ad)
  - a portfolio of job samples that show your capabilities, if possible
  - a log/record of dates, jobs applied for, and interviews (use for interview follow-up)

During the interview

The interview is your chance to convince the employer that you are the best candidate. Be prepared to talk in a confident way about yourself and your career goals.

- Enter confidently. Your body language will show your attitude towards the job.
- Let the interviewer guide the interview. Wait for, but don't expect, an offer to shake hands (then do it firmly). Don't sit down until you are invited to do so.

- Remember your interviewer's name.
- Relax, sit naturally.
- Avoid "yes" and "no" responses. Expand on your answers. Questions are usually designed to encourage you to talk.
- Listen carefully to the interviewer's questions so that you avoid evasive replies.
- Be sensitive to the interviewer's reactions to you; adjust your approach if necessary.
- Look at the interviewer. Direct eye contact signifies confidence.
- Smile!
- Keep the discussion to job-related topics. Home or social concerns have no place here.
- Answer questions about interests and hobbies openly.
- Do not chew gum.
- Be positive and honest about your capabilities but do not be too modest. Include the fact that you learn new skills easily.
- Speak positively of former employers and work experiences.
- Use your school record, summer job, and volunteer experiences as examples of work experience.
- Be prepared to be tested when skills are part of the job.
- Do not drink alcohol if you are invited to a job interview at lunch.

The issue of salary is a sensitive one, and some employers do not discuss it during the first interview. The following should be helpful, however:

- Know, before going to an interview, what you are prepared to accept.
- Allow the prospective employer to raise the subject. If it looks as though you are going to be offered the job and salary has not been mentioned, then raise the subject yourself.

Employers today are concerned with quality and service. Applicants who demonstrate an understanding of this are more likely to succeed.

Answering and asking questions You will be asked questions, of course, and these will vary from job to job. The following are some typical ones that you would be well advised to review and be prepared to answer before you go for your interview:

- What are your best personal qualities?
- What was your greatest achievement at school? College?
- What is your weakest skill area? Your strongest skill area? (Be very honest; this answer could be the determining factor that gets you the job.)
- Were your grades in school an accurate reflection of your capabilities?
- What are your limitations?
- Why do you want to work for this company/organization?
- What do you know about the company/organization?
- Why are you interested in this job?

- What qualities do you think are necessary for this job?
- What would you like to be doing five years from now?
- How long would you stay with us if the job were offered to you?
- If you could have any position, what would it be? Why?
- Why do you think we should hire you?
- How long would it take for you to make a positive contribution?
- Why did you leave your previous job?
- What did you like least about your previous job?
- What is your opinion of the company where you last worked?
- How do you handle deadlines and working under pressure?
- How would you deal with a colleague who constantly interrupted you while you were involved in a job/task?
- Do you have references? Which one would you prefer me to contact and why?

You will also be invited to ask questions. Again, be prepared. Even if your interviewer seems to have dealt with all the information you require, try to ask at least one relevant question when invited to do so. These are questions you might consider:

- What promotional and career opportunities does the company offer?
- Does the company provide a training program for new employees?
- Does the company encourage and sponsor advanced education?
- What are your expectations of the person chosen for this position?
- Will I be working as part of a small or a large team?

Not all interviews are the same, of course. You may find it informative to refer to Unit 7, H9 and H10, on the subject of how to conduct an interview, so that you are aware of what an employer is trying to find out about you.

The end of the interview Leave the interviewer with a good impression:

- Thank the interviewer.
- Ask for a date by which you can expect an answer. (If you do not hear within 10 days, write or call.)
- If it is clear at the conclusion of the interview that you have not been successful, be polite as you leave.

J19   SERIAL/TEAM INTERVIEWS

This interviewing process involves an interview team made up of two or more interviewers. The candidate moves from one interviewer to another, meeting a few or several interviewers for an hour each, often within the same day. During the process there may be testing, tours, or even a working breakfast or lunch involved. Large companies routinely hiring in big numbers and multi-faceted organizations such as financial institutions, the police, federal government, law firms, and new companies are known for using this hiring method.

J20   VIDEO INTERVIEWS

Two-way voice and image communication means an employer in one area (e.g., Vancouver) can meet and evaluate a job candidate in another area (e.g., Winnipeg) without the expense of travel.

In variations of this technique, an employer can view (on a secure website or CD-ROM) the videos of candidates answering preset questions. Candidates can also make their own video presentations introducing themselves and selling their qualifications to far-away employers.

J21   INTERVIEW FOLLOW-UP

Evaluate yourself after each interview by asking yourself these questions:

◆ Was my research of the company adequate?

◆ Did I show confidence?

◆ How did I deal with the questions?

Be honest in your appraisal, work on any weaknesses, and be better prepared for the next interview.

◆ Consider sending a follow-up letter to the interviewer, expressing your thanks for the interview and indicating that you are looking forward to

441 College Avenue
Brandon, MB   R7A 1E8
January 28, 20--

Mr. Jack Wallace, Manager
Human Resources Department
East/West Enterprises Ltd.
3419 McDonald Avenue
Brandon, MB   R7B 0B5

Dear Mr. Wallace:

Thank you for the time you spent with me today at the interview. It was a pleasure to meet you and to find out so much about your organization. The possibility of working for such a dynamic company is most exciting.

I look forward to hearing from you very soon and, I hope, to become a part of East/West Enterprises Ltd. in the near future.

Sincerely,

Marnie Bell

Marnie Bell

Follow-up letter to interviewer

a reply. Use the letter to further emphasize important skills you could bring to the job and add any relevant information that perhaps you feel did not come across strongly during the interview.

If you are offered the job, congratulations! If you are unsuccessful, try not to be discouraged. Consider phoning the employer and asking for an evaluation of your performance at the interview. Use this feedback to better prepare yourself for future job searches.

J22 Success on the Job

Constantly improving technology and the increasing availability of knowledge and data make it essential for workers who wish to progress to prepare for two or three career options and to keep abreast of the job market. Bear in mind that the key qualities of a desirable employee are genuine interest, willingness to learn, co-operation, and initiative. Demonstrate these qualities and encourage your professional growth by

◆ finding a mentor, a role model who will guide you along your career path

◆ taking relevant courses

◆ identifying your weaknesses and planning to correct them (e.g., speaking skills, language skills, team-player qualities)

◆ subscribing to work-related magazines

◆ joining professional organizations

◆ keeping up to date with technological advances

◆ welcoming new challenges

Business and industry need skilled employees. Workers today need and want educational programs that allow them to upgrade their skills while accommodating their busy work schedules.

Online learning (distance learning/education) and testing programs are available through local community colleges and private business schools. Today's workplace offers online training programs for job reinforcement and career advancement.

The worker who gains new skills and is willing to change career goals to adapt to the job market will always have the greatest potential for success.

Give the job a fair chance. If you do not like your job, stay at least a year to gain the experience, and then look for another more challenging or suitable position. Keep your résumé updated on a regular basis; add new skills, courses, employment history, references, etc.

V

NOTE Never leave a job unless you have another one to go to!

Go to www.gov.on.ca and click on "Finding a job"; here you can find information on training opportunities, looking for a job, and other topics.

For other career-related resources, employer lists, university lists, and various commercial job searches on the internet, go to www. careerresource.net.

TIP Small-business enterprise centres are available to assist entrepreneurs with starting a small business. Below is a list of some provincial economic development departments.

Ministry of Economic Development and Trade (Ontario)
www.ontariocanada.com/ontcan/en/home.jsp

Nova Scotia Economic Development
www.gov.ns.ca/econ

Alberta Economic Development Authority
www.alberta-canada.com/aeda/index.cfm

Training and Employment Development (New Brunswick)
www.gnb.ca/0105/index-e.asp

Manitoba Industry, Economic Development, and Mines
www.gov.mb.ca/itm

J23   JOB SEARCH/TRAINING WEBSITES

◆ www.distancestudies.com

◆ jobfutures.ca

◆ www.jobbank.gc.ca

◆ www.monster.ca

◆ www.workopolis.com

J24   TOP TEN JOBS*

Sales representatives
Engineers
Technicians
Production operators
Positions in skilled manual trades (primarily carpenters,
   welders, and plumbers)
IT staff (primarily programmers/developers)
Administrative assistants/personal assistants
Drivers
Accountants
Management/executives

*Top ten jobs that employers have difficulty in filling, according to a Manpower Inc. survey of 33 000 employers in 23 countries.

J

J25 WOMEN IN THE WORKPLACE

NOTE This information is drawn from Statistics Canada's Women in Canada Report:

◆ The number of women enrolled in community college has increased only slightly over the past three decades, with women making up 54 percent of the total number of full-time students in 2000.

◆ In 2001, 8 percent of women had completed a trade certificate or diploma compared to 14 percent of men.

◆ The number of working women with young children (under three) doubled to 65 percent from 1976 to 2004.

◆ The average annual pre-tax income for women was $24 400 in 2003, up 13 percent from 1997.

◆ The number of working women climbed to 58 percent from 42 percent in 1976.

◆ Just under one-third (31 percent) of women were described as low income compared to 28 percent of men.

WORDS OF WISDOM

*The best way to appreciate your job
is to imagine yourself without one!*

····APPENDIX·····

ABBREVIATIONS
    Academic Degrees
    Business Terms

BUSINESS/FINANCIAL TERMS

INSURANCE TERMS

LEGAL TERMS

REAL ESTATE TERMS

FOREIGN WORDS AND PHRASES

OTHER TERMS

HOLIDAYS
    National
    Provincial
    U.S. National Holidays

METRIC SYSTEM
    Most Frequently Used Metric Measurements
    Conversion Chart for Commonly Used Measures
    Some Easy-to-Remember Measurements
    Metric Equivalents

ROMAN NUMERALS

TIME ZONES AND AREA CODES
    Canada
    United States
    International Times
    World Time Zones
    Daylight Saving Time (DST)

This appendix contains important business-related reference material to supplement the information provided by this textbook.

▶ ABBREVIATIONS

Acceptable abbreviations for academic degrees, as well as for Canadian provinces and U.S. states, are listed here.

ACADEMIC DEGREES

Bachelor of Arts	B.A.
Bachelor of Commerce	B.Com. or B.Comm.
Bachelor of Dental Surgery	B.D.S.
Bachelor of Engineering	B.E.
Bachelor of Education	B.Ed.
Bachelor of Fine Arts	B.F.A.
Bachelor of Journalism	B.J.

(continued . . .)

Bachelor of Laws	LL.B.
Bachelor of Library Science	B.L.S.
Bachelor of Music	B.Mus.
Bachelor of Philosophy	B.Ph.
Bachelor of Pharmacy	B.Pharm.
Bachelor of Science	B.S. or B.Sc.
Bachelor of Social Work	B.S.W.
Bachelor of Theology	B.Th.
Master of Arts	M.A.
Master of Applied Science	M.A.Sc.
Master of Business Administration	M.B.A.
Master of Dental Surgery	M.D.S.
Master of Forestry	M.F.
Master of Music	M.Mus.
Master of Philosophy	M.Phil.
Master of Science	M.Sc.
Master of Surgery	M.Ch.
Doctor of Divinity	D.D.
Doctor of Dental Surgery	D.D.S.
Doctor of Education	Ed.D.
Doctor of Literature	D.Lit.
Doctor of Library Science	D.L.S.
Doctor of Philosophy	Ph.D. or D.Ph.
Doctor of Science	D.Sc.
Doctor of Theology	D.Th.
Doctor of Veterinary Medicine	D.V.M.
Doctor of Veterinary Science	D.V.Sc.

See Unit 1, T110, for college diploma designations.

BUSINESS TERMS

For a list of standard business abbreviations, see Unit 1, T100.

▶ BUSINESS/FINANCIAL TERMS

Commonly used expressions that do not appear elsewhere in this handbook are listed below:

Agent: A person authorized to act for or in the place of another.

Amortize: To set money aside in a special account or fund for the repayment of a debt in a specified period of time.

Audit: Official examination of accounts and records of an organization.

Bill of sale: Written evidence of transfer of ownership.

Bond: Certificate acknowledging a loan.

Cartel: Group of businesses formed to regulate prices, production, and marketing of goods.

CEO: Chief Executive Officer.

Chattel mortgage: Personal property used as security for a debt.

CMA: Canadian Medical Association, Certified Management Accountant.

Collateral: Property offered as security for a loan.

Compound interest: Interest calculated on the principal plus the interest earned.

Contract: Legally binding agreement.

Debenture: Another term for *bond*, a certificate acknowledging a loan.

Depreciation: The diminishing in value of assets over a period of time.

Drawing account: A business account that enables the user to withdraw funds in advance.

Equity: The dollar value of a business or property in excess of amounts owed in relation to it.

Franchise: Authorization to sell a company's products or services.

GM: General manager.

Inventory: List of stock of a business.

Liability: A debt for goods, services, or cash provided and owed to a business or individual.

Liable: Responsible or bound by law to pay a debt or obligation.

Lien: Signifies the right to another's property until debt has been cleared.

M&A: merger and acquisition, i.e., corporate deals.

Notary public: Person authorized to perform legal formalities.

Outsourcing: The sending of work to another location/company.

PAC: Pre-authorized contribution plan.

PAD: Pre-authorized debit plan.

Patent: Protection of an invention.

Power of attorney: Legal authority to act on another's behalf.

Promissory note (p.n., P/N): A written promise to pay or repay a loan at a future time.

Share: Document proving part-ownership of a corporation.

Sight draft: An order to pay on presentation of the draft.

SOHO: Small office/home office.

Statute of limitations: A law placing a specific time limit on the enforcement of claims.

APPENDIX

Title: The written right to possession of property.

Void: Not legally enforceable.

Voucher: A receipt or record of a business transaction.

Warranty: Guarantee of quality of goods purchased.

Write-off: Removal of a bad debt from an account.

▶ INSURANCE TERMS

Adjuster: A person who adjusts claims for the insurance company.

Auxiliary: Helping, assisting, or additional.

Coinsurance: Joint insurance.

Compliance: The act of complying or doing as another wishes.

Comprehensive: Including other coverage.

Demerit: Mark against a person's record.

Disclaimer: Refuse to recognize; deny connection with.

Discretion: The freedom to judge or choose; good judgment.

Eligibility: Qualification for insurance.

Endowment: The money or property given to provide income.

Forfeit: Damages, loss, or penalty.

Immune: Exempt; not liable for some duty or obligation.

Indemnify: To compensate for damage, loss, or expense incurred.

Indemnity: The payment for damage, loss, or expense incurred.

Infirm: Weak or feeble.

Insolvency: Inability to pay one's debts; bankruptcy.

Insurable: Capable of being insured.

Longevity: Long life.

Monetary: Referring to the money of a country; a money award.

Precedence: The act or fact of preceding; of greater importance.

Prudent: Describes one who plans carefully ahead of time.

NOTE The Financial Services Commission of Ontario (FSCO) Insurance Ombudsman will investigate consumer complaints, but consumers must first contact an insurance company's ombudsman liaison officer.

A list of all firms and their liaison officers is available at www.fsco.gov.on.ca

▶ LEGAL TERMS

Affidavit: A statement in writing that is sworn to be true.

Barrister: A legal representative (lawyer).

Contingency fee: A fee paid to a lawyer based on the percentage of the amount of money recovered in a legal action.

Decedent/Deceased: A person who is dead.

Decree: A decision ordered or settled by law.

Defendant: The person who is accused in a lawsuit.

Dissolution: The breaking up or termination of a legal bond (e.g., the breaking up of a partnership agreement).

Executor: The person named in a will to carry out the terms of the will.

Garnishee: To hold assets by legal authority.

Garnishment: A legal action where possessions belonging to the defendant must be held until the plaintiff's claims are settled.

Judicial: Having to do with the administration of justice.

Notarial certificate: A document that contains facts that are sworn to be true and is witnessed and signed by a person legally authorized to certify the information in the document.

Notary public: A person who is legally authorized to act on behalf of others and certify documents.

Plaintiff: A person who brings legal action against the defendant.

Proxy: Someone authorized or substituted to act or vote for a person in their absence.

Solicitor: A legal representative (lawyer).

Substantiate: To prove or establish the truth.

Summons: Notify formally to appear before a court or a judge.

▶ REAL ESTATE TERMS

Amortization: The number of years it will take to pay off the entire amount of a mortgage.

Appraisal: An estimate of a property's market value. This amount is used by lenders to determine the amount of a mortgage or loan.

Assessment: The value of a property set by the local municipality. The assessment is used to calculate property taxes.

Assumable mortgage: A mortgage held on a property by a seller that can be taken over by the buyer. The buyer then assumes responsibility for making payments. An assumable mortgage can make a property more attractive to potential buyers.

Blended mortgage payments: Equal or regular mortgage payments consisting of both a principal and an interest component.

Bridge financing: Money borrowed against a homeowner's equity in a property (usually for a short term) to help finance the purchase or to make improvements to a property being sold.

Broker: A real estate professional licensed to facilitate the sale, lease, or exchange of a property.

Buy-down: A situation where the seller reduces the interest rate on a mortgage by paying the difference between the reduced rate and the market rate directly to the lender. A buy-down can make a property more attractive to potential buyers.

Closed mortgage: A mortgage that cannot be prepaid, renegotiated, or refinanced during its term without signing penalties.

CMHC: Canada Mortgage and Housing Corporation is the federal Crown corporation that administers the *National Housing Act*.

Conventional mortgage: A first mortgage issued for up to 75 percent of the property's appraised value or purchase price, whichever is lower.

Debt service ratio: The percentage of a borrower's gross income that can be used for housing costs (including mortgage payments and taxes). This is used to determine the amount of a monthly mortgage payment the borrower can afford.

Easement: A legal right to use or cross (right of way) another person's land for limited purpose. A utility's right to run wires or lay pipe across a property is a common example.

Encroachment: An intrusion onto an adjoining property. A neighbour's fence, shed, or overhanging roofline that partially intrudes onto a property are examples.

Equity: The value of property beyond what may be owed on the property, e.g., a house worth $200 000 with an outstanding mortgage of $100 000, creating equity of $100 000.

First mortgage: The first security registered on a property. Additional mortgages secured against the property are termed "secondary."

Gross debt service ratio (GDSR): The percentage of pre-tax income needed to cover payments related to housing, including mortgage, taxes, and other household costs.

High-ratio mortgage: A mortgage for more than 75 percent of a property's appraised value or purchase price.

Listing agreement: The contract between the listing broker and an owner, authorizing the agent to facilitate the sale or lease of a property.

Mortgage: A contract between a borrower and a lender where the borrower pledges a property as security to guarantee repayment of the mortgage debt.

Mortgage term: The length of time a lender will loan mortgage funds to a borrower. Most terms run from 6 months to 5 years, after which the borrower will either pay off the balance or renegotiate the mortgage for another term. Payment is calculated using the interest rate offered for the term, the amount of the mortgage, and the amortization period.

Multiple Listing Service (MLS): A comprehensive system for relaying information to agents about properties for sale.

Open mortgage: A loan in which the borrower can repay all or part of the debt without being charged a penalty (as distinct from a closed mortgage).

P.I.T. (principal, interest, and taxes): The regular mortgage payment that includes payment against a portion of the principal, the interest, and the municipal property taxes.

Pre-approved loan or mortgage: One that is approved, based on the borrower's financial circumstances, prior to the purchase, which will be made possible by the loan.

Term: The length of time a specific interest rate is paid on a mortgage.

Total debt service ratio (TDSR): The percentage of pre-tax income required to cover all payments for housing and all other debts, e.g., personal loans.

NOTE   This information was provided by local agents and the Ontario Real Estate Association (OREA) for the benefit of consumers in the real estate market.

▶ FOREIGN WORDS AND PHRASES

Many foreign words and phrases have been assimilated into English usage. Some of the more frequently used ones appear below.

ad hoc	temporary; for a specific purpose
ad infinitum	without limit or end
ad nauseam	to the point of disgust
ad valorem	according to value
bona fide	in good faith
caveat emptor	let the buyer beware
carte blanche	full discretionary powers
circa	about
coup d'état	a sudden and decisive political measure
cum laude	with honour, praise
exempli gratia (e.g.)	for example
esprit de corps	team spirit, team work, co-operation
et cetera (etc.)	and so forth
ex officio	by virtue of an office
fait accompli	something already done
faux pas	false step, error
id est (i.e.)	that is
incognito	in disguise
in toto	altogether, entirely
je ne sais quoi	indefinable quality
kudos	praise
laissez faire	the principle of letting people do as they please
modus operandi	method of operating
modus vivendi	way of life

(continued . . .)

APPENDIX

nota bene (N.B.)	note well
ne plus ultra	the highest degree
non sequitur	does not follow, irrelevant
objet d'art	a work of art
per annum	each year
per capita	each person
per diem	each day
per se	itself
persona non grata	an unacceptable person
pièce de résistance	an outstanding item or event
prix fixe	set price for a complete meal
pro forma	done as a matter of form
pro rata	in proportion to
raison d'être	reason for being
répondez s'il vous plaît (R.S.V.P.)	please reply
sine qua non	something essential
status quo	current state of affairs
verbatim	word for word
via	by the way of (a route)
videlicet (viz.)	namely

▶ OTHER TERMS

AIDS	acquired immune deficiency syndrome
ATM	automated teller machine
AV	audio-visual
CD	compact disc
GNP	gross national product
PR	public relations
R&D	research and development
SRO	standing room only/sold right out

▶ HOLIDAYS

Statutory national and provincial holidays for Canada and the United States are listed here.

NATIONAL

New Year's Day	January 1
Good Friday	Varies
Victoria Day	Monday prior and closest to May 24
Canada Day	July 1
Labour Day	First Monday in September
Thanksgiving Day	Second Monday in October
Christmas Day	December 25

Government offices are also closed on Boxing Day (December 26), Easter Monday, and Remembrance Day (November 11). Banks are also closed on Remembrance Day.

PROVINCIAL (IN ADDITION TO NATIONAL HOLIDAYS)

Alberta	Boxing Day	December 26
British Columbia	British Columbia Day	First Monday in August
	Boxing Day	December 26
Manitoba	Civic Holiday	First Monday in August
	Boxing Day	December 26
New Brunswick	Boxing Day	December 26
Newfoundland and	St. Patrick's Day	March 17
Labrador	St. George's Day	April 23
	Commonwealth Day	May 24
	Discovery Day	June 26
	Memorial Day	July 1
	Orangeman's Day	July 12
	Boxing Day	December 26
Northwest Territories	Civic Holiday	First Monday in August
	Boxing Day	December 26
Nova Scotia	Boxing Day	December 26
Nunavut	Civic Holiday	First Monday in August
	Remembrance Day	November 11
Ontario	Civic Holiday (Simcoe Day in Toronto and some other municipalities)	First Monday in August
	Boxing Day	December 26
Prince Edward Island	Boxing Day	December 26
Quebec	St-Jean-Baptiste Day	June 24
Saskatchewan	Civic Holiday	First Monday in August
	Boxing Day	December 26
Yukon	Discovery Day	Third Monday in August

U.S. NATIONAL HOLIDAYS

New Year's Day	January 1
Martin Luther King Day	Third Monday in January
Presidents' Day	Third Monday in February
Good Friday	Varies
Memorial Day	Last Monday in May
Independence Day	July 4
Labor Day	First Monday in September
Columbus Day	Second Monday in October
Veterans' Day	November 11
Thanksgiving Day	Fourth Thursday in November
Christmas Day	December 25

▶ METRIC SYSTEM

The metric system adopted by Canada is Le Système international d'unités, or SI. Because the system is international, units, prefixes, and symbols must be used properly. Rules for keying metric expressions can be found in Unit 14, "Keying and Formatting Documents for Processing," K72. To obtain publications on metric practices, contact the Canadian Standards Association, 178 Rexdale Blvd., Toronto, ON M9W 1R3.

MOST FREQUENTLY USED METRIC MEASUREMENTS

Quantity	Unit	Symbol
Length	millimetre	mm
	centimetre	cm
	metre	m
	kilometre	km
	(1 m = 100 cm or 1000 mm)	
Area	square centimetre	cm^2
	square metre	m^2
	square kilometre	km^2
	hectare	ha
Volume	cubic centimetre	cm^3
	cubic decimetre	dm^3
	cubic metre	m^3
	(1 m^3 = 1 000 000 cm^3)	
	millilitre	mL
	litre	L
	(1 L = 1000 mL)	
Mass	milligram	mg
	gram	g
	kilogram	kg
	tonne	t
	(1 kg = 1000 g)	
Time	second	s
	minute	min
	hour	h
Speed	metres per second	m/s
	kilometres per hour	km/h
Temperature	degree Celsius	°C

CONVERSION CHART FOR COMMONLY USED MEASURES

Length	1 inch	= 2.54 cm or 25.4 mm
	1 foot	= 0.305 m
	1 yard	= 0.914 m
	1 mile	= 1.609 km
Area	1 square inch	= 6.452 cm^2
	1 square foot	= 0.093 m^2
	1 square yard	= 0.836 m^2
	1 acre	= 0.405 ha (hectare)
	1 square mile	= 2.590 km^2 (259 ha)

(continued . . .)

Volume	1 fluid ounce	= 28.413 cm^3 (28.4 mL)
	1 pint (imperial)	= 0.568 dm^3 (0.57 L)
	1 quart	= 1.137 dm^3 (1.14 L)
	1 gallon	= 4.546 dm^3 (4.546 L)
	1 cubic inch	= 16.387 cm^3
	1 cubic foot	= 28.317 dm^3 (28.32 L)
	1 cubic yard	= 0.765 m^3
Mass	1 ounce	= 28.350 g
	1 pound	= 0.454 kg
	1 ton (short 2000 lb.)	= 907.185 kg
Speed	1 mile per hour	= 0.447 m/s
		= 1.609 km/h

Temperature: $^5/_9 \times$ (No. of degrees Fahrenheit − 32) = degrees Celsius

or

Converting °F to °C	*Converting °C to °F*
Subtract 32	Multiply by 1.8
Divide by 1.8	Add 32
Example: 80°F	*Example:* 27°C
80 − 32 = 48	27 × 1.8 = 48.6
48 ÷ 1.8 = 26.66°C	48.6 + 32 = 80.6°F

SOME EASY-TO-REMEMBER MEASUREMENTS

◆ The standard doorway is about 2 m high and 0.75 m wide.

◆ An average chair seat is roughly 0.5 m high.

◆ A paper clip is about 3 cm long.

◆ There are about 200 mL in a cup of coffee.

◆ The width of a small fingernail is 1 cm.

◆ A coin is approximately 1 mm thick.

METRIC EQUIVALENTS

A few common comparisons are listed for quick reference.

1 centimetre	= 0.3937 inch
1 inch	= 2.54 centimetres
1 litre	= 35 ounces
1 pint	= 0.571 litre
1 metre	= 1.0936 yards
1 yard	= 0.9144 metre
1 kilogram	= 2.20 pounds
1 pound	= 0.4536 kilogram
80 km/h	= 50 mph
100° Celsius	= 212° Fahrenheit
0° Celsius	= 32° Fahrenheit

APPENDIX

▶ ROMAN NUMERALS

◆ Use uppercase numerals for major divisions in outlines and in literary publications (volumes, books, chapters, appendices, etc.).

◆ Use lowercase numerals for preliminary pages in reports and subsections.

Arabic	Roman	Arabic	Roman
1	I	30	XXX
2	II	40	XL
3	III	50	L
4	IV	60	LX
5	V	70	LXX
6	VI	80	LXXX
7	VII	90	XC
8	VIII	100	C
9	IX	200	CC
10	X	300	CCC
11	XI	400	CD
12	XII	500	D
13	XIII	600	DC
14	XIV	900	CM
15	XV	1 000	M
16	XVI	5 000	$\overline{V}$*
17	XVII	8 000	$\overline{VIII}$*
18	XVIII	10 000	$\overline{X}$*
19	XIX	30 000	$\overline{XXX}$*
20	XX	50 000	$\overline{L}$*

Build combinations of roman numerals by prefixing or annexing letters. A letter prefixed to another is subtracted from it; a letter annexed is added:

$$49 = \overbrace{L - X}^{40} + IX = XLIX$$

$$62 = \overbrace{L + X}^{60} + II = LXII$$

Do not repeat a roman numeral more than three times:

337 = CCCXXXVII
437 = CDXXXVII not CCCCXXXVII
1988 = MCMLXXXVIII
1990 = MCMXC
2000 = MM
2004 = MMIV
2008 = MMVIII

▶ Time Zones and Area Codes

CANADA

Canada is divided into six time zones. There is one hour's difference between each zone as you move across the country. Newfoundland time, however, is only one-half hour different from Atlantic time.

Subtract one hour for each zone moving from east to west. Add one hour for each zone moving from west to east.

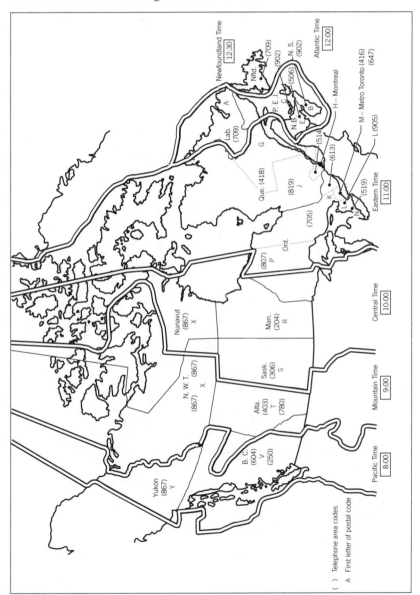

Canadian time zones and telephone area and postal codes

NOTE See Unit 4, TT13, for more information on area code overlays.

NOTE Eastern Labrador observes NST. Most of Saskatchewan does not observe Daylight Saving Time.

UNITED STATES

The continental United States is divided into four time zones, with one hour's difference between adjacent zones.

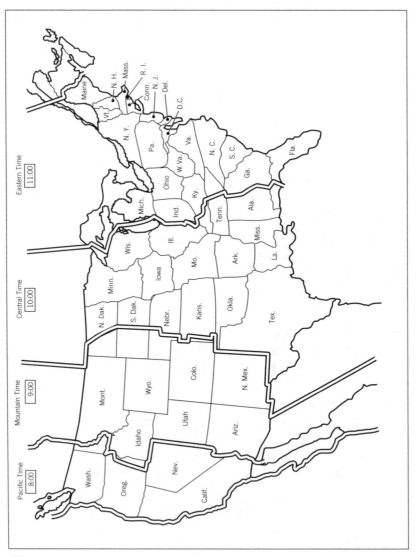

U.S. time zones

INTERNATIONAL TIMES

Add or subtract from Eastern Standard Time the hours shown to find Standard times in these countries.

(Ottawa, Monday 6 p.m. = Tokyo, Japan, Tuesday 8 a.m.)

Argentina	+	2	India	+	$10\frac{1}{2}$
Australia (East)	+	16	Iran	+	$8\frac{1}{2}$
(West)	+	13	Iraq	+	8
Austria	+	6	Israel	+	7
Belgium	+	6	Italy	+	6
Bermuda	+	1	Japan	+	14
Bolivia	+	1	Korea	+	$13\frac{1}{2}$
Bosnia-Herzegovina	+	6	Kuwait	+	8
Brazil	+	2	Netherlands	+	6
Bulgaria	+	7	New Zealand	+	17
Chile	+	1	Norway	+	6
China	+	13	Philippines	+	13
Colombia		0	Poland	+	6
Costa Rica	−	1	Portugal	+	5
Croatia	+	6	Russia	+	8
Cuba		0	Singapore	+	$12\frac{1}{2}$
Czech Republic	+	6	Slovak Republic	+	6
Denmark	+	6	South Africa	+	7
Egypt	+	7	Spain	+	6
Finland	+	7	Sweden	+	6
France	+	6	Switzerland	+	6
Germany	+	6	Syria	+	7
Ghana	+	6	Turkey	+	7
Great Britain	+	5	Ukraine	+	8
Greece	+	7	Uruguay	+	2
Hawaii	−	5	Venezuela	+	$\frac{1}{2}$
Hong Kong	+	13	Zimbabwe	+	7
Hungary	+	6			

WORLD TIME ZONES

Given a 24-hour day and 360 degrees of longitude around the earth, the world's 24 time zones are on average 15 degrees wide. The individual zone boundaries are not straight, however, because they have been adjusted for the convenience and desires of local populations.

Specialized world time-zone clocks are available from manufacturers; these clocks can be customized for time zone display, digital time zone, military time zone, etc. They can also obtain synchronized time using GPS (global positioning system), IRIG-B (missile and space), CDMA (cell phone towers), and the NTP (ethernet) time protocol.

DAYLIGHT SAVING TIME (DST)

Approximately 70 countries utilize daylight saving time. Equatorial and tropical countries (lower latitudes) do not observe DST.

For additional information: www.worldtimezones.com

WORDS OF WISDOM

You may be disappointed if you fail,
but you are doomed if you don't try!

Information that appears on the Text Enrichment Site for this text at www.pearsoned.ca/text/campbell is indicated by a reference to *TES*.

a, 17, 20–21, 44
a lot, 23
a part, 23
a while, 23
abbreviations
    academic degrees, 69, 549–550
    in addresses, 69
    alphabet sequencing, 215
    broadcasting stations, 69
    business terms, 70–71
    Canada Post, 333
    capitalization and, 73
    company names, 71
    compass points, 71
    dates, 71–72
    figures, use of, 77
    metric measurements, 72
    organization names, 71
    period, use of, 63–64
    places, 72, 333–334
    plural form, 43
    publication terms, 72
    in tables, 369
    times, 71–72
    titles (people), 72
    use of, 69
abstract nouns, 41
academic degrees, 69, 73–74,
    214–215, 549–550
academic field, 73–74
accede, 4
accent, 4
accept, 4, 17
acceptance, 131
access, 308
access, 4
accompanied by, 25
accompanying prepositions,
    24–25
according to, 25
account for, 25
account to, 25
accounting
    accounting records, 493–495
    banking services, 508
    budgets, 500
    described, 493
    double entry, 495
    financial statements. *See*
        financial statements
    fundamental accounting
        equation, 497
    journals, 494
    ledger, 495
    ledger accounts, 494–495
    source documents (forms),
        493–494
    statement of account, 495
    trial balance, 495
accounting equation, 497
accounting records, 493–495
accounting software, 293, 371,
    499–500
accounting systems, 499–500

accounts, 501–502
accounts payable, 497
accounts receivable, 497
acid-test ratio, 498
acknowledgment letter, 86
acronyms, 215
active voice, 38, 46
actively managed funds, 524
acts, 75
ad, 4
A.D., 71
ad hoc committee, 266
adapt, 5
AdAware, 155
add, 4
addition, 4
addresses
    abbreviations in, 69
    capitalization and, 74
    comma in, 58–59
    envelope addressing. *See*
        envelope addressing
    forms of address. *See* forms
        of address
    French addresses, 343
    inside address, placement,
        342–343
    numbers in, 78
    return address, 459
    word division, 82
adept, 5
adjective-adverb confusion, 39
adjectives
    versus adverbs, 50
    comparative form, 48–49
    compound adjectives, 49, 61
    degrees of comparison, 48–49
    described, 48
    independent adjectives,
        separation of, 57–58
    irregular adjectives, 49
    linking verbs, 49
    superlative form, 49
adjoin, 5
adjourn, 5
adjusted chequebook balance,
    507
adjusted statement balance, 507
adopt, 5
ADSL, 426
adverbs
    versus adjectives, 50
    conjunctive adverbs, 50, 51
    described, 49
    identification of, 50
adverse, 5
advertisements (recruitment),
    189–190
advertising trademarks, 74
advice, 5
advise, 5
adware, 153
aerogrammes, 462
affect, 5, 17
afterthoughts, 59

age guidelines, 208
agenda, 253–254, 266
ages, 78
aggressive individuals, 137
AGP, 308
agree on/upon, 25
agree to, 25
agree with, 25
aid, 5
aide, 5
ail, 5
air letters, 462
air miles, 269
air travel
    airfares, 269–270
    baggage, 271
    business or executive class, 269
    cancellation, 270–271
    chartered planes, 272
    check-in considerations, 271
    confirmation, 270–271
    discounted fares, 269–270
    economy class, 269
    first class, 269
    frequent-flyer plans/air miles,
        269
    making calls, 270
    meals, 270
    reservations, 268–269
    scheduled flight, 270
    transportation to and from
        airport, 271
airfares, 269–270
airlines, 468
aisle, 5
ale, 5
alertness, 135
all ready, 23
all right, 23
all together, 23
all ways, 23
allot, 23
allowed, 5
almanacs, *TES*
aloud, 5
alpha-numeric filing, 223
alphabet (in records
    management), 212
alphabet sequencing
    abbreviations, 215
    acronyms, 215
    ARMA rules, 214, 219
    associations, 217
    banks, 217
    boards, 218
    colleges, 217
    committees, 218
    compass points in names, 217
    degrees, 214–215
    described, 213
    estates, 218
    geographic names, 216
    governments and their
        divisions, 218
    hyphenated names, 216

identical names, 218–219
initials, 215
names of companies, 214
names of individuals, 214
numbers, 217
organizations, 217
prefixes, 215–216
punctuation, 216
religious institutions, 217
schools, 217
societies, 217
symbols, 216
telephone directory, 219
titles, 214–215
trustees, 218
universities, 217
alphabetic directory (White
   Pages), 144
alphabetic document file,
   219–220
alphabetic filing, 221
alphabetical directory, 431
already, 23
alright, 23
altar, 5
alter, 5
alternate, 5
alternative, 5
altogether, 23
always, 23
a.m., 71
amendment, 255–256, 266
American Management
   Association, 327
among, 17
amortization formula, 486–487
ampersand, 69, 219
an, 17, 20–21, 44
analog copying process, 241
analog systems, 236, 389
and etc., 17
angry individuals, 137
anniversaries, 78
annotating mail, 456
announcement of meeting,
   251–252
anonymous FTP, 421
answering calls, 135
anthologies, 364
anti-harassment policies, 128
anti-virus programs, 155,
   299–300, 306
any body, 23
any more, 23
any time, 23
any way, 23
anybody, 23
anymore, 23
anyplace, 17
anytime, 23
anyway, 18, 23
anyways, 18, 23
anywhere, 17
apart, 23
APEX (Advance Purchase
   EXcursion), 270
apology letter, 86–87
apostrophe
   compound words, 53
   contractions, 52
   gerunds, 54

measurement-related
   expressions, 54
omissions, 52
ownership, indication of, 54
plural possessive, 53
in plurals, 52
possessives, 52–53
as single quotation mark, 54
time-related expressions, 54
appearance, 117, 118
appendix, 109, 360
applicants. *See* recruitment of
   staff
application form, 190, 540–541
application letter, 532–534
applications software. *See*
   software
appointment schedule, 171
appositives, 57
appraise, 5
apprise, 5
archive file, 421
are, 6
area code overlays, 140
arm movement, 176
ARMA rules, 214, 219
armed forces titles, 99
articles
   definite article, 44
   indefinite article, 44
   misused articles, 17
   preceding nouns, 44
artificial intelligence, 308
artwork, 402–404
as, 20
as regards, 18
ascender, 409
ascent, 4
ASCII, 308
assent, 4
assistance, 6
assistance, offers of, 117
assistants, 6
associations, 217
assumptions, 121
astronomical bodies, 74
asynchronous communications,
   162
at, 18
atlases, *TES*
attachment notation, 346
attachments, 85
attendance, 6
attendants, 6
attention line, 343
attractive documents, 378–379
audio conferencing, 263–264
audio-plus conferencing, 264
auto transport, 273
automated banking machine
   (ABM), 508
automated filing equipment, 236
automated teller machine (ATM),
   277, 508
automated voice-response
   telephone systems, 160–161
automatic bill payment, 508–509
automatic changer, 389
automatic features, 383
automatic PBX, 146
automatic selector, 389

auxiliary guides, 220
auxiliary verbs, 47
averages, 490–491
averse, 5
awhile, 23

backup
   computer files, 306
   copies, 232
   disk backup, 386
baggage
   air travel, 271
   train travel, 273
bail, 6
balance, 405–406
balanced funds, 524
balanced structure, 38
bale, 6
bank cards, 510, 513
bank reconciliation, 506–508
banking
   accounting services, 508
   accounts, types of, 501–502
   automated teller machine
     (ATM), 508
   automatic bill payment,
     508–509
   bank cards, 510, 513
   cheques, 503–506
   credit card, 509–510
   credit card protection, 510
   debit cards, 508
   deposits, 502–503
   drafts, 510–511
   electronic funds transfer, 508,
     511
   financial advice, 511
   financial institutions, 500–501
   foreign currency, 511
   investments, 511
   letters of credit, 511–512
   loans, 512
   Mondex Smart Card, 511
   money orders, 512
   mortgages, 512
   overdraft protection, 512
   package services, 512
   payroll services, 512
   reconciliation, 506–508
   retirement savings plans, 512
   safety deposit boxes, 513
   service charges, 506
   by telephone and online, 509,
     511
   term deposits, 513
   traveller's cheques, 513
   withdrawals, 503
banks, 217
banners, 409
bar code, 290, 315, 452
barcoding, 230
bare, 6
base number, 479
bases, 6
basis, 6
B2B funds, 524
B.C., 71
bear, 6
bedroom (train), 272
behind, 18
berry, 6

berth, 6
beside, 6, 18
besides, 6, 18
between, 17
biannual, 6
bias, 32
bibliographic text services, 413
bibliography, 109, 360, 367–368
biennial, 6
the bill (for meal), 130
bill of lading, 448, 471
bill to a third number calls, 141, 142
billing
  forms, 448–449
  math applications, 481–482
binary, 308
binding, 408
biographical references, 428–429
biometrics, 279
BIOS, 309
birth, 6
bit, 309
bit streams, 309
bitmap, 309
blade servers, 309
blank endorsement, 504
bloc, 6
block, 6
blogs, 426
blue chips, 524
board, 6
boards, 218, 309
body
  of letter, 344
  of report, 108, 356–367
body language, 118, 132
body text
  commonly used typefaces, 401
  display text, 400
  format, 400
  text content, 399–400
  type selection, 401–402
  type styles, 400
  typefaces, 400
  typography, language of, 400–401
Bon Voyage, But ..., 278
bona fide occupational requirement, 208
bond paper, 408
bonds, 522
book paper, 408
book research, 107
book retrieval, 415
books, 365
bookshelf printer, 303
boot process, 309
bored, 6
borrowing stored materials, 229–230
bound reports, 356
brace brackets, 63
brake, 7
break, 7
break-even point, 489
brevity, 85
bring, 18
broadcasting stations, 69
browser, 426, 428
budgets, 500

buffer, 309
bug, 309, 393
bulleted lists, 360
bulletin board, 157
burnout, 23
bury, 6
bus network configuration, 322–323
bus parcel express (BPX), 468
business abroad, 132–133
business cards, 132
business chequing account, 501
business directories, 430–431
business etiquette
  abroad, 132–133
  cell phone etiquette, 147
  current, 128–129
  dining etiquette, *TES*
  email etiquette/netiquette, 153
business forms. *See* forms
business information, 425
business itinerary, 275, 276
business letters
  see also letter formatting
  acknowledgment letter, 86
  apology letter, 86–87
  appearance, 85
  application letter, 532–534
  brevity, 85
  cancellation of contract, 88
  collection letter, 87
  colons in, 55
  complaint letter, 88
  condolence letter, 96
  congratulatory letter, 89
  covering letter with sales information, 96
  development, 84
  donation (response to request for), 89
  ending, 84
  five Cs, 84
  form letter, 86, 90, 349–350
  gratitude or thank-you letter, 90–91
  honesty, 85
  inquiry letter, 91
  introduction, 84
  introduction letter, 91–92
  job recommendation letter, 92
  job refusal letter, 93
  job rejection letter, 93–94
  job resignation letter, 94
  letter of reference, 92
  letter samples, 86–96
  logical development, 84–85
  negative news, 85
  order letter, 94
  paragraphs in, 40
  payment letter, 95
  preparation for writing, 84
  proofreading, 85
  reference letter, 92
  reply to sympathy letter, 96
  request for job recommendation/reference letter, 92
  reservations letter, 95
  response to unsolicited job application, 94
  sales letter, 95–96
  shortcuts, 85–86

speeding up letter production, 384
sympathy letter, 96
use of, 83
"you" approach, 85
business math applications. *See* math applications
business process reengineering, 323
business-related software. *See* software
business reply cards and envelopes, 462
business telephone systems and equipment
  cell phone etiquette, 147
  cell phones, 147
  centralized answering, 145–146
  computer-based telephone systems, 146–147
  digital subscriber line (DSL), 149
  internet/phone line, 149
  key telephone systems, 146
  message services, 148
  modularity, 146
  pagers, 149
  telemarketing fraud, 148
  telephone-answering services, 149
  videophone, *TES,* 148
  virtual private network (VPN), 149
  voice-mail systems, 148
business terms
  abbreviations for, 70–71
  commonly used expressions, 550–552
but, 22
buy, 7
by, 7
bye, 7
byte, 309

cache, 309
cache, 7
CAD/CAM, 309
CAD programs, 295
calculators
  percentage increases and decreases, 478–479
  percentage key, 476–477
  touch fingering, 474–475
  use of, 474–475
call letters, 69
calling card, 141, 142
calls, 86
  see also telephone calls
can, 18
Canada Revenue Agency (CRA), 278, 279, 468, 472, 515, 517
Canada Employment Centres, 530
Canada Labour Code, 185
Canada Pension Plan, 515
Canada Post, 151, 468
  see also Canadian postal services
Canada Post preferred style, 331, 332–333, 333, 342
  see also envelope addressing

Canada Postal Guide, 434, 459, 461, 465, 468
canada411.ca, 144
Canadian Air Transport Security Authority (CATSA), 280
Canadian Centre for Occupational Health and Safety, 175, 185
Canadian Charter of Rights and Freedoms, 188
Canadian facts
  government of Canada, 435–436
  government services, 436–437
  history, 435
  Maple Leaf Flag, 437
  National Anthem, 438
  origin of name, 435
  Prime Ministers of Canada, 437
  Service Canada, 437
Canadian Human Rights Act
  appeals, 209
  complaints, 209
  described, 205
  discrimination, 206–207
  exceptions, 208
  fines, 209
  harassment, 207
  right to protection, 209
  sexual harassment, 207–208
Canadian Human Rights Commission, 208–209
Canadian postal services
  aerogrammes, 462
  alternatives to, 468–469
  business reply cards and envelopes, 462
  cards (international), 466
  change of address cards, 463
  COD, 463
  copy of signature, 465
  coverage for loss or damage, 463
  customs declaration, 467
  duty-free importations by mail, 468
  Electronic Shipping Tools (EST), 463
  expedited parcel, 462, 466
  franked mail, 464
  international destinations, 466–468
  international parcels service, 466–467
  letter-post, 465
  lettermail, 461
  letters (international), 466
  lock boxes, 464
  Members of Parliament mailing privileges, 464
  on-demand pickup, 464
  parcel services, 462
  post office boxes, 464
  postal code products, 463
  postal service within Canada, 461–465
  postcards (international), 466
  Priority Courier, 464
  publications, 461
  registered mail, 464–465
  scheduled pickup service, 464

small packet, 465, 466
  special Canada Post services, 462–465, 466, 467
  tax-exempt importations by mail, 468
  unaddressed mail, 461
  to the United States, 465–466
  volume electronic mail, 463
  Xpresspost-International, 467
  Xpresspost-USA, 465–466
Canadian provinces and territories, 333
Canadian time zones, 561–562
Canadian Venture Exchange (CDNX), 524
cancellation
  air travel, 270–271
  of contract, 88
  train travel, 273
cancelled cheques, 506
CANPASS, 279
canvas, 7
canvass, 7
capable of, 25
capital, 7
capitalization
  abbreviations, 73
  academic field, 73–74
  addresses, 74
  advertising trademarks, 74
  astronomical bodies, 74
  basic guide, 73
  dates, 74
  geographic terms, 74
  government, 75
  historical periods, 74
  holidays, 74
  institutions, 75
  languages, 75
  nationalities, 75
  organization names, 75
  political references, 75
  publications, 75
  punctuation marks, 75–76
  races, 75
  religious references, 76
  seasons, 74
  titles (people), 76
  use of, 72–73
Capitol, 7
car rentals, 273
carat, 7
career counselling services, 529
career planning
  job search. *See* job search
  success on the job, 546–547
  top ten jobs, 547
  women in the workplace, 548
caret, 7
Carpal Tunnel Syndrome (CPI), 175, 176
carrot, 7
cascade, 309
case
  incorrect, 39
  nominative case, 39, 44
  objective case, 39, 44
  possessive case, 39, 44
  pronouns, 44
cash, 7
cash discounts, 483–484

cash payments (disbursements) journal, 494
cash receipts journal, 494
cast, 7
caste, 7
cause for termination, 198–199
CD disk care, 385–386
CD-R, 393
CD-ROM, 302
CD-RW (compact disk read/write), 302, 393
ce endings, 27
cell phone etiquette, 147
cell phones, 143, 147
census, 7
cent, 7
central processing units. *See* CPUs
centralized answering services, 145–146
centralized copying services, 244–245
centralized departments, 392
centralized recording units, 389
Centrex, 146
cereal, 7
certified cheques, 505
Certified Financial Planner (CFP), 525
chain discounts, 484
chair position, 176
chairperson, 254, 256
chairs, 179
change of address cards, 463
charge-out procedures, 229–230
charter flight, 270
chartered planes, 272
checkmark, 23
cheques
  cancelled cheques, 506
  certified cheques, 505
  cheque clearing, 504
  dishonoured (irregular) cheques, 506
  endorsement, 504–505
  NSF cheques, 506
  post-dated cheques, 505–506
  preparation of, 503–504
  special types of, 505–506
  stale-dated cheques, 506
  stopped cheques, 505
  voucher cheques, 503, 504
child care, 208
China, names in, 125, 132
choose, 8
chose, 8
chronological file, 229
chronological résumés, 536–537, 540
circular files, 235
cite, 8
city directories, 431
civic titles, 72
classified business directory, 431
classified directory (Yellow Pages), 144
clauses
  dependent (subordinate), 36
  independent clauses, 56
  independent (main), 36
  intervening, 34–35
  introductory clauses, 56

non-restrictive clauses, 57
  in sentences, 36
cleaning the disk, 386
clear, 84
clichés to avoid, 3–4
click, 309
client/customer service excellence.
    See public relations
client-server, 309
client/visitor interaction, 125
clipboard, 309
clothing, 129, 132
  see also dress
co-operation, 117
co-operative attitude, 118
co-ordinating conjunctions, 51
co-ordination, excessive, 38
coach, 272
coarse, 8
COD, 463, 471
codec, 264
coding, 227, 232
coherent, 84
collating, 408
collect calls, 141, 142
collect on delivery (COD), 463, 471
collecting, 449–450
collection letter, 87
collections, 364
collective nouns, 41
college diplomas, 73–74
colleges, 194, 217, 529
colon
  in business letters, 55
  capitalization after, 75
  with direct quotations, 54–55
  introductory statements
    followed by lists or series, 55
  in ratios, 55
  in references to publications, 55
  in times, 55
colour, 179, 180, 403–404
colour printers, 407
coloured labels, 231
come, 18
comedy, 121
comma
  in addresses, 58–59
  after introductory words,
    phrases or clauses, 56
  with afterthoughts, 59
  appositives, setting off, 57
  avoiding problems, 60
  in compound sentences, 56
  and conjunctive adverbs, 50
  with contrasting expressions,
    59
  in dates, 58
  in direct address, 59
  with direct quotations, 59
  incorrect usage, 60
  independent adjectives,
    separation of, 57–58
  with interruptions, 59
  items in a series, separation of,
    58
  in money amounts, 81
  in names, 59
  non-restrictive phrases and
    clauses, setting off, 57
  numbers, use with, 77

omissions, 59
  repeated words or numbers,
    setting off, 59
  setting off parenthetical
    expressions, 56–57
  between statement and
    question, 59
  subordinate clauses, setting off,
    57
  in titles, 59
  use of, 55
comma fault, 38
command-driven software
    program, 393
commercial copying services, 247
commercial databases, 413, 414
commercial drafts, 510–511
commercial printers, 407
commissions, 482, 513
committees, 218
common equivalents, 480
common gateway interface
    (CGI), 426
common nouns, 41, 73
common stocks, 522
communicating computers, 155
communicating skills, 120–121
communications
  asynchronous
    communications, 162
  business abroad, 132
  communicating skills, 120–121
  computers, 305–306
  electronic mail. *See* electronic
    mail
  with employees, 201
  links, 315
  oral communications. *See* oral
    expression
  responding to, 122
  synchronous communications,
    162
  written communications. *See*
    written expression
communications software, 293,
    317
companies. *See* organizations
company contact, direct, 529
company name in closing, 344
comparative form, 48–49
comparisons, 483
compass points, 71, 74, 217
compatibility, 309
complaint letter, 88
complaints handling, 125
complement, 35
complement, 8
complex sentences, 37
compliment, 8
compliment slip, 86
complimentary closing, 344
complimentary closings, 103
comply with, 25
compound adjectives, 49, 61
compound-complex sentences, 37
compound interest, 485
compound sentences, 37, 56,
    66–67
compound subject, 34
compound words, 53
compressed format, 421

compulsory payroll deductions,
    515–516
computer accounting systems,
    499–500
computer-based message systems,
    151–161
  see also electronic mail
computer-based telephone
    systems, 146–147
computer conferencing, 265
computer output to laser disk
    (COLD), 237
computer programs. *See* software
computer software. *See* software
computer teleconferencing, 157
computer to fax, 158
computerized lists, 228
computers
  arithmetic/logic unit, 287–288
  bus speed, 288
  choosing a computer system,
    292
  communicating computers, 155
  communications, 305–306
  components, 287–292
  computer literacy, 308
  control unit, 288
  CPUs, 180, 287–288
  desktop publishing (DTP)
    hardware, 397
  and ergonomics, 176–178
  graphical user interface (GUI),
    287
  information security, 307
  input devices, 289–292
  keyboards, 177, 289–290, 380
  maintenance, 306–307
  memory, 288
  monitors, 176–177, 289
  mouse, 178, 291, 380
  networked computers, 155
  non-keyboard input devices
    and methods, 290–292
  operating systems, 287
  Pentium III or P4, 288
  plotters, 305
  portable computers, 286–287
  preparation of conferences and
    conventions, 262
  primary storage unit (memory),
    287
  printers, 303–304
  processing power, 288
  random access memory (RAM),
    288
  read-only memory (ROM), 288
  removal of sensitive
    information, 307
  retrieval, 300–303
  software. *See* software
  start-up time, 154
  storage, 300–303
  storage space, 288–289
  terms, 308–313
  turning off your PC, 307
  types of, 286–287
concise, 84
*Concise Oxford Dictionary of
    Current English*, 27
concur in, 25
concur with, 25

condolence letter, 96
conducting a meeting, 254–256
conference calls, 142–143
conferences and conventions
    computer conferencing, 265
    duration of, 250
    equipment needs, 262
    meaning of, 249
    preparation of materials, 262
    preregistration, 263
    program, 261
    publicity, 261–262
    registration, 263
    report of the proceedings, 263
    site, 262
    teleconferences. *See*
        teleconferences
    wrap-up, 263
confidant(e), 8
confident, 8
configuration, 310
conflict resolution, 128, 203–204
conform to, 25
confused words, 4–16
congratulatory letter, 89
conjugation of verbs, 45–46
conjunctions, 51, 56
conjunctive adverbs, 50, 51
connecting flight, 270
connectives, 34, 50
conscience, 8
conscious, 8
constellations, 74
consul, 8
consultants, 392
contact lenses, 175
contents page, 355
Continental Plan, 275
continuous loop, 393
contract cancellation, 88
contract workers, 201
contractions, 52
contrast, 406
contrasting expressions, 59
convenience photocopiers, 242
conversation, 120
conversion (documents), 381
conversion (math)
    common equivalents, 480
    decimal to percentage, 477
    fraction to percentage, 477
    fractions into decimals, 476
    metric measurements, 558–559
    percentage to decimal, 477
    whole numbers to decimals, 476
cookie, 426
copiers. *See* photocopying
copula verbs, 48
copy centre request form, 245
copy notation, 346
copy of signature, 465
copying equipment, 247–248
copying processes
    analog copying process, 241
    centralized copying services,
        244–245
    choices, 241
    choosing copying equipment,
        247–248
    commercial copying services,
        247

copyright concerns, 247
    described, 315
    digital cameras, 246
    digital copying process, 241
    digital duplicators, 246
    finishing equipment, 247
    imaging technologies, 241
    intelligent copiers, 245–246
    offset duplicating, 246
    photocopying, 241–244
    photography, 246
    phototypesetting, 244
    specialized copiers, 245–246
Copyright Act, 247
copyright concerns, 127, 247, 428
copyright symbol, 247
core, 8
corps, 8
corpse, 8
correct, 84
correlative conjunctions, 51
correspondence
    business letters. *See* business
        letters
    dealing with, 170–171
    mail-handling techniques,
        456–461
correspondence, 8
correspondents, 8
cost of goods sold, 496
council, 8
counsel, 8
counselling, 203–204
country names, 72, 74
courier to fax for courier or postal
    delivery, 159
couriers, 468–469
course, 8
courteous, 84
courtesy, 117
cover paper, 408
cover sheet
    fax, 159
    reports, 108
coverage for loss or damage
    (mail), 463
covering letter with sales
    information, 96
cpi, 393
cps, 393
CPUs, 180, 287–288
crash, 310
credible, 8
credit card, 141, 277, 509–510
credit card protection, 510
credit invoice, 449
creditable, 8
crop, 409
cross-referencing, 227–228
cross-referencing folders, 228
cross-referencing sheets, 227, 228
CRT displays, 289, 310
currant, 8
current, 8
current assets, 497
current liabilities, 497
current ratio, 498
currently, 19
Curriculum Vitae. *See* résumés
cursor control keys, 289, 383
customization, 381

customs, 280–281
customs charges, 472
customs declaration, 467
cyberspace, 426
cyberworld, 426

daily planning, 166–167
dash, 60
data backups, 303
data processing, 315
data sheet. *See* résumés
data warehouse, 325–326
databases, 168, 237–238,
    293–294, 413–414, 416
date-stamp, 456
dates
    abbreviations, 71–72
    capitalization, 74
    comma, use of, 58
    current date, using software,
        58
    en dash, 60
    on letters, 341
    numbers in, 78–79
    numeric dates, 372–373
    word division, 82
daylight saving time (DST), 564
DDE, 310, 393
de-emphasis, 62
debit cards, 508
decent, 9
decentralized departments, 392
decimal filing, 223
decimal places, 475
decimals, 64, 79, 370, 475, 477
decision making, 132, 172–173
default format settings, 330
default settings, 384
defective, 9
defer, 9
defer to, 9
deferred sales charge (DSC), 525
deficient, 9
definite article, 44
degrees. *See* academic degrees
delivery of speech, 111
delivery receipt, 447–448
demonstrative pronouns, 45
Department of Foreign Affairs
    and International Trade
    (DFAIT), 278
dependent clauses, 36
deposit slips, 502
deposits, 502–503
descender, 409
descent, 9
descriptive expressions, 38
desert, 9
design
    balance, 405–406
    of business forms, 451
    contrast, 406
    DTP layout screen, 404–405
    graphic lines, 405
    graphics placement, 406
    hints, 406
    meaning of, 404
    principles of design, 405–406
    proportion, 405
    rhythm, 406
    text placement, 406

unity, 406
webpage design, 423
designated-purpose keys, 289
desk calendar, 229
desks, 179, 181
desktop accessory packages, 294
desktop dictation units, 388–389
desktop publishing (DTP)
advantages, 396
artwork, preparation of,
402–404
body text, 399–402
colour, 403–404
described, 395
disadvantages, 396
finalizing design and layout,
404–406
graphic lines, 405
graphics, preparation of,
402–404
hardware, 397
ideas for, 409
illustration software, 398
layout screen, 404–405
planning the publication,
398–399
portable document format
(PDF), 408–409
preliminary page designs, 399
printing and finishing final
version, 406–408
producing a document,
398–409
skills for, 396–397
software, 397–398
systematic approach, 398
terms, 409–410
text, preparation of, 399–402
typography, language of,
400–401
use of, 396
word-processing software, 398
desktop publishing software, 294,
378
desktop sorter, TES
dessert, 9
destruction (records), 233
detachable palm rest, 177
development, 84
device, 9
devise, 9
Dewey decimal system, 415
dial-up modem, 426
dial-up phone number, 426
Dialog, 413
dialog box, 310
dictation equipment
centralized recording units, 389
desktop units, 388–389
hand-held portable units, 388
machine/microtranscription, 390
productivity techniques, 390
transcription units, 390
types of, 388–389
dictation techniques, 114–115
dictionaries, 429–430
die stamps, 451
differ, 9
different from, 19, 25
difficult callers, 137–138
difficult visitors, 125–126

digital cameras, 246, 290
digital copying process, 241
digital duplicators, 246
digital subscriber line (DSL), 149
digital systems, 236, 389
digital writing system, 290
digitized photos, 279
dining etiquette, TES
dining out
acceptance, 131
the bill, 130
group dining, 130
guidelines, 129
invitations, 130–131
regrets, 131
smoking, 129
tipping, 130
diploma programs, 73–74
diplomatic titles, 99
direct address, 59
Direct Broadcast Video (DBV),
265
direct dialing, 141, 142
direct flight, 270
direct imaging, 407
direct object, 35
direct quotations, 54–55, 59, 65–66
directories, 430–431
disbursements journal, 494
disbursing, 450
discounts, 483–484, 489
discreet, 9
discreetness, 138
discrete, 9
discrete media recorder, 389
discrimination, 32, 128, 206–207
discussions, 120–121
dishonoured (irregular) cheques,
506
disk backup, 386
disk care, 385–386
disk cleanup, 306
disk management
naming files, 386–387
working with folders, 387
dismissal, 198–199
display text, 400
display type, 409
dissent, 9
distant learning, 326
distributing mail, 457
diverse workforce, 128
diversified funds, 525
dividends, 525
document-based management
systems (DBMS), 237
document processing
automatic features, use of, 383
cost-effectiveness, 382–385
default settings, 384
document-processing cycle,
380–381
inputting, 380–381
integrated software packages,
382
letter production, speeding up,
384
machine dictation equipment,
388–390
macros, use of, 384–385
moving around the screen, 383

organization of activities,
391–392
originating text for, 388–390
paper-handling devices, 388
printer use, 383–384
printers, 388
reports, productive production
of, 384
service bureaus and
consultants, 392
spell checker, proper use of, 384
storage, 385–387
technological changes, 392–393
templates, 384
temporary document-processing
help, 392
terms, 393–394
use of system to full potential,
383–385
word-processing software,
381–382
document-processing cycle,
380–381
document production
artwork, preparation of,
402–404
body text, 399–402
colour, 403–404
finalizing design and layout,
404–406
graphic lines, 405
graphics, preparation of,
402–404
multi-media document
production, 395
planning the publication,
398–399
portable document format
(PDF), 408–409
preliminary page designs, 399
printing and finishing final
version, 406–408
systematic approach, 398
text, preparation of, 399–402
typography, language of,
400–401
document records
borrowing stored materials,
229–230
charge-out procedures, 229–230
coding, 227
cross-referencing, 227–228
document filing tips, 230–231
follow-up systems, 228–229
management of, 226–231
organization and supplies,
219–220
releasing, 226
reminder (tickler) systems,
228–229
unnecessary records storage,
383
document style manuals, 379
documents, attractiveness of,
378–379
doing business abroad, 132
dollar signs, 370
domain, 426
domain name, 156
Domain Name System (DNS),
156, 426

domestic drafts, 511
donation (response to request for), 89
don't, 22
dot.com, 156
double endorsement, 504
double entry, 495
double negative words, 22
downloading, 310, 420, 421, 426
downtime, 310, 393
DPI (dots per inch), 409
drafts (banking), 510–511
draw programs, 295
drawing room (train), 272
dress, 117, 129, 132
drop capital, 409
drop shadows, 405
DSL (digital subscriber line), 149
DTP. *See* desktop publishing (DTP)
dumb terminal, 393
dump, 310
duplex numeric filing, 223
duplication of effort, 383
dusting, 306
duty-free importations by mail, 468
DVD, 310

e-audio books, 416–417
e-learning, 326
early mailing, 459
eating out. *See* dining out
EbscoHost, 413
ebusiness, 317–318
editing
  basic word-processing features, 381
  document style manuals, 379
  making documents attractive, 378–379
  meaning of, 374
  productivity tips, 378
  versus proofreading, 374–375
  recurring errors, 375–376
  text editing, 394
edition, 4
education information, 425
education titles, 99–100
educational technologies, 326
effect, 5, 17
effective communication. *See* oral expression; written expression
effective discussions, 120–121
effective interest rate, 486
efficiency. *See* time management
electronic business, 317–318
electronic data interchange (EDI), 238, 310, 317–318, 452–453, 471–472
electronic forms software, 451–452
electronic funds transfer, 508, 511
electronic information retrieval (databases), 416
electronic information sources
  databases, 413–414
  electronic reference sources, 412
electronic mail
  advantages of, 151–152

computer-based message systems, 151–161
computer teleconferencing, 157
  described, 393
  disadvantages, 152
  electronic mail-handling systems, 460–461
  email services. *See* email services
  etiquette/netiquette, 153
  as evaluation tool, 152
  facsimile transmission, 158–159
  internet/email messaging, 156
  intranets, 150
  malware, 153
  messages, 85
  networked computers, 155
  personal email, 153
  planning, 152–153
  spam mail, 154–155
  spyware, 154
  unfamiliar email messages, 153
  use of, 150–151
  viruses, 153
  voice mail, 160–161
  volume electronic mail, 463
electronic/online job application, 541
electronic organizers, 170
electronic PBX, 145
electronic publishing, 395
electronic records
  coding, 232
  control, 232–233
  described, 231
  legal admissibility of, 238–239
  management of, 231–233
  other systems, 237–238
  record identification, 232
  storage, *TES,* 231–232
electronic reference sources, 412
electronic reminder systems, 229
Electronic Shipping Tools (EST), 463
electronic signature, 290
electronic surveillance, 327
elevators, leaving, 128
elicit, 9
eligible, 9
ellipsis mark, 64
em-dash, 60, 409
em space, 410
email
  see also electronic mail
  address, 427
  described, 156, 393
  etiquette/netiquette, 153
  as evaluation tool, 152
  format, 156
  malware, 153
  networked computers, 155
  versus personal contact, 161
  personal email, 153
  planning, 152–153
  spam mail, 154–155
  spyware, 154
  time-saving tips, 168–170
  unfamiliar email messages, 153
email messaging, 156
email services
  internet protocols/servers, 163–164

management of email, 161
personal digital assistants (PDAs), 163
use of, 161
VoIP (Voice over Internet Protocol), 162
email services asynchronous *versus* synchronous communications, 162
emanate, 9
embedded object, 310, 393
emigrant, 9
eminent, 9
emphasis
  italics, 68
  question mark, 65
  quotation marks, 66
  in sentence construction, 38
  underscore, 67
employee assistance plan (EAP), 205
employee evaluation
  dismissal, 198–199
  employee records, 199
  payment policy, 199–201
  performance review, 195–197
  promotion policy, 197
  resignation, 199
  transfer policy, 197
employee monitoring, 327
employee motivation, 201
employee records, 199
Employee's Tax Deduction Declaration (TD1), 516
employer's legal financial obligations, 517–518
employment agencies, 204, 529
employment equity plans, 189
employment insurance, 515–516
Employment Standards Act, 199
employment standards legislation, 210
en-dash, 60, 410
en space, 410
enclosure notation, 346
encyclopedias, 425, 432
ending, 84
endless loop, 389
endnotes, 109, 362–364
endorsement of cheques, 504–505
English language usage and style, 432
ensuite (train), 272
ensure, 9
enunciation, 109
envelop, 10
envelope, 10
envelope addressing
  Canada Post abbreviations, 333
  folding and inserting correspondence, 335
  general guidelines, 332
  international addresses, 334
  labels, 337
  places (abbreviations), 333–334
  preferred style, 331, 332–333
  production hints, 334–335
  speedy sealing and stamping by hand, 336
  standard-sized envelopes, 336–337

window envelopes, 335–336
envelope feeders, 388
Environment Canada, 185
environmental issues, 425
equal pay guidelines, 208
equality of opportunity, 197
equipment manufacturers, 194
equity-income funds, 525
er endings, 27
ergonomics
　arm and wrist movement, 176
　chair and sitting position, 176
　chairs, 179
　colour, 180
　computer considerations,
　　176–178
　described, 175
　eyes, 175
　heating, ventilation, and air
　　conditioning (HVAC), 178
　and human resources
　　management, 201
　keyboarding techniques, 176
　keyboards, 177
　lighting, 178
　monitors, 176–177
　mouse, 178
　noise, 178
　reducing risk, 176
　tips, 175
　workstation, 176, 179–180
essay format. *See* report format
estates, 218
estimating answers, 481
etc., 17
ethics, 127
etiquette
　business etiquette. *See* business
　　etiquette
　netiquette, 153, 427
　table etiquette, *TES*
every day, 23
every one, 24
every which way, 19
everyday, 23
everyone, 24
exceed, 4
except, 4, 17
exception processing, 317
excess, 4
excessive co-ordination, 38
excessive paper use, 383
exclamation mark, 60–61, 76
exclusive language, 32
expansion slot, 310
expedited parcel, 462, 466
expense report, 278, 283, 500
expenses, 496
expert systems, 310
Explorer, 310
external hard drives, 303
external networks, 426
extranet, 427
eye contact, 132
eyes, ergonomics and, 175
eyestrain, 383

facsimile cover sheet, 159
facsimile transmission, 158–159,
　305
facts, 121

facts about Canada. *See*
　Canadian facts
fair, 10
fair-treatment policies, 128
FAQ, 427
fare, 10
farther, 10
fatigue, 383
favour (thank-you letter), 90
fax cover sheet, 159
fax features, 158
fax machines, 158, 305
fax numbers, 82
fax-response capabilities, 161
fax to fax, 158
fax transmission, 158–159
feat, 10
federal government references,
　432–433
feedback, 203
feet, 10
female individuals, addressing, 97
feminine suffixes, 32
field, 310
figures. *See* numbers
file, 310
file cabinets, 234–235
file naming, 386–387
filename, 24
filing notation/path and
　filename, 346–347
filing tips, 230–231
fill, 405
final report, 108
finance information, 425
financial advice, 511
financial institutions, 500–501
financial management
　accounting, 493–500
　banking, 500–513
　financial marketplace, 519–522
　identity theft, 523–524
　investment terms, 524–525
　payroll, 513–518
　petty cash, 518–519
financial management software,
　293
financial marketplace, 519–522
financial references, 432
Financial Services Commission of
　Ontario (FSCO) Insurance
　Ombudsman, 552
financial statements
　analysis, 498–499
　balance sheet, 496–498
　comparison of operating
　　results, 483
　formatting, 371
　income statement, 496
　liquidity, 498
　performance, 498
　profitability, 498–499
　use of, 495
financial terms, 550–552
find and replace, 381, 393
fingernails, 117
finishing, 408
finishing equipment, 247
finishing final version, 406–408
firewalls, 421–422
first impressions, 117

five-language talking translators,
　326
fixed assets, 497
flames, 427
flat databases, 293
flatbed scanner, 291
flights, types of, 270
folder labels, 220
folder tabs, 220
folder tabs with top cuts, *TES*
folders
　for computer documents, 387
　cross-referencing folders, 228
　described, 220
　for mail-handling, 459
　suspension folders, 220
folding correspondence, 335
follow-up
　job interviews, 193, 545–546
　meeting, 261
follow-up systems, 228–229
font style, 400
fonts, 330–331, 381, 400
footers, 360, 381, 393
footnotes, 109, 362–363, 365
foreign currency, 277, 511
foreign currency exchange,
　484–485
foreign transactions, 509–510
foreign words and phrases, 16,
　43, 68, 555–556
foreword, 10
form letter, 86, 90, 349–350
form of proxy, 257
formal invitations, 130
formal meetings, 249–250,
　254–256, 260
　see also meetings
formally, 10
format, 331
formatting
　basic word-processing
　　features, 381
　body text, in DTP, 400
　described, 393
　editing, 373–380
　formatting techniques. *See*
　　formatting techniques
　keying from recorded tapes,
　　378
　keying from written notes,
　　378
　page placement information,
　　330–331
　proofreading, 373–380
formatting techniques
　email, 156
　envelope addressing, 331–337
　essays, 352–368
　financial statements, 371
　legal documents, 371
　letters. *See* letter formatting
　manuscripts, 352–368
　memorandums, 351–352
　metric expressions, 371–373
　reports, 352–368
　spacing rules, 373, 374
　tables (tabulation), 368–371
formerly, 10
forms
　application form, 540–541

basic business activities, 441–450
  bill of lading, 448
  billing, 448–449
  collecting, 449–450
  for computer use, 451–452
  credit invoice, 449
  delivery receipt, 447–448
  described, 440–441
  design of, 451
  disbursing, 450
  electronic forms software, 451–452
  forms-related technologies, 452–453
  government forms, 454
  inventory control forms, 444–445
  inventory record, 444–445
  invoice, 448–449
  mailing sets, 452
  preprinted forms, 450–451
  pro bill form, 471
  producing, 445
  production order, 445–446
  purchase order, 443
  purchase requisition, 442
  purchasing forms, 442–443
  receiving forms, 443–444
  receiving report, 444
  replacements for, 451
  sales order, 446–447
  selling, 446–447
  shipping, 447–448
  shipping memo, 447–448
  source documents (forms), 493–494
  statement of account, 449–450
  stock requisition, 445
  voice-activated forms, 453
  work order, 445–446
forms control, 453–454
forms of address
  addressee name unknown, 97
  armed forces, 99
  chart, 99–102
  complimentary closings, 103
  diplomatic titles, 99
  education, 99–100
  examples, 96–97
  gender of addressee unknown, 97
  government titles, 100
  individuals, 97
  judiciary, 101
  no social title, 97
  organizations, 98
  professional titles, 101
  religious titles, 101–102
  salutations, 103
forms-related technologies
  bar code, 452
  electronic data interchange (EDI), 452–453
  imaging, 453
  pen-based computers, 453
  voice-activated forms, 453
forms software, 294–295
forth, 10
forward, 10
fourth, 10

fractions, 62, 79, 476, 477
franked mail, 464
franking machine, 336
freeware, 420–421
freight forwarders, 470–471
frequent-flyer plans, 269
frequently called numbers, 138
frequently confused words, 4–16
frequently misspelled words, 28–29
fringe benefits, 200–201
from, 19
front-line reception. *See* public relations
FTP client, 163
FTP (File Transfer Protocol), 163, 427
FTP server, 163
FTP sites, 420
FTPSpace, 420
full block style, 338
full endorsement, 504–505
full footnote, 365
full text services, 413
function key, 58
function keys, 289
functional résumés, 536
fundamental accounting equation, 497
further, 10

Gage Canadian Dictionary, 27
ge endings, 27
gender discrimination, 32
gender equity, 128–129
gender-inclusive language, 32, 128
gender role stereotyping, 32, 128
general journal, 494
geographic filing, 221–222
geographic names, 216
geographic terms, 74
gerund, 39, 48, 54
GIF format, 403
gift giving and receiving abroad, 133
gifts
  custom duties on, 468
  thank-you letter, 90
gigabyte, 310
glasses, 175
global domain, 427
global find and replace, 393
global positioning system (GPS), 284
glossary, 368
go, 18
golf, 10
good, 19
good hosts, 133
good manners, 117
  see also business etiquette
goods and services tax (GST), 468, 489–490
government
  bodies, 75
  and divisions, alphabet sequencing of, 218
  forms, 454
  franked mail, 464
  information, 425
  offices, holiday closing, 556

officials, greeting, 125
pages (telephone directories), 144
references, 432–433
services, 436–437
titles, 100
government of Canada, 435–436
government pension, 515
grammar and usage
  components of, 33
  consistency in, 37
  paragraph, 40
  parts of speech, 40–51
  sentences, 33–39
grammar check, 381
graphic design, 404–406
  see also design
graphic lines, *TES,* 405
graphical user interface (GUI), 287, 310
graphics, 381, 402–404
graphics placement, 406
graphics (reports), 361
graphics software, 295
graphics tablet, 290
gratitude letter, 90–91
greetings
  names, abroad, 132
  in public, 128
  visitors, 124–125
gross earnings, 513–514
gross profit, 496
gross profit margin, 498
gross sales, 496
groundwood, 408
group dining, 130
group fare, 270
groupware, 295–296, 322
growth funds, 525
guaranteed bookings, 274
guaranteed investment certificates (GICs), 520
guessed, 10
guest, 10
guides, 220
gulf, 10

hackneyed expressions, 3–4
hail, 10
hair, 117
hale, 10
halftone, 410
hall, 10
hand-held portable dictation units, 388
hand stamping, 336
hand-held scanner, 291
handouts, 113
handshakes, 127, 128, 132
handwriting recognition, 290
hanging indent, 393
harassment, 207
hard copy, 310, 393
hard disks, 301
hard-drive virus scanning, 306
hardly, 22
harmonized sales tax (HST), 468
hasn't, 22
haul, 10
have, 19
headers, 360, 381, 393

headings (reports), 358–359
health in the workplace, 181–182
health information, 425
health requirements, 280
hear, 10
heating, ventilation, and air
  conditioning (HVAC), 178
here, 10
hierarchical network
  configuration, 322
hierarchy, 310
high school, 24
high speed hookups, 305
historical periods, 74
hole, 11
holidays, 74, 132, 556–557
holy, 11
holy days, 132
Home Buyer's Plan, 521
homepage, 427
honesty, 85
hosting visitors, 133
hostname, 427
hotel accommodations, 273–275
hotel terms, 274–275
hour, 6
hourly wage system, 514
HTML (Hypertext Markup
  Language), 427
HTTP (Hypertext Transfer
  Protocol), 163, 421, 427
human resources management
  Canadian Human Rights Act,
    205–209
  employee assistance plan
    (EAP), 205
  employee evaluation, 195–201
  employee records, 199
  employment standards
    legislation, 210
  flexibility of, 187
  human resources planning, 187
  payment policy, 199–201
  recruitment, 187–195
  supervising the staff, 201–204
  temporary help, 204–205
  unionized environment, 205
  working environment
    (ergonomics), 201
human resources planning, 187
human rights complaints, 209
human rights legislation, 188
Human Rights Tribunal, 209
hyphen
  capitalization after, 76
  compound adjectives, 61
  in fractions, 62
  in numbers, 62
  prefixes, 62
  spelled-out numbers, 77
  suffixes, 62
  use of, 61
  word division, 62
hyphenated names, 216
hyphenated words, 42
hyphenation, 382

icon, 310, 427
ideas, receptiveness to, 117
identical names, 218–219
identifying yourself, 135–136

identity theft, 523–524
I'll, 5
illegible, 9
illicit, 9
illustration software, 398
image processing, 236, 291, 315
image technology, 236–237
imaging technologies, 241, 453
IMAP (Internet Message Access
  Protocol), 163
IMAP server, 163
immigrant, 9
imminent, 9
imperative mood, 46
impersonal (indefinite)
  pronouns, 45
in, 19
in all directions, 19
in back of, 18
in front of, 18
in-house networks, 150
in-house printing, 407
in-house training, 194
in regard to, 20
in to, 19–20, 24
inanimate objects, 54
incite, 11
inclusive language, 32
income statement, 496
income tax deductions, 516
incoming mail, 456–457
incorrect case, 39
indefinite article, 44
indefinite pronouns, 45
independent adjectives, 57–58
independent clauses, 36, 56
index, 360, 368
index cards, 228
index fund, 525
index icon, 419
indexing, 213
indicative mood, 46
indirect object, 35
individual names, 214
individual ownership, 54
individuals, addressing, 97
infectious diseases, 280
informal meetings, 249–250, 254
  see also meetings
informal reports, 355
informality, 132
Information Fatigue Syndrome
  (IFS), 176
information processing, 314–315
information processing
  technologies, 315–316
information report, 106
information security, 307
information sources
  biographical references,
    428–429
  business directories, 430–431
  city directories, 431
  dictionaries, 429–430
  directories, 430–431
  electronic information sources,
    412–414
  encyclopedias, 432
  English language usage and
    style, 432
  facts about Canada, 435–438

financial references, 432
government references, 432–433
internet, 417–428
libraries, 415–417
office handbooks, 433–434
postal information, 434
print information sources,
  428–434
telephone directories, 434
initial public offering (IPO), 525
initials, 215
input devices, 289–292
inputting, 380–381
inquiry letter, 91
inserting correspondence, 335
inset information, 348
inside address, 342–343
insight, 11
institutions, 75
insurance complaints, 552
insurance terms, 552
insure, 9
integrated office
  advantages of, 318–320
  described, 323
  electronic business, 317–318
  electronic surveillance, 327
  impact on people, 324–325
  information processing,
    314–315
  networks, 320–323
  re-engineering, 323
  return on investment (ROI), 324
  typical integrated office
    applications, 316–317
  workplace management, 324
integrated services data network
  (ISDN), 264
integrated software, 296
integrated software packages, 382
intelligent copiers, 245–246, 407
intelligent printers, 407
intelligent terminal, 394
interactive processing, 310
interest
  amortization formula, 486–487
  compound interest, 485
  credit card, 509
  described, 485
  effective interest rate, 486
  simple interest, 485
  tables, 485
interface, 311
interjections, 51, 61
international addresses, 334
International Air Transportation
  Association (IATA), 269
international draft, 511
International Health Regulations,
  280
international mail, 466–468
international parcels service,
  466–467
international shipping, 472
international times, 563
international travel
  CANPASS, 279
  customs, 280–281
  digitized photos, 279
  guidelines, 278
  health requirements, 280

NEXUS, 279–280
passport, 279
security measures, 280
travel documents, 279–280
visa, 280
international visitors, 125
internet
access, 417
advantages, 423–424
banking, 509
best of the web, 425–426
blogs, 426
business and finance information, 425
business traveller information, 282–283
common file extensions, 420
computer terminology dictionary, 313
copyright, 428
disadvantages, 424–425
downloading files, 420, 421
education information, 425
electronic/online job application, 541
email. See email
email address, 427
encyclopedias, 425
environmental issues, 425
fare finders, 282
firewalls, 421–422
freeware, 420–421
FTP sites, 420
government information, 425
health and medical information, 425
high speed hookups, 305
home and small business use, 417
index icon, 419
as information source, 417–428
internet service providers (ISPs), 417–418
intranets, 150, 423, 427
job search, 530–531
job search/training websites, 547
keyboard, 177
mortgage calculation, 488
national libraries, 426
netiquette, 153, 427
newspapers, 426
online résumés builder, 538
phone directory (canada411.ca), 144
phones, 325
posting résumés on, 530–531
references, 365, 428
search engines, 419, 427
search tips, 419–420
shareware, 420–421
sitekits, 423
spyware, 154
telephony, 325
terms, 426–428
travel reservations online, 282
URLs, 418–419
Usenet/Netnews, 422
web graphics, 402–403
webpage creation, 422–423
webpage design, 423
website addresses, 418–419

World Wide Web, 417
internet/phone line, 149
internet protocols/servers, 163–164
internet service providers (ISPs), 417–418, 427
interoffice memorandums, 104, 351–352
interpersonal skills
communicating, 120–121
communications, 121–122
described, 117
on the job, 118–119
listening skills, 122–123
professional image, 118
professionalism, 118–119
interrogative pronouns, 45
interruptions, 59
interview. See job interview
into, 19–20, 24
intranet services, 427
intranets, 150, 423, 427
see also computer-based message systems
intransitive verbs, 48
introduction letter, 91–92
introductions
being introduced, 126–127
in business letter, 84
guidelines, 126
handshakes, 127
lists or series, 55
making introductions, 126–127
of speakers, 110
introductory
statements followed by lists or series, 55
words, phrases and clauses, 56
inventory control, 444–445
inventory record, 444–445
inventory turnover ratio, 498
investment account, 502
investment terms, 524–525
investments, 511
invitations, 130–131
invoice, 448–449
invoicing math applications, 481–482
Inwats (INcoming WATS-Code 800/Toll Free), 143
IP (Internet Protocol), 163
IP Telephony, 162, 325
irate callers, 137–138
irregular adjectives, 49
irregular cheques, 506
irregular verbs, 46, 47
ISA, 311
isle, 5
italics, 67, 68
items in series, 58
itinerary, 275, 276
its, 11
it's, 11

jewelry, 117
job analysis, 187–188
job applicants. See recruitment of staff
job application
application form, 540–541
application letter, 532–534

electronic/online application, 541
interview, 541–546
résumés, 534–540
job descriptions, 188
job interview
closure, 192
conducting, 191–192
described, 541
end of the interview, 544
follow-up, 193, 545–546
give opportunity to respond, 192
during the interview, 542–544
job details, 192
making applicant comfortable, 191–192
preparation, 191, 541–542
recording reactions, 192
serial/team interviews, 544
video interviews, 545
job performance review, 195–197
job recommendation letter, 92
job refusal letter, 93
job rejection letter, 93–94
job request form, 391
job resignation letter, 94
job search
agencies, 529
application. See job application
Canada Employment Centres, 530
career counselling services, 529
direct company contact, 529
internet, 530–531
newspapers, 528
personal contacts, 527–528
posting résumés on internet, 530–531
preparation, 527
professional associations and unions, 530
schools, colleges and universities, 529
sources, 527–531
tips, 527
websites, 547
joint account, 502
joint ownership, 54
journal research, 107
journals, 494
JPEG, 403
judiciary, 101
junk mail, 154–155

"keep lines together" feature, 359
kerning, 400
key, 11
key operators, 244
key telephone systems, 146
keyboarding techniques, 176
keyboards, 177, 289–290, 380
keying and formatting
basic word-processing features, 381
editing, 373–380
formatting techniques. See formatting techniques
keying from recorded tapes, 378
keying from written notes, 378
page placement information, 330–331

proofreading, 373–380
kilobyte (KB), 311
kissing, 128
knew, 11

labels, 337
land-border document, 279
language
  body language, 118, 132
  exclusive language, 32
  gender-inclusive language, 32, 128
  identifying yourself, 135–136
  inclusive language, 32
  in presentations, 113
  profanities, 118
  usage, abroad, 132
languages (national)
  capitalization, 75
  five-language talking translators, 326
  names, 73
LANs, 295, 320–321
laptops, 286
last, 11
later, 11
lateral move, 197
laterally rolling modular filing systems, 235
latest, 11
Latin nouns, 43
Latin phrases, 16
latter, 11
lay, 11, 20
layering, *TES,* 405
layout
  graphic lines, 405
  graphics placement, 406
  meaning of, 404
  screen, 404–405
  text placement, 406
LCD displays, 289, 311
lead, 11
leading, 400–401
lean, 11
learning management software, 326
leased, 11
least, 11
leaving messages, 139
led, 11
ledger, 495
ledger accounts, 494–495
legal admissibility (records), 238–239
legal documents, 371
legal terms, 552–553
legislation, 75
lessen, 11
lesson, 11
letter formatting
  additional letter and punctuation styles, 340
  attention line, 343
  basic letter and punctuation styles, 338–339
  body of letter, 344
  company name in closing, 344
  complimentary closing, 344
  copy notation, 346
  date, 341

displayed information, 347–349
enclosure/attachment notation, 346
filing notation/path and filename, 346–347
form letters, 349–350
full block style, 338
identification line, 344–345
illustration of, 337–338
inside address, 342–343
letter placement, 341–346
letterhead, 341
mailing or other special notations, 341–342
mixed punctuation, 338
modified block style, 338
multi-page letters, 347
open punctuation, 338
postscript, 346
reference initials, 345
salutation, 343–344
small stationery, 350–351
special effects, 349
subject line, 344
letter of reference, 92
letter-post, 465
letter quality (LQ), 393
letter samples
  acknowledgment letter, 86
  apology letter, 86–87
  cancellation of contract, 88
  collection letter, 87
  complaint letter, 88
  condolence letter, 96
  congratulatory letter, 89
  covering letter with sales information, 96
  donation (response to request for), 89
  form letter, 90
  gratitude or thank-you letter, 90–91
  inquiry letter, 91
  introduction letter, 91–92
  job recommendation letter, 92
  job refusal letter, 93
  job rejection letter, 93–94
  job resignation letter, 94
  letter of reference, 92
  order letter, 94
  payment letter, 95
  reference letter, 92
  reply to sympathy letter, 96
  request for job recommendation/reference letter, 92
  reservations letter, 95
  response to unsolicited job application, 94
  sales letter, 95–96
  sympathy letter, 96
letterhead, 341
lettermail, 461
letters (alphabet), 43, 68, 139, 222–224
letters of credit, 277, 511–512
letters (written). *See* business letters; letter samples
libraries
  book retrieval, 415
  classification systems, 415

electronic information retrieval (databases), 416
national libraries, 426
non-print media retrieval, 415
virtual books, 416–417
library catalogue, 415
Library of Congress system, 415
lie, 11, 20
lien, 11
light pen, 290
lightening, 12
lighting, 178
lightning, 12
like, 20
line drawing, 382
line numbering, 382
lines, *TES,* 405
linked object, 393
linking verbs, 48, 49
liquidity, 498
listening skills
  attention, 122
  attentive listening, 122
  becoming a better listener, 123
  good listener techniques, 122–123
  importance of, 122
  improvement of, 121
  interest, 122
  as interpersonal skill, 117
  learning, 122
  motivation, 122
  poor listening skills, 122
  roadblocks to effective listening, 123
lists
  bulleted lists, 360
  introduction of, 55
  items in a list, 347
  numbered lists, 360
loan, 12
loans, 512
local dial-up phone number, 427
lock boxes, 464
logical operators, 382
lone, 12
long-distance calls
  alternative, 140
  bill to a third number calls, 141, 142
  calling card, 141, 142
  collect calls, 141, 142
  credit card, 141
  direct dialing, 141, 142
  discount plans, 141
  information about, 140
  inquiries, 141
  North America, 140–142
  operator assisted, 142
  overseas calls, 142
  packages, 141
  person to person calls, 142
  rates, 140
  special needs service, 142
  station to station, 141
  station to station calls, 142
  time differences, 140–141
  time zones, 141
long quotations, 65, 362
long-term deposits, 520

long-term liabilities, 497
loose, 12
lose, 12
lower back pain, 178
lower berth, 272

M-O, 302
machine dictation equipment,
   388–390
machine/microtranscription, 390
machine-readable labels, 230
macros, 382, 384–385
magazine references, 365
magazine research, 107
magnetic disk or tape, 291, 301
magnetic ink character
   recognition (MICR), 291
mail-filtering programs, 155
mail-handling systems, 460–461
mail-handling techniques
   equipment, 459–461
   incoming mail, 456–457
   outgoing mail, 457–459
mail openers, 460
mailbox, 24
mailing notations, 341–342
mailing sets, 452
main clauses, 36
main guides, 220
mainframes, 286
major database services, 413
making calls, 138
male individuals, addressing, 97
mall, 12
malware, 153
management. *See* supervising the
   staff
management expense ratio
   (MER), 525
mandatory retirement, 208
mannerisms, 119
manners. *See* business etiquette
manual mail-handling systems,
   460
manual PBX, 145
manual selector, 389
manuscript format. *See* report
   format
Maple Leaf Flag, 437
margin, 487–489
marine calls, 143
markdown, 489
markup, 487–489
mastheads, 410
maternity care, 208
math
   calculators, using, 474–475
   common equivalents, 480
   conversions. *See* conversion
      (math)
   decimals, 475, 477
   fractions, 476, 477
   percentage increases and
      decreases, 478–480
   percentages, 476–480
   typical business math
      applications. *See* math
      applications
math applications
   billing (invoicing), 481–482
   commissions, 482

comparisons, 483
discounts, 483–484, 489
estimating answers, 481
foreign currency exchange,
   484–485
interest, 485–487
mortgage payments, 486–487,
   488
pricing goods for sale, 487–489
sales taxes, 489–490
spreadsheets, 492
statistical data, 490–492
verification of answers, 481
maul, 12
may, 18
may be, 24
maybe, 24
McAfee Antivirus, 155
meals, 251
mean, 490–491
measurement-related
   expressions, 54
medal, 12
meddle, 12
median, 491
medical information, 425
meetings
   agenda, 253–254
   announcement of, 251–252
   conducting a meeting, 254–256
   follow-up, 261
   formal meetings, 249–250,
      254–256, 260
   informal meetings, 249–250, 254
   last-minute preparations, 254
   meals, 251
   meaning of, 249
   minutes, 257–260
   net meetings, 265
   parliamentary procedure,
      255–256
   planning a meeting, 250–254
   point of order, 256
   presenting a motion, 255–256
   proxies, 256–257
   recording a meeting, 257–260
   room layout, 251
   virtual meetings. *See*
      teleconferences
megabyte (MB), 311
megahertz (MHz), 311
Members of Parliament mailing
   privileges, 464
memorandums, 104, 351–352
memory aids, 26
memory card, 290
memory sticks, 301
men, and manners, 128–129
menu-driven software, 394
merge, 382
merged documents, 350
merged text, 394
merit, 197
message services, 148
messages
   email, 85
   leaving messages, 139
   recorded messages, 139
   taking messages, 136–137
   voice mail, 160–161
metric equivalents, 559

metric measurements, 72,
   371–373, 558
metric symbols, 79
metric system, 370, 557–559
microcomputers, 286
microfilm devices, 301
microforms, 301
micrographics, *TES,* 236, 238–239
Microsoft Media Center, 327
Microsoft Windows, 287
microtranscription, 390
middleware, 296
might, 12
military titles, 72
miner, 12
minicomputers, 286
minimum wage, 200
minor, 12
minutes
   approval of, 259–260
   described, 257–258
   example, from formal meeting,
      260
   notes for, 258–259
   production of, 259–260
   tape-recording, 259
misspelled words, 28–29
misused words, 17–21
mite, 12
mixed numbers, 79
mixed punctuation, 338
mobile calls, 143
mobile carriage filing systems,
   TES, 235
mobile managers, 326
mobiles, 143
mode, 491
modem, 264, 305, 394, 427
Modified American Plan (MAP),
   275
modified block style, 338
modifiers, positioning of, 38
modularity, 146
Mondex Smart Card, 511
money amounts, 63, 79–80, 82
money orders, 464, 512
monitoring calls, 136
monitoring employees, 327
monitors, 176–177, 289
mood, 46–47, 135
moral, 12
moral issues, 127
morale, 12
mortgage payments, 486–487, 488
mortgages, 512
motel accommodations, 273–275
motherboard, 311
motions, 255–256
motivation, 201
mouse, 178, 291, 380
multi-media document
   production, 395
multi-page letters, 347
multi-tasking, 311, 427
multi-user, 311
mutual funds, 521–522

names
   abbreviations, 71
   alphabet sequencing. *See*
      alphabet sequencing

in China, 125
commas in, 59
country names, 74
language names, 73
minor words in, 75
organization names, 71, 75
place names, 72, 74
remembering names, 127
usage and greetings, abroad, 132
word division, 82
NASDAQ, 525
National Anthem, 438
national holidays, 556
National Institute for
    Occupational Safety and
    Health (NIOSH), 175
national libraries, 426
National Transportation Agency
    of Canada, 269
nationalities, 75
NC, 427
near-letter quality (NLQ), 394
negative feedback, 203–204
negative images, 117
negative news, 85
negative words, 22
neither, 22
neither ... nor, 22
net income, 496
net meetings, 249, 265
net profit margin, 499
net sales, 496
netiquette, 153, 427
network configurations, 321–323
network light, 154
networked computers, 155
networks, 295, 320–323, 394, 426
never, 22
new, 11
new technologies, 325–327
    see also integrated office
New York Stock Exchange
    (NYSE), 525
newspaper article research, 107
newspaper job ads, 528
newspaper references, 365
newspaper-style columns, 382
newspapers (online), 426
newsprint, 408
NEXUS, 279–280
900 services, 143
976 services, 143
no, 22
no body, 24
no one, 20
nobody, 22, 24
noise, 178
nominative case, 39, 44
non-keyboard input devices and
    methods, 290–292
non-print media retrieval, 415
non-print sources, 365
non-restrictive phrases, 57
non-selector, 389
none, 20, 22
nonstop flight, 270
Norton Antivirus, 155
not, 22
notebooks, 286
notes receivable, 497
nothing, 22

Notice of Meeting form, 251, 252
nouns
    abstract nouns, 41
    articles preceding nouns, 44
    collective nouns, 41
    common nouns, 41, 73
    compound nouns, 42
    described, 40
    foreign nouns, 43
    forms of, 41
    hyphenated, 42
    Latin nouns, 43
    as object, 35–36
    plural form, 41–43, 53
    possessive form, 43–44
    proper nouns, 41
    singular nouns, 52–53
    as subjects, 33–35
    types of, 41
    usage of, 41
nowhere, 22
NSF cheques, 506
numbered lists, 360
numbered sentences, 347
numbering notes, 363
numbering pages, 360
numbering systems, 359
numbers
    in addresses, 78
    ages, 78
    alphabet sequencing, 217
    anniversaries, 78
    base number, 479
    comma, use of, 77
    in dates, 78–79
    decimals, 64, 79, 370, 475, 477
    document numbers, 79
    dollar signs, 370
    figures *versus* words, 77
    fractions, 79, 476, 477
    general guidelines, 77
    hyphens, 62
    italicized, 68
    metric symbols, 79, 372
    mixed numbers, 79
    money amounts, 63, 79–80, 82
    numeric filing, 224–225
    percentages, 80, 476–480
    plural form, 43, 77
    proportions, 80
    ratios, 80
    repeated numbers, 59
    Roman numerals, 109, 560
    spelling out, 77
    style mechanics, 77
    in subject filing, 222–224
    in tables, 370
    temperatures, 80
    times, 80
    totals, 370
    whole numbers, 370
    word division, 82
numeric filing, 224–225
numeric keypad, 290

object
    described, 35
    direct object, 35
    indirect object, 35
    of preposition, 35
object complement, 36

objective case, 39, 44
*Occupational Health and Safety
    Act* (OHSA), *TES,* 185
of, 19
off, 19
office handbooks, 433–434
office layout and landscaping,
    180–181
office management, 167–168
office suites, 296
office technology, 173
Official Airline Guide (OAG), 268
Official Hotel and Resort Guide,
    274
offset duplicating, 246
offset paper, 408
old-fashioned expressions, 3–4
OLE, 311, 394
omissions, 52, 59, 64
on, 20
on-demand pickup, 464
on to, 20
one-column format, 406
one-way video, 265
online, 311
    see also internet
online banking, 509, 511
only, 22
onscreen proofreading, 375
onto, 20
open database connectivity
    (ODBC), 311
open door policy, 167
open (mail), 456
open mind, 117
open plan office concept, 180
open punctuation, 338
opening doors, 128
operating systems, 287, 311
operator assisted long-distance
    calls, 142
operator's daily log, 391
optical character recognition
    (OCR), 394, 453
optical disks, 236–237, 301–303
optical mark reading (OMR), 291
oral expression
    business abroad, 132
    considerations, 109
    dictation techniques, 114–115
    enunciation, 109
    pitch, 109
    presentations, 110–113
    pronunciation, 109
    rate, 109
    tone, 109
    volume, 109
oral reports, 110–112
order letter, 94
organizations
    addressing, 98
    alphabet sequencing, 217
    names, 71, 75, 214
orientation, 193
orphan, 359
our, 6
OUT guides, *TES,* 230
outgoing mail, 457–459
outlines
    reports, 107
    software functions, 107

speeches, 110
output, 394
outsourcing data, 239
Outwats (OUTgoing WATS), 143
overdo, 12
overdraft protection, 512
overdue, 12
overseas calls
    bill to a third number calls, 142
    calling card, 142
    collect calls, 142
    direct dial, 142
    operator assisted, 142
    person to person calls, 142
    special needs service, 142
    station to station calls, 142
overseas mail, 466–468
overseas ringing, 140–141
owner's equity, 498
ownership, indication of, 54

package services (banking), 512
packed, 12
pact, 12
page layout, 404–406
page numbering, 360
page placement information,
    330–331
pagers, 149
pail, 12
paint programs, 295
pair, 13
pale, 12
Palm-held, 326
palmtops, 286
paper feeders, 388
paper finishes, 408
paper-handling devices, 388
paper sizes, 330
paper (stock), 407–408
paper types, 408
paragraph, 40
parallel port, 311
parallel structure, 38
parcel services, 462
parcel size, *TES*
parcels, 459
pare, 13
parentheses, 62–63
parenthetical expressions
    commas to set off, 56–57
    dash, use of, 60
parliamentary procedure,
    255–256, 266
parts of speech
    adjectives, 48–49
    adverbs, 49–50
    conjunctions, 51
    described, 40
    interjections, 51
    nouns, 40–44
    prepositions, 50–51
    pronouns, 44–45
    verbs, 45–48
passed, 13
passive voice, 46
passport, 279
Passport Office, 279
past, 13
past tense, 46
patience, 13

patients, 13
pay scales, 200
paying the bill, 130
payment letter, 95
payment policy, 199–201
payroll
    deductions, 515–516
    described, 513
    employer's legal financial
        obligations, 517–518
    gross earnings, calculation of,
        513–514
    making payroll payment, 517
    preparation, 514–515
    severance pay, 516
    vacation pay, 516
payroll journal, 494, 514
payroll services, 512
PBX (private branch exchange),
    145–146
PC cleaning, 307
PDAs (personal digital
    assistants). *See* personal
    digital assistants (PDAs)
PDF documents, 408–409, 427
peace, 13
peak, 13
pear, 13
peek, 13
peer to peer, 322
pen-based computers, 453
per, 20, 21
per se, 16
percentage increases and
    decreases, 478–480
percentage key, 476–477
percentage signs, 370
percentages, 80, 476–480
perfectionism, 383
performance, 324, 498
performance appraisal form, 196
performance review, 195–197
period
    abbreviations, 63–64
    capitalization after, 76
    decimals, 64
    and introductory statements, 55
    omissions, 64
    use of, 63–64
periodic transfer, 233
peripherals, 311, 394
perpetual transfer, 233
person to person calls, 142
personal, 13
personal call-management
    software, 169
personal chequing account, 501
personal computers (PCs), 286
personal contact, 161
personal contacts, 527–528
personal digital assistants (PDAs),
    147, 163, 286–287, 311
personal email, 153
personal identity theft
    prevention, 524
personal notepad and file, 157
personal pronouns, 44
personal telephone directory, 145
personnel, 13
perspective, 13
peruse, 13

petty cash, 518–519
phone calls. *See* telephone calls
phone numbers, 82
phone techniques. *See* telephone
    techniques
photo printer, 304
photo scanner, 291
photocopying
    convenience photocopiers, 242
    copyrighted materials, 127
    economic use, 243
    key operators, 244
    monitoring copier use, 243–244
    photocopier features, 242
    quality copies, 242–243
    types of photocopying
        equipment, 241–242
photography, 246
phototypesetting, 244
phrases
    intervening, 34–35
    introductory phrases, 56
    non-restrictive phrases, 57
    parenthetical phrases, 56
    in sentences, 36
physical presentation, 117
PICS (Platform for Internet
    Content Selections), 427
piece, 13
piecework rates, 513
pitch, 109
place names, 72, 74, 333–334
plaintiff, 13
plaintive, 13
plan to, 25
planets, 74
planning a meeting, 250–254
planning the publication, 398–399
planning your day, 166–167
plotters, 305
plurals
    apostrophes, 52
    figures, 77
    nouns, 41–43, 53
    words, 43
p.m., 71
point of order, 256, 266
point of presence, 163, 427
point-of-sale terminals, 291
point sizes, 330–331
point-to-multipoint video
    conferencing, 264
point to point network
    configuration, 322
point-to-point video conferencing,
    264
points, 401
political references, 75
poor, 13
POP (point of presence), 163
POP (Post Office Protocol), 163
POP server, 163
pop-ups, 154
portable computers, 286–287
portable document format (PDF),
    408–409
positioning tables, 369
positive feedback, 203
possessive case, 39, 44
possessive form
    apostrophes and, 52–53

compound words, 53
and inanimate objects, 54
nouns, 43–44, 52–53
plural possessive, 53
pronouns, 54
singular possessive, 52–53
post-dated cheques, 505–506
post office boxes, 464
postage scales, 460
postal code directory, 431
Postal Code Directory, 434, 457–459
postal code products, 463
postal information, 434
postal services
airlines, 468
alternatives to Canada Post
service, 468–469
bus parcel express (BPX), 468
Canadian postal services. *See*
Canadian postal services
couriers, 468–469
incoming mail, 456–457
mail-handling equipment,
459–461
mail-handling systems, 460–461
mail-handling techniques,
456–461
outgoing mail, 457–459
standard courier services, 469
taxis, 469
postscript, 346
potential, 324
pour, 13
power station, 327
PPM, 394
practising presentations, 111
pray, 13
pre-authorized contribution plan
(PAC), 525
precede, 13
predicate, 35
preface, 108, 353–355
preferred stocks, 522
prefixes, 30–31, 62, 215–216
preliminary page designs, 399
prepositions
accompanying prepositions,
24–25
common prepositions, 51
described, 50
object of, 35
unnecessary, 25
unnecessary prepositions, 25
preprinted forms, 450–451
preprinted stickers, *TES*, 451
preregistration, 263
present participle tense, 46
present tense, 46
presentation graphics software,
295
presentations
effective oral presentations,
112–113
handouts, 113
introducing a speaker, 110
language, 113
physical setting, 112
rate of speaking, 112
speech, 110–112
speech plan, 112–113
thanking a speaker, 110

tips, 111–112
visual cues, 113
presently, 19
press releases, 104–105
prey, 13
pricing goods for sale
break-even point, 489
margin, 487–489
markdown, 489
markup, 487–489
primary research data, 106
Prime Ministers of Canada, 437
principal, 13
principle, 13
print information sources
biographical references,
428–429
business directories, 430–431
city directories, 431
dictionaries, 429–430
directories, 430–431
encyclopedias, 432
English language usage and
style, 432
financial references, 432
government references, 432–433
office handbooks, 433–434
postal information, 434
telephone directories, 434
printer port, 311
printers, 303–304, 383–384, 388
printing final version, 406–408
Priority Courier, 462, 464
private branch exchange (PBX),
145–146
Private Communication
Technology (PCT), 163
private systems, 389
procedures manuals, 172
proceed, 13
process colour separation, 410
producing, 445
production order, 445–446
productivity, 324, 390
profanities, 118
professional associations, 530
professional image, 118
professional titles, 72, 101
professionalism, 118–119
profitability, 498–499
program, 261
progressive present tense, 46
promotion of event, 261–262
promotion policy, 197
pronoun-antecedent non-
agreement, 39
pronouns
case, 44
demonstrative pronouns, 45
described, 44
impersonal (indefinite)
pronouns, 45
interrogative pronouns, 45
as object, 35–36
personal pronouns, 44
possessive pronouns, 54
reflexive pronouns, 45
relative pronouns, 45
as subjects, 33–35
types of, 44–45
pronunciation, 109

proofreading, 85, 113, 375
proofreading marks, 376–377
proper nouns, 41
properties, 311
proportion, 405, 492
proportional spacing, 373
proportions, 80
ProQuest, 413
prospective, 13
protocols, 311
provinces, 333
provincial economic development
departments, 547
provincial government
publications, 433
provincial health insurance, 516
provincial holidays, 557
provincial sales tax, 489–490
proxies, 256–257, 266
public relations
client/visitor interaction, 125
complaints handling, 125
conflict resolution, 128
difficult visitors, 125–126
dining out, 129–131
discrimination, 128
dressing for the job, 129
ethics, 127
gender equity, 128–129
gender role stereotyping, 128
greeting visitors, 124–125
introductions, 126–127
remembering names, 127
public speaking. *See*
presentations
publication terms, 72
publications
capitalization, 75
desktop publishing. *See* desktop
publishing (DTP)
mailing, 461
titles of. *See* titles (works)
publicity, 261–262
punctuality, 132
punctuation
alphabet sequencing, 216
apostrophe, 52–54
brace brackets, 63
capitalization, 75–76
colon, 54–55
comma, 55–60
dash, 60
ellipsis mark, 64
exclamation mark, 60–61
hyphen, 61–62
italics, 68
parentheses, 62–63
period, 63–64
question mark, 64–65
quotation marks, 65–66
right diagonal, 64
semicolon, 66–67
slash, 64
spacing rules, 373, 374
square brackets, 63
underlining, 67
underscore, 67
use of, 52
punctuation styles (letters),
338–340
purchase order, 443

purchase requisition, 442
purchases journal, 494
purchasing, 442–443
purchasing system, 440
purge, 394
pursue, 13

quality copies, 242–243
quay, 11
Quebec Pension Plan, 515
query string, 427
question mark
  capitalization after, 76
  use of, 64–65
  when not to use, 65
quick ratio, 498
quiet, 14
quit, 14
quite, 14
quorum, 266
quotation marks
  capitalization after, 76
  direct quotations, 65–66
  punctuating with, 66
  single quotation mark, 54, 65
  special emphasis, 66
  with titles, 66
quotations
  complete sentences, 361
  direct quotations, 54–55, 59,
    65–66
  long quotations, 65, 362
  parts of sentences, 361–362
  in reports, 361–362
  short quotations, 361
quoted information, 348

races, 75
radio, 136
radio frequency (RF) wireless
    keyboards, 290
RAID, 311
rail fares, 272
rain, 14
random access memory (RAM),
    288
rate, 109
ratios, 55, 80, 492, 498–499
re endings, 27
re-engineering, 323
read-only memory (ROM), 288
reading efficiency, 174–175
reading mail, 456
reading rate, 173–174
reading skills, 173–175
real, 14, 21
real estate terms, 553–555
really, 21
receipt, 14
receiving, 443–444
receiving report, 444
recent, 14
recipe, 14
reconciliation, 506–508
recorded messages, 139
recorded tapes, 378
recording a meeting, 257–260
  see also minutes
records. *See* document records
records and information
    management (RIM)

alphabet, 212
alphabetic document file, parts
    of, 219–220
alphabetic sequencing. *See*
    alphabet sequencing
automated filing equipment, 236
basic document records
    organization and supplies,
    219–220
described, 212, 238, 315
document-based management
    systems (DBMS), 237
document records,
    management of, 226–231
electronic records, 231–233
electronic records systems,
    237–238
image technology, 236–237
indexing, 213
legal admissibility, 238–239
outsourcing data, 239
privacy, 239
records management program,
    238–239
records management systems,
    221–226
records retention, 233–234
records storage equipment,
    234–235
records cycle, 225
records management. *See* records
    and information
    management (RIM)
records management program,
    238–239
records management systems
  alphabetic filing, 221
  geographic filing, 221–222
  numeric filing, 224–225
  records cycle, 225
  subject filing, 222–224
records retention, 233–234
records retention schedule, 233
records storage equipment,
    234–235
recruitment of staff
  advertisements, 189–190
  application form, 190
  follow-up to interview, 193
  interview, 191–192
  job analysis, 187–188
  job descriptions, 188
  orientation, 193
  procedure, 188–189
  retraining, 193–194
  screening, 190–191
  sources of applicants, 189–190
  staff procedural manual,
    194–195
  tests, 193
  training, 193–194
recurring references, 366
redlining, 382
reel, 14
reference initials, 345
reference letter, 92
reference sources. *See* information
    sources
references
  anthologies, 364
  bibliography, 368

books, 365
  constructing, 364–367
  internet, 365, 428
  magazines, 365
  newspapers, 365
  non-print sources, 365
  other references, 366
  to publications, 55
  recurring references, 366
  shortened references, 366
  in tables, 370–371
references (job), 539
reflexive pronouns, 45
registered education savings
    plans (RESPs), 520
registered mail, 464–465
registered retirement income
    funds (RRIFs), 521
registered retirement savings
    plans (RRSPs), 520–521
registration, 263
regrets, 131
regular parcel, 462
regular verbs, 45, 47
reign, 14
rein, 14
relational databases, 293
relative pronouns, 45
releasing documents, 226
religious institutions, 217
religious references, 76
religious titles, 101–102
remembering names, 127
reminder (tickler) systems,
    228–229
remittances, 517
rental cars, 273
repeated words or numbers, 59
repetitive motion injuries, 175
repetitive strain injuries, 175
Repetitive Stress Injury (RSI),
    176
reply to sympathy letter, 96
report format
  bibliography, 367–368
  body of report, 356–367
  bound reports, 356
  contents page, 355
  displayed information, 360–361
  double spacing, 356
  ending the pages, 359
  endnotes, 362–363
  footnotes, 362–363
  formal guidelines, 352–353
  glossary, 368
  graphics, 361
  headings, 358–359
  index, 368
  keying endnotes, 363–364
  keying footnotes, 363
  keying textnotes, 364
  numbering notes, 363
  numbering systems, 359
  numbering the pages, 360
  placement guide, 356–357
  preface, 353–355
  quoted material, 361–362
  references, 364–367
  spacing and indents, 357–358
  special effects, 361
  starting lines, 357

textnotes, 362–363
title page, 353
reports
  appendix, 109
  bibliography, 109
  body of report, 108
  categories of, 106
  conference proceedings, 263
  cover sheet, 108
  endnotes, 109
  final report, 108
  footnotes, 109
  format of. *See* report format
  informal reports, 355
  information report, 106
  oral reports, 110–112
  outlines, 107
  parts of, 108–109
  preface, 108
  preparation of, 106
  productive production of, 384
  research, 106–107
  research report, 106
  rough draft, 107–108
  summary, 108
  table of contents, 108
  textnotes, 109
  title page, 108
request for job recommendation/
  reference letter, 92
research
  see also information sources
  book research, 107
  described, 106
  journals, 107
  magazines, 107
  newspaper articles, 107
  primary research data, 106
  secondary research data, 106
research report, 106
resent, 14
reservations letter, 95
resignation, 199
resolution, 266, 410
response
  donation request, 89
  to invitations, 131
  to sympathy letter, 96
  to unsolicited job application,
    94
restaurant terms, 274–275
restrictive appositives, 57
restrictive endorsement, 505
résumés
  accomplishments, 537
  business experience, 538
  chronological résumés,
    536–537, 540
  described, 534
  education, 539
  functional résumés, 536
  getting started, 535
  interests, 539
  marketable skills, 537
  online résumés builder, 538
  personal information, 537
  posting online, 530–531
  presentation, 535–536
  references, 539
  types of, 536–537
retirement savings plans, 512

retraining, 193–194
retrieval, 300–303
return address, 459
return on investment (ROI), 324
returning calls, 139
rewriteable DVD, 303
rewriteable (erasable), 302
rhythm, 406
rich text, 427
right, 14
right diagonal, 64
ring network configuration, 321
RISC (reduced instruction set
  computing), 312
rite, 14
Robert's Rules of Order, 256
robots, 312
role, 14
roll, 14
Roman numerals, 109, 560
roomette, 272
root, 14
root word, 30
rotary (circular) files, 235
rough draft, 107–108
route, 14
router, 305
RRSP Home Buyer's Plan, 521
rubber stamps, 451
rules, 119
run-around, 410

safety deposit boxes, 513
safety in the workplace, 183–184
sail, 14
salaries, 514
sale, 14
sales information, in covering
  letter, 96
sales journal, 494
sales letter, 95–96
sales order, 446–447
sales slip, 446
sales system, 441
sales tax licence number, 490
sales taxes, 489–490
salutations, 103, 343–344
sample letters. *See* letter samples
sans-serif, 401
satellite centres, 392
scale, 410
scanner, 291, 380
scarcely, 22
scene, 14
scent, 7
scheduled flight, 270
scheduled pickup service, 464
scheduled tasks, 306
scheduling appointments, 171
schools, 194, 217, 529
screening calls, 138, 405
screening job applicants, 190–191
scroll arrows, 312
scroll bar, 312
scroll box, 312
sealing envelopes, 336
search engines, 419, 427
seasons, 74
seat saver, 270
secondary research data, 106
security, 201

security measures, 280
seeing as how, 21
seen, 14
selling, 446–447
semicolon
  in compound sentences, 66–67
  and conjunctive adverbs, 50, 51
  decreasing use in business
    communications, 67
  items in a series, 58
  in a series, 67
seminars, 194
seniority, 197
senses, 7
sent, 7
sentence
  clauses, 36
  complex sentences, 37
  compound-complex sentences,
    37
  compound sentences, 37, 56,
    66–67
  construction hints, 37–38
  flaws to avoid, 38–39
  numbered sentences, 347
  object, 35–36
  parallel (balanced) structure,
    38
  parts of, 33–36
  phrases, 36
  predicate, 35
  quoting, 361–362
  simple sentences, 37
  subject, 33–35
  topic sentence, 40
  transitional sentence, 40
  types of sentences, 37
sentence fragment, 38
separation certificate, 518
sequential numeric system,
  224–225
serial, 7
serial port, 312
serial/team interviews, 544
series
  introduction of series, 55
  items in series, 58
  semicolon, use of, 67
serif, 401
service bureaus, 392
Service Canada, 437
service charges, 506
severance pay, 516
sew, 14
sexual harassment, 128, 207–208
shading/fill, 312, 405
shall, 21
shared-logic system, 320
shared-resource system, 320
shareholder's equity, 498
shareware, 296, 420–421
sheet-fed scanner, 291
shelves, *TES,* 235
shifted constructions, 39
shipper's responsibilities, 471
shipping documentation, 471
shipping forms, 447–448, 471
shipping memo, 447–448
shipping services
  charges for, 470
  documentation, 471

electronic data interchange (EDI), 471–472
freight forwarders, 470–471
international shipping, 472
pro bill form, 471
shipper's responsibilities, 471
transportation mode, choice of, 470
shoes, 132
short quotations, 361
short-term deposits, 520
shortcut, 24
shortened references, 366
should of, 21
shredders, 233–234, 307, 388
SI Metric System, 371
sight, 8
silent *e*, 27
simple average, 491
simple fractions, 79
simple interest, 485
simple sentences, 37
simple subject, 34
since, 21
single quotation mark, 54
single quotation marks, 65
single units, 392
singular nouns, 52–53
singular possessive, 52–53
site, 8
sitekits, 423
sitting position, 176
slash, 64
sleep mode, 312
small-business enterprise centres, 547
small packet, 465, 466
smart cards, 325, 511
smart (intelligent) terminal, 394
smartphones, 326
smoking, 129
SMTP (Simple Mail Transfer Protocol), 163
snail mail, 428
so, 14
social etiquette, 117
social skills, 117
social titles, 72, 97
societies, 217
soft copy (readout), 312
soft skills, 117
software
  accounting and financial management software, 293
  accounting software, 371, 499–500
  anti-virus programs, 155, 299–300
  choosing software, 300
  command-driven software program, 393
  communications software, 293, 317
  databases, 168, 237–238, 293–294
  desktop accessory packages, 294
  for desktop publishing (DTP), 397–398
  desktop publishing software, 294, 378

electronic forms software, 451–452
email software, 156
forms software, 294–295
freeware, 420–421
graphics software, 295
groupware, 295–296, 322
illustration software, 398
integrated office applications, 316–317
integrated software, 296
integrated software packages, 382
learning management software, 326
mail-filtering programs, 155
menu-driven software, 394
middleware, 296
shareware, 296, 420–421
spreadsheets, 296–297, 369, 492
time-management software, 170
time-saving tips, 168–170
utilities, 299
word-processing software, 300, 381–382, 398
see also software functions
software functions
  additional features, 381–382
  basic word-processing features, 381
  calculating ability, 381
  conversion of documents, 381
  current date, 58
  customization, 381
  em-dash, 60
  find and replace, 381
  fonts, 381
  footers, 381
  function key, 58
  grammar check, 381
  graphics, 381
  headers, 381
  hyphenation, 382
  "keep lines together" feature, 359
  line drawing, 382
  line numbering, 382
  logical operators, 382
  macros, 382
  merge, 382
  newspaper-style columns, 382
  outlines, 107
  redlining, 382
  sorting, 382
  spell checker, 382, 384
  split screen, 382
  styles feature, 108
  syntax checker, 382
  table of contents feature, 108
  thesaurus, 382
  widow/orphan protection, 82, 359
  windowing, 382
  WYSIWYG (What You *See* Is What You Get), 382
sole, 14
some place, 21
some time, 24
sometimes, 24
somewhere, 21

sort (mail), 456
sorting, 382
soul, 14
source documents (forms), 493–494
source file, 312
space management, 180–181
spacing rules, 373, 374
spam mail, 154–155, 428
speakers
  introducing, 110
  thank-you letter for, 91
  thanking, 110
speaking notes, 111
special discounts, 483
special effects, 349, 361
special filing equipment, 235
special guides, 220
special needs service, 142
special negatives, 22
specialized copiers, 245–246
specialized directories, 430
speech plan, 112–113
speeches
  see also presentations
  closing, 112
  delivery of, 111
  getting started, 110
  outline, 110
  practising, 111
  presentation tips, 111–112
  speaking notes, 111
  writing the speech, 110
spell checker, 28, 382, 384
spelling
  frequently misspelled words, 28–29
  rules, 26–27
  word variants, 27–28
split keyboard, *TES*
split screen, 382
spoken word. *See* oral expression
spreadsheet formulas, 297–298
spreadsheet graphics, 298, 299
spreadsheets, 296–297, 369, 492
SpySweeper, 155
spyware, 153, 154
square brackets, 63
staff procedural manual, 194–195
staff selection procedures, 188
stair, 14
stale-dated cheques, 506
stalk, 15
stamping, 336
standard courier services, 469
standard punctuation, 338
standard-sized envelopes, 336–337, 459
standing up, 128
star network configuration, 322
stare, 14
stars, 74
start-stop transmission, 162
statement of account, 449–450, 495
states, 333–334
station to station calls, 141, 142
stationary, 15
stationery, 15
statistical data
  averages, 490–491

mean, 490–491
median, 491
mode, 491
proportion, 492
ratio, 492
Statistics Canada, 548
status, 132
status bar, 312
status function, 157
statute, 15
statutory holidays, 556–557
Stentor Canadian Network
    Management, 148
stereotypes, 32
stickers, *TES*, 451
stock, 15
stock (paper), 407–408
stock requisition, 445
stocks, 522
stopped cheques, 505
storage
    CD disk care, 385–386
    choosing, 302
    cleaning the disk, 386
    computer-based storage
        capacities, 303
    disk backup, 386
    disk care, 385–386
    disk management, 386–387
    hard disks, 301
    magnetic tape, 301
    memory sticks, 301
    microfilm devices
        (microforms), 301
    optical disks, 301–302
    write-protecting disks, 386
straight, 15
strait, 15
strange icons, 154
street directory, 431
stress, 38
stress management, 182–183
style manuals, 379
style mechanics
    abbreviations, 69–72
    capitalization, 72–76
    numbers, 77
    use of, 68–69
    word division, 81–82
style sheet, 410
styles feature, 108
sub-domains, 156
subfolder, 312
subject
    compound subject, 34
    with intervening phrase or
        clause, 34–35
    joined by connectives, 34
    of sentence, 33–35
    simple subject, 34
    and verb agreement, 33, 39
subject filing, 222–224
subject line, 344
subject-numeric filing, 224
subject-verb non-agreement, 39
subjunctive mood, 47
subordinate clauses, 36, 57
subordinate conjunctions, 51
subsidiary ledgers, 495
substance abuse, 184
suffixes, 26–27, 31, 32, 62

suite, 15
summary, 108
Super APEX, 270
superior to, 25
superlative form, 49
supervising the staff
    conflict resolution, 203–204
    motivation, 201
    qualities of good supervisor,
        201–202
    team approach, 202–203
surfing the net, 428
surrounded by, 25
suspension folders, 220
sweet, 15
symbols, 77, 216, 371–372, 373
sympathy letter, 96
synchronous communications, 162
syntax checker, 382

T4 (withholding statement), 517
table etiquette, *TES*
table of contents, 108, 355
tabled motion, 256, 266
tables (tabulation), 368–371
tabulated information, 348,
    360–361
tact, 117, 138
tags, 428
tail, 15
take, 18
taking messages, 136–137
tale, 15
task review, 306
taskbar, 312
tax-exempt importations by mail,
    468
taxis, 469
TCP/IP, 163
TCP (Transmission Control
    Protocol), 163
team approach, 202–203
team interviews, 544
tear, 15
technological changes, 392–393
teleconferences
    audio conferencing, 263–264
    audio-plus conferencing, 264
    described, 263
    meaning of, 249
    preparation for, 265
    use of, 250
    video conferencing, 264–265
teleconferencing, computer, 157
telemarketing fraud, 148
telephone-answering services, 149
telephone banking, 509
telephone calls
    from aircraft, 270
    versus letter, 86
    personal call-management
        software, 169
    time-saving tips, 168–170
telephone company system, 389
telephone directories
    alphabet sequencing, 219
    alphabetic directory (White
        Pages), 144
    classified directory (Yellow
        Pages), 144
    described, 434

government pages, 144
    on internet, 144
    long-distance information, 140
    personal directory, 145
telephone equipment. *See*
    business telephone systems
    and equipment
telephone hookup, 389
telephone number directory, 431
telephone numbers, 82
telephone services
    alternative long-distance
        services, 140
    area code overlays, 140
    conference calls, 142–143
    long-distance calls, North
        America, 140–142
    marine calls, 143
    mobile calls, 143
    900 services, 143
    976 services, 143
    overseas calls, 142
    special types of calls, 142–143
    telephone directories, 140,
        143–145
    311 service, 143
    toll-free service, 143
    TT26 WATS service, 143
    211 service, 143
telephone systems. *See* business
    telephone systems and
    equipment
telephone techniques
    alertness, 135
    answering calls, 135
    difficult callers, 137–138
    discreetness, 138
    identifying yourself, 135–136
    leaving messages, 139
    making calls, 138
    monitoring calls, 136
    mood of answerer, 135
    recorded messages, creating,
        139
    returning calls, 139
    screening calls, 138
    tact, 138
    taking messages, 136–137
    transferring calls, 136
temperatures, 80
templates, 384, 394, 410
temporary document-processing
    help, 392
temporary help, 204–205
temporary workers, 201
tendonitis, 175
tenses, 46
tension neck syndrome, 175
term deposits, 513
terminal digit filing, 225
termination of employment,
    198–199
terminology
    business terms, 550–552
    computer terms, 308–313
    desktop publishing (DTP)
        terms, 409–410
    document processing terms,
        393–394
    financial terms, 550–552
    hotel terms, 274–275

insurance terms, 552
internet terms, 426–428
investment terms, 524–525
legal terms, 552–553
real estate terms, 553–555
restaurant terms, 274–275
terms. *See* terminology
territories, 333
tests, 193
text, 394
text, body. *See* body text
text content, 399–400
text editing, 394
text placement, 406
text wrap, 410
textnotes, 109, 362–363, 364
than, 15, 21
thank-you letter, 90–91, 133
thanking a speaker, 110
that, 57
The Net system, 148
their, 15
then, 15, 21
there, 15
there are, 21
there is, 21
thesaurus, 382
they're, 15
thoracic outlet syndrome, 175
thorough, 15
311 service, 143
threw, 15
through, 15
tickler file, 229
tickler systems, 228–229
TIFF files (tagged image file
    format), 410
time differences, 140–141
time management
    appointment schedule, 171
    computer software time-saving
        tips, 168–170
    correspondence, dealing with,
        170–171
    decision making, 172–173
    email time-saving tips, 168–170
    office management, 167–168
    office technology, 173
    planning your day, 166–167
    procedures manuals, 172
    reading skills, 173–175
    scheduling appointments, 171
    starting point, 166
    telephone time-saving tips,
        168–170
    time-saving tips, 167–170
time-management software, 170
time-related expressions, 54
time-saving tips
    computer software, 168–170
    email, 168–170
    office management, 167–168
    telephone, 168–170
time zones
    abbreviation, 72
    Canada, 561–562
    long-distance calls, 141
    United States, 562
    world time zones, 563
times
    abbreviations, 71–72

colon, use of, 55
daylight saving time (DST), 564
figures or words, 80
international times, 563
numeric times, 372–373
in tables, 370
tipping, 130, 133
title page, 353
title page (report), 108
titles (people)
    abbreviations, 72
    alphabet sequencing, 214–215
    armed forces, 99
    capitalization, 76
    diplomatic titles, 99
    education, 99–100
    forms of address chart, 99–102
    government, 75
    government titles, 100
    judiciary, 101
    professional titles, 101
    religious titles, 101–102
    social titles, 97
titles (works)
    all capitals, 68
    commas in, 59
    italics, 68
    quotation marks with, 66
to, 18, 21
tolerance, 119
toll-free service, 143
tone, 109, 135–136
too, 21
toolbar, 312
toolbox, 312
tooltip, 312
topic sentence, 40
Toronto Stock Exchange (TSX),
    525
totally connected (point to point),
    322
totals, 370
touch fingering, 474–475
touch-sensitive screen, 291
Touch-Tone, 24
trackball, 290
tracking function, 157
trade discounts, 483
trade show. *See* conferences and
    conventions
trademarks, 74
train travel, 272–273
training, 193–194
training websites, 547
transcribing unit, 394
transcription units, 390
transfer methods (records), 233
transfer policy, 197
transferring calls, 136
transitional sentence, 40
transitive verbs, 47
translators, 326
travel agents, 268
travel arrangements
    air travel, 268–272
    booking online, 282
    business traveller information
        online, 282–283
    customs, 280–281
    electronic business kit, 275
    expense report, 278

foreign currency, 277
global positioning system
    (GPS), 284
health requirements, 280
hotel/motel accommodation,
    273–275
international travel, 278–283
itinerary, 275, 276
making travel arrangements,
    281–283
preparation guidelines, 281–282
rental cars, 273
security measures, 280
support staff responsibilities,
    275–277
train travel, 272–273
travel agents, 268
travel documents, 279–280
travel funds, 277
travel insurance, 278
worksheet, *TES*
travel documents, 279–280
travel funds, 277
travel insurance, 278
traveller's cheques, 277, 513
traveller's electronic business
    kit, 275
treaties, 75
trial balance, 495
Trojan horses, 153
trustees, 218
try to, 25
TT26 WATS service, 143
turnaround time, 312, 394
turnover, 24
two, 21
two-column format, 406
two-point punctuation, 338
211 service, 143
type styles, 400
typefaces, 400, 401–402
typography, 400–401

unable, 22
unaddressed mail, 461
underscore, 67–68
unions
    job search and, 530
    payment policy and, 200
    working in unionized
        environment, 205
United States
    mail to, 465–466
    national holidays, 557
    states, districts and territories,
        333–334
    time zones, 562
    U.S. dollar account, 502
unity, 406
universities, 217, 529
university degrees, 74
unnecessary prepositions, 25
unnecessary records storage, 383
unsolicited job application,
    response to, 94
unwilling, 22
upload, 428
upper berth, 272
uptime, 312
URLs, 418–419, 428
U.S. dollar account, 502

usage. *See* grammar and usage
USB, 313
USB ports, 301
Usenet/Netnews, 422
user-friendly, 313
utilities, 299

vacation pay, 516
vendors, 194
verb phrase, 35
verbatim, 16
verbs
  auxiliary verbs, 47
  conjugation, 45–46
  copula verbs, 48
  described, 45
  gerund, 39, 48, 54
  intransitive verbs, 48
  irregular verbs, 46, 47
  linking verbs, 48, 49
  mood, 46–47
  as predicate, 35
  regular verbs, 45, 47
  and subject agreement, 33, 39
  tenses, 46
  transitive verbs, 47
  types of, 47–48
  voice, 46
verification of answers, 481
verses, 15
versus, 15
vice versa, 16
video conferencing, 264–265, 305–306
video input, 292
video interviews, 545
videophone, *TES,* 148
violence in the workplace, 184
virtual books, 416–417
virtual meetings. *See* teleconferences
virtual private network (VPN), 149
virus protection, 155, 299–300
virus scanner, 154
virus scanning, 306
viruses, 153, 155
vis-à-vis, 16
visa, 280
visitors
  client/visitor interaction, 125
  difficult visitors, 125–126
  government officials, 125
  greeting, 124–125
  hosting visitors, 133
  international visitors, 125
visual cues, 113
voice
  active voice, 38, 46
  described, 46
  passive voice, 46
voice-activated forms, 453
voice mail
  automated voice-response telephone systems, 160–161
  changing recorded messages, 161
  incoming messages, 160
  outgoing messages, 160
  versus personal contact, 161
  planning, 152–153

systems, 148
use of, 160
voice messaging, 306
Voice over Internet Protocol (VoIP), 162, 164, 325
voice processing, 315
voice recognition, 292, 381
voice technology, 162
voice (tone), 135–136
VoIP (Voice over Internet Protocol), 162, 164, 325
volume, 109
volume electronic mail, 463
voluntary payroll deductions, 516
Volunteer Opportunities Exchange (VOE), 539
voucher cheques, 503, 504
VPN (virtual private network), 149
VRML (Visual Reality Modelling Language), 428

wages, 514
waist, 16
wait, 16
waive, 16
WANs, 295, 320–321
ware, 16
waste, 16
wave, 16
waybill, 471
weak, 16
wear, 16
weather, 16
web browser, 428
web graphics, 402–403
web server, 428
WebCrawler, 428
weblog, 426
webpage, 428
webpage creation, 422–423
webpage design, 423
website, 428
website addresses, 418–419
Webster's New World Dictionary, 27
week, 16
weight, 16
weighted average, 491
well, 19
were, 16
what, 45
whatever, 45
where, 16
whether, 16
which, 21, 45, 57
whichever, 45
White Pages, 144
WHMIS (Workplace Hazardous Materials Information System), 184–185
who, 21, 45
whoever, 45
whole, 11
whole numbers, 370
wholly, 11
whomever, 45
who's, 16
whose, 16
Wide-Area Transmission Service, 143
widow/orphan protection, 82, 359

WiFi (wireless fidelity), 164
wild-card searches, 420
will, 21
window envelopes, 335–336
windowing, 313, 382
wiping, 313
with regards, 18
withdrawals, 503
without, 22
wizards, 394
women, and manners, 128–129
Women in Canada Report, 548
women in the workplace, 548
word choice
  accompanying prepositions, 24–25
  clichés to avoid, 3–4
  double negative words, 22
  frequently confused words, 4–16
  gender-inclusive language, 32
  importance of, 3
  Latin phrases, 16
  misused words, 17–21
  one word *versus* two, 23–24
  and sentence construction, 37
  spelling, 25–29
  unnecessary prepositions, 25
  word meanings, 30–31
word division
  hyphens, 62
  never divide, 81
  related expressions, 82
  where to divide, 81–82
word-processing software, 300, 315, 330, 381–382, 398
  see also document processing; software functions
word variants, 27–28
words
  with accompanying prepositions, 24–25
  compound words, 42, 53
  double negative words, 22
  ending in *er* and *re,* 27
  foreign words and phrases, 68
  frequently confused words, 4–16
  to identify letters, 139
  introductory words, 56
  italicized, 68
  meanings, 30–31
  misused words, 17–21
  one word *versus* two, 23–24
  parenthetical words, 56
  plural form, 43
  prefixes, 30–31
  repeated words, 59
  root word, 30
  suffixes, 26–27, 31, 32
  with unnecessary prepositions, 25
work injury problems, 175
work order, 445–446
work relationships, 119
work surfaces, 179
workers' compensation, 517
working capital, 498
working conditions, 201
working environment. *See* ergonomics

working memory, 288
workplace, 24
workplace health, 181–182
workplace identity theft
    prevention, 523–524
workplace management, 324
workplace safety, 183–184
workplace violence, 184
worksheet, 24
workshops, 194
workstation, 176, 179–180
workstation, 24
workstation design, *TES,* 179–180
World Equity Benchmark Shares
    (WEBS), 525
World Health Organization

(WHO), 280
world time zones, 563
World Wide Web, 417
WORM disks, 302
wouldn't, 22
wraparound, 410
wright, 14
wrist movement, 176
write-protecting disks, 386
written expression
    business abroad, 132
    business letters, 83–96
    forms of address, 96–103
    memorandums, 104
    press releases, 104–105
    reports, 106–109

responding to, 122
written notes, 378
WYSIWYG (What You *See* Is
    What You Get), 382, 410

x-height, 410
Xpresspost, 462
Xpresspost-International, 467
Xpresspost-USA, 465–466

yearbooks, *TES*
Yellow Pages, 144
you, 29
"you" approach, 85
your, 16, 29
you're, 16